Celtic Coinage: New Discoveries, New Discussion

Edited by

Philip de Jersey

BAR International Series 1532
2006

Published in 2016 by
BAR Publishing, Oxford

BAR International Series 1532

Celtic Coinage: New Discoveries, New Discussion

ISBN 978 1 84171 967 2

BAR Publishing is the trading name of British Archaeological Reports (Oxford) Ltd. British Archaeological Reports was first incorporated in 1974 to publish the BAR Series, International and British. In 1992 Hadrian Books Ltd became part of the BAR group. This volume was originally published by Archaeopress in conjunction with British Archaeological Reports (Oxford) Ltd / Hadrian Books Ltd, the Series principal publisher, in 2006. This present volume is published by BAR Publishing, 2016.

Printed in England

BAR
PUBLISHING

BAR titles are available from:

BAR Publishing
122 Banbury Rd, Oxford, OX2 7BP, UK
EMAIL info@barpublishing.com
PHONE +44 (0)1865 310431
FAX +44 (0)1865 316916
www.barpublishing.com

Contents

List of contributors

Miranda Aldhouse-Green
Department of Social Science
University of Wales, Newport
Caerleon Campus
PO Box 179
Newport
NP18 1YG
miranda.aldhouse-green@newport.ac.uk

John Creighton
Department of Archaeology
University of Reading
Whiteknights
PO Box 227
Reading
RG6 6AB
lascretn@reading.ac.uk

Mark Curteis
Essex Record Office
Wharf Road
Chelmsford
CM2 6YT
Mark.Curteis@essexcc.gov.uk

Philip de Jersey
Institute of Archaeology
36 Beaumont Street
Oxford
OX1 2PG
philip.dejersey@arch.ox.ac.uk

Megan Dennis
Norfolk Landscape Archaeology
Union House
Gressenhall
Dereham
NR20 4DR
megan.dennis@norfolk.gov.uk

Gavin Edwards
Manor House Museum
Castle Yard
Ilkley
LS29 9DT
g.edwards@bradford.gov.uk

Brigitte Fischer
63 rue de la Glacière
75013 Paris
France

Colin Haselgrove
School of Archaeology and Ancient History
University of Leicester
University Road
Leicester
LE1 7RH
cch7@le.ac.uk

Rainer Kretz
rainer@kretz8.wanadoo.co.uk

Jeffrey May
jeffrey@jmay.fsworld.co.uk

Chris Rudd
PO Box 222
Aylsham
Norfolk
NR11 6TY
chrisrudd@celticcoins.com

John Talbot
john.talbot@talbot7.com

Robert Van Arsdell
Barre Books
158 North Main Street
Barre
Vermont 05641
USA
vanarsdl@charter.net

Imogen Wellington
imogen.wellington@lycos.co.uk

Mike Williams
maw@globalnet.co.uk

Introduction: retrospect and prospect

Philip de Jersey

The papers collected in this volume were, with a couple of exceptions, presented at a conference on Celtic coinage held at the Ashmolean Museum and the Institute of Archaeology, Oxford, on 6th – 7th December 2001. With seventeen speakers and an audience of ninety, this was by far the largest gathering devoted specifically to Celtic numismatics since the 1989 Oxford conference published by Mays (1992), and indeed must have been one of the largest meetings devoted to Celtic coinage ever to have taken place.

The current popularity of research into Celtic numismatics has been caused by a combination of several factors. In retrospect, 1989 marked something of a turning point in the subject. As well as the Oxford conference, the same year saw the publication of R. D. Van Arsdell's *Celtic Coinage of Britain*: the first entirely new catalogue of British Celtic coinage for nearly forty years, with the effect of a large stone thrown into a quiet, if not quite stagnant pond. Despite criticism of various aspects of Van Arsdell's catalogue, it has rapidly become the standard typological reference for the series. At approximately the same time, Derek Harrison began to work on updating the records of the Celtic Coin Index (Harrison 1992), about which more below; and a number of postgraduate students under the direction of Jeffrey May at Nottingham University began to work on various aspects of the British Celtic series.

Little of this new work could have been done without significant additions to the corpus of data, of course, and perhaps the biggest change to have occurred in the past fifteen years is the huge increase in the number of recorded coins, nearly all of which have been found by metal detectorists. The relationship between archaeologists and detectorists has had, at least until very recently, a long and often acrimonious history, familiar to most readers here. It is probably true to say that for Celtic coinage at least, the relationship was at a particularly low ebb in the mid and late 1980s, following episodes such as the ransacking of Wanborough temple. By the end of that decade the situation had barely improved except for the work of a few individuals, notably Tony Gregory in Norfolk (see the obituary reproduced in Mays 1992, 70-71), who to his everlasting credit appreciated that the only way to build a productive relationship between the two sides was to get them talking to each other; an approach which has slowly become the norm rather than the exception. While there are still those on each side stubbornly clinging to the bad old days, the creation of the Portable Antiquities Scheme (PAS) marks another significant step towards integrating the important contribution of detectorists with more conventional archaeological records.

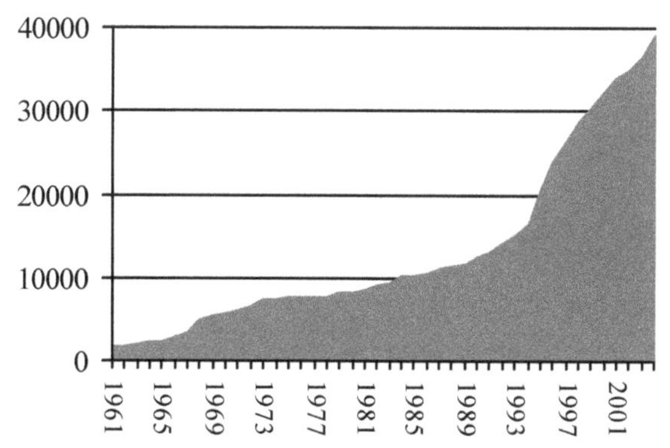

Figure 1. Cumulative total of coins recorded in the CCI, 1961-2004.

Throughout this period the Celtic Coin Index (CCI) has consistently encouraged detectorists to report their finds, with some success (Figure 1). Its over-riding principle has been to record everything shown to it, on the basis that it is better to record material which would otherwise be lost to scholarship, rather than to refuse to record it because there may be some suspicion that it was illegally recovered. While this position can quite legitimately be criticized, the alternative fails on several counts: not only does it lose information, often irretrievably, but an approach which leans more towards the stick than the carrot also provides very little opportunity to improve the situation through dialogue between the two sides. As a repository for *all* available information on finds of Iron Age coins in Britain, the Celtic

Coin Index continues to play an important role in making large quantities of new data available to researchers.

Unlike the PAS, the CCI also records unprovenanced finds. Most of these are gathered from the catalogues and lists of dealers. With the notable exception of Chris Rudd, who deserves much praise for the quantity and quality of data he has recorded since 1992, very few dealers routinely record or publish the findspots of the coins they buy and sell. This problem has been exacerbated in the past five or six years by the growth of online auctions, and in particular by eBay. Information associated with coins which appear for sale on the website is not retained there beyond a maximum of ninety days after the close of the auction, and thus this potentially important information is ephemeral in comparison to even the poorest quality dealer's catalogue. Between 1998 and 2004 the CCI has recorded more than 1300 British Celtic coins on eBay; this is certainly an underestimate of the actual total offered for sale, probably in excess of 2500 coins, since it is not possible to keep track of all sales throughout the year, some coins are advertised without images, or under misleading or incorrect categories, and many coins of very poor quality have not been recorded. But even coins of poor quality had a findspot at some point, and the loss of this information is a problem which needs to be addressed. The relative anonymity of buyers and sellers on eBay further complicates the situation, but it is encouraging to note that various interested parties are working towards a more rigorous policing of the sale of coins, and other antiquities, on the site.

Despite these various lacunae in data collection, the total number of coins recorded since the late 1980s has increased by some 250%. In terms of new coinages, this includes one or more examples of an extraordinary 300 types not recorded by Van Arsdell (1989; new data from E. Cottam, de Jersey and Rudd, forthcoming). Discussion of these newly recorded coinages is obviously one of the themes to have emerged in the past fifteen years, and indeed they form a significant component of several papers in this volume (Talbot, Kretz, de Jersey, Van Arsdell). Among the most interesting groups of new types are the coins which Chris Rudd, in particular, has ascribed to the Belgae, in the hinterland of the Solent. This view came in for some criticism at the 2001 conference (Van Arsdell, this volume) and Chris Rudd has been given the opportunity to present his side of the argument in further detail here. A number of other areas with coinage which seems to have been exposed to Belgic influence are discussed by de Jersey, in the course of an analysis of the c. 330 Belgic imports so far found in Britain, and both of Colin Haselgrove's papers demonstrate that we cannot possibly hope to understand the development of the British series without a full appreciation of what was going on in Belgic Gaul.

The huge quantity of finds made in the Chichester area during the 1990s, which has directly influenced this debate, encapsulates all the controversies and difficulties in recording which were alluded to above. Anecdotal evidence suggests that at least one temple site was among those producing significant quantities of finds, which under the terms of the 1996 Treasure Act should therefore have been declared. Leaving aside for a moment the obvious archaeological implications, how should we deal as numismatists with material which we suspect may have come from this site? We cannot realistically ignore it; if we report the finder (or, more likely, the dealer who buys and sells it), we can wave goodbye to any prospect of getting better co-operation in the future; if we publish it, are we tacitly condoning the continued, possibly illegal excavation of the site? There are clearly conflicts here between the benefits to numismatic scholarship, as well as the improvement of our wider understanding of the late Iron Age, and the need to be seen to be acting entirely within the letter of the law. These conflicts may ultimately be irreconcilable, but it is important that they are debated, because one of the possible outcomes is that provenances will simply never be recorded, particularly by dealers, because to do so only invites trouble. That would represent a significant step backwards.

A very similar problem has recently been faced by curators at Birmingham Museum, relating to the publication of coins possibly found at Wanborough temple in Surrey (Symons 1997; responses in Anon. (Jones) 1998). When, if ever, does it become acceptable to refer to coins from illegally excavated hoards? Some criticism has been made of the CCI because its online record lists a large quantity of Icenian silver more or less certainly from the so-called "bowl hoard", apparently discovered at Snettisham in 1991. The circumstances of its discovery have been briefly discussed by a distinguished former curator of the British Museum (Ian Stead, *The Salisbury Hoard* (1998), pp. 147-148), who raises the very same questions about the status of the find and how we should discuss it. It is difficult to see how suppressing the provenance of these coins in the CCI makes any useful contribution to scholarship; it is certainly far too late to make any difference to the illegal behaviour of the finder(s) of the hoard, and can acknowledging the likely origin of these coins really be interpreted as condoning illegal excavation in the future?

However we view the possible numismatic responses to these problems, there is clearly a grave risk of losing valuable archaeological information from illicit excavation, whether in the micro-context of a hoard or on a larger scale at, for example, temple or settlement sites. The usual defence of metal detectorists – that their finds are predominantly from the topsoil – may absolve them from the charge of damaging stratigraphy, but in many cases it ignores the potential information to be gained from the horizontal relationships between finds, as exemplified by classic studies such as Brown at Saham Toney (*Britannia* 17, 1986). Some detectorists do record this information, of course, and before archaeologists get too smug about the superiority of their techniques, they should perhaps acknowledge that the routine practice of stripping the topsoil with a JCB is every bit as destructive, if not more so, than typical detecting practice.

Despite the potential lack of useful contextual information, a number of archaeologists have continued to focus their research on the evidence provided by excavated coinage, as exemplified since the 1980s by the work of Colin Haselgrove. His former students Imogen Wellington and Mark Curteis have adopted a similar approach, demonstrating how useful information can be teased out of what sometimes seems to be unpromising archaeological data. Unfortunately it remains the case that much Iron Age coinage is stubbornly resistant to being found in sealed Iron Age contexts, and with a gradual decline in the number of large-scale research excavations, we increasingly have to make do with the scraps thrown up by rescue work.

At the opposite end of the spectrum lies a more purely numismatic approach. This is currently no better exemplified than by the work of John Sills, whose paper on the Tayac hoard presented at the 2001 conference is subsumed within his massive work on *Gaulish and early British gold coinage* (Spink, 2003). Sills demonstrates convincingly that if archaeologists are to make full and valid use of Iron Age coinage, they must first have a firm grasp of the numismatic principles behind it: envisaging the typological development of a particular stater type as a rather vague, ill-defined process extending over one or two generations may be a serious distortion of reality, as evidenced by the reconstruction of a die-chain which may indicate one or two bursts of production, each lasting perhaps just a matter of weeks or months. Of course not all archaeologists are guilty of treating the numismatic evidence in such a cavalier fashion – Colin Haselgrove in particular has long warned of just such an approach – but we should all be aware of the possible pitfalls, just as numismatists must learn to accept that dating from secure archaeological contexts can be relatively precise, however much it may inconvenience their own interpretations.

Other approaches to the subject have come to the fore during the past fifteen years. John Creighton has adopted a particularly innovative approach, bringing a quite different interpretation to the analysis of the imagery of British Celtic coinage. The fullest expression of his ideas, in *Coins and Power in Late Iron Age Britain* (2000), demonstrates how seemingly arcane numismatic detail can have an impact on much wider questions of the nature of political development in Britain before the Roman conquest. Whether or not we agree that Tincomarus, Cunobelin *et alii* may have been educated at Rome, it is encouraging to see authors pushing the boundaries of what Iron Age coinage can tell us.

Several other scholars have focused primarily on the imagery of coinage: Aldhouse-Green (this volume) considers the relationships between the imagery on coins and that on other, contemporary media, while Fischer (this volume) provides a welcome continental example, analysing the coin imagery associated with wine. Jonathan Williams's conference paper (published in the *British Numismatic Journal* 71 (2001), 1-17) concentrated on the adoption of writing and the significance of its appearance in the British series. The literal meaning of a number of inscriptions still remains uncertain, as shown in this volume by Rainer Kretz, working on the silver coinage of Tasciovanos. Focusing on another aspect of British Iron Age silver, John Talbot makes a major contribution to the study of the early East Anglian series; the influence of metal-detecting and better recording is clearly demonstrated by the increase in these coins from the 77 known to Tony Gregory (1992) to the 638 which form the basis of the paper presented here.

Two particular finds are published here in detail: Jeffrey May tackles the possible coin weight from Rotherwick, initially reported as the first Iron Age die found in Britain; and Gavin Edwards and Megan Dennis discuss the small but intriguing hoard found at Silsden in West Yorkshire. Despite, or perhaps because of, the increase in finds recorded over the past 15 – 20 years, the publication of Celtic hoards has signally failed to keep pace with the rate of discovery. A quick calculation, based on the records of the CCI, short notices in the *Numismatic Chronicle* and, more recently, summary accounts in the Treasure Trove reviews suggests that between 1989 and 2003 at least eighty and probably as many as one hundred Iron Age coin hoards have been recovered (counting multiple finds, such as East Leicestershire, as one). Of these, about ten have been fully published. Of course this process takes some time, and it is obvious that for the larger hoards at least there will be an unavoidable interval of some years before the material is ready for publication. But clearly some effort needs to be made to address this problem, because a few lines in the Treasure Reviews does not provide a remotely adequate level of publication; and nor is the rate in the number of hoards recorded likely to decline in the near future. We have some eleven volumes of *Coin Hoards from Roman Britain*, not to mention Anne Robertson's *Inventory of Romano-British Coin Hoards* (2000); is it not time for the Iron Age to catch up?

Although relatively few hoards have been published between 1989 and 2004, it is evident that a great deal of valuable numismatic scholarship has been produced during this period. Some of this work has already been mentioned; the bibliography appended to this discussion provides details of virtually all the significant work on British Iron Age coinage of the past fifteen years. Among the most important contributions not so far mentioned is the long-awaited British Museum catalogue, brought to fruition by Richard Hobbs (1996) after many years of false starts. At the opposite end of the publishing spectrum, more than seventy short articles on a huge variety of Celtic numismatic topics have appeared in the pages of Chris Rudd's Lists since 1997. This is an extremely effective way of circulating up to the minute news and research to a wide audience, and Chris Rudd again deserves our appreciation for developing this opportunity.

What, then, does the future hold? It is somewhat ironic that at the time of writing this account of the great developments of the past fifteen years, the CCI itself lacks any long-term funding; the PAS is safe for a few years, although that ominous phrase "for the foreseeable future" lurks in the background. It is frustrating, to say the least, that while great improvements in the recording of data are readily demonstrated, along with the dissemination of that data to scholars and to the wider public, so this relatively simple process of recording and dissemination is somehow not enough: instead we are forced to come up with ever more challenging "deliverables", to justify our existence every one or two years. The simple fact is that hundreds of thousands of archaeological items – including perhaps 7000 – 10 000 Iron Age coins in any one year – are being dug up, and we have a duty to record these items as best we can, so that we can work on them and work on conveying their historical significance to a wider audience. It's not a particularly expensive process, but convincing the various funding bodies of the importance of this work seems to become harder, and more time-consuming, every year.

We should not end this brief review on a downbeat note,

however. The past fifteen years have seen a huge increase in finds of Celtic coinage, and a huge increase in the work done on them. Some of this new research is presented here; other work is at this very moment being mulled over, formed into shape and prepared for publication. New types of coinage will continue to be discovered, and new avenues of research will be developed to investigate them; the study of Celtic coinage will continue to thrive.

Acknowledgements
I am grateful to Emma Durham, Laura Ugolini, Alison Wilkins and Debbie Day for their assistance in ensuring that the 2001 conference ran smoothly, and to The British Academy for financial support.

Bibliography of British Celtic coinage, 1989 – 2004

The bibliography below aims to list all the significant work on British Celtic coinage published between 1989 and 2004. It focuses primarily on work of *numismatic* interest, and is not intended to provide a gazetteer of finds from this period; therefore it does not generally include lists of unillustrated coins, such as recorded annually in some of the county archaeological journals, nor does it include passing mention of Iron Age coins in popular archaeological titles, or vague references of the nature of "a coin of the Iceni was found about 5km away". Significant reports of excavated coins are however included, and all references, including those omitted here, can be consulted in the online bibliography maintained at http://web.arch.ox.ac.uk/coins/ccirdng.htm. The most important continental publications dealing with the Gallo-Belgic coinages are included in the following list, but the reader is directed to John Sills's *Gaulish and early British gold coinage* (2003) for fuller coverage of the relevant continental literature. Where the subject of the cited reference is unclear from the title alone, brief details are provided in square brackets.

Ainsworth, K. and May, J. 2003: An Iron Age coin die from near Alton, Hampshire. *Current Archaeology* 188 (November 2003), 326. [Gallo-Belgic B reverse]

Allen, D. F. (ed. J. Kent and M. Mays) 1990: *Celtic coins in the British Museum II: the silver coins of North Italy, South and central France, Switzerland and South Germany* (London, British Museum Press).

Allen, D. F. (ed. M. Mays) 1995: *Celtic coins in the British Museum III: bronze coins of Gaul* (London, British Museum Press).

Anheuser, K. and Northover, P. 1994: Silver plating on Roman and Celtic coins from Britain - a technical study. *British Numismatic Journal* 64, 22-32.

Anon. 1990: A variant of Van Arsdell 409-1. *Spink Numismatic Circular* 98, 159.

Anon. 1994: Treasure trove: time for change. *Coin News* 30/12 (Dec. 1994), 19. [bowl hoard inquest]

Anon. 1995-96: New false Celtic gold coins. *Bulletin on Counterfeits* 20/2, 10-11. [Gallo-Belgic D and E]

Anon. 1996: Coin hoards 1996. *Numismatic Chronicle* 156, 249-332. [pp. 280-82 for British Celtic]

Anon. 1997: Coin hoards 1997. *Numismatic Chronicle* 157, 213-248. [pp. 217-21 for British Celtic]

Anon. 1997: The 1998 Standard Catalogue, a concordance for the Celtic section. *Spink Numismatic Circular* 105, 318-21.

Anon. [Jones, P.] 1998: Wanborough temple coins, again. *Bulletin of the Surrey Archaeological Society* 317, 11-12. [re Symons (1998)]

Anon. [Jones, P.] 1998: Wanborough coins. *Bulletin of the Surrey Archaeological Society* 318, 10-11. [re Symons (1998)]

Anon. 1998: Coin hoards 1998. *Numismatic Chronicle* 158, 287-331. [pp. 289-91 for British Celtic]

Anon. 1998: The Burnham Market Celtic hoard. *Treasure Hunting* December 1998, 38-39. [c. 200 Icenian coins]

Anon. 1998: *Treasure Trove Reviewing Committee. Annual Report 1996-97* (Department for Culture, Media and Sport). [pp. 10-13, reports of nine hoards]

Anon. 1999: *Portable Antiquities Annual Report 1997-98* (Department for Culture, Media and Sport). [IA finds at pp. 7, 16]

Anon. 1999: Iron Age coins from Sittingbourne area. *Kent Archaeological Review* 136, 134-35. [3 G-B E, Vosenos quarter in ?hoard]

Anon. [S. Hurter?] 1999: Ashmore replicas part III. *Bulletin on Counterfeits* 24, 21-23. [nos. 106 (Cunobelin quarter), 122 (V353 quarter), 123 (Corio quarter), 127 (Tasciovanus quarter)]

Anon. 1999: Coin hoards 1999. *Numismatic Chronicle* 159, 339-347. [pp. 339-41 for British Celtic]

Anon. 2000: Coin hoards 2000. *Numismatic Chronicle* 160, 309-367. [pp. 309-12 for British Celtic]

Anon. 2000: *Portable Antiquities. Annual Report 1998-99* (Department for Culture, Media and Sport). [IA coins p. 18]

Anon. 2000: *Treasure Annual Report 1997-1998* (Department of Culture, Media and Sport). [IA hoards, pp. 24-29]

Anon. 2000: Rare coin hoard finds good home in Chelmsford. *Essex Journal* 35/1, 23. [hds from Great Waltham and Great Leighs]

Anon. ['Roman Ron'] 2000: Home and away. *Treasure Hunting* August 2000, 20-24. [pp. 23-24, information on Joist Fen hoard, c. 1960]

Anon. 2001: Coin hoards 2001. *Numismatic Chronicle* 161, 329-359. [pp. 329-31 for British Celtic]

Anon. 2002: Coin hoards 2002. *Numismatic Chronicle* 162, 385-419. [pp. 385-87 for British Celtic]

Anon. 2003: *Portable Antiquities Scheme Annual Report 2001/02-2002/03* (Department for Culture, Media and Sport). [pp. 24, 57, Beverley/Driffield hoards]

Anon. 2004: *Portable Antiquities Scheme Annual Report 2003/04* (Department for Culture, Media and Sport). [IA coins, pp. 36, 47-48]

Aves, N. 1999: Building a numismatic library. Part III - Celtic. *Coins and Antiquities* May 1999, 50-54.

Barker, P. 1999: From the mists of time. *The Searcher* April 1999, 16-17. [?hoard of 3 G-B E, Vosenos quarter stater]

Bean, S. C. 1991: The "sons of Commius" reconsidered. *Celtic Coin Bulletin* 1, 1-6.

Bean, S. C. 1991: Two unpublished types of Celtic coin. *Celtic Coin Bulletin* 1, 7-8. [North Thames bronzes]

Bean, S. C. 1992: British Celtic coins added to the Finney collection, 1991: some further observations. *Spink Numismatic Circular* 100, 303.

Bean, S. C. 1993: Early British Celtic staters: British A (VA 200-1, 202-1) and British C (VA 1220). *Spink Numismatic Circular* 101, 286-88.

Bean, S. C. 1993: The coinage of the British Atrebates: the sons of Commius. In *Proceedings of the XIth International Numismatic Congress, Brussels, 1991* (vol. II) (Louvain), 1-5.

Bean, S. C. 1994: The earliest staters from the area of the Dobunni? *British Numismatic Journal* 64, 126-27.

Bean, S. C. 1996: Review of M. G. O'Connell and Joanna Bird with Clive Cheesman, "The Roman temple at Wanborough", in Surrey Archaeological Collections 82 (1994). *Numismatic Chronicle* 156, 348-54.

Bean, S. C. 1996: A new stater of the Iceni? *Spink Numismatic Circular* 104, 367.

Bean, S. C. 1997: The application of metallurgical analyses in numismatics: some cautionary tales. In A. Sinclair, E. Slater and J. Gowlett (eds.), *Archaeological Sciences 1995* (Oxbow Monograph 64), 112-15.

Bean, S. C. 1997: Tincomaros but no Tincommius: clearing the Atrebatic waters. *Spink Numismatic Circular* 105, 238-39.

Bean, S. C. 2000: An unpublished type of Tincomaros. *Chris Rudd list* 50, 4-5.

Bean, S. C. 2000: *The coinage of the Atrebates and Regni* (Oxford, OUSA Monograph 50, Studies in Celtic Coinage 4).

Besly, E. 1995: Short cross and other medieval coins from Llanfaes, Anglesey. *British Numismatic Journal* 65, 46-82. [including bronze of Carnutes, p. 62, and update of Boon's (1988) list of Celtic coins in Wales, p. 47 n.4]

Bland, R. (ed.) 2000: *Treasure Annual Report 1998-1999* (Department for Culture, Media and Sport). [IA hoards, pp. 98-108]

Bland, R. and Voden-Decker, L. (eds.) 2002: Treasure Annual Report 2000 (Department for Culture, Media and Sport). [IA hoards, pp. 106-10]

Bland, R. and Voden-Decker, L. (eds.) 2003: *Treasure Annual Report 2001* (Department for Culture, Media and Sport). [IA hoards, pp. 90-91]

Booth, J. 1997: *SCBI 48. Northern Museums. Ancient British, Anglo-Saxon, Norman and Plantagenet coins to 1279* (Oxford, OUP/Spink). [including 140 Celtic]

Briggs, D. 1995: Coinage. In M. J. Green (ed.), *The Celtic World* (London, Routledge), 244-53.

Briggs, D. 1997: Review of D. F. Allen (ed. M. Mays), "Catalogue of Celtic coins in the British Museum III: bronze coins of Gaul". *Numismatic Chronicle* 157, 263-64.

Briggs, D., Haselgrove, C. and King, C. 1992: Iron Age and Roman coins from Hayling Island temple. *British Numismatic Journal* 62, 1-62.

Burnett, A. 1989: Review of R. D. Van Arsdell, "Celtic Coinage of Britain". *British Numismatic Journal* 59, 235-37.

Burnett, A. 1990: Celtic coinage in Britain III: the Waltham St Lawrence treasure trove. *British Numismatic Journal* 60, 13-28.

Burnett, A. 1992: A new Iron Age issue from near Chichester. *Spink Numismatic Circular* 100, 340-42.

Burnett, A. 1994: Somerton, Suffolk, treasure trove. *British Numismatic Journal* 64, 127-28.

Burnett, A. 1995: 'Gallo-Belgic' coins and Britain. In B. Raftery (ed.), *Sites and sights of the Iron Age* (Oxbow Monograph 56), 5-11.

Burnett, A. and Cowell, M. 1988: Celtic coinage in Britain II. *British Numismatic Journal* 58, 1-10.

Chadburn, A. 1990: A hoard of Iron Age silver coins from Fring, Norfolk, and some observations on the Icenian coin series. *British Numismatic Journal* 60, 1-12.

Chadburn, A. 1991: A new Celtic coin from East Anglia. *Britannia* 22, 207-08.

Chadburn, A. 1991: Some observations on the Icenian uninscribed gold series. *Celtic Coin Bulletin* 1, 9-13.

Chadburn, A. 1991: New links between the Icenian coins of AESV and SAENV. *Celtic Coin Bulletin* 1, 14-18.

Chadburn, A. 1992: A preliminary analysis of the hoard of

Icenian coins from Field Baulk, March, Cambridgeshire. In M. Mays (ed.), *Celtic coinage: Britain and beyond* (Oxford, BAR 222), 73-81.

Chadburn, A. 1995: Wolves, crescents, stars and horses: the Iceni and their coins with particular reference to Norfolk. *The Quarterly* (The Journal of the Norfolk Archaeological and Historical Research Group) 17, 3-12.

Chadburn, A. 1996: Iron Age coins. In R. P. J. Jackson and T. W. Potter, *Excavations at Stonea, Cambridgeshire 1980-85* (London, BMP), 264-86.

Chadburn, A. 1999: Tasking the Iron Age: the Iceni and minting. In J. Davies and T. Williamson (eds.), *Land of the Iceni* (Centre of East Anglian Studies, University of Norwich), 162-72.

Chadburn, A. 2003: Iron Age coins. In C. Evans, "Britons and Romans at Chatteris: investigations at Langwood Farm, Cambridgeshire". *Britannia* 34, 213-16. [17 coins; discussion at pp. 254-58]

Chadburn, A. and Gurney, D. 1991: The Fring coin hoard. *Norfolk Archaeology* 69, 218-25.

Cheesman, C. 1994: The coins. In M. G. O'Connell and J. Bird, "The Roman temple at Wanborough excavation, 1985-86". *Surrey Archaeological Collections* 82, 31-92.

Cheesman, C. 1998: Correspondence. *Spink Numismatic Circular* 106, 208-09. [derivation of Tincomarus]

Cheesman, C. 1998: Tincomarus Commi filius. *Britannia* 29, 309-15.

Clogg, P. and Haselgrove, C. 1995: The composition of Iron Age struck 'bronze' coinage in eastern England. *Oxford Journal of Archaeology* 14, 41-62.

Cottam, G. 1992: Van Arsdell type 355 - Commios or Tincommios? *Spink Numismatic Circular* 100, 303.

Cottam, G. 1992: A possible minim coinage of Vep Corf. *Spink Numismatic Circular* 100, 305.

Cottam, G. 1993: Correspondence. *Spink Numismatic Circular* 101, 243. [Yarmouth staters]

Cottam, G. 1996: Further confirmation of a Kentish alliance? - light shed by a new bronze unit of Verica. *British Numismatic Journal* 66, 113-16.

Cottam, G. 1997: An overstruck silver unit of Verica. *British Numismatic Journal* 67, 95-97.

Cottam, G. 1999: The 'cock bronzes' and other related Iron Age bronze coins found predominantly in West Sussex and Hampshire. *British Numismatic Journal* 69, 1-18.

Cottam, G. 2001: Plated Iron Age coins: official issues or contemporary forgeries? *Oxford Journal of Archaeology* 20, 377-90.

Cottam, G. 2001: Review of S. C. Bean, "The coinage of the Atrebates and Regni". *British Numismatic Journal* 71, 200-01.

Cottam, G. 2003: An unusual contemporary forgery. *Chris Rudd list* 71, 5-6.

Cotton, J. and Wood, B. 1996: Recent prehistoric finds from the Thames foreshore and beyond in Greater London. *Transactions of the London and Middlesex Archaeological Society* 47, 1-33. [pp. 23-29, potin hoards and single finds]

Cowell, M. 1992: An analytical survey of the British Celtic gold coinage. In M. Mays (ed.), *Celtic coinage: Britain and beyond* (Oxford, BAR 222), 207-33.

Creighton, J. 1992: The decline and fall of the Icenian monetary system. In M. Mays (ed.), *Celtic coinage: Britain and beyond* (Oxford, BAR 222), 83-92.

Creighton, J. 1994: A time of change: the Iron Age to Roman monetary transition in East Anglia. *Oxford Journal of Archaeology* 13, 325-34.

Creighton, J. 1995: Visions of power: imagery and symbols in late Iron Age Britain. *Britannia* 26, 285-301.

Creighton, J. 2000: *Coins and power in late Iron Age Britain* (Cambridge, CUP).

Cuddeford, M. J. 1994: A new variety of Cunobelin quarter stater. *Spink Numismatic Circular* 102, 305.

Cuddeford, M. J. 1995: Cunobelin "AGR" variety confirmed. *Spink Numismatic Circular* 103, 5.

Cuddeford, M. J. 1997: Corieltauvian scyphate quarter staters. *Caesaromagus* (Journal of the Essex Numismatic Society) 71, 2-6.

Cuddeford, M. J. 1998: A Tasciovanus quarter stater. *Spink Numismatic Circular* 106, 7.

Cuddeford, M. J. 2000: Two new legend varieties for Cunobelinos. *Spink Numismatic Circular* 108, 106. [V2083 and V1667 (ie Dubnovellaunos)]

Cuddeford, M. J. 2002: Some Celtic observations. *Chris Rudd list* 64, 8-9. [scyphate interpretation]

Curnow, P. E. 1990: The coins. In D. S. Neal, A. Wardle and J. Hunn, *Excavation of the Iron Age, Roman and medieval settlement at Gorhambury, St Albans* (HBMC, English Heritage Archaeological Report 14), 105-12. [including 14 Celtic]

Curteis, M. 1996: An analysis of the circulation patterns of Iron Age coins from Northamptonshire. *Britannia* 27, 17-42.

Curteis, M., Jackson, D. and Markham, P. 1998-99: Titchmarsh Late Iron Age and Roman settlement. *Northamptonshire Archaeology* 28, 164-75. [27 Celtic coins, pp. 168-70]

Davies, J. A. 1997: Iron Age coins. In S. M. Elsdon, *Old Sleaford revealed* (Oxford, Oxbow Monograph 91 [78 on cover], Nottingham Studies in Archaeology 2), 175.

Davies, J. A. 1998: Hoards of the Boudican revolt. *Coins and Antiquities* December 1998, 27-29.

Davies, J. A. 1999: Patterns, power and political progress in Iron Age Norfolk. In J. Davies and T. Williamson (eds.), *Land of the Iceni* (Centre of East Anglian Studies, University of Norwich), 14-43.

De Bernardo Stempel, P. 1991: Die Spräche altbritannischer Münzlegenden. *Zeitschrift für celtische Philologie* 44, 36-55.

de Jersey, P. 1992: Celtic coins (Coin Register 1992). *British Numismatic Journal* 62, 204-17.

de Jersey, P. 1993: A new quarter stater for British G? *Spink Numismatic Circular* 101, 236-37.

de Jersey, P. 1993: Some modern Corieltauvian forgeries. *Spink Numismatic Circular* 101, 347-48.

de Jersey, P. 1993: Celtic coins (Coin Register 1993). *British Numismatic Journal* 63, 136-44.

de Jersey, P. 1994: Gazetteer of findspots of Dobunnic coins. In *The Coinage of the Dobunni* (Oxford, OUCA Monograph 38, Studies in Celtic Coinage 1), 67-84.

de Jersey, P. 1994: Correspondence. *Spink Numismatic Circular* 102, 165-66. [Cantiian trophy types and Gallo-Belgic D]

de Jersey, P. 1994: Celtic coins (Coin Register 1994). *British Numismatic Journal* 64, 137-43.

de Jersey, P. 1995: Deliberate defacement of a continental Celtic coin. *Spink Numismatic Circular* 103, 53.

de Jersey, P. 1995: A new Celtic minim. *Spink Numismatic Circular* 103, 89-90.

de Jersey, P. 1995: Correspondence. *Spink Numismatic Circular* 103, 92. [Cantiian trophy types]

de Jersey, P. 1995: Celtic coins (Coin Register 1995). *British Numismatic Journal* 65, 227-34.

de Jersey, P. 1996: The Savernake stater (British MB) and a new, associated quarter stater. *Spink Numismatic Circular* 104, 161-63.

de Jersey, P. 1996: *Celtic coinage in Britain* (Shire Archaeology 72).

de Jersey, P. 1996: Celtic coins (Coin Register 1996). *British Numismatic Journal* 66, 143-47.

de Jersey, P. 1997: Armorica and Britain: the numismatic evidence. In B. W. Cunliffe and P. de Jersey, *Armorica and Britain: cross Channel relationships in the late first millennium BC* (Oxford, OUCA monograph 45, Studies in Celtic coinage 3), 72-103.

de Jersey, P. 1997: Who made money in Celtic Britain? *Chris Rudd list* 26.

de Jersey, P. 1997: Counting the coinage. *Sussex Past and Present* 81, 6-7. [work of CCI, map of Sussex finds]

de Jersey, P. 1997: SA and SAM: one and the same? *Spink Numismatic Circular* 105, 114-15.

de Jersey, P. 1997: Cast away riches: estimating the volume of Celtic coinage found in Britain. *The Yorkshire Numismatist* 3, 1-13.

de Jersey, P. 1997: Review of R. Hobbs, "British Iron Age coins in the British Museum". *Numismatic Chronicle* 157, 265-68.

de Jersey, P. 1997: Mint sites of Celtic Britain. *Chris Rudd list* 28, 1-2.

de Jersey, P. 1997: Celtic coins (Coin Register 1997). *British Numismatic Journal* 67, 125-30.

de Jersey, P. 1998: Striking Celtic coins. *Chris Rudd list* 30, 1-2.

de Jersey, P. 1998: Abingdon Zoo: a new Celtic silver unit from Berkshire. *Spink Numismatic Circular* 106, 150-51.

de Jersey, P. 1998: An introduction to Cunobelin's gold. *Chris Rudd list* 35, 2-3.

de Jersey, P. 1998: Casting Celtic coins. *Chris Rudd list* 38, 2-3.

de Jersey, P. 1998: Introduction à l'étude des monnaies celtiques de Grande-Bretagne. *Annales de la Société Bretonne de Numismatique et d'Histoire* 1998, 3-9.

de Jersey, P. 1998: Celtic coins (Coin Register 1998). *British Numismatic Journal* 68, 163-66.

de Jersey, P. 1999: The Celtic Coin Index. *Coins and Antiquities* January 1999, 34-35.

de Jersey, P. 1999: Exotic Celtic coinage in Britain. *Oxford Journal of Archaeology* 18, 189-216.

de Jersey, P. 1999: Exotic Gaulish imports. *Chris Rudd list* 46, 2-3.

de Jersey, P. 1999: The stater of Volisios Cartivellaunos. *Spink Numismatic Circular* 107, 208-09.

de Jersey, P. 1999: Celtic coins (Coin Register 1999). *British Numismatic Journal* 69, 227-30.

de Jersey, P. 2000: Durotrigan cast bronze. *Chris Rudd list* 49, 5-7. [Downton hoard] de Jersey, P. 2000: Iron Age coins from the Danebury Environs. In B. W. Cunliffe, *The Danebury Environs Programme. The prehistory of a Wessex landscape, volume I. Introduction* (Oxford, EH/OUCA), 215-18.

de Jersey, P. 2000: Biga and better: Cunobelin's first gold. *Chris Rudd list* 54, 2-3.

de Jersey, P. 2000: Celtic coins (Coin Register 2000). *British Numismatic Journal* 70, 156-58.

de Jersey, P. 2001: Where and when? *Chris Rudd list* 56, 2-7. [regional classification and chronology]

de Jersey, P. 2001: Cunobelin's silver. *Britannia* 32, 1-44.

de Jersey, P. 2001: The volume of Celtic coinage found in Britain. *Chris Rudd list* 60, 2-4.

de Jersey, P. 2001: Celtic coins (Coin Register 2001). *British Numismatic Journal* 71, 177-80.

de Jersey, P. 2002: Volisios Dumnovellaunos and Co. *Chris Rudd list* 63, 2-3.

de Jersey, P. 2002: Cunobelin's silver. *Chris Rudd list* 63, 5-9.

de Jersey, P. 2002: Two Celtic oddities. *Spink Numismatic Circular* 110, 264-65.

de Jersey, P. 2002: AGR, and life after Cunobelin. *Chris Rudd list* 64, 5-8.

de Jersey, P. 2002: Cartimandua and Cartivellaunos. *Chris Rudd list* 66, 2-3. [also in *Treasure Hunting*, August 2002]

de Jersey, P. 2002: Celtic coins (Coin Register 2002). *British Numismatic Journal* 72, 191-94.

de Jersey, P. 2003: ALIIFF SCAVO and ALE SCA. *Chris Rudd list* 70, 4-6.

de Jersey, P. 2003: Minimum impact. *Chris Rudd list* 71, 2-4. [are minims associated with temple sites?]

de Jersey, P. 2003: Celtic coinage. In C. Alfaro and A. Burnett (eds.), *A survey of numismatic research 1996-2001* (Madrid, International Numismatic Commission/IAPN Special Publication no. 14), 219-36.

de Jersey, P. 2004: A mystery bronze. *Chris Rudd list* 73, 2-3. [?Gaulish bronze from Kirmington]

de Jersey, P. 2004: Review of J. Sills, "Gaulish and early British gold coinage". *Spink Numismatic Circular* 112, 13-14.

de Jersey, P. 2004: Sam. *Chris Rudd list* 74, 2-4.

de Jersey, P. 2004: A new Celtic inscription? *Chris Rudd list* 75, 6-7. [CAT on unit of Dias]

de Jersey, P. 2004: Celtic coins (Coin Register 2004). *British Numismatic Journal* 74, 201-03.

de Jersey, P. and Newman, J. 1995: Staters of Cunobelin from Shotley, Suffolk. *British Numismatic Journal* 65, 214-15.

de Jersey, P. and Newman, J. 1997: Iron Age coins from Barham, Suffolk. *British Numismatic Journal* 67, 93-95. [mostly Bury types, including distribution map]

de Jersey, P. and Newman, J. 2000: A hoard of Iron Age coins from near Woodbridge, Suffolk. *British Numismatic Journal* 70, 139-41. [mostly Clacton staters and quarters, including distribution map]

de Jersey, P. and Wickenden, N. 2004: A hoard of staters of Cunobelin and Dubnovellaunos from Great Waltham, Essex. *British Numismatic Journal* 74, 175-78.

Delestrée, L.-P. 1996: Quarts de statères dits «au bateau» en Gaule Belgique. *Revue Numismatique* 151, 29-50.

Delestrée, L.-P. 1997: Les monnayages d'or de la Gaule Belgique derivés du statère «à flan large». *Revue Numismatique* 152, 91-120.

Delestrée, L.-P. 2003: Un nouveau bronze de l'île de Bretagne en Gaule Belgique. *Cahiers Numismatiques* 40 (June, no. 156), 39-40. [Chichester cock bronze]

Delestrée, L.-P., Gendre, P. and Boisard, C. 2003: Monnaies celtiques de Bretagne insulaire trouvées en Gaule du Nord. *Cahiers Numismatiques* 40 (March 2003, no. 155), 11-19.

De Michaeli, C. 1992: The shape of the dies of the early staters of the Corieltauvi. *The Yorkshire Numismatist* 2, 5-9.

Dennis, M. 2002: Die alignments in Celtic coins? *Chris Rudd list* 62, 2-5.

Dennis, M. 2003: Review of S. C. Bean, The coinage of the Atrebates and Regni (2000). *Numismatic Chronicle* 163, 408-10.

Diack, M., Mason, S. and Perkins, D. 2000: North Foreland. *Current Archaeology* 168 (vol. 14, no. 12), 472-73. [illus. of hoard of 64 potins from settlement exc.]

Dobinson, C. and Denison, S. 1995: *Metal detecting and archaeology in England* (English Heritage/CBA).

Dunger, G. T. 1999: Unrecorded Celtic quarter staters from the Winchester area. *Spink Numismatic Circular* 107, 247. [new ?Atrebatic uninscribed]

Elsdon, S. M. 1997: *Old Sleaford revealed* (Oxford, Oxbow Monograph 91 [78 on cover], Nottingham Studies in Archaeology 2). [including chapter on mint debris, several other references to IA coinage]

Finn, P. 2000: Ashmore replicas - revisited. *Spink Numismatic Circular* 108, 50-54. [modern Celtic forgeries]

Fitzpatrick, A. 1990: A hoard of Iron Age class II potin coins from New Addington, Surrey. *Surrey Archaeological Collections* 80, 147-52.

Fitzpatrick, A. 1992: The roles of Celtic coinage in south east England. In M. Mays (ed.), *Celtic coinage: Britain and beyond* (Oxford, BAR 222), 1-32.

Fitzpatrick, A. 1993: Iron Age coin. In P. Cox and C. Hearne, *Redeemed from the Heath: the archaeology of the Wytch Farm Oilfield (1987-90)* (Dorset Natural History and Archaeological Society monograph 9), 157.

Fitzpatrick, A. 1996: The hoard of Iron Age class II potin coins from New Addington, Surrey: an addendum. *Surrey Archaeological Collections* 83, 238-39.

Fitzpatrick, A. 1996: The Celtic coin. In L. Cooper, "A Roman cemetery in Newarke Street, Leicester", *Transactions of the Leicestershire Archaeological and Historical Society* 70, 69. [probable Cunobelin bronze, residual in pit]

Fitzpatrick, A. 1997: Celtic coin. In A. P. Fitzpatrick, *Archaeological excavations on the route of the A27 Westhampnett bypass, West Sussex, 1992. Volume 2: the late Iron Age, Romano-British and Anglo-Saxon cemeteries* (Wessex Archaeology Report no. 12), 87-89. [British O quarter; other mentions throughout exc. report, indexed]

Forrest, R. 1994: Even more fakes, forgeries and fantasies. *Coin News* 30/7 (July 1994), 35-36. [line drawing of one IA]

Forrest, R. 1995: From Period Coins to Ashmore replicas. *Coin News* 32/10 (Oct. 1995), 36-39. [p. 39, six IA fakes]

Fournier, J. 1997: Un poincon monétaire gaulois pour statères unifaces belges. *Bulletin de la Societe Francaise de Numismatique* 52, 192-93.

Futcher, G. 1999: A field of "Golden Buttons". *Treasure Hunting* April 1999, 40-42. [hoard of 25 British Q, 33 G-B E]

Gannon, A., Voden-Decker, L. and Bland, R. (eds.) 2004: *Treasure Annual Report 2002* (Department for Culture, Media and Sport). [IA hoards, pp. 126-27]

Goodburn, R. 1989: British coins. In I. Stead and V. Rigby, *Verulamium: the King Harry Lane site* (English Heritage Archaeological Report 12), 12, 87.

Goodburn, R. 1992: The Celtic coins. In P. Crummy, Colchester Archaeological Report 6: excavations at Culver Street, the Gilberd School, and other sites in Colchester 1971-85 (Colchester Archaeological Trust), 294-95.

Graham, D. 2000: A Roman coin deposit on Frensham Common. *Bulletin of the Surrey Archaeological Society* 338, 6-7. [series of small votive pots, including nearly 400 coins, mostly Roman bronze but also IA quarter staters]

Green, M. 1992: The iconography of Celtic coins. In M. Mays (ed.), *Celtic coinage: Britain and beyond* (Oxford, BAR 222), 151-63.

Green, M. 1998: God in Man's image: thoughts on the genesis and affiliations of some Romano-British cult-imagery. *Britannia* 29, 17-30. [imagery on coins, pp. 21-22, including ram-headed snakes, boars]

Gregory, A. 1991: *Excavations in Thetford, 1980-1982, Fison Way. Vol. I* (East Anglian Archaeology Report 53).

Gregory, A. 1992: Snettisham and Bury: some new light on the earliest Icenian coinage. In M. Mays (ed.), *Celtic coinage: Britain and beyond* (Oxford, BAR 222), 47-68.

Gregory, A. 2001: Iron Age coins. In M. Flitcroft, *Excavation of a Romano-British settlement on the A149 Snettisham bypass, 1989* (East Anglian Archaeology 93), 51. [incl unique Norfolk wolf quarter; passing mention also at pp. 5, 15]

Gunstone, A. J. H. 1992: *SCBI 42. South-eastern museums. Ancient British, Anglo-Saxon and later coins to 1279.* (London, OUP/Spink). [including 451 IA coins]

Hamilton, S. 1998: Using elderly data bases. Iron Age pit deposits at the Caburn, East Sussex, and related sites. *Sussex Archaeological Collections* 136, 23-39. [brief mentions of potins from pit 37, pp. 28, 29, 31, 32, 33]

Hanworth, R. 1998: Wanborough coins. *Bulletin of the Surrey Archaeological Society* 319, 12-13. [re Symons (1998)]

Harrison, D. 1989: Celtic coins (Coin Register 1989). *British Numismatic Journal* 59, 222-27.

Harrison, D. 1990: Celtic coins (Coin Register 1990). *British Numismatic Journal* 60, 145-57.

Harrison, D. 1991: Celtic coins (Coin Register 1991). *British Numismatic Journal* 61, 143-49.

Harrison, D. 1992: The Celtic Coin Index. In M. Mays (ed.), *Celtic coinage: Britain and beyond* (Oxford, BAR 222), xv-xvi.

Haselgrove, C. 1989: Celtic coins found in Britain 1982-1987. *Bulletin of the Institute of Archaeology, University of London* 26, 1-75.

Haselgrove, C. 1989: Iron Age coin deposition at Harlow temple, Essex. *Oxford Journal of Archaeology* 8, 73-88.

Haselgrove, C. 1989: The Iron Age coins. In T. W. Potter and S. Trow (eds.), *Puckeridge-Braughing, Hertfordshire: the Ermine Street excavations 1971-2* (*Hertfordshire Archaeology* 10), 21-29.

Haselgrove, C. 1990: After Mack: Van Arsdell's insular Celtic coins. *Antiquity* 64, 416-18.

Haselgrove, C. 1992: Iron Age coinage and archaeology. In M. Mays (ed.), *Celtic coinage: Britain and beyond* (Oxford, BAR 222), 123-37.

Haselgrove, C. 1993: The development of British Iron-Age

coinage. *Numismatic Chronicle* 153, 31-63.

Haselgrove, C. 1994: Coinage and currency in Iron Age Wessex. In A. P. Fitzpatrick and E. L. Morris (eds.), *The Iron Age in Wessex: recent work* (AFEAF/Trust for Wessex Archaeology), 22-25.

Haselgrove, C. 1995: Potin coinage in Iron Age Britain, archaeology and chronology. In K. Gruel *et al.*, *Les potins gaulois* (*Gallia* 52), 117-27.

Haselgrove, C. 1996: Iron Age coinage: recent work. In T. C. Champion and J. Collis (eds.), *The Iron Age. Recent trends* (Sheffield), 67-85.

Haselgrove, C. 1997: Review of R. Hobbs, "British Iron Age coins in the British Museum". *Britannia* 28, 501-03.

Haselgrove, C. 1999: The development of Iron Age coinage in Belgic Gaul. *Numismatic Chronicle* 159, 111-68.

Hobbs, R. 1996: *British Iron Age coins in the British Museum* (London, British Museum Press).

Hobbs, R. 2000: The Portable Antiquities Scheme. Latest news. *The Searcher* 174 (Feb. 2000), 53-54. [p. 54, new reading of Prasutagus legend]

Holman, D. 1996: The coin. In K. Parfitt, *Iron Age burials from Mill Hill, Deal* (London, British Museum Press), 112-13. [Eppillus bronze]

Holman, D. 1998: Three further coins of SAM. *Spink Numismatic Circular* 106, 204.

Holman, D. 1999: *Sego* and *Duno*: reassessment and reinterpretation. *British Numismatic Journal* 69, 196-98.

Holman, D. 2000: Iron Age coinage in Kent: a review of current knowledge. *Archaeologia Cantiana* 120, 205-33.

Hooker, J. 2003: The meaning of the boar. *Chris Rudd list* 69, 2-4.

Hunt, A. T. 1998: Further finds from an unrecorded Romano-Celtic settlement. *Treasure Hunting* December 1998, 64-65. [Atrebatic, Durotrigan and continental coins from Isle of Wight]

Hunter, F. 1994: Celtic chicanery questioned. *Spink Numismatic Circular* 102, 259. ["carnyx" on Whaddon Chase stater]

Hunter, F. 1997: Iron Age coins in Scotland. *Proceedings of the Society of Antiquaries of Scotland* 127, 513-25. [also includes discussion of finds in northern England]

Hurst, D. 2001: Dobunnic tribal centres, commodities and trade: the South Worcestershire hoard, salt and pottery. *West Midlands Archaeology* 44, 84-93. [brief mention of hoard, discussion of location of Dobunni]

Hurter, S. 1995-96: Ashmore replicas, part I. *Bulletin on Counterfeits* 20/2, 19-28. [incl 5 British Celtic]

Hutcheson, N. 2004: *Later Iron Age Norfolk. Metalwork, landscape and society* (Oxford, BAR 361).

Ikins, T. G. 1995: Volisios, Vodesios, Vodenios - votive inscriptions on coins of ancient Britain. *Spink Numismatic Circular* 103, 182-83.

Kent, J. 1990: Review of R. D. Van Arsdell, "Celtic coinage of Britain". *Numismatic Chronicle* 150, 266-68.

Kiernan, P. 2001: The ritual mutilation of coins on Romano-British sites. *British Numismatic Journal* 71, 18-33. [includes Hayling Island coins, Durotrigan hoard]

King, A. and Soffe, G. 1998: Internal organisation and deposition at the Iron Age temple on Hayling Island. *Hampshire Studies 1998* (*Proceedings of the Hampshire Field Club and Archaeological Society* 53), 35-47.

Kretz, R. 1997: Correspondence. *Spink Numismatic Circular* 105, 377. [derivation of Tincomaros]

Kretz, R. 1998: The early gold staters of Tasciovanus - a reappraisal of the first series. *Spink Numismatic Circular* 106, 2-7.

Kretz, R. 1998: From Kentish lad to Essex man. The enigma of Dubnovellaunos. *Chris Rudd list* 31, 1-6.

Kretz, R. 1998: Correspondence. *Spink Numismatic Circular* 106, 358-59. [derivation of Tincomaros]

Kretz, R. 1999: On the track of the Norfolk wolf. *Chris Rudd list* 48, 3-9.

Kretz, R. 2000: The early gold staters of Tasciovanos - a postscript. *Spink Numismatic Circular* 108, 49. [1st series 'anomaly']

Kretz, R. 2000: The 'RICON' staters of Tasciovanos. *Spink Numismatic Circular* 108, 97-102.

Kretz, R. 2001: The quarter staters of Tasciovanos. *Spink Numismatic Circular* 109, 6-10.

Kretz, R. 2001: Tasciovanos' second coinage staters - a first classification. *Spink Numismatic Circular* 109, 234-43.

Kretz, R. 2002: The problem of Andoco... *Spink Numismatic Circular* 110, 267-71.

Laing, L. 1991: Types and prototypes in insular Celtic coinage. *Celtic Coin Bulletin* 1, 19-24.

Laing, L. 2000: Celtic coin motifs in other media. *Chris Rudd list* 51, 2-3.

Lesbre, R. 1998: Connaissez-vous Boudicca? *Cahiers Numismatiques* 35 (no. 138), 7-8. [illus. of VA792]

McFadden, E. J. 1993: New detail on a Celtic gold stater of the Cheriton type. *Classical Numismatic Review* 18/4, 5. [modern fake]

Martin, E. 1999: Suffolk in the Iron Age. In J. Davies and T. Williamson (eds.), *Land of the Iceni* (Centre of East Anglian Studies, University of Norwich), 45-99.

May, J. 1991: Iron Age coins from the site of the Romano-British temple at Thistleton: an interim note. *Celtic Coin Bulletin* 1, 25-27.

May, J. 1991: A new East Midlands inscription. *Celtic Coin Bulletin* 1, 28-30. [CAT]

May, J. 1992: Iron Age coins in Yorkshire. In M. Mays (ed.), *Celtic coinage: Britain and beyond* (Oxford, BAR 222), 93-111.

May, J. 1992: The earliest gold coinages of the Corieltauvi? In M. Mays (ed.), *Celtic coinage: Britain and beyond* (Oxford, BAR 222), 113-21. [scyphate quarters]

May, J. 1992: The order of the prototype gold staters of the Corieltauvi. *The Yorkshire Numismatist* 2, 1-4.

May, J. 1993: Coinage, settlement and society in the Late Iron Age of East Midland England. In *Proceedings of the XIth International Numismatic Congress, Brussels, 1991* (vol. II) (Louvain), 7-10.

May, J. 1994: Test cuts on a Corieltauvian stater? *Spink Numismatic Circular* 102, 3.

May, J. 1994: Coinage and the settlements of the Corieltauvi in east Midland Britain. *British Numismatic Journal* 64, 1-21.

May, J. 1996: Coins. In J. May, *Dragonby I* (Oxford, Oxbow Monograph 61), 217-22.

May, J. 1997: Lindsey sycphates. *Chris Rudd list* 29, 1-2.

May, J. 1998: Boudica - Britain's first Queen Victoria. *Chris Rudd list* 30, 3.

May, J. 1998: North East coast staters. *Chris Rudd list* 36, 2-3.

May, J. 1999: Minting coins in Iron Age Britain. *Coins and Antiquities* May 1999, 57-60.

May, J. 2000: Dumno Tigir Seno staters. *Chris Rudd list* 49, 4-5.

May, J. 2001: Review of J. Creighton, "Coins and Power in Late Iron Age Britain". *British Numismatic Journal* 71, 199-200.

May, J. 2002: Detective work on a domino stater by a consortium of sleuths. *Chris Rudd list* 64, 3-5.

Mays, M. 1992: Inscriptions on British Celtic coins. *Numismatic Chronicle* 152, 57-82.

Mays, M. (ed.) 1992: *Celtic coinage: Britain and beyond* (Oxford, BAR 222).

Mays, M. 1997: Review of R. Hobbs, "British Iron Age coins in the British Museum". *British Numismatic Journal* 67, 149-50.

Nash, D. 1998: Iron Age coins. In C. P. Clarke, *Excavations to the south of Chigwell Roman villa, Essex, 1977-81* (*East Anglian Archaeology* 83), 71. [five coins, one stratified in residual context]

Nash, D. and Sellwood, L. 1995: The Celtic coins. In K. Blockley, M. Blockley, P. Blockley, S. Frere and S. Stow (eds.), *Excavations in the Marlowe Car Park and surrounding areas. Part II: the finds* (The Archaeology of Canterbury volume V) (Canterbury Archaeological Trust), 922-26.

Northover, P. 1992: Materials issues in the Celtic coinage. In M. Mays (ed.), *Celtic coinage: Britain and beyond* (Oxford, BAR 222), 235-99.

O'Bee, M. 2002: The second coin of ATT. *Spink Numismatic Circular* 110, 62. [reprinted in *Chris Rudd list* 63 (2002), 9-10]

O'Bee, M. 2003: The third trefoil stater. *Chris Rudd list* 68, 3-4.

Orna-Ornstein, J. 1999: National treasures. *The Searcher* 167 (July 1999), 34-36. [pp. 34-35, brief details of Alton hoards]

Orton, C. 1997: Testing significance or testing credulity? *Oxford Journal of Archaeology* 16, 219-25. [Iceni hoards]

Overbeck, B. 1997: Keltisches Münzwesen. In International Numismatic Commission, *A survey of numismatic research 1990-1995* (Berlin, IAPN special publication 13), 143-64 [especially pp. 148-49]

Parkhouse, J. (ed.) 1997: Archaeological notes from the Buckinghamshire County Museum. *Records of Buckinghamshire* 39, 163-170. [p. 163, hoard of 15 Whaddon Chase staters and 23 British QB staters from Buckingham area]

Popescu, A. 2001: Coin finds from Norfolk, 2000. *Norfolk Archaeology* 43, 688-93. [pp. 688-90, 21 IA coins]

Popescu, A. 2002: Coin finds from Norfolk, 2001. *Norfolk Archaeology* 44, 137-49. [pp. 138, 142, 21 IA coins]

Priest, V., Clay, P. and Hill, J. 2003: Iron Age gold from Leicestershire. *Current Archaeology* 188 (November 2003), 358-62. [including J. Williams, 'The coins and the helmet', pp. 361-62]

Reynolds, J. 1997: The statistical analysis. In S. M. Elsdon, *Old Sleaford revealed* (Oxford, Oxbow Monograph 91 [78 on cover], Nottingham Studies in Archaeology 2), 56-59. [IA mint debris]

Robbins, K. and Bayley, J. 1997: Metallurgical analysis of coin pellet moulds and crucible fragments. In S. M. Elsdon, *Old Sleaford revealed* (Oxford, Oxbow Monograph 91 [78 on cover], Nottingham Studies in Archaeology 2), 59-64.

Robertson, A. (ed. R. Hobbs and T. V. Buttrey) 2000: *An inventory of Romano-British coin hoards* (London, RNS special publication 20). [pp. 438-39, index of hoards incl Celtic]

Robinson, P. 1991: A Durotrigian coin from Stonehenge. *Wiltshire Archaeological Magazine* 84, 119-20.

Robinson, P. 1993: Iron Age coins from Cunetio and Mildenhall. *Wiltshire Archaeological Magazine* 86, 147-49.

Robinson, P. 2000: The Dobunnic branched emblem, again. *Chris Rudd list 53*, 3.

Ross, A. 1999: The Bury diadem. *Chris Rudd list* 41, 3. [VA 80]

Roy, G. and Dunn, A. 1998: The Chessington hoard. *Treasure Hunting* December 1998, 29-30. [G-B A and C]

Rudd, C. 1991: The hidden treasure house: the Celtic coins of Britain. *Coin News* 28/10 (Oct. 1991), 42-45. [introductory]

Rudd, C. 1991: The flying farmer. *Coin News* 28/11 (Nov. 1991), 38-39. [Henry Mossop]

Rudd, C. 1992: The Nottingham Celts. *Coin News* 29/1 (Jan. 1992), 38-39. [work of J. May *et al.*]

Rudd, C. 1992: VA 1235-1: anatomy of a Celtic stater. *Coin News* 29/4 (Apr. 1992), 41-42.

Rudd, C. 1992: The Bristol forger. *Coin News* 29/9 (Sept. 1992), 33-34.

Rudd, C. 1992: Golden Locketts: ten stunning Celtic gold staters from the Richard Lockett collection. *Coin News* 29/10 (Oct. 1992), 36-37.

Rudd, C. 1993: South Worcestershire hoard of Celtic coins. *The Searcher* 9/2 (Nov. 1993), 8.

Rudd, C. 1994: War trumpet or snake? *Spink Numismatic Circular* 102, 262. ["carnyx" on Whaddon Chase stater]

Rudd, C. 1996: Coin hoards rename Celtic king. *Coin News* 33/7 (July 1996), 16. [Alton hoards, Tincomarus]

Rudd, C. 1998: Celtic coinage of Britain. *Coin Yearbook 1998*, 93-95. [introductory]

Rudd, C. 1998: Britain's first coins. *Coins and Antiquities* November 1998, 51-60.

Rudd, C. 1998: Duck Helmet. *Coin News* 35/5 (May 1998), 35. [new silver type]

Rudd, C. 1998: Verica and the fortune teller. *Coin News* 35/10 (Oct. 1998), 30. [V533 silver unit]

Rudd, C. 1998: Cunobelin and the shining one. *Coin News* 35/11 (Nov. 1998), 31. [V1963 bronze unit]

Rudd, C. 1998: Coins of King Prasutagus in Celtic hoard. *Coin News* 35/12 (Dec. 1998), 29. [SW Norfolk hoard]

Rudd, C. 1999: The hidden faces of Tasciovanus. *Coin News* 36/1 (Jan. 1999), 25.

Rudd, C. 1999: Esup R Asu and the owl. *Coin News* 36/2 (Feb. 1999), 25. [V924 silver unit]

Rudd, C. 1999: Norfolk god or Norfolk queen? *Coin News* 36/4 (Apr. 1999), 31. [V792 silver unit]

Rudd, C. 1999: The Burnham Market hoard. *Chris Rudd list* 41, 2. [also known as SW Norfolk hoard]

Rudd, C. 1999: Dating coins of the Eceni. *Chris Rudd list* 41, 4-5.

Rudd, C. 1999: A day in Oxford. *Chris Rudd list* 45, 2. [summary of papers given at Oxford conference, 5.5.1999]

Rudd, C. 1999: The minting process. *Chris Rudd list* 47, 2-3. [illustrations from Musée de Bretagne, Rennes catalogue]

Rudd, C. 2000: The Forncett hoard. *Chris Rudd list* 50, 6-7. [336 Iceni AR + 45 denarii]

Rudd, C. 2000: Husband of British queen changes his name. *Coin News* 37/3 (Mar. 2000), 27. [Prasutagus/Esuprastus]

Rudd, C. 2000: The face that launched 80,000 deaths. *Coin News* (Oct. 2000), 23-24. [illus of Bury A, VA 78]

Rudd, C. 2000: Were Celtic moneyers on drugs? The Celator (July 2000), 34-35, 38. [discussion of Creighton 2000]

Rudd, C. 2001: Tribal or regional? *Chris Rudd list* 55, 2-3. [use of tribal names, alternatives]

Rudd, C. 2001: The Boudica myth. *Chris Rudd list* 58, 5-11.

Rudd, C. 2001: Hengistbury Hairy. *The Celator* (Apr. 2001), 17-20. [Durotrigan cast bronze]

Rudd, C. 2002: Baby wolf found in Norfolk. *Coin News* 39/1 (Jan. 2002), 8. [Norfolk wolf quarter stater]

Rudd, C. 2002: A gripping idea. *Chris Rudd list* 65, 2-3. [interpretation of AGR]

Rudd, C. 2002: Solidu, king of Kent. *Chris Rudd list* 66, 4-7.

Rudd, C. 2002: Caesar and Hitler and Gallic War gold staters. *The Celator* (Dec. 2002), 21. [role of G-B E]

Rudd, C. 2003: A new Ale Sca type. *Chris Rudd list* 67, 3.

Rudd, C. 2003: Birdman, fact or fiction? *Coin News* 40/4 (Apr. 2003), 23-24. [evidence for feathers as IA decoration]

Rudd, C. 2003: First gold Lat Ison stater. *Chris Rudd list* 69, 8-9.

Rudd, C. 2003: Celtic treasure unearthed in Leicestershire. *Coin News* 40/6 (June 2003), 23-24. [E Leics. hoards]

Rudd, C. 2003: Celtic cow bone hoard. *Treasure Hunting* Nov. 2003, 15-18. [Sedgeford hoard]

Rudd, C. 2003: Celtic cash cow hoard. *Coin News* 40/10 (Oct. 2003), 22-23. [Sedgeford hoard]

Rudd, C. 2003: Druids and coins. *Chris Rudd list* 72, 2-4.

Rudd, C. 2003: Ash and the Dobunnic tree. *Chris Rudd list* 72, 7-15.

Rudd, C. 2004: Forger's die found in Hampshire. *The Searcher* 222 (Feb. 2004), 60-63.

Rudd, C. 2004: Celtic hoard may be linked to Caesar. *Treasure Hunting* (June 2004), 38-40. [Thurnham hoard; also *Coin News* 41/3 (Mar. 2004), 24-25]

Rudd, C. 2004: Aedic is Anted. *Chris Rudd list* 76, 6-7.

Rudd, C. 2004: Embargoed – State stops export of Celtic coin. *Coin News* 41/8 (Aug. 2004), 23-24. [Aliiff Scavo silver]

Rudd, C. 2004: Celtic gold hoards lost by slave traders? *The Searcher* 20/4 (Nov. 2004), 52-53. [Beverley/Driffield hoards; also in *World Coin News* (Sept. 2004), 28-30; *Treasure Hunting* (Nov. 2004), 34]

Rudling, D. 1991: Two Iron Age silver coins found in East Sussex. *Sussex Archaeological Collections* 129, 245.

Rudling, D. 1992: An Iron Age gold coin from South Malling. *Sussex Archaeological Collections* 130, 238. [G-B E stater]

Rudling, D. 1999: Pits and potin coins: a report on a new potin coin find from the Caburn. In P. Drewett and S. Hamilton, 'Marking time and making space. Excavations and landscape studies at the Caburn hillfort, East Sussex, 1996-98', *Sussex Archaeological Collections* 137, 7-37. [pp. 28-29, including illus. of cl. IL potin]

Rudling, D. 2001: Loose change. *Sussex Past and Present* 93, 10-11. [coins at Fishbourne, including Tincomarus quarter and minim]

Rudling, D. 2003: All change. *Sussex Past and Present* 99, 6-7. [coins at Fishbourne, incl Carthage bronze and V562 minim]

Scheers, S. 1992: Celtic coin types in Britain and their Mediterranean origins. In M. Mays (ed.), *Celtic coinage: Britain and beyond* (Oxford, BAR 222), 33-46.

Sellwood, L. 1993: The Celtic coins. In A. Woodward and P. Leach, *The Uley shrines. Excavation of a large ritual complex on West Hill, Uley, Gloucestershire: 1977-9* (London, English Heritage Archaeological Report 17), 82. [three Dobunnic silver coins; also discussion at pp. 21, 23, 80, 83, 85, 328 and fiche 1]

Sills, J. 1991: Interpreting the coin legends of the Corieltauvi. *Celtic Coin Bulletin* 1, 31-32.

Sills, J. 1995: The Volisios legend on coins of the Corieltauvi. *Spink Numismatic Circular* 103, 260.

Sills, J. 1996: The summer of 54 BC. *Spink Numismatic Circular* 104, 334-35.

Sills, J. 1997: The earliest British coins: dating the undated. *Chris Rudd list* 27.

Sills, J. 1997: Coinage of the British coalition against Caesar. *Spink Numismatic Circular* 105, 324-26.

Sills, J. 1998: The ABC of Westerham gold. *Chris Rudd list* 33, 2-4.

Sills, J. 1999: Early Corieltauvian gold. *Chris Rudd list* 43, 2-4.

Sills, J. 1999: A Philip III stater from Kent. *Chris Rudd list* 46, 4.

Sills, J. 1999: Three Philippus imitations from Essex. *Chris Rudd list* 46, 5-6.

Sills, J. 2000: The Ingoldisthorpe stater and the study of Iron Age coins. *Chris Rudd list* 49, 2-3.

Sills, J. 2000: The silver coinage of Bodvoc. *Chris Rudd list* 52, 2-3.

Sills, J. 2000: Review of J. Creighton, "Coins and power in late Iron Age Britain". *Spink Numismatic Circular* 108, 162-63.

Sills, J. 2000: Crossed lines staters. *Chris Rudd list* 53, 2-3. [Gallo-Belgic B]

Sills, J. 2001: A new trumpet type half stater. *Chris Rudd list* 58, 4-5.

Sills, J. 2003: Imitation Philippi from Britain. *Chris Rudd list* 69, 4-6.

Sills, J. 2003: Celtic or Roman? AGR and ESVPRASTO. *Chris Rudd list* 70, 2-4.

Sills, J. 2003: *Gaulish and early British gold coinage* (London, Spink).

Sills, J. 2003: Dobunnic staters: a new sequence. *Chris Rudd list* 72, 4-7.

Sitch, B. 1993: Thomas Sheppard, the Morfitts of Atwick and Allen coin number 223. *Yorkshire Archaeological Journal* 65, 11-19.

Smith, J. B. 1998: More votive finds from Woodeaton, Oxfordshire. *Oxoniensia* 63, 147-85. [pp. 177, 182-183, sheet bronze with impression of Cunobelin classic stater]

Stead, I. M. 1991: The Snettisham treasure: excavations in

1990. *Antiquity* 65, 447-65.

Stead, I. M. 1998: *The Salisbury hoard* (Stroud, Tempus). [coin from Berkshire, p. 120; Iceni hoards, p. 135; Essendon coins, pp. 144-45; Snettisham bowl hoard, pp. 146-48, 149; Wanborough, p. 149]

Stevens, W. F. 1999: The production of Celtic coins in Britain - how and where? *Coin News* 36/7 (July 1999), 24-25.

Stevens, W. F. 2000: Celtic coinage in late Iron Age Britain. *Coin News* 37/9 (Sept. 2000), 23-25.

Stevens, W. F. 2001: Uffington and all that. *Coin News* 38/1 (Jan. 2001), 21-23. [horses and other animal imagery]

Stevens, W. F. 2001: The circle and the wheel. *Coin News* 38/3 (Mar. 2001), 26-28. ['solar and agrarian symbolism']

Stevens, W. F. 2002: Every picture coins a story – part I. *Coin News* 39/6 (June 2002), 25-27. [introductory]

Stevens, W. F. 2002: Every picture coins a story – part II. *Coin News* 39/7 (July 2002), 26-28. [introductory]

Stevens, W. F. 2002: Every picture coins a story – part III. *Coin News* 39/8 (Aug. 2002), 35-36. [introductory]

Stevens, W. F. 2002: Tribal emblems on late Iron Age coinage – numismatic statements of tribal unity. *Coin News* 39/11 (Nov. 2002), 23-24.

Stevens, W. F. 2003: Heads it is... or from a head to a wreath and back again. *Coin News* 40/9 (Sept. 2003), 22-24. [heads in profile on IA coinage]

Stevens, W. F. 2004: Face value... the cult of the head and other Celtic beliefs represented on late Iron Age tribal coinage. *Coin News* 41/1 (Jan. 2004), 27-29.

Stevens, W. F. 2004: Cunobelin – king of the Britons – his power and prestige as reflected in his coinage. *Coin News* 41/6 (June 2004), 23-25.

Symons, D. 1989: A silver unit of Andoco. *Spink Numismatic Circular* 97, 289.

Symons, D. 1990: Two Celtic coins from the Kidderminster area. *Transactions of the Worcestershire Archaeological Society* series 3, 12, 67-71. [fragmentary Dobunnic stater, quarter stater of Cunobelin]

Symons, D. 1990: Celtic coinage of Britain: some amendments and additions. *Spink Numismatic Circular* 98, 48-50.

Symons, D. 1990: Further Celtic coins from the Finney collection. *Spink Numismatic Circular* 98, 268-72.

Symons, D. 1991: Recent additions to the Finney collection. *Spink Numismatic Circular* 99, 112-13.

Symons, D. 1992: British Celtic coins added to the Finney collection, 1991. *Spink Numismatic Circular* 100, 226-27.

Symons, D. 1992: Some new forgeries of Celtic coins. *Spink Numismatic Circular* 100, 149.

Symons, D. 1993: The Finney collection - British Celtic acquisitions, 1992. *Spink Numismatic Circular* 101, 188-89.

Symons, D. 1997: Some Iron Age coins from Wanborough temple. *Bulletin of the Surrey Archaeological Society* 312, 8-9. [list of 22 coins more or less certainly from Wanborough, in Birmingham Museum]

Symons, D. 1998: Q. "When is a horse not a horse?". *Spink Numismatic Circular* 106, 260-61.

Symons, D. 1999: Iron Age coins. In P. J. Watson, D. J. Symons, P. J. Wise and T. Bridges, "Antiquities from Surrey in West Midlands Museums", *Surrey Archaeological Collections* 86, 262-63. [Finney collection, certainly or probably from Wanborough]

Symons, D. 1999: Iron Age coins. In P. J. Watson, D. J. Symons, P. J. Wise, T. Bridges and S. Lamb, "Antiquities from Norfolk in West Midlands Museums", *Norfolk Archaeology* 43, 336-37. [Finney collection]

Symons, D. 2000: Iron Age coin. In P. J. Watson, P. J. Wise, D. J. Symons, D. A. Ford and T. Bridges, "Antiquities from Yorkshire in West Midlands Museums", *Yorkshire Archaeological Journal* 72, 3-4. [Dumnoc Tigir Seno stater, ex Lightcliffe?]

Symons, D. and Watson, P. 1998: Worcestershire material added to the collections of the department of antiquities, Birmingham Museum and Art Gallery - 1975-1998. *The Recorder* (newsletter of the Worcestershire Archaeological Society) 57, 11-12. [3 EISV staters, 1 VEP CORF]

Talbot, J. 2002: New East Anglian stater. *Chris Rudd list* 61, 2-3.

Talbot, J. 2003: A new example of the 'Eyelash Crescent' Iceni stater. *Chris Rudd list* 69, 6-7.

Tindall, A. 1993: An Iron Age coin from near Nantwich. *Cheshire Past* 2, 5. [uninscribed silver unit of Corieltauvi]

Trott, K. and Tomalin, D. 2003: The maritime role of the island of Vectis in the British pre-Roman Iron Age. *International Journal of Nautical Archaeology* 32, 158-181. [several mentions, maps of coinage]

Van Arsdell, R. D. 1989: *Celtic coinage of Britain* (Spink).

Van Arsdell, R. D. 1989: Take out the gold, but keep the colour. *Spink Numismatic Circular* 97, 82-83.

Van Arsdell, R. D. 1989: The quarter staters of Commius. *Spink Numismatic Circular* 97, 115.

Van Arsdell, R. D. 1989: Celtic chicanery II - the hidden face on an Atrebatic stater. *Spink Numismatic Circular* 97, 152.

Van Arsdell, R. D. 1989: The face on the defaced die staters. *Spink Numismatic Circular* 97, 190-91.

Van Arsdell, R. D. 1989: The silver minims of Commius. *Spink Numismatic Circular* 97, 289.

Van Arsdell, R. D. 1989: A new (but illegible) inscription on a Cantiian stater. *Spink Numismatic Circular* 97, 323.

Van Arsdell, R. D. 1989: The Badbury-Shapwick hoard and the date of the Maiden Castle coins from Sir Mortimer Wheeler's 1934-37 excavations. *Oxford Journal of Archaeology* 8, 347-51.

Van Arsdell, R. D. 1991: The Thurrock type coin. In N. Sharples, *Maiden Castle: excavations and field survey 1985-6* (HBMC Archaeological Report 19), 155-56.

Van Arsdell, R. D. 1991: Coins. In B. W. Cunliffe and C. Poole, *Danebury volume 5. The excavations, 1979-88: the finds* (CBA Research Report 73), 320-28.

Van Arsdell, R. D. 1992: Money supply and credit in Iron Age Britain. In M. Mays (ed.), *Celtic coinage: Britain and beyond* (Oxford, BAR 222), 139-50.

Van Arsdell, R. D. 1992: Inscription on Cunobeline ship type confirmed. *Spink Numismatic Circular* 100, 45.

Van Arsdell, R. D. 1992: Three new Celtic staters. *Spink Numismatic Circular* 100, 80. [V346, V725, V759]

Van Arsdell, R. D. 1992: Metallurgical and metrological analysis of pre-dynastic staters in Britain I - the Corieltauvi. *Spink Numismatic Circular* 100, 151.

Van Arsdell, R. D. 1992: The coinage of Queen Boudicca, an update. *Spink Numismatic Circular* 100, 306-07.

Van Arsdell, R. D. 1992: Trade routes in Celtic Britain via trend surface analysis. *Spink Numismatic Circular* 100, 346-49.

Van Arsdell, R. D. 1993: Die-cutting expertise in Celtic Britain. *Spink Numismatic Circular* 101, 153.

Van Arsdell, R. D. 1993: An anomalous Yarmouth stater. *Spink Numismatic Circular* 101, 155-56.

Van Arsdell, R. D. 1993: Metallurgical and metrological analysis of pre-dynastic staters in Britain II - the Atrebates. *Spink Numismatic Circular* 101, 117.

Van Arsdell, R. D. 1993: Bad day at Flat Rock. *Spink Numismatic Circular* 101, 283. [flan production techniques]

Van Arsdell, R. D. 1993: Coin scales in late pre-Roman Iron Age Britain.*Oxford Journal of Archaeology* 12, 361-65.

Van Arsdell, R. D. 1993: The recently stolen Holdenhurst hoard and coins from the Bushe-Fox excavations at Hengistbury - corrections to the record. *Spink Numismatic Circular* 101, 350.

Van Arsdell, R. D. 1994: Money supply and coin circulation in Dobunnic territory. In *The Coinage of the Dobunni* (Oxford, OUCA Monograph 38, Studies in Celtic Coinage 1), 1-65.

Van Arsdell, R. D. 1994: Two new Cantian coins. *Spink Numismatic Circular* 102, 6.

Van Arsdell, R. D. 1994: Celtic chicanery IV - the war trumpet. *Spink Numismatic Circular* 102, 103.

Van Arsdell, R. D. 1994: The Wanborough "hoard": a reconstruction. *Spink Numismatic Circular* 102, 209-10.

Van Arsdell, R. D. 1994: Clashed dies and the organization of Verica's mint. *Spink Numismatic Circular* 102, 402-03.

Van Arsdell, R. D. 1995: Some recent discoveries. *Spink Numismatic Circular* 103, 3. [V145, V147, "carnyx"]

Van Arsdell, R. D. 1995: A Boudiccan coin from the German Limes. *Spink Numismatic Circular* 103, 87.

Van Arsdell, R. D. 1996: A statistical analysis of Icenian coin hoards. *Oxford Journal of Archaeology* 15, 235-43.

Van Arsdell, R. D. 1996: Muddying the Atrebatic waters. *Spink Numismatic Circular* 104, 444.

Van Arsdell, R. D. 1998: It's 1960 again - is everyone feeling much better now? *Spink Numismatic Circular* 106, 104-05.

Van Arsdell, R. D. 2001: Appreciating Celtic coins. *Chris Rudd list* 57, 4-5. [reprinted from Van Arsdell 1989]

Van Arsdell, R. D. 2002: Celtic Coinage 2001. *Spink Numismatic Circular* 110, 12. [review of conference]

Van Arsdell, R. D. and Northover, P. 2004: Ancient British coins. In R. Havis and H. Brooks (eds.), *Excavations at Stansted Airport, 1986-91. Volume 1: Prehistoric and Romano-British* (East Anglian Archaeology Report 107), 115-20. [potin hoard, not illustrated]

Walbank, J. 1999: Yorkshire's golden harvest. *The Searcher* 165 (May 1999), 43-44. [Silsden hoard]

Walker, C. 2004: Concerning a silver unit of Verica ruler of the Atrebates. *Spink Numismatic Circular* 112, 295-96. [V505, alleged constellation of Leo in lion's mane]

Ward, A. 1992: Treasure Trove and the law of theft. *International Journal of Cultural Property* 1, 195-98. [case of R v. Hancock, Wanborough silver coins; not seen]

Watson, J., Seymour, D. J., [sic - Symons] Wise, P. J., Bridges, T. and Lamb, S. 1997: Antiquities from Sussex in West Midlands Museums. *Sussex Archaeological Collections* 135, M17-20. [not checked, but includes IA coins]

Watson, J., Symons, D. J., Ford, D. A. and Wise, P. J. 1994-97: Antiquities from Berkshire in West Midlands Museums.

Berkshire Archaeological Journal 75, 121-24. [coins from Finney legacy to Birmingham, listed by Symons, pp. 123-24]

Watson, J., Symons, D. J., Wise, P. J., Bridges, T. and Lamb, S. 1996-97: Antiquities from Northamptonshire in West Midlands Museums. *Northamptonshire Archaeology* 27, 184-85. [p. 184, quarter stater of Tasciovanus]

Watson, J., Wise, P. J., Symons, D. J. and Bridges, T. 1997: Antiquities from Oxfordshire in West Midlands Museums. *Oxoniensia* 62, 309-13. [two coins from Finney legacy to Birmingham, listed by Symons, pp. 310-11]

Wellington, I. 1999: An addition to the Trinovantian coinage. *Spink Numismatic Circular* 107, 47. [North Thames bronze]

Wellington, I. 2001: Iron Age coinage on the Isle of Wight. *Oxford Journal of Archaeology* 20, 39-57.

Wellington, I. 2003: Cross-Channel relations and the lightweight silver coinages of central southern Britain. In Humphrey, J. (ed.), *Re-searching the Iron Age* (University of Leicester, School of Archaeology and Ancient History, Leicester Archaeology Monographs 11), 35-43.

Wickenden, N. 1999: The Great Leighs Gallo-Belgic hoard. *Coins and Antiquities* January 1999, 39-40.

Williams, D. 2000: A newly-discovered Roman temple and its environs: excavations at Wanborough in 1999. *Bulletin of the Surrey Archaeological Society* 336, 2-6. [?44 IA coins, Tincomarus silver and Verica gold illustrated]

Williams, D. 2000: Wanborough Roman temple. *Current Archaeology* 14 (no. 167), 434-37. [photos of ten Atrebatic coins]

Williams, J. H. C. 1994: Ancient British forger's coin-die. *British Museum Magazine* 20 (Winter 1994), 20. [Gallo-Belgic C obverse? see May, this volume]

Williams, J. H. C. 1998: Imitation or invention? A new coin of Tasciovanus. *Spink Numismatic Circular* 106, 350-51.

Williams, J. H. C. 1998: Delete-undelete: Mack 280 and early British silver. *Numismatic Chronicle* 158, 53-61. [type now known to bear inscription of Addedomaros]

Williams, J. H. C. 2000: Iron Age coin adds new king to history of Britain. *British Museum Magazine* 37 (summer 2000), 5. [coins apparently reading Esuprasto]

Williams, J. H. C. 2000: The silver coins from East Anglia attributed to King Prasutagus of the Iceni - a new reading of the obverse inscription. *Numismatic Chronicle* 160, 276-81.

Williams, J. H. C. 2001: Coin inscriptions and the origin of writing in pre-Roman Britain. *British Numismatic Journal* 71, 1-17.

Williams, J. H. C. 2002: Pottery stamps, coin designs, and writing in late Iron Age Britain. In A. E. Cooley (ed.), *Becoming Roman, writing Latin? Literacy and epigraphy in the Roman West* (Portsmouth, Rhode Island; Journal of Roman Archaeology Supplement 48), 135-49.

Williams, J. H. C. 2003: Iron-Age and Roman coins. *British Numismatic Journal* 73, 44-57.

Williams, J. H. C. and Hobbs, R. 2003: Coin hoards and ritual in Iron Age Leicestershire. *Minerva* 14/4 (July/Aug. 2003), 55-56.

Wilthew, P. 1991: Examination and analysis of coin pellet moulds from Rochester. In A. C. Harrison, "Excavation of a Belgic and Roman site at 50-54 High Street, Rochester", *Archaeologia Cantiana* 109, 49-50.

Wise, P. J. 1995: The Bedworth hoard of Celtic coins. *British Numismatic Journal* 65, 215-17.

Early potin coinage in Britain: an update

Colin Haselgrove

Less than 20 years ago, it was generally thought that the Kentish Flat-Linear potin series, starting c. 100 BC or a little earlier, represented the earliest British base metal coinage, the only coinage in use before this period being Gallo-Belgic gold types (e.g. Haselgrove 1988). In 1987, however, a hoard of 2000 coins was found at Corringham, near Thurrock (Essex), which was dramatically to alter this perception. The coins in the hoard belonged to a hitherto unrecognised potin series, the earliest examples of which still bore clear affinities with their ultimate prototype – the late third or early second century BC bronze coinage of the Greek city of Massalia (Marseille) in southern France, from which the potin coinages of central Gaul are also derived (Allen 1980). Prior to 1987, potins resembling those in the Thurrock find had from time to time been found in Britain, including a similar, smaller hoard found in 1979 near Folkestone (Holman forthcoming), but these were assumed to be imports from central Gaul (Allen 1971; Haselgrove 1988), which they closely resembled.

The Thurrock hoard is still not fully published, but Van Arsdell included a typology of the contents in his 1989 catalogue. He suggested that the coinage was local to Essex and had been inspired by early Flat-Linear types (Van Arsdell 1989, 320-21). Following the publication of his catalogue, new finds began to be regularly reported, whilst a number of previous discoveries were now recognised to be of this type. By the early 1990s, there was enough information for me to put forward an alternative model for the series, as part of a more general review of potin coinage in Britain (Haselgrove 1995). Noting that the main concentration of findspots of Thurrock potins was in Kent rather than north of the Thames in Essex, I suggested that Kent was in fact their home. Moreover, given the resemblance that the best specimens bore to the bronze coinage of Massalia or close Gaulish copies such as LT 5284, I also argued that the Thurrock potins were more likely to be the prototypes for the Flat-Linear Kentish types – which must therefore have succeeded them – rather than vice versa (*ibid.*, 118-19, Fig 55).

The only archaeological dating for the Thurrock types was provided by a coin found in the 1984-85 excavations at Maiden Castle, Dorset (Sharples 1991, 155). This was recovered from a horizon containing pottery dated to the late second century BC. Since this was earlier than the date that Van Arsdell (1989) had proposed for the series, the excavator suggested that there might have been a recording error (Sharples 1991), although I personally could see no reason to discount the on-site interpretation. Moreover, a certain amount of support for an early dating was provided by the Flat-Linear potins, which regularly occur in stratified contexts dating before the mid first century BC (Haselgrove 1988; 1995, 121-24). If these derived from the Thurrock types, the latter should be earlier still.

On balance, I therefore felt justified proposing a late second century BC date for the Thurrock types, at the same time suggesting that there might be a connection between their adoption and the import of Gallo-Belgic A and B gold staters and quarter-staters from northern France at broadly the same period (Haselgrove 1995, 124). One other point was the existence of an apparently separate series of early Massalia imitations from the Paris area of northern France (Mitard 1978). At the time, this series was dated to the period of the Gallic war, in keeping with the very late chronology for potin coinage then in vogue among French numismatists. However, there were hints that it might in fact be rather earlier, in which case some kind of relationship to the Kentish series could not be entirely ruled out (Haselgrove 1995, 120).

In the intervening ten years, important new publications with a bearing on these issues have appeared on both sides of the Channel. In Britain, Holman (2000) has carried out a much-needed new study of the Iron Age coinages of Kent, whilst de Jersey (1999) has undertaken a survey of exotic Iron Age imports, including Gaulish imitations of Massalia bronzes. In France, an earlier chronology for potin has gained widespread acceptance, following a groundbreaking study by Guichard *et al.* (1993), and there is now very little doubt that potin was introduced into Belgic Gaul before the mid second century BC (Pion 1996; Haselgrove 1999). Delestrée (1999) has reviewed the Paris Basin series itself, whilst Sills (2003) has comprehensively reassessed the earliest gold coinages on both sides of the Channel.

In this paper, I propose to take a fresh look at the attribution and dating of both the British and the French series of early Massalia potins in the light of the information that is now available, beginning with the Thurrock types. I will then turn to the more complex issue of whether the Thurrock and Flat-Linear potin types had similar or different functions and the likely chronological relationship of both series to the earliest gold coinages used in Britain.

Attribution and typology

As of December 2001, the Celtic Coin Index (CCI) had records of finds of Thurrock potins from a total of 117 different parishes, of which over three-fifths are in Kent (61.5%). By number, the disparity is much greater still: many of the Kentish finds are multiple, comprising several coins and involving a number of locations in the same parish, whereas with the exception of Thurrock, finds from elsewhere in England are of one or two coins at most. Coins are attested from a minimum of 222 locations, of which all but forty-six are in Kent (79.3%). As Figure 1 shows, the main concentration of findspots is in east Kent, east of the river Stour including the Island of Thanet, with a secondary cluster of finds around the Medway valley and along the edge of the North Downs. By number of coins, the focus on east Kent is much greater, with 406 Thurrock coins recorded from findspots east of the river Stour, against only forty examples from the rest of the county (Holman 2000, 221, Table 2).

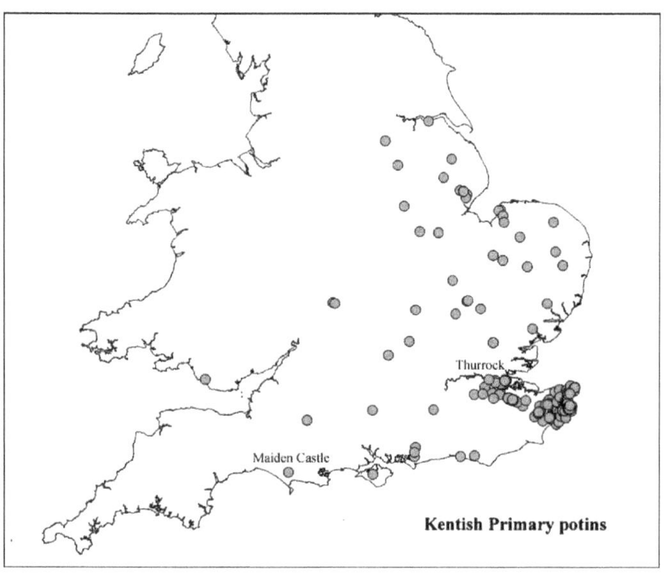

Figure 1. The distribution of Kentish Primary potins in Britain (based on data from the CCI).

We must allow for a certain amount of bias towards Kent in general and the east of the county in particular, due to Holman's work in recording finds made there since the early 1990s, when the Kent Iron Age Coin project was set up (*ibid.*, 205). Between 1992-2001, more coins were reported to the CCI from Kent than from the other 'high-density' counties of Essex, West Sussex and Hertfordshire combined (de Jersey 2003). The establishment of the Portable Antiquities Scheme is starting to redress this imbalance in recording, but it will take time (Worrell forthcoming).

Even allowing for over-representation of Kentish provenances, there is little doubt that the Thurrock series had its home in Kent, most probably in east Kent, which was certainly the primary focus of deposition. This view obtains further support from the numbers of coins that have been found relative to other Kentish types. As Holman (2000, Table 2) shows, Thurrocks have easily overtaken Flat-Linear potins – known since the nineteenth century – as the commonest Iron Age coin find in Kent; a total of 343 Flat-Linear potins are known from finds in the county (counting hoards as one coin), as against 446 Thurrock potins. Moreover, whilst the latter figure includes a few coins once thought to be Gaulish and now reattributed, e.g. two from the excavations in Canterbury, the vast majority are new detector finds. Why this prolific series should have remained essentially 'undetected' until the late twentieth century is a question to which I return below.

Although their chronology is yet to be discussed, I propose here to adopt Holman's terminology (*ibid.*, 206) and henceforth refer to the Thurrock potins as the 'Kentish Primary series'. This not only more accurately reflects the apparent area of origin, but is also less open to confusion than 'early Massalia imitations', the term used in Haselgrove (1995). In that article, I suggested that the Flat-Linear potin series proper, beginning with Allen's (1971) type B, derived from the Kentish Primary series, via the coins that Allen classified as type A. The early class A coins (VA 102) are cast in relief and have other features which point to their derivation from the earlier, better style Kentish Primary types, which if true might mean that the two series overlapped chronologically. The later class A types have designs scribed into the mould with a stylus, probably for ease of production but possibly under the influence of the well-known Gaulish series with an outlined helmeted head (LT 7388-7405).

Whilst the typological arguments appear still to hold good, the question of the geographical origins of the Flat-Linear series has become more complex. When I last wrote about the topic, the distribution of the Class A types appeared to focus on the Medway region (Haselgrove 1995, fig. 55). This made me wonder whether the Flat-Linear types might in fact have originated on the western margins of the Kentish Primary series. If so, the two series could well have evolved in parallel for a period, as the process of derivation seemed to require. In the intervening period, however, several Class A coins have been recorded in east Kent (information from CCI), where the other early Flat-Linear types are also fairly common (D. Holman, pers. comm.), which might suggest geographical continuity there.

On the other hand, the overall total for Flat-Linear potins is higher in east Kent too (Holman 2000). The Flat-Linear coins were certainly used extensively in the area to the east of the river Stour, but it may be that in this case the apparent focus on east Kent *is* misleading. As Holman has noted, Kentish Primary predominate 2:1 over Flat-Linear I coins in east Kent, but this ratio is reversed in the Medway zone, whilst west of the Darent, they are in a minority of 1:4 (albeit based on far fewer findspots). The trend is similar for the Flat-Linear II coins; from being in a minority of 1:5 in east Kent, the ratio falls to 1:2 in central Kent, whilst west of the

Darent, they are in the majority by as much as 6:1 (Holman 2000, 220-24).

Assuming that these figures have not been seriously distorted by differences in the relative volumes of the two series, they reinforce an apparent geographical trend about which I had previously commented. Over time, the centre of gravity of potin circulation in Britain appears to shift from east to west, up the Thames estuary (Haselgrove 1988, 116; 1995, 125), and it is possible that some of the Flat-Linear II coins may have been issued north of the Thames (Haselgrove 1988, 117; Holman 2000, 224).[1] They would thus have overlapped in date with the earliest uninscribed Kentish struck bronze issues, neatly explaining why the two groups show similar patterns of datable associations (Haselgrove 1995, 122, fig. 58).

Equally, whatever caused the export of Flat-Linear I potins from their presumptive home territory in either eastern or central Kent to areas like east Sussex and the lower Thames Valley, this apparently happened independently of the dispersal of Kentish Primary potins outside their core circulation. As Figure 1 shows, the majority of findspots for the latter series outside south-east England are in East Anglia and the East Midlands, with a lesser scatter along the South Coast; there is also a noticeable void in the Thames Valley. By contrast, the Flat-Linear coins, whilst also common enough finds along the South Coast (though not on the same sites), tend not to occur north of the Wash and in northern East Anglia.

The various close imitations of Massalia bronzes (cast or struck) imported in Britain display the same focus on east Kent as the early British potins (de Jersey 1999). There may be some recording bias, but as de Jersey notes (*ibid.*, 203), their distribution does differ from other, later central Gaulish imports found in Britain, suggesting that the difference is a real one. The precise origin of most of these 'Massalia' bronzes is uncertain, but amongst them are types which could have provided the immediate inspiration for the Kentish Primary series, such as a pair of bronze coins of heavy weight, in excellent style, apparently struck onto cast flans found at Worth; although not potins as such, their shiny black appearance suggests a high tin alloy (Holman 2005, 271). Whatever their derivation, the presence of these 'Massalia' bronzes in Britain should probably be seen in the same context as other pre-Roman imports of Greek and Punic bronzes, of which there is mounting evidence. The Worth finds also include potins with slight stylistic differences to the Kentish Primary series, which may therefore belong to the Paris Basin series (*ibid.*).

Despite their shared focus on eastern and central Kent, the Kentish Primary and Flat-Linear potin types are otherwise mutually exclusive to quite a remarkable degree. Both series were hoarded, but *not* together. Similarly, whilst from Allen type B onward, the Flat-Linear potins are among the commonest Iron Age coin types found in excavations in Britain (Haselgrove 1987), I know of only three sites, all in east Kent and examined below, with excavated coins belonging to both series. I may have overlooked some other instances, but not, I believe, many. There are metal-detector finds of both types from the same location, but in most cases, the nature of the association - if any - is unknown. The one major exception is Worth, where some 70 Kentish Primary and 24 Flat-Linear potins have been found along with other types, associated with an Iron Age site underlying the late Roman temple (Holman 2005).

Based on the typological and distributional evidence, it still seems to me most likely that the Kentish Primary series represents an earlier stratum of coinage, from which the Flat-Linear types evolved and diverged. We must now however consider what archaeological evidence for their date has come to light since the mid 1990s.

Archaeological evidence for the dating of the Kentish Primary series

A later third or early second century BC upper limit for the Kentish Primary series is given by the medium bronze coins of Massalia from which all the butting-bull potin series derive. The parent type is not well dated however, whilst the exact prototype is anyway in doubt, so that in practice the date given by the inception of other imitations like the Paris Basin types may be as useful. The lower limit is likely to be within the second century BC, given the predominantly late middle Iron Age associations of the early Flat-Linear types B-H, which were themselves supplanted by types J-L before the mid first century BC (Haselgrove 1995, 121-22, fig. 57). Due to the theoretical possibility of overlap between the Kentish Primaries and the Flat-Linear I types, as well as the suspected persistence of some 'middle Iron Age' ceramic traditions into the first century BC, this date, too, is at best approximate.

What further help can site evidence provide? In contrast to a decade ago, when only one excavated find was recorded, Kentish Primaries are now known from eleven sites where there has been some excavation. Apart from an unstratified discovery made during the excavations of the mid to late Iron Age settlement and Roman villa at Stanwick (Northamptonshire) (Curteis 2001),[2] the additional finds are all in east Kent, three on Thanet, the others close by (Figure 2). Most of the coins are new discoveries (from Ickham, Manston, Margate, Newington, North Foreland, Sutton, and Worth), but they include three that were originally identified as Gaulish imports (from Canterbury and Richborough). The Ickham coin is from a Roman watermill in the old course of the Little Stour and can be discounted for dating purposes; it came from a superficial layer (Haselgrove forthcoming 1). The excavation yielded numerous Roman issues of Flavian and later date, but only one other certain Iron Age coin: an uninscribed Kentish struck bronze (Allen LY7).

Both Primary potins from Canterbury are from late Roman contexts, one from the 1950s excavations on the city wall (Haselgrove 1987, 451, CA69), the other from the Marlowe site (*ibid.*, 450, CA 54). The late Iron Age occupation at Canterbury is not thought to have started before the mid first century BC (e.g. Haselgrove 1987, 139-45; Macpherson-Grant 1991, 44-48), reflected in a complete absence of Flat-Linear potins before types J-L and clear preponderance of Flat-Linear II varieties (Haselgrove 1988, 115-16). At least 155 Iron Age coins are recorded from various excavations within the later walled area (Holman 2005), nearly half of which are Flat-Linear potins (45%), so the very low representation of Kentish Primaries seems likely to be of chronological significance.

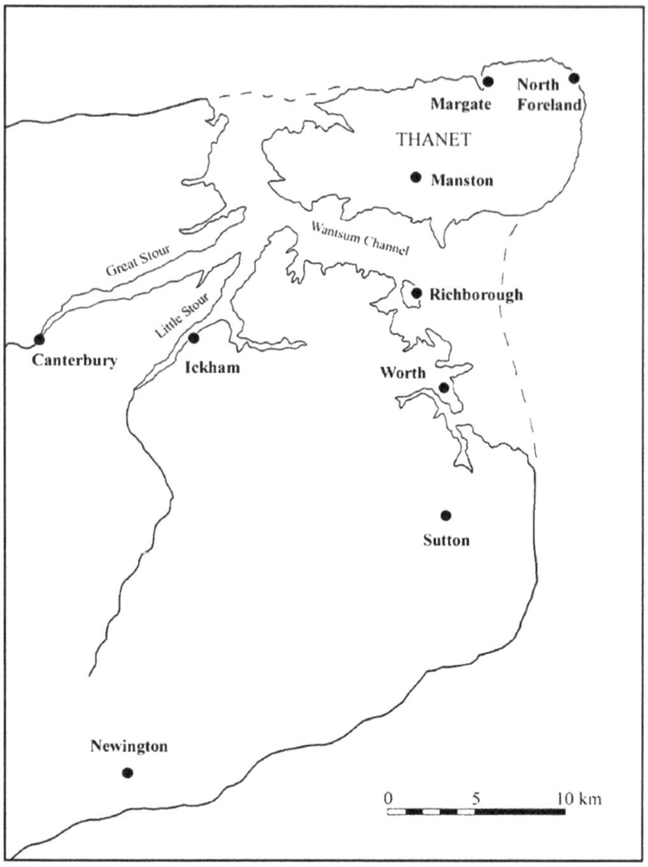

Figure 2. Excavated sites with Kentish Primary potin finds on Thanet and in east Kent. The modern coastline is shown with dashed lines. The edges of the Wantsum Channel are based on Hearne et al. *1995, fig. 2.*

None of the 23 coins from Richborough is recorded to context. There are middle Iron Age enclosures beneath the Roman fort, but their exact date and function is uncertain (Cunliffe 1968). The majority of Iron Age coin losses appear to relate to the early Roman military occupation, leaving a small group of earlier types, which might well be associated with the previous use of the site (Haselgrove 1987, 153: a Kentish Primary potin; two Belgic and one central Gaulish potin; a Flat-Linear I potin (type L); and conceivably some of the uninscribed Kentish and Belgic bronzes.

There have been unstratified finds of Kentish Primaries at three sites occupied in the middle and/or late Iron Age. One was found on the surface in the vicinity of Dollands Moor, Newington, where a late Iron Age enclosure complex succeeded an early Iron Age open settlement (Bennett 1988, 10-12; Cunliffe 2005). The absence of middle Iron Age pottery implies a gap between the two phases, but how far this carried on into the later Iron Age is unclear. The only other coin from the excavations was a bronze unit of Amminius, from a shallow gully of early Roman date (Haselgrove forthcoming 2). At Sutton, two Kentish Primaries and Flat-Linear I and II potins have been found in the same field as a site occupied in the middle and late Iron Age (D. Holman, pers. comm.); among the excavation finds were a quarter-stater of 'helmet' type (Delestrée 1996; Sills 2003, 255) and a further Flat-Linear I potin.

The extensively excavated hilltop site at North Foreland has a long history of use going back to the Bronze Age (Diack *et al.* 2000). The main periods of Iron Age settlement seem to be at the start of the period, and again in the mid to late Iron Age (c. 250/200-100/50 BC), after which the site was largely abandoned. A Primary potin was found at the base of the topsoil within one of three Bronze Age ring ditches. In another part of the site, a hoard of over 60 Flat-Linear I potins was excavated from an elongated pit. There is no other dating evidence, but the hoard has a relatively early-looking composition compared to other Flat-Linear I hoards (there are similarities to the one found in 1853 in Quex Park, Birchington; Allen 1971), implying that the North Foreland find is contemporary with the mid to late Iron Age settlement. Given that Kentish Primaries were also present on the site, their absence from the hoard might therefore be relevant.

Two other Iron Age sites have yielded stratified finds, but they add little to the overall picture. The elevated site at Fort Hill, Margate was extensively occupied in the earlier Iron Age (Perkins 1999, 375) and there are also middle Iron Age features (D. Holman, pers. comm.), suggesting that the overall sequence may be similar to North Foreland. However, the relevant find – two Kentish Primaries fused together – came from an undated pit. The site at Manston International Business Park is an enclosure dating to the end of the Iron Age (Perkins *et al.* 1998). Four Kentish Primary potins were found together in a single pit, provisionally dated by pottery to the earlier first century AD, and a fifth was recovered from the top layer of the late Iron Age enclosure ditch (D. Holman, pers. comm.). The date of these contexts is clearly at odds with the absence of Kentish Primaries from the Canterbury sequence and will bear further scrutiny when the Manston excavations are published.

Holman (2005) has recently discussed the coins from Worth. The late Roman temple lies within an earlier oval ditched enclosure, which was probably constructed in the first century BC. Other evidence of pre-Roman activity included pits containing early to middle Iron Age pottery and quantities of mid to late Iron Age pottery spread across the site (*ibid.*, 267-69). The nature of the Iron Age activity is unclear, but that some of it was of ritual character seems likely, given the number of coins (204). No less than one-third of these are Kentish Primaries (34.3%), slightly in advance of the east Kentish mean (Holman 2000, 221, Table 2). The 24 Flat-Linear potins are predominantly early – over half are of types A-D (54.2%) – and only one is of Flat-Linear II type (Holman 2005, 270). Other early types include the imported Gaulish potins mentioned above. In general, mid to later first century BC coins are under-represented, suggesting a decline in activity at this time, before losses recovered to their previous level in the earlier first century AD (*ibid.* , 272).

In sum, the archaeological finds discussed here offer little definite help with the detailed chronology of the Kentish Primary potins, being divided fairly evenly between sites with little or no occupation after the mid first century BC (Margate, North Foreland); sites not occupied until this date (Canterbury, Manston); and sites with activity in both periods (Sutton, Worth). Richborough appears to fall in the first category, whilst at Newington, there is some doubt over the extent of mid to late Iron Age activity. The stratified finds from Manston are difficult to reconcile with an early chronology for the series, but nor are they easy to accept as near contemporary losses. This would require the Kentish Primary series to be a free-standing and typologically backward-looking development, broadly contemporary with the Flat-Linear II series and/or the earliest Kentish struck bronze types, but if so, we are entitled to ask why these other types – but not the Kentish Primaries – occur regularly in stratified contexts of the expected date (cf. Haselgrove 1995, 122, fig. 58).

This leaves the Kentish Primary coin found at Maiden Castle in 1984-85. Its problems have already been rehearsed, but there is one further aspect to consider here. The coin was excavated from a silt layer believed to seal Phase 6E (Sharples 1991). Both Phase 6E (for which a third century BC date was assigned) and the subsequent Phase 6F with its coin were lacking in closely dateable material. However, archaeomagnetic dating indicated that a hearth belonging to the latter phase was last used c. 200-150 BC. Sharples's comment on the date of the hearth is worth reproducing: 'This would fit with the date for Phase 6E and is perhaps more accurate that the late second century BC date suggested for the ceramic assemblage,' adding that 'these dates are clearly incompatible with the early first century date for the potin coin' (Sharples 1991, 241). At the time, I myself thought that the date for the hearth was impossibly early for the coin, particularly if the silt deposit was laid down at the start of Phase 6F, but now that we know that the Massalia potins in the Paris Basin are of similar date, the matter deserves reconsideration. It is to this new French evidence that we must now turn.

The archaeological dating of the Paris Basin potins

Whilst the recent discovery in east Kent of Massalia bronzes in good style has greatly increased the likelihood that the Kentish potins are an independent development, the date of the Paris Basin series remains a useful indicator for when the butting-bull type first began to be imitated in areas far removed from the Mediterranean.

The case for dating the Paris Basin series (LT 5284) before the first century BC until recently rested on their apparent association with early wheel-made pottery at Epiais-Rhus (Haselgrove 1995), but this evidence is far from conclusive owing to the way in which this site is recorded and published (cf. Lardy *et al.* 1987). Although Epiais-Rhus is still among the principal findspots, with over 100 examples, LT 5284 is now recorded from more than 30 sites in the Paris region, several of which have been extensively excavated. The core of the distribution apparently lies north of the river Seine, in the region bounded by its tributaries, the Epte and the Marne (Bourgeois 1999, 193, fig. 143; Delestrée 1999, 18-19).

The most important new finds are those from Bobigny, La Vache-à-L'Aise and Fontenay-en-Parisis, La Lampe (both in Seine-St-Denis), and from Bennecourt (Yvelines). We may begin with Bobigny, where the phasing has been studied as part of a chronological seriation of Iron Age burials and settlement deposits in the Paris Basin (Marion 2004). Over half the 33 potins found at this substantial rural site are LT 5284.[3] According to Delestrée (1999), nine potins were found in La Tène C2 contexts (Phases 2-5), all of them either LT 5284 or Scheers 203; twelve in contexts assigned to the final period of Iron Age occupation (Phase 6, La Tène D1a); and ten in unphased Iron Age deposits. The early date for Scheers 203 ties in with the Aisne Valley chronology, where the series is represented (at Acy-Romance) in contexts dating to the latter part of La Tène C2 (Pion 1996), as indeed is the outlined helmeted head type (LT 7388-7404).

Delestrée's total for the earlier phases at Bobigny differs by one from that given by Marion (2004, 467-68), who only identifies some of the coins. According to Marion, two were found in Phase 2 contexts (type unspecified); one in Phase 4 (identified as LT 5284); and seven in Phase 5 (including four LT 5284 and one Scheers 203). He assigns Bobigny Phase 2 to his Etape 7, which he equates to the start of La Tène C2 or possibly even the end of La Tène C1 (*ibid.*, 273-74). Phase 5 is attributed to Etape 8, equated to the end of La Tène C2, but perhaps overlapping with the start of La Tène D1a in Pion's (1996) Aisne Valley chronology. Phase 4 is not assimilated to the periodisation, but would represent an intermediate stage of La Tène C2 (*ibid.*, 467).[4]

At the religious sanctuary at Bennecourt (Bourgeois 1999), one example each of LT 5284 and Scheers 203 were found in the infill of the second stage of the enclosure ditch, together with several examples of the so-called 'chevrons' series (Scheers 206-I). This phase of the sanctuary is attributed to La Tène D1a. Three further examples of Scheers 206-I were found in the remnants of the ditch belonging to the first phase of the enclosure, which is dated to La Tène C2. The 'chevrons' types are considered by Delestrée (1999, 24) to represent a schematic interpretation of LT 5284, which if true, must place the appearance of the prototype itself no later than La Tène C2. The distribution of Scheers 206-I is closely complementary to that of Scheers 203 (Bourgeois 1999, figs 141-142), which might well reinforce the idea that together they represent a second stage of potin coinage, derived from the early Massalia imitations.

Based on the Bennecourt and Bobigny evidence alone, it would be difficult to argue for widespread circulation of potins much before the mid second century BC. All but two of the relevant finds from Bobigny are from the later part of La Tène C2 (eight coins) or from La Tène D1a contexts (twelve coins); and the two unidentified examples from Phase 2 could after all be intrusive. The Bennecourt evidence shows a similar increase from La Tène C2 (three coins) to La Tène D1a (sixteen coins), although here the truncated nature of the deposits associated with the first enclosure must also be a factor. The evidence from Epiais-Rhus would also tend to point to La Tène D1a rather than any earlier, as wheel-made pottery is still virtually non-existent in La Tène C2.

The clinching evidence for the early dating of LT 5284 is provided by the third site, at Fontenay-en-Parisis. This appears to be a rural settlement, although it has also been proposed as a sanctuary (Delestrée 1999). All twelve potins found in this excavation were LT 5284. Ten of them were found in a ditch, nine along a stretch of only 3 m, whilst the other two came from the lower fills of storage pits, sited some 150 m away from the ditch (*ibid.*, 22). The ditch yielded a substantial assemblage of brooches, glass bracelets, and pottery, allowing Marion (2004, 334) to attribute its fill to Etape 7, the start of La Tène C2 or possibly even the end of La Tène C1, or in other words, no later than the beginning of the second century BC, possibly even slightly earlier. In practice, we may assume that the two unidentified potins from Bobigny Phase 2 are also LT 5284, since Delestrée (1999, 23) presents these as corroborating the evidence from Fontenay-en-Parisis in dating the series to the start of the second century BC.

There is no longer any real doubt then that the imitation of Massalia bronzes occurred at a very early date in northern France, perhaps even contemporary with the prototype. This being so, we may seriously entertain the possibility of an equally early date for the Kentish Primary series, although there is clearly no need for these developments to be directly connected. However, before returning to the relationship between the Kentish series and other early coinages in south-east England, we may examine the evidence that we have for the use and circulation of LT 5284 and what – if Delestrée (1999) is right – are amongst its earliest derivatives, such as Scheers 203 and 206.

A recent analysis of the findspots of Belgic potins has shown that the overwhelming majority are from known sites, or from other archaeologically-significant contexts such as wet places (the average is 82%). When only exact findspots are considered, the proportion from known sites climbs to 98% (Haselgrove 2005, Table 5). This contrasts with the contemporary gold coinages, for which the equivalent figures are 35% and 76%, partly because they include many poorly-recorded older finds, partly because gold coins clearly were frequently deposited in locations without any obvious physical remains, whether as single coins or as hoards. A similar pattern has been noted for gold finds in Britain (Haselgrove 1987). All told, potins occur on more sites than Belgic coins in any other metal and on nearly twice as many sites as gold.

Approximately three-quarters of LT 5284 findspots are known sites (76.5%), a little below the potin average, and lower than the figure for either Scheers 203 (90.2%) or Scheers 206 (83.7%), if these do represent a second stage of development. As many as three-fifths of the sites yielding LT 5284 apparently had a religious function (61.5%) – the highest proportion for any major Belgic coinage – but not out of keeping with the settlement pattern in western Belgic Gaul, where cult sites and sanctuaries probably served to integrate society politically and economically in the same way as major fortified settlements (*oppida*) elsewhere. Rural settlements account for another quarter of LT 5284 findspots (23.1%), followed by *oppida* (11.5%). Conversely, LT 5284 hardly ever occurs on nucleated settlements and other types of site that tend to be late in date. The full figures are given in Haselgrove (2005, Table 7). Unlike the Kentish Primary potins, there are no known hoards of LT 5284 *per se*, although the numbers from sites can be substantial (Delestrée 1999, 18).

The provenances of Scheers 203 and 206 are fairly similar to LT 5284, with more finds at religious sites than anywhere else (albeit including more wet sites), and a fair number from rural settlements. They differ however from the presumed prototype in being represented on a wider spectrum of site types, a tendency that becomes even more pronounced for the potin series that were current during La Tène D1b and D2a (c. 120-60 BC). They also differ from one another in that Scheers 203, which has much the closer distribution to LT 5284 but which extends further into southern Belgic Gaul, is far better represented than either LT 5284 or Scheers 206 at *oppida*. This makes sense chronologically, as *oppida* were an earlier development in the east of the Paris basin than to the west or north (Haselgrove 2005).

In summary, all three potin series occur most frequently in a religious context, whilst the predominance of rural sites among the minority of settlement finds is not unexpected, given that Belgic society was still essentially rurally based in the early to mid second century BC. The site associations imply that LT 5284 went out of use before the two series with which it circulated, confirming that it is the earliest of the three. All three series occur at fewer sites than the potin types that were current in the late second and earlier first century BC. This might well indicate that the use of potin was initially restricted to a relatively small segment of Belgic society, and/or that it was less frequently deposited at this period than later, a trend we also find with the earliest gold coinages (Haselgrove 2005). At this point, we will return to Britain.

Functional rather than chronological differences?

I have already commented on the striking lack of association between the Kentish Primary series and the Flat-Linear types. At face value, the most probable explanation is chronological, with the Kentish Primary coins representing an essentially earlier development. There may have been some overlap in date between the two, but it ought not to have lasted long, otherwise we might expect some direct associations between the types, for instance in the hoards. Geography may also be a factor, with the centre of gravity of the Flat-Linear series possibly to the west of the Kentish primaries, which is something that the current high level of recording in east Kent may be masking.

Another possibility that must be considered is that of functional differences between the two series. To reconcile the hoarding of the Flat-Linear I coins with the quantity of Flat-Linear II finds from settlements, Collis (1974) suggested that over time a downgrading in the status of potin had occurred, from a relatively high value medium to one that was used more as small change. However, since Collis wrote, two Flat-Linear II hoards have been found – at New Addington and Stansted – whilst there are numerous Flat-Linear I coins from settlement deposits, so the picture is clearly more complex (Haselgrove 1988). It is certainly possible that the function of potins did change over time, leading to altered patterns of deposition, especially in the early stages as communities became habituated to the idea of using coinage. Cultural attitudes and practices may also have varied geographically.

As in northern France, we can investigate this question by examining where the different types of insular potins are found. A difference that does need to be stressed is the tiny proportion of Primary potins from known sites (14.0%), lower than the figure for any Belgic gold coinage, let alone continental potins (Haselgrove 2005). The figures for Flat-Linear I (72.6%) and II potins (88.3%) on the other hand are far closer to the Belgic pattern; indeed where the exact provenance is known, all but two Flat-Linear II findspots

(New Addington and a multiple find from Bardwell) are known sites, as are all but four Flat-Linear I findspots.

A large proportion of the Kentish Primaries do have exact findspots (P. de Jersey, pers comm.) and the problem may simply be that we do not yet have the relevant data. A fair number of locations have yielded multiple coin finds, whether solely of Kentish Primaries or a mixture of types, some of which probably are sites, although in other cases, the coins appear over large areas with no clear concentration, as at Ringwould and Waldershare Park (D. Holman, pers. comm.), and may therefore represent another kind of depositional practice. It may even be that the reason that the Kentish primary series evaded detection for so long is its general avoidance of sites in the accepted sense, coupled with its unprepossessing appearance which led to fewer casual finds being reported than for other Iron Age types. Be that as it may, the sample of find sites for Kentish Primaries (34) is far smaller and probably less robust than for either Flat-Linear I (113) or Flat-Linear II (51) coins. In addition, more than half of the supposed site finds of Primary potins are recorded to parish only (55.9%), leaving some doubt as to whether they are actually from the archaeological site in question, as for instance with coins from Colchester and Caerwent.

These lacunae notwithstanding, the site frequencies for Primary potins and Flat-Linear I types are remarkably similar (Figure 3). In each case, rural settlements predominate and – perhaps surprisingly – the proportion of hoards is also almost identical.[5] The one marked difference is the higher proportion of Flat-Linear I wet finds, mostly from the Thames foreshore in the London area, but including also finds in the Great Stour and the Medway. The apparently higher incidence of Primary potins from formal religious sites may however be illusory: three of the find sites are far from definite and the function of the other two ('Eastry', Worth) is open to debate (Holman 2005).

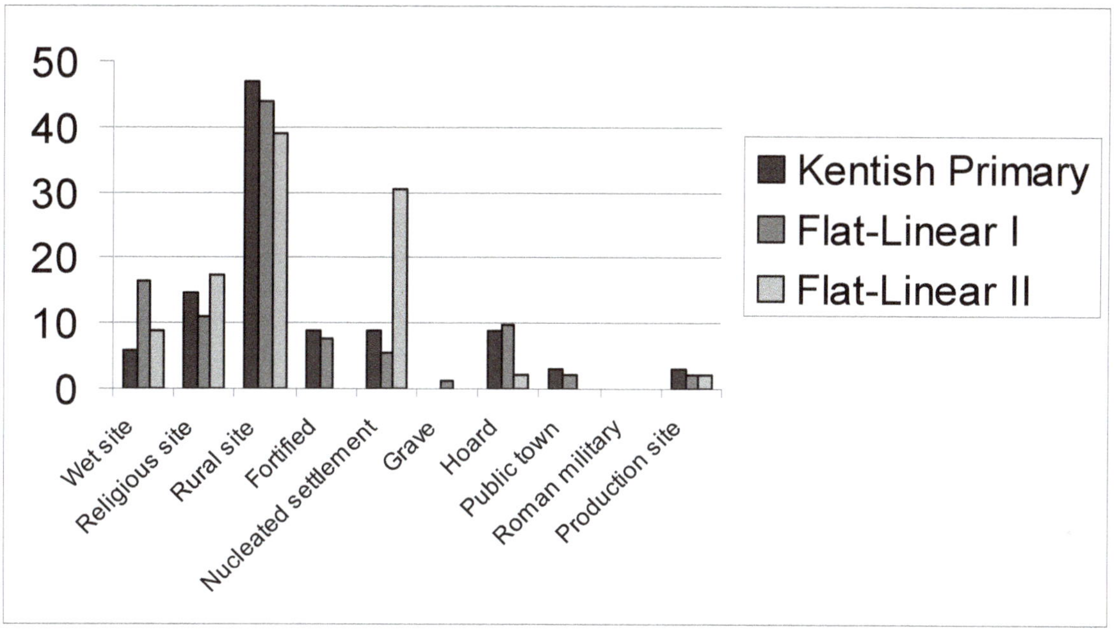

Figure 3. Frequencies of archaeological site types yielding the three main series of British potin coinage.

If we consider only the definite findspots for Kentish Primaries (cf. Haselgrove 1987, 42-43 F1), the proportion of rural settlements rises to over half (53.3%), which well may be a truer reflection of the overall situation. Rural sites also account for a high proportion of Flat-Linear II provenances, but there is a sharp increase in finds from nucleated settlements and significantly there are none from hillforts. There is also less background 'noise' from other types of site, implying that Flat-Linear II coins had a more restricted sphere of circulation than the earlier potins (cf. Haselgrove 1988).

Standing back from the detail, we can see that there is little in the site evidence to suggest that the Kentish Primaries and Flat-Linear types had distinctive functions. The main differences seem likely to be chronological and geographical in origin. Only the two earlier series occur on hillforts, many of which went out of use around the end of the second or start of the first century BC. This coincides with the appearance of the first unenclosed nucleated settlements, as at Baldock, especially north of the Thames, where a significant proportion of the Flat-Linear II coins are found.

At face value, the main difference between the three British series and those from the Paris Basin is the more overtly religious dimension to the deposition of Belgic potins. Formal religious sites do not seem to have been a feature of Iron Age Britain in the same way as they were in much of Belgic Gaul (Haselgrove 2005); indeed, the one major exception, at Hayling Island, stands out for its continental affinities. In this respect, it is interesting that four of the cult places where Flat-Linear potins have been found are actually in northern France, not southern Britain. The potins are fairly late varieties – type L at Chilly (Somme) and Fesques (Seine-Maritime); and Flat-Linear II types at Bailleul-sur-Therain (Oise) and Limetz-Villez – but nevertheless provide a valuable reminder that cross-Channel interaction at this period was two-way.

The lack of potin coins from formal religious shrines in Britain should not be read as necessarily indicating that most of the finds represent losses from use. It is now widely accepted that many coins – and other objects – found on Iron Age settlements, even rural ones, were deposited as offerings in the course of domestic rituals (e.g. Hill 1995; Haselgrove 2005; Haselgrove and Wigg-Wolf 2005). There is also evidence on both sides of the Channel to suggest that wet places and other naturally-significant locations such as hilltops and caves were often used for ritual purposes, attracting offerings of coins and other valuable objects. The Snettisham hoards – including one containing Flat-Linear I potins (Haselgrove 1990) – fall into this category (Hutcheson 2004), as do the spectacular finds unearthed near Market Harborough (Priest *et al.* 2003). It seems likely that a similar explanation applies to many smaller or single finds of coins in wet places and other locations that are not sites in the accepted sense, especially for gold and in the earliest stages of coin use (Haselgrove 2005), but also potentially with coinage in other metals.

It thus remains to be seen whether with additional data, the proportion of non-site finds of Primary potins is maintained. If so, the implied contrast with Belgic Gaul, where a majority of the earliest potins are from indisputable religious sites, may be more apparent than real. Indeed one of many explanations suggested for Gaulish potins is that they were – or at least started out life as – religious tokens that were issued to individuals to enable them to participate in specific rites or ceremonies (Gruel 1989), although such a view seems a difficult to reconcile with their often very extensive distribution patterns. It is however to the relationship between the adoption of potin in Kent and the earliest gold coinages of south-east England that I will now turn in order to conclude this review.

The relationship to gold coinage

In his recent study of early gold coinage in south-east England, John Sills (2003, 347-49) notes that the distribution of the Primary potins in Kent is almost identical to that of imported Gallo-Belgic C staters (Scheers 9) and early Gallo-Belgic D quarter-staters (Scheers 13-I-II). Whilst noting that the distribution of the earlier Flat-Linear I coins (types A-K) is also very similar, Sills suggested that the Primary potins might be contemporary with, or slightly later than, Class 3 Gallo-Belgic C staters (essentially Scheers 9-III), which he, like me, attributes to the late second century BC (*ibid.*, 330; Haselgrove 1999, 134-36). Gallo-Belgic C or early D and Kentish Primary potins do occasionally occur on the same site, as at Sutton, Worth and 'Eastry' (Holman 2005), but each time, the apparent association is neutralised by the presence of Flat-Linear I potins on the same site, with which the gold might instead be contemporary.

Now that we know that the Paris Basin potins were in existence by the early second century BC at latest and that the Kentish Primary series might not be significantly later in date, we need to ask whether there might instead be a relationship with any of the Gallo-Belgic gold coinages imported into south-east England prior to the late second century BC. These begin with the Somme valley series of half- and quarter-staters and other early Philippus types that were current in Belgic Gaul in the third century BC (Sills 2003). From the number of known sub-types, it seems likely that these early gold coins were much commoner than the record suggests, but were rarely deposited, a feature we find with other first-generation gold coinages.

It is immediately apparent that the British distribution of these early Somme Valley coins is very similar to the core area of potin circulation in central and especially eastern Kent (Sills 2003, 64 map 10). The enhanced recording in east Kent may be a factor, but probably not enough totally to distort the picture. In addition, at least three-quarters of the British findspots of these early gold types are at non-site locations (77.8%), albeit on a very small sample. The proportion may well be higher, since neither of the possible site finds is securely attested and the coins from Waltham St Lawrence were apparently residual in a later coin deposit.

These first-generation imports were followed in the second century BC by Gallo-Belgic A and B. This time, only the early Gallo-Belgic Ba quarter-staters have a predominantly Kentish distribution (Sills 2003, 169-70, map 21). Gallo-Belgic A – although including east Kent – is found regularly over a much larger area, whilst the distribution of that of Gallo-Belgic Bb is essentially complementary to both Kentish potin series (*ibid.*, 182, map 22). In other respects, however, Gallo-Belgic A and B display various similarities to the Primary potins: the total number of findspots is now far higher, as is the incidence of multiple finds/hoards, whilst the proportion of non-site finds remains very high (86.6% for Gallo-Belgic A; 79.6% for Gallo-Belgic B).

With the introduction of Gallo-Belgic C, the focus of attention reverts to Kent, but at the same time, the pattern of deposition starts to change (Haselgrove 2005). Fewer Gallo-Belgic C staters are found singly (50% against 70.5% for Gallo-Belgic A) and twice as many as multiple finds/hoards (30.3% against 16%). There is also a modest increase in site finds (from 13.4 to 19.7%), but mainly in wet places and at definite cult sites, rather than in settlements.[6] With Gallo-Belgic D quarter-staters, the number of site finds climbs sharply, to over half (52.8%), but again mostly at wet and cult sites (Haselgrove 2005). Gallo-Belgic D continued to be minted later than Gallo-Belgic C (Haselgrove 1999; Sills 2003), which is reflected in an increased number of finds from nucleated settlements.

It is clear then that the imported gold follows the Primary potins in apparently avoiding known archaeological sites, suggesting that gold and potin were initially subject to fairly similar depositional rules. The Flat-Linear potins, however, have a more site-orientated distribution, but it is not until the first century BC that we start to see changes in the treatment of the gold, with a movement from non-site locations to wet places and more obviously identifiable cult sites. It is possible that with the passage of time, potin was increasingly incorporated into domestic rituals enacted on settlement sites, whereas larger-scale observances at communal ceremonial sites and cult places mainly employed gold.

As we have seen, the earliest gold imports and the Primary potins share similar distributions and need not be far apart in date; indeed, they could even overlap. One way of interpreting this distributional co-incidence is to suggest that the communities who were the first to use gold coins in Britain also became the first to mint their own coinage. Why they should have produced potin rather than gold is unclear, but the same phenomenon is found in parts of Gaul, for instance in Champagne, where no gold was minted until the late second century BC, but there was a plentiful potin coinage (Haselgrove 1999). Given its silvery appearance and high weight, the explanation may quite simply be that Iron Age societies put a greater value on potin than we would expect from its base composition and that the role of the two metals was initially not that different (Haselgrove 1988, 118-119). If so, this might explain why some peoples opted to issue gold, and others to mint potin.

It is possible that cultural preferences lie behind not only the initial adoption of potin in Britain, but also the shape of subsequent developments, with the inhabitants of eastern and central Kent continuing to favour this medium throughout the second century BC, whilst their neighbours in south-east England increasingly espoused the use of imported gold, whilst also in some cases importing potins from eastern Kent.[7] Given its location and external contacts, there is no good reason why the gold should mainly pass this region by during the second century BC, especially when the area east of the Medway is one of the few areas where we find Gaulish base metal imports in any number (Holman 2000). Equally, when the peoples of south-east England did eventually start to mint their own gold coinages modelled on Gallo-Belgic C, this did not include the inhabitants of eastern Kent, who instead imported Gallo-Belgic C and early D from the Continent, yielding the distribution noted by Sills (2003).

Conclusion

There are grounds then to suggest that, as in many areas of Belgic Gaul, political or social circumstances caused the peoples of Thanet and east Kent to start producing potin coinage in the early second century BC, or possibly even slightly earlier. Recent excavations reveal that the coastal strip was densely occupied at this period, with a mixture of small farmsteads and occasional larger unenclosed settlements. Their inhabitants had close ties to the continent and were introduced to the idea of coinage in the third century BC, as the presence of the early Somme Valley issues shows. With the adoption of the Flat-Linear types, the use of potin coinage appears to have gradually expanded into central Kent and also eventually to the north of the Thames, but the majority of insular communities do not seem to have taken to the idea culturally, preferring imported Gallo-Belgic gold.

The peoples of east Kent had extensive maritime contacts within Britain and this apparently led to the export of a certain number of gold and potin coins along the south and east coasts of England during the second and early first century BC, as at Maiden Castle and Snettisham. It seems likely that these coins were used as gifts or in other forms of occasional social or political transactions between the leading groups in each region, rather than for economic purposes in a modern sense. In a few cases, however, notably in East Sussex, potins seem to have been imported in some quantity and even adapted to local rituals and cultural practices, as at the Caburn (cf. Drewett and Hamilton 1999), hinting at much closer cultural or political ties.

There is still much that we do not know about the early phases of coinage in Britain and I make no apology for concluding with a series of questions. For a start, why was coin production confined to this one relatively small region for such a long period, whilst coinage itself was used over an increasingly large area? Why too was there was such rigid adherence to the original design and why did other peoples in south-east England not produce their own potin coinages, or adopt different types, as happened in Belgic Gaul? And why if gold and potin both had high social values, why was the former imported in such large quantities, but not the latter, especially when there is evidence both from both sides of the Channel that potin was frequently used in long-distance transactions?

To some extent, the answer to this last question may lie in differing regional depositional practices, with certain types of coin being recycled for their metal content, whilst other were employed as offerings to the gods. Intensive patterns of interaction may simply not be reflected in the evidence at our disposal. It is not that long ago, after all, that we were ignorant of the entire Primary series. In the future, we certainly need to pay more attention to the cultural factors involved in the formation of the numismatic record, rather than regarding this as largely a matter of chance. More generally, we should stop treating Iron Age coinage as a familiar medium just because it shares the same basic form as our own, when all the indications are that it was used in ways that would make little sense to a twenty-first century observer, and by people whose beliefs and institutions and priorities had much less in common with our own than we are prepared to admit.

Acknowledgements

I very grateful to David Holman and Philip de Jersey for their generous help in providing information and answering numerous queries relating to this paper. Any errors remain my responsibility alone.

Notes

[1] This does not include type M, which has more than half of its findspots south of the Thames and is common at Canterbury.

[2] Stanwick was apparently quite a substantial settlement in the middle Iron Age, but seems to have been in decline in the late Iron Age (J. Taylor, pers. comm.).

[3] In this analysis, the term rural settlement is used to cover a spectrum of sites, ranging from what were probably farmsteads occupied by a singe household to larger much larger aggregations such as Bobigny and Acy-Romance (Aisne).

[4] Depending on whose scheme is adopted, the approximate dates of these periods are as follows: La Tène C1: 270/250-200/180 BC; La Tène C2: 200/180-150/130 BC; La Tène D1a 150/130-120/100 BC.

[5] The Kentish Primary figures include a possible third hoard from Gravesend (Holman 2000, 206) together with a small number of finds noted by the author but not yet recorded in

the CCI. The site frequencies for Flat-Linear I and II coins are based primarily on the data provided in Haselgrove (1988), updated to take account of more recently published finds.

[6] Within the general category of wet finds, coastal deposition is much more frequent in Britain than in northern France, although it does occur there too.

[7] It is noticeable that many site finds of Primary potins outside Kent are from sites that served as local or regional centres, as at Colchester, Maiden Castle, Stonea Grange, Stanwick (Northants.), and perhaps the predecessor of Caerwent, and/or from sites involved in long-distance exchange, as at Merthyr Mawr (Glamorgan) and South Ferriby, opposite the important gateway site at Redcliff on the Humber.

Bibliography

Allen, D. F. 1971: British potin coins: a review. In D. Hill and M. Jesson (eds), *The Iron Age and its hillforts* (Southampton), 127-154.

Allen, D. F. 1980: *The coins of the Ancient Celts* (Edinburgh).

Bennett, P. 1988: Archaeology and the Channel tunnel. *Archaeologia Cantiana* 106, 1-24.

Bourgeois, L. 1999: *Le sanctuaire rural de Bennecourt (Yvelines)* (Paris, Documents d'Archéologie Française 77).

Collis, J. R. 1974: A functionalist approach to pre-Roman coinage. In P. J. Casey and R. Reece (eds), *Coins and the archaeologist* (Oxford, BAR 4), 1-11.

Cunliffe, B. W. 1968: *Excavation of the Roman fort at Richborough, Kent, V* (Oxford, Reports of the Research Committee, Society of Antiquaries of London, 23).

Cunliffe, B. W. 2005 (4th ed.): *Iron Age communities in Britain* (London, Routledge).

Curteis, M. 2001: *The Iron Age coinages of the south Midlands, with particular reference to distribution and deposition*. Unpublished Ph.D. thesis, University of Durham.

de Jersey, P. 1999: Exotic Celtic coinage in Britain. *Oxford Journal of Archaeology* 18, 189-216.

de Jersey, P. 2003: *Spatial variation in the recording of Celtic coins* (Unpublished report to English Heritage, January 2003).

Delestrée, L-P. 1996: L'ensemble des quarts de statères dits «au bateau» en Gaule Belgique. *Revue Numismatique* 151, 29-50.

Delestrée, L-P. 1999: Les bronzes coulées imités de Marseille dans la région parisienne. *Cahiers Numismatiques* 141, 17-25.

Diack, M., Mason, S., and Perkins, D. 2000: North Foreland. *Current Archaeology* 168, 472-473.

Drewett, P. and Hamilton, S. 1999: Marking time and making space: excavations and landscape studies at the Caburn hillfort, East Sussex, 1996-98. *Sussex Archaeological Collections* 137, 7-37.

Gruel, K. 1989: *La Monnaie chez les Gaulois* (Paris).

Guichard, V., Pion, P., Malacher, F., and Collis, J. 1993: A propos de la circulation monétaire en Gaule chevelue au IIe et Ier siècles av. J.-C. *Revue Archéologique du Centre de la France* 32, 26-55.

Haselgrove, C. 1987: *Iron Age coinage in south-east England: the archaeological context* (Oxford, BAR 174).

Haselgrove, C. 1988: The archaeology of British potin coinage. *Archaeological Journal* 145, 99-122, M1/01-08.

Haselgrove, C. 1995: Potin coinage in Iron Age Britain; archaeology and chronology. In *Les potins gaulois: typologie, diffusion, chronologie, état de la question (Gallia* 52), 117-127.

Haselgrove, C. 1999: The development of Iron Age coinage in Belgic Gaul. *Numismatic Chronicle* 159, 111-168.

Haselgrove, C. 2005: A new approach to analysing the circulation of Iron Age coinage. *Numismatic Chronicle* 165, 129-174.

Haselgrove C. forthcoming 1: Ickham, Kent, 1974 excavations. Iron Age coins. Canterbury Archaeological Trust.

Haselgrove C. forthcoming 2: Newington, Kent, Channel Tunnel site. Iron Age coins. Canterbury Archaeological Trust.

Haselgrove, C. and Wigg-Wolf, D. (eds) 2005: *Iron Age coinage and ritual practices* (Mainz, Studien zu Fundmünzen der Antike 20).

Hearne, C. M., Perkins, D. R. J. and Andrews, P. 1995: The Sandwich Bay Wastewater Treatment Scheme archaeological project, 1992-1994. *Archaeologia Cantiana* 115, 239-343.

Hill, J. D. 1995: *Ritual and Rubbish in the Iron Age of Wessex* (Oxford, BAR 242).

Holman, D. 2000: Iron Age coinage in Kent: a review of current knowledge. *Archaeologia Cantiana* 120, 205-233.

Holman, D. 2005: Iron Age coinage from Worth and other possible evidence of ritual deposition in Kent. In C. Haselgrove and D. Wigg-Wolf (eds), *Iron Age coinage and ritual practices* (Mainz, Studien zu Fundmünzen der Antike 20), 265-285.

Hutcheson, N. 2004: *Later Iron Age Norfolk. Metalwork,*

landscape and society (Oxford, BAR 361).

Lardy, J.-M., Meyer, H., Rebour, V. and Vanpeene, N. 1997: Monnaies celtiques en situation stratigraphique sur le site d'Epiais-Rhus (Val d'Oise). In J.-L. Brunaux and K. Gruel (eds), *Monnaies Gauloises découvertes en fouilles* (Paris, Dossier de Protohistoire 1), 152-210.

Macpherson-Grant, N. 1991: A reappraisal of prehistoric pottery from Canterbury. *Canterbury's Archaeology* 1990-91, 38-49.

Marion, S. 2004: *Recherches sur l'âge du Fer en Ile-de-France. Entre Hallstatt final et La Tène finale. Analyse des sites fouillés. Chronologie et société.* (Oxford, BAR S1231).

Mitard, P.-H. 1978: Les pseudo-potins des Mandubii découverts dans le Vexin français. *Bulletin de la Société Française de Numismatique* 33, 321-322.

Perkins, D. 1999: Early Iron Age settlement: Margate. *Archaeologia Cantiana* 119, 375-376.

Perkins, D., Boast, E., Wilson, T. and Macpherson-Grant, N. 1998: Kent international business park, Manston: excavations and evaluations 1994-1997, Report 1. *Archaeologia Cantiana* 118, 217-255.

Pion, P. 1996: *Les habitats Laténiens tardifs de la Vallée de l'Aisne: contribution à la périodisation de la fin du second Âge du Fer en Gaule nord-orientale.* Unpublished Ph.D. thesis, University of Paris I.

Priest, V., Clay, P. and Hill, J. D. 2003: Iron Age gold from Leicestershire. *Current Archaeology* 188, 358-360.

Sharples, N. 1991: *Maiden Castle: excavations and field survey 1985-6* (London, English Heritage Archaeological Report 19).

Sills, J. 2003: *Gaulish and early British gold coinage* (London, Spink).

Van Arsdell, R. D. 1989: *Celtic coinage of Britain* (London, Spink).

Worrell, S. forthcoming: Detecting the later Iron Age: a view from the Portable Antiquities. In C. Haselgrove and T. Moore (eds), *The later Iron Age in Britain and beyond* (Oxford, Oxbow).

Metaphors, meaning & money: contextualising some symbols on Iron Age coins

Miranda Aldhouse-Green

> 'The images, or types, on coins are no mere decorations invented by the idle imagination of an artist, but are ideas of great emotional significance'
>
> (Desmonde 1962, 67)

So wrote the social philosopher Desmonde in his book, published in 1962, entitled *Magic, Myth and Money. The Origin of Money in Religious Ritual*. In a paper published in *Britannia*, Hilary Cool (2000, 29-40) discussed the religious significance of certain precious metal hoards deposited in Britain during the Roman period, which include coins and snake-jewellery. In examining the second-century Snettisham 'jeweller's' hoard, Cool suggests (2000, 37; following Johns 1997, 81-84) that the denarii found in the cache should be 'looked on not as coins but as discs with images'. It is my view that we may appropriately apply such an approach to studies of Iron Age coins and, if we do so, then it makes sense to examine coin iconography within the broader framework of coeval and later imagery occurring in other media: rock, carved stone and metal.

This paper addresses a particular schema identifiable in a great deal of coin art, namely the presentation of 'surreal' motifs, that is images based upon realism but altered, distorted or otherwise rendered fantastic. The repertoire includes antlered anthropomorphic figures, human-faced animals, exaggerated features, triplism, gender-bending and sinistrality, all motifs that can be traced on other, non-coin, iconography in the Iron Age and/or Roman period in north-west Europe. The contextualization of figural coin art, in terms of its relationship to macro-imagery, is important, for it serves to embed visual expression - through the medium of coin – within a much wider spectrum of depictive currency that must be viewed as contingent upon an existing socio-symbolic matrix. Coins are not isolated types of object but may, instead, be understood as fora for complex sets of meanings that may reflect and endorse religious and social experience and, perhaps, even serve to influence the playing-out of political negotiations and power-games, in precisely the same manner as more monumental imagery (Aldhouse-Green 2004). Indeed, in so far as coins circulate – in a way that neither figurines nor stone statuary do – coin images, despite their small size, may impact upon their users with more influence than 'static' iconography: coins go to people rather than people to coins, unlike the pilgrim-visitations to sacred places, for instance. Like jewellery, coins may be treated as highly personal objects, 'worn' on the body in bags or pouches and, in this way, they may carry a profound and intimate meaning for both possessor and giver. Indeed, this kind of significance for coins may be read into a group of stone figures, interpreted as 'benefactors', from the early Gallo-Roman healing sanctuary of *Fontes Sequanae* in Burgundy (Aldhouse-Green 1999, fig. 4, pls. 8 & 9), each of whom holds a bag of coins (Figure 1), presumably to signify their patronage of the sacred precinct and their devotion to the presiding deity, Sequana.

Figure 1. Stone image of a 'benefactor' with bag of money, from the Gallo-Roman healing sanctuary of Fontes Sequanae, *near Dijon (Anne Leaver).*

An important issue of contextualization concerns the repetition of motifs across the boundary of *romanitas*. It is possible to track patterns of imagery on Iron Age coins not only to other media but also across time-zones and culture-zones. Thus, a number of themes, of which the antlered human construct is a classic example, appear on pre-Roman coinage, on other contemporary figural iconography and – much more commonly – in Gallo-Roman imagery. In some instances, a subtle change between pre-Roman coin-motifs and Gallo-British Roman period imagery may be identified. A case in point is the image of the warrior horsewoman (Figure 2), a recurrent theme of Iron Age coin reverses, particularly in Breton issues. Although apparently disappearing within the Gallo-Roman artistic repertoire, she may be discernible instead in the image of the horse-goddess Epona, having lost her military persona, at least overtly (Green 1998a, 182-183). She enjoyed her greatest popularity among cavalry troops on the Rhine frontier and this perhaps betrays her military origins. That such a view may have validity is suggested by the presence, on Iron Age coin imagery, of mares and suckling foals (Gruel 1989, 90; Figure 3), a very common feature of Epona iconography, particularly in Burgundy (Green 1989, figs. 6-7; Figure 4).

Figure 2. Coin reverse depicting a female charioteer driving a human-headed horse, issued in eastern Armorica (Paul Jenkins).

Figure 3. Coin reverse depicting a mare and suckling foal (Lengyel 1954, no. 182).

Figure 4. Epona with foal (Brazey, Burgundy) (author).

Monsters in microcosm

'What comes after them is the stuff of fables – Hellusii and Oxiones with the faces and features of men, but the bodies and limbs of animals. On such unverifiable stories I will express no opinion.'

(Tacitus *Germania* XLVI)

Here, Tacitus was describing tales he had heard of fabulous half-people living on the edges of Germania. In so doing, he was perpetuating longstanding myths current in Classical antiquity, namely the portrayal of monstrous beings encountered by travellers to the edge of the known world (King 1995). In 1982, George Boon of the National Museum of Wales, Cardiff, published a British silver coin dated to *c.* AD 10 - 20 in the NMW collections, first provenanced to Petersfield but later ascribed to the Midlands (Boon 1982). The image on the obverse will be familiar to many readers (Figure 5): briefly, it comprises a human head with mask-like features; knobbly antlers and a wheel-decorated headdress, surrounded by 'astral' symbols.

Figure 5. Obverse of silver coin depicting an antlered human head; British Midlands (National Museum of Wales).

While the coin image is – to my knowledge – unique, its theme resonates strongly with iconography in other media from both Iron Age and Roman contexts. A rapid survey of the comparanda throws up antlered human forms as a recurrent motif in Iron Age rock-art from Val Camonica (Aldhouse-Green 2001a, fig. 7.2; Figure 6), on the Gundestrup Cauldron (*op. cit.*, fig. 7.3; Olmsted 1979, pl. 2A; Kaul *et al.* 1991, fig. 221; Figure 7) and – much more commonly – in bronze and stone cult-iconography within temperate Gaul and even, occasionally, in Britain (Aldhouse-Green 2001a, figs. 7.5-7.8).

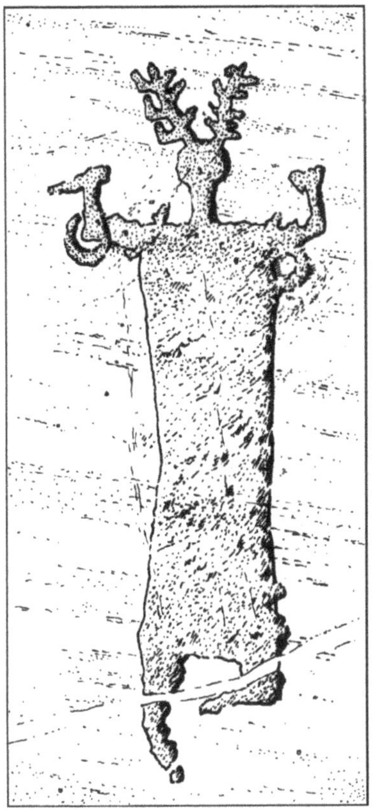

Figure 6. Carving of antler-headed human figure, from Val Camonica, North Italy; c. 4th century BC (Anne Leaver).

Figure 7. Antlered human figure from one of the inner plates of the Gundestrup cauldron, Jutland. 2nd – 1st century BC (Anne Leaver).

Figure 8. Carving of a bearded human head with torcs hanging from its antlers; above is an inscription 'Cernunno'. Dated to the reign of Tiberius, c. AD 26, the stone was found in Paris, and is part of a columnar monument dedicated by the Nautes Parisiacae *(Réunion des Musées Nationaux).*

An early Gallo-Roman carving from Paris (Espérandieu 1911, no. 3133; Figure 8) even gives a name to the image – Cernunnos – although it is far from clear whether we can properly apply this name or title to other antlered beings. Interestingly, the late Iron Age antlered faces on the British coin and on the Gundestrup cauldron would appear to be masked, and the wheel-surmounted headgear worn by the coin image lends credence to its interpretation as liturgical regalia: two of the chain-headdresses from the Wanborough temple (Figure 9) are crowned with similar spoked wheels (O'Connell & Bird 1994, 102, pl. 16). Features on certain Gallo-Roman iconography also suggest that clergy rather than deities may be depicted: the images from Savigny, near Autun in Burgundy (Thévenot 1968, 144-149) and Sommerécourt (Haute-Marne) (Espérandieu 1915, no. 4839) are fitted with pairs of holes for the insertion of detachable antlers, a device perhaps to signify seasonal or gender change. In the latter respect, it is worth noting the presence, in Gallo-Roman imagery, of females wearing antlers (Green 1995, 168); a motif that denies realism not only in so far as the mixing of human and animal is concerned, but in ascribing the male feature of antlers to a female image (in life, reindeer are the only members of the deer family where the females bear antlers).

The antlered image is important, for it is one of very few figural motifs common in the Gallo-British repertoire of Roman imperial religious art whose genesis can be traced back to Iron Age European origins. In recent papers for *TRAC* (Aldhouse-Green 2001a) and for an international colloquium on problems of artistic practice in the Roman provinces (Aldhouse-Green 2003), I explored the manipulation of imagery like this, in terms of power-negotiations and resistance to the dislocative impact (however peaceful and welcomed) of full-scale *romanitas* on Gallo-British communities. In his discussions of image selection for British coinage, John Creighton (2000) has argued with conviction for determination factors associated with becoming Roman, but I would suggest that such motifs as the antlered head on the Midlands coin has more to do with staying non-Roman. Could an image such as this exemplify the subtle harnessing of visual expression to present a re-assertion or maintenance of independent identity? Given the essentially realistic perspective underpinning Classical iconography, it may be that deliberate contravention of 'norms', as presented in monstrous beings, might be read in terms of alternative cosmovision, itself reflective of political as well as spiritual self-determination. Both Jane Webster (2003) and I (1998b, 2003) have presented arguments in favour of acknowledging the factor of resistance to Roman *mores* and values in non-Classical figural expression. The retention of Iron Age fantasy into Roman period imagery may thus be understood as a statement of resistance in two ways: firstly in its denial of realism and secondly in its persistence after the Roman conquest.

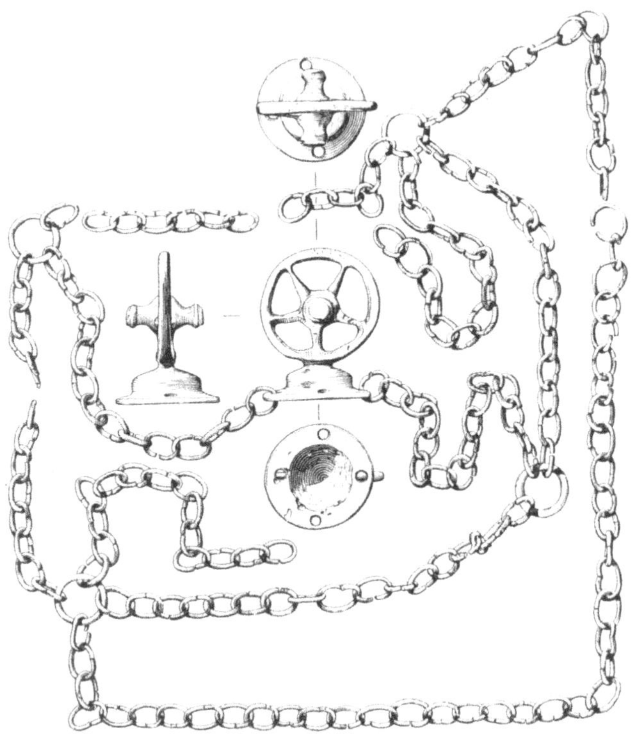

Figure 9. Wheel-decorated copper-alloy chain headdress, from the Wanborough Roman temple, Surrey (Surrey Archaeological Collections).

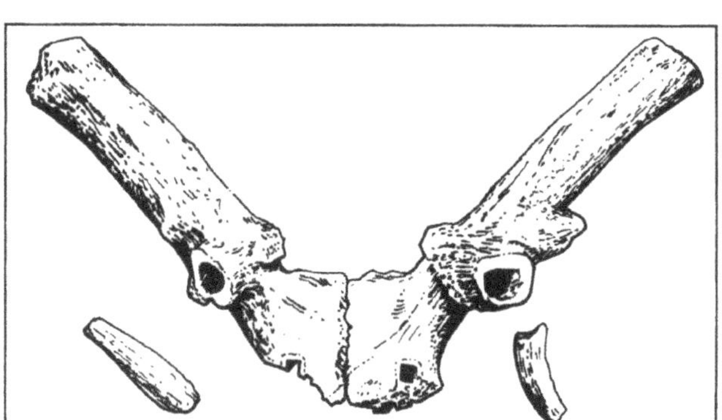

Figure 10. Pair of red-deer antlers, frontal bone pierced as if for attachment; from a Romano-British pit at Hook's Cross, Hertfordshire (Anne Leaver, drawn from transparency supplied by the excavator, Tony Rook).

Three further issues concerning antlered images may be relevant to the current enquiry, of which the first pertains to the wearing of antler-headdresses: occurrences of modified pairs of antlers, suggestive of their use as headgear, are recorded in both Gaul and Britain. Ten pierced skull-caps of antlered deer come from a Middle Iron Age sanctuary at Digeon (Somme) in northern France (Meniel 1987, 125); a similar find comes from a Romano-British pit with second-century ceramics at Hook's Cross in Hertfordshire (Aldhouse-Green 2001a, fig. 7.9; Tony Rook pers. comm.; Figure 10). Secondly, although not depicted on the Midlands coin, antlered images frequently appear in a cross-legged seating position (Figure 11) and this may itself have significance: both Athenaeus (IV, 36) and Diodorus Siculus (V, 28, 4) make reference to the Gauls' propensity for sitting on the ground while feasting, and both allude to the importance of communal drinking, Athenaeus commenting upon the socio-symbolic importance of seating-position. Such descriptions resonate with drink-practice in some traditional societies cited by anthropologists: in a paper on ritual aspects of kava-drinking among Polynesians in Tonga, Elizabeth Bott discusses the ceremonial aspects of corporate alcohol consumption, the ranking significance of where people sit relative to each other, and the cross-legged seating-attitude of the participants (Bott 1987, 184). She emphasizes that precise seating position was a crucial part of the ceremony. The same is true of certain Amazonian psychotropic consumption rituals (Vitebsky 1995).

Figure 11. Gallo-Roman carving of an antlered human figure, depicted seated cross-legged, with bowl or cauldron before him; from Vendeouvres (Indre) (Anne Leaver).

It is possible that we can relate such perspectives to Iron Age and Gallo-Roman iconography and that the cross-legged attitude of antlered beings has something to do with commensality or feasting rituals, particularly with drinking, with sharing ingestion experience, trance and communion with the spirits. Certainly wine as a trance-agent is well-recognised in Central Asian rituals associated with Sufism (Rozwadowski 2001, 72). In terms of coin imagery, it may be relevant to note the presence both of cauldrons and amphorae on certain issues (Gruel 1989, 97, 99; Figures 12-13). John Collis and Vincent Guichard (pers. comm.), among others, have noted the possible significance of the huge quantities of wine consumed in late Iron Age contexts (see

Fischer, this volume), such as at Bibracte and Corent. Cauldrons may have been powerful symbols of hidden knowledge (Davidson 1989, 73), associated not only with shared feasting but with divination and sacrifice.

Figure 12. Armorican coin depicting cauldron (Lengyel 1954, no. 71).

Figure 13. Coin of the Arverni depicting amphora (Lengyel 1954, no. 84).

Finally, reference should be made to the close association between antlered images and torcs, even though the head on the Midlands coin does not show a neckring. On some Iron Age imagery – as at Val Camonica and Gundestrup – and on Gallo-Roman figures – as at Autun – pairs of torcs are depicted in association with stag-men. Additionally, the copper-alloy figure from Bouray, Essonne (Figure 14), though without antlers, has the ears of a deer, sits cross-legged and wears a torc (Joffroy 1979, no. 78; Green 1997, fig. 8). Creighton (2000) has drawn attention to the apparent symbolic linkage between torcs and coins in Iron Age Britain, and the same is true for Gaul (witness the association in the Tayac hoard from Aquitania, where there is both a physical and metrological linkage between the great gold torc and the coins found with it (Allen 1980, 33; Gruel 1989, 121).

Torcs are best interpreted as iconic indicators of status, but in certain circumstances they may carry additional significance in terms of connections with the spirit world, and therefore perhaps with priesthood or shamanhood. There are several reasons for presenting this suggestion: torcs may be understood, perhaps, as symbolic of bondage, of subservience and submission, and here it may be useful to cite Tacitus's comment on ritual custom among the Germanic Semnones:

'No one may enter the sacred grove unless he is bound with a cord. By this he acknowledges his own inferiority and the power of the deity. Should he chance to fall, he must not get up on his feet again. He must roll out over the ground. All this complex of superstition reflects the belief that in that grove the nation had its birth, and that there dwells the god who rules over all while the rest of the world is subject to his sway.'

(Tacitus *Germania* XXXIX)

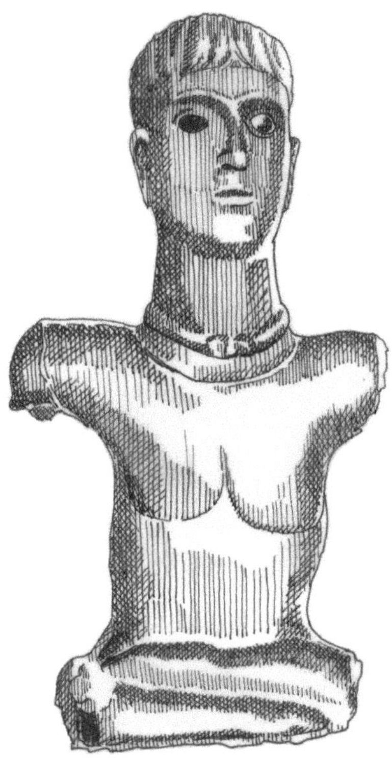

Figure 14. Copper-alloy statuette of an anthropomorphic being wearing torc and seated cross-legged; from Bouray (Essonne), France. 2nd – 1st century BC (Paul Jenkins).

Although no more than conjecture, we might speculate as to whether torcs may have such symbolic associations. Study of the way human bodies were sometimes treated in the later Iron Age (Aldhouse-Green 2005) reveals that bondage and physical restraint were closely linked with sacrificial and other cult-practice in the north-western European Iron Age. The ceremonial significance of torcs is likewise indicated by their presence on pre-Roman stone images on which little other detail is carved: the Alésia figure (Green 1989, fig. 3; Figure 15) is a case in point, and the repeated presence of torcs on the outer plates of the Gundestrup Cauldron is probably meaningful (Olmsted 1979, pl. 4b & c; pl. 55, f & g). The depiction of torcs on some Gallic coinage is important: Katherine Gruel (1989, 152) illustrates one on which a human figure carries a spear in one hand and a large torc in the other (Figure 16); on another, similar, issue, a person with hair in two braids sits cross-legged, bearing a torc in the right hand (Gruel 1989, 103; Figure 17), in exactly the attitude of the Gundestrup antlered figure. Issues from the region of Amiens depict warrior-horsewomen brandishing torcs as though they were weapons (Duval 1987, 49-51).

Figure 15. Late Iron stone figure wearing torc, from Alésia, Burgundy (author).

Figure 16. Obverse of potin of the Remi, showing figure with spear and torc (Institute of Archaeology, Oxford).

Mindful of a suggestion made earlier, namely that such coin horsewomen might be the ancestresses of the Gallo-Roman horse-goddess Epona, it is of interest that the carved stone image of the goddess from Alesia depicts her with an attribute that may be a twisted torc in her hand (Green 1996, 79, pl. 50; Figure 18). Other coins depict harpy-like creatures in robes that look like wings and with beak-like faces, grasping huge buffer-torcs in their talons (Gruel 1989, 101). This kind of imagery, together with the undeniably close relationship between torcs and antlers on iconography, leads me to wonder whether each symbol was, perhaps, an empowering, authoritative emblem, 'spirit-currency' that opened gateways between worlds.

Figure 17. Obverse of potin of the Remi, showing cross-legged figure with torc (Institute of Archaeology, Oxford).

Figure 18. Stone statuette of the Gallo-Roman goddess Epona, with a torc or wreath in her right hand, from Alésia (Paul Jenkins).

The winged monster just cited brings me to a hybrid human/animal occurring repeatedly on coins, over several tribal regions: the human-headed horse (Figure 2), its form perhaps inspired by the centaur of Greek myth, one of a number of Classical monsters which, according to Helen King, 'violate the boundaries' by mixing human and animal and exploring similarity and difference (King 1995, 139). Similarly Michael Shanks argues that blending species serves to create disorder and the 'dissonance of equivalence' (Shanks 1996, 380-81). Does such an occurrence on Iron Age coins also present a denial of 'civilizing' order? I have argued elsewhere (1997, 906) for the significance of the motif in terms of the chaos and anarchy engendered by warfare: many human-faced coin horses are depicted drawing chariots driven by naked females (Gruel 1989, 93; Duval 1987, pl. opp. 44).

In the light of observations made earlier in this paper, it is interesting to note that the chariot-driver of these hybrid horses may bear a torc in one hand and the horse itself may also wear a neckring (though this last may be no more than harness gear). Should we interpret these animals as spirit-horses, perhaps dead ancestors carrying the living into battle and evocative of earthly destruction? Do such boundary-crossers, perhaps, exhibit the liminality of war, danger and the paradox of energy and death? The motif of the human-faced horse is not confined to numismatic art but is also found in a sepulchral context at Reinheim in Germany. Here, in the fourth century BC, a woman was interred with sumptuous grave-furniture, including a wine-flagon with a horse perched on its lid (Green 1996, fig. 87; Megaw 1970, no. 73; Figure 19). The creature is a complex blend of human and animal: it has a bearded human face, a horse's body but with rounded ears more reminiscent of a leopard, and while three of its feet end in hooves, the right foreleg appears to end in toes (Aldhouse-Green 2001b).

Figure 19. Human-headed horse on the lid of a wine-flagon deposited in a woman's grave at Reinheim, Germany; 4th century BC (Anne Leaver).

As is tentatively suggested for the coin horses, it may be appropriate to read the Reinheim beast, within a funerary context, as having metaphoric meaning associated with death. If this were so, then other imagery within the grave falls into place: the woman was interred with a set of ring-jewellery depicting a woman, her hands folded across her stomach, in the attitude of a laid-out corpse, surmounted by a bird of prey (Figure 20).

Figure 20. Terminal of a piece of gold ring-jewellery buried with a woman at Reinheim, Germany in the 4th century BC. The image is of a woman laid out as a corpse, with a bird of prey perched on her head (Paul Jenkins).

Figure 21. Gold coin from Normandy depicting a horse ridden by a huge bird of prey (Lengyel 1954, no. 69).

It makes sense to interpret this figure as an image of the deceased, in the process of apotheosis, the bird, perhaps, representative both of death and transference to spirit. In this connection, it is interesting to reflect upon the coin images depicting horses ridden by great birds, for instance in Normandy (Duval 1987, 20-21, no. 1; Figure 21), of which more anon. Horses may have been charged with transformative meaning perhaps, in part at least, because they may have been perceived as liminal creatures, useful to humans but retaining their essential wildness (Aldhouse-Green 2001b; Figure 22). Among certain traditional shamanistic societies, the horse has a special symbolic role in so far as it represents a high status consonant with the speed at which it can convey the shaman between the layers of the cosmos (Dowson & Porr 2001). Furthermore, I was interested to read that, in Gaelic tradition, horses are particularly credited with 'second sight', because of their apparent sensitivity to precognition: in the words of John MacInnes, 'the horse is the seer of the animal kingdom' (MacInnes 1989, 14). If horses were associated with such vaticinatory qualities in Iron Age antiquity - qualities which they therefore shared with shamanic prophets - then such perceptions may have contributed both to their importance for coin imagery and for their human-headed imagery (Aldhouse-Green and Aldhouse-Green 2005, 127-131).

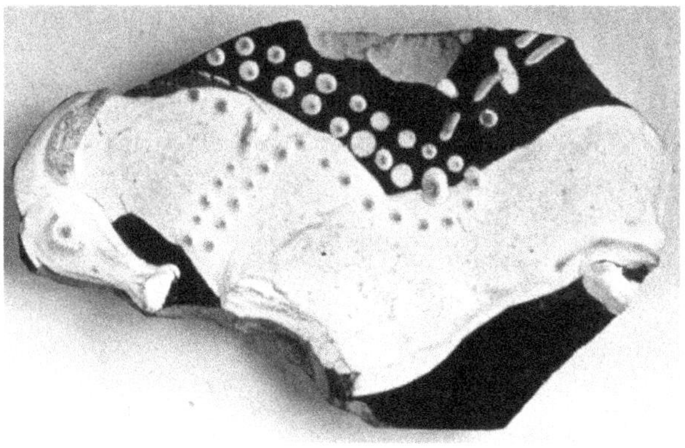

Figure 22. Sherd of colour-coated pottery depicting a white horse; from the Roman town of Wroxeter, Shropshire (author).

Through a glass darkly: disproportion & exaggeration

The coin just mentioned is singular, not simply in so far as it depicts a bird riding a horse but also because the bird is hugely disproportionate in terms of realistic dimorphism. Such discrepant treatment focuses attention on a further feature linking coin imagery to that of other coeval and later media: unrealistic exaggeration and multiplication of animal body-parts, the treatment of motifs that, like monsters, fall within the schema of surreality. The most common example of exaggeration is the extended dorsal crest on coin boar-figures (Gruel 1989, 109; Van Arsdell 1989, 108; Figure 23), but a similar approach to image-making can be discerned in the treatment of antlers (Green 1986, 10; Figure 24).

Figure 23. Bronze coin of the Veliocasses depicting a boar with exaggerated dorsal bristles (Institute of Archaeology, Oxford).

Figure 24. Silver coin found at Maidstone, Kent, depicting stag and boar (National Museum of Wales).

Precisely the same form of distortion can be identified on figural metalwork and stonework of the Iron Age and Roman periods. Countless boar images exhibit this pattern of treatment: for example, from religious hoards at Neuvy-en-Sullias, Loiret (Green 1992, fig. 5.9; Figure 25), and from Hounslow in south-east England (*op. cit.*, fig. 5.12) and Báta in Hungary (Megaw and Megaw 1989, 161, fig. 248). So do stag images, most evocatively at Val Camonica (Priuli 1996, 100, fig. 176). James Blackmore (1996) and others (Lorblanchet and Bahn 1993) draw attention to the persistent theme of this kind of exaggeration in 'shamanistic' transcendental art, past and present: Blackmore, in particular, looks at the way in which a dead or spirit giraffe is typically depicted with erect dorsal ridge, to signify its otherworldly status, perhaps because of observation that the animal's hair erects during death-trauma. What is more, this raising of the dorsal ridge may be to do with dream-visions: dogs and cats erect their back hair while dreaming. Perhaps we should approach the treatment of horses' manes on coins in the same way: there is a pattern of depiction showing the mane as a row of large dots (Duval 1987, 56, 63) that is precisely similar to the treatment of the mane on the weird half-horse, half-bull creatures on the Capel Garmon firedog, ritually deposited in a North Welsh peat-bog beneath a large stone in the late Iron Age (Savory 1976, pl. VI).

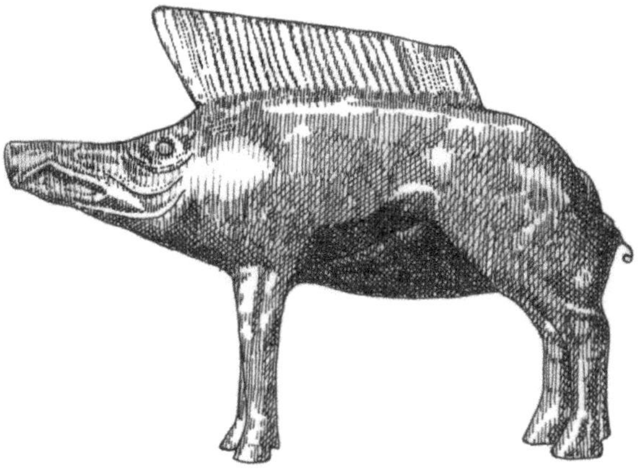

Figure 25. Almost life-size bronze boar-statuette found in a hoard of religious imagery, including a horse, stag and other boars, from a shrine of the Roman conquest period at Neuvy-en-Sullias, Loiret (Paul Jenkins).

Multiplication may be part of the same kind of surreal attitude: the triple-tailed horse is a numismatic commonplace, but other forms of multiplication are also manifest: the Bratislava coin (Figure 26) with its row of three phalli or teats is a case-in-point (Green 1997, 903, fig. 2). That this horse may be a 'death' animal is, perhaps, reflected in the presence of a row of dots beneath its tail, which may be interpreted as depicting defecation; loss of bowel-control may occur as part of the stress of the dying process, and is displayed on certain Iron Age Iberian ceramics from Numancia apparently representing human and animal sacrifice (Sopeña Genzor 2000; Aldhouse-Green 2001c, 47). The coin motif already mentioned, of a horse ridden by a disproportionately large bird of prey may, perhaps, be similarly interpreted as an image of death.

Figure 26. Silver coin from Bratislava, Bohemia, depicting a 'spirit-horse' (Nick Griffiths).

Gender-bending and sinistrality

The final theme I would like briefly to explore in this paper is the treatment of gender on coins and other iconography. The motif of the naked horsewoman or female chariot-driver has already been touched upon once or twice, particularly with regard to the human-faced horse, but I should like now specifically to engage with the issues perhaps underpinning such depiction since it may be appropriate to acknowledge a multi-layered set of meanings. Firstly, the very representation of females in a 'warrior' context is interesting, especially if viewed through the prism of resistant, independent iconographies here suggested (Green 1998a), for such a theme runs counter to the *mores* of the Roman world.

Secondly, there is the issue of nakedness: female nudity which, in a battle-context, might be regarded as shocking to Roman sensibilities. But nakedness may have been charged with special meaning, over and above the contesting of *romanitas*. Chris Tilley (1999, 257) has suggested that nakedness may be associated with liminality and acknowledgement of the symbolic boundary of skin; in the context of Peruvian Moche tradition, Erica Hill (2000, 317-326) draws attention to the effect of stripping people for human sacrifice, arguing that such action serves to deny individuality but to emphasise the concept of corporeality. Certainly, a significant number of Iron Age bog-bodies went into the marsh naked, and the woman from Haraldskaer in Denmark, who died in the fifth century BC, was interred naked but with her clothes placed nearby (Aldhouse-Green 2001c, 202; Hvass 1998). Not only are the coin women naked but they may occur in attitudes of frenzy, almost as if possessed or in an ecstatic state (Figure 27). Were these images deliberately selected as statements of "unroman-ness"?

Figure 27. Coin of eastern Armorica depicting frenzied horsewoman (Lengyel 1954, no. 196).

The third issue relates to sinistrality: on some coins, the woman holds a sword in her left hand and her shield in the right (Figure 28): it is possible to argue that, once more, there is an intention to contravene the norm of righthandedness. If we glance at non-coin iconography, we find some parallel material: the little Romano-British stone figure from Lemington, on the Cotswolds, depicts a woman - not naked, it is true - but with a spear in her left hand (Green 1995, 75; Figure 29).

Figure 28. Coin of eastern Armorica, depicting a naked horsewoman, with sword in left hand and shield in right (Lengyel 1954, no. 197).

Paying the ferryman: magic, myth & money

In conclusion, we should return to our starting-point, namely the function of Iron Age coins as vehicles for the conveyance of images. There is no doubt that motifs on coins were designed to be read; their small size is no inhibition to such a function: Iron Age decorated metalwork, particularly on jewellery, is full of minute images that were nonetheless charged with meaning and, in turn, served to empower the objects they adorned and their possessors. Should we read special meaning into coinage? Perhaps it is important to appreciate that all money is intrinsically magical: after all, unlike an axe or a weapon, a coin means something other than itself, depending for its power on human cognitive investment, together with notions of fidelity and trust between individuals, groups of people and between humans and the gods. In Classical contexts, as in medieval Europe, money was inextricably bound up with religion: we need only to cite the temple treasuries of ancient Greece, the creation of the goddess Moneta in Rome, or the moneychangers' booths in the temple at Jerusalem that so incensed Christ. Small wonder, then, that Iron Age coins on the one hand comprised symbols in themselves and, on the other, served to carry powerful messages that both reinforced and created relationships in both terrestrial and spiritual domains. The fantastic, surreal motifs examined in this paper are of particular interest, for they resonate within a broader canvas of monsters, shape-shifters and spirit-beings whose polysemic character reflected their ability to migrate between worlds, layers of being and states of becoming.

Figure 29. Romano-British stone carving of a robed female figure, with a spear in her left hand and a casket or bucket beneath her right; from Lemington, Gloucestershire (The National Trust).

It is fitting to end with allusion to a direct connection between money and transference between earth and spirit worlds in an ancient European context: the ritual of paying the ferryman, Charon, the sinister boatman of Classical tradition, who rowed dead souls across the Styx to the Otherworld and for whom a coin was placed in the mouths of corpses to pay for their crossing. In Book VI of the *Aeneid*, an account of the Trojan hero Aeneas's journey to the underworld to visit his father, Anchises, Charon is described in graphic detail by Virgil as a liminal, transformative being:

'A dreadful ferryman looks after the river crossing,
Charon: appallingly filthy he is, with a bush of unkempt
White beard upon his chin, with eyes like jets of fire;
And a dirty cloak draggles down, knotted about his shoulders.
He poles the boat, he looks after the sails, he is all the crew
Of that rust-coloured wherry which takes the dead across -
An ancient now, but a god's old age is green and sappy.'

(Virgil *Aeneid* VI, lines 298-304; trans. C. D. Lewis, in Chisholm & Ferguson 1981)

Bibliography

Aldhouse-Green, M. J. 1999: *Pilgrims in Stone. Stone Images from the Gallo-Roman Sanctuary of Fontes Sequanae* (Oxford, British Archaeological Reports S754).

Aldhouse-Green, M. J. 2001a: Animal iconographies. Metaphor, meaning and identity (or Why Chinese Dragons Don't Have Wings). In G. Davies, A. Gardner and K. Lockyear (eds), *TRAC 2000. Proceedings of the Tenth Annual Theoretical Archaeology Conference London 2000* (Oxford, Oxbow), 80-93.

Aldhouse-Green, M. J. 2001b: Cosmovision and metaphor: monsters and shamans in Gallo-British cult-expression. *European Journal of Archaeology* 4(2), 201-230.

Aldhouse-Green, M. J. 2001c: *Dying for the Gods. Human Sacrifice in Iron Age and Roman Europe* (Stroud, Tempus).

Aldhouse-Green, M. J. 2003: Alternative iconographies: metaphors of resistance in Romano-British cult-imagery. In P. Noelke (ed.), *Romanisation und Resistenz in Plastik, Architektur und Inschfriften der Provinzen des Imperium Romanum: neue Funde und Forschungen. Akten des VII Internationalen Colloquiums über Probleme des Provinzialrömischen Kunstschaffens* (Mainz, Zabern), 39-48.

Aldhouse-Green, M. J. 2004: *An archaeology of images* (London, Routledge).

Aldhouse-Green, M. J 2005: Ritual bondage, violence, slavery and sacrifice in later European prehistory. In M. Parker Pearson and I. J. N. Thorpe (eds), *Violence and Slavery in prehistory: proceedings of a Prehistoric Society conference at Sheffield University* (Oxford, BAR S1374), 155-163.

Aldhouse-Green, M. J. and Aldhouse-Green, S. 2005: *The quest for the shaman* (London, Thames and Hudson).

Allen, D. F. 1980: *The Coins of the ancient Celts* (Edinburgh, Edinburgh University Press).

Blackmore, J. 1996: Outlining a 'new' region: the rock art of the Omburo Ost, Namibia. Paper delivered at the Theoretical Archaeology Group Conference, University of Liverpool, December 1996.

Boon, G. C. 1982: A coin with the head of the Cernunnos. *Seaby's Coin and Medal Bulletin* 769, 276-282.

Bott, E. 1987: The Kava Ceremonial as a dream structure. In M. Douglas (ed.), *Constructive Drinking. Perspectives on Drink from Anthropology* (Cambridge), 182-204.

Chisholm, K. and Ferguson, J. (eds) 1981: *Rome. The Augustan Age* (Oxford, OUP/Open University Press).

Cool, H. E. M. 2000: The significance of snake jewellery hoards. *Britannia* 31, 29-40.

Creighton, J. 2000: *Coins and Power in Late Iron Age Britain* (Cambridge, CUP).

Davidson, H. E. 1989: The Seer's Thumb. In H. E. Davidson (ed.), *The Seer in Celtic and Other Traditions* (Edinburgh, John Donald), 66-78.

Desmonde, W. H. 1962: *Magic, Myth and Money. The Origin of Money in Religious Ritual* (New York, The Free Press of Glencoe Inc.).

Dowson, T. and Porr, M. 2001: Special objects – special creatures. Shamanistic imagery and the Aurignacian of South-West Germany. In N. Price (ed.), *The Archaeology of Shamanism* (London, Routledge), 163-177.

Duval, P.-M. 1987: *Monnaies gauloises et mythes celtiques* (Paris, Hermann).

Espérandieu, E. 1911: *Recueil Général des Bas-Reliefs de la Gaule Romaine et Pré-Romaine IV* (Paris, Leroux).

Espérandieu, E. 1915: *Recueil Général des Bas-Reliefs de la Gaule Romaine et Pré-Romaine VI* (Paris, Leroux).

Green, M. J. 1986: *The Gods of the Celts* (Gloucester, Alan Sutton).

Green, M. J. 1989: *Symbol and Image in Celtic Religious Art* (London, Routledge).

Green, M. J. 1992: *Animals in Celtic life and myth* (London, Routledge).

Green, M. J. 1995: *Celtic Goddesses. Warriors, Virgins and Mothers* (London, British Museum Press).

Green, M. J. 1996: *Celtic art: reading the messages* (London, Weidenfeld and Nicolson).

Green, M. J. 1997: Images in opposition: polarity, ambivalence and liminality in cult representation. *Antiquity* 71, no. 274, 898-911.

Green, M. J. 1998a: Some Gallo-British goddesses: iconography and meaning. In L. Goodison and C. Morris (eds), *Ancient Goddesses. The Myths and the Evidence* (London, British Museum Press), 180-195.

Green, M. J. 1998b: God in man's image: thoughts on the genesis and affiliations of some Romano-British cult-imagery. *Britannia* 29, 17-30.

Gruel, K. 1989: *La monnaie chez les Gaulois* (Paris, Errance).

Hill, E. 2000: The embodied sacrifice. *Cambridge Archaeological Journal* 10:2, 317-326.

Hvass, L. 1998: *Dronning Gunhild - et moselig fra jernalderen* (Vejle, Sesam).

Joffroy, R. 1979: *Musée des Antiquités Nationales, Saint-Germain-en-Laye* (Paris, Editions de la Réunion des Musées Nationaux).

Johns, C. M. 1997: *The Snettisham Roman Jeweller's Hoard* (London, British Museum Press).

Kaul, F., Marazov, I., Best, J. and de Vries, N. 1991: *Thracian Tales on the Gundestrup Cauldron* (Amsterdam, Najade Press).

King, H. 1995: Half-human creatures. In J. Cherry (ed.), *Mythical Beasts* (London, British Museum Press), 138-167.

Lengyel, L. 1954: *L'art gaulois dans les médailles* (Montrouge-Seine, Corvina).

Lorblanchet, M. and Bahn, P. G. (eds) 1993: *Rock-Art Studies: The Post-Stylistic era or where do we go from here?* (Oxford, Oxbow Monograph 35).

MacInnes, J. 1989: The Seer in Gaelic Tradition. In H. E. Davidson (ed.), *The Seer in Celtic and other Traditions* (Edinburgh, John Donald), 10-24.

Mattingly, H. (transl.) 1948: *Tacitus on Britain and Germany* (West Drayton, Penguin).

Megaw, J. V. S. 1970: *Art of the European Iron Age* (New York, Harper and Row).

Megaw, R. and Megaw, V. 1989: *Celtic Art. From its beginnings to the Book of Kells* (London, Thames and Hudson).

Meniel, P. 1987: *Chasse et élevage chez les Gaulois* (Paris, Errance).

O'Connell, M. G. & Bird, J. 1994: The Roman temple at Wanborough, excavation 1985-1986. *Surrey Archaeological Collections* 82, 1-168.

Olmsted, G. S. 1979: *The Gundestrup Cauldron* (Brussels, Collection Latomus Monograph 162).

Price, N. (ed.) 2001: *The Archaeology of Shamanism* (London, Routledge).

Priuli, A. 1996: *Le Più Antiche Manifestazioni Spirituali Arte Rupestre Paleoiconografia Camuna e delle Genti Alpine* (Torino, Collana, I Grandi Libri).

Rozwadowski, A. 2001: Sun Gods or shamans? Interpreting the 'solar-headed' petroglyphs of Central Asia. In N. Price (ed.), *The archaeology of Shamanism* (London, Routledge), 64-86.

Savory, H. N. 1976: *Guide Catalogue of the Iron Age Collections* (Cardiff, National Museum of Wales).

Shanks, M. 1996: Style and design of a perfume jar from an Archaic Greek city state. In R. W. Preucel and I. Hodder (eds), *Contemporary Archaeology in Theory: a reader* (Oxford, Basil Blackwell), 364-393.

Sopeña Genzor, G. 2000: Apuntes sobre ritos funerales en Celtiberia. In G. Ruiz Zapatero and A. Jimeno Martínez (eds), *Numancia y el Mundo Celtibérico 'Paisaje Social y Simbólico en la Europa Céltica'* (Soria, Fundación Duques de Soria, Curso de Arqueologia July 2000).

Thévenot, E. 1968: *Divinités et sanctuaires de la Gaule* (Paris, Payot).

Tilley, C. 1999: *Metaphor and material culture* (Oxford, Basil Blackwell).

Van Arsdell, R. D. 1989: *Celtic Coinage of Britain* (London, Spink).

Vitebsky, P. 1995: *The Shaman* (London, Macmillan).

Webster, J. 2003: Art as resistance and negotiation. In S. Scott and J. Webster (eds), *Roman Imperialism and Provincial Art* (Cambridge, CUP), 24-51.

Coinage and wine in Gaul

Brigitte Fischer

'Lève-toi, remplissons notre coupe de vin,
Avant qu'on n'ait rempli la coupe de la vie'
(Omar Khayam)

The beginning of wine-making in Gaul is a subject of much debate. Some authorities believe it existed a long time before the Roman conquest, others that it appeared only after the conquest. Whichever the case, one fact is certain: wine-drinking goes back to the remote past of the country, since the thousands of sherds of imported Etruscan amphorae in Lattes (Hérault) and Saint-Blaise (Bouches-du-Rhône), for example, can be dated to the end of the seventh century BC (Tchernia 1986, 91).

It is well known that Celtic coins in general, and Gaulish coins in particular, provide evidence for various aspects of life during the period in which they were in use. We also know that the wine trade, well attested by archaeology, was an extremely important feature of society and the economy during the protohistoric period. The purpose of this article is thus to assess the importance of vine and wine in the iconography of the Gaulish coinage.

The first Celtic imitations of Greek staters were accurate copies of their models, and thus we do not expect to find great evidence of originality among them. Nor, perhaps more surprisingly, do we find designs related to wine and the wine trade among the next generations of gold coins. In fact the coin types related to these subjects are very rare and late. They are chiefly to be found in the centre of Gaul. The peoples who made them include the Arverni, the Turones, the Carnutes and the Aulerci Eburovices, as well as the Meldi, who were located at the limit between the Celtic and the Belgic worlds (Figure 1). These tribes are close to each other. They nearly all have common borders and, if the Bituriges, who do not use this iconography, had not barred the way, these tribes would have constituted a large block in the heart of Gaul.

The lack of designs related to wine on the Biturigan coinage presumably cannot be explained by the temperance of this people, since numerous sherds of amphorae have been found in the territory. In Bourges, for example, the ancient *Avaricum*, a significant trade in amphorae from Italy is known as early as the second century BC (Barthélemy-Sylvand 2000-01, 77). Important *oppida*, such as Levroux (Indre) and Châteaumeillant (*Mediolanum*, Cher), typically have a layer of Italic amphorae, dated around the third and second centuries BC (*ibid.*, 78). For unknown reasons, the Bituriges preferred simpler designs on their coinage: on the obverses, human heads, and on the reverses, various animals – horses, birds, and wild pigs. None of this decoration is related to vine-growing or wine.

During the Gallic War, the Arverni minted two series of gold staters which show an amphora engraved under the belly of the horse. One series is sometimes uninscribed, on other occasions inscribed: in the example shown here, the word CAS is engraved on the obverse (Figure 2). The other series is in the name of Vercingetorix (Figure 3). The reverses of all of these coins are very similar. Their western neighbours, the Turones, struck bronzes inscribed TVRONOS/TRICCOS. This coinage, which is dated after the Roman conquest, can be divided into two series. For one of them, several *denarii* were imitated on both obverse and reverse. On the other series (Figure 4), the head on the obverse seems close to the *denarius* minted by the Pomponia *gens*, struck in 118 BC (Seaby 1978, 77; *Pomponia* 6). The reverse is wholly Gaulish: it features a standing bull facing right, with a beaded circle, with a pellet at its centre, above the animal, and an amphora as high as the bull standing in front of it. Several coinages are decorated with a bull of this type, especially in the east of Gaul (e.g. LT XXIX 7187/7186, 7191).

The Carnutes also struck late bronzes which are deeply romanized, and decorated with motifs related to wine. This coinage can be divided into two series. A human head in Roman style is engraved on the obverse of both, in front of which is the inscription CATAL. On one of the series, behind the head, at the end of a long stem, there is a leaf divided in three parts which seems to be a stylised vine leaf (Figure 5). A Roman *denarius*, minted by the Plaetoria *gens* and dated around 67 BC (Seaby 1978, 73; *Plaetoria* 4), has been closely imitated on the reverse. The inscription engraved around the prototype has not been reproduced on the Gaulish coin; an S-shaped hook has been added on each side of the bird's head, as well as a *lituus* to the left, but the most important addition is an amphora to the right of the eagle.

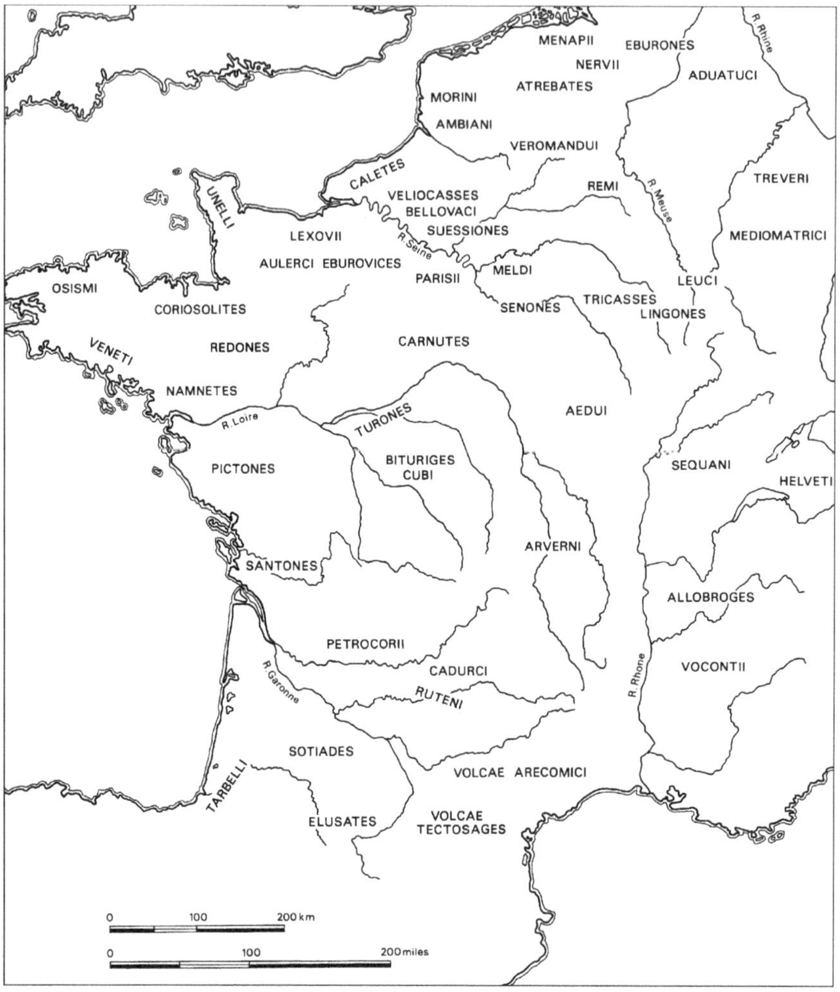

Figure 1. Map of the Gallic peoples (after Allen 1995, map 3).

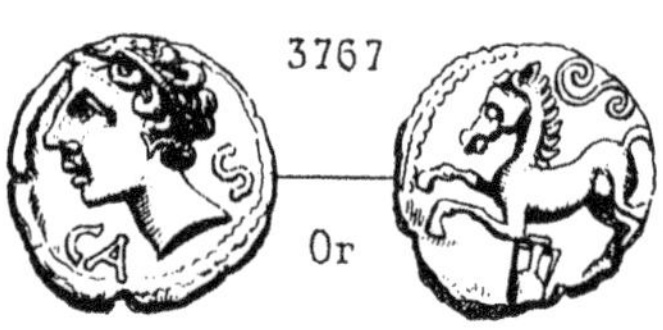

Figure 2. Gold stater of the Arverni, BN 3767.

Figure 3. Gold stater of the Arverni, BN 3774.

Figure 4. Bronze unit of the Turones, BMC III, 145.

Figure 5. Bronze unit of the Carnutes, BN 6330.

Although the Aulerci Eburovices did not engrave amphorae on their coins, they still paid attention to the vine, since it decorates the obverse of some of their bronze coins, in front of the human face (Figure 6). This side seems to be imitated from a *denarius* of the Caecilia *gens*, dated between 82 and 80 BC (Seaby 1978, 20; *Caecilia* 30). On the Gaulish imitation, the artist added superb vine branches to the head visible on the Roman coin. The leaves are perfect, but the grapes, instead of being in bunches, are all grouped by three, which is a deeply symbolic number. On the reverse there is a galloping horse facing right. Two S-shaped hooks and a small circle are engraved above the horse's back, and a hanging leaf at the end of a long stem stands in front of its chest. This is probably a vine leaf. This coinage was also struck after the Roman conquest.

The Meldi, located in the northern part of the country, around Melun (*Metlosedum*), minted various silver and bronze coins which are related to vine and wine. On the obverse, silver coins are decorated with a human bust and the neck is adorned with a pearl necklace. There are borders of leaves around the edge of the obverse (Figure 7). On the reverse, there is a galloping horse to the right, sometimes with a tall male figure standing in front of the animal. A large vine, with its roots, rises behind the horse. Grapes are grouped three by three along the stem.

A good image of the vine is to be seen on bronze coins of the Meldi. The obverse is decorated with a head facing left. The inscription ARCANTODAN ROVECA is engraved on some coins, while on others, behind the head, there is a vine leaf and a bunch of grapes (Figure 8). A winged lion running to the right is visible on the reverse. Above the lion there are two S-shaped hooks, and there are bunches of grapes and vine-branches beneath the exergual line.

The most surprising bronze coinage shows a head facing left on the obverse. The word ROVECA is inscribed in front of the face. Two small ringed pellets are visible under this head, one on each side (Figure 9). The neck is decorated with a torc, and there is a small oblique line at the bottom of the neck. Beneath this line is a small amphora on its side. On the reverse there is a horse galloping to the left, with a small ringed pellet above and below. The inscription POOYIKA is engraved around the bottom part of the coin.

Figure 6. Bronze unit of the Aulerci Eburovices, BN 7042.

Figure 7. Silver coins of the Meldi, Lyons 1000-01.

Figure 8. Bronze unit of the Meldi (Hucher 1868, pl. 48.1).

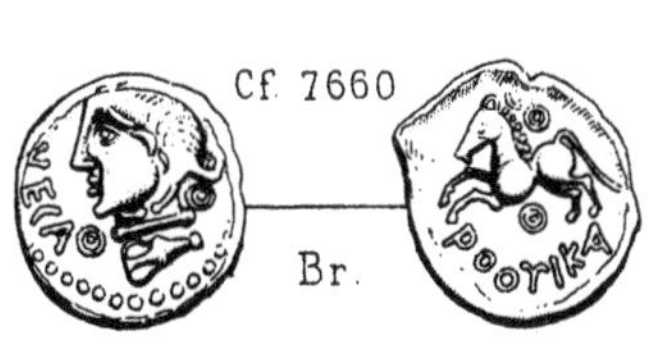

Figure 9. Bronze unit of the Meldi, BN 7660.

At this point we can summarize some facts about these various coinages:

- the peoples who struck these coins related to vine and wine are located in Celtic Gaul, except the Meldi, who are on the margins of Celtic and Belgic Gaul. So relatively few peoples are concerned with this iconography, and most of them have common borders.
- the coins are made of gold, silver (one type only) and bronze. There are no known cast coins.
- all these coins were minted either during the conquest or not long after it.

Some negative observations are also worth making:

- *Narbonnensis*, which is an extensive region and where wine-making originated, does not show any decoration related to wine on its numerous coins.
- in the '*denarius* zone', in the east of Gaul, where the wine trade was so important - especially in the Rhône and Saône valleys - there is again no wine iconography on the coinage. But thousands and thousands of amphorae sherds have been found in various places in this region, such as Mont-Beuvray (Larochemillay, Nièvre), Joeuvres and Essalois (Loire).

The presence of amphorae on Arvernian gold staters and on the obverse of the Meldi bronzes, immediately beneath the human face, shows how very important wine was. However, if the wine trade was so economically and socially significant in Gaul, how can we explain that so few peoples evoked it on their coins, and when they did, why was this decoration used at such a late period? The vines and grapes on the coins are obviously related to wine, but no more precise information can be drawn from these motifs. The amphorae, however, are a different matter. Might we be able to identify the various types shown on the Gaulish coins, and thus through knowledge of their origin and chronology gain useful information about trade routes and wine-making in Gaul?

In fact after comparing the amphorae on coins with the genuine items, and following discussion with amphorae specialists, it is apparent that the amphorae on coins are not true representations of these containers. Instead the coin engravers tended to choose one type, and then added features of another type to it. On some staters of Vercingetorix, for example, the representation of Massaliot amphorae is very close to the original (Figures 10-11). However, these amphorae were not made between about 125 and 40 BC (Bats 1993, 60), a period which of course encompasses the production of these staters. In his study of Marseilles, Rome and Gaul from the third to the first century BC, Christian Goudineau has commented that 'from the mid-second century Italian wine replaced that of Marseilles. It totally replaced it... from around 100 BC' (Goudineau 1983, 80). The narrow amphorae which are engraved on the Arvernian staters are close to the Greco-Italic amphorae (Figures 12-13). But, at this time, the Dressel I type was imported in huge quantities nearly everywhere in Gaul: sherds of this type amount to more than 90% of the total quantity of sherds recovered from contexts of this period.

Figure 10. Gold stater of the Arverni, Péronne 108.

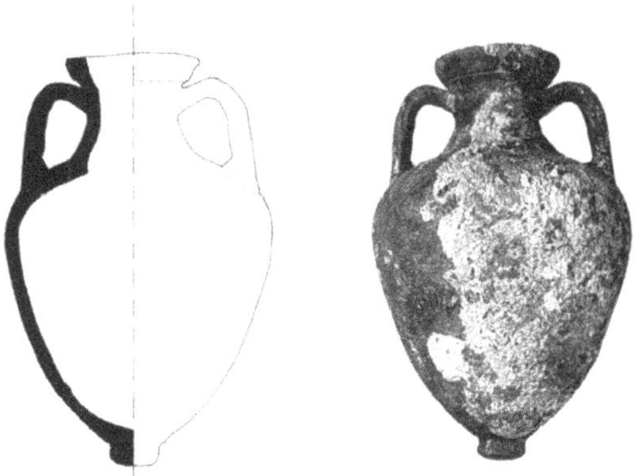

Figure 11. Massiliot amphora (after Sciallano and Sibella 1991, 27).

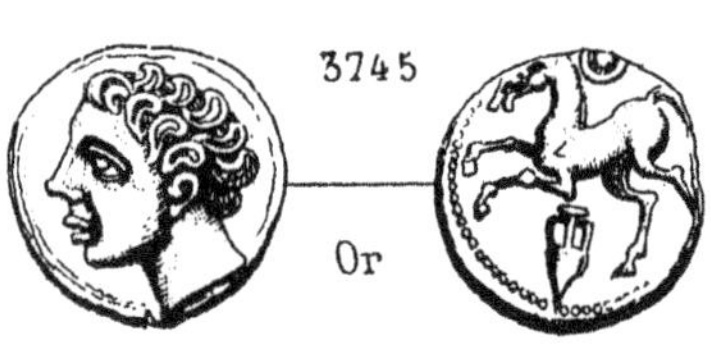

Figure 12. Gold stater of the Arverni, BN 3745.

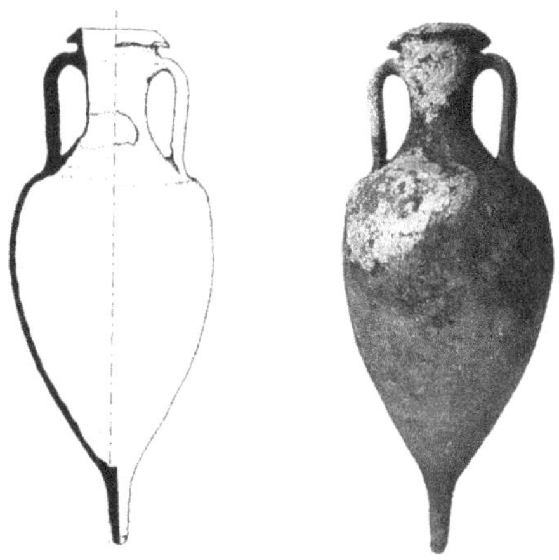

Figure 13. Greco-Italic amphora (after Sciallano and Sibella 1991, 30).

In a recent article, Loughton and Jones (2000) have stressed the exceptional importance of the wine trade in the Arvernian territory. They suggest that it started at the turn of the third and second centuries BC, and increased tremendously during the course of the second century BC. Its decline began around 80/70 BC. In the department of Puy-de-Dôme alone, amphorae have been found on 117 sites (Figure 14). This is nearly as many as in the south of France and in the areas supplying metal ores, where wine-drinking was exceptionally popular (Figure 15). In contrast, in Berry (the Biturigan territory), Greco-Italic amphorae are very rare; in Auvergne (the Arvernian territory) they are found even on medium-size settlement sites, and there wine-drinking seems to have been common among a great part of the population. The authors of this study point out that such a significant trade, which lasted more than one century, in a time of major social, political and economic change, must have required a remarkable degree of organization and a steady market (Loughton and Jones 2000, 69, 72, 79).

At the time of the Gallic War, when these staters were struck, Greco-Italic amphorae were no longer imported. They are not usually found in contexts of this period, although there may be some residual sherds in levels dated after 120 BC. This is somewhat unexpected, and it indicates that the Arverni did not show on their coins the amphorae which were in use at that time. Instead the artists engraved much older amphorae on their staters, made half a century or even a century before. As we have seen, that period was the peak of the wine trade in the Arvernian territory. So, might we suggest that although the amphorae were related to wine, of course, they were also – and perhaps more importantly – symbolic of the peak of this important trade, and therefore of prosperity? Wine was a fundamental element of wealth. Diodorus of Sicily famously wrote of the Gauls that 'They have a furious passion for drinking and get altogether beyond themselves... for one amphora of wine they receive one slave, thus exchanging the drink for the cupbearer' (Diodorus, V, 26, 3). In exchange for wine the Romans also received metal ores, which is why amphorae are so commonly found in mining regions (Laubenheimer 1990, 74-75; Tchernia 1986, 88). Tchernia (*ibid.*) stresses this point: 'Le goût des Gaulois pour le vin était presque proverbial dans l'Antiquité...'. It was a prestige item. It was an essential element of the gifts exchanged between princes and nobles, and of the huge assemblies and celebrations they must have organized. Archaeological excavations have proved that numerous amphorae were opened at the same time, and that the wine was drunk within a short time by many people (Poux and Selles 1998, 221-222).

In this world, political power and wealth were strictly associated. This fact is obvious on the bronze coin of the Carnutes, on which the amphora added to the Roman prototype is engraved on the right side of the eagle, symbol of power. A *lituus* is visible on the left side of the bird of prey, demonstrating a religious association (Figure 16): wine was also used in religious celebrations. In an article about Italic wine among the Carnutes, Poux and Selles studied the amphorae excavated at Chartres (Eure-et-Loir), ancient *Autricum.* In spite of the very limited research work which has been carried out there, hundreds of amphorae of various types were discovered. The authors note the prominent role of the Carnutes in religion (Poux and Selles 1998, 222), recalling Caesar's comment in *De Bello Gallico* (VI, 13): 'These Druids, at a certain time of the year, meet within the borders of the Carnutes, whose territory is reckoned as the centre of all Gaul, and sit in conclave in a consecrated spot.' It would seem that this tribe, so important from the religious point of view, also used much wine.

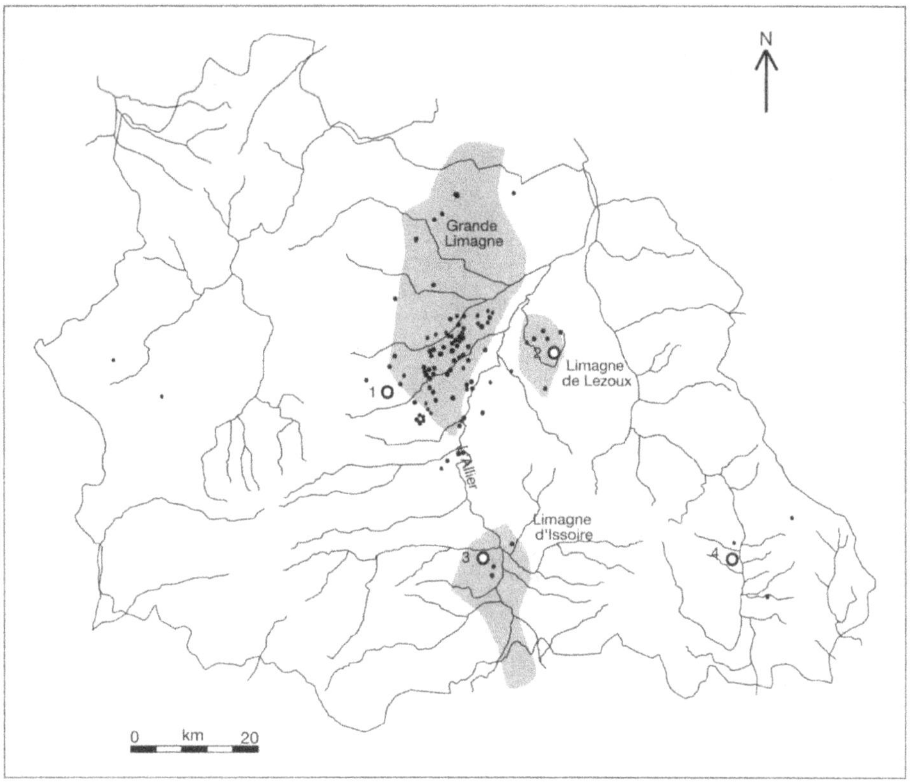

Figure 14. Distribution of Republican amphorae in the department of Puy-de-Dôme (after Loughton and Jones 2000, fig. 4).

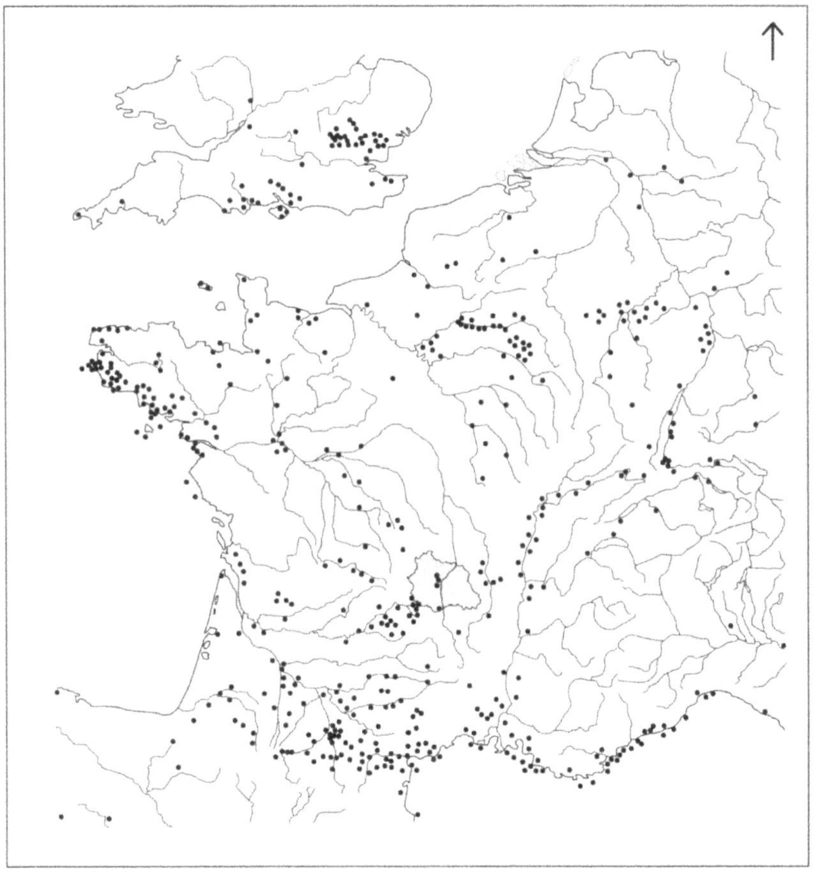

Figure 15. Distribution of Republican amphorae in western Europe (after Loughton and Jones 2000, fig. 3, based on Fitzpatrick 1985, fig. 3).

On the bronze coin of the Turones, the amphora is associated with the standing bull and it is as high as the animal, probably to show its importance (Figure 17). A careful observation of the bull reveals that it is not an ordinary animal. In the middle of his body there is a small piece of material which hangs on each side of his belly. This ornament is typical of the animals used for sacrifice, and, again, this scene reminds us of the sacred world.

Figure 16. Bronze unit of the Carnutes, BMC III, S123.

Figure 17. Bronze unit of the Turones, BN 6999.

Consider the cult of Dionysus, evoked by Franke and Marathaki (1999, 41) in their work on wine and coinage in Greece. The authors write that originally, 'Songs, pantomine and choruses were first consecrated to this god'. They add: 'Before a performance began, there was a sacrifice to him. This ceremony was finally followed by a public drinking contest... At the 'City' Dionysia in March, the cult statue was brought from the neighbouring community of Eleutherae in a great procession with sacrificial bulls, wine and drinking vessels... At the feast given afterwards, there was a lot of merry drinking'. Could it be such a ceremony which is represented on the reverse of the Turones bronze?

The relatively plain iconography of the Meldi bronze coin is of little use in drawing further conclusions, although at least it shows the exceptional significance of the amphora, which is engraved under the head on the obverse of the coin (Figure 18).

On these three bronze series, it is hard to detect the precise type of the amphora. No known pottery can be identified as being the prototype, but a relationship is to be found between the amphorae engraved on the Turones, Meldi and, to a lesser extent Carnutes coins with an amphora which decorates a Bithynian tetradrachm of Heraclea (Figure 19). On the reverse of this coin, dated between 289 and 281 BC, the seated figure of Dionysus holds a very similar amphora at arm's length (Franke and Marathaki 1999, figs. 115, 128).

The motif of the giant vine on a silver coin of the Meldi also takes us back to Greece (Figure 20). The branches, with their leaves and grapes grouped in threes, are symmetrically engraved. This type, which is exceptional in terms of its style and arrangement, appeared three centuries earlier in Euboea. The city of Histiaea minted a silver drachm, dated between 369 and 338 BC, which shows a bull, symbol of the town, in front of a high vine with symmetrical branches, just like the branches on the Gaulish coin (Franke and Marathaki 1999, figs. 60, 76; Figure 21).

Figure 18. Bronze unit of the Meldi, BN 7660.

Figure 19. Silver tetradrachm, Bythinia, Heraclea (Franke and Marathaki 1999, fig. 115).

Figure 20. Silver coin of the Meldi, BN 7698.

Figure 21. Silver drachm, Histiaea, Euboea (Franke and Marathaki 1999, fig. 60).

We know that the Gauls copied the Greeks in many aspects of coin production: not only the concept of money, but obviously at first they also closely imitated the staters of Philip II of Macedon, and adopted the same metrology. At the end of their coinage, when many Greek motifs had been replaced by locally-derived decoration, several Gaulish tribes returned to Greek monetary iconography, as we can see here from these representations of wine and amphorae. It is interesting to note that the Meldi, who used motifs related to wine more than any other people, are also one of the last tribes to use the Greek alphabet along with the Latin one.

Marc Bar (1987, 82) has written that only the Meldi established a cooperative relationship with Caesar: 'Il semble donc qu'ils aient accepté l'offre de César moyennant son aide technique et aussi la fourniture de vin campanien (voir... du cheval gaulois de leurs monnaies d'argent et de bronze, le cep de vigne avec feuilles et fruits)'. Our conclusions are identical to his own views, when he writes that 'Même les personnifications qui sont inspirées de celles de deniers romains paraissent choisies pour leur caractère grec' (*ibid.*, 85). In Belgic Gaul, at the time of Caesar, he identifies '...une avide recherche de nouveaux types monétaires empruntés au répertoire romain, mais aussi à celui des Grecs occidentaux...' (*ibid.*, 2). The study of this relationship between old Greek coins and late Gaulish coins deserves much attention: it may yet reveal further, surprising information.

Acknowledgements
I would like to thank my colleagues C. Bémont, A. Hesnard and S. Humbert for their advice on amphorae, and D. Gerin for information on Greek numismatics.

Bibliography

Allen, D. (ed. Mays, M.) 1995: *Catalogue of Celtic coins in the British Museum. Volume III, Bronze coins of Gaul* (London, BMP).

Bar, M. 1987: Les modalités de l'influence de l'hellénisme sur les monnaies gallo-belges du temps de César. *Cercle d'études numismatiques* 24, 1-12, 35-43, 67-77, 81-90.

Barthélemy-Sylvand, C. 2000-01: Les amphores: chronologie des importations. *Cahiers d'archéologie et d'histoire du Berry* 144/145, 69-78.

Bats, M. 1993: Amphores massaliètes. In M. Py (ed.), *Dictionnaire des céramiques antiques (VIIème s. av. n.è.-VIIème s. de n.è.) en Méditerranée nord-occidentale (Provence, Languedoc, Ampurdan)* (Lattes, Lattara 6), 60-63.

de La Tour, H. 1892 (updated by Fischer, B., 1999): *Atlas de monnaies gauloises* (Paris).

Empereur, J.-Y. and Hesnard, A. 1987: Les amphores hellénistiques. In P. Lévêque and J.-P. Morel (eds), *Céramiques hellénistiques et romaines II (Paris, Annales littéraires de l'Université de Besançon* 331), 10-71.

Franke, P. R. and Marathaki, I. 1999: *Wine and Coins in Ancient Greece* (Athens, The Hatzimichalis Estate).

Goudineau, C. 1983: Marseilles, Rome and Gaul from the third to the first century B.C. In P. Garnsey, K. Hopkins and C. R. Whittaker (eds), *Trade in the ancient economy* (London, Chatto and Windus), 76-86.

Laubenheimer, F. 1990: *Le temps des amphores en Gaule. Vins, huiles et sauces* (Paris, Errance).

Loughton, M. E. and Jones, S. 2000: Les amphores républicaines en Auvergne (Puy-de-Dôme): importation et diffusion avant la Conquête. *Revue archéologique du Centre de la France* 39, 63-81.

Poux, M. and Selles, H. 1998: Vin italique en pays carnute. A propos d'un lot d'amphores Dressel 1 découvert à Chartres, rue Sainte-Thérèse. In L. Rivet (ed.), *Société Française d'Etude de la Céramique Antique en Gaule, Actes du Congrès d'Istres, 21-24 mai 1998*, 207-223.

Sciallano, M. and Sibella, P. 1991: *Amphores, comment les identifier?* (Aix-en-Provence, Edisud).

Seaby, H. A. 1978 (3rd ed., revised by D. R. Sear and R. Loosley): *Roman Silver Coins, volume I. The Republic to Augustus* (London, Seaby).

Tchernia, A. 1986: *Le vin de l'Italie romaine. Essai d'histoire économique d'après les amphores* (Rome, Ecole française de Rome 261).

Shamanic practices and trance imagery in the Iron Age

Mike Williams and John Creighton

Shamanism is a widespread phenomenon amongst many traditional communities around the world (Vitebsky 1995). Although having different cultural manifestations, the central premise is to establish contact with the supernatural realm through the ecstatic experiences of a professional and inspired intermediary, the shaman. However, it is not just a contemporary phenomenon, but also one with extreme time-depth. Historical sources of Siberian practices, where the name originates, date back to the 16th century; but archaeological evidence has suggested the practice goes back into the Palaeolithic.

Given its longevity, it is perhaps surprising that shamanism has only recently become a topic for archaeological enquiry, and is gradually forming a new framework within which to interpret the material evidence for past societies. Many avenues have been explored, such as the evidence for narcotics and hallucinogens (Sherratt 1991), the acoustic properties of ancient monuments and their relation to entering trance-states (Watson 2001), and, perhaps the most widely known example, the application of shamanic metaphors to parietal rock art (Chippendale and Taçon 1998). It was within this context that one of the authors wrote an article, subsequently developed, suggesting that the early imagery on northern European Iron Age coinage might be related to metaphors taken from the trance-world of shamanic visions (Creighton 1995, 2000). So far the idea has been treated as a curiosity in the main; although it aroused surprisingly vitriolic reactions from a small number of researchers, which was also the experience for those who first started talking about shamanism and rock art in the late 1980s. We would like to take this opportunity, therefore, to situate the idea about Iron Age coinage within a broader discussion of some of the phenomena that occur in late prehistory in northern Europe, in order to demonstrate that this idea is not perhaps quite as strange as it first appears.

The first and most important point to emphasise is that if we do adopt shamanism as a means of interpreting the past then nothing can fall outside of its influence. Shamanism forms a cosmology, that is an all-encompassing way of interpreting the world. Accordingly, if it existed in the Iron Age, everything would have been understood according to the cosmology: not only burial and ritual, but also things which we perceive as everyday objects, such as the theme for this volume, coins.

Since shamanism is a way of interpreting the world, it encompasses rather than replaces religion. Various manifestations of its basic form are found on all inhabited continents, from the Indians of southern America to the tribes of Siberia and from the Inuit of the Arctic to the Aboriginals of Australia. Whilst each express shamanism in their own particular way, there are several themes that seem to be held in common throughout these groups. Taking a very reductionist approach, shamanism views the cosmos as divided into three: an *upperworld*, a *middleworld,* and a *lowerworld* (Eliade 1964). The middleworld is what we may call reality, the space inhabited by people and things. The upper and lowerworlds are places inhabited by spirits and the ancestors. Often they are joined by a central pillar, an *axis mundi*, which can take the form of a tree or a river (for examples from northern Europe see Bäckman and Hultkrantz 1978; Terebikhin 1993; Pentikäinen 1998). Although there is a clear similarity to the Christian tradition of heaven and hell, in a shamanic cosmology there is no moral association attributed to either realm. Access to the upper and lowerworlds is the responsibility of the shaman, male or female, who enters these realms by inducing a trance, either through drumming, taking drugs or limiting their external stimuli. Once in the otherworld, the shaman perceives himself or herself speaking with the spirits or the ancestors before returning to the community. In so doing, the shaman learns of things that could not otherwise be known: restricted knowledge. This trance journey to the otherworlds is one of the most enduring facets of shamanism world-wide.

Although shamanic societies usually limit entry to the otherworlds to a shaman, the ability to enter trance is achievable by anybody using similar techniques to the shamans, such as repetitive drumming or drug ingestion. In the northern countries, for example, dried fly agaric is often used to promote trance (Bäckman and Hultkrantz 1978; Czigány 1980). When in trance, a person's awareness is shifted from a normal state of consciousness, which is the usual state whilst awake, to an alternative state of consciousness. Whilst in this alternative state, people may initially feel more alert and experience sharper sensory perceptions. This stems from a slowing of brain-wave patterns from what is known as a beta to an alpha level. Eventually, people's brain waves will slow even further so that they reach a theta level, and this accords with trance (Winkelman 1986).

As the brain waves slow and people enter trance, other phenomena occur and these have been outlined by David Lewis-Williams and Thomas Dowson (1988) in a three-stage neuropsychological model. When first entering an alternative state of consciousness, people begin to see spots of light before their eyes, despite sitting in darkness or with their eyes closed. These naturally form into geometric images called entoptics (Stage 1). These entoptic images are completely cross-cultural and common to all people, and generally comprise grids, parallel lines, dots or flecks, zigzags, nested curves and filigrees.

After a time, the entoptic patterns can change into recognisable images. However, the immediate disposition of the person entering the alternative state may affect the type of image seen. For example, if a person is hungry, a curved pattern may become an orange or, if they are fearful, it may become a bomb. The change to such recognisable imagery forms the second part of the neuropsychological model (Stage 2). The third stage is reached when these images seem to dissolve into a vortex or tunnel. This is caused by certain cells in the brain being especially susceptible to tunnel imagery. To the person in the trance, they feel as if they are passing through the tunnel and will eventually emerge to be confronted with especially vivid imagery. To a shaman, passing through the tunnel equates to the journey to the otherworlds and the images at its end represent the realm of spirits and the ancestors (Stage 3).

This three-stage model has been applied to a variety of archaeological media but particularly to rock art. Lewis-Williams and Dowson (1988), for example, illustrated their ideas with reference to Palaeolithic cave art where the three stages of entering an alternative state of consciousness seem to be reflected by the images painted on the walls. Since then, there is little rock art that has not been subjected to a similar analysis, often with variable results (examples from Europe include Bradley 1989; 1997; Patton 1990; Lewis-Williams and Dowson 1993; Dronfield 1996; Clottes and Lewis-Williams 1998; and Lewis-Williams 2002). The implication for the universality of shamanism, stemming from the neuropsychology of our brains, is that the phenomenon has much broader relevance for understanding northern European prehistory. Shamanism is not a unique phenomenon marginalised in the northern Eurasian tundra, rather shamanism is a ubiquitous, almost innate way for humans to understand the world.

The possibilities that this observation brings have not been lost on archaeologists. More and more researchers are using elements of the shamanic cosmology to explain aspects of the archaeological record, and a series of examples follow where the application of a shamanic cosmology has thrown new light on later prehistory. The archaeological data will concentrate upon regions of northern Europe in the Iron Age, and shamanic parallels will be largely restricted to examples from the societies of northern Europe and Siberian Russia. This not only provides a geographical proximity to the archaeology but also allows for the possibility that Iron Age people may have had direct contact with the prehistoric shamanic culture of northern Scandinavia and, through them, to much of the northern Eurasian tradition.

To many shamanic communities, the middleworld, that is the world we all inhabit, is often divided according to the cardinal points. These points represent both actual directions – north, south, east and west – but also an inner cosmology where east corresponds to birth and the beginning of life and west to the end of life and death. These attributes arise from the daily journey of the sun, with its symbolic 'birth' in the east and its 'death' in the west. This concern with the cardinal points also informs the layout of many traditional dwellings in northern Europe and Siberia. These are often orientated with their entrances or prominent windows to the east. These face the rising sun and thereby acknowledge the return of its life-giving rays each morning. As the sun dawns in the world, it also dawns in people's homes, and the house becomes a world in miniature. Representations of this cosmology can also be seen on objects used in the trance process, such as the Saami drums from Lapland, which often show the community of the Saami village organised around the central cardinal points (Manker 1938; 1950).

Such principles may prove illuminating for the Iron Age where many structures are also orientated with their entrances facing east (Oswald 1997). Possibly the reasons for the alignment are similar to those in shamanic societies and Iron Age people also thought of the east as representing a life-giving direction. By aligning their houses to the east, people may have been arranging them according to their cosmological understanding of the world. Furthermore, other structures, such as the Scottish roundhouses, seem to have been organised so that anyone entering is forced to walk around the interior space in a certain way, often sun-wise (Giles and Parker Pearson 1999). This may have had particular relevance given that the sun was important in the alignment of the house entrance. Once again, people were mirroring the wider arrangement of the world in their houses.

In addition to arranging the exterior of their houses to reflect their cosmology, the shamanic peoples of northern Europe and Siberia also organise the interior of their dwellings according to their view of the world. Often, these are divided between northern and southern parts and, following the idea that the sun journeys daily through the realms of life and death, the south is associated with life, since this is where the sun shines brightest, and the north is associated with death, since this is where the sun disappears into the lowerworld. Iron Age roundhouses also seem to be organised around a north-south divide with artefacts usually being recorded in the south but not in the north. Since the northern part of the houses were empty of finds, possibly this was an area for sleeping, whereas the southern part, where many artefacts occur, was the area for living. Remembering the division of north and south in the houses of shamanic societies corresponding to the division between life and death, similar themes may be apparent in the roundhouses. The southern part of the roundhouse where people lived may have been associated with life, and the northern part that people slept in may have been associated with death (Parker Pearson 1996; 1999; Fitzpatrick 1997). The analogy between sleep and death is straightforward but, in some Scottish examples, burials have also been found in the northern part of roundhouses, seemingly emphasising the connection with death (Parker Pearson et al. 2002).

The seemingly blank area within the northern part of houses is often repeated on a larger scale in settlement arrangements and especially within the hillforts of southern Britain. For example, Danebury, our most comprehensively excavated hillfort, is roughly divided into northern and southern parts by the main east-west road running through its centre (Cunliffe 1984; 1995). Although approximate, this division seems to be reflected in the internal layout, with grain storage pits to the north and granaries to the south. Storage pits seem to fit the imagery of death well. The pits were hidden, possibly covered, and the grain they held was kept underground, in an otherworldly realm. The addition of human remains in the pits seems only to emphasise this connection. Conversely, the granaries held their wares raised up for all to see; this grain was most definitely in the world of the living. Upon entering the hillfort, the realm of death would be to the north. This may help to explain another facet of the archaeological record: why the dead found on the hillforts are often aligned with their heads to the north (Whimster 1981). They were aligned toward the direction associated with death. It may be more than coincidence that shamanic societies also see the north as the direction of death.

It is not just artificial structures that are given significance within shamanic cosmologies, but also certain natural places. For example, the Saami people, among other things, recognise certain rocks that are sacred to them, where they leave offerings of fish oil and reindeer antlers. The rocks themselves were not worshipped but provided an interface to the otherworlds, a place where the spirits were close (Vorren 1987; Mulk 1994). The recognition that some natural places were considered special and provided interfaces to the otherworld might help explain some aspects of the archaeological record. For example, many researchers are now noticing that metalworking in the Iron Age seems to have occurred in unusual places and are making links with ethnographic parallels in many traditional African societies (Budd and Taylor 1995; Hingley 1997). In Zimbabwe, for example, metal is not so much made as is born, and the smelting furnaces often take on the outward appearance of pregnant women (Childs 1991). Smelting is seen as a sexual activity with the resultant birth of the metal. Similar imagery may also be found in the Iron Age. For example, at Maiden Castle in southern Britain metalworking took place on the eastern boundary entrance following the hillfort's abandonment, and similarly at Hodde in Denmark, metalworking took place on the boundary of the settlement (Wheeler 1943; Hvass 1985). This boundary location is a common feature for metalworking in the Iron Age and may correspond to ideas of liminality and possibly of birth that are evident in the African examples. This may be best represented at the Titelberg hillfort in Luxembourg where a building was used as a foundry and possible mint during the Iron Age. When that foundry was abandoned several items were placed in the smelter pit: coin moulds, crucible fragments, slag but, perhaps most significantly, also deposited was a one year old child, tightly curled into a foetal position (Rowlett et al. 1982). The association between birth and the metalworking process seems to have been writ large.

If metalwork is birthed rather than made, this implies that it assumed a life of its own and that the metal artefacts we find were actually treated as if they were alive. This is also a feature of shamanic societies called animism. Every physical feature of their world is imbued with life and a soul. Every animal, tree, and object is alive and has a soul that can be directly approached and spoken to. For example, when the Inuit of Greenland kill a polar bear they must honour the passing of the bear's soul. So they skin the bear and hang the skin by their dwelling. Since bears are said to like metal artefacts, next to the bear are hung several items that people think the bear might appreciate. After a set number of days, the bear's soul departs taking with it the souls of the metal artefacts that have been hung next to it. Since the bear has been honoured, or perhaps bribed, it will depart happily and will not stay to cause trouble for the people (Rasmussen 1908). What is striking in this example, however, is that it is not just the bear that is alive and has a soul, but also the metal objects that are hung next to it. In other places, artefacts, including those made of metal, are deposited at locations that are thought to be interfaces to the otherworlds, such as the Saami rocks noted above (Zachrisson 1984).

If we are to infer a similar approach for metalwork in the prehistoric period then, at the end of its life, we should see metalwork deposited in places where its soul can easily make the journey to the otherworld. For much of the late Bronze and Iron Age, metalwork is very rarely found in settlement sites, nor for much of the period is it found in burial sites. Most metalwork is either deposited underground or is deposited in wet places such as rivers, lakes and bogs (Fitzpatrick 1984). In virtually all northern shamanic societies wet places, and especially rivers, are seen as gateways to the otherworlds. In the Iron Age it may be that by placing the metalwork into the water the artefact is being taken out of the realm of the living and is passing over into the realm of the dead. That many of the objects were deliberately broken or damaged before deposition completes this transformation (cf. Bradley 1998).

So far, the shamanic cosmology has only been discussed with reference to structures, places and things, but it can also relate to that other form of archaeological evidence: human bodies, or to be more specific the so-called bog bodies of north-western Europe. Initially, what is most striking about the bog bodies is the apparent savagery in which many were killed. Where post-mortems have taken place, most of the injuries seem to have occurred around the head: strangulation, cut throats, bashed skulls and, in two cases, decapitation (van der Sanden 1996). In addition, some of the bodies seem to have suffered a number of these injuries. However, the violence inflicted on the bodies does not stop there. Many were fixed into the bog with stakes or were weighted down with pieces of wood or stones (*ibid.*). This action seems particularly superfluous after the extreme violence that was used to kill the person in the first place.

Many of the bog bodies met their deaths naked or semi-clothed. Some had only a token item of clothing, such as the fox fur armband worn by Lindow Man or the peaked cap worn by Tollund Man (Budworth et al. 1986; Fischer 1999). Others were wrapped in capes or were deposited with, but were not wearing, selected items of clothing. Some of the bodies had been scalped or shaven, and sometimes over only half the head. Conversely, one body, that of Elling Woman, had a very elaborate coiffure (Fischer 1999).

Although very few of the bodies were deposited with anything that might be identified as grave goods, there are indications that some of the people killed may have held a high status during their lives. Some bodies were well nourished and even plump. With others, the fineness of the hands and fingers suggests that they had undertaken very little manual work during their lives. But there are other features that suggest that such people may have been perceived as different. Lindow Man for example, had a deformity of his thumb that gave him an extra digit and may have even worn body paint (Buckland et al. 1994; Brothwell and Bourke 1995).

The final meals of the bog bodies are also striking. Many ate gruel or cakes made up from many different types of seeds. Possibly more significant is the final meal of Grauballe Man, which was contaminated with ergot, a natural hallucinogenic drug sufficient to send him into a deep coma (Helbæk 1958). Other bodies also showed strange additions to their diet, such as the mistletoe pollen grains found in the stomach of Lindow Man (Scaife 1986). Since the evidence suggests that the body was not deposited during the mistletoe flowering season, it is possible that these grains represent the ingestion of mistletoe berries. This could not have represented a normal diet since mistletoe is, of course, poisonous.

The bog bodies are clearly a striking group of people, but who were they? Why did they come to be in the bogs in the first place? Many have pointed to the Classical texts that speak of such deaths as punishment for deeds such as adultery or homosexuality (Munksgaard 1984). It seems convincing but does not sit easily with the care that some bodies received after death. Many bodies were wrapped in capes, Borremose Woman was laid on a bed of birch-bark and cotton grass, and Tollund Man was left as if he were quietly sleeping (Fischer 1979; 1999). Even if these features can be explained away, were the bogs really suitable locations for depositing criminals? We must remember the other items deposited into these bogs: weapons, jewellery and unique and outstanding objects such as the Gundestrup cauldron (Levy 1982). Could it be that the people killed and buried in the bogs were considered as special as the metalwork also deposited: a rite of death as special as the people receiving it? But if they were so special, then who were they? This is where it is necessary to take a closer look at the ethnographic records of actual shamans in northern Eurasia, to see if they can provide any clues. However, rather than focus specifically on any one ethnic group, we will highlight certain aspects shared by shamans across many groups.

Upon initiation, the shaman is often dismembered. This can take many forms, and it should be stressed that it occurs in the spiritual rather than physical realms. It is often marked by an extreme level of violence and in making sure that all signs of life are completely extinguished (Eliade 1958; Halifax 1982). Some shamans may be tied up or weighted down during their journeys. Many are set free during the time that they are away, ostensibly with the aid of the spirits (Siikala 1978). Shamans may journey naked. Since they leave this world they have no need of clothing for warmth, and there are many accounts of shamans controlling their own body temperatures (*ibid.*). Some shamans perceive their power as located within their heads and, more particularly, within their hair. The hair of a shaman is considered particularly efficacious and to remove it could be seen as sharing in their power. Other shamans emphasise their calling with elaborate headwear or hats (Donner 1920). The shaman's status in their communities is ambiguous and they are simultaneously feared, respected, relied upon, yet shunned (Lewis 1986; 1989). But lastly, and perhaps most strikingly, some of the shamans stood out from their people, either through having extra bones, particularly finger and toe bones, or by bearing tattoos (Basilov 1997).

The characteristics of shamans that match those of the bog bodies have been deliberately selected to emphasise their apparent similarities: the violence of their journeys; their binding; their indifferent need for clothes; the preoccupation with the head and their hair; the wearing of hats; and, as discussed earlier, their use of drugs. Bog bodies and shamans seem similar people. However, the violence and death meted out to the shamans occurs in the other worlds, whilst they are in trance, whereas for the bog bodies the violence occurred in this world and it ended their lives. However, possibly this provides the key to explaining the bog bodies. If they are seen as the Iron Age equivalent to the ethnographic shamans, possibly their deaths provided a vivid display of what it was to travel to the otherworlds. Their extreme manner of death was a dramatic performance of a journey to the otherworld, deliberately orchestrated to make an impact on those watching it (Williams 2003). That bogs were selected as the backdrop to such a journey in the Iron Age should come as no surprise. The importance attributed to these liminal places in the later prehistoric period has already been stressed. Once again, water represented the entrance to the otherworld.

If the bog bodies were undertaking a shamanic journey, they may be expected to keep returning and aiding the land of the living, albeit in spirit form. This may help explain why the bodies were fixed to the bog in the first place. Possibly the body provided a physical anchor to which the soul would return, and perhaps the valuable offerings found in the bogs were also in remembrance of these people and the role that they had taken on.

Whereas bog bodies are naturally restricted to regions where fen predominated, it may be that the pit bodies found at sites such as Danebury represent a similar group of people. The discovery of dismembered corpses in disused grain storage pits has been interpreted in the past as being indicative of criminals or deviants, disposed of outside the normal burial rite. However, perhaps these too are the remains of the Iron Age equivalent to shamans, left in the pits to mark their final trip to the lowerworld. In terms of pathological evidence for the method of death and evidence for the binding of bodies, there are many similarities (Cunliffe 1992; 1993).

We hope to have shown above how a shamanic interpretation of late northern European prehistory is starting to take shape in people's interpretation of material evidence. However, if a shamanic cosmology did exist, then it would have informed every aspect of people's lives. The shaman, mediating between the different worlds, and between the living and the ancestors, may have been a significant individual within society. Their position and authority relied upon them relating their experiences and using their travel between worlds to benefit the community. As such, many of the images and ideas of the otherworlds would have been openly expressed, whether metaphorically in stories or directly in visual media. It is within this context that we have other powers at play, namely the issuing and circulation of coinage, and the power relations that the use of this medium sought to establish or maintain. In what follows, we will first explain why the imagery on the coinage looks as if it may relate to metaphors drawn from trance imagery. Then we will interpret its potential implications.

We have shown that, when shamans had trances, their vocalisation and representations of their travels in the other realms are communicated to others. Furthermore, as individuals go into a trance there are some very specific experiences that are cross-culturally common to all people. Therefore, when we identify these features amongst prehistoric representations (whether on rock, paintings, or plastic media such as coins), we have some indication that the trance experience may be taking place somewhere within society. In northern Europe, we have the development of gold coinage, principally derived from the gold coinage of Philip II of Macedon (Figure 1). The completely naturalistic imagery of the Hellenistic world gradually gave way to various forms of abstraction or elaboration; so that in Armorica horses sprouted human-style heads, whereas in south-west Britain they dissolved into a series of dots. These regional derivations were distinctive and helped to create local identity such that many people denote the extent of various tribes by tracing the extent of various groups of coin issues. But what is striking to us is that each of these separate strands of development draws upon forms of abstraction/elaboration which relate directly to that experienced by people entering a trance; and specifically those relating to shamanic practice.

If we explicitly follow Lewis-Williams and Thomas Dowson's (1988) three-stage neuropsychological model of the trance experience, mentioned above, we can trace images from each stage appearing on the coinage of northern Europe. We have noted above that, as the brain waves start to slow, images appear which have their origin in the physical structure of the eyeball and neurological structure of the brain. These various images – grids, parallel lines, dots or flecks, zigzags, nested curves and filigrees – will tend to move, replicating, fragmenting, rotating and forming complex patterns (Figure 2). As has been noted for many years, the coinage of northern Europe is dominated by dots, star bursts and a plethora of other tiny images that Allen once dismissed as 'fill-in ornaments' (Allen 1980, 149).

As the trance deepens the brain attempts to interpret these stimuli, and this is where culturally specific images start to appear (Figure 3). How these images are interpreted depends upon the mind-set of the individual. Many shamans identify themselves with one or another sacred animal, and on Southern African rock art, for example, we can see grid patterns blending into and forming the pattern on a giraffe's hide. On northern European coin, as the horse becomes more and more abstract, it dissolves into potential entoptic forms, such as the dots on the coinage of the Durotriges (SW Britain), or the crescents on the coinage of the Corieltauvi (NE Britain). If a shaman was so minded to see a horse, then in this case the crescents would coalesce to form this image and yet there would still be other entoptics floating around the field of vision.

The final stage of trance is the deepest, and one where a series of curious phenomena are described. The first is the transition into this state, which, as we noted above, is often described as being in a tunnel of light. This is where the hallucination is at its most vivid, and iconic images appear, such as fully formed horses and people (Figure 4). The British Ma coin is curious here. In the south of Britain, where this comes from, previous issues had shown relatively abstract horses. It is this coin and British L that revert to the first vaguely naturalistic horse, and at the same time it shows it appearing in front of a spiral of light.

The spiral of light is the same as the tunnel of light that shamans journey through and practitioners often describe this as flying or swimming, whilst feeling a sense of weightlessness. Furthermore, representations of shamans sometimes have wings added to them. They interpret the sensation as their spirit travelling to other realms, whilst they remain attached to their corporeal body, which remains put. Sometimes a link or ribbon is described, pulling at the back of the spirit head and leading back to the body itself. This is not unrelated to the 'out-of body' experiences and 'near death experiences', which are occasionally related in hospitals (Mitchell 1985).

A final transition occurs in some societies, where shamans perceive themselves becoming their spirit animal, changing into an eland, bear, or whatever other animal happens to be particularly culturally important to the community. In terms of representation, this is where we often find part human and part animal images appearing, showing this transition. The combinations of human and horse appear on various coins, most notably the Treveran and Armorican human headed horses, but also the curious coin of the Ambiani showing a horse climbing in one ear and out the other, or the coin of the Iceni, integrating the name of *ANTED* with the legs of the horse. We also get other animals, such as the 'birdman' from the Rhineland. Certainly both horses and birds were culturally very important, and we find examples of coins framing these within a temple, just as contemporary Roman coins framed deities in temples. A combination of these ideas help explain the flying horses, which may be a representation of a transformed shaman.

Many sculptural artefacts dating to the Iron Age or early Roman period have been found which also show this dualism. Perhaps the most famous is the statuette from Bouray in France of the cross-legged male, though curiously one of his feet has a deer's hoof (Joffroy 1979). Many of these images have been discussed by Green (1997). Traditionally they have been interpreted as gods and goddesses, but it may be that they represent the transition as the shaman enters the spirit world to mediate between the worlds on behalf of the community.

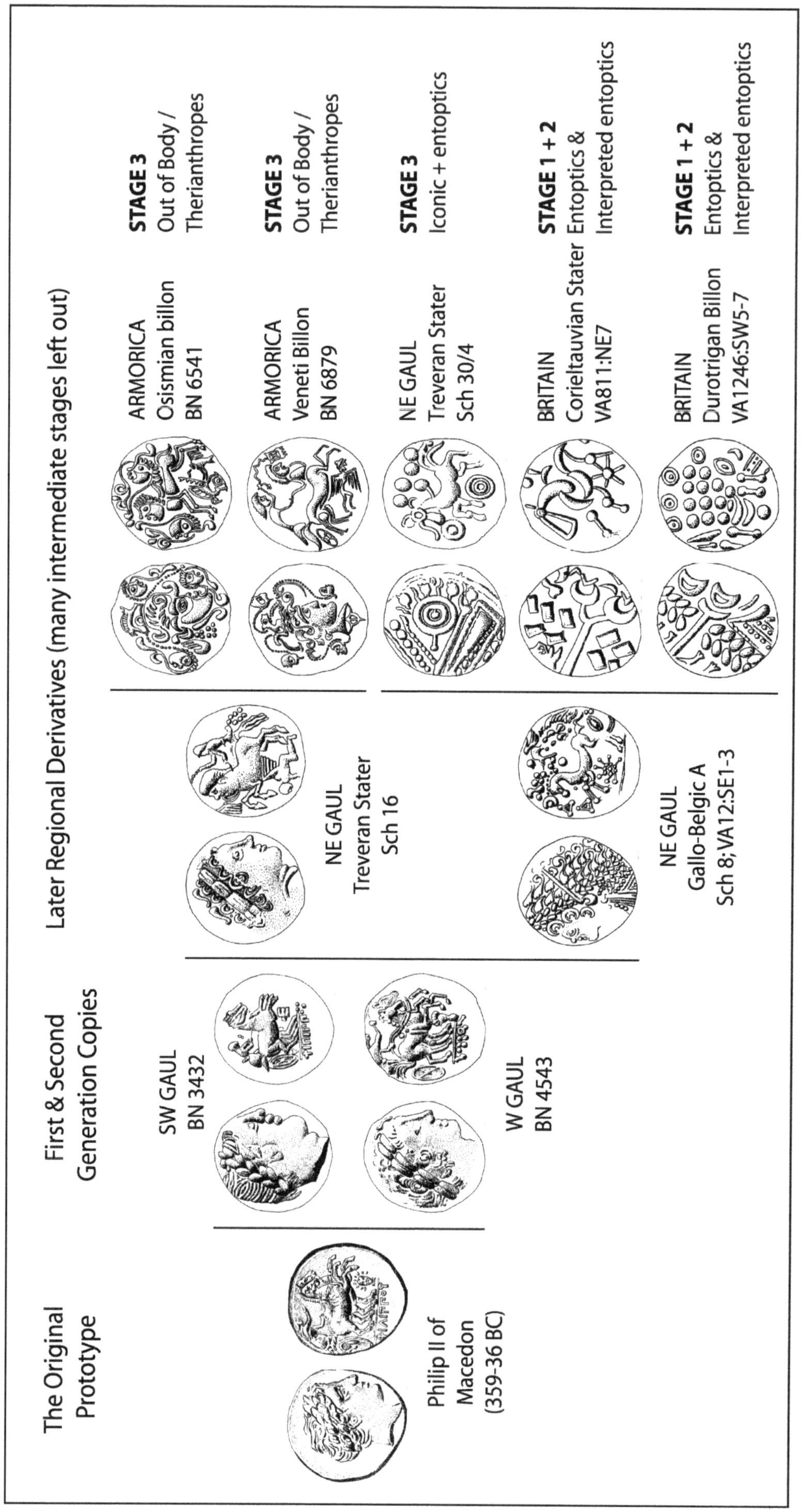

Figure 1. The regional development of gold in northern Europe.

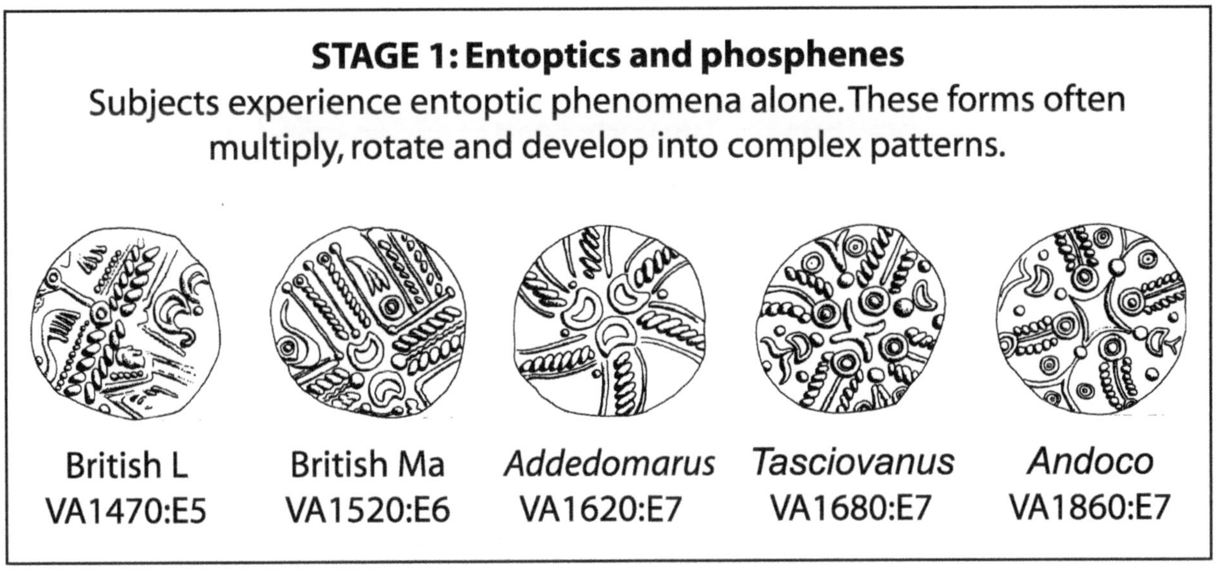

Figure 2. Stage 1 – Entoptics and phosphenes.

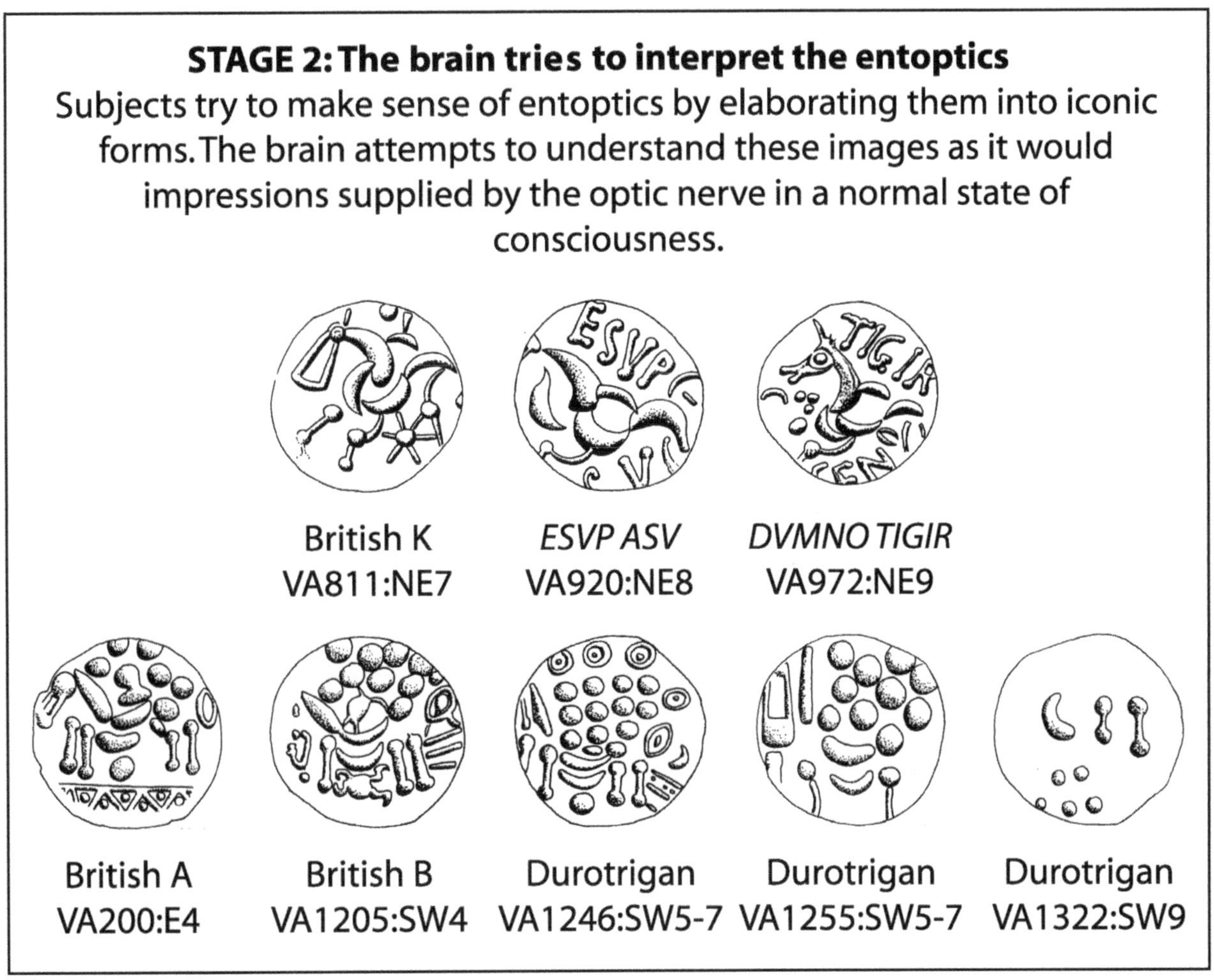

Figure 3. Stage 2 – the brain tries to interpret the entoptics.

Much prehistoric rock-art has been accepted as probably relating to shamanic imagery, even though much of it only contains collections that may be entoptic patterning. On Iron Age coinage, by contrast, are images that potentially relate to all stages of the trance. It seems that a coin has been taken from the Hellenistic world, and the imagery transformed bit by bit, using a visual language of power that meant something to the populace in northern Europe. This does not mean that the people who made the coins had trances. It just means that in the language of power at the time, the metaphors surrounding the trance experience were likely to be current.

STAGE 3a: The Vortex and iconic images

A major change occurs with individuals experiencing a vortex or rotating tunnel around them. Within this the first spontaneously produced iconic hallucinations appear.

Eburones BN 8859 | *British Ma* VA1520:E6 | *Addedomarus* VA1620:SE7

STAGE 3b: Weightlessness and 'Out of Body' experience

Subjects often perceive a sensation of weightlessness, expressed in terms of flying or diving under the water. Related to this are impressions of the spirit-body becoming dissociated from the 'real' body, as it then drifts off, the back of the spirit head often linked to the 'real' body with a chord.

Rhineland Sch. 56 | SE Britain VA165:SE7 | Armorica BN 6879 | Armorica BN 6879 | Armorica BN 6541

STAGE 3c: Therianthropes (Animism)

Shamans often imagine themselves transforming into a particular animal, usually one of particular symbolic importance to that culture/group.

HORSES

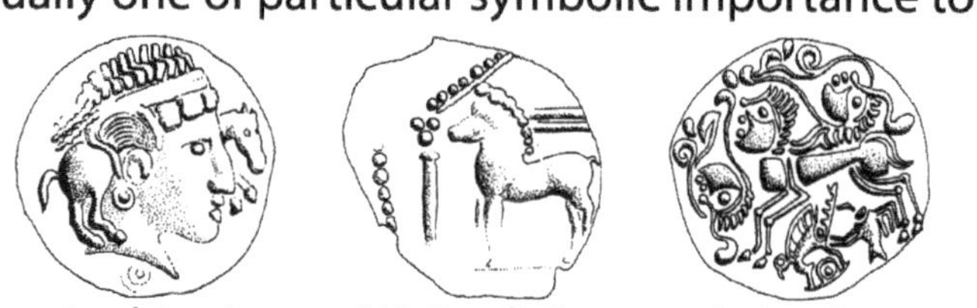

Ambiani Sch. 4/1 | W. Gaulish BN 7050 | Osismian BN 6541

ANTED VA711:EA8 | Veniti BN 6879 | Treveran Sch. 16

BIRDS

Rhineland Sch. 56

Carnutes BN 7100

Figure 4. Stage 3 – the vortex and full iconic hallucination

As the work takes place to create a coherent interpretation of later northern European prehistory, which involves an appreciation of shamanic cosmologies, coinage will need to be built into the narrative as will other material culture. Coinage has often carried images relating to power, whether temporal or divine, and therefore imagery relating to the mediation between the various spirit worlds would not be at all out of place.

It may be that the bog bodies and burials in pits were Iron Age shamans who made their final journey into the lowerworld. Perhaps some of them did envision themselves changing into the culturally powerful form of a horse as they did so. If so, it would help explain two curious features in the archaeological record. At Danebury, utilising the pits where some of these human bodies were found, a detailed analysis considered the highly structured ritualised deposition of bones from other species. It emerged that the bones of wild animals, domesticated animals, and humans were all deposited in different ways in different positions in the stratigraphic sequence. Curiously, horses were treated in exactly the same way as the human corpses, as if equivalence was being made. Furthermore, at the cemetery in Mill Hill, Deal, amongst all the other inhumations, one stood out as being identical to all the rest except in one respect: it was a horse buried and not a human (Parfitt 1995: Grave 53). This might make us mindful of a Saami practice whereby horses were sacrificed and placed in the earth to symbolise the journey of Ruto, a god-like shamanic figure, in his ride from this world into the lowerworld.

Whatever the specific beliefs of Iron Age people, the transformation away from this type of imagery at the very end of the Iron Age in northern Europe, with the adoption of naturalistic imagery from the Classical world, represents a fundamental change in the imagery of power. Trance-informed imagery, if this is what it was, was displaced as the new world order of the Principate came to dominate the South East, with its very different power structures.

Bibliography

Allen, D. F. (ed. Nash, D.) 1980: *The coins of the ancient Celts* (Edinburgh, EUP).

Bäckman, L. and Hultkrantz, Å. 1978: *Studies in Lapp Shamanism* (Stockholm, Stockholm Studies in Comparative Religion 16).

Basilov, V. 1997: Chosen by the spirits. In M. Mandelstam Balzer (ed.), *Shamanic Worlds: rituals and lore of Siberian and Central Asia* (London, North Castle Books) 3-48.

Bradley, R. 1989: Deaths and entrances: a contextual analysis of Megalithic art. *Current Anthropology* 30, 68-75.

Bradley, R. 1997: Working the land: imagining the landscape. *Archaeological Dialogues* 4, 39-52.

Bradley, R. 1998 (2nd ed.): *The Passage of Arms: an archaeological analysis of prehistoric hoards and votive deposits* (Oxford, Oxbow).

Brothwell, D. and Bourke, J. 1995: The human remains from Lindow Moss 1987-8. In R. Turner and R. Scaife (eds), *Bog Bodies: new discoveries and new perspectives* (London, BMP) 52-61.

Buckland, P., Housley, R. and Pyatt, F. 1994: Paint, date, bog stratigraphy and murder: some comments on Lindow Men. In R. Luff and P. Rowley-Conwy (eds), *Whither environmental archaeology?* (Oxford, Oxbow) 7-12.

Budd, P. and Taylor, T. 1995: The Faerie Smith meets the bronze industry: magic versus science in the interpretation of prehistoric metalworking. *World Archaeology* 27, 133-143.

Budworth, G., McCord, M., Priston, A. and Stead, I. 1986: The artefacts. In I. Stead, J. Bourke and D. Brothwell (eds), *Lindow Man – the body in the bog* (London, BMP) 38-40.

Childs, S. T. 1991: Style, technology, and iron smelting furnaces in Bantu-speaking Africa. *Journal of Anthropological Archaeology* 10, 332-359.

Chippendale, C. and Taçon, P. (eds) 1998: *The Archaeology of Rock-art* (Cambridge, CUP).

Clottes, J. and Lewis-Williams, J. D. 1998: *The Shamans of prehistory: trance and magic in the Painted Caves* (New York, Harry N. Abrams).

Creighton, J. 1995: Visions of power: imagery and symbols in Late Iron Age Britain. *Britannia* 26, 285-301.

Creighton, J. 2000: *Coins and Power in Late Iron Age Britain* (Cambridge, CUP).

Cunliffe, B. 1984: *Danebury: An Iron Age Hillfort in Hampshire. Volume 1 - the excavations 1969-1978: the site.* (London, Council for British Archaeology Research Report 52).

Cunliffe, B. 1992: Pits, preconceptions and propitiation in the British Iron Age. *Oxford Journal of Archaeology* 11, 69-83.

Cunliffe, B. 1993: *Fertility, propitiation and the Gods in the British Iron Age* (Amsterdam, Universiteit van Amsterdam).

Cunliffe, B. 1995: *Danebury: An Iron Age Hillfort in Hampshire. Volume 6: A Hillfort community in perspective* (York, Council for British Archaeology Research Report 102).

Czigány, L. 1980: The use of hallucinogens and the shamanistic tradition of the Finno-Ugrian people. *The Slavonic and East European Review* 58, 212-17.

Donner, K. 1920: Ornements de la tête et de la chevelure. Quelques mots sur leur signification. *Journal de la Société Finno-Ougrienne* 37, 1-23.

Dronfield, J. 1996: Entering alternative realities: cognition, art and architecture in Irish Passage Tombs. *Cambridge Journal of Archaeology* 6, 37-72.

Eliade, M. 1958: *Rites and symbols of initiation: the mysteries of birth and rebirth* (New York, Harper Torchbooks).

Eliade, M. 1964: *Shamanism: archaic techniques of ecstasy* (London, Arkana).

Fischer, C. 1979: Moseligene fra Bjældskovdal. *Kuml* 1979, 7-44.

Fischer, C. 1999: The Tollund Man and the Elling Woman and other bog bodies from central Jutland. In B. Coles, J. Coles and M. Schou Jørgensen (eds), *Bog Bodies, Sacred Sites and Wetland Archaeology* (Exeter, Wetland Archaeology Research Project) 93-97.

Fitzpatrick, A. 1984: The deposition of La Tène Iron Age metalwork in watery contexts in Southern England. In B. Cunliffe and D. Miles (eds), *Aspects of the Iron Age in Central Southern Britain* (Oxford, OUCA) 178-190.

Fitzpatrick, A. 1997: Everyday life in Iron Age Wessex. In A. Gwilt and C. Haselgrove (eds), *Reconstructing Iron Age societies: new approaches to the British Iron Age* (Oxford, Oxbow Monograph 71) 73-86.

Giles, M. and Parker Pearson, M. 1999: Learning to live in the Iron Age: dwelling and praxis. In B. Bevan (ed.), *Northern Exposure: The Iron Age in Northern Britain* (Leicester, Leicester Archaeology Monographs 4) 217-31.

Green, M. 1997: Images in opposition: polarity, ambivalence and liminality in cult representation. *Antiquity* 71, 898-911.

Halifax, J. 1982: *Shaman: The wounded healer* (London, Thames and Hudson).

Helbæk, H. 1958: Grauballemandens sidste måltid. *Kuml* 1958, 83-116.

Hill, J. D. 1995: *Ritual and rubbish in the Iron Age of Wessex: a study on the formation of a specific archaeological record* (Oxford, BAR 242).

Hingley, R. 1997: Iron working and regeneration: a study of the symbolic meaning of metalworking in Iron Age Britain. In A. Gwilt and C. Haselgrove (eds), *Reconstructing Iron Age societies: new approaches to the British Iron Age* (Oxford, Oxbow Monograph 71) 9-18.

Hvass, S. 1985: *Hodde. Et vestjysk landsbysamfund fra ældre jernalder* (København, Universitetsforlaget i København Arkæologiske Studier Volume VII).

Joffroy, R. 1979: *Musée des Antiquités Nationales, St-Germain-en-Laye* (Paris, Editions de la Réunion des Musées Nationaux).

Levy, J. 1982: *Social and religious organization in Bronze Age Denmark: an analysis of ritual hoard finds* (Oxford, BAR S124).

Lewis, I. 1986: *Religion in context: cults and charisma* (Cambridge, CUP).

Lewis, I. 1989 (2nd ed.): *Ecstatic religion: a study of Shamanism and spirit possession* (London, Routledge).

Lewis-Williams, J. D. 2002: *The mind in the cave: exploring consciousness and prehistoric art* (London, Thames and Hudson).

Lewis-Williams, J. D. and Dowson, T. 1988: The signs of all times: entoptic phenomena in Upper Palaeolithic art. *Current Anthropology* 29, 201-45.

Lewis-Williams, J. D. and Dowson, T. 1993: On vision and power in the Neolithic: evidence from the decorated monuments. *Current Anthropology* 34, 55-65.

Manker, E. 1938: *Die Lappische Zaubertrommel 1: Die Trommel als Denkmal Materieller Kultur* (Stockholm, Nordiska Museet, Acta Lapponica 1).

Manker, E. 1950: *Die Lappische Zaubertrommel 2: Die Trommel als Urkunde Geistigen Lebens* (Stockholm, Nordiska Museet, Acta Lapponica 6).

Mitchell, J. 1985: *Out-of-Body experiences: how science is helping us to understand the experience of living beyond the body* (Wellingborough, Turnstone Press).

Mulk, I.-M. 1994: Sacrificial places and their meaning in Saami society. In D. Carmichael, J. Hubert, B. Reeves and A. Schanche (eds), *Sacred sites, sacred places* (London, Routledge) 121-131.

Munksgaard, E. 1984: Bog bodies – a brief survey of interpretations. *Journal of Danish Archaeology* 3, 120-123.

Oswald, A. 1997: A doorway on the past: practical and mystic concerns in the orientation of roundhouse doorways. In A. Gwilt and C. Haselgrove (eds), *Reconstructing Iron Age societies: new approaches to the British Iron Age* (Oxford, Oxbow Monograph 71) 87-95.

Parfitt, K. 1995: *Iron Age burials from Mill Hill, Deal* (London, BMP).

Parker Pearson, M. 1996: Food, fertility and front doors in the first millennium BC. In T. Champion and J. Collis (eds), *The Iron Age in Britain and Ireland: recent trends* (Sheffield, J R Collis Publications) 117-32.

Parker Pearson, M. 1999: Food, sex and death: cosmologies in the British Iron Age with particular reference to East Yorkshire. *Cambridge Archaeological Journal* 9, 43-69.

Parker Pearson, M., Marshall, P., Mulville, J. and Smith, H. 2002: The dead beneath their feet: housewarming c. 1000 BC – roundhouse rituals at Cladh Hallan. *Past* 40, 1-2.

Patton, M. 1990: On entoptic images in context: art, monuments, and society in Neolithic Brittany. *Current Anthropology* 31, 554-8.

Pentikäinen, J. 1998 (3rd ed.): *Shamanism and culture* (Tampere, Etnika).

Rasmussen, K. 1908: *The People of the Polar North: a record* (Compiled from the Danish Originals and Edited by G. Herring) (London, Kegan, Paul, Trench, Trübner and Co.).

Rowlett, R., Thomas, H., Sander-Jørgensen Rowlett E. and Stout, S. 1982: Stratified house floors on the Titelberg, Luxembourg. *Journal of Field Archaeology* 9, 301-12.

Scaife, R. 1986: Pollen in human palaeofaeces; and a preliminary investigation of the stomach and gut contents of Lindow Man. In I. Stead, J. Bourke and D. Brothwell (eds), *Lindow Man – the body in the bog* (London, BMP) 126-35.

Sherratt, A. 1991: Sacred and profane substances: the ritual use of narcotics in later Neolithic Europe. In P. Garwood, D. Jennings, R. Skeates and J. Toms (eds), *Sacred and profane - proceedings of a conference on archaeology, ritual and religion, Oxford, 1989* (Oxford, OUCA Monograph 32) 50-64.

Siikala, 1978: *The rite technique of the Siberian shaman* (Helsinki, Suomalainen Tiedeakatemia).

Terebikhin, N. 1993: Cultural geography and the cosmology of the Saami. *Acta Borealia* 10, 3-17.

van der Sanden, W. 1996: *Through nature to eternity: the bog bodies of Northwest Europe* (Amsterdam, Batavian Lion International).

Vitebsky, P. 1995: *The Shaman: voyages of the soul, trance, ecstasy and healing from Siberia to the Amazon* (London, Duncan Baird Publishers).

Vorren, Ø. 1987: Sacrificial sites, types and function. In T. Ahlbäck (ed.), *Saami Religion* (Åbo, The Donner Institute for Research in Religious and Cultural History) 94-109.

Watson, A. 2001: The sounds of transformation: acoustics, monuments and ritual in the British Neolithic. In N. Price (ed.), *The Archaeology of Shamanism* (London, Routledge) 178-92.

Wheeler, R. E. M. 1943: *Maiden Castle, Dorset* (London, Reports of the Research Committee of the Society of Antiquaries of London 12).

Whimster, R. 1981: *Burial practices in Iron Age Britain: a discussion and gazetteer of the evidence c. 700 BC – AD 43* (Oxford, BAR 90).

Williams, M. 2003: Tales from the dead: remembering the bog bodies in the Iron Age of north-western Europe. In H. Williams (ed.), *Archaeologies of remembrance: death and memory in past societies* (New York, Kluwer Academic) 89-112.

Winkelman, M. 1986: Trance states: a theoretical model and cross-cultural analysis. *Ethos* 14, 174-203.

Zachrisson, I. 1984: *De Samiska Metalldepåerna År 1000-1350 i Ljuset av Fyndet från Mörtträsket, Lappland* (Umeå, University of Umeå).

Distribution and ritual deposition of Iron Age coins in the South Midlands

Mark Curteis

Introduction

The last decade has seen major advances in both archaeological excavation technique and in the detail of recording. The latter includes not only excavated material, but also casual and metal detecting finds where object, find spot and associated data are now often recorded with some precision.

During this period archaeologists have reassessed 'ritual deposition', looking at the structure of material assemblages (e.g. Hill 1994, 1995) and determining that such structuring is often deliberate, and not representative of random rubbish disposal. Such studies have also looked at site morphology and, in particular, the positioning of special deposits within sites. However, although the emphasis given to such hypotheses is both worthwhile and valid, it has tended to leave specific artefact studies under-represented.

This paper examines Iron Age coins as an artefact group and uses the new data and information available to help illuminate how, and why, they ultimately come to be buried in archaeological contexts. First, the distribution of Iron Age coins is looked at from a regional perspective, before focusing in on the distribution of coins at site level and finally the depositional context itself. The area examined for the study incorporates the modern counties of Oxfordshire, Northamptonshire, Bedfordshire, Buckinghamshire, Cambridgeshire and Hertfordshire (Figure 1).

Distribution studies

Although it has had its detractors (e.g. Collis 1981), the plotting of regional distribution maps of Iron Age coins is a well-established tool in trying to identify areas of political, cultural or socio-economic unity, i.e. what are normally termed tribal areas (e.g. Allen 1944, Cunliffe 1981). It has been over a decade since the last major distribution study (Van Arsdell 1989) and during this time a very large number of new coin finds have been made, allowing for greater resolution on resulting distribution maps. This new data has allowed existing hypotheses drawn from distributions plots to be questioned and new hypotheses developed. In this section I will summarize the distribution of the main coin series in the study area.

The first Celtic coins to appear in any quantity in Britain are the large flan staters and quarter staters known as Gallo-Belgic A, imported from Belgic Gaul. The series is thought to date from around the start of the second century BC (Haselgrove 1999, 125). Roughly contemporary with Gallo-Belgic A was Gallo-Belgic B, followed by Gallo-Belgic C, D, E and F. It has been suggested that Gallo-Belgic E was issued in quantity to pay British mercenaries in the Gallic struggle against Caesar (e.g. Scheers 1972), although recent developments in dating the Gallo-Belgic E series (Haselgrove 1999) may argue against this hypothesis.

The find locations for Gallo-Belgic A staters within the study area (Figure 2) are either on, or to the south of, the line formed by the Icknield Way and the Chiltern Ridge, with a single exception from Over in Cambridgeshire. Nash (1987, 110) notes the main focus of the coinage is in northern Kent and the lower Thames Valley. The northern distribution of the series can now be more clearly defined.

Gallo-Belgic B issues appear to have a similar distribution to Gallo-Belgic A. The similarity in distribution between the types is likely to be a chronological effect and may suggest that during the period in which these coin types were in circulation the cultures using, or depositing, them did not extend beyond the Chilterns. This is contrary to the opinion of Allen (1960, 103) who believed that the distributions of Gallo-Belgic A and B were separate.

Gallo-Belgic C are spread across the study area with only two of the seven find spots to the south of the Icknield Way; suggesting that by the time these coins were in circulation the culture using the staters had spread to encompass much of the area. Previous studies (e.g. Fitzpatrick 1992, 7) had suggested the distribution to be the same as Gallo Belgic A and B.

Although the absolute numbers of Gallo-Belgic C issues are

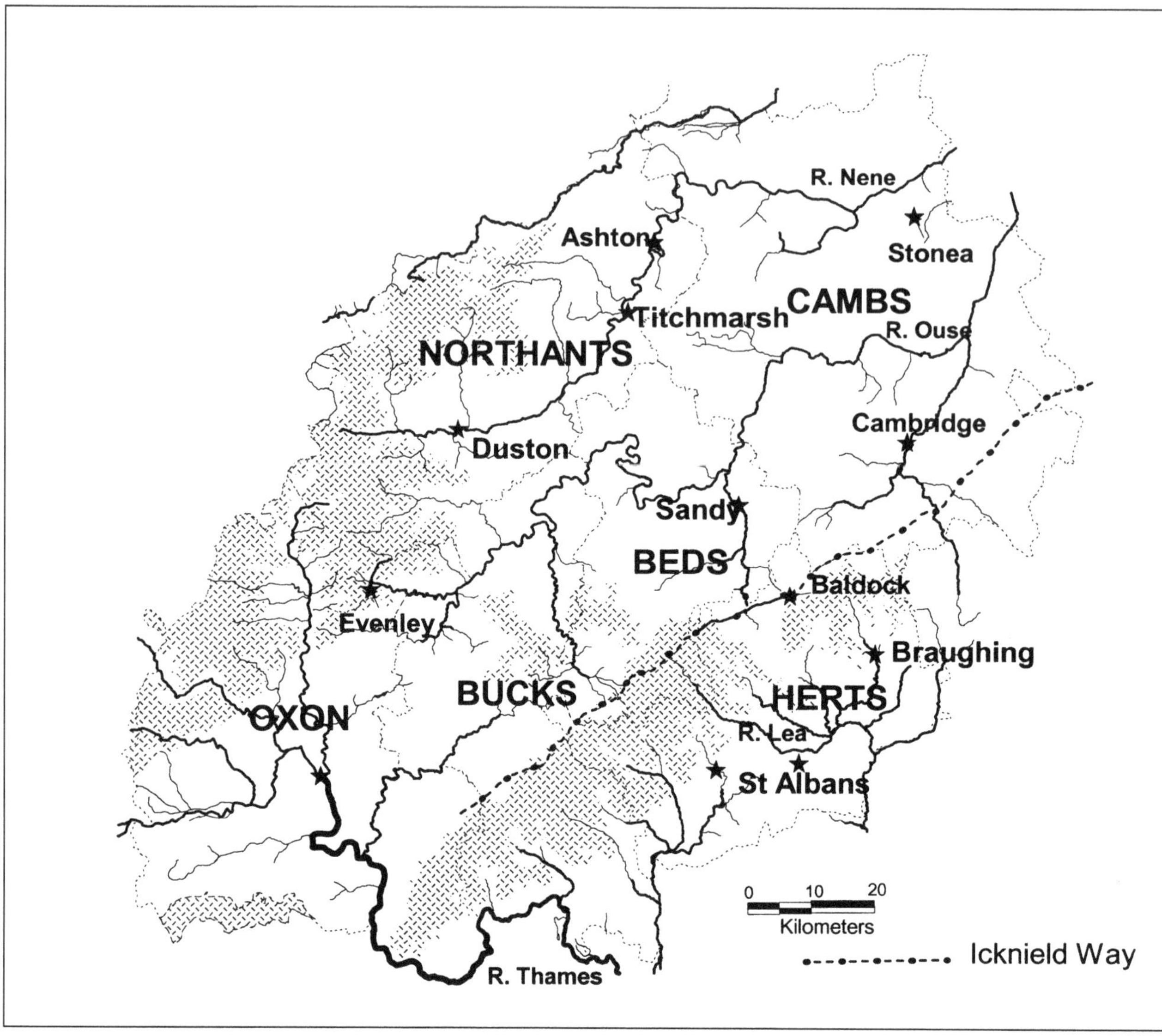

Figure 1. The study area.

low, when compared to Gallo-Belgic A and B, a void is indicated in west Oxfordshire. Previous distribution maps (Cunliffe 1981, fig. 42 and Van Arsdell 1989, map 6) suggest this area is beyond the distribution previously perceived for the issue, which appears to focus on north Kent. The find spot in north Cambridgeshire corroborates evidence that the distribution continued northwards to the Wash, while the example recorded from Northamptonshire marks the north-westerly limit.

The Gallo-Belgic D quarter staters have a similar distribution to those of Gallo-Belgic C, with the addition of a find spot in east Cambridgeshire. The issue had conventionally been given a southern coastal distribution (e.g. Allen 1960, 111 and Nash 1987, 112). The distribution of the comparatively plentiful Gallo-Belgic E staters is more extensive than that of Gallo-Belgic D. The find spots in Cambridgeshire indicate that coin-using cultures now existed up to the north of the county, and other distribution maps (Cunliffe 1981, fig. 44 and Van Arsdell 1989, map 7) confirm the distribution into Lincolnshire. As with the other issues, west Oxfordshire appears to remain outside the sphere of circulation, and consequently within a different cultural zone.

The divergent distribution patterns between Gallo-Belgic C, D and E could argue against Burnett's (1995, 6) hypothesis (drawn from metallurgical analyses by Cowell 1992), which overlaps Gallo-Belgic D with C and E, and using data from the Weybourne and Fring hoards (both of which link Gallo-Belgic D and E), suggests that Gallo-Belgic D may be the smaller denomination associated with both Gallo-Belgic C and E. Our distribution pattern would appear to indicate that Gallo-Belgic D is more likely to be associated with Gallo-Belgic C than E. The distributions reflect the picture seen for Gallo-Belgic C, D and E on the continent (Haselgrove 1999, 140-141).

The preceding discussion of Gallo-Belgic types shows the potential value of distribution plots, against which particular hypotheses can be developed to explain the observed phenomena; in this case a hypothesis to show a chronological spread in coin use throughout the South Midlands, which in turn helps to more clearly define a chronological series.

Distribution studies have often been used to locate tribal areas (e.g. Sellwood 1984). For example, if we draw a distribution map of coins belonging to the Western Series (after Haselgrove 1987), which are generally attributed to the Dobunni (Figure 3), it can be observed that, within the study area, the issues are concentrated in Oxfordshire, notably to the west of the Thames-Cherwell line. Sellwood (1984, 195) has suggested that this line forms the eastern and southern boundaries of the Dobunnic territory, while Van Arsdell (Van Arsdell 1994, 24-25) would suggest a line roughly between Marlborough and Grim's Ditch. The evidence here would seem to suggest that the area south of the Thames, in the area of our study, is also in Dobunnic territory, extending across the Vale of the White Horse to the Ridgeway. A large number of coins have been found in the area of the White Horse and the associated hillfort, perhaps indicating a ritual boundary zone (see below), the latter perhaps accounting for the chalk figure at this point. Very few issues associated with eastern tribes cross this boundary.

Concentrations of these coins are also found in Northamptonshire, particularly at Duston and Evenley, but at both these sites types attributed to the Catuvellauni predominate. Both sites are near to major rivers, and may have been trading centres. While Duston is likely to be in Catuvellaunian territory, Evenley is more marginal, away from the main concentrations of Catuvellaunian coinage, and lying on the extreme edge of the main area of Dobunnic coin distribution.

Hodder (1979) has suggested that markets frequently grow up on tribal borders, where trading can occur outside the inner sphere of social relations. It has also been observed (Brunaux 1988, 3) that there is a strong correlation between tribal boundaries and sanctuaries, and it is possible that the tribal boundary was symbolically marked and venerated in a comparable, but greater, way to which settlement boundaries have been shown to have been marked in England. Consequently, along boundaries we should expect to see concentrations of coins and other items of material culture focusing on shrines, temples and other areas of ritual activity. This is contrary to Van Arsdell (Van Arsdell 1994, 25) who suggests that tribes were separated by areas of 'no man's land', in which material finds are rare. Romano-Celtic temples with evidence for pre-conquest ritual activity are known along the Ouse at Cosgrove, Old Stratford, Thornborough and probably at Evenley, which has produced over 70 Iron Age coins and Roman votive material. The evidence may suggest this section of the Ouse, as well as the lower part of the Cherwell, formed the boundary. We might also identify a boundary line following the Thames southwards to Abingdon, along the river Ock, which is overlooked by the Iron Age and Roman sanctuaries at Frilford, and continuing in the direction of the Ridgeway and Uffington.

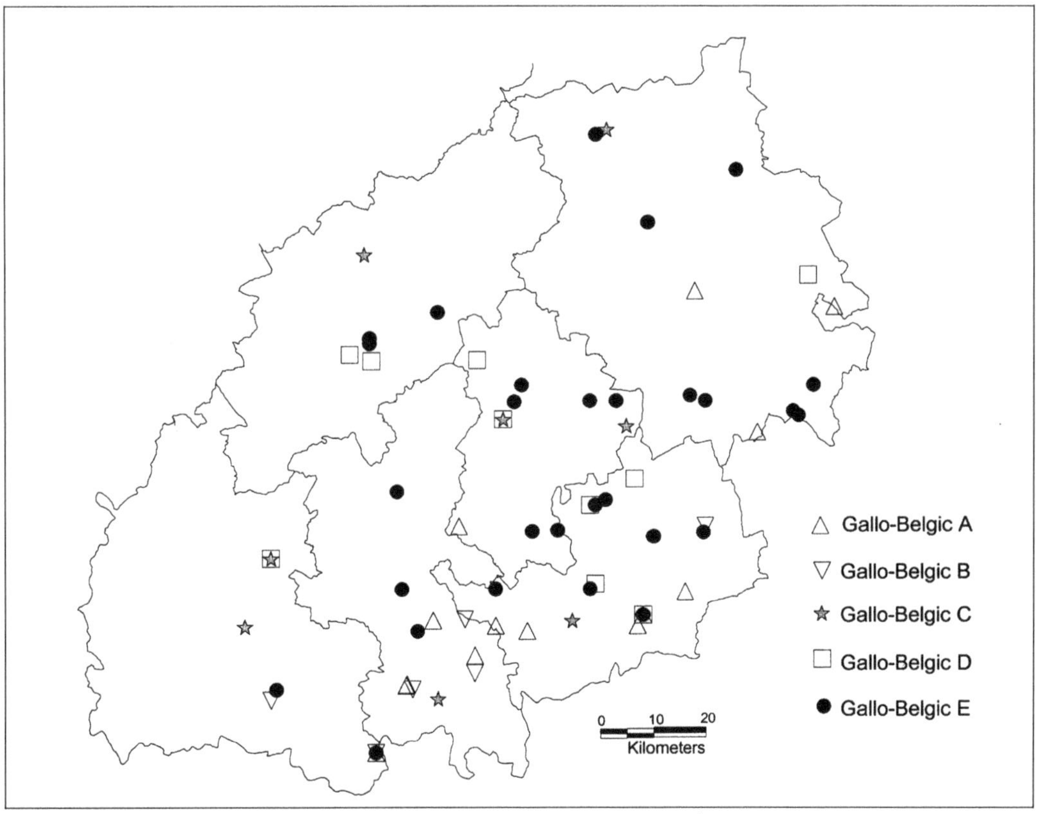

Figure 2. Findspots of Gallo-Belgic issues.

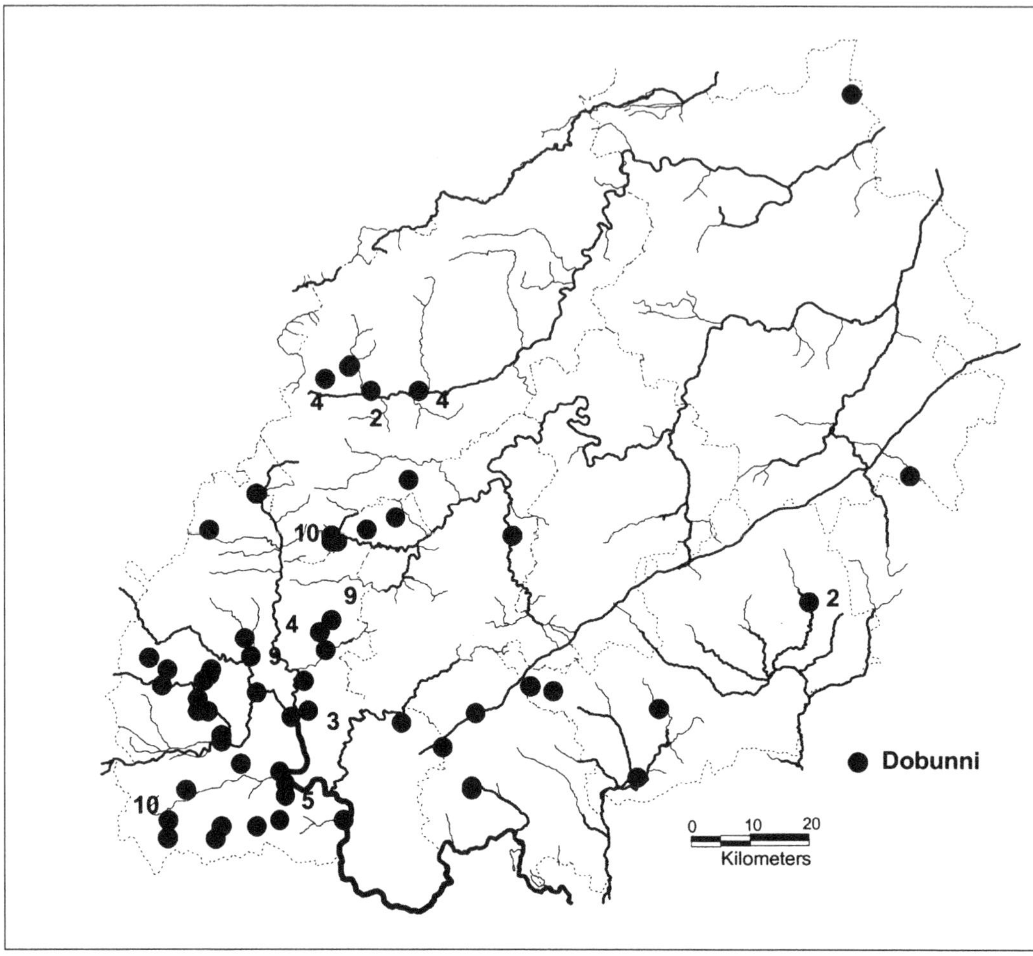

Figure 3. Findspots of coins of the Dobunni.

A number of arguments can be put forward to explain the penetration of Dobunnic coins as far as Duston or even Cambridgeshire. The Dobunnic coins are of a similar weight and module to Catuvellaunian silver, so an argument can be made to suggest that if a coin of a neighbouring tribe was available it might circulate outside its intended official area of use. Most of the Dobunnic coins found beyond Oxfordshire are late issues. We must not forget the possibility that Iron Age coins were moved around by the Roman army after the invasion. Wigg (1996) has shown in his study of northern Gaul that the Roman army used other available currencies to supplement their own official issues; alternatively soldiers may have simply carried them as curiosities, which may account for stray finds such as the coin of Tasciovanus from South Shields.

A further use of coin distribution studies is to help define areas over which named individuals had control. Addedomaros and Dubnovellaunus, for example, are thought to have been broadly contemporary, but little is known about the relative extent of their territories. The coins inscribed in the name of Addedomaros have been shown to concentrate in Essex and Hertfordshire, but they also spread into East Anglia and the Midlands (after Van Arsdell 1989, map 68).

Addedomaros types have only been recorded in the central and southern part of the present study area, with voids in north and west Northamptonshire, the coins not reaching beyond the Nene valley, or into north Bedfordshire or Cambridgeshire (Figure 4). The types are clearly concentrated in the region of the Chilterns, perhaps pointing to this area as their place of origin. If Van Arsdell (1989) is correct in dividing the coinage of Addedomaros up into three phases, then all the coins of the first series lie on or south of the Chilterns. Only the later varieties extend beyond this area, suggesting expansion.

Although there is an overlap along the central axis of the study area, notably at Baldock and Braughing, the issues of Dubnovellaunus mainly lie in the eastern half of the region. Such a picture is not surprising after the work of Rodwell (1976), which shows issues of Dubnovellaunus to be heavily concentrated in north Essex. It can now be shown in some detail that the circulations of the inscribed coinages of both rulers are different, but with an overlap along their conjoining margins.

Distribution studies can also be used to define subdivisions within larger tribal areas. The status of Andoco, Dias and Rues in this area has long been a subject of debate. Allen (1967, 4) noted the general resemblance of the coins of Rues to those of Tasciovanus, and also of Dias, and concluded they must be of similar date. Although an attempt has been made (Van Arsdell 1989) to place these three rulers, assuming that the inscriptions refer to personal names, in a single chronological sequence, it has also been suggested (de Jersey 1996, 35; Curteis 1997, 22) that they may have been associates or subordinates of Tasciovanus, perhaps occupying small areas or *pagi* within the territory under his control.

Another hint of a situation where Tasciovanus acted as an overlord is provided by the inscription RICON or RICONI which appears on some staters. Allen (1944, 17) has given the most universally accepted view that such a legend may be the Celtic form of the Latin 'rex', emphasizing Tasciovanus's position as the head of the tribe. The distribution of coins with legends linking them to Dias, Andoco, Rues and also the Ricon legend is shown in Figures 5 and 6. The issues of Rues appear superficially to be spread over much the same area as those of Tasciovanus, yet they are almost completely absent from Northamptonshire, Cambridgeshire and Oxfordshire. They are concentrated in north Hertfordshire and east Bedfordshire, particularly in the area of Sandy and Braughing. The concentration of ten finds at Sandy, comprising 14% of all issues of Rues from the study area, is particularly significant. The other major concentration of twelve examples from St Albans has been artificially increased by the inclusion of a hoard of ten coins from a grave in the King Harry Lane cemetery (Goodburn 1989, 87).

The rarer issues of Dias are also diffused throughout much of the study area where issues of Tasciovanus predominate. However, they are clearly concentrated at Braughing and Puckeridge, which account for 33% of all the Dias types from the region.

The issues of Andoco, which also spread across much of the geographical area covered by the issues of Tasciovanus, are concentrated in Hertfordshire and south Bedfordshire. The greatest concentrations are at Braughing/Puckeridge where the assemblage forms 18% of the total number of coins of Andoco, and Baldock where the recovered assemblage represents 16%. The concentration of these types at Baldock is significantly higher than for Rues (7%) and Dias (7%). If the hypothesis of Dias, Rues and Andoco as ruling sub-tribal areas or *pagi* under the overall authority of a greater ruler (Tasciovanus) is correct, then we could see Rues having his centre of authority at Sandy, Dias at Braughing/Puckeridge, and Andoco at Baldock.

On the same basis the largest concentrations of the issues of Tasciovanus are at St Albans and Braughing/Puckeridge. The Tasciovanus assemblage forms 27% of the site total for Iron Age coinage at St Albans, and 22% of the total at Braughing/Puckeridge. These results would indicate that at least during the later part of the reign of Tasciovanus, his power base, and also presumably the tribal capital, was at St Albans.

The distribution of the coins bearing the RICON inscription (Figure 6) covers much the same geographical area as all the coins inscribed in the name of Tasciovanus. However, unlike the issues of Rues, Dias and Andoco, these coins are found in Oxfordshire to the west of the Thames.

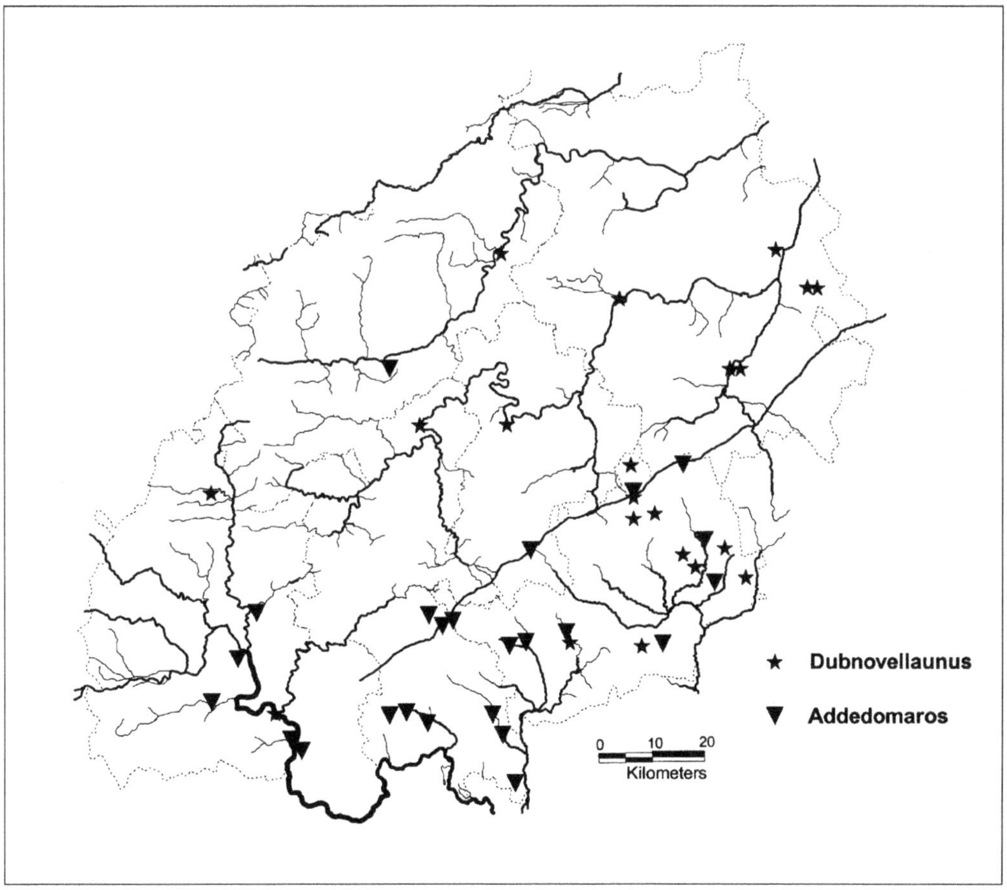

Figure 4. Distribution of coins of Addedomaros and Dubnovellaunus.

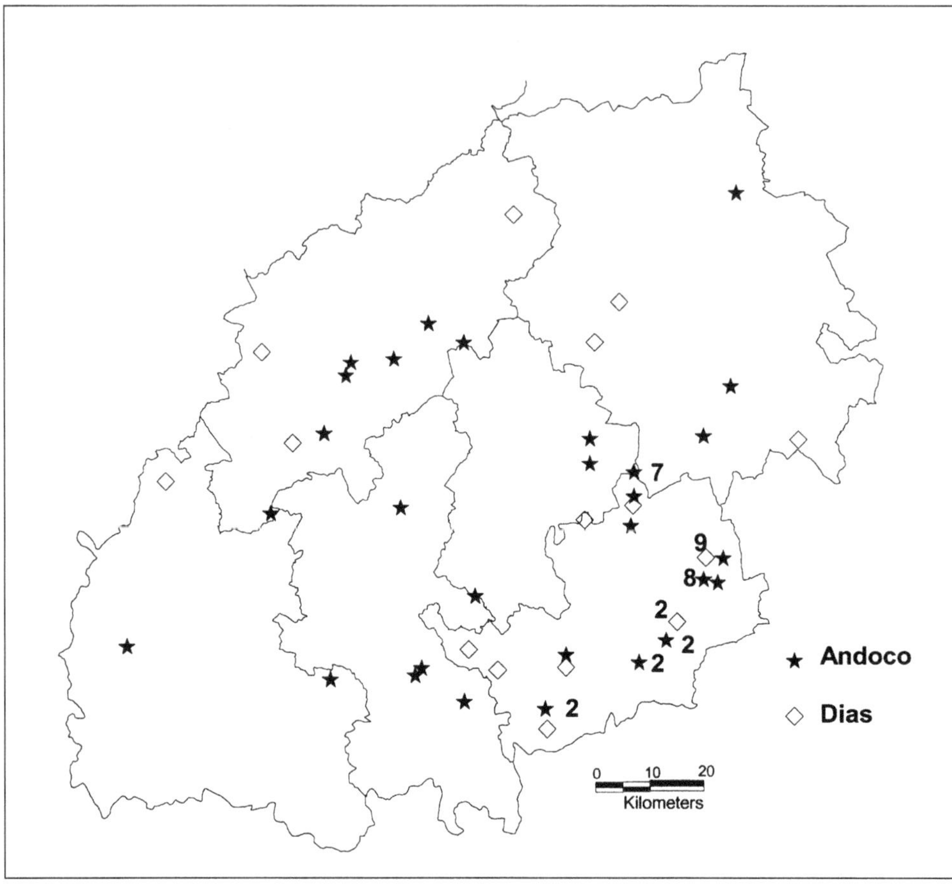

Figure 5. Distribution of coins of Dias and Andoco.

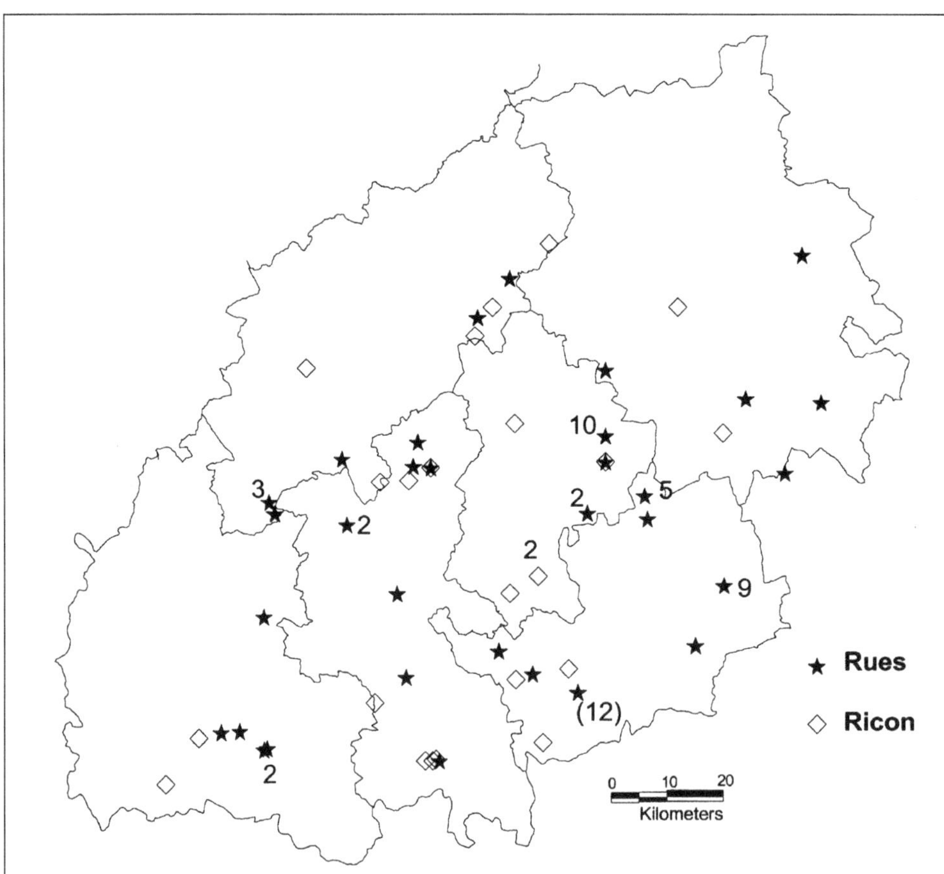

Figure 6. Distribution of coins of Rues, and coins inscribed 'RICON'.

These results suggest that the word RICON(I) is indeed a title. The issues are only produced in gold, not in a base metal; gold may perhaps have been seen as the appropriate medium for such a proclamation. They have a wider geographical spread than any of the issues of the sub-ordinates. They cannot be seen to concentrate at any particular settlement.

Distribution plots are not the only way of looking at regional trends. Histograms can be used to enable site chronology and political orientation to be determined when compared to the regional background. Figure 7 shows the coin loss profile for Northamptonshire. The peaks and troughs for both major and minor coin producing sites are similar, and indicate that sites such as Evenley and Duston, with extensive coin lists, are not skewing the profile.

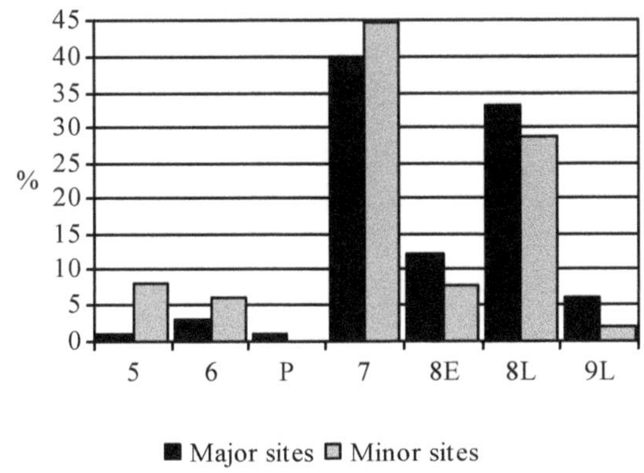

Figure 7. Coin loss in Northamptonshire.

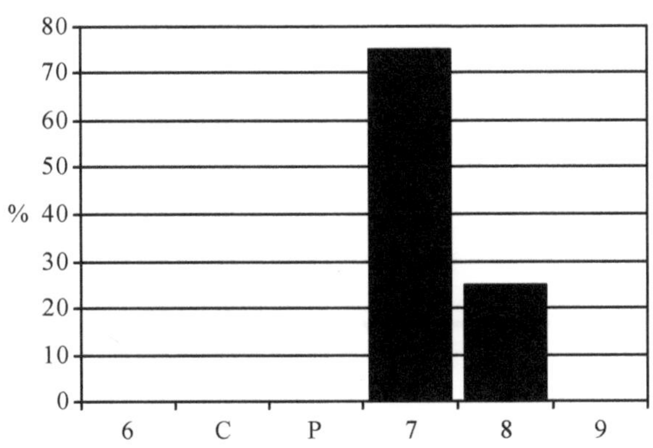

Figure 8. Coin loss at Weekley (n = 8).

Weekley is a partially excavated, late pre-Roman Iron Age and Roman settlement in central Northamptonshire (Jackson and Dix 1987). The assemblage (Figure 8), although only eight coins, is worthy of further comment. Six of these coins are eastern or south-eastern (i.e. Trinovantian or Catuvellaunian) issues and belong to Phase 7 (see Haselgrove 1987 for details of phasing). The other two coins, from Phase 8, are ascribed to the Corieltauvi. Eastern series coins, especially the regionally numerous developed coinage of Cunobelin, are notably absent. This may suggest either that the site declined in Phase 8, or perhaps, that it came under a different sphere of influence in this period, changing from Catuvellaunian to Corieltauvian control; the site is near a proposed boundary between the two tribes and would certainly fall within a boundary zone. A decline would seem unlikely because the site later developed into a Roman settlement of regional significance. There is also archaeological evidence here to support the boundary theory (Gwilt 1995). A change of political control in the area is confirmed by the coin list at Titchmarsh, about 10km further along the river Nene (Curteis 2000), which parallels that of Weekley. In contrast, at Cherry Hinton, Cambridgeshire, which potentially may lie in the vicinity of an Icenian/Catuvellaunian boundary, all the coin finds up to phase 7 are Icenian while all the later coins are eastern issues. Perhaps we may be seeing Catuvellaunian expansion in the east but slight retraction to the north? Such analyses reinforce the point that boundaries were not always static but were sometimes in a state of flux.

The various distribution studies described above have shown previous studies to be incorrect mainly because their conclusions were based on a comparative lack of data. This highlights the problem of drawing conclusions from incomplete databases, and although we continually add more find spots to the database we can never be sure that future finds will not render particular conclusions, based on distribution analyses, obsolete. Consequently it is important to continually reappraise distributions as new data becomes available.

Site based and contextual analyses

The detail of recording on archaeological excavations has developed significantly over the last couple of decades, and as techniques have developed more precise contextual information has been collected. The wealth of contextual data now available has recently led a number of researchers to examine the nature of archaeological deposits, in order to try to unravel site formation processes, particularly with regard to how artefacts actually enter the archaeological record. Up until the 1990s small finds, including coins, were generally seen by archaeologists as useful chronological indicators, possibly with future exhibition possibilities. With the exception of pioneering work on Iron Age coinages (such as Haselgrove 1987) there was little consideration of the context of deposition.

The detailed study by Hill (1995) of all classes of material found in pits and ditches clearly demonstrated that such material is composed of complex and highly structured patterns; it does not merely represent a random act of rubbish disposal, but instead should be seen as a ritual act. Just as the position of material within a feature has been identified as non-random, the position of features containing structured deposits within the sites has also been recognised as highly significant (Brunaux 1988; Hill 1994). Consequently the layout of a settlement and the organization of the deposits within it have come to be seen as structured and symbolic, "but not just symbolic: the irregular ritual deposits in different parts of the settlement served to physically engrave the cosmological concerns of ritual onto the spaces in and through which Iron Age peoples lived" (Hill 1994, 6).

Coin deposition has often been seen to reflect accidental loss resulting from purely economic factors (e.g. Casey 1974). However, during the 1980s coinage deposited off-site was seen in an increasingly 'ritual' perspective. Late Iron Age shrines were often seen to have deposits of coinage (Brunaux 1988; Haselgrove 1989), while the gold coinages, almost exclusively known from off-site contexts, also began to be interpreted in a symbolic way. How can coins, with little intrinsic but high symbolic value, be seen in terms of structured deposition, and what can this tell us about the function of coins?

To provide an answer to these questions a detailed analysis must be made of the archaeological contexts from which coins are derived. The South Midlands area examined for this study includes a number of relatively well explored late Iron Age settlements which provide useful information.

If the features on site are examined chronologically (Figure 9), it can be observed that the majority of Iron Age coins originate from deposits dated to the late Iron Age, the period in which they had obvious meaning and currency to the people who used them. As time progresses there are fewer and fewer coins recovered from features. However, even if we take into account the early Roman period being perhaps two or even three times shorter than the late Iron Age, there is apparently no rapid discard of coins in the decades following the invasion, as they lost their original purpose. This could indicate that whatever meaning the coins had in society did not terminate following the invasion, and that the fall-off in deposition is simply a reflection of the availability of Iron Age coinage.

An analysis of the feature types from which the coins have been recovered clearly shows that in the LPRIA coins were most commonly deposited in ditches, followed by pits and alluvium.

The ditch has been shown to have functioned as a strongly symbolic division of space between what was enclosed and that which was outside. The results showing that coins were predominantly deposited in such features indicate that the ditch was a medium specifically selected for such deposition, and that such an act was a deliberate action to enhance the symbolic importance of the ditch or other feature, rather than an accidental, random loss.

The second most common place for coins to be deposited is the pit. It has been recognised for some time that grain storage pits often had 'special deposits' at their bases, and the nature of Iron Age chthonic beliefs may be an important consideration in the interpretation of material in pits.

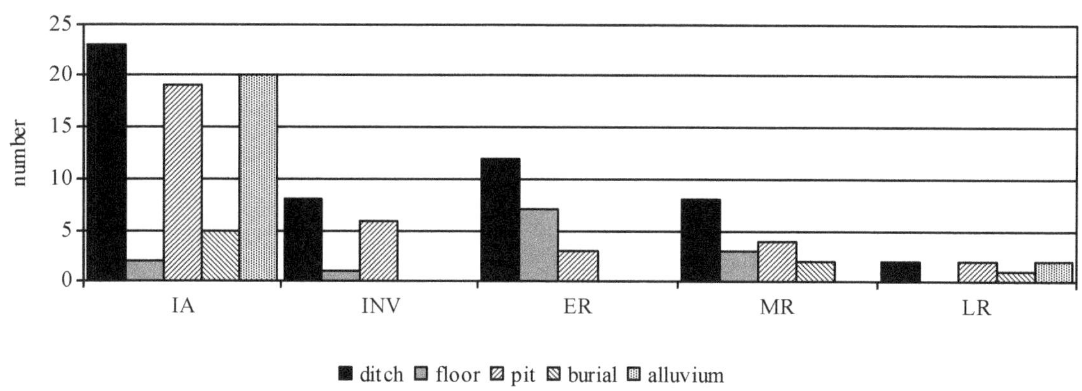

Figure 9. Deposition of coins by date (IA: Iron Age; INV: Invasion Period; ER: Early Roman (AD 43 – 100); MR: Middle Roman (AD 100 – 300); LR: Late Roman (AD 300 – 450).

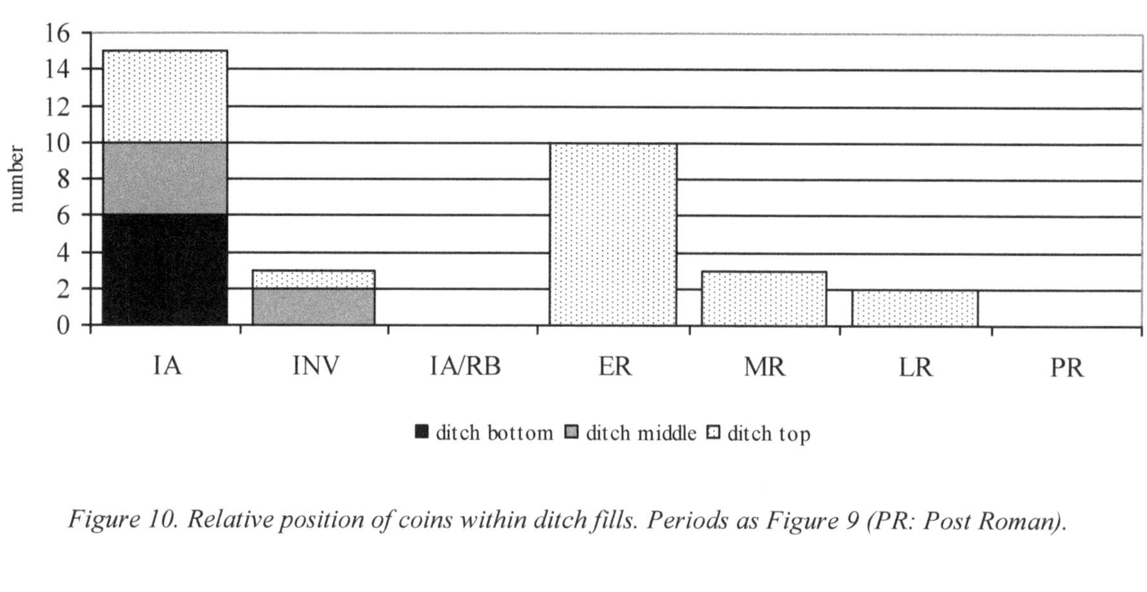

Figure 10. Relative position of coins within ditch fills. Periods as Figure 9 (PR: Post Roman).

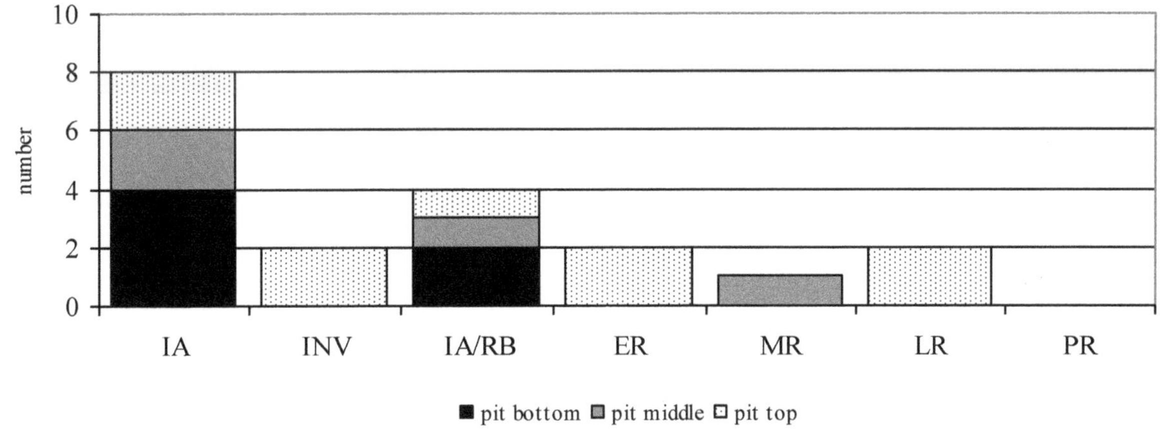

Figure 11. Relative positions of coins within pit fills. Periods as Figure 9.

Alluvium (i.e. areas that would have been stream beds or wetlands in the late Iron Age), would seem a very appropriate place for the deposition of coins, considering the popularity of votive deposition in watery contexts during the Iron Age. This practice has been demonstrated in relation to gold coinage (Curteis 1996), and we can now add that a proportion of the base metal coinage may also have been deposited in a similar way.

Burial contexts also appear to have been chosen for coin deposition, to a certain extent. However, the only LPRIA context associated with a primary burial context is the hoard of ten coins in a single grave at King Harry Lane, St Albans. In all the other cases the coin comes from the grave fill, the grave pit perhaps then being seen in a similar way, both functionally and symbolically, to other pits. This could be taken to suggest that coins were not functional items for the journey to, or use in, the afterlife in the same way as conventional grave goods or, significantly, Roman coins during the Roman period.

Immediately after the invasion the pattern of deposition dramatically changes, thereby emphasising that the picture we see reflects deliberate and structured activity, not a simple picture of random loss and deposition. In Roman period contexts the majority of coin finds still come from ditches. However, the idea of a pit being seen as a preferred depositional environment almost entirely disappears following the invasion, although pits still continued to be a common feature on all types of site. A similar change in depositional practice is also seen in alluvial deposits, which also sharply decline following the invasion.

A greater proportion of coin finds following the invasion may be residual, and residuality is a function of deposition likely to increase with time. Yet, as will be seen below, a major component of the Iron Age coin assemblage recovered from Roman deposits can be seen as deliberate deposition. An example from the study area is Brigstock, Northants., (Greenfield 1963), where a gold stater was found lying on the floor of the Roman shrine alongside Roman votive material, suggesting that it was not accidentally redeposited from an earlier feature, but was regarded, and used, in a votive way.

Many studies on structured deposits (e.g. Hill 1995, Parker-Pearson 1999, Fitzpatrick 1997) have emphasised the position of certain material within pits and ditches, noting that different categories of material come from different positions in the fill. It would appear that the relative positioning of coins within features (Figures 10 and 11) was deliberate and, as with the choice of feature, is emphasised by change following the Roman invasion. Prior to the invasion coins were deposited throughout the fills of pits and ditches, with a slight emphasis on the lower fill. Following the invasion the coins come entirely from the tops of ditches, including ditches of Roman date, where they may have functioned as termination deposits. This may suggest that there was some curation of Iron Age coinage during the Roman period. If the features had been filled in a non-structured way we would expect coinage to be much more evenly spread throughout the fills.

The character of specialized Iron Age religious sites in Britain, and continuity into the Roman period

It is well-known that the largest collections of archaeological site and metal detecting finds of Iron Age coins come from specialized religious sites. The best known British examples are Wanborough, Hayling Island and Harlow. There are also numerous examples from north-west Gaul, including Bois-l'Abbé, Vendeuil-Caply and Estrées-Saint-Denis (Delestrée 1996).

An analysis of Iron Age/Roman specialised religious sites, or temples (Table 1), shows that they tend to have many geographical and physical characteristics in common. The architecture of settlement gateways was often elaborate, thus emphasizing the crossing of such a boundary, while the ditch terminals either side of an entrance were often the location for ritual deposits, e.g. at Gussage All Saints (Hill 1994, 6-7). At the majority of sites there is evidence of ritual activity in the area before the late Iron Age, and long or round barrows can seen to be commonly associated with later religious sites. Religious use of the site usually extended into the Roman period and this is reflected in the occurrence of specific Roman votive objects; often it is the Roman evidence that has led to an Iron Age religious site being identified.

Unusually large pits or hollows (natural or man-made), containing deposits of carefully selected material, are frequently associated with these sites, either below or next to the structure of the shrine or temple, where they may have functioned as the focus for the religious activity. These material assemblages can often be identified as votive because of the unusual and high status nature of the finds they contain.

Brooches are always found at religious sites and, frequently, toilet articles. Weaponry is associated with the sites to a lesser extent but there is clearly an association when weapons are rarely found on domestic settlements; it may be that it depends on the nature of the deity being worshipped. Stone tools are also commonly found on religious sites and they are more likely to come from Iron Age and Roman than Neolithic or Bronze Age contexts, which may suggest that the material has been especially collected for votive use.

It can be demonstrated (see below) that many sites which have produced multiple finds of Iron Age coins have characteristics that closely reflect the template summarised above, suggesting that such coin-rich sites had a major religious or ritual component.

Site analysis

In the South Midlands there are a number of well-known and archaeologically well-explored and recorded Iron Age and Roman sites which have produced several Iron Age coins. Some of these sites are discussed below.

Verlamion

In the 1930s Wheeler drew attention to a complex system of late Iron Age earthworks which appear to focus on Verlamion (Wheeler and Wheeler 1936, 10-16). Many of the earthworks define enclosures or drove ways, while some, such as New Dyke and Devil's Ditch, appear to be major land boundaries.

	Fison Way	Brigstock	Gournay	Harlow	Hayling Island	Thornborough	Wanborough	Woodeaton	Uley
Iron Age structure	no	yes	no	yes	no	yes	yes	yes	yes
Roman temple	yes	yes	yes	yes	yes	yes	yes	yes	yes
IA artefacts	yes	yes	yes	yes	yes	yes	yes	yes	yes
Elaborate gate	?	yes	yes	yes	yes	yes	yes	yes	yes
Gate deposits	yes	yes	yes	yes	yes	yes	yes	yes	yes
Gate facing	E	E	E	E	E	E	E	E	E
Votive assemblages	yes	yes	yes	yes	yes	yes	yes	yes	yes
Large pit/hollow	?	yes	yes	yes	yes	?	?	?	yes
Human bone	yes	yes	yes	yes	yes	yes	yes	yes	yes
Brooches	yes	yes	yes	yes	yes	yes	yes	yes	yes
Toilet articles	yes	yes	yes	yes	yes	yes	yes	no	yes
Weaponry	yes	yes	yes	no	yes	yes	no	no	yes
Metalworking	no	yes	yes	no	yes	no	no	no	yes
Stone tools	yes	yes	?	yes	yes	yes	yes	yes	yes
IA coins	yes	yes	yes	yes	yes	yes	yes	yes	yes
Quantity Roman coins	yes	yes	yes	yes	yes	yes	yes	yes	yes
RB votive items	yes	yes	yes	yes	yes	yes	yes	yes	yes

Table 1. Summary of specialised religious sites which have produced Iron Age coins.

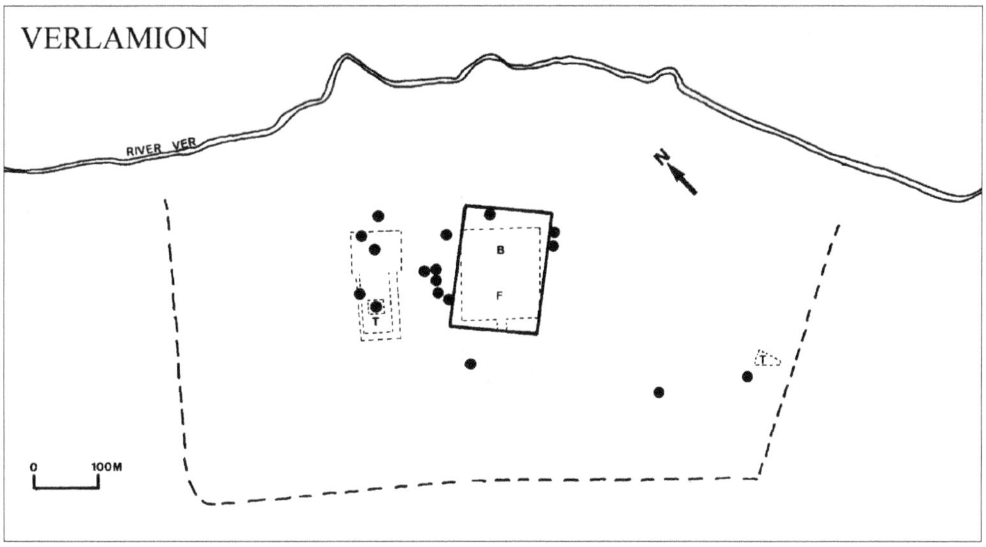

Figure 12. Plan of Verlamion, showing position of coin finds and the St Michael's enclosure. The position of Roman temples (T) and the basilica (B) and forum (F) complexes are also shown. The dashed line defines the town in the late first century AD.

The majority of the enclosures were positioned on the edge of a plateau above the river Ver. The one exception to a plateau edge location is a ditched enclosure, known as St Michael's enclosure. It is unusual both in its large size and in being positioned on a low level gravel terrace on the flood plain. The enclosure is separated from the river by a marsh and is clearly exceptional, as emphasized by the status of the Roman use for the site as the forum and basilica complex.

St Michael's enclosure is unusual not only for its coin finds (Figure 12), most of which come from the west of the enclosure, where metalworking is known to have taken place. Pellet mould fragments have also been found in the vicinity of the enclosure, mostly to the west. Pellet moulds are also known to be associated with the important religious and metalworking centre at Fison Way, Norfolk (Gregory 1992). The linking of religion and metalworking has many parallels and it is a characteristic associated with many temple sites. It is probable that metalworking may have been seen as a magical transformation or metamorphosis of metal, and consequently that the process required overseeing by the gods. Metalworking and multiple coin finds are also associated elsewhere in the South Midlands, notably at Ashton, Northamptonshire and Cow Roast, Hertfordshire. Evidence for ritual activity has been identified at both sites.

To the west of St Michael's enclosure at Verlamion a large temple complex developed during the Roman period, its significance being such that a theatre was later added. The number of Iron Age coins, one of which was found below the *cella* itself, and pre-conquest brooches, strongly suggest that the Romano-British temple had an Iron Age precedent. It can be postulated that a cult site grew up at Verlamion, based upon the presence of the marsh and nearby river. The close association with a major boundary, formed by the dykes and perhaps the river itself, provided the necessary requirements for an important cult site to develop.

The cult and ceremonial centre represented by the temple and the enclosure was of such significance that it became the heart of the Roman *municipium*, the enclosure itself being replaced by the forum and basilica, which hints at the function of the enclosure as a ceremonial area of territorial importance. There are close parallels with Gosbecks, Colchester, which also appears to have been an important Iron Age religious centre; during the Roman period it possessed a temple and theatre complex, and there is also a large rectilinear enclosure adjoining the temple, interpreted as 'Cunobelin's farm' (Crummy 1997, 17).

At Gorhambury (Neal *et al.* 1990) excavations revealed what has been interpreted as an elite farmstead, positioned on the plateau edge c. 1.5 km north-east of the St Michael's enclosure. It may indicate that the leading elite had decided to take up residence around Verlamion to reinforce links between the enactment of religious festivals and the reproduction of political power (Haselgrove and Millett 1997, 284-85). By the end of the Iron Age the site (Figure 13) consisted of a double enclosure which could only be entered by crossing the New Dyke, which forms part of the Verlamion dyke system. Each of the two enclosures would have to be entered through substantial gateways. As with the other sites under discussion the location of the coins is not random and a patterning is clearly visible.

Fourteen coins were excavated here. The three recovered from the boundary ditches were in the ditch terminals, emphasising the crossing of the boundary. Significantly, two were closely associated in the south ditch terminal at the entrance to enclosure while the other, from the entrance to enclosure B, was found in the north ditch terminal. Late Iron Age people did differentiate north/south and east/west when making special deposits and here we may be seeing a deliberate transposition in the selection of terminal between the two enclosures, perhaps intending to symbolically demarcate a change in activity between enclosures A and B. The larger number of coins from enclosure B would suggest that it was here that ritual activity was particularly focused.

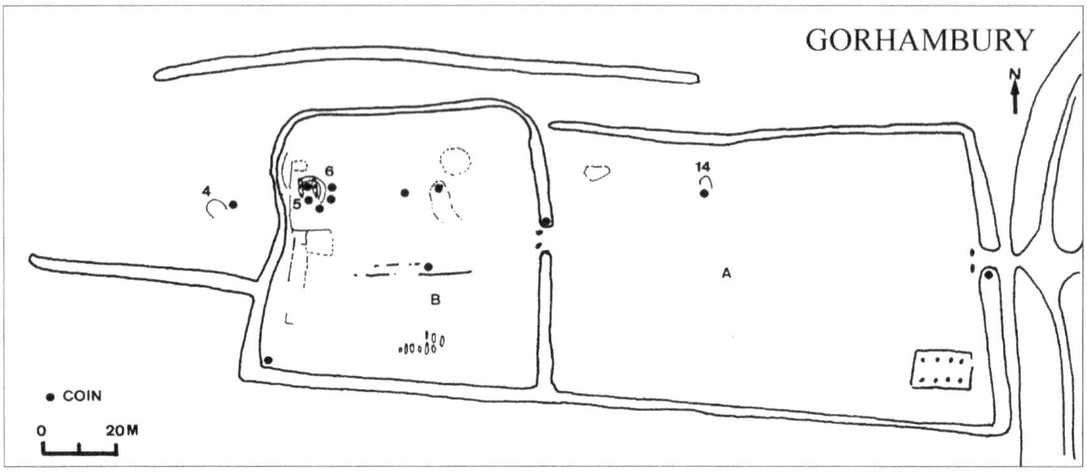

Figure 13. Position of coin finds at Gorhambury.

In enclosure B the majority of coins from the site were associated with buildings 5 and 6. They lay immediately to the north of the later villa complex. Neither of these buildings could be satisfactorily interpreted by the excavator although building 5 was interpreted as a granary. It was replaced by building 6, a circular structure with a central hearth, a cist and shallow pit. Two Republican *denarii* were also found in the same area, coins which are generally rare as site finds. The concentration of Iron Age and Republican coins, together with the unusual form of the buildings, would suggest that the buildings were not of a basic agricultural utilitarian type, but of some status and significance.

The number of Iron Age coins around buildings 5 and 6 is further emphasized by the complete absence of any other metallic small finds from the area, indicating that the buildings were not used as receptacles for rubbish; this suggests that the coins must have been selected in preference to other material. If we view enclosure B as a ritual enclosure containing a shrine (buildings 5/6), then a special deposit should be sought in the entrance way which is elaborated as at known religious sites. Indeed the southern terminal contained numerous small finds, including three brooches, a crescent pendent and a signet ring. The archaeological data from enclosure B is summarised in Table 2.

Pre Iron Age	Roman temple	Location	IA structure	IA artefacts	Elaborate gate	Gate deposits	Gate facing	Votive assemblages	Large pit/hollow	Human bone	Brooches	Toilet articles	Weaponry	Metalworking	Stone tools	Iron Age coins	Quantity Roman coins	RB votive items
yes	no	S	yes	yes	yes	yes	E	yes	yes	yes	yes	yes	no	yes	yes	yes	yes	yes

Table 2. Gorhambury compared to characteristics of known Iron Age religious sites.

Enclosure B at Gorhambury can be seen to fulfil many of the characteristics we have noted as being present at the majority of specialized Iron Age cult sites (Table 2). The Roman objects that may be of a votive nature include a cast bronze eagle's wing, and the hand of a figurine holding a bunch of grapes. The only obvious category of material lacking is weaponry, but here we could be dealing with a peaceful water cult. In all other respects the main difference between this and certain cult sites is that in this case a villa was constructed during the Roman period rather than a temple.

Baldock

Baldock (Stead and Rigby 1986; Burleigh 1995) seems to have been a focus for burial and ritual activity within a complex of settlement, cemeteries and burials lying on the northern spine of the Chilterns, in north Hertfordshire. The site, in a prominent position on the edge of the Chilterns, is located by the springs of the river Ivel. The juxtaposition of these springs and the proximity of the Icknield Way may provide a ritual reason for the foundation of the settlement.

An elite burial, found as part of an excavation of an area known as BAL1 (Figure 14), was placed under a barrow at the centre of a square ditched enclosure. Opposite this burial enclosure, on the other side of the road, was a smaller cremation enclosure which later became incorporated within an extensive Roman inhumation cemetery. Both the major and minor burial enclosures lie on a crossroads formed by the main Welwyn/Verlamion road and a trackway. The crossroads was positioned by a large solution hollow which was extended in size during the Iron Age and Roman periods, until it encroached on the main burial enclosure. In the hollow was a series of carefully constructed cobbled floors separated by layers containing charcoal, human bone and a rich variety of small finds. It has been suggested (M. Stevenson, pers. comm.) that the character of the material in the hollow implies it was a focus for ritual activity, and it is unlikely that its position by the crossroads and proximity with an elite burial was accidental.

Seven coins were recovered from late Iron Age and Roman layers within the hollow, the highest concentration of non-hoard coins from any feature excavated to date in the South Midlands. All of the layers were notable for their wealth of finds, which included three brooches, worked flint, finger-rings, slag and imported pottery.

The association of Iron Age coins in features that also contain a variety of other small finds can be seen as part of a recurring pattern. Attention is particularly drawn to the association of coins with personal items (such as brooches, jewellery and toilet articles), with metalworking debris, and with the presence of worked flint. The association of these deposits with hollows also recurs elsewhere. It is interesting that the feature which lies on the opposite corner of the crossroads contains the second largest concentration of non-hoard coins in the South Midlands. Such a high concentration of coins in two closely connected features is exceptional. This feature represents an area of disturbance and 'extremely unusual activity'. It has been postulated that this was an area where particular ritual ceremonies took place, the resulting ceremonial material perhaps being removed and placed in the solution hollow (M. Stevenson, pers. comm.). As with the material associated with the coins in the solution hollow, the contexts containing coins recovered from this area were similarly rich in finds (including four brooches), and with similar artefactual associations.

About 100m to the south-east of BAL1 is an area excavated between 1968 and 1971, known as Site A (Stead and Rigby 1986; Figure 15). In general the site consists of LPRIA and Roman enclosures, including two small burial enclosures, pits, ditches and track ways. More coins were found when parts of the site were re-excavated by Burleigh in 1983 (M. Stevenson, pers. comm.). There is a notable concentration of six coins around the entrance to an enclosure dated to the second century AD. The enclosure overlay a smaller LPRIA enclosure (the narrower ditches on Figure 15), the latter incorporating an area on which the circular building was later constructed. It is probable that the entrance to the earlier enclosure was in a similar position to that of the later one.

The entrance to the enclosure was marked by a substantial gateway, indicated by four large post-holes. One of the coins was recovered from the northern ditch terminal. A quantity of other small finds came from the same context. It is likely that the assemblage was a deliberate votive deposit, indicated by the quality and quantity of finds it contained. The ditch terminal on the south side of the entrance was unexcavated. The entrance structure stood over a large hollow.

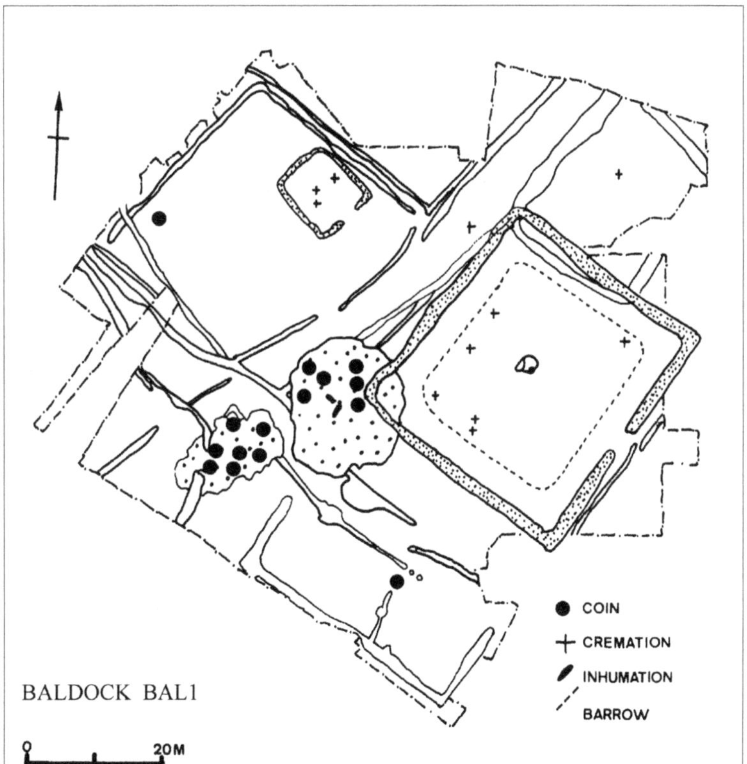

Figure 14. Plan of Baldock site BAL1, showing position of coin finds.

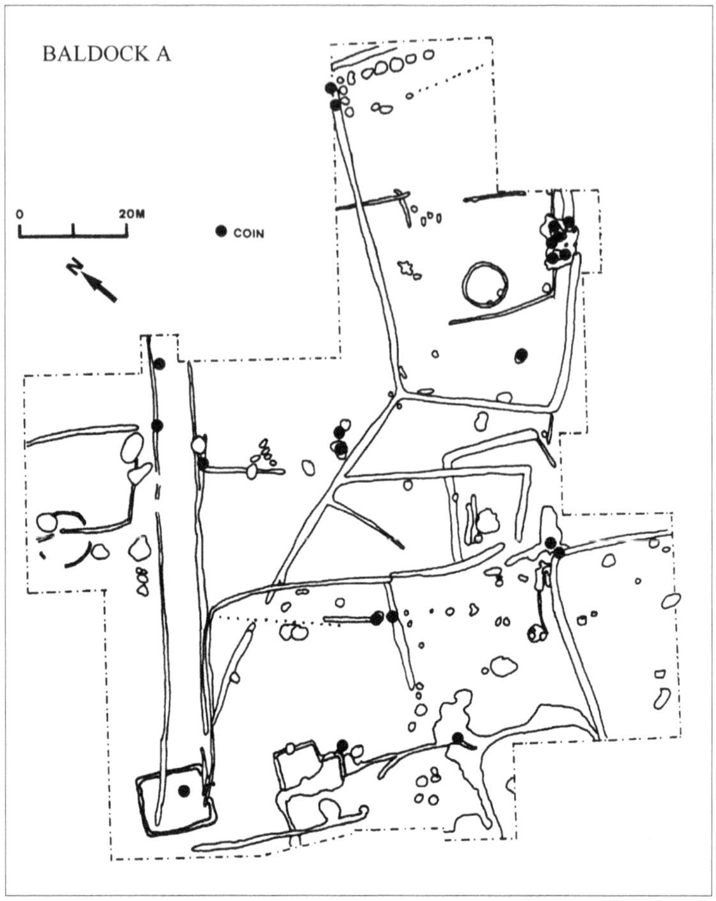

Figure 15. Plan of Baldock A, showing position of coin finds.

Just as the solution hollow on BAL1 seems to been seen and treated in a special way, it is unlikely that the presence of a large hollow underlying the entrance is coincidental. Along with a coin, this hollow also contained several unusual finds including part of a rare mould-blown glass face-flask. Cut into the hollow on its southern side, immediately inside the entrance, was a well containing a very large amount of votive material including a model spear, a ritual rattle, a bronze statue fragment, and a bronze working crucible and two coins. The well was mirrored on the north side of the entrance by a shallow pit, dated to the LPRIA by the excavator. This pit contained another two coins and a quantity of imported and decorated LPRIA pottery. The number of coins from the entrance way, and the other rich assemblage of finds, are clearly concentrated around, and symbolically mark the entrance.

Another two coins were recovered from near the top of the enclosure ditch, but only one coin was located within the enclosure, although this was found to contain a wealth of other small finds including more than 32 spear heads and two votive axes. Consequently, it would appear that the enclosure ditch, and the entrance in particular, were seen as more suitable contexts for the deposition of coins than the enclosed area itself.

The very large quantity of small finds generally suggests that the circular building was a shrine, and the ditch marked the sacred area surrounding it. If we compare the characteristics of the site with the characteristics of specialized religious sites (Table 3) the match is perfect.

Across the whole site the number of contexts that contain Iron Age coins and a rich assemblage of other finds is notable, but the contexts that contain both Iron Age coins and jewellery and toilet utensils are particularly striking, and should perhaps be taken to indicate a link between the two categories of find; this might suggest that votive deposits were personal and made by an individual, not by the community, as appears to have been the case before the LPRIA period. Table 4 shows the incidence of features containing various categories of metallic small finds, compared with those containing coins.

The table shows that although iron is the most common small find material found in features, iron objects are rarely associated with coins. The rarer copper alloy small finds are much more likely to be associated with coins in features: toilet utensils occur in over 14% of features that also contain coins, compared with only 6% for iron objects. Jewellery stands out as having a still closer association with coinage, with more than one-fifth (21%) of the features containing jewellery also containing coins. The close association of coins and these items suggests that in deliberate acts of deposition coins, jewellery and personal items must all have been seen to have had compatible votive importance.

Yet there are parts of Baldock where excavation has revealed extensive LPRIA activity but where very few, if any, Iron Age coins have been recovered. These include extensive cemeteries, and notably the large area of the Hartsfield School playing area, where pottery assemblages suggest intense LPRIA activity. This would suggest that the areas where a number of coins were recovered are exceptional, and of a different status to other parts of the settlement. This is a picture seen across the South Midlands, where notable LPRIA sites have been excavated but no coins recovered, and includes sites where the presence of a Roman villa would suggest an Iron Age settlement of similar status.

It is often the case that where Iron Age coins have been found during the excavation of Roman villas they very rarely come from the site of the main building: for example, Piddington and Stanwick (both in Northamptonshire), Gorhambury, Herts. (Neal *et al.* 1990) and Bancroft, Bucks. (Williams and Zeepvat 1994). The only villas within the study area where an Iron Age coin is closely associated with the villa itself are at Shakenoak, where the coin was associated with the fill of a niched cellar which was interpreted by its excavators (Brodribb *et al.* 1971) as a shrine or chapel, and at Park Street, St Albans (O'Neill 1945; Saunders 1961). This may suggest that the LPRIA, or Roman, elite did not either use Iron Age coins or consider their homes an appropriate place to deposit (or discard) them. The evidence that coins are very infrequently found in Iron Age or Roman domestic contexts reinforces our argument for a ritual use being a main function of coins, or at least, the reason for their entry into the archaeological record.

Pre Iron Age	Roman temple	Location	IA structure	IA artefacts	Elaborate gate	Gate deposits	Gate facing	Votive assemblages	Large pit/hollow	Human bone	Brooches	Toilet articles	Weaponry	Metalworking	Stone tools	Iron Age coins	Quantity Roman coins	RB votive items
yes	yes	yes	yes	yes	yes	yes	E	yes	yes	yes	yes	yes	yes	yes	yes	yes	yes	yes

Table 3. Characteristics of structure and deposits of sacred area, Baldock Site A.

Skeleton Green, Puckeridge

The association of Iron Age coins with rich small find assemblages, especially those including personal items and imported pottery, stands out at Skeleton Green (Partridge 1981), as at Baldock. It is worth noting that the association of rich deposits with Iron Age coins continues into the Roman period. This may suggest that the votive or ritual significance attached to coins also continued into the Roman period, just as areas of ritual importance show continuity.

Table 5 shows, even more strongly than at Baldock, the close association of coins with personal items. Here 75% of features that contain toilet instruments also contain coins. Again, this very high correlation can be compared with the relatively common finds of iron objects, where only a third of features with iron objects contain coins. Such a correlation clearly indicates that the association of coins and other classes of find, particularly toilet instruments, is unlikely to be accidental.

At Skeleton Green 47% of Iron Age coins come from Iron Age deposits, compared to 43% from pre-conquest deposits at Baldock Site A. The Skeleton Green deposits were sealed by a flood silt in the mid-first century AD, thereby reducing the possibility of the coins in Roman features being accidental deposits as a result of the disturbance of Iron Age features. Thus at other sites, such as Baldock, coins in post-conquest features cannot necessarily be assumed to be secondary (cf. Haselgrove 1987), and this is substantiated by the continuing association of coins and certain categories of small find in deposits during the Roman period.

The above site analyses suggest that coin deposition was non-random and highly structured. The position of a coin within a site with particular religious elements, and the type of feature, were both specifically identified for deposition.

Symbolism

If we are correct in the supposition that the majority of coins were deliberately deposited, then it may follow that the symbolism on the coins also played a role in the choice of coins for deposition. The commoner figure types from the seventeen most prolific sites in the South Midlands have been analysed here: in order to minimize chronological bias only the issues of Tasciovanus and Cunobelin have been considered, both of which are common over much of the region. With the exception of the goat and ram all the types appear on coins of both issuers. Several figure types are linked together because they are often linked on obverse and reverse sides of a coin, and therefore a symbolic connection between the two may be inferred.

Precious metal hoards are not included. The figure types used on the gold coinage are almost entirely composed of horse or mounted warrior motifs and could skew resulting profiles. The selection of these motifs on gold coins does however show the importance of, and the close connection between, horse and mounted warriors, both of which must have been seen as potent symbols of power.

The analysis shows that although warrior, bull and boar types are common at most sites, while the sphinx and goat/ram types are rare (which may reflect the relative numbers of the original issues), the proportion of each type present does vary. At most sites one figure type is particularly predominant, or another type completely absent (Table 6).

No. of features excavated on site A	544
No. of features containing coins	16
No. of features containing coins and bronze finds	7
No. of features containing toilet utensils	21
No. of features containing coins and toilet utensils	3
No. of features containing brooches	52
No. of features containing brooches and coins	5
No. of features containing other jewellery	14
No. of features containing coins and jewellery	3
No. of features containing ironwork	54
No. of features containing ironwork and coins	3
Percentage of features with toilet utensils that also have coins	14%
Percentage of features with brooches that also have coins	10%
Percentage of features with other jewellery that also have coins	21%
Percentage of features with iron objects that also have coins	6%

Table 4. Analysis of metallic small finds from Baldock site A.

The results are inconclusive but the evidence does suggest there was some pre-selection of type. For example, it is notable that the two sites in the list that have large Roman buildings of the type conventionally termed 'villa' (Stanwick and Gorhambury) are the only two sites were the warrior figure type predominates. Coins with warrior symbolism may indeed be seen as more appropriate for deposition in and around buildings that were associated with a warrior elite. It is particularly notable that the ten coins of the same type placed in a primary position in the burial in the King Harry Lane cemetery depict mounted warriors. The two temple sites in the sample (Thornborough and Evenley) have produced different profiles, possibly reflecting different aspects of the deities worshipped.

An argument could be made to suggest that individual mints produced different figure types which were then distributed to different areas. Yet plots of VER and CAM legend coins show little variation across the study area. Similarly, distribution plots of individual issues (which the author has produced for most of the issues of Tasciovanus and Cunobelin) show no obvious geographical grouping, suggesting that if they were produced by localized or mobile mints then this had little effect on distribution within the study area.

Another aspect of figurative symbolism where there may be a positive relationship is between a depicted animal and the archaeologically recovered bone assemblage. The results of the analysis (Table 7) indicate that there could be a relationship but it appears to be inversely proportional for the largest bone assemblages. At Baldock, sheep bones predominate but coins depicting ovicaprids are rare and, similarly at Skeleton Green, pig bone predominates but coins depicting pig are less well represented. This may suggest some disproportionality in depositional practice: coins perhaps being used to represent animals where the appropriate animal is absent.

No. of features containing coins	37
No. of features containing toilet utensils	8
No. of features containing coins and toilet utensils	6
No. of features containing brooches	55
No. of features containing brooches and coins	23
No. of features containing other jewellery	7
No. of features containing coins and jewellery	3
No. of features containing ironwork	38
No. of features containing ironwork and coins	12
Percentage of features with toilet utensils that also have coins	75%
Percentage of features with brooches that also have coins	42%
Percentage of features with other jewellery that also have coins	43%
Percentage of features with iron objects that also have coins	32%

Table 5. Analysis of metallic small finds from Skeleton Green.

An analysis of context type also suggests a deliberate selection of figure type. For example, the figure types from layers (bulls, boars and warriors), are significantly less likely to come from pits. A possible explanation for this is that coins from layers were actually placed on or above the ground rather than within it, and therefore may in some instances equate with sky gods or goddesses while those from pits are more obviously associated with earth and chthonic gods.

All figure types are found in ditches, but warrior types are notably absent from pits. As previously mentioned, this may be a function of the warrior motif being seen in connection with the sky, rather than with chthonic gods. The warrior motif is also associated with alluvium (i.e. water deposits); there may be a link with the horse and horse/warrior motifs seen on gold coins, which were often associated with sources of water.

Site	Predominant figure type
Odell	Pegasus/Victory
Sandy	Boar
Baldock A	Bull
Baldock 12/13	Pegasus/Victory
Baldock BAL1	Boar
Gorhambury	Warrior
Puckeridge Ermine St A	Pegasus/Victory
Puckeridge Smiths	Bull/Warrior
Puckeridge Roundabout	Boar
Skeleton Green	Bull
St Albans Hills Field	Pegasus/Victory
Stanwick villa	Warrior
Thornborough	Pegasus/Victory
Wellbury	Bull
Ashwell	Bull
Evenley	Bull
H. Wycombe field 207A	Sphinx

Table 6. Predominant image type in major assemblages.

	Gorhambury	Skeleton Green	Baldock
Pig/Sow/Boar bones	27%	40%	11%
Sheep/Goat/Ram bones	26%	20%	57%
Cow/Bull bones	46%	30%	26%
Pig/Sow/Boar coins	0% (0)	14% (2)	27% (3)
Sheep/Goat/Ram coins	25% (1)	7% (1)	9% (1)
Cow/Bull coins	75% (3)	79% (11)	64% (7)

Table 7. Relative percentages of minimum numbers of animals compared with coins.

Conclusions

The results show that distribution studies remain a powerful tool in elucidating the primary circulation areas of coins and hence areas of political unity, the position of possible boundaries between such areas, possible issuing authority, relative chronology and the significance of metallic composition. The geographical location of many of the coins near water sources, such as spring lines, can also help to determine possible functional aspects.

Histograms are another way of looking at regional trends, and they may enable individual site chronology and political orientation to be determined when compared to the regional background. The coin lists at Weekley and Titchmarsh, for example, suggest a change in political control, and reinforce the point that boundaries were not static, but were in a state of flux. More work on potential boundary settlements may reveal other sites like Weekley.

The results of the various analyses described above indicate that previous studies may have been incorrect mainly because their conclusions were based on a comparative lack of data. This highlights the problem of drawing conclusions from incomplete databases, and although we continue to add more findspots to the data we can never be sure that future finds will not render particular distribution studies obsolete. Consequently it is important to reappraise distributions as new data become available.

The site-based contextual analyses suggest that Iron Age coins were not randomly distributed around sites or concentrated in areas that would appear to be shops or markets. They are preferentially positioned at entrances, and in enclosure ditches most notably where the ditch delimits an area of high status activity, particularly that used for religious practices. The connection between coins and religious practice is further highlighted when we consider that many sites producing coins can be seen to have a strong religious element, indicated by both their form and associated material assemblages.

Along with type of site and context, the position within the context also seems to have been the product of a conscious decision. The deliberate nature of this act is indicated by change following the Roman invasion, after which pits are no longer considered appropriate for deposition and coins appear to be used as termination deposits, only appearing in the top of features.

The votive significance of coins is further emphasized by the rich nature of the material with which they were associated. The associated material often includes brooches, jewellery and toilet instruments, indicating that such offerings were made by the individual and not by the community. Such association would also appear to be deliberate.

Preliminary analyses indicate that the symbolic representation on coins may be significant in selecting coins for deposition and that this too is dictated by context and site type. There would also appear to be an inverse relationship with the animal bones deposited on sites. The numbers we are dealing with, however, are small and the inconclusive results highlight the need for more detailed data in order to help resolve such questions.

In summary it may be concluded that Iron Age coins tend to enter archaeological deposits in a deliberate and votive way. They may have been chosen on the basis of their imagery before being deliberately deposited in selected contexts, often with other specially selected material, and this function continued into the Roman period.

Bibliography

Allen, D. F. 1944: The Belgic dynasties of Britain and their coins. *Archaeologia* 90, 1-46.

Allen, D. F. 1960: The origins of coinage in Britain: a reappraisal. In S. S. Frere (ed.), *Problems of the Iron Age in Southern Britain* (London, University of London, Institute of Archaeology, Occasional Paper 11) 97-308.

Allen, D. F. 1967: Celtic coins from the Romano-British temple at Harlow. *British Numismatic Journal* 36, 1-7.

Brodribb, A. Hands, A. and Walker, D. 1971: *Excavations at Shakenoak Farm, near Wilcote, Oxfordshire. Pt 2, Sites B and H* (Oxford, A. R. Hands).

Brunaux, J.-L. 1988: *The Celtic Gauls: gods, rites and sanctuaries* (London, Seaby).

Burleigh, G. 1995: A late Iron Age oppidum at Baldock, Hertfordshire. In R. Holgate, R., *Chiltern Archaeology: recent work: a handbook for the next decade* (Dunstable, Book Castle), 103-112.

Burnett, A. M. 1995: 'Gallo-Belgic' coins and Britain. In B. Raftery, V. Megaw and V. Rigby (eds), *Sites and sights of the iron age: essays on fieldwork and museum research presented to Ian Mathieson Stead* (Oxford, Oxbow Monograph 56), 5-11.

Casey, P. J. 1974: The interpretation of Romano-British site finds. In P. J. Casey and R. Reece (eds), *Coins and the archaeologist* (Oxford, BAR 4), 37-51.

Collis, J. 1981: Coinage, oppida, and the rise of Belgic power: a reply. In B. W. Cunliffe (ed.), *Coinage and society in Britain and Gaul: some current problems* (London, CBA Research Report 38), 53-55.

Cowell, M. R. 1992: An analytical survey of the British Celtic gold coinage. In M. Mays (ed.), *Celtic coinage: Britain and beyond* (Oxford, BAR 222), 207-233.

Crummy, P. 1997: *City of victory: the story of Colchester, Britain's first Roman town* (Colchester, Colchester Archaeological Trust).

Cunliffe, B. W. (ed.) 1981: *Coinage and society in Britain and Gaul: some current problems* (London, CBA Research Report 38).

Curteis, M. 1996: An analysis of the circulation patterns of Iron Age coins from Northamptonshire. *Britannia* 27, 17-42.

Curteis, M. 1997: Iron Age coinage. *The Archaeologist* 28 (Spring 1997), 21-22.

Curteis, M. 2000: Titchmarsh late Iron Age and Roman settlement. *Northamptonshire Archaeology* 28, 164-174.

de Jersey, P. 1996: *Celtic coinage in Britain* (Princes Risborough, Shire).

Delestrée, L.-P. 1996: *Monnayages et peuples gaulois du nord-ouest* (Paris, Errance).

Fitzpatrick, A. P. 1992: The roles of Celtic coinage in south east England. In M. Mays (ed.), *Celtic coinage: Britain and beyond* (Oxford, BAR 222), 1-32.

Fitzpatrick, A. P. 1997: Everyday life in Iron Age Wessex. In A. Gwilt and C. Haselgrove (eds), *Reconstructing Iron Age societies* (Oxford, Oxbow Monograph 71), 73-86.

Goodburn, R. 1989: British coins. In I. Stead and V. Rigby, *Verulamium: The King Harry Lane site* (London, English Heritage Archaeological Report 12), 87.

Greenfield, E. 1963: The Romano-British shrines at Brigstock, Northants. *Antiquaries Journal* 43, 228-263.

Gregory, A. 1992: *Excavations in Thetford 1980-1982, Fison Way* (Dereham, East Anglian Archaeology Report 53).

Gwilt, A. 1995: *Sacralised cultural contact and innovation at a border?* Lecture delivered at TAG conference, Reading.

Haselgrove, C. 1987: *Iron Age coinage in south-east England: the archaeological context* (Oxford, BAR 174).

Haselgrove, C. 1989: Iron Age coin deposition at Harlow temple, Essex. *Oxford Journal of Archaeology* 8(1), 73-88.

Haselgrove, C. 1999: The development of Iron Age coinage

in Belgic Gaul. *Numismatic Chronicle* 159, 111-168.

Haselgrove, C. and Millett, M. 1997: Verlamion reconsidered. In A. Gwilt and C. Haselgrove (eds), *Reconstructing Iron Age societies* (Oxford, Oxbow Monograph 71), 282-296.

Hill, J. D. 1994: Why we should not take the data from Iron Age settlements for granted: recent studies of intra-settlement patterning. In A. P. Fitzpatrick and E. L. Morris (eds), *The Iron Age in Wessex: recent work* (Salisbury, Trust for Wessex Archaeology), 4-8.

Hill, J. D. 1995: *Ritual and rubbish in the Iron Age of Wessex* (Oxford, BAR 242).

Hodder, I. M. 1979: Pre-Roman and Romano-British tribal economies. In B. C. Burnham and H. B. Johnson (eds), *Invasion and response: the case of Roman Britain* (Oxford, BAR 73), 189-196.

Jackson, D. A. and Dix, B. 1987: Late Iron Age and Roman settlement at Weekley, Northamptonshire. *Northamptonshire Archaeology* 21, 41-94.

Nash, D. 1987: *Coinage in the Celtic world* (London, Seaby).

Neal, D., Wardle, A. and Hunn, J. 1990: *Excavation of the Iron Age, Roman and medieval settlement at Gorhambury, St Albans* (London, English Heritage Archaeological Report 14).

O'Neill, H. 1945: The Roman villa at Park Street near St Albans, Herts: report on the excavations of 1943-45. *Archaeological Journal* 102, 21-110.

Parker Pearson, M. 1999: Food, sex and death: cosmologies in the British Iron Age with particular reference to East Yorkshire. *Cambridge Archaeological Journal* 9:1, 43-69.

Partridge, C. 1981: *Skeleton Green. A late Iron-Age and Romano-British site* (London, Britannia Monograph 2).

Rodwell, W. 1976: Coinage, oppida and the rise of Belgic power in south-eastern England. In B. W. Cunliffe and T. Rowley (eds), *Oppida: the beginnings of urbanism in barbarian Europe* (Oxford, BAR S11), 181-367.

Saunders, A. D. 1961: Excavations at Park Street, 1954-57. *Archaeological Journal* 118, 100-135.

Scheers, S. 1972: Coinage and currency of the Belgic tribes during the Gallic War. *British Numismatic Journal* 41, 1-6.

Sellwood, L. 1984: Tribal boundaries viewed from the perspective of numismatic evidence. In B. W. Cunliffe and D. Miles (eds), *Aspects of the Iron Age in central southern Britain* (Oxford, OUCA Monograph 2), 191-204.

Stead, I. M. and Rigby, V. 1986: *Baldock: the excavation of a Roman and pre-Roman settlement: 1968-72* (London, Britannia Monograph 7).

Van Arsdell, R. D. 1989: *Celtic coinage of Britain* (London, Spink).

Van Arsdell, R. D. 1994: *The coinage of the Dobunni: money supply and coin circulation in Dobunnic territory* (Oxford, OUCA Monograph 38).

Wheeler, R. E. M. and Wheeler, T. V. 1936: *Verulamium, a Belgic and two Roman cities* (London, Society of Antiquaries Research Report 11).

Wigg, D. G. 1996: The function of the last Celtic coinages in Northern Gaul. In C. E. King and D. G. Wigg, (eds), *Coin use in the Roman world. The 13th Oxford symposium on coinage and monetary history* (Berlin, Gebr. Mann Verlag), 415-436.

Williams, J. and Zeepvat, R. 1994: *Bancroft: the late Bronze Age and Iron Age settlements and Roman temple-mausoleum* (Aylesbury, Buckinghamshire Archaeological Society).

The role of Iron Age coinage in archaeological contexts

Imogen Wellington

Introduction

What was the function of Iron Age coinage? In Britain, we usually consider coins as a discrete category of artefact, minted for a single function (whatever that was), and study them accordingly. However, when the findspots of coinage are inspected it is clear that different denominations and types of coinage were deposited in very different ways, and the archaeological contexts in which they are found change over time. Should they still be considered as a separate type of artefact, as implied in this volume? This paper aims to consider the role of different denominations of coinage in the later Iron Age of southern England and northern France by looking at the archaeological record.

There has been surprisingly little work on the function of Iron Age coinage in western Europe. Most archaeologists concentrate on the dating of these coins, and amongst those who do consider coinage beyond its ability to date a context with (sometimes questionable) accuracy, the monetary function of an individual coin is rarely questioned. Coinage either indicates the beginnings of a market economy (e.g. Allen 1971) or it is a symbol of gift exchange, illustrated by using anthropological models. However, the use of anthropology presents its own assumptions. Both of these current orthodoxies, the economic and gift-exchange models, need to be reassessed in the light of new evidence.

The vast majority of numismatic articles concentrate on chronology and typology. This is important, but the numismatic perspective of Iron Age coinage and the 'just another form of material culture' view of coins common in archaeological circles are becoming increasingly divergent. The function and role of coinage is a difficult question, and apart from a few honourable engagements with the subject (discussed below) there is a policy of 'if it is ignored it will go away'. This is a problem that can only be addressed by considering the numismatic aspects in conjunction with the contextualisation of archaeological discoveries.

Previous work on the function of coinage is not widespread but has taken place. The initial attempt to move away from the economic and historical model favoured by Mack (1975) and Allen (e.g. 1960) was taken by Collis (1971, 1974). His archaeology driven approach differed from the prevailing 'invasion led' theories in vogue at the time, and introduced the idea of coinage as reflecting "social and economic relationships" (1971, 73).

Although Collis maintained the prevailing political and monetary interpretations of the inscribed coinage (e.g. 1971, 75), he did introduce the idea of non-economic functions in the gold and high value silver coinages, an idea reiterated by Allen (1976). The functions of bronze and potin coinages were still linked to the introduction of market transactions (Collis 1971, 77), although an important distinction was made between the findspots, and therefore functions of different denominations. In Collis's later paper he argued for the changing function of potin coinage over time (1988, 8) which was elaborated on and extended by Haselgrove (1988).

Non-economic functions for coinage were championed by Haselgrove (1979) and Hodder (1979) in a volume edited by Burnham and Johnson (1979). Hodder used the example of Polanyi (1957) to propose an 'embedded' primitive economy for pre-Conquest Britain (1979, 190), using anthropological models. He suggested that the exchange of coinage need not have been through economic media, but in a social gift-exchange network, an idea which still garners much support. Hodder saw the bronze coinage as acting "as payment in the form of tribute and obligations and as a local standard" (1979, 191). Haselgrove also used the work of Polanyi to consider the possibilities of non-economic coin use in the later Iron Age, concentrating on the use of coinage as a means of payment and for the storage of wealth (1979, 202).

The use of anthropological approaches was also seen in Roymans and van der Sanden (1980) who considered the non-economic role of Iron Age coinage in the north-east of Belgic Gaul, a groundbreaking study, but one which had its most attentive audience in the Netherlands. It had little impact on French numismatics, which continued in a very functional and monetary vein in this period. Roymans expanded his consideration of gold coinage and its role in conjunction with social elites as part of his wider archaeological study (1990), where he linked the use of gold coins to the establishment and maintenance of social networks at the highest levels of societies.

Haselgrove extended his 1979 work by considering coinage in its archaeological context (1987), conducting the most geographically expansive survey to date of the archaeological findspots of coinage in south-eastern Britain. The introduction of metal-detection and increase in excavation has greatly increased the quantity of coinage which is now available, but the majority of his assertions are still valid. Haselgrove recognised several important archaeological patterns; the tendency of gold to be found away from settlements and individually (1987, 113, 119), the domination of silver on ritual sites (*ibid.*, 130) and the association of struck bronze coinage and settlement sites in eastern England; as well as re-emphasising the possibility of non-economic coin use.

On the continent, Iron Age coinage is usually assumed to be primarily monetary (e.g. the influential work of Colbert de Beaulieu, i.e. 1973). Amongst French numismatists economic functionalism still largely prevails. Nash (1978, 1981) suggested a range of other functions for the use of coinage in central Gaul, concentrating on mercenary payments, and the use of coinage to pay for clients and troops, but also emphasising the importance of coinage as a ritual deposit (e.g. 1981, 14). One exception to this was the work of Gruel (1989), who did promote some interesting ideas on the ritual functions of coinage, and linked the production of potin coins with temples (1989, 123). She also looked at the transformations in ritual deposition at the time of the Conquest, which led to a great intensification in coin deposition on temples (1989, 125). These arguments have only recently been considered by other French scholars (e.g. Delestrée 1996).

A primarily economic function for coinage had also been assumed by Cunliffe (1981) and subsequently by Van Arsdell (e.g. 1992) although this assumes the presence of certain economic factors, and is increasingly unsustainable in the light of new archaeological discoveries. Certainly this extremely functional approach is now at odds with the way the rest of the archaeological record is now considered.[1] It is dangerous to project economic models backwards, and recent work by Aarts (2001) has suggested that it is increasingly doubtful that the model of a fully monetised society can even be projected backwards onto the Roman world in the north-western provinces, let alone the Iron Age.[2]

The most recent specific consideration of the function of coinage in Britain was that by Fitzpatrick (1992), who reviewed the role of the coinage of south-eastern England from the earliest Gallo-Belgic types to the later 'dynastic' coins. Fitzpatrick's approach emphasised the importance of cross-Channel links, and considered coinage (in this case the Gallo-Belgic series) was used to "articulate clientage and dependency in an overtly militaristic society and to maintain traditional, ancestral, familial links" (1992, 19).

This approach was also taken in Creighton's recent (2000) review of the interaction with Rome before the Claudian conquest, although this work concentrated largely on the iconography and images on late Iron Age coinage. The anthropological approach is becoming increasingly popular in continental numismatics, but many British studies are more traditional in approach (forming a dichotomy with the archaeology). Fitzpatrick's general view of coinage is not an economic one, and the use of coinage in votive contexts as well as the changing role of coinage over time are considered. However, these points deserve further exploration in the light of recent discoveries.

The main continental debates at the moment are chronological, and the majority of recent continental scholarship has concentrated on the quantification and organisation of different coin series. Most of the important recent studies concentrate on restricted geographical areas (e.g. Guichard et al 1993, Delmaire 1996, Delestrée 1996, de Jersey 1994). Recent synthetic articles (e.g. Haselgrove 1999) show the complicated web of coin issues, and do indicate the difficulty of pan-regional studies across even Belgic Gaul.

The use of coinage to identify political groups and boundaries is a recent development (e.g. Gruel 2002, Ginoux and Poux 2002) although this work rarely articulates or explores the assumption that coinage was primarily used to reinforce chief/client relationships. Recent work on ritual deposition of coinage (e.g. Delestrée 1996, 2001) has been heavily numismatic, and considerations of the coins role have yet to be fully integrated in France. However, the most recent Dutch survey (Aarts 2001) considers the function of coinage, and the author sees "coins as exchange goods – not as the means to facilitate the exchange of other goods" (*ibid.*, 112), which is a key distinction, and one which is often insufficiently clarified in Britain.

As in Britain, continental archaeologists use coinage primarily as a dating tool, but the use of coinage to identify tribal groups is profoundly unfashionable in British archaeology. This is partly due to a stronger history of text based archaeology on the continent[3] (primarily using Caesar's *Gallic Wars*) and the epigraphy of the coins themselves. However, there is an ongoing numismatic tendency on both sides of the Channel to project the shifting tribal groups of the Gallic Wars backwards as static social and material culture boundaries (e.g. Van Arsdell 1989). This can no longer be sustained when we consider the distribution of material culture even 100 years before the Gallic Wars. These groups seem to have been extremely fluid entities, and were possibly only assembled at times of stress, with smaller family groups predominating much of the time. Throughout both northern France and southern Britain the coinage is dominated by small-scale localised issues for most of the late Iron Age.[4] It is only in the latest inscribed stages of coinage that the Gallic War tribal groupings have much relevance.

The function of coinage in north-eastern France

It is becoming clear that there is considerable divergence in the find-spots of different coin denominations in north-eastern France. Archaeological discoveries are beginning to show distinct patterns of deposition, and the regional nature of many of the coin types is being highlighted by the increased volume of finds. When we look at the coinage in a wider context, it is clear that there are major regional variations in coin findspots. This is clearly connected to the high level of regional diversity we see in other aspects of the archaeological record in the later Iron Age. It would be stranger if the coinage did not fit into this pattern.

The coins from several departments have been analysed. However, there are problems with the data which should be considered. The information has been gathered from several sources, including Scheers (1977), the *Carte Archéologique de la Gaule* volumes, published site reports and unpublished archive information. They do contain few metal-detected finds, which have made such a difference north of the Channel.[5] This will therefore limit the quantity of coinage, but in terms of findspots, and contextualising coinage, it is a less significant problem, as many Continental metal detected finds have no context. Many of the large finds in northern Gaul are antiquarian, and the records for many of these finds are very bad. The two World Wars played havoc with the numismatic record, both archaeologically and in terms of finds held in museums (see Hill 1919 for an illustration of the problem).

Bearing these points in mind, where are coins found? The coins from four of the *departments* in the north-east of France have been analysed, and some interesting patterns have resulted. Archaeologically the areas do have some important differences. The Nord and Pas-de-Calais have little archaeological evidence for elites or centralised social networks in the north of the regions (usually articulated by the presence of *oppida*, rich burials and sanctuaries) although there are a few *oppida* in the south of the area (Fichtl 2000). The situation is different in Seine-Maritime, which has a significant number of *oppida* along the Seine and Channel coast, and a few early sanctuaries such as Fesques (Mantel 1997). The Oise has had a high level of archaeological activity and the numismatic record is dominated by finds from the numerous cult sites, and the area has *oppida,* sanctuaries and high-status settlements in the middle and late Iron Age.[6]

It is clear that the quantities of coinage in the different areas are very different, and although it is hard to assess, it seems likely that this reflects the original volume of coin density as well as standards of recording. In the northern areas, the numismatic record is dominated by gold coins, although much of this comes from large hoards. Even with these hoards removed, gold is still dominant, a distinct difference from the Oise and Seine-Maritime areas. The absolute quantities of coinage are comparable, although they are deposited in very different contexts.

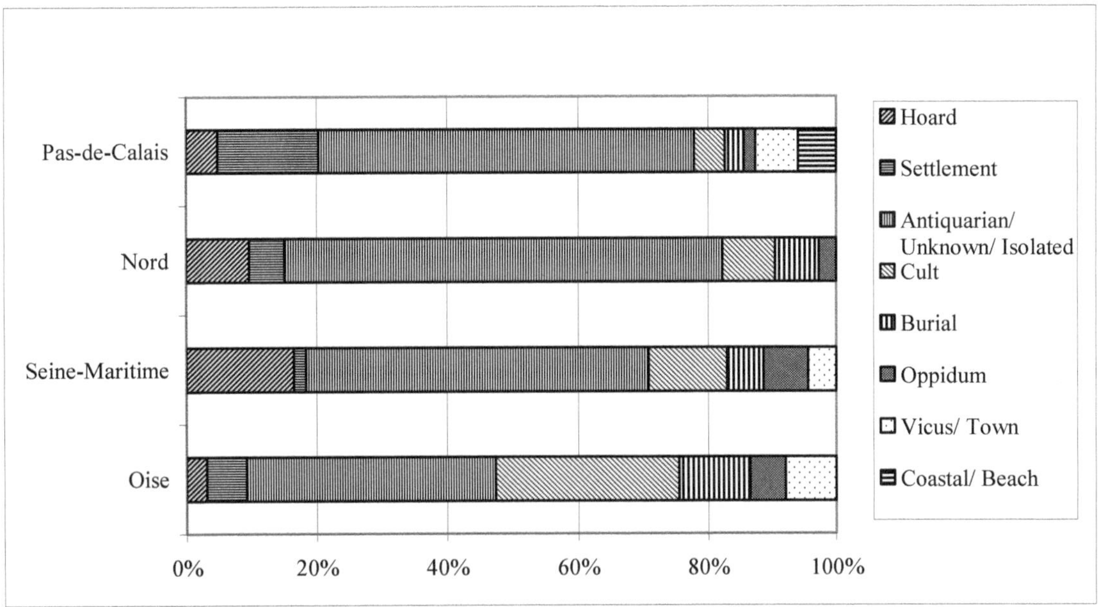

Figure 1. The contexts of coin discoveries.

The graph above represents each *incidence* of Iron Age coin deposition in a region, not each coin. As we will see below, this can be misleading, as it masks the actual numbers of coins, as well as the predominance of certain metals in certain contexts. A small number of sites have the majority of the coinage, while the vast majority of the antiquarian/ unknown/ isolated and settlement finds are of single coins. These categories do not distinguish Iron Age sites, and only 7% of the settlement finds from the Pas-de-Calais are from unambiguously Iron Age contexts. Most of the coins are in post-Iron Age contexts, with settlement finds being predominantly Roman in date, implying some continuity of circulation (especially amongst the bronze coinage). There is also a marked trend of deliberate selection of antiquarian coins for placement in Merovingian burials, which is an interesting phenomenon in its own right, but consequently over half of the burial finds do not reflect Iron Age use. We do not know the source of these coins, but it does illustrate the apparently easy availability of Iron Age coinage in the early medieval period.

There are some localised differences in the archaeology of coin using sites. A greater incidence of cult activity is evident in the more southerly areas, which ties into the Picardy sanctuary tradition, in which coinage plays a major part (Delestrée 1996). These sites have not been found in the far north-east of France. Oppida are a more common focus of coin deposition in the southern areas, but there are very few of them in the Nord/Pas-de-Calais. However, considering the quantity of oppida along the Seine, comparatively few of them produce much coinage in comparison with those from central Gaul and along the Aisne Valley (see below). Considering the archaeological differences, those we see in the regional distribution of findspots are not great. When we consider the actual numbers of coinage the picture does change dramatically, and we begin to see clear regional trends.

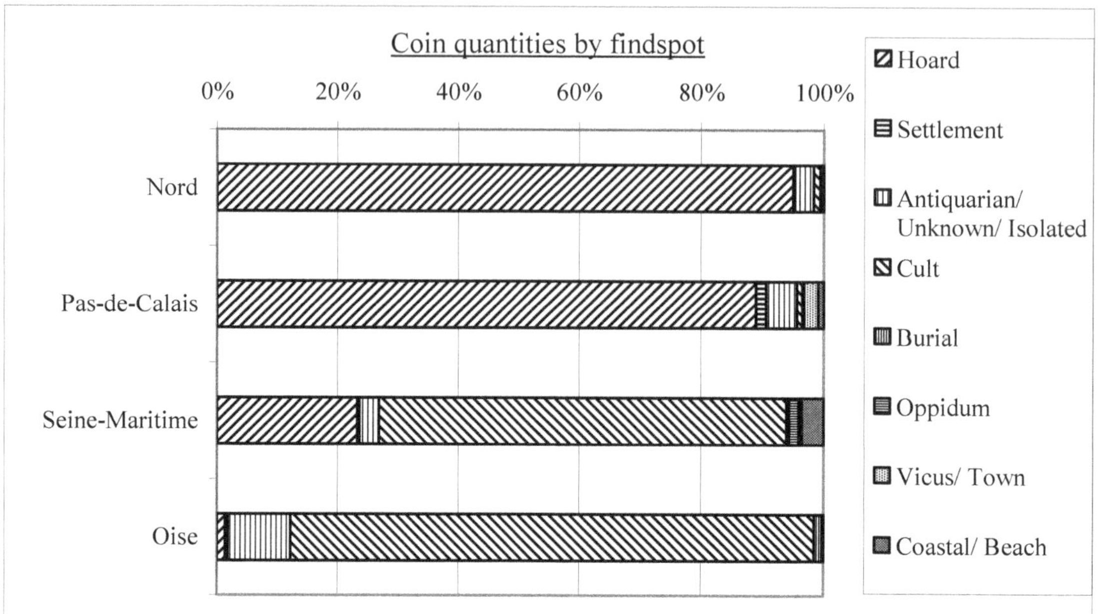

Figure 2. Total coin quantities by type of find/department.

As we can see in Figure 2, which shows the actual number of coins lost per context, there is a major difference in the places where coins are being deposited in any quantity. Although when the data is displayed by findspot, the antiquarian and isolated finds predominate, it is clear that when the actual number of coins are considered a small group of sites dominate the record.

In the Nord and Pas-de-Calais the total quantities of coinage are dominated by a couple of very large hoards, while in the southern areas the effect of large votive sites such as Bois l'Abbé is felt. This is an interesting difference in patterns of deposition, and an important contrast in the function of coinage in society. Votive sites do not appear in any significant numbers in the Nord or Pas-de-Calais areas; those which do exist are mostly around the southern boundaries of the regions, and are clearly part of the Somme group of votive sites (see Wellington 2005).

However, these graphs do mask some important differences in the contexts in which different denominations of coinage are found. The different denominations of coinage are found in very different contexts, and in differing quantities. In the northern regions fairly early gold dominates the absolute quantities of coinage, largely due to a couple of very big hoards, while in the Oise and Seine-Maritime regions coinage is dominated by the very late struck bronze deposits from cult sites.

Nord

In terms of absolute quantities of coinage, the Iron Age coins from the Nord region are dominated by gold. This is largely caused by a single hoard containing c. 15-18 litres of staters (estimated at 5000 coins for the purpose of this analysis) from Ledringham near Dunkirk.[7] Looking at the individual metals we can see differences between the contexts in which we find coins. The contexts of gold coins are dominated by individual and antiquarian finds, with a small quantity of hoards, *oppida* and wet contexts forming the rest of the record. They are not found on settlements or in urban contexts, despite the increase in the excavation of these types of site recently. When we look at absolute quantities, we can see that the single large hoard is dominant. With this extremely unusual find removed the 97 coins which are found in individual or antiquarian contexts would actually form 65% of the total number of coins.

Only 13 find-spots are known for silver coins, mostly antiquarian or unknown, making it hard to draw any major conclusions. Silver is also found on the few southern cult sites, which fits in with the finds from Picardy. Potin coins are also rare; neither silver nor potin coins were struck in the area, and out of the total of 41 coins, nearly half come from unknown or antiquarian sources. Although a small number of potin coins are known from settlements, such as Hornaing (which produced one potin and one struck bronze coin), none are stratified to pre-Conquest levels, and the majority come from Roman layers, probably suggesting movement of coinage after the conquest. Most potin coins come from cult sites, and it seems likely that they ended up there as unusual late deposits. It seems clear that whatever the function of potin in this area, these were not common coins, and appear in the archaeological record as an occasional curiosity rather than a widespread find, as sites to the south suggest.[8]

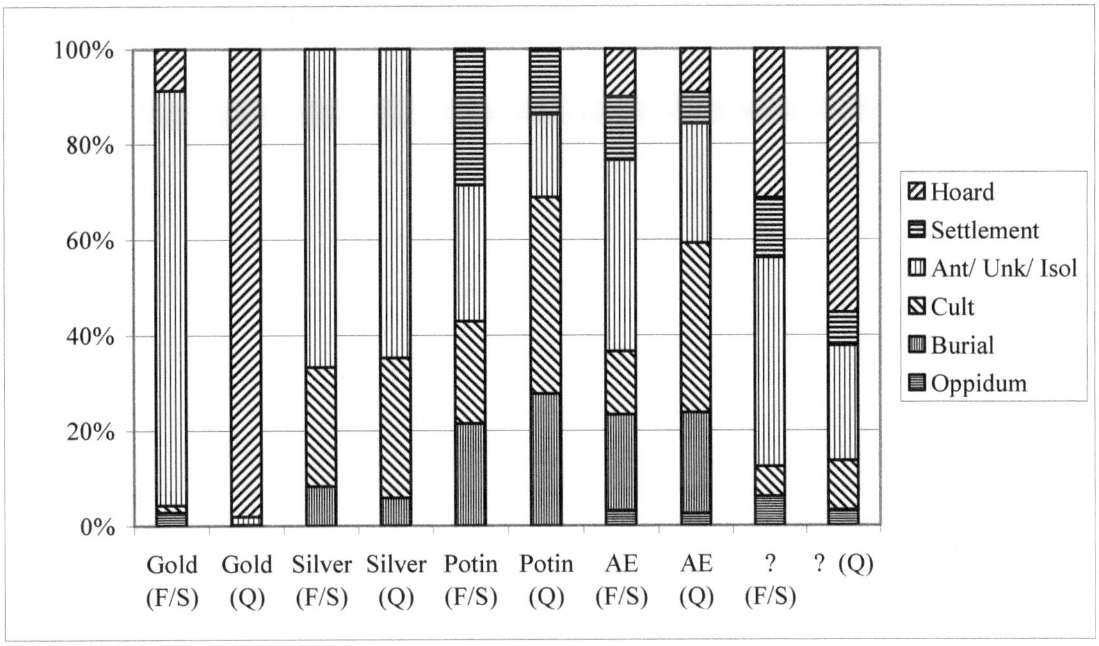

Figure 3. Coin findspots in Nord.
F/S: findspots; Q: quantity

Struck bronze is more numerous than either potin or silver, with at least 78 coins known. With the exception of a few struck bronze coins in early Roman hoards the coins are found on the same sites as potin. This suggests that potin and struck bronze arrived in the area together and were used in the same way once they reached the dèpartment. This would also indicate that the potin which reached the Nord did so at a late date, and has taken on the function of struck bronze. The plotting of finds at the oppida of the Aisne Valley would suggest that the massive expansion in struck bronze production took place in the LT D2a period, either side of the Gallic Wars (Guichard et al. 1993). At the same period potin ceases to be struck and although potin does remain in circulation in large quantities in the areas to the south, it is discovered in the same type of contexts as struck bronze from the LT D2a onwards. This similarity of deposition indicates that both potin and struck bronze are reaching the Nord very late, probably after the Roman conquest.

Pas-de-Calais

The predominance of gold is also found in this *department*, and again we can see the effect of a few large hoards. The number of single or double finds of gold are high in this area, with the majority of the rest of the gold being found in larger groups. This is broadly comparable to the Nord, although there is a higher proportion of gold found in urban contexts in the Pas-de-Calais. However, there are more urban contexts to consider, as major Roman centres such as Arras have recently been the focus of intensive digging programmes.[9] The difference in distribution is probably due to the nature of excavation in the department. Coastal and wet locations have produced a significant quantity of coinage, but this is largely due to a series of deposits at Sangatte and Wissant, which have produced coinage since the sixteenth century, and have been recorded more assiduously than many other antiquarian finds.

The overall quantity of silver, potin and struck bronze is higher in this department than the Nord. This can be ascribed to more coin production in the area itself, but proximity to the very rich coin producing areas of the Somme and Aisne is also worth considering. Silver in the Pas-de-Calais is largely hoarded, and the metal seems to have been treated in a similar way to gold, which is relatively unusual for silver coinage in the Iron Age, which usually seems to cluster on votive sites and 'unusual' contexts.

Potin coins are found across a wide range of contexts, none particularly predominating, but compared to other departments they are found in fairly high number on Roman period settlements and urban sites. This would again suggest a late appearance in the area. Cult deposits of potin coins are also present in the department, which does tie in better with sites further to the south of known Iron Age date (see below).

The struck bronze coinage from the Pas-de-Calais has been discovered in overwhelmingly late archaeological contexts. Over 50% of it is from Roman settlement layers or Roman urban contexts, such as Vaulx-Vracourt, Thérouanne, Arras and Boulogne. The north of the area does not seem to have got (or perhaps deposited?) much Iron Age coinage. In the Iron Age the south of the Pas-de-Calais was clearly closely related to Picardy, and the kinds of archaeological finds which the southern Pas-de-Calais produces support this. Apart from the cult deposits, where there is significantly more struck bronze deposited than potin (indicating later deposition), the coins appear on the same kinds of sites; settlements, urban contexts and unknown/ antiquarian finds.

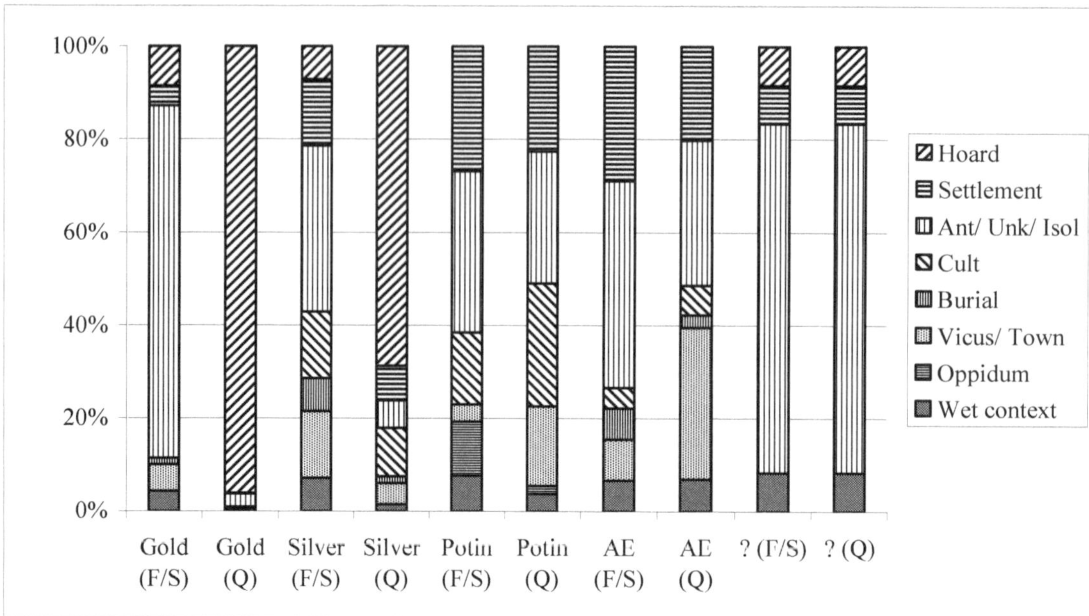

Figure 4. Coin findspots in Pas-de-Calais.
F/S: findspots; Q: quantity

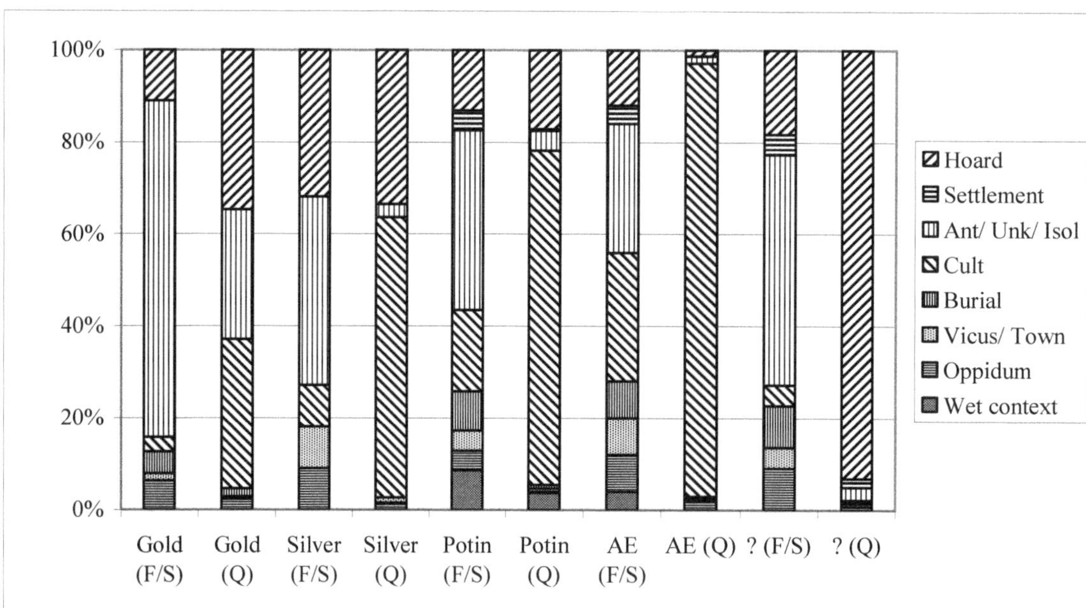

Figure 5. Coin findspots in Seine-Maritime.
F/S: findspots; Q: quantity

Neither potin nor struck bronze coinage appears to have played an important pre-Conquest role in the area, and it is probable that the bulk of these coins arrived in the area in the early Roman period. This is a major difference in coin use when compared with the areas to the south, and it fits in with other forms of archaeological evidence. The settlement record is more akin to the decentralised patterns found in the north of modern Belgium and the Low Countries, areas where the appearance of potin and struck bronze are also very late, and possibly post-Conquest (Roymans and van der Sanden 1980; Roymans 1990).

Seine-Maritime

This distribution pattern is quite different in the Seine-Maritime department. The quantity of precious metal hoarding is much lower, and the amount of coinage found in votive contexts is much higher. The archaeological record is significantly different in this area, with more oppida, nucleated settlements and large cult sites. The different coin metals are deposited in very different contexts from those found in the Nord and Pas-de-Calais.

Gold is hoarded, but in much smaller quantities, and Seine-Maritime lacks the very large hoards which dominate the numismatic record of the Nord and Pas-de-Calais areas. The majority of gold coinage is deposited singly or in very small groups, a pattern which has been suggested as ritual in nature (Aarts 2001). Almost a third of gold coinage has been found on cult sites, which is unusual for northern France, but this is solely due to two large sanctuary sites, Fesques (Mantel 1997) and Bois l'Abbé (Delestrée 1996) which have produced many coins.

These two sites have also produced all of the silver coinage from cult sites, which forms over half of the total silver finds from the department. Silver is also hoarded in the area, with the same number of findspots as gold coinage. It seems likely that silver was used mainly on votive sites, or hoarded (perhaps ritually?).

In terms of findspots, again potin and struck bronze are found on similar sites, and in a broad range of contexts. However, there is much more struck bronze (1735 coins to 306), and the quantities show a different picture. The vast majority of struck bronze coinage is found on votive sites (again, Fesques and Bois l'Abbé predominate). The presence of large quantities of struck bronze coinage on votive sites is a phenomenon which is found all over Picardy, and is connected to the dramatic increase in minting and ritual deposition of coinage in the mid first century BC.

Oise

Despite the Oise being in the core area of northern Gallic coin production, and one of the early centres of coin use, the lack of hoards mean that the actual number of precious metal coins is low. The higher quantity of the other coin types which are present in comparison to most of the other areas suggests that potin and struck bronze played a more important role in this area. Potin coinage appears at a very early date, and perhaps to some extent negated the use of precious metal on such a wide scale. This is similar to the pattern from Seine-Maritime. Of course, it is equally likely that the depositional practices utilised for the precious metal coinage of the area precludes archaeological discovery (e.g. reminting old types or deposition at wet locations) and we are not finding such a high percentage of precious metal coinage for this reason.

The effect of cult sites is also magnified in the Oise. While hoards are not a major factor in the region outside of the gold coinage (and even with the gold, they only form 40% of the total coins), there are many finds of coins from cult sites. There are more votive sites in the Oise, and the record is not dominated by a few large sites, as we see in Seine-Maritime. However, the quantities of coinage found on these sites are impressive, and it is clear that the vast majority of coins were deposited on votive sites such as Vendeuil-Caply and Champlieu, a significant difference from the more northerly departments.

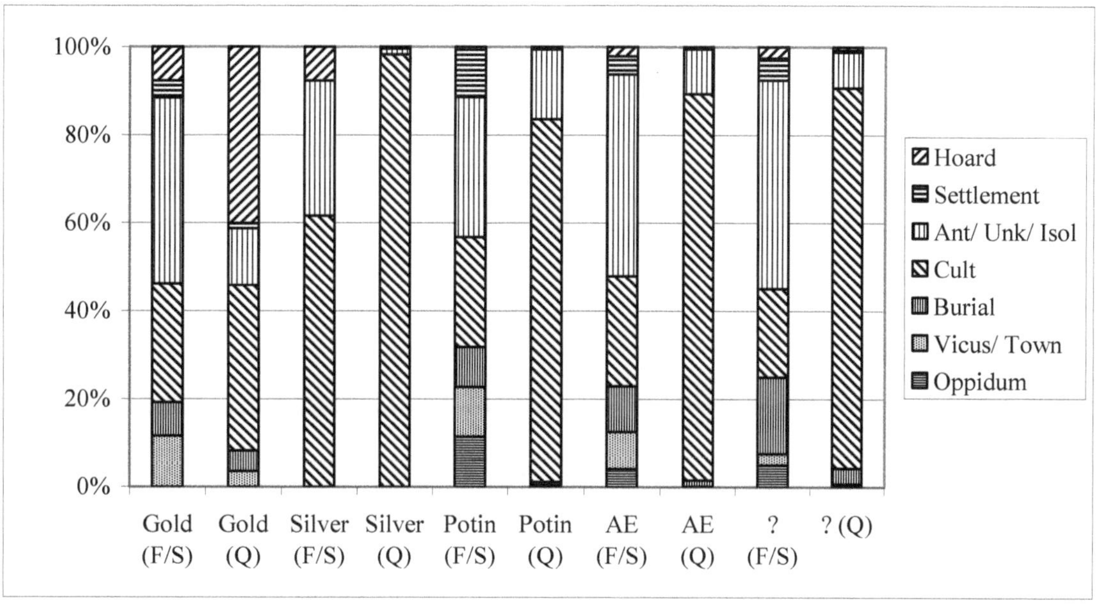

Figure 6. Coin findspots in Oise.
F/S: findspots; Q: quantity

Considering the precious metal coinage, both the gold and the silver have distinct distributions. As mentioned above, the gold coins are the only ones which are hoarded in any significant quantity, and a high percentage of coins (38%) are still found in isolated contexts. However, little gold coinage is known from the Oise (under 100 coins compared to several thousand from most of the other departments).

Assuming that gold coinage was deposited and not recycled in place of hoarding, it does not seem to have been a major component of the numismatic assemblage after the early stages of coinage. Instead the Oise has a strong silver tradition and many potin coins, which seem to come into circulation early, and are clearly minted in the area.

The distribution of silver coinage in the Oise is striking. Delestrée (forthcoming) has suggested that many of the sanctuaires of Picardy minted coinage, and the evidence from the findspots indicates that there is a strong case for the minting and use of silver predominantly on votive sites in the area. However, many of the silver coins are relatively small, and it is possible that they are only easily recovered in excavations,[10] as much of the archaeological excavation has been focussed on sanctuaries in the area. This is also a problem in southern Britain (see below). Still, 98.3% of silver coins come from votive contexts, so for the moment, we must assume that in this area these coins rarely found their way away from the votive sites, and were primarily a kind of 'temple token'.

Potin and struck bronze coins have nearly identical findspots and are found in very similar quantities in the different types of site. Although the findspots are fairly varied, with settlements, antiquarian finds, cult sites, urban sites, burial contexts and wet contexts having approximately the same proportions (although rather more of the struck bronze coins are from antiquarian sources) we see a change when looking at the quantities.

The vast majority of coins come from cult sites (82% of potin, 88% of struck bronze). There are only 14 coin producing cult sites in this area, but the majority of them have produced large quantities of coinage, especially potin and struck bronze, which were deposited in large quantities in the first and second quarters of the first century BC. This is connected to the great expansion of coin minting, and the two perhaps bear more connection than the traditional view of an intensification of minting at the time of the Gallic Wars for economic and clientage purposes would suggest. It also seems likely that the majority of the unknown coins from the area were actually potin and struck bronze, as the graph matches up with those two metal groups.

Geographical differences in coin function

It is clear from the consideration of coin findspots that the use of coinage cannot usually be accurately generalised about on a supra-local level, especially outside of the direct zone of production. The types of coin in use over time also differ, so in some ways the picture presented above is misleading. While the comparison of the findspots of gold and struck bronze are interesting, the actual incidents may be separated by a significant chronological margin. However, bearing these factors in mind, I believe that it is possible to begin to consider the way in which coinage was used in the later Iron Age.

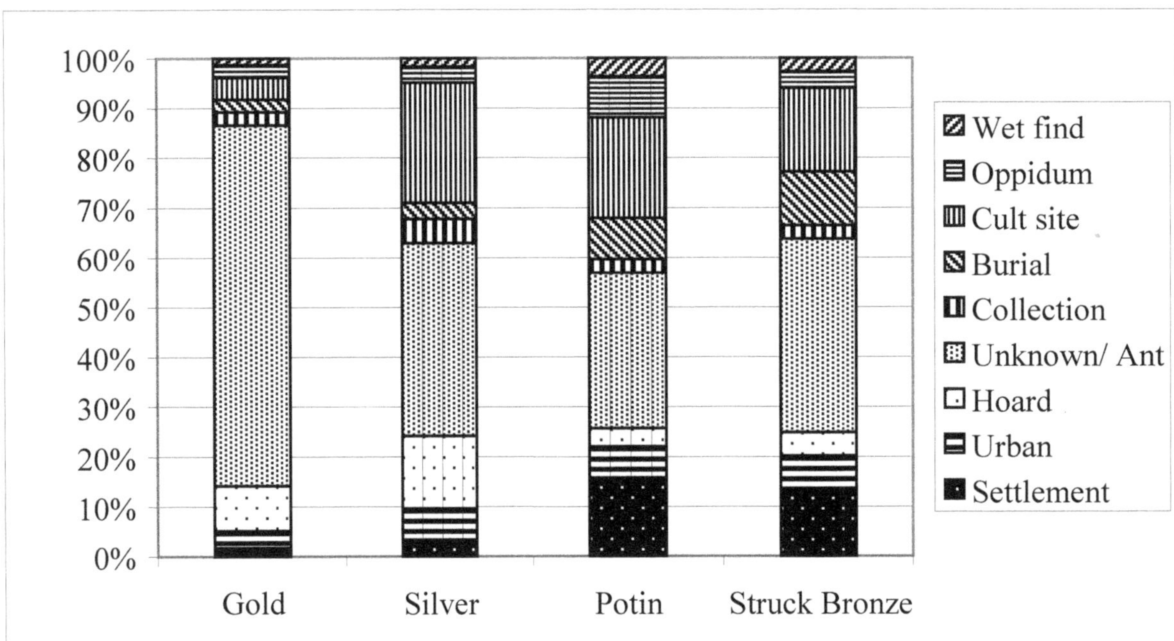

Figure 7. Total coin findspots, by metal type.

Gold

One generalisation that can be made is that gold is found individually in large quantities throughout the study area. It is also frequently hoarded in some *departments* (notably the Nord and Pas-de-Calais), while in Picardy it is found on early votive sites.[11] Most of the gold dates to the third to early first centuries BC, gold was the earliest coin type to be widely used in northern Europe, and it seems likely that the hoarding and individual deposition of gold is (at least in part) early. Other authors have dwelt on the importance of liminality, and the possibility of gold being deposited singly in important ritual locations such as boundaries (Haselgrove 1987), but this is not unique to coinage. I believe that the early gold should be considered as part of a wider phenomenon of metalwork deposition, with weaponry and such enigmatic objects as 'currency bars' forming part of the same process (e.g. Bradley 1998; Hingley 1993; Fitzpatrick 1984).

Gold is not unique in this deposition, nor in the process of hoarding, and it seems likely from the evidence, that instead of having any special function, gold coinage (and in some areas silver coinage) functioned as another form of elite exchange good, albeit an extremely portable and convenient one. Gold seems likely to have maintained this function over several centuries. Not only are the earlier types of gold found in hoards and individually, but the process clearly continued in areas which were very late to adopt coinage (such as the Dutch river area: Roymans 1990). This perhaps suggests a very static function for gold in much of north-eastern Europe, Britain included, with the only major exception being Picardy, and its gold deposition on sanctuaries, and perhaps these functioned as tribal treasuries in their earlier phases. However, areas which seem to have made a deliberate attempt not to use gold coinage would argue against this. Perhaps the use of coinage was rejected by conservative elements in some groups, despite its convenience?

Silver

The deposition and indeed presence of silver coinage varies geographically. The minting and use of silver coin is patchy to the north of Burgundy, and is only really found on any scale in a few areas (Seine-Maritime, the Oise, the middle Aisne, central southern England and in north-western France). Where silver coinage is a significant part of the coin pool, it is found predominantly on votive sites and in votive contexts. The rarity of silver coinages in north-western Europe, and the lack of availability of the raw metal made silver an unusual commodity for most of the late Iron Age. The predominance of votive deposits suggests that it functioned in a non-monetary way until the latest phases of the Iron Age. At this time interaction with central Gaul and the Roman world would have introduced a ready supply of *denarii* and *quinarii*, and silver seems to have become a trading currency on major sites, such as those of the Aisne valley.

Excavations carried out in the last twenty years have produced a large quantity of silver coinage from votive contexts, and in Seine-Maritime and western Picardy there is a localised domination of silver on ritual sites. Outside these areas, even where we find a reasonable quantity of silver, such as on the *oppida* of Villeneuve-Saint-Gemain and Pommiers in the Aisne valley, it is still greatly outnumbered by the vast numbers of potin and struck bronze coins respectively on the two sites (Guichard et al. 1993).

Potin

Potin coinage has been the subject of a major chronological reassessment in the last decade (summarised in Gruel 1995 and Haselgrove 1988) which changed it from a post-Gallic Wars small change currency, to one of the earliest coinages struck in northern France (and by implication Britain). However, despite this recent work, the function of potin is not clear. The conclusion from these reviews, and also considering recent finds, is that in the early stages of use potin coinage is found largely on votive sites in Picardy and Seine-Maritime. Along the Aisne valley, the Ardennes and the Paris region it is found in settlement and burial contexts (Lambot and Delestrée 1991; Haselgrove 1999; Ginoux and Poux 2002).

It appears to undergo a change of function during the period of its circulation, with potins being amongst the earliest coins to be found in stratified contexts, usually on votive sites (e.g. Gournay-sur-Aronde) and settlement sites. The later finds of potin coinage come from the same layers as struck bronze, and where potin is found in later contexts, it seems likely that it was used in the same way as bronze. In this way many of the potin types have surprising longevity. Even so, with regard to some types the earliest dating must be questioned, and there is still the problem of the speed of diffusion of the coin type from the areas where it was first minted (such as Picardy and perhaps Kent).

The point of transition from potin to struck bronze coinage is neatly illustrated (for the Aisne area at least) by the finds from the short-lived *oppida* of the lower Aisne Valley. As shown by Guichard et al (1993) the earlier sites of Condé-sur-Suippe and Villeneuve-Saint-Germain[12] are dominated by potin coinage (93.1% and 80.7% respectively), while the later site of Pommiers is dominated by struck bronze (81.1%). The three sites also neatly illustrate the growing intensity of coin minting in the later Iron Age. Condé has 58 excavated coins and Villeneuve has 758, while the antiquarian excavations at Pommiers[13] produced 2230. Presumably large-scale excavations at Pommiers would increase this number even more.

In the Aisne Valley at least, it seems likely that there was a major change in the Gallic War period which caused the change from potin to struck bronze. The reason is impossible to guess; perhaps there was pressure on tin sources, or the influence of the regions to the south, with their struck coinages? It is interesting that the transition comes so late here, in other areas of northern France the transition to struck bronze seems to have happened earlier, in the early first century BC, as illustrated by finds from sanctuaries in the Seine-Maritime and Picardy areas. Again it illustrates the regionality of coin use in the Iron Age, and the essential futility of broad generalisations.

Struck bronze

Coins minted in struck bronze are late in date compared to the other types of coinage which we find in northern France. Although any reason that can be suggested for the introduction of struck bronze can only be speculation at this stage, it is incontestable that in the post Gallic-Wars period its minting rapidly increases to the point where struck bronze dominates the coin pool across a wide range of sites types. This can be seen at sites such as the *oppidum* of Pommiers, and many of the sanctuary sites of north-eastern France and the Low Countries (e.g. Empel; Roymans and Derks 1994). Many of the large issues of struck bronze are post-Conquest, and the minting of coinage in the post Gallic-Wars period rapidly becomes exclusively in this metal or brass (which has been considered here under bronze for the sake of clarity).

Many of the most common and widespread post Gallic-War types of struck bronze[14] are clearly struck by groups with the approval (or at least sanction) of the official sources, and were struck until the earliest Augustan period. These coins should perhaps be considered less as 'Iron Age' coinage than as a local "Roman provincial" issue corresponding to a shortage of small change in a relatively non-monetised and recently conquered part of the Roman Empire.

They do indicate the importance of coin minting for the local groups, and suggests that by the middle of the first century BC the production of coinage was an important part of the identification of a group or polity (or indeed tribe). This seems to have been fulfilled in gold in the pre-Conquest period, but with the lack of precious metals after the Gallic Wars struck bronze was the dominant coin metal. The minting of all provincial coinage in the area definitely ceases with the Batavian revolt, and this was evidently part of the increasingly centralised control which the area came under in the Flavian period.

Although struck bronze coinage has often been seen as 'small change' the large quantities found in ritual contexts, combined with the large quantities on *oppida* suggests that the main reasons behind minting are those of prestige and social identification. Struck bronze (in common with all Iron Age coinage apart from gold) is usually found in an extremely restricted geographical area, which is at odds with the idea of market function where coins are diffused over a wide area. In only a few cases do we find issues over a wide area, and these are usually the brass issues, or those which would have appealed to Roman military users, such as the triple bust (REMO/REMO) issue.[15]

The function of coinage in southern Britain

Moving across the Channel to consider southern Britain, the traditional perception of Iron Age coinage has been dramatically changed by the quantity of coinage found since the advent of metal-detection. In Britain, there have been concerted recent attempts to catalogue these coins,[16] and it is now clear that instead of being a minor curiosity, coinage was used in southern Britain in large quantities.

Can (and indeed should?) the introduction and use of Iron Age coinage in Britain be considered in the same way as the coinage of north-eastern France. While there are many similarities in the actual coin types, with some issues being found on both sides of the Channel (a cause of debate, e.g. Burnett 1995), and others being from clearly related series, there are also important geographical differences which suggest different functions for British coinage.

There are major differences in the archaeological record of southern Britain and northern France in the late Iron Age. Another important caveat is the chronological difference between the Caesarian conquest of Gaul and the Claudian conquest of Britain. During this time there were significant changes and developments in the British and Gallic coinages which make direct comparison invalid.[17] As we saw above, the continental coins are found in very different locations in the different areas, and there is significant continuity of local coin use (of restricted coin series) until the Augustan period. This is not present in Britain, where local coin minting rapidly ends after the Claudian conquest. Therefore we find fewer Iron Age coins in Roman contexts in Britain.

Oppida are also problematic in Britain. In southern Belgic Gaul they play an important part in the production of coinage, while in areas where there are few *oppida* (such as the Nord and Pas-de-Calais) there is less coin production, which is undoubtedly related. The association of coinage and *oppida* is not new. Both Rodwell (1976) and Collis (1981) have discussed the matter, the latter considering the problems inherent in associating the production of coinage solely with oppida and other major sites. It is now debatable whether any sites in Britain can be compared with the major oppida of central and northern Gaul,[18] although this is a matter of significant debate in itself, and one which I will not discuss here.

However, there are similarities with the finds of coinage in north-eastern France. As in northern Gaul, few coins have been found in archaeologically excavated contexts in Britain. Very few precious metal Iron Age coins have been discovered on settlement sites along the south coast, although late struck bronze coins are found on settlements in the south Midlands area (Curteis 2001). Gold is hoarded in Britain, and is also found individually in large quantities. In north-western Europe, the deposition patterns of gold coinage appear to be supra-local, with the individual finds being normal in all areas. Hoarding is more patchy, but is still frequent in most areas and can be found across southern Britain.

	Silver/ billon	% of silver on site	Uninscribed south coast silver	Uninscribed SC silver as %	Total coin on site
Hayling Island	85	59.3	36	21.82	165
Waltham St-Lawrence	119	68	11	6.29	175
Farley Heath	14	43.8	9	28.13	32
Lancing Down	12	85.7	1	7.14	14?
Danebury	67	89.3	6	8.45	75
Wanborough	762	83.7	45	60	910

Table 1. Silver coins on votive sites in southern Britain.

Silver is found along the south coast of England in some quantity. Recent discoveries have revealed a plethora of small issues of silver coins; some clearly related to continental examples.[19] The distribution of early silver is probably related to availability of the metal, as it seems likely that south-western silver resources were exploited in the late Iron Age (see Todd 1996 for the Roman exploitation). From the known archaeological contexts (which are not numerous) it would seem that in the west (the 'Durotrigan' area) silver took on the role of gold, being hoarded in the same manner as gold is outside the area. In central southern Britain much silver is found on votive sites (Table 1), along with continental issues at a few sites such as Hayling Island (Briggs et al. 1992).

Potin

Potin coinage first appears in south-eastern England, mostly in Kent. Coins are found in the rest of southern Britain, but their minting remained primarily in the south-eastern area. A rapid adoption north of the Channel is supported by Haselgrove (1995) but not by Van Arsdell (1989), with the earliest date currently suggested being in the LT C2 period. Although these coins were originally seen as a curiosity, they are now appearing in large hoards, with the earlier 'Massalia imitation' types having a wider distribution than the 'Thurrock' types. Neither of these types are found in large numbers outside of hoards (the only stratified example is from Maiden Castle in Dorset (Sharples 1991), well outside the normal distribution area). A bullion or wealth storage function may be suggested by this, as potin may have had a high value in the Iron Age. Traditionally the coins have been seen as small-change (e.g. Allen 1976), but tin was not a common metal in the Iron Age, and the coins would have originally had a silvered appearance, so this was probably not the case.

A major shift in deposition can be seen with the later 'Kentish flat-linear' potins. These are found in large numbers in stratified contexts on settlement sites (the contexts up to 1996 are listed in Haselgrove 1996, 126), and more have been found since. The only site to have produced both types of potin is North Foreland (Kent) and they are not from the same context. Differences in appearance, weight, manufacturing technique and findspot make it hard to link these disparate series in anything bar their metal content (and even this has only undergone preliminary investigation). The presence of later potin types on settlement sites suggests a function akin to struck bronze, and they are found in late contexts. The earlier types have a distribution and deposition akin to gold, so a major change seems to have taken place during the first century BC. This may be chronologically linked to the transition to struck bronze in Gaul, and may suggest interesting cross-Channel contacts. Perhaps a scarcity of struck bronze led to a localised solution in Kent in the form of the flat-linear coins?

Struck bronze

The adoption of struck bronze in Britain post-dates its introduction in Belgic Gaul, and is placed by Haselgrove (1993) in the mid to late first century BC (around 50-20 BC). It was adopted with different degrees of enthusiasm in different areas. Struck bronze was introduced in south-east England and rapidly became the most numerous coin type. However, on the south coast and in the south-west it was far less popular, with a debased billon coinage continuing in the south-west in preference (likely to have been connected to the availability of silver ore, and close contacts with the Armorican peninsula[20]). In the first century BC small silver issues dominated the south coast and (with the possible exception of the enigmatic Chichester 'cock bronzes' Burnett 1992; Cottam 1999) although struck bronze was used as part of tri-metallic sets, silver continued to be far more important than it was in the south-east. Only in the latest periods is struck bronze found in any quantities.

Struck bronze seems to be connected to large centres, such as Camulodunum and Verlamio[21] and the issue of large tri-metallic inscribed coin series on these and other sites clearly indicates that coinage was important to the identification of a group or polity, as it was in Gaul. Only the struck bronze makes it onto settlement sites in any appreciable quantities, mostly sites dating to the early first century AD, suggesting different functions (though one issuer) for the different metals. Struck bronze seems to be mostly issued by larger authorities and not minted on a small scale. It continues to be deposited on sites after the conquest for a short period as in Gaul. The British struck bronze coinage suggests votive deposition on sites as much as any market function, and it is found in large quantities on votive sites north of the Thames (95% of the coinage from Harlow temple is struck bronze: France and Gobel 1985).

Conclusion

There are still problems which need to be addressed when considering the function of Iron Age coinage in north-western Europe. I have only looked at a small geographical area, and by wider study different functions and uses of coinage will undoubtedly present themselves. Above all the use of coinage shows great flexibility in different areas, with the metals and denominations differing across sometimes restricted regions. Availability of ores is a factor which deserves more intensive work, as it must have played an important role in the choice of coinage, constraining certain areas to producing certain types of coinage.[22] The ideas which I have presented here are less applicable to the Armorican and south-west English peninsulas due to the different denominations and predominance of silver in these areas.

But, if the coins have different functions, why is the iconography often related? I do not consider the minting of coins in different metals for different purposes while having a similar iconography a problem. In the cases where tri-metallic sets are in use (the Gallic War period in Gaul and in the early first century AD in southern Britain), they are very late, and exist in a time when the elite was under considerable pressure. Whatever the function of different types of coinage, it is clear that they were minted by a restricted sector of society, and were probably minted at a restricted series of sites.[23] Centralised minting does not mean identical function, and it is illustrated by the range of different types of artefact produced at the oppida of northern Gaul.

I believe that the different metals should be considered in different ways, and that archaeology indicates a flexible and variable function, both chronologically and geographically. Gold coinage (and potin in some areas) seems to have been a coinage largely reserved for individual deposits and hoarding, with a small and localised tradition of sanctuary deposition in Picardy. Silver was an important votive deposit, which was also a primary coin type in a few areas. The use of silver seems to have been a matter of regional choice and availability of the metal, and it was also minted on sanctuaries as well as on *oppida*. Potin was introduced early, is found largely on votive sites (and in hoards in south-eastern Britain) and underwent a major change in function with the introduction of struck bronze. Struck bronze is minted on large centralised sites, and rapidly dominated the coin pool in most areas, being found on a wide range of sites, and continuing in use after the Roman conquest in both Gaul and Britain, despite the chronological difference.

There are still many unanswered questions about the function of coinage in the late Iron Age, and these can only be approached with more archaeological excavation. The pattern is also extremely regional, and in many areas the distribution and stratigraphic context of coinage is still obscure. With further excavation, the picture will hopefully become less opaque.

Acknowledgements
Many thanks to Colin Haselgrove and Jonathan Williams who have read and commented on drafts of this paper, and Philip de Jersey and J.D. Hill who have discussed the matter of coin function with me. I would also like to thank the staff of the Service Regional d'Archéologie units of the Nord-Pas-de-Calais, Picardy and Haute-Normandie who have kindly made unpublished information available and helped me during my time in France. Any errors, of course, remain my own.

Notes

[1] Structured deposition on settlement sites has now become the orthodoxy, rather than the exception in British excavation reports.

[2] Hopkins (1980), in his famous reassessment of Roman trade and taxation, did not believe that the Roman monetary economy was ever more than skin deep. There is a misguided tendency amongst prehistorians to treat the Roman Empire and the modern world as synonymous in their use of coinage.

[3] This is possibly related to the structure of academic departments in Britain, with classical text-led archaeology and traditional approaches rather on the decline (rightly or wrongly) in British archaeology departments.

[4] The few larger issues on both sides of the channel are rare, and are mostly late in date (e.g. the issues of Cunobelin and those inscribed Germanus Indutilli L.). The exceptions to this are tend to be gold or potin coinage (e.g. the Scheers 191 potin series which is found in very large numbers and over an unusually wide geographic and chronological area).

[5] de Jersey (1997) quantified the amount of Iron Age coinage found in Britain using the records from the Celtic Coin Index which includes metal detected finds. This contained records of 23,301 coins in February 1997, and the number has increased by more than 15000 since.

[6] For a further discussion of this matter see Wellington (2005).

[7] The Ledringhem hoard is relatively well published, but only a fraction of it survived (see Leclercq 1978 for information on this section). Original reports indicate an extremely large hoard (Cousin 1856:352, CAG 59:295), the small part which was examined consisted of Scheers 24 and 29 coins (Leclercq 1978:754).

[8] In the Ardennes and Aisne Valley sites such as Acy-Romance (Lambot & Méniel 1992, Lambot 2000) and settlements in the Aisne Valley (Haselgrove 1996) have potin coinage from early stratified contexts. The lack of this evidence from the Nord suggests that potin was not used on settlements in the Iron Age, but was largely deposited on votive sites.

[9] These are largely unpublished at present.

[10] The 'petit argent lamellaires', which are part of the same family as the Hampshire thin silver types found north of the Channel (Allen 1965, Gruel & Taccoën 1992).

[11] Although the example of the Oise has been used here, it is clear that the same phenomenon of early gold deposition on cult sites is also present elsewhere in Picardy, an example being the recent excavations at Ribemont-sur-Ancre which have produced very early gold (Brunaux 1999, Delestrée 2001).

[12] The dating of the Aisne Valley sites has been the source of some controversy. Condé-sur-Suippe is fairly incontestably the earliest, with occupation in the LTD1b period, from c. 120-80 BC. The other two sites are more problematic. The principle excavator of Villeneuve-Saint-Germain maintains that the site post-dates Pommiers (Debord 1993, 1995, 2002) but the majority of recent scholars and the overwhelming evidence of the material indicate that Villeneuve-Saint-Germain is the earlier of the two. The main phase of occupation dates to the LTD2a period, c. 80-55 BC, and the site has been linked to Caesar's Noviodunum (Haselgrove 1996; Debord 2002) although there is also limited activity after the Conquest. Pommiers dates from the later first century BC (LTD2b) to the earliest Gallo-Roman period.

[13] The antiquarian excavations were over a wide area. The 1987-1988 ERA 12 excavations were small-scale.

[14] Such as the REMO/REMO issue of the Remi in the lower Seine basin and the AVAVCIA and GERMANVS INDVTILLI L. brass issues, probably struck by the Treveri.

[15] These coins are very iconographically Roman (therefore presumably an appealing substitute for the official coinage) and were issued by one of the prominent client groups.

[16] The major centres are the Celtic Coin Index at the University of Oxford, and the Portable Antiquities Scheme, based at regional museums. Both have produced large quantities of Iron Age coins in recent years. For a quantification of Iron Age coinage, using the data from the CCI, see note 3. More Iron Age coinage is recorded in southern Britain than in northern France, which does seem unlikely in reality.

[17] Such as the deliberate removal of precious metals from the coin pool and the favouring of a few big issues of brass coinage in northern Gaul, and the continuation of precious metal coinage, and introduction of tri-metallic coin sets in Britain. The increasingly Romanised iconography of the later British Iron Age coins is also an interesting factor (see Creighton 2000 for a discussion of the iconography of late Iron Age coinage in Britain).

[18] Indeed, Hill (1995) believes that the British sites can be interpreted as centres for communal rituals and festivals, and not elite centres at all.

[19] The issues include the Hampshire Thin silver group (BM 2782-2787) discussed by Allen (1965) in conjunction with continental examples, and the rather nebulous 'Danebury group' (BM 376-409). The continental discoveries have been updated by Gruel and Taccoën (1992), the continental coins found in Britain by de Jersey (1999), and the central southern British ones by Williams (1998) and Wellington (2003).

[20] For further consideration of the coinage of the south-west and its social relations with Armorica, see de Jersey 1994 and Cunliffe and de Jersey 1997.

[21] References for these sites are numerous, a few are listed here: Frere 1983, Reece 1985, Haselgrove 1987, Stead and Rigby 1989, Haselgrove and Millett 1997, Niblett 1999.

[22] Nash (1981, 11) pointed this out for central Gaul, suggesting that in the area of the Bituriges Cubi, silver coin production was based at Argentomagus (St. Marcel, Indre) due to the proximity of sources of silver ore. This is likely to be true for other areas.

[23] Discoveries of coin dies have been interesting. In Gaul, coin dies have been found mostly on major fortified sites, such as Mont Beuvray (Delestrée & Duval 1977)and Corent (Malacher 1987). Ritual deposition seems likely for some other examples, such as the die found down a cleft on the fortified plateau of Larina (Hières-sur-Amby, Isère) with other votive offerings (Perrin 1990) and the die from the temple site of Halloy-en-Pernois (Fournier *et al.* 1989). This would indicate that coin production was based at major coin depositing sites, indicating that coins are not getting far from their point of origin. However, generalisations cannot be made using such a small data-set.

Bibliography

Aarts, J. 2001*: Coins or money? Exploring the monetization and functions of Roman coinage in Belgic Gaul and Lower Germany. 50BC - AD 450* (Amsterdam, Vrije Universiteit).

Allen, D. F. 1960: The origins of coinage in Britain: a reappraisal. In S. S. Frere (ed.), *Problems of the Iron Age in southern Britain* (London, University of London., Occasional Paper 11) 97-308.

Allen, D. F. 1965: Les pièces d'argent minces du comté de Hampshire: nouveau lien entre la Gaule celtique et la Grande-Bretagne. *Revue Numismatique* series 6, vol. 7, 79-93.

Allen, D. F. 1976: Wealth, money and coinage in a Celtic society. In J. V. S. Megaw (ed.), *To illustrate the monuments* (London Thames and Hudson) 199-208.

Bradley, R. 1998 (2nd ed.): *The passage of arms* (Oxford, Oxbow).

Briggs, D., Haselgrove, C. and King, C. 1992: Iron Age and Roman coins from Hayling Island Temple. *British Numismatic Journal* 62, 1-62.

Brunaux, J.-L. (ed.) 1999: Ribemont-sur-Ancre (Somme). Bilan préliminaire et nouvelles hypothéses. *Gallia* 56, 177-283.

Burnett, A. M. 1992: A new Iron Age issue from near Chichester. *Spink Numismatic Circular* 100, 340-342.

Burnett, A. M. 1995: "Gallo-Belgic" coins and Britain. In B. Raftery, J. V. S. Megaw and V. Rigby (eds), *Sites and sights of the Iron Age* (Oxford, Oxbow Monograph 56) 5-11.

Burnham, B. C. and Johnson, H. B. (eds) 1979: *Invasion and response, the case of Roman Britain* (Oxford, BAR 73).

Collis, J. 1971: Functional and theoretical interpretations of British coinage. *World Archaeology* 3, 71-84.

Cottam, G. L. 1999: The 'Cock Bronzes' and other related Iron Age bronze coins found predominantly in West Sussex and Hampshire. *British Numismatic Journal* 69, 1-18.

Cousin, L. 1857: Note. *Mémoires de la Société. Dunkerquoise* 4, 1856-57, 352.

Creighton, J. 2000: *Coins and Power in Late Iron Age Britain* (Cambridge, CUP).

Cunliffe, B. W. 1981: Money and society in pre-Roman Britain. In B. W. Cunliffe (ed.), *Coinage and society in Britain and Gaul: some current problems* (London, CBA Research Report 38) 29-39.

Cunliffe, B. W. and de Jersey, P. 1997: *Armorica and Britain. Cross-channel relationships in the late first millennium BC* (Oxford, OUCA Monograph 45).

Curteis, M. E. 2001: *The Iron Age coinages of the South Midlands, with particular reference to distribution and deposition.* Unpublished PhD thesis, University of Durham.

Debord, J. 1993: Les artisans gaulois de Villeneuve-Saint-Germain (Aisne). Structures, production, occupation du sol. *Revue Archéologique de Picardie* 3:4, 71-110.

Debord, J. 1995: A propos de la chronologie des sites de Pommiers et de Villeneuve-Saint-Germain (Aisne). *Revue Archéologique de Picardie* 1:2, 205-208.

Debord, J. 2002: Novodunum Suessionum: Pommiers ou Villeneuve-Saint-Germain. *Mémoires du Soissonnais* series 5, vol. 2, 7-30.

de Jersey, P. 1994: *Coinage in Iron Age Armorica* (Oxford,

OUCA Monograph 39).

de Jersey, P. 1997: Cast away riches: estimating the volume of Celtic coinage found in Britain. *The Yorkshire Numismatist* 3, 1-15.

de Jersey, P. 1999: Exotic Celtic Coinage in Britain. *Oxford Journal of Archaeology* 18:2, 189-216.

Delestrée, L.-P. 1996: *Monnayages et peuples gaulois du Nord-Ouest* (Paris, Errance).

Delestrée, L.-P. 2001: L'or du trophée laténien de Ribemont-sur-Ancre (Somme), témoin d'une bataille oubliée. *Revue Numismatique* 156, 175-213.

Delestrée, L.-P. and Duval, A. 1977: Un coin monétaire inédit du Mont Beuvray. *Antiquités Nationales* 9, 45-47.

Delmaire, R. 1996: De la monnaie gauloise à la monnaie romaine: l'exemple de la région du Nord-Pas-de-Calais. *Revue du Nord* 78, 9-14.

Fichtl, S. 2000: *La ville celtique: les oppida de 150 av. J.-C. à 15 ap. J.-C.* (Paris, Errance).

Fitzpatrick, A. P. 1984: The deposition of La Tène Iron Age metalwork in watery contexts in southern England. In B. W. Cunliffe and D. Miles (eds), *Aspects of the Iron Age in Central Southern Britain* (Oxford, OUCA Monograph 2) 178-190.

Fitzpatrick, A. P. 1992: The roles of Celtic coinage in south east England. In M. Mays (ed.), *Celtic Coinage: Britain and beyond* (Oxford, BAR 222) 1-32.

Fournier, C., Fournier, J. and Fournier, J. 1989: Le poinçon monétaire gaulois d'Halloy-Les-Pernois (Somme). *Revue Archéologique de Picardie* 1:2, 119.

France, N. E. and Gobel, B. M. 1985: *The Romano-British Temple at Harlow* (West Essex Archaeology Group).

Ginoux, N. and Poux, M. 2002: Les Parisii, entre Gaule Belgique et Gaule Celtique: peuplement et territoire. In D. Garcia and F. Verdin (eds), *Territoires celtiques* (Société Archéologique Champenoise) 226-243.

Gruel, K. 1989: *La monnaie chez les Gaulois* (Paris, Errance).

Gruel, K. (ed.) 1995: Les potins gaulois: typologie, diffusion, chronologie. État de la question à partir de plusieurs contributions. *Gallia* 52, 1-144.

Gruel, K. 2002: Monnaies et territoires. In D. Garcia and F. Verdin (eds), *Territoires celtiques* (Société Archéologique Champenoise) 205-212.

Gruel, K. and Taccoën, A. 1992: Petit numéraire de billon émis durant et après la conquête romaine dans l'Ouest de la Gaule. In M. Mays (ed.), *Celtic Coinage: Britain and beyond* (Oxford, BAR 222) 165-188.

Guichard, V., Pion, P., Malacher, F. and Collis, J. 1993: A propos de la circulation monétaire en Gaule chevelue aux IIe et Ier siècles av. J.-C. *Revue Archéologique du Centre de la France* 32, 25-56.

Haselgrove, C. C. 1979: The significance of coinage in pre-conquest Britain. In B. C. Burnham and H. B. Johnson (eds), *Invasion and response, the case of Roman Britain* (Oxford, BAR 73) 197-207.

Haselgrove, C. C. 1987: *Iron Age coinage in south-east England: the archaeological context* (Oxford, BAR 174).

Haselgrove, C. C. 1988: The archaeology of British potin coinage. *Archaeological Journal* 145, 99-122.

Haselgrove, C. C. 1995: Potin coinage in Iron Age Britain, archaeology and chronology. *Gallia* 52, 117-127.

Haselgrove, C. C. 1999: The development of Iron Age coinage in Belgic Gaul. *Numismatic Chronicle* 159, 111-168.

Hill, G. F. 1919: A find of ancient British gold coins. *Numismatic Chronicle* ser. 4 vol. 19, 172-178.

Hill, J. D. 1995: How should we understand Iron Age societies and hillforts? A contextual study from southern Britain. In J. D. Hill and C. Cumberpatch (eds), *Different Iron Ages: studies in the Iron Age in temperate Europe* (Oxford, BAR S602) 45-66.

Hingley, R. 1993: Iron Age 'Currency Bars'. The archaeological and social context. *Archaeological Journal* 147, 91-117.

Hodder, I. 1979: Pre-Roman and Romano-British Tribal Economies. In B. C. Burnham and H. B. Johnson (eds), *Invasion and response, the case of Roman Britain* (Oxford, BAR 73) 189-196.

Hopkins, K. 1980: Taxes and trades in the Roman Empire (200 BC - AD 400). *Journal of Roman Studies* 70, 101-125.

Lambot, B. and Delestrée, L.-P. 1991: Des séries de potin du Belgium antérieurs au début du 1er siècle avant J.-C. *Bulletin de la Société Archéologique Champenoise* 84, 67-79.

Lambot, B. and Méniel, P. 1992: *Le site protohistorique d'Acy-Romance (Ardennes). I. L'habitat gaulois 1988-1990* (Reims, Société Archéologique Champenoise).

Lambot, B. and Méniel, P. 2000: Le centre communautaire et cultuel du village gaulois d'Acy-Romance dans son contexte régional. In S. Verger (ed.), *Rites et espaces en pays celte et méditerranéen* (Rome, Ecole Française de Rome 276) 7-139.

Leclercq, P. 1978: Le trésor gaulois de Ledringhem. Essai d'interprétation. In *Tresors, Monnaies et Archéologie du Nord de la France* (Revue du Nord, numero spécial) 753-759.

Mack, R. P. 1975 (3rd ed.): *The coinage of ancient Britain* (London, Spink & Seaby).

Malacher, F. 1987: Découverte d'un coin monétaire à Corent (Puy-de-Dôme). *Bulletin de la Société Française de Numismatique* 42:9, 275-276.

Mantel, E. 1997: *Le sanctuaire de Fesques: "Le Mont du Val aux Moines", Seine-Maritime* (Nord-Ouest Archéologie 8).

Nash, D. 1978: *Settlement and coinage in central Gaul, c.200-50 B. C.* (Oxford, BAR S39).

Nash, D. 1981: Coinage and state development in central Gaul. In B. W. Cunliffe (ed.), *Coinage and society in Britain and Gaul: some current problems* (London, CBA Research Report 38) 10-17.

Perrin, F. 1990: *Un dépôt d'objets gaulois à Larina, Hières-sur-Amby, Isère* (Lyon, Circonscription des Antiquités Historiques, Documents d'Archéologie en Rhône-Alpes 4).

Polanyi, K., Arensberg, C. M. and Pearson H. W. 1957: *Trade and market in the early empires* (New York, Free Press).

Rodwell, W. 1976: Coinage, oppida and the rise of Belgic power in south-eastern Britain. In B. W. Cunliffe and R. T. Rowley (eds), *Oppida: the beginnings of urbanization in barbarian Europe* (Oxford, BAR S11) 181-367.

Roymans, N. 1990: *Tribal societies in northern Gaul: an anthropological perspective* (Amsterdam, University of Amsterdam).

Roymans, N. and Derks, T. 1994: *De Tempel van Empel. Een Hercules-heiligdom in het woongebied van de Bataven* (Stichting Brabantse Regionale Geschiedbeoefening, Graven naar het Brabantse verleden 2).

Roymans, N. and van der Sanden, W. 1980: Celtic coins from the Netherlands and their archaeological context. *Berichten van de Rijksdienst voor het Oudheidkundig Bodemonderzoek* 30, 173-254.

Scheers, S. 1977: *Traité de Numismatique Celtique II, La Gaule Belgique* (Paris, Les Belles Lettres).

Sharples, N. M. 1991: *Maiden Castle: excavation and field survey 1985-6* (London, English Heritage Archaeological Reports 19).

Todd, M. 1996: Pretia Victoriae? Roman lead and silver mining on the Mendip Hills, Somerset, England. *Münstersche Beiträge zur antiken Handelsgeschichte* 15:1, 130-148.

Todd, M. 2002: Mining, bullion and the balance of payments in the Roman West. *Laverna* 2002, 81-90.

Van Arsdell, R. D. 1989: *Celtic coinage of Britain* (London, Spink).

Van Arsdell, R. D. 1992: Money supply and credit in Iron Age Britain. In M. Mays (ed.), *Celtic Coinage: Britain and beyond* (Oxford, BAR 222) 139-150.

Wellington, I. J. 2003: Cross-Channel relations and the lightweight silver coinages of central southern Britain. In J. Humphrey (ed.), *Re-searching the Iron Age* (University of Leicester, School of Archaeology and Ancient History, Leicester Archaeology Monographs 11), 35-43.

Wellington, I. J. 2005: Placing coinage and ritual sites in their archaeological contexts: the example of northern France. In C. Haselgrove and D. Wigg,-Wolf (eds), *Iron Age coinage and ritual practices* (Mainz, Studien zu Fundmünzen der Antike 20), 227-245.

Williams, J. H. C. 1998: Delete-Undelete: Mack 280 and Early British Silver. *Numismatic Chronicle* 158, 53-61.

The impact of the Roman conquest on indigenous coinages in Belgic Gaul and southern Britain

Colin Haselgrove

Introduction

This paper examines some effects of the Roman conquest on indigenous coinages in Belgic Gaul and southern Britain.[1] Several factors make this an instructive comparison. At the time of their initial contact with Rome, peoples in both provinces had been using coinages based on a common prototype for at least a century, and shared other cultural and political links. There were also peoples on both sides of the Channel – those inhabiting the coastal areas in the far north of Belgic Gaul, and the Britons living to the north-west of the Severn and Humber – who had previously rejected the adoption of coinage. Their reaction to Roman coinage is thus likely to have been quite different to that of indigenous peoples who were already habituated to the idea of coin-based transactions, albeit in a different monetary system.

This paper will focus on two main themes: the changes in coin production that took place in Belgic Gaul and southern Britain following their respective Roman conquests; and what coin deposition can tell us about changes in indigenous coin use and the penetration of Roman coinage. First, however, we have to confront the problem that Roman expansion has traditionally provided the major fixed points for dating Iron Age coinage on both sides of the Channel. This means that before we even start to analyse the material, we have in effect already assumed that certain changes were linked to the arrival of the Romans. Without independent dating evidence, this can only be a circular argument. I will start therefore by discussing this link between explanation and chronology, from which archaeology is now gradually releasing us by furnishing the required evidence. There are also important structural differences between northern Gaul and Britain at the time of their respective conquests, which need to be reviewed before subsequent developments can be compared.

Chronology and interpretation

For many years, the absolute chronology of Belgic coinages relied on the framework set out by the late J-B. Colbert de Beaulieu (1966), which placed the majority of Gaulish coinages in the late second and first centuries BC. A central tenet of his scheme was the proposition that cast potin coinage did not appear before the Gallic war, while the minting of gold ceased immediately afterwards. Within this framework, closer dating of series depended on asserting links between specific sites, hoards or coin types, and known people or historical events, or by arguing that borrowing from Roman coins had occurred. In Belgic Gaul, however, definite copying of Roman prototypes is confined to a few, mostly inscribed, silver and bronze issues, which are clearly late in the sequence anyway, while the main 'fixed point' used elsewhere in Gaul – provided by the prolific coin finds from the battlefield at Alésia where Caesar defeated Vercingetorix in 52 BC – is of limited relevance to the north of the country.

In constructing her chronology for Belgic coinage, Simone Scheers, like Colbert de Beaulieu, relied on the pivot provided by the Gallic war, especially for the gold. Arguing that the similarities between the later gold coinages reflected an attempt at monetary harmonisation by the Belgic peoples who opposed the Roman invasion in 57 BC, she proceeded to equate specific issues with the events recorded by Caesar (Scheers 1972; 1977). Other factors which seemed to support this view included the scale of the issues; the sharp fall in weight and purity between classes; and the number of hoards containing these types. In the absence of significant evidence to the contrary, this hypothesis rapidly won general acceptance (e.g. Kent 1978) and has provided a point of departure for most subsequent work on the subject.

Over the last two decades, however, new finds – especially from excavations – have rendered first the detail, and increasingly the substance, of Scheers's chronology open to question. This fresh evidence has been set out elsewhere (Guichard *et al.* 1993; Haselgrove 1987; 1995; 1999; Pion 1996; 2000; Wigg and Riederer 1998) and need not be reiterated here. It is now clear that potin coinage appeared in Belgic Gaul more than a century before the Gallic war, while some gold series attributed to the invasion evidently began earlier and lasted longer than Scheers believed. As we will see below, the archaeological evidence also provides a different – if not yet always very clear – picture of coin production in the decades following the Roman invasion. The prolific Cricirv series (Scheers 27), for example, which was once unhesitatingly ascribed to the period c. 57 – 50 BC, is not known from stratified contexts predating c. 30 BC and is probably later than the war (Pion 1996; Haselgrove 1999). In retrospect, the nature of our previous error is clear enough: coin chronology was allowed to become wholly dependent on interpretation, rather than vice versa. Whilst this was largely unavoidable at the time, we need to ensure that lessons are learnt. These are, first, that we should be cautious in seeking to push the dating of Iron Age coinages beyond the limits of the available evidence; and second, that we also need to be careful about the assumptions we make in analysing the numismatic data, and expose these to critical scrutiny.

In southern Britain, the problem of dating coinages belonging to the period of the Roman invasion is less acute. By AD 43, the inhabitants of all but one of the main coin-using regions had been inscribing coins for some generations, while various types copy issues of Augustus and his successors as Roman emperor (Haselgrove 1987; Creighton 2000). Several rulers in south-east England are named in the classical texts as well as on coins, placing a limit on their reigns. Cunobelinus, the ruler of the principal eastern kingdom, whose capital was at *Camulodunum* (Colchester), was certainly dead by AD 43. Verica, the ruler of the southern kingdom – assuming that he is the Βερικος named by Cassius Dio (*Histories* 60, 19, 1) – had apparently been driven from his territory, and is credited with persuading Claudius to mount the invasion. Another ruler whose name appears on coins, Adminius, had previously surrendered to Caligula (Suetonius, *Caligula*, 44, 2).

A number of uncertainties remain, as we shall see below, particularly in relation to the latest coinages issued by the some of the outlying peoples. Far more problematic however is the absolute dating of the coinages that predate the later first century BC, for which we have very little archaeological evidence.[2] On balance, a long chronology seems to me the more probable (Haselgrove 1993; 1999), and I am sceptical – for the reasons I have just set out – of recent attempts to link the minting of various uninscribed British gold coinages directly with Julius Caesar's invasions of 55 and 54 BC, or of their Gallo-Belgic predecessors with other military emergencies such as the late second century BC migrations of the Cimbri and the Teutones (e.g. Sills 1996; 1997a; 1997b; 2000a).[3]

Structural differences

There are important structural differences between the situations in 57 – 51 BC when Caesar conquered Belgic Gaul, and in AD 43 – 47 when Claudius's army conquered southern Britain. These apply to the conquerors as well as to the indigenous peoples they annexed, and have a significant bearing on the comparisons I shall be drawing. In the century that elapsed between the two conquests, the competitive politics of the late Republic had given way to a centralised imperial administration, a far-reaching cultural and ideological revolution had taken place, and the Roman monetary system had itself been comprehensively reformed in Augustus's reign.

Caesar's army operated with the assistance of large auxiliary contingents drawn from allied Gaulish peoples, some of whom like the Remi and Treveri were themselves inhabitants of Belgic Gaul. It is widely believed that such auxiliaries were paid for by their own peoples, in their own coinage, both during and after Caesar's campaigns (e.g. Nash 1978; Crawford 1985).[4] If these troops spent periods garrisoning native fortresses (*oppida*) in other regions, this could well have distorted the circulation pattern of the coinages in question. In contrast, the auxiliaries belonging to the Claudian army in Britain, were recruited outside the province and were paid in Roman coin, even if they also made use of locally-available issues, so that the numismatic record generated by the armies of Caesar and Claudius will have been both qualitatively and quantitatively different.

The process of conquest and its aftermath also differed significantly. Having suffered a drawn-out series of campaigns, in the course of which Caesar undoubtedly did strip many of the portable valuables from the peoples who opposed him or later rebelled (Suetonius, *Julius Caesar*, 54; Haselgrove 1984), Belgic Gaul was left largely to its own devices until c. 20 BC. Not until the onset of the Augustan campaigns in Germany were Roman legionaries stationed permanently in the province and then primarily on the Rhine frontier.[5] Britain, on the other hand, had a large garrison from the start, with troops being quartered in the territories of virtually all the major coin-using peoples (e.g. Millett 1990), although by the Flavian period, the bulk of the army was concentrated in the North and West. In comparison to Belgic Gaul, the process of conquest seems to have been relatively painless, although meeting strong resistance in certain regions.

The two provinces also differed in their exposure to the Roman world prior to the invasions. There is no evidence of direct contact between Belgic Gaul and the Roman authorities prior to 57 BC. A fair amount of Italian wine and other imports did reach southern Belgic Gaul from the late second century BC onward, but these could have arrived through the intermediary of Gaulish traders, or in social and diplomatic exchanges between the leading peoples (Haselgrove 1996). Southern Britain, on the other hand, from c. 20 BC onward, was exposed to increasing cultural, diplomatic and economic influence from the developing province of Belgic Gaul. In Roman terms, British rulers who submitted to Caesar in 54 BC were as much a part of the empire as their neighbours across the Channel (Creighton 2000). The extent to which these client rulers and other 'free' peoples within the empire were initially absolved from the requirement to pay tax is a further complicating factor.

There were also substantial differences between the currency systems in use at the time of the invasions. Most Belgic peoples favoured gold and potin; silver coinage – the mainstay of the Roman system – was relatively rare,[6] while the use of legends and bronze was just starting. By contrast, by AD 43 most of the coin-using peoples of Britain possessed inscribed coinages of gold and silver, and in eastern England, copper, bronze and even brass denominations (Clogg and Haselgrove 1995).[7] Moreover, from the Augustan period onward, rulers in south-east

England made use of an increasingly Romanized repertoire of designs and symbols on their coin types (e.g. Williams 2005), a phenomenon which is seen in other client peoples around the edge of the empire at this time, including Belgic Gaul (Creighton 2000). From the coin distributions, it is also clear that the polities controlled by the leading rulers in south-east England were more centralised than their counterparts in Belgic Gaul a century earlier, although to the north and west, there is evidence of a more fluid political structure closer to that which obtained among most northern Gaulish peoples in Caesar's time.

Belgic coin production in the later first century BC

A comparison of coin lists from sites which were first occupied in La Tène D2b[8] with those attributable to earlier periods indicates that the character of Belgic coinage altered significantly in the mid first century BC (Guichard *et al.* 1993; Haselgrove 1999; Pion 2000), although the lack of precision of archaeological dating makes it difficult to distinguish changes during the Gallic war from ones that occurred in its wake. Key developments included a massive increase in struck bronze coinage; the demise of potin and diminution in the importance of gold; and the widespread adoption of legends, some series bearing dual inscriptions in Greek and Latin characters, although most had Roman letters only. The amount of non-Belgic coinage in circulation also increased. Prior to the mid first century BC, struck bronze was virtually restricted to western Picardy, although it was starting to be used in the territories of the Suessiones and the Remi, along with crude inscriptions (Haselgrove 1999, 145-149).

It is clear that gold did not abruptly disappear with the conquest and was occasionally minted decades later (Haselgrove 1984; 1999). Among the most prominent mid first century BC gold series are the later classes of 'eye' staters minted by the Remi and the Treveri, the former inscribed Vocarant or Lvcotios (Scheers 30-II, -III), the latter Pottina (Scheers 30-V).[9] The legends are in well-formed Roman letters. All three types were apparently minted on a massive scale, although with a lower gold content than their uninscribed predecessors (Scheers 30-I, -IV), achieved by using poorer alloys (Classes II-III) or by reducing the weight (Class V). Although there is no archaeological evidence to indicate precisely when minting began and how long it lasted,[10] general site associations point to all three types having circulated primarily on sites first occupied in the later first century BC (Haselgrove 2005).

The 'epsilon' staters minted by the Nervii and inscribed Viros (Scheers 29-IV) are probably of similar, or slightly later date. They too are lighter and richer in copper than their uninscribed predecessors (c. 30%). Examples were present in the Kwaremont hoard, which has Roman coins of the early first century AD (Scheers 1977, 887). The name occurs on a bronze coinage from the same region, featuring an equestrian type (Scheers 29a), which has links with coinage minted by the Atrebates and the Treveri in the 40s or 30s BC. The legend Viros and that of Lvc(otios) also occur on debased quarter-staters (Doyen 1987-I, II), with which the staters are presumably associated.

Other late Belgic gold coinages were on a smaller scale and have related silver and bronze issues. These include another Treveran series, inscribed Arda (Scheers 30a), and the southern Belgic coinages of Cricirv and Roveca (Scheers 27-28). Several of Arda's silver and bronze types copy Roman or Numidian prototypes dating to the 40s BC,[11] although his gold has more traditional designs (Scheers 30-VI).[12] Evidence from the tribal *oppidum* at the Titelberg indicates that the bronze issues post-date another Romanized Treveran type naming Caesar's general A. Hirtius (Scheers 162-I), which implies a date for Arda's reign centering on the 30s BC.[13] His gold and silver was struck to the same weight standard as previous precious metal issues in the region (Scheers 30-V; Scheers 55), but the gold is baser.[14]

As Creighton (forthcoming) has argued, the symbolism employed on Arda's coins, particularly the equestrian imagery, recalls the iconography exploited by Octavian's adherents during his power struggle with Mark Antony. After Gaul fell under Octavian's control in 40 BC, it seems likely that rather than stationing large Roman forces in the north, the future emperor Augustus installed some of his own clients – members of the Gaulish elite whose patron he had become after Caesar's death – as rulers of strategically important peoples like the Treveri and the Atrebates, through whose lands ran the road network established by Agrippa between 39 – 37 BC (Wightman 1985). This would fit well with the dating proposed for Arda's coinage. Creighton (2000) suggests that Gauls like Arda acquired their familiarity with the symbolism employed by Octavian's faction through being taken to Rome as hostages by Caesar when they were young. Auxiliary service with the Roman army during and after the civil war is another possibility (Loscheider 1998, 173-183).

The equestrian type found on the Viros bronzes (Scheers 29a) recurs on two other Belgic series: the Atrebates bronzes inscribed Andobru/Garmanos (Scheers 46) and their silver coins inscribed Carsicios/Commios (Scheers 47). The two series are linked by their legends to another silver type inscribed Garmanos/Commios (Scheers 45). This Commios is assumed to be the individual whom Caesar made king of the Atrebates in 57 BC and who later joined in the revolt of 52 BC;[15] the others may be younger members of the same dynasty (Creighton 2000; forthcoming). In Britain, a similar equestrian type appears on the gold coinage of yet another member of the Commian dynasty, Tincomaros, who ruled the southern kingdom in the last quarter of the first century BC.[16]

The trimetallic series inscribed Cricirv and Roveca, issued by the Suessiones and the Meldi respectively, are closely related. In both cases, the gold is descended from the southern Belgic triple-tailed horse series (Scheers 26), while the silver takes its weight standard from a group of silver coins found in the same region (Scheers 48). Cricirv and Roveca seem to be broad contemporaries of Arda, but their imagery is more diverse. The head on Cricirv's silver is inspired by Massaliote drachms, possibly via southern Gaulish imitations, while the head on one of Roveca's bronzes copies a Roman *denarius* (Scheers 28-V). The lion on the reverse of another bronze (Scheers 28-IV) resembles ones depicted on several other Belgic bronzes at this period. One difference between the two series is that Cricirv employs Latin lettering only, whereas Roveca has dual legends in Greek and Latin, a feature the series shares with the stylistically similar Epenos bronzes (Scheers 143), which are found in the same area and probably came from the same mint.

The only other Belgic groups to issue post-conquest silver coinages were the Tungri, who apparently minted a lightweight *quinarius* type inscribed Annaroveci (Scheers 1996); and the inhabitants of the eastern Dutch river delta region, who produced a debased series with a triquetrum design (Roymans 2001).[17] The latter coinage is derived from the earlier Mardorf group in the middle Rhineland and eventually degenerated into billon issues containing only a small percentage of precious metal. The Dutch river delta area has no previous history of coin production and Roymans (2001) suggests that the series was minted following the migration of a group of the Chatti into the region (Tacitus *Germania* 29, 1; *Hist.* 4, 12). The billon coins are frequently found at Augustan military sites, suggesting that they were still current when the Roman campaigns in Germany began. The Tungri were presumably settled on the left bank of the Meuse, sometime after the conquest, in land previously occupied by the Eburones and the Atuatuci, who disappear from history after their defeat by Caesar (Wightman 1985, 13).

The Remi were one of a handful of Belgic peoples outside western Picardy who had started to use struck bronze before the invasion (Haselgrove 1999, 147-149) and afterwards they were the only ones to strike extensive coinages bearing the tribal name. The Remo/Remo type (Scheers 146) depicts a Roman-style Victory driving a chariot on the reverse, which might be an allusion to Caesar's defeat of the Belgic coalition in 57 BC,[18] whilst the heavier Atisios Remos series (Scheers 147) has the legend on one side only and bears a lion on the reverse. From their different styles, the two series are thought to have been issued by separate mints, with the Remo/Remo coins being found on over twice the number of sites. The coin lists from sites like Reims and Château Porcien which were not occupied before La Tène D2b are dominated by inscribed bronze issues, to the detriment of potin (Delestrée 1996), suggesting a very rapid alteration in the status of the latter.

The change was apparently almost as rapid in those areas of Belgic Gaul with no history of struck bronze prior to Caesar. In the territory of the Nervii, potin is already a minor component of coin assemblages at sites founded in the later first century BC (Scheers 1996). Apart from the Viros series, the principal Nervian bronze coinages are the stylistically related Vercio type (Scheers 145) and the 'au rameau' types (Scheers 190-I, II), some of which are inscribed Varticeo.[19] The picture is similar in Treveran territory and in that of their neighbours, the Mediomatrici, whose bronzes employ imagery reminiscent of other post-conquest series: the helmeted head on the Medioma coins (Scheers 138) recalls the Garmanos coins (Scheers 45-46), while one of the reverse types (Class II) depicts a winged horse in similar style to the winged lion on some Roveca bronzes (Scheers 28-I). The early Arc Ambacti coins depict a lion (Scheers 139-II), while the later ones imitate the unwreathed head found on issues of Octavian from 36 BC onward (Scheers 139-I).

The longer tradition of struck bronze coinage makes developments in western Belgic Gaul less easy to follow. Certain series such as the 'running/squatting person' coinage (Scheers 163), which start in the late second or early first century BC, apparently carried on after the conquest, marked only by the acquisition of legends. The period is characterised by the proliferation of minor issues, often unknown beyond the confines of a single site or district. The situation is particularly complex in the Somme basin, where there is a plethora of inter-related bronze types, generally with animal designs on one side if not both, most of which are still uninscribed (Delestrée 1996, 100-102).

Definite post-conquest coinages in western Belgic Gaul include the Romanized Svticos/Ratvmacos and Eccaios series (Scheers 164, 176), both of which include issues copying a *denarius* of c. 46 BC (Crawford 458/1).[20] A second Eccaios type (Scheers 176-II) has a rearing equestrian design reminiscent of the Arda silver. Another interesting type is the heavy bronze coin inscribed C. Iuli Telidhi (Delestrée 1996, 111); its reverse is copied from the elephant *denarius* of Julius Caesar, while the obverse derives from the earlier 'à l'astre' series (Scheers 25). Other instances of borrowing include Scheers 59, on which the head copies a *denarius* of C. Calpurnius Piso (Crawford 340/1); and two types derived from an Iberian silver issue (Delestrée 1996, 24; Scheers 104).

The Iron Age coin types found in early Gallo-Roman deposits tend to be the same as those present in La Tène D2b deposits, reinforcing the impression given by borrowing from Roman types that minting declined rapidly after Augustus initiated his reorganisation of the Gallic provinces in 27 BC. A few series can however be dated later. The first of these is the well-known Germanvs Indvtilli L type (Scheers 216), which is the most widely distributed of all later Belgic coinages. Another important series began with coins inscribed Avavcia (Scheers 217-Ia), followed by uninscribed issues (Classes Ib-III). A cluster of finds in the territory of the Tungri may betray the area of origin, but the main body of finds are from Augustan forts on both banks of the Rhine.[21]

A smaller and more localised group of bronzes found in Bellovacan territory is probably later still, since the reverse of one type (Scheers 214-I) depicts an altar taken from the Lyons first Altar series, dating between c. 7 – 3 BC (van Heesch 1999). This appears to confirm that the Roman authorities had still not suppressed the freedom of individual Belgic *civitates* to mint coins if they so determined. In practice, few of them now chose to do so, and any local minting which did take place after this date, as in parts of Belgic Gaul during the Claudian period, was to produce imitations of Roman coin types (Nash 1978; Wigg 1996).

Standing back from the evidence, we can summarise the main points to have emerged so far. Away from the Dutch river delta and the territory of the Tungri – where there were special circumstances – most peoples who minted coinage after the conquest were using it before 57 BC, both in precious and in base metals. Many of these series were however much more localised than the pre-war issues, although a few enjoyed wider circulation, like the Remo/Remo types of the Remi, or the late Germanvs Indvtilli L issues.

Gold coinages minted after the conquest were generally in

poorer alloy or of lower weight, and the biggest issues were confined to the territories of Roman allies such as the Remi and the Treveri, who presumably retained the largest precious metal stocks. Minting in silver – despite its importance in the Roman system – seems to be limited to those peoples who had a tradition of silver coinage prior to the conquest. The majority of coin types minted were in bronze, either because treasuries were too depleted by the war and by the obligation to pay tribute to strike gold or silver, or because bronze was in fact more appropriate for many of the purposes for which new coinage was now required.[22]

Unlike the gold, which followed traditional designs, silver and bronze issues show more Roman influence, a phenomenon found on the coinages of various client rulers around the fringes of the Roman empire (Creighton 2000). A personal link with Augustus would explain the choice of imagery on the coinage of rulers like Arda and Garmanos, whilst the more limited copying of Roman prototypes found in other regions indicates that there too, whoever chose the coin types – presumably members of the elite – was open to Roman ideological influence (Wigg 1999).

Post-conquest coin circulation and deposition in Belgic Gaul

At many major sites which were occupied in the mid to late first century BC, there is a noticeable augmentation in the number of coins from other areas of Gaul, typified by a group of 39 coins found at the entrance to the western Belgic *oppidum* of La Chaussée-Tirancourt: 69% of these coins are non-Belgic, including five Togirix silver (LT 5550) and 14 Massaliote obols (Delestrée 1997; 1999, 27-28). The Togirix type is also common at Pommiers (cf. Guichard *et al.* 1993). The widespread dispersion of Atevla/Vlatos *quinarii* (Scheers 41) is another facet of the same phenomenon.[23]

Roman coins, however, remained notably rare,[24] even at sites which are likely to have been garrisoned by the Roman army at some period between Caesar and Augustus. At Pommiers, they represent a mere 1.4% in an assemblage which goes down to the end of the first century BC (Guichard *et al.* 1993) (Table 1).[25] At the Titelberg, they account for under 5% of the finds in pre-Augustan contexts (Metzler 1995) and there were none at all in the group from La Chaussée-Tirancourt, despite the presence of items of military equipment (Delestrée 1997). This in turn reinforces the idea that Belgic Gaul was garrisoned largely by auxiliary forces who were paid in their own coinage (Wightman 1975; Nash 1978). Belgic Gaul is also virtually devoid of the large mixed Gaulish and Roman silver hoards found throughout central and north-west Gaul in the 40s and 30s BC (e.g. Allen 1980).

From c. 15 BC, when Roman troops were first stationed permanently on the Rhine and following the opening of the mints at Nîmes and Lyons, the quantity of Roman coinage in the frontier region started to increase rapidly. At the Titelberg, where there was certainly military activity around this time, the proportion of Roman coins rises to 53% (Table 1). At the legionary fortress of Oberaden, occupied for only 3 or 4 years between 11 – 8/7 BC, virtually all the coinage is Roman (Ilisch 1992). The rapid turnover of bronze at successive forts provides an indication of the volume of Roman coinage reaching the military zone (van Heesch 1999; Wigg 1997), although the silver does not seem to have been replaced in circulation anything like as quickly as the bronze, leading Wigg (1999) to speculate that however military pay was calculated, the soldiers actually received mainly bronze coins.

In the adjoining territory of the Tungri, Augustan coins outnumber indigenous issues at Tongres and most other early sites in the region, and the ratio of Lyons first and second Atlar series coins is similar to that in the military zone (van Heesch 1999). This points to a relatively uninterrupted flow of Roman coinage into the territory, which was in any case on the periphery of the main coin-using area of northern Gaul, having no bronze coinage of its own prior to the late Avavcia issues. However, in the adjoining territory of the Nervii, the pattern is reversed, with Iron Age coins outnumbering early Roman issues even at official foundations like Bavai, already a flourishing centre in the Augustan period and on the main road network.

Away from the military zone, in the interior of Gaul, Roman coinage seems to have entered circulation relatively slowly to judge from the few sites where information on finds from successive stratified horizons is readily available.[26] These include Besançon (Guilhot and Guy 1992) and Roanne (Lavendhomme and Guichard 1997) in Celtic Gaul, both already important settlements in the Iron Age and the former later a *civitas* capital; and the religious sites of Champlieu (Huysecom 1982) and Vendeuil Caply (Delestrée 1985) in western Belgic Gaul.

At Besançon, the first Roman coins occur in the early Augustan period and increase gradually thereafter, only becoming the majority in the Tiberian period or later (Table 1). At Roanne, the pattern is similar: Roman issues are found in pre-conquest layers, but levels are low until c. AD 15 – 30, when there is a marked rise. However, even we make allowance for an increasing proportion of the Iron Age coins in the later contexts being residual, the impression from both sites is that the transition to exclusively Roman coin use was not completed before the Flavian period at the earliest, whereas at sites in the military zone like Hofheim, this seems to have happened by the Claudian period (Wigg 1999).

At the religious sanctuaries of Champlieu and Vendeuil-Caply, Roman issues are completely absent from deposits pre-dating the very end of the first century BC (Table 1). A similar pattern is evident at the Martberg in the territory of the Treveri, where Roman coins first appear in a layer which was sealed no earlier than c. 10 BC (Wigg 2000), and at other western Belgic sanctuaries like Gournay-sur-Aronde (Brunaux 1987) and Fesques (Mantel 1997).[27] Equally, the main increase in the deposition of Roman coins at Champlieu and Vendeuil-Caply does not occur before the Tiberian period at the earliest, recalling the pattern at Besançon and Roanne.[28]

The frequency of Roman coins in later first century AD contexts at Champlieu and Vendeuil Caply is decidedly lower than at the two civil settlements. The same is true of Bois-L'Abbé, where a mere 9.6% of the coins recovered within the *cella* of the main temple are Roman, although monetary offerings continued at least until Claudius's reign (Delestrée 1996). Although residuality is undoubtedly a factor at these religious sites, another possibility is that this pattern may reflect a reluctance by the dedicators to use Roman coins as offerings even when these became more readily available. Some support for this view comes from the work of Wigg (2000), who noted that the ratio of *quinarii* to *denarii* is higher on civilian sites than at forts, and highest of all at temples like the Martberg or Möhn. This could well indicate a conservative attitude on the part of the civilian population – and especially the religious authorities – who preferred smaller coins that were closer to native monetary traditions.

A different view is put forward by Crawford (1985, 275), who contends that coin use in the interior of Gaul was already fundamentally Roman by the Augustan period, with actual high-value Roman coins circulating alongside the native bronze issues, attributing a lack of Roman coins in hoards – which would fill out the picture given by site finds – to the *pax Augusta*.[29] However, the loss pattern for single gold coins is in fact similar to that for site finds. *Aurei* of Tiberius outnumber those of Augustus and the late Republic, whilst the numbers for Nero and the Flavians are higher still (Callu and Loriot 1990).[30] The coins themselves must have been deposited somewhat later than their date of issue. Interestingly, the density of first century AD *aurei* in Belgic Gaul is twice that for Celtic Gaul, partly no doubt because the former includes the military zone, but also perhaps because gold had ceased to be the preferred metal for coinage in most of Celtic Gaul before the conquest took place.[31]

	Iron Age	Roman	% Roman
Pommiers			
All	2027	29	1.4
Titelberg			
LT D2	230	11	5
c. 25 – 5 BC	93	106	53
Oberaden			
All	9	319	97
Besançon			
LT D1	27	-	-
LT D2	28	-	-
c. 30 – 1 BC	39	7	15
c. AD 1 – 20	26	17	40
c. AD 20 – 65	11	19	63
c. AD 65 – 120	6	26	81
Roanne			
LT D1	73	-	-
LT D2	59	8	12
c. 10 BC – AD 15	31	9	23
c. AD 15 – 30	5	11	69
c. AD 30 – 70	1	10	91
Champlieu			
LT D2	13	-	-
c. 10 BC – AD 30	14	7	33
c. AD 30 – 120	8	15	65
Vendeuil-Caply			
LT D2	21	-	-
LT D2 to c. AD 15	48	3	6
c. AD 50 – 75	16	16	50

Table 1. Selected coin groups from central and northern Gaul (sources as text).

Some additional evidence comes from religious sites, which have the highest loss rate for native gold and silver after the conquest. Accepting that temple offerings may well be biased against Roman coinage, it is nevertheless noteworthy that only two of 14 precious metal hoards of Augustan or earlier date found at Bois-L'Abbé contained Roman silver: one comprising 18 republican *denarii*,[32] the other a mixed hoard which belongs to a sub-group of three which Delestrée (1996, 38-39) interprets as being of military origin.[33] This compares to three hoards with Massaliote obols. And at the other temples mentioned above, only three of the 15 Roman coins lost prior to c. AD 15 – 30 were silver (20%), and none gold.[34]

Far from circulating freely among the civilian population, the penetration of Roman coinage into the interior of Gaul appears to be minimal prior to Tiberius's reign, leaving us to consider how the native Belgic coinages were used in the intervening period. One way to do this is to examine the types of sites on which they are found (Haselgrove 2005). Here I shall present this information for eight post-conquest series, including at least one from each of the main coin-using areas within Belgic Gaul.[35] The types are the Viricius series from the coastal region (Scheers 109); the Cricirv and Remo/Remo bronzes from southern Belgic Gaul (Scheers 27, 146); the Arda bronzes of the Treveri (Scheers 30a); the 'rameau' bronzes of the Nervii (Scheers 190, I-II); the triquetrum coinage of the Dutch river delta; and the Germanvs Indvtilli L and Avavcia types (Scheers 216-217). For ease of reference, the proportions of different types of site shown in Figures 1 and 2 are normalised as percentages.[36]

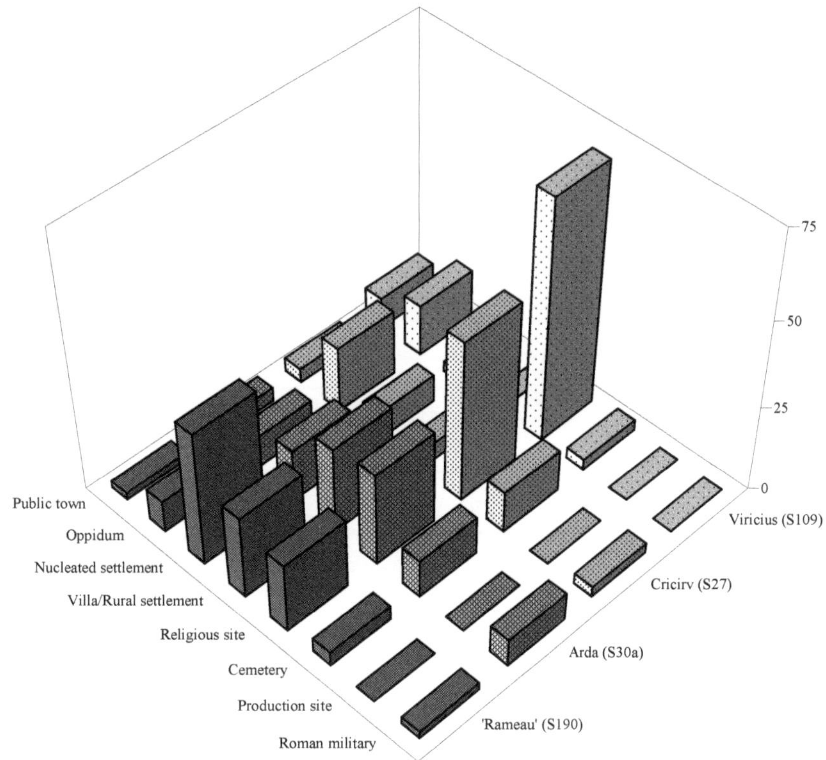

Figure 1. The incidence of selected Belgic coinages on different types of archaeological sites. The figures are percentages (source: Haselgrove 2005).

In order to interpret the figures, three preliminary points must be made. First, the patterns are influenced by the character of the settlement pattern in different parts of Belgic Gaul, which varies from one area to another, especially between south and north (Haselgrove 1996; Roymans 1996). Inevitably, therefore, coin types that travelled further, like Scheers 216, will have more generalised site associations. Second, the figures take no account of the number of coins deposited at a particular site. At some temples and *oppida*, finds of a single coin type can run into hundreds, but here such occurrences are given equal weight to a single find from another site. Third, since the figures partly derive their meaning from comparisons with earlier Belgic series, we must not overlook the degree to which settlement patterns were themselves disrupted by the conquest (Haselgrove 1996).

All eight series display a strong association with religious sites, lending support to the view that after the conquest, coin offerings at temples and sanctuaries took over ritual functions previously fulfilled by other objects such as weaponry. Only Scheers 190 does not occur at more religious sites than any other site type, almost certainly a function of the generally late date of construction of formal temples in northern Belgic Gaul. The increased intensity of offerings on religious sites compared to the pre-conquest period is particularly striking in western and southern Belgic Gaul and, in the case of the former, seems to underline the central role of such sites in the political integration of the peoples who collectively called themselves Belgae (Caesar, *BG* V, 12; 24). As Delestrée (1996) suggests, some western Belgic coinages were almost certainly minted at religious sites, perhaps even specifically for use as offerings.

A marked increase in finds from *oppida* and commensurate decline in coins from rural settlements compared to the pre-conquest period is apparent in southern and, to a lesser extent, western Belgic Gaul. This presumably reflects the concentration of population – and thus of activities in which coinage was used – at fortified sites during the first century BC. Initially, the military crises of the period were the driving factor in this shift, but later it could reflect a greater willingness on the part of the Remi and their clients to espouse an urban lifestyle after the conquest. It was not until the late first century BC, that rural site numbers start to rise again in southern Belgic Gaul (Haselgrove 1996). In contrast, the Treveri seem to have reverted to an essentially rurally-based settlement pattern after the crisis had passed, shown by the numerous finds of Arda bronzes on villas and other rural sites.[37] Placing of coin offerings in graves also increased significantly among the pro-Roman peoples of southern and eastern Belgic Gaul, which may reflect the influence of Roman beliefs and practices.

Further north, the 'rameau' bronzes are closely associated with the nucleated settlements which started to develop in the later first century BC in the zone behind the Rhine frontier – a trend which is also apparent for the Arda types. The overall number of findspots in Nervian territory also fell drastically compared to the pre-conquest period, for which there are several possible explanations: a fall in population levels as a result of the devastating defeat inflicted by Caesar in 57 BC (*BG* II, 28); a reduction in the velocity of coin circulation after the conquest (Pion 2000); or the movement of people into larger centres in the wake of the crisis, or as a consequence of economic growth induced by the need to supply the army in the Augustan period. The proportion of finds from rural settlements in Nervian territory – although lower than before – is still higher than in many areas, reflecting the essentially decentralised character of the northern Belgic peoples.

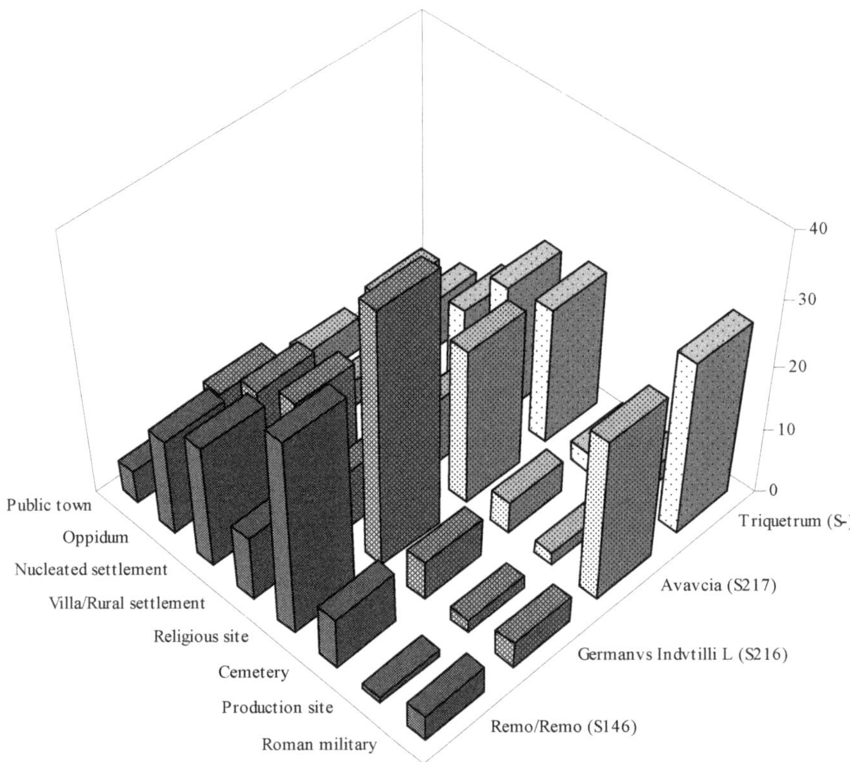

Figure 2. The incidence of selected Belgic and Gallo-Roman coinages on different types of archaeological sites. The figures are percentages (source: Haselgrove 2005).

The late Germanvs Indvtilli L series (Scheers 216) occurs on a wider range of sites than any of the earlier types, although religious sites are still the commonest single category. There is a strong emphasis on *civitas* capitals, both existing *oppida* and new foundations, with secondary centres not far behind, a pattern which might support the idea that Scheers 216 enjoyed some degree of official recognition. Its similarity to Augustan *quadrantes* minted at Lyons – down to the choice of brass and not bronze – certainly implies that they were used as an equivalent, whether or not this was the issuers' intention.[38] The low proportion of rural finds is as we would expect if transactions involving coinage were mainly concentrated at larger settlements.

Like other series minted in the interior of Belgic Gaul, Scheers 216 is found on many Augustan forts in Germany, but never in quantity.[39] This distinguishes it from the Avavcia and triquetrum coins, which are strongly associated with military sites on both banks of the Rhine (Figure 2). At some sites, finds of Scheers 217 run into hundreds, although the triquetrum coins usually occur in lower numbers (Wigg 1996). Despite the large amount of official bronze reaching the military zone, there was clearly a shortage of small denominations, as shown by the frequent practice of halving larger bronzes. It is also possible that Gaulish camp followers and traders preferred the smaller coins to which they were accustomed at home. Availability was probably therefore the main factor in the use of the Avavcia and triquetrum coins at the forts.[40] Many of the copies of official bronzes produced in northern Gaul during the Claudian period were similarly light weight pieces which were evidently intended to fulfil a need for coins smaller than the *as* (Wigg 1999).

The more widespread series also occur occasionally at

specialised manufacturing sites (Figure 2), reflecting the growth in industrial production in the early Roman period, partly linked to the army. Outside the military zone, there is however a contrast between the findspots of the Avavcia and the triquetrum coins, which reflects the social and cultural differences between the peoples of the Rhine delta area and those living in the Romanized territories further west. The Avavcia coins have a similar ratio of rural settlement findspots to nucleated settlements to the various Nervian bronze types, and a similar proportion of religious site finds, whereas the ratio is reversed for the triquetrum types, reflecting the decentralised character of the peoples inhabiting the river delta (Roymans 2001).[41]

Across Belgic Gaul, the evidence points to a significant intensification of coin use after the conquest, as well as increased offerings on religious sites. Contrary to this view, Pion (2000) has argued that velocity of coin circulation actually fell in the later first century BC. While my own feeling is that Pion relies too much on the small area excavated at Pommiers in 1987-88, it is certainly true that most post-conquest bronzes do not travel as far as the earlier potin series. A reduction in circulation velocity might also help explain the lack of later first century BC finds at rural sites in some areas, although I suspect that this is a consequence firstly of more transactions in which coins were employed being focused at the major sites, and secondly of a change in the nature of votive offerings, from private dedications on settlements to public offerings at formal cult places.

Was there coin production in Britain after the conquest?
In the circumstances that prevailed in Belgic Gaul in the mid-first century BC, it would have been surprising if indigenous minting had not continued. It is thus something of a paradox that in Britain, where a number of client rulers are known to have maintained their autonomy for at least a generation (Millett 1990), it is difficult to identify any indigenous coinages minted after AD 43. The one generally-agreed exception is a light silver type from East Anglia (BM 4577-4580), which bears a Julio-Claudian head,[42] and comes at the very end of the regional sequence, although its attribution to Prasutagus, the mid-first century AD ruler of the Iceni – which seemed to provide clinching evidence – is no longer secure (Williams 2000).[43]

While the British client rulers might simply have had no reason or desire to issue coins, it is worth exploring whether the supposed lack of post-conquest minting in southern Britain is indeed genuine. Even with the supposedly well dated coinages of the eastern and southern kingdoms, there are other possibilities we should consider. First, there is the long held assumption that the flight of British rulers like Verica and Adminius to the Roman court provides a *terminus ante quem* for their coinage (e.g. Haselgrove 1987, 92). It is however conceivable that they were reinstated after AD 43 and resumed minting, if only on a modest scale. Verica, for example, copies various late issues of Tiberius and Gaius,[44] and whilst we know that he was succeeded by [T]ogidubnus, we do not know when. Verica's later issues are well represented in post-conquest deposits such as Waltham St Lawrence and Wanborough (Haselgrove 1987; Cheeseman 1994). Whilst the coins of Epaticcus – who is thought to be responsible for expelling Verica – and Cara[tacus] are assumed to be the latest British issues in these deposits, this need not necessarily follow.[45]

Cunobelinus was dead by AD 43, but we cannot exclude the possibility that some of his issues are posthumous and were minted after the invasion. This might help explain the rarity of his later issues in late Iron Age – as opposed to early Roman – deposits (Haselgrove 1987). Equally, whilst some of Cunobelinus's sons opposed the Roman invasion, other sons or relatives could have sided with Rome and profited afterwards by being recognised as client rulers of parts of his kingdom. Perhaps the best candidate is Solidv, one of whose issues apparently copies a coin of Gaius,[46] and who seems to have succeeded Adminius in Kent (Rudd 2002). Another candidate is Agr,[47] whose coinage in Cunobelinus's tradition is found mainly in southern East Anglia. It has been suggested (de Jersey 2002) that this individual could be another offspring of Cunobelinus, with the Roman name Agrippa (or Agrippina), who perhaps succeeded to part of his territory north of the Thames.

Outside the eastern and southern kingdoms, the idea that coin production ceased immediately after the Roman invasion is more an article of faith than grounded in solid fact. There are a number of possible examples of post-conquest minting, of which I will discuss two here. The first comes from the client kingdom of the Iceni, where there are several large, superficially similar, silver hoards. Rather than all of these hoards dating to the Boudiccan revolt, as was long assumed, these can be placed in a sequence, corroborated by the Roman coins present in many of them (Creighton 1994) implying that they span the whole period from c. AD 43 – 60,[48] and incidentally demonstrating increased penetration of Roman coinage into the region at this time. The Esvprasto coins (BM 4577-4580) only occur in one of the two latest hoards – confirming their very late dating – whilst the proportion of later Icenian types increases through time at the expense of earlier ones, suggesting that at least some of the series inscribed Ecen, Ed, Ece, Saenv, Aesv and Aliff Scavo/Ale Sca (BM 4033-4572, 4576) were not minted until after the conquest, or at least, were still being put into circulation then.[49]

The second example comes from the east Midlands. May (1992, 103-105) has observed that some uncommon gold and silver types attributed to the Corieltauvi, which bear the legend Volisios paired with other names,[50] seem to concentrate on the banks of the Humber and in the valleys of west Yorkshire, outside the Corieltauvian heartland, occurring only infrequently in the core territory. The Volisios coins form the dominant Iron Age constituent of two mixed hoards from Lightcliffe and Honley, the former deposited no earlier than the reign of Caius, the latter after AD 69.[51] A third hoard recently found at Silsden (Edwards and Dennis, this volume) contained a single Volisios coin, alongside six Corieltauvian staters of Esvprasv and twenty staters of Cunobelinus and Epaticcus, but with no Roman coinage. The late date, the rarity of at least two of the three Volisios series, and their focus on an area beyond Corieltauvian core territory and outside the zone under Roman military control until c. AD 71 – 72 , all hint strongly at the possibility of post-conquest minting.[52]

Without going into all possible examples,[53] it thus seems that we need to reconsider the question of post-conquest minting in Britain. In contrast to Belgic Gaul, this does not seem to be accompanied by major changes in the character of the coinage. There is no evidence of late bronze coinages among peoples who only had silver or gold, while the Humber basin is the only area with a late coinage without a previous history of minting. Apart from the Agr quarter-staters and the Volisios staters, the main candidates as post-conquest issues are all silver – unless of course, we include the copying of Claudian bronzes, which certainly took place in Britain until the mid-Neronian period. Most of this appears to have been in a military context, but some copies may be of civilian origin (Kenyon 1987; Wigg 1996).

Roman impact on coin circulation in Britain

We can be confident that the impact of the Roman monetary system on most of southern Britain was much more rapid and immediate than it was in Belgic Gaul. For a start, large quantities of Roman coinage were brought in at the outset by the army, as well as by officials and traders. Second, the swiftly-evolving military dispositions of the Claudian-Neronian period (Millett 1990) ensured rapid distribution of Roman coinage within the new province, although there was presumably some imbalance between the client states and other peoples. Finally, in the south-east at least, the Britons who used coinage were already ideologically habituated to Roman-style imagery, and some actual Roman coins must have reached Britain before AD 43.[54]

The rapid influx of Roman coinage into Britain from AD 43 is apparent both from the hoard record and from site finds. New finds of hoards containing Roman coinage up to the Flavian period have not altered the basic pattern noted by Kent (1973), whereby mixed hoards are the norm in the client kingdoms of southern England and East Anglia, as well as in the outlying districts to the west and north, whereas in the intervening regions, hoards with Roman coins only are the rule.[55] From his analysis of the hoard data, Creighton (1992) identified a peak in the number of *denarii* in circulation in Britain in the mid first century AD, followed by a period of relative scarcity until the late first century AD, when numbers increase again. This Claudian peak in supply might, he suggests, be a product of two factors: British silver having been exchanged for Roman coins; and the loans which Claudius made to the British elite (Dio, *Histories*, 62.2.1), assuming that these were made in cash.

Two Roman hoards dating to Domitian's reign recently found at Stillington in eastern England provide a nice example of the rapid integration of Roman coinage into local customs on the part of the British elite (Denison 1999). The two hoards, one of 123 *aurei*, the other of seven *denarii*, were buried close to a spring and a prehistoric long barrow, at what therefore seems to have been a native cult site, indicating a continuity of the practice of depositing gold coinage at sacred sites, which in southern Britain can be traced back to at least to the early first century BC (Haselgrove 2005).[56]

At military sites and official foundations and other important settlements like London, which was situated on the boundary between several different peoples (Millett 1990), Roman coinage predominated from the start. As Table 2 shows, hardly any British coinage was deposited within the colony established at Colchester (*Camulodunon*), when the legionary fortress was vacated, even though this lay within an important British *oppidum* (e.g. Crummy 1987), while at nearby Sheepen, which was heavily involved in commerce with the army, there was a very rapid increase in Roman coin after AD 43. Interestingly, there is some suggestion of spatial separation between Iron Age and Roman coin losses within the Sheepen complex (Haselgrove 1987). On the other hand, the scarcity of cut larger Roman denominations at Sheepen compared to the Claudian fort of Hofheim in Germany is presumably explained by the availability of British bronze coins to act as divisions. At the military supply base and entry port of Richborough in east Kent, the proportion of Roman coinage is even higher than at the Colchester *colonia*.[57]

Within the early town at St Albans (*Verlamion*), also a pre-Roman royal site, the incidence of British coin loss in the early phases is a little higher than at Colchester.[58] Reece (1985, 15-17) has noted that the supply of Roman coinage to St Albans lags behind other British sites, not catching up until the Flavian period. It is likely that the town lay within territory initially placed under a pro-Roman client ruler (cf. Creighton 2000), which might help explain this shortfall. British coin loss is also noticeably higher in the suburban areas than in the town centre (Haselgrove 1987, 176), perhaps suggesting a preference for Roman coinage in the latter area, where incoming colonists and traders, and members of the pro-Roman establishment, presumably resided.

As on the other side of the Channel, there was a sharp rise in offerings on religious sites after the conquest. Most of the coins were British, and the same conservative attitude to Roman coins seems to have existed as in Belgic Gaul (Table 2). At Harlow, the later types of Cunobelinus are often in mint condition, perhaps indicating that they were used as offerings because they were superfluous in their original role. Hayling Island has a similar phase of intensified offerings in the decades leading up to the Flavian rebuilding of the temple, but although the dynasty ruling the southern kingdom had close links to the continent, these do not seem to have led to any more Roman coinage being deposited there after the conquest than at Harlow. Moreover, the *denarii* from Hayling Island were all plated (Briggs *et al.* 1992), as were many British issues, indicating that a similar process of selection favouring valueless coinage as offerings may have been operating there.[59] At Fishbourne, the Roman palace of the British client ruler [T]ogidubnus, coin use seems to have been Roman from the start, with hardly any British coins having been found in the excavations.

At Canterbury and Baldock, one a civitas capital, the other a moderately successful small town, the transition to Roman coinage appears to be slower (Table 2), reminiscent of the interior of Gaul. The nature of the excavated areas may be a contributory factor, as may the size of the coin samples. The Marlowe site at Canterbury shows a low density of occupation and a relatively slow rate of development (Blockley *et al.* 1995), although the absence of a Roman street grid until the Flavian period is not particularly unusual in Romano-British towns. The area, which includes a bath complex, is situated next to a large religious and ceremonial precinct, of which it may conceivably have formed a part. If so, we may again be seeing the influence of religious conservatism on the choice of coins for offerings. In the Iron Age, Baldock was an important ritual and mortuary centre associated with the source of the river Ivel, which may similarly have affected the character of the coin deposits there (Curteis 2005).

	Iron Age	Roman	% Roman
Colchester – Colonia			
All pre-Nero	6	110	95
Colchester – Sheepen			
LIA	16	-	-
c. AD 43 – 60	74	83	53
c. AD 61 – 65	13	21	62
Richborough			
All pre-Nero	21	588	97
St Albans			
All pre-Nero	14	112	89
Harlow			
LIA	10	-	-
LIA to c. AD 70	49	8	14
c. AD 70 – 100	19	4	17
c. AD 100 – 200	31	16	34
Hayling Island			
LIA to c. AD 70	46	8	15
c. AD 70 – 200	41	37	47
Fishbourne			
All pre-Nero	-	76	100
Baldock			
LIA	4	-	-
c. AD 43 – 70	8	4	33
c. AD 70 – 120	4	1	20
Canterbury – Marlowe			
LIA to c. AD 70	13	2	13
c. AD 70 – 125	20	7	26

Table 2. Selected coin groups from southern Britain (sources as text).

Over south-east England as a whole, the evidence suggests that the deposition of Iron Age coinage rose sharply immediately after the conquest, only to fall back again rapidly in the Flavian period. Table 3 shows the incidence of Iron Age coin finds from successive horizons, expressed in terms of an annual loss rate. By the second century AD, the quantity of Iron Age coinage being lost afresh was clearly negligible, once account is taken of residuality. Indeed, if we remove from the calculation the finds from Harlow and Hayling Island – where many of the coins associated with the stone temples are clearly residual from earlier activity – the annual loss rate for the second century AD is a mere 0.5 coins per year.

Looking at the types of site with finds, the most obvious feature is the high proportion of nucleated settlements. As in Belgic Gaul, this reflects a growth of secondary centres at nodal points along the new road network, especially in areas where settlement was relatively decentralised prior to the conquest. In such areas, there was a net movement of people into such centres, or a shift in the locus of transactions using coinage to these sites. Many of the new settlements were involved in industrial production, whether for the military or for the civilian market. It is noticeable however that coin use at the equivalent sites in the southern kingdom seems to have been Roman from the start (Haselgrove 1987, 208). Along with the evidence from Fishbourne, this might suggest an early switch to the use of Roman coinage for everyday transactions in this client kingdom, although local precious metal issues evidently continued to function as an acceptable medium for storing wealth until the Flavian period at least, as the mixed hoards from the region attest.

Many Roman military sites also yield Iron Age coins, if only in small quantities (Figure 3). As in Belgic Gaul, indigenous bronze coinage was used wherever it existed, helping to compensate for the shortage of official issues, especially small denominations. There is also an increase in cemetery finds, which were previously very rare in Britain. The incidence of coins from religious sites founded after the conquest is however relatively low, when compared to existing sites like Harlow or Hayling Island. Interestingly, there are more finds of gold (mostly plated) and silver types from public towns than from villas, especially south of the Thames, whereas for bronze, the pattern is the opposite. The incidence of genuine gold coins is slightly greater at cemeteries, temples and villas, although not by very much.

Analysis by Creighton (1992) indicates that the highest proportion of early Roman silver coinage in site assemblages, excluding forts, occurs in regions where there was no bronze coinage before the conquest; the opposite trend is found in areas which had base metal coinage. This perhaps implies a cultural resistance to the adoption of bronze in the areas which previous only had precious metal coinage, reminiscent of the preference for *quinarii* in Belgic Gaul. It also suggests a higher degree of post-conquest monetarization of areas which were already habituated to low-value coinage. This pattern can be traced through to Hadrian, after which the distinction disappears.

Period	*No. of stratified coins*	*Loss rate (coins/year)*
c. 50-1 BC	13	0.3
c. AD 1-40	69	1.7
c. AD 40-70	236	7.9
c. AD 70-100	67	2.2
c. AD 100-200	126	1.3

Table 3. Relative loss rates of British coinage in south-east England through time (source: Haselgrove 1987).

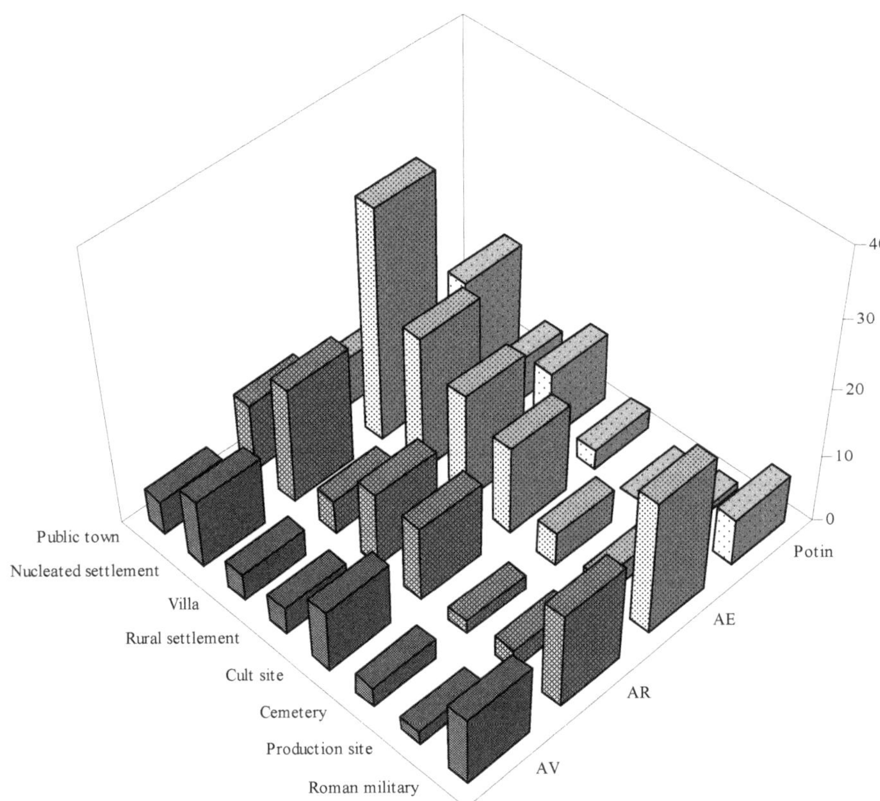

Figure 3. The frequency of types of Romano-British sites with Iron Age gold, silver, bronze or potin coin finds (source: Haselgrove 1987).

There is little evidence for penetration of Roman coinage into previously non coin-using areas of Britain until after they too had been brought under military control. Large-scale excavations at Stanwick in northern England, very probably the capital of the pro-Roman client ruler of the Brigantes, yielded only two early Roman coins and one Corieltauvian issue (Haselgrove forthcoming) to set beside an unparalleled assemblage of imported glass and pottery, which included vessel types rarely found outside the Mediterranean.[60] The overall distribution of Claudian bronzes in northern England is centred on military sites of Flavian date, although there is a thin scatter of coins from sites without known military associations. Most of the latter are, however, single finds, recalling the pattern in Wales and south-west England, and suggesting gradual introduction of coinage, via the military (Kenyon forthcoming). Moreover, up until the Antonine period, the proportion of Roman silver from civilian settlements in the zone with no previous indigenous coinage is higher than in lowland Britain (Creighton 1992), suggesting that they were primarily valued as bullion.

In sum, although the Roman invasion initially led to an intensification of indigenous coin use, British coinage started to disappear from circulation during the Flavian period, as Roman coinage increased in volume. Equally, although we have probably underestimated the amount of post-conquest minting, this was never on a large scale and was probably relatively short-lived. This need occasion no surprise. In Roman terms, south-east England at least was part of the Roman world from 54 BC, and many of its client rulers under Augustus and Tiberius must have been personally familiar with Roman coinage. In the absence of regular supplies of Roman coinage, they struck imitative issues, often drawing on classical imagery, but generally following local traditions with regard to weight and metal.[61] After AD 43, however, the rapid influx of Roman coinage into the province and the loans made to members of the elite rapidly rendered minting redundant. In the peripheral areas, the process was possibly further speeded up by the Boudiccan revolt, after which the Roman authorities decided upon a policy of annexing all former client territories as soon as the opportunity arose.

Conclusion

Both in northern Gaul and in Britain, it is clear that, initially at least, the Roman authorities adopted a 'laissez faire' attitude to indigenous coinages. Even with precious metals which the state had a strong interest in acquiring, it seems that apart from booty taken at the time of the invasion – no doubt often in considerable quantities – the Roman authorities were normally content to allow taxation to exert its more gradual effect on conquered peoples and – after their eventual annexation – client states as well. In both provinces, native coin use and deposition seems have intensified after the conquest, while in Belgic Gaul large-scale minting of bronze coinage continued for well over a generation and Roman coinage did not have a significant impact outside the military zone until the Tiberian period. The one area of more rapid change was in the sphere of coin iconography, reflecting the readiness of the Belgic elites to adapt ideologically to Roman rule (Wigg 1999; Creighton 2000).

In Britain, the transition to Roman coin use was more rapid due both to the immediate reality of the military occupation and the longer history of exposure to Roman goods and ideas prior to AD 43. Even so, there is evidence of similar conservative attitudes to Roman coinage on the part both of coin users and of the religious authorities, while at some sites, British and Roman coin use seems to have remained largely mutually exclusive in the decades following the conquest. By the Flavian period, however, the rate of indigenous coin loss was falling significantly and by the end of the century, its demise was complete on both sides of the Channel.

At a methodological level, this paper has identified the need for further work in two main areas. First, there needs to be further analysis of stratified coin sequences, as only this can provide reliable comparative data on the incidence of indigenous and Roman issues deposited in successive periods and at different types of site. Unfortunately, the structure of most excavation reports inhibits analysis of monetary transition, with Iron Age and Roman coins generally being published separately, with little regard to their stratigraphic context.

Second, we need to consider religious and symbolic attitudes to coinage and to the metals from which it was minted, as these could well explain why peoples from similar cultural or economic backgrounds reacted quite differently to Roman coinage and concepts of coin use. Moralising though he was, Tacitus's comment on the lack of interest of the Germans in possessing gold and silver, and the preference of frontier peoples for familiar types and for silver coins over gold (*Germania* 5) is sufficiently close in time and space to Gaul or Britain to show that we ignore such matters at our peril.

There is a growing comparative literature on how traditional societies have reacted to the introduction of universal money (e.g. Parry and Bloch 1989). This might provide valuable insights for understanding Roman monetary impact on Iron Age societies, both those who already possessed coinages of their own, and those who had apparently rejected the concept. The time has come for us to build some of these anthropological ideas into our approach and seek to establish which, if any, of them might be relevant in an archaeological context, rather than relying on the limited classical texts – underpinned by our own ethnocentric concepts of monetary economy – for constructing our narratives, as we have tended to do in the past.

Notes

[1] This paper is a revised version of one first delivered at the 2nd Trier Symposium on Ancient Economic History "Die Entstehung eines europäischen Wirtschaftraumes".

[2] An exception being the Kentish flat linear potin series, which occurs frequently in settlement deposits (Haselgrove 1988); see also Haselgrove this volume.

[3] Although payments to the army were the principal mechanism by which Roman coinage entered circulation (Crawford 1985; Wigg 1997), we are too ready to assume that paying for warrior services and military emergencies were the main occasions for striking Iron Age gold coinage (e.g. Nash 1987), when we actually know very little about any of its functions. Whilst certain issues do show signs of having been produced at great speed (e.g. Allen 1972; Sills 2000b), military necessity is not the only reason for this to have occurred.

[4] From the reign of Augustus, auxiliaries were paid in Roman coinage (Wolters 1988). See also note 3.

[5] Further revolts by Belgic peoples were suppressed in 46 BC and 30 – 29 BC (e.g. Wightman 1985).

[6] The main exception is along the Rhine, where a number of peoples employed silver coinages on the light Gaulish quinarius standard.

[7] Certain parts of southern Britain, such as Wiltshire, had apparently ceased minting coinage by the time of the Roman conquest, a phenomenon we also find in territories along the upper Rhine and in southern Germany.

[8] The inception of La Tène D2b is now generally set around 60/55 BC. The earliest Gallo-Roman assemblages appear in the decade beginning c. 30 BC (Haselgrove 1999, 116-118).

[9] The 'eye' staters are now thought to have been issued by both the Remi (Classes I-III) and the Treveri (Classes IV-VI) (Delestrée 1996; Pion 1996).

[10] The discovery of a Pottina stater on the surface at Camp C at Alésia (Fischer 1994) suggests that this type was in existence by 52 BC, whilst the absence of Vocarant and Lvcotios coins from the oppidum at Saint Thomas implies that these types are no earlier than the 50s BC (Haselgrove 1999, 137 and note 119). A starting date in the Gallic War thus seems more than likely, whilst the number of dies employed would allow all three series to be of considerable duration.

[11] The obverse of Arda's earliest silver type (Silver-I) is hubbed from a quinarius of Juba I, dated 48 – 46 BC (Loscheider 1998, 173-5), while one of his bronzes (Scheers 30a-II) takes its obverse from the denarius of Terentius Varro (Crawford 1974, 447/1a, dated c. 49 BC).

[12] As Creighton (2000) notes, the use of conservative designs for gold as opposed to more Romanized silver and bronze types, need not indicate an earlier date: a similar phenomenon recurs in the coinage of British rulers like Tincomaros or Tasciovanus. Such conservatism may be linked to the ideological significance and social functions of gold coinage as opposed to coinage in other metals.

[13] For the relative dating of the Hirtius and Arda types, see Metzler (1995).

[14] The silver is struck on the reduced Gaulish quinarius standard (Loscheider 1998, 203-210), established in the Moselle region since the early first century BC (Wigg and Riederer 1998).

[15] BG IV, 21 etc. An example of Scheers 45 was apparently found at Alésia, although it is not listed in the original publication (Fischer 1994; and pers. comm.).

[16] Creighton (2000) suggests that after Commios came to terms with Mark Antony in 51 BC (BG VIII, 23), he was sent to southern Britain, where he became ruler of the British Atrebates. This would explain why the name occurs on later, insular varieties of the southern Belgic triple-tailed horse series (Scheers 26, British QA). Alternatively, the Commios of the British staters may be a son (Hobbs 1996, 17).

[17] Although the extensive quinarius series inscribed Atevla/Vlatos (Scheers 41) is usually attributed to Belgic Gaul, its origin is more likely to be in east central France, or possibly west of the Seine, where the related Senodon/Caledu types (Scheers 42) seem to cluster (Haselgrove 2005). Both types occur frequently in the mixed Gaulish and Roman silver hoards deposited in the 40s or early 30s BC across a broad swathe of central and north-western Gaul.

[18] The Remo/Remo type is usually thought to have commenced during the Gallic war. Two coins of this type are recorded from the Alésia ditches, but if so they are not now among the coins preserved in Paris (Fischer 1994). De Saulcy's notes only mention an unstratified example from Mont Réa. The type is however absent from Saint Thomas, where occupation ceased at the La Tène D2a-D2b transition (cf. Delestrée 1996, 133-134), while at the Titelberg, almost twice as many examples came from the early Roman levels than from the La Tène D2b deposits, suggesting that the type may in fact not have come into existence until the post-war period.

[19] Colbert de Beaulieu (1962) suggests that Varticeo is the Nervian leader, Vertico, who defected to the Romans in 54 BC (Caesar, BG V, 45). Van Heesch (1999) suggests that all three Nervian types are in fact of Augustan date, owing to the lack of stratified examples from earlier contexts. In my view, the typological links of the Viros and Vercio coins with the Treveran types and the continuity of the rameau coins with the earlier potin issues in the same region (Scheers 190-II, IV) makes a slightly earlier dating more likely.

[20] The legend Veliocassi on the reverse of Scheers 164-IV indicates a link to the people of the same name, confirmed by the distribution.

[21] The small number of finds from Oberaden compared to later military sites like Haltern led Wigg (1996) to date the Avavcia series to the last decade BC. Scheers (1996) suggests however that the inscribed coins are a decade or two earlier, since they closely resemble the Annaroveci quinarii from the same region. This could well be correct, since at the Hunerberg fortress at Nijmegen, occupied in the penultimate decade BC, inscribed Avaucia coins outnumber the uninscribed varieties.

[22] Another possibility – that Roman gold and silver was already a significant factor in circulation in Belgic Gaul in the decades following the conquest – is discussed below.

[23] See note 17.

[24] Roman coins occasionally reached the area before the conquest. Probable examples include a countermarked quinarius of 99 BC (Crawford 331/1) found with early Belgic issues in the pit which underlies Temple III (Fosse A) at Gournay-sur-Aronde (Brunaux 1987). The middle Rhineland Nauheim series (Scheers 56) borrows from a denarius of c. 100 BC (Crawford 327/1).

[25] This excludes the hoard of c. 100 Roman and Gaulish silver found at Pommiers in 1875, which contained at least 5 denarii down to 63 BC, along with central Gaulish types, including 2 Togirix (Haselgrove 1999, 160, n. 231). All the Gaulish types are ones present in the Alésia ditches, making it likely that the hoard was deposited during the Gallic War or very shortly thereafter.

[26] All too often, Iron Age and Roman coins are reported on by different specialists and no attempt is made to integrate

the data, nor is information given about the context of individual coin finds.

[27] At Gournay, a single second Altar series *as* was found in the demolition levels associated with Temple 3, which yielded 10 Iron Age coins; at Fesques, the groups from pits 300 and 318, which terminate in the Augustan period, contained 5.6% and 1.4% of Roman coins respectively.

[28] Four-fifths of the Augustan coins (79%) from Champlieu belong to the final Lyon second Altar series, c. AD 12 – 14. At Vendeuil-Caply, second Altar series or later issues similarly predominate among the stratified Roman bronze.

[29] As Wigg (1999) points out, hoards might not in any case be a good indicator of how far Roman coinage had penetrated into an indigenous cultural milieu, since at this era, they could easily reflect a military presence. Three hoards from the Somme-Pas-de-Calais area all terminating with Roman issues of 32 – 31 BC — from Dury, Fonquevilliers, and Tilly-Capelle — provide a case in point, as they are often linked to the campaign conducted by C. Carrinas, governor of Gaul in 30 – 29 BC, against the Morini and their allies (e.g. Wightman 1985, 45).

[30] The increase in Neronian gold is mostly confined to Belgic Gaul, although not to the military zone, whereas Flavian finds are more evenly distributed. One region of Belgic Gaul that stands out against the general trend is Somme-Pas-de-Calais, which in addition to the three early hoards mentioned above (note 29), has a higher proportion of Augustan aurei than elsewhere.

[31] Continuity of native depositional traditions may also be a factor. The Tilly-Capelle hoard, for example, was deposited in a marsh like many Iron Age hoards in the area.

[32] Delestrée (1996, 40), as yet unpublished. A second unpublished hoard contained 65 denarii and 7 asses down to Claudius.

[33] Hoard 1976-1-244, which contained 4 Roman silver coins down to 39 BC (Crawford 529/4b) and 24 Gaulish silver (Delestrée (1996, 36). It is thought that the hoards, which all come from the same Julio-Claudian horizon, were originally suspended from the roof. None appear to have been assembled later than c. 30 BC, while the earliest might even be pre-conquest.

[34] These figures do not include the Roman coins from the Martberg, which are not yet published in detail. This site is in any case much closer to the military zone and may have had more direct access to Roman coin supplies. At Bois-L'Abbé, 20 of the Roman coins down to Claudius found singly in the *cella* area were of silver (40%).

[35] The data used here were collected as part of a wider study of coin circulation on archaeological sites in Belgic Gaul (Haselgrove 2005).

[36] I have not included information for every minor category of site: Scheers 27 and 146, for example, occur sporadically in Merovingian graves. The total for religious sites includes small temples and wet cult places, as well as larger sanctuary complexes.

[37] The percentage of the later Arda coins from fortified sites is significantly lower than for the slightly earlier Hirtius types (Haselgrove 2005).

[38] The weight (2.75 – 3.0g) is slightly lighter than the apparent prototype (RIC I^2 Augustus 227-8), but identical to many Belgic bronzes, implying that the issuers adopted an indigenous standard. As David Wigg (pers. comm.) has pointed out, the prototype is itself something of an oddity – the *quadrans* was normally a copper coin – and may itself have been struck at an auxiliary mint, rather than at Lyons.

[39] The higher proportion of Arda bronzes from military sites presumably reflects the proximity of the Treveri to the Rhine frontier.

[40] Van Heesch (1999, 350) has speculated that local authorities may even have recycled the larger bronze denominations to mint smaller units like the Avavcia bronzes (Scheers 217) and light-weight imitations of the Roman types, contributing to the rapid turnover of official coins at this period.

[41] A far higher proportion of the triquetrum coins come from wet cult sites than from formal temples, another indicator of the differences between the two zones.

[42] The most plausible prototypes for the portrait are issues of Nero (Hobbs 1996, 31).

[43] The obverse legend is now read as Sub Esvprasto, rather than Sub Ri Prasto, making the attribution of the type to King Prasutagus more difficult, though not impossible. It also opens up a potential link with the east Midlands coinage inscribed Esvprasv (Williams 2000).

[44] The reverse of BM 1420 is copied from RIC I^2 Tiberius 25-30, AD 36-37; the obverse of BM 1421-1449 apparently derives from RIC I^2 Gaius 58, AD 37-41.

[45] Both hoards contained numerous coins of Epaticcus in relatively unworn condition (Cheeseman 1994, 53), together with a few of Cara[tacus] – apparently the son of Cunobelinus, who opposed the Roman invasion. The condition of Epaticcus's coins might simply indicate that they were rapidly withdrawn from circulation, rather than that they are necessarily later than all the Verica types.

[46] The silver unit BM 1894-1895, which also apparently copies RIC I^2 Gaius 58. Rudd (2002) plausibly interprets the legend Cuno on the reverse of this type as a patronymic. A silver minim type inscribed Sol is also known.

[47] The gold quarter stater BM 1854-1855 and the silver unit BM 1899.

[48] But see also Orton 1997.

[49] The effect might also be due to systematic withdrawal of older, purer silver coins from circulation over a period of time. The apparent introduction of the tribal name on the coinage in the conquest period is reminiscent of the situation

in Gaul a century earlier. For the late Aliff Scavo/Ale Sca series, see de Jersey (2003).

[50] The Volisios legend occurs paired with Dvmnocoveros (BM 3330- 3341), Dvmnovellavnos (BM 3342-3346) and Cartivellavnos (BM 3347-3348; de Jersey 1999). All three series probably originally consisted of sets of gold staters and silver units and half units, but whilst the Dvmnocoveros coins are fairly common, only staters and silver half-units are known for the other two Volisios types.

[51] Roman coins apparently predominated in both hoards, if the surviving coins are a fair guide (May 1992, 103). Creighton (1992, 96) notes that the Roman coins in the hoards have an 'archaic' structure, suggesting that little new coinage was being sent beyond the frontier at this stage.

[52] Research in progress by Geoff Cottam suggests that the Corieltauvian series is divided into at least two parallel streams, with Esvprasv coming at the end of one of them (Sills 2003).

[53] For other potentially late issues, see Haselgrove 1987, 233-266.

[54] As indicated by the copying of certain types. Possible examples of Roman coins in stratified pre-conquest contexts are known at Hayling Island temple (Briggs *et al.* 1992, 39-40) and at Elm's Farm, Humberstone (Charles *et al.* 2000). It is however very unlikely that Roman coinage got into general circulation before the conquest, a point born out by the lack of *quinarii* in Britain compared to Gaul, and many imports may simply have been melted down for recoining.

[55] A number of the hoards ending with issues of Cunobelinus, Verica and their contemporaries were presumably deposited after AD 43, but appear fairly evenly spread throughout the different tribal territories.

[56] Compare also the Tilly-Capelle hoard from Pas-de-Calais, note 31 above.

[57] As the Richborough finds show, the Roman army which arrived in Britain was carrying virtually no bronze coinage older than Gaius with it. A few Gaulish coins found at the site may reflect continued use of native coinage by the Roman army in the Rhineland, but are more probably a function of the quantity of imported coinage in circulation in east Kent at this period (Haselgrove 1987). 75% of the Claudian bronzes are imitations (Wigg 1997).

[58] At St Albans, the ratio of British to early Roman issues is 1:8, compared to 1:18 at Colchester colonia.

[59] Alternatively, precious metal offerings may later have been collected up, perhaps even to finance the building of the stone temple.

[60] Arguably imported coins may have been recycled for metal, but this, too, would imply virtually no monetary impact.

[61] Occasional experiments, such as the introduction of brass units or larger bronze denominations, which may have been inspired by the Roman monetary system, do not seem to have been followed up.

Bibliography

Allen, D. F. 1972: The fibula of Criciru. *Germania* 50, 122-132.

Allen, D. F. 1980: *The coins of the ancient Celts* (Edinburgh, Edinburgh University Press).

Blockley, K., Blockley, M., Frere, S. S. and Stow, S. 1995: *Excavations in the Marlowe car park and surrounding areas* (The Archaeology of Canterbury V) (Canterbury).

Briggs, D., Haselgrove, C., and King, C. E. 1994: The Iron Age and Roman coins from Hayling Island temple. *British Numismatic Journal* 62, 1-62.

Brunaux, J-L. 1987: Les monnaies du site de Gournay-sur-Aronde. In J.-L. Brunaux and K. Gruel (eds), *Monnaies gauloises découvertes en fouilles* (Paris, Dossier de Protohistoire 1), 14-32.

Callu, J-P. and Loriot, X. 1990 (eds): *L'or monnayé II. La dispersion des aurei en Gaule Romaine sous l'empire* (Juan-les-Pins, Cahiers Ernest-Babelon 3).

Charles, B., Parkinson, A. and Foreman, S. 2000: A Bronze Age ditch and Iron Age settlement from Elms Farm, Humberstone, Leicester. *Transactions of the Leicestershire Archaeological and Historical Society* 74, 113-220.

Cheeseman, C. 1994: The coins. In M. G. O'Connell and J. Bird, The Roman temple at Wanborough, excavation 1985-1986. *Surrey Archaeological Collections* 82, 31-92.

Clogg, P. W. and Haselgrove, C. 1995: The composition of Iron Age struck 'bronze' coinage in Eastern England. *Oxford Journal of Archaeology* 14, 41-62.

Colbert de Beaulieu, J-B. 1962: Les monnaies gauloises au nom des chefs mentionnés dans les commentaires de César. *Latomus* 58, 419-446.

Colbert de Beaulieu, J-B. 1966: Umlauf und Chronologie der gallo-keltischen Münzen. *Jahrbuch für Numismatik und Geldgeschichte* 16, 45-62.

Crawford, M. H. 1974: *Roman Republican Coinage* (Cambridge, CUP).

Crawford, M. H. 1985: *Coinage and money under the Roman Republic* (London, Methuen).

Creighton, J. 1992: *The circulation of money in Roman Britain from the first to third century*. Unpublished Ph.D. dissertation, University of Durham.

Creighton, J. 1994: A time of change: the Iron Age to Roman monetary transition in East Anglia. *Oxford Journal of Archaeology* 13, 325-334.

Creighton, J. 2000: *Coins and power in late Iron Age Britain* (Cambridge, CUP).

Creighton, J. forthcoming: Links between the classical imagery in post-Caesarian Belgica and the rest of the Roman world. In J. Metzler and D. Wigg (eds), *Die Kelten und Rom: neue numismatische Forschungen* (Mainz, Studien zu Fundmünzen der Antike 19).

Crummy, N. (ed.) 1987: *Colchester Archaeological Report 4: the coins from the excavations in Colchester 1971-9* (Colchester).

Curteis, M. 2005: Ritual coin deposition on Iron Age settlements in the south Midlands. In C. Haselgrove and D. Wigg-Wolf (eds), *Iron Age coinage and ritual practices* (Mainz, Studien zu Fundmünzen der Antike 20), 207-225.

de Jersey, P. 1999: The stater of Volisios Cartivellaunos. *Spink Numismatic Circular* 107, 208-209.

de Jersey, P. 2002: AGR, and life after Cunobelin. *Chris Rudd List* 64, 5-8.

de Jersey, P. 2003: ALIFF SCAVO and ALE SCA. *Chris Rudd List* 70, 4-6.

Delestrée, L-P. 1985: Les monnaies gauloises du temple des Châtelets, à Vendeuil-Caply (Oise). *Revue Archéologique de Picardie* 1-2, 51-64.

Delestrée, L-P. 1996: *Monnayages et peuples gaulois du Nord-Ouest* (Paris, Errance).

Delestrée, L-P. 1997: Le numéraire gaulois, témoin d'une présence militaire sur le site fortifié de la Chaussée-Tirancourt. *Cahiers Numismatiques* 34, 5-13.

Delestrée, L-P. 1999: La Romanization et la fin du monnayage celtique dans le Nord de la Gaule. *Revue Numismatique* 154, 15-40.

Denison, S. 1999: Roman gold mixed with native religion. *British Archaeology* 48, 5.

Doyen, J. 1987: Les subdivisions "aux segments de cercles" du type BN 8030: état de la question. In *Mélanges offerts au Docteur J.-B. Colbert de Beaulieu* (Paris, Le Léopard d'Or), 315-330.

Fischer, B. 1994: Les monnaies gauloises d'Alésia: enseignements et questions. In M. Reddé and S. von Schnurbein (eds), *Fouilles du siège d'Alésia: rapport triennal 1992-1994* (Dijon), 82-94.

Guichard, V., Pion, P., Malacher, F., and Collis, J. 1993: A propos de la circulation monétaire en Gaule chevelue au IIe et Ier siècles av. J-C. *Revue Archéologique du Centre de la France* 32, 26-55.

Guilhot, J-O. and Guy, C. 1992: *Les fouilles du parking de la Mairie à Besançon* (Besançon).

Haselgrove, C. 1984: Warfare and its aftermath as reflected in the precious metal coinage of Belgic Gaul. *Oxford Journal of Archaeology* 3, 81-105.

Haselgrove, C. 1987: *Iron Age coinage in south-east England: the archaeological context* (Oxford, BAR 174).

Haselgrove, C. 1993: The development of British Iron Age coinage. *Numismatic Chronicle* 153, 31-64.

Haselgrove, C. 1995: Les potins "au personnage courant". *Gallia* 52, 51-59.

Haselgrove, C. 1996: Roman impact on rural settlement and society in southern Picardy. In N. Roymans (ed.), *From the sword to the plough: three studies on the earliest Romanization of Northern Gaul* (Amsterdam Archaeological Studies 1), 127-187.

Haselgrove, C. 1999: The development of Iron Age coinage in Belgic Gaul. *Numismatic Chronicle* 159, 111-168.

Haselgrove, C. 2005: A new approach to analysing the circulation of Iron Age coinage. *Numismatic Chronicle* 165, 129-174.

Haselgrove, C. forthcoming: The Iron Age and Augustan coins. In C. Haselgrove (ed.), *Cartimandua's Capital? Excavations and fieldwork at the Iron Age and early Roman site at Stanwick, North Yorkshire 1984-89* (London, Britannia Monographs).

Hobbs, R. 1996: *British Iron Age coins in the British Museum* (London, BMP).

Huysecom, E. 1982: Contribution à l'étude des monnaies Celtiques II. *Revue Belge de Numismatique* 128, 27-38.

Ilisch, P. 1992: Die Münzen aus den Ausgrabungen im Römerlager Oberaden. In J.-S. Kühlborn (ed.), *Das Römerlager in Oberaden III* (Münster, Bodenaltertümer Westfalens 27), 175-201.

Kent, J. P. C. 1973: Les relations entre le monnayage des Romains et ceux du peuples voisins de l'ouest. *Cercles d'Etudes Numismatiques* 10, 2-11.

Kent, J. P. C. 1978: The origins and development of Celtic gold coinage in Britain. In *Actes du Congrès International d'Archéologie; Rouen, 3, 4, 5 juillet 1975* (Rouen), 313-324.

Kenyon, R. 1987: The Claudian coinage. In N. Crummy (ed.), *Colchester Archaeological Report 4: the coins from the excavations in Colchester 1971-9* (Colchester), 24-41.

Kenyon, R. forthcoming: The Claudian copy. In C. Haselgrove (ed.), *Cartimandua's Capital? Excavations and fieldwork at the Iron Age and early Roman site at Stanwick, North Yorkshire 1984-89* (London, Britannia Monographs).

Lavendhomme, M.-O. and Guichard, V., 1997: *Rodumna (Roanne, Loire), le village gaulois* (Paris, Documents d'Archéologie Française 62).

Loscheider, R. 1998: Untersuchungen zum Spätlatènezeitlichen Münzwesen des Trevererlandes. *Archaeologia Mosellana* 3, 61-226.

May, J. 1992: Iron Age coins in Yorkshire. In M. Mays (ed.), *Celtic coinage: Britain and beyond; the eleventh Oxford Symposium on coinage and monetary history* (Oxford, British Archaeological Reports 222), 93-111.

Mantel, E. 1997: *Le Sanctuaire de Fesques* (Berck-sur-Mer, Nord-Ouest Archéologie 8).

Metzler, J. 1995: *Das Treverische Oppidum auf dem Titelberg* (Luxembourg, Dossiers d'Archéologie du Musée Nationale d'Histoire et d'Art 3).

Millett, M. 1990: *The Romanization of Britain* (Cambridge, CUP).

Nash, D. 1978: Plus ça change ..: currency in central Gaul from Julius Caesar to Nero. In R. A. G. Carson and C. M. Kraay (eds), *Scripta nummaria Romana: essays presented to Humphrey Sutherland* (London, Spink), 12-31.

Orton, C. 1997: Testing significance or testing credulity? *Oxford Journal of Archaeology* 16, 219-225.

Parry, J. and Bloch, M. 1989: Introduction. In J. Parry and M. Bloch (eds), *Money and the Morality of Exchange* (Cambridge, CUP), 1-32.

Pion, P. 1996: *Les habitats Latèniens tardifs de la Vallée de l'Aisne: contribution à la périodisation de la fin du second Âge du Fer en Gaule nord-orientale.* Unpublished Ph.D. dissertation, University of Paris I.

Pion, P. 2000: Charakteristika und Entwicklung des Münzumlaufs in Nord-Ost-Gallien im zweiten und ersten Jahrhundert vor Christus. In B. Kluge and B. Weissner (eds), *Akten. XII. Internationaler Numismatischer Kongress, Berlin 1997*, 418-424.

Reece, R. 1972: A short survey of the Roman coins found on fourteen sites in Britain. *Britannia* 3, 269-276.

Reece, R. 1985: The coins. In S. S. Frere, *Verulamium Excavations, Vol. III* (Oxford University Committee for Archaeology Monograph 1), 3-17.

Roymans, N. 1996: The sword or the plough. Regional dynamics in the romanisation of Belgic Gaul and the Rhineland area. In N. Roymans (ed.), *From the sword to the plough: three studies on the earliest Romanization of Northern Gaul* (Amsterdam Archaeological Studies 1), 9-126.

Roymans, N. 2001: The lower Rhine *Triquetrum* coinages and the ethnogenesis of the Batavi. In T. Grünewald (ed.), *Germania inferior. Besiedlung, Gesellschaft and Wirtscaft an der Grenze der römisch-germanischen Welt* (Berlin, RGA-E 28), 93-145.

Rudd, C. 2002: Solidu, King of Kent. *Chris Rudd List* 66, 4-7.

Scheers, S. 1972: Coinage and currency of the Belgic tribes during the Gallic War. *British Numismatic Journal* 41, 1-6.

Scheers, S. 1977: *Traité de Numismatique Celtique II: La Gaule Belgique* (Paris, Les Belles Lettres).

Scheers, S. 1996: Frappe et circulation monétaire sur le territoire de la future *Civitas Tungrorum*. *Revue Belge de Numismatique* 142, 5-51.

Sills, J. 1996: The summer of 54 BC. *Spink Numismatic Circular* 104, 334-335.

Sills, J. 1997a: The earliest British coins: dating the undated. *Chris Rudd List* 27, 2-5.

Sills, J. 1997b: Coinage of the British coalition against Caesar. *Spink Numismatic Circular* 105, 324-326.

Sills, J. 2000a: The Ingoldisthorpe stater and the study of Iron Age coins. *Chris Rudd List* 49, 2-3.

Sills, J. 2000b: Crossed lined staters. *Chris Rudd List* 53, 2-3.

Sills, J. 2003: Celtic or Roman? AGR and ESVPRASTO. *Chris Rudd List* 70, 2-4.

Sutherland, C. H. V. 1984 (2nd ed.): *The Roman Imperial Coinage, Volume 1: from 31 BC to AD 69* (London, Spink).

van Heesch, J. 1998: *De Muntcirculatie Tijdens de Romeinse Tijd in het Noordwesten van Gallia Belgica* (Brussels, Koninklijke Muse voor Kunst en Geschiedenis Monografie van Nationale Archeologie 11).

van Heesch, J. 1999: Augustan bronze coins in the north-west of Gaul. In W. Schlüter and R. Wiegels (eds), *Rom, Germanien und die Ausgrabungen von Kalkriese*, (Osnabrück, Universitätsverlag Rasch), 347-361.

Wigg, D. 1996: The function of the last Celtic coinages from Germany. In C. E. King and D. Wigg (eds), *Coin finds and coin use in the ancient world* (Berlin, Studien zu Fundmünzen der Antike 10), 415-436.

Wigg, D. 1997: Coin supply and the Roman army. In W. Groenman-van Waateringe (ed.), *Roman Frontier Studies 1995* (Oxford, Oxbow Monograph 91), 281-8.

Wigg, D. 1999: The development of the monetary economy in north Gaul in the late La Tène and early Roman period. In J. Creighton and R. Wilson (eds), *Roman Germany: studies in cultural interaction* (Journal of Roman Archaeology Supplement 32), 99-124.

Wigg, D. 2000: The Martberg on the lower Mosel and the development of the coin-using economy in North Gaul in the late La Tène and early Roman period. In B. Kluge and B. Weissner (eds), *Akten. XII. Internationaler Numismatischer*

Kongress, Berlin 1997, 447-452.

Wigg, D. and Riederer, J. 1998: Die Chronologie der Keltischen Münzprägung am Mittelrhein. In U. Peter (ed.), *Stephanos nomismatikos. Edith Schonert Geiss zum 65. Geburtstag* (Berlin, Akademie Verlag), 661-74.

Wightman, E. M. 1985: *Gallia Belgica* (London, Batsford).

Williams, J. H. C. 2000: The silver coins from East Anglia attributed to King Prasutagus of the Iceni - a new reading of the obverse inscription. *Numismatic Chron*icle 160, 276-281.

Williams, J. H. C. 2005: 'The newer rite is here'; vinous symbolism on British Iron age coins. In C. Haselgrove and D. Wigg-Wolf (eds), *Iron Age coinage and ritual practices* (Mainz, Studien zu Fundmünzen der Antike 20), 25-41.

Wolters, R. 1988: Keltische münzen in römischen Militärstationen und die Besoldung römischer Hilfstruppen in spätrepublikanischer und frühaugusteischerzeit. *Tyche* 3, 261-272.

Belgic coins in Britain

Philip de Jersey

This paper is the third of three pieces of work examining imported Iron Age coinage in Britain. Previous articles have focused on Armorican imports (de Jersey 1997) and "exotic" imports (de Jersey 1999); here, our concern is with coins originating in Belgic Gaul.

Definitions

For the purposes of this paper, Belgic Gaul has essentially a numismatic definition, corresponding almost exactly to the region studied by Simone Scheers in her fundamental survey of Belgic coinage (1977). Haselgrove (1999), in an attempt to overcome the perennial difficulties of tribal nomenclature, has usefully divided this area into western, southern, central and eastern zones (Figure 1), and these will be followed with only very minor modification here. Some acknowledgement of the supposed tribal areas is required, however, not least because despite the valiant efforts of Delestrée and Tache (2002) they are still virtually ubiquitous in publications describing the coins of Belgic Gaul.

The western zone is roughly equivalent to Caesar's Belgium, incorporating the territories of the Ambiani, the Bellovaci, the Atrebates, the Caleti and the Veliocasses. It is also taken here to include the territories of the Lexovii and the Aulerci Eburovices, which although lying on the 'wrong' side of the Seine, have bronze coinages which seem to be more closely related to Belgica than to Armorica, to the west. The southern zone is dominated by the Remi and the Suessiones. To their north, the Nervii are the principal tribe of the central zone, accompanied by a number of smaller tribes of which only the Aduatuci and the Eburones have much relevance to the coins found in Britain. The eastern zone – reaching and at some periods probably extending beyond the Rhine – consists chiefly of the Treveri, the Mediomatrici and the Leuci.

The development of coinage throughout this region has been admirably set out by Haselgrove (1999). Some elements of this development, although they impinge on Britain, are beyond the scope of this paper: in particular, no attempt has been made here to discuss the importation of the various gold coinages commonly known as Gallo-Belgic A – F, and the rarer early imports which Allen (1960, 169ff.) labelled Gallo-Belgic XA and XB. The early gold coinages produced in Belgica, including Gallo-Belgic XA, XB and A – D, have been discussed at length by Sills (2003), and there is little point in repeating here his full treatment of the British examples. Some consideration will be given, however, to the other Belgic gold and base gold coinages which have been imported into Britain, albeit in small numbers, and which are not included in Sills's monumental survey. Our main concern though is with the Belgic bronze coinages, imported into Britain in significant numbers during the late Iron Age.

The coins

The appendix to this article lists some 327 'stray finds', from 105 locations, plus the Belgic coins from four or five small, generally rather badly recorded hoards. Of the 327 stray finds, 22 (6.7%) are in gold (including base gold and plated), 12 (3.7%) are in silver or silver-plated, and the bulk – 293 coins, or 89.6% – are bronze. The bronze coins can be further subdivided into 87 cast (29.7% of the bronze coinage) and 206 struck (70.3%).

Gold

As indicated above, the various coinages conventionally described as Gallo-Belgic A – F and Gallo-Belgic XA and XB have not been included in this survey. However, other gold types from Belgica were occasionally imported into Britain. The commonest (Figure 2) is a rather problematic base gold quarter stater (Scheers 152; see Doyen 1987), possibly issued by the Remi or the Suessiones: there are probably at least eight from Britain, plus a small hoard of another eight of doubtful provenance.

The style of the horse on some of these coins is not entirely dissimilar to early British uninscribed quarter staters, and it is not impossible that this conferred a measure of acceptability on them. Scheers 152 was a long-lived coinage, if we accept the archaeological dating proposed by Haselgrove (1999, 140), who notes that it "first appeared during La Tène D1b [c. 120 – 90 BC], had its *floruit* during La Tène D2a [c. 90 – 60 BC], and was still current at the start of La Tène D2b [c. 40 – 30 BC]." Most British examples are in base gold and are perhaps most likely to have entered the country late in this long period. No other Belgic gold type is represented in Britain by more than three or four examples, and it seems reasonable to assume that none of these other coinages arrived in very significant numbers, even allowing for melting down and other routes to non-recovery. The distribution of these gold imports, together with the silver and bronze, will be considered below.

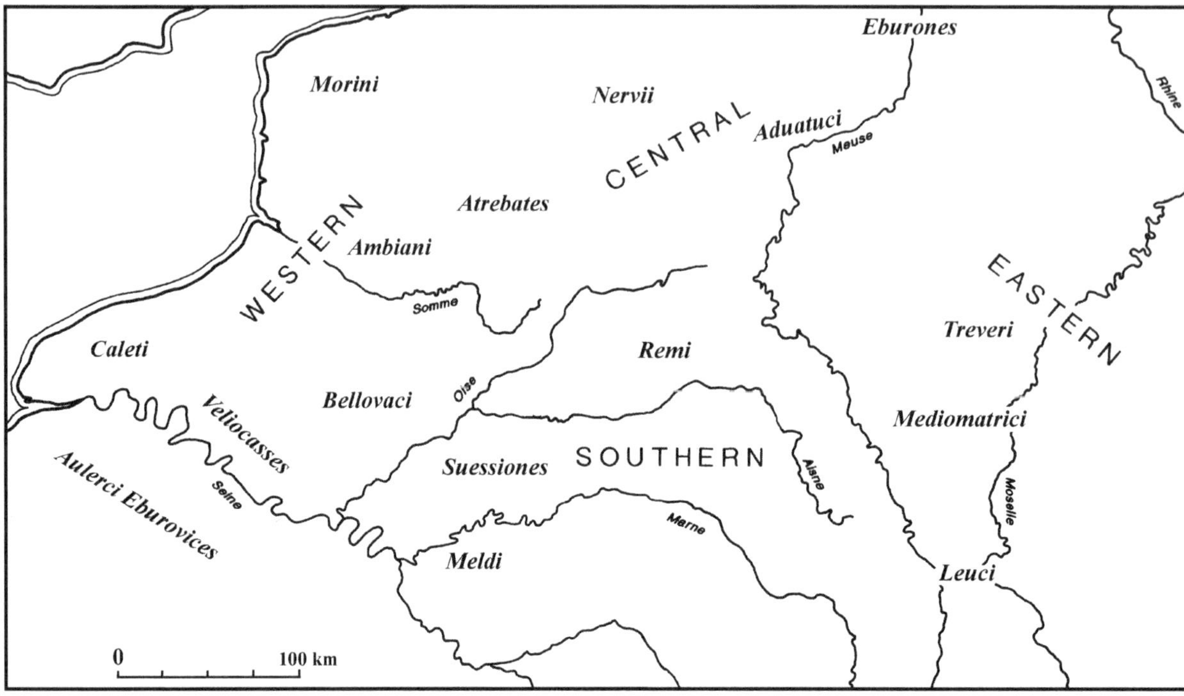

Figure 1. Regions and tribes of Belgic Gaul (after Haselgrove 1999, fig. 1, and Delestrée and Tache 2002, 16, with additions).

Figure 2. Base gold quarter stater, Scheers 152 (CCI 01.0926, Maldon, Essex). Twice actual size.

Silver

Silver coinage was never very common in Belgic Gaul (Scheers 1977, 110), and its rarity there is reflected by the small numbers found in Britain. Six of the twelve recorded coins are *quinarii* inscribed ATEVLA VLATOS (Scheers 41), and four of these are plated coins found at Hayling Island temple. The source of this post-conquest coinage, which occurs across Belgic Gaul, has never been satisfactorily identified, and Delestrée and Tache (2002, 125) have suggested that it may have been particularly associated with Roman auxiliary camps, hence its wide circulation during the second half of the first century BC.

Of the other six miscellaneous silver types, the most interesting (Figure 3) is the curious overstruck unit with a pseudo-legend, apparently found at Wanborough in Wiltshire, and possibly in association with uninscribed Dobunnic silver (Allen 1961, 111, 130). This coin was initially taken to be British – it was slotted into Mack (1964) at 396a – but in fact the type is known in some quantity from the late Iron Age site of Villeneuve-Saint-Germain, Aisne. Debord (1987, 238-239) notes examples overstruck on *quinarii* of the Aedui (LT XVI 5138), and on the well-known Kaletedu issue usually attributed to the Lingones (LT XXXII 8291); the undertype of the Wanborough example is not clear. He suggests (*ibid.*, 241) that the type must have been produced at Villeneuve-Saint-Germain, between c. 50 and 20 BC, and that the unusual practice of overstriking may reflect the lack of available silver resources. This is in some conflict with the archaeologically-derived dating of the site (Haselgrove 1999, 144-145), which suggests an earlier *floruit*, between 90 and 60 BC, although this has relatively little relevance to the single British example. If the Wanborough coin is a genuinely British find, and there is no particular reason to doubt it, then it seems to be the only provenanced example not to have been found at Villeneuve-Saint-Germain.

Figure 3. Villeneuve-Saint-Germain overstruck silve unit (CCI 61.0063, Wanborough, Wiltshire). Twice actual size.

Bronze

The great majority of Belgic coins in Britain are in bronze, approximately two-thirds struck and one-third cast. Most are comparatively well-known types, and thus warrant little further discussion here. However, it may be useful to break down the overall figure into various categories, thus shedding a little more light on the nature of the imported bronze.

Table 1 shows the breakdown of the bronze coinage by tribe and region. As already indicated, some of these tribal attributions are questionable, and so the division by geographical region – which combines types that can be fairly satisfactorily assigned to a particular region, but not to the tribe within that region – might be more useful. It is immediately obvious that the western zone supplies more than half (57.2%) of the Belgic bronze coinage found in Britain, and of those western zone coins about three-quarters are traditionally attributed to the Ambiani, or what Delestrée and Tache (2002, 12-13) have recently termed the "fonds commun des Ambiani".

	Number of coins	Number as % of all bronze
SOUTH	**54**	**22.2**
Meldi	3	1.2
Remi	21	8.6
Suessiones	30	12.3
WEST	**139**	**57.2**
Ambiani	108	44.4
Atrebates	5	2.1
Aulerci Eburovices	3	1.2
Bellovaci	6	2.5
Caleti	1	0.4
Lexovii	1	0.4
Veliocasses	15	6.2
CENTRAL	**24**	**9.9**
Aduatuci	22	9.1
Nervii	2	0.8
EAST	**13**	**5.3**
Leuci	13	5.3
GERMANVS IND.	**13**	**5.3**
TOTAL	243	100.0

Table 1. Imported Belgic bronze in Britain. Figures do not include uncertainly attributed or unidentified coins.

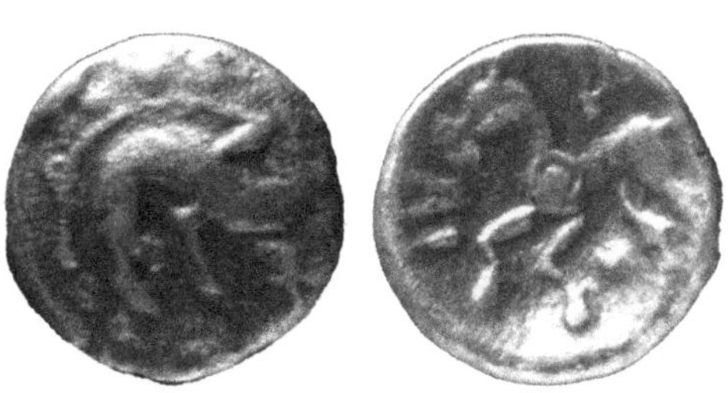

Figure 4. Bronze unit, Scheers 80g (CCI 95.0721, Cambridge). Twice actual size.

Within this group, by far the commonest issues (Figure 4) are the various subtypes of Scheers 80, mostly with a representation of a boar (occasionally a horse) on the obverse and a horse on the reverse, together accounting for some 36 finds. No other Belgic import – from the western zone or elsewhere – achieves a similar presence in Britain. The other relatively common imports include three cast bronze types: Scheers 190, perhaps of the Aduatuci or the Nervii (17 examples); Scheers 186, the well-known issue of the Leuci with a boar standard reverse (12 examples); and Scheers 198, another familiar type with stylized head and boar, traditionally attributed to the Bellovaci, but more recently (Allen 1995, 95) reassigned to the Suessiones (20 examples). These four types between them account for more than a third of all the stray finds of Belgic bronze in Britain. Various types of Remic bronze (Scheers 146, which is struck, and Scheers 191, 194 and 195, which are cast) are also relatively well-represented. Finally, there are fourteen recorded examples of the very late bronze (technically brass) issue inscribed GERMANVS INDVTILLI L, which copies a *quadrans* of Augustus of c. 15 – 8 BC (Scheers 216). Some of the types most commonly found in Britain are relatively early: Haselgrove (1999, 133) states that Scheers 186 and 191 were the principal potin types of southern and eastern Gaul "during the last quarter of the second century BC", and that Scheers 190 was in circulation by c. 90 BC (*ibid.*, 146). The actual date of their arrival in Britain remains largely unknown, given the lack of significant contextual information (see below).

Perhaps the most interesting of the bronze imports are those coins which can be shown to have exerted a strong stylistic influence on other British coinages. A detailed consideration of all the potential stylistic links between Belgic and British coinage is beyond the scope of this paper, but it is worth examining some specific examples here.

In the north Thames region at least three 'new' inter-related bronze types seem to show some connection to coinages from Belgic Gaul, although the links are complex and not yet entirely clear. Two of these were published by Bean (1991), although with the benefit of many further discoveries in the past decade the descriptions of the types need some revision. As Bean suspected, the object he described as a 'spear-headed staff' behind the horse on one type (*ibid.*, fig. 1) is actually an etiolated horse-rider (see BMC 2491, a particularly clear example; Figure 5). Although neither Scheers (1977) nor Delestrée and Tache (2002) illustrate any Belgic types with quite the same form of rider, there are numerous examples within the Belgic coinage which might have provided inspiration for the reverse of the British type, the closest of which is perhaps the VIROS bronze of the Nervii (Scheers 29a; BMC III, 41; DT 625).

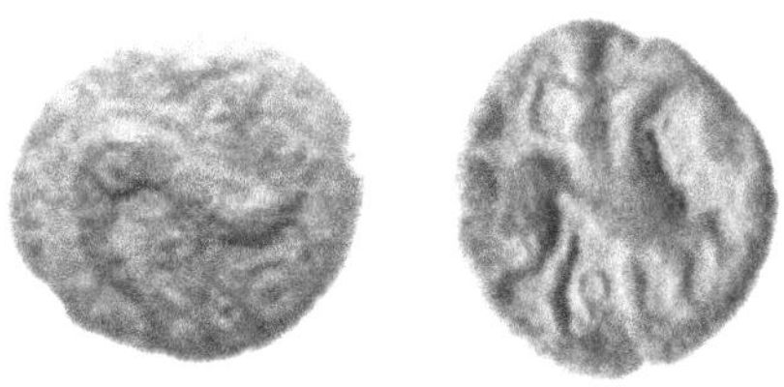

Figure 5. Bronze unit, BMC 2491 (CCI 96.1910, unprovenanced). Twice actual size.

The obverse of the British type seems to feature some kind of mythical creature, perhaps part dragon and part snake, standing on two back legs (it has no front legs) and turning its neck and head backwards. It is not dissimilar to Scheers 89, a rare bronze unit perhaps of the Ambiani, which in turn has a horse on the reverse with the very distinctive form of hooves and legs found on the second of these north Thames types, Evans G12 (BMC 405; Figure 6).

Figure 6. Bronze unit, Evans G12 (CCI 01.1607, unprovenanced). Twice actual size.

As the classification suggests, this bronze has been known for some considerable time (Evans 1864, 120-121), but until recently it was widely considered to be a Belgic type. More than 40 examples are now recorded in Britain, predominantly from the eastern part of the north Thames territories, and there can be little doubt that it has an insular origin. While there do not appear to be any exact matches in the Belgic series for the two boars around a wheel on the obverse, the reverse is linked not only to the Ambianic bronze mentioned above, but possibly to Scheers 217 cl. III, traditionally attributed to the Aduatuci. An association with Scheers 217 cl. III is also cited for the two bronze units catalogued as BMC III, 42-43, although these two coins have a very different style of horse to the example illustrated by Scheers (1977, pl. XXVI.747), and – despite the basic similarity of the obverses, with what appear to be four horse heads revolving clockwise – there must be some question as to whether they are really the same type (Figure 7). It is not impossible that BMC III, 42, from Braughing (Hertfordshire), and three other British finds (Chelmsford and Maldon in Essex, and Maidstone in Kent), are actually insular productions, rather than imports, perhaps drawing on both the Aduatuci and the Ambiani issues cited here for their inspiration. On the other hand, Scheers (1982, 96 no. 79) and Delestrée (1996, 96 no. 64) illustrate coins very similar to the putative British variety from the sanctuary sites of Chilly and Digeon respectively; so might it be Belgic after all? It may be simply impossible to tell at present for some of these rarer types, which could be at home on either side of the Channel.

Figure 7. Bronze unit, BMC III, 42 (CCI 69.0641, Braughing, Herts.). Twice actual size.

The third related north Thames type (Bean 1991, fig. 2; BMC illustrated as 407, details given as 403; Figure 8) may represent a step further away from possible Belgic prototypes, since although it seems to share the same crooked legs and relatively large hooves with the other two insular types, there are fewer obvious parallels to continental issues.

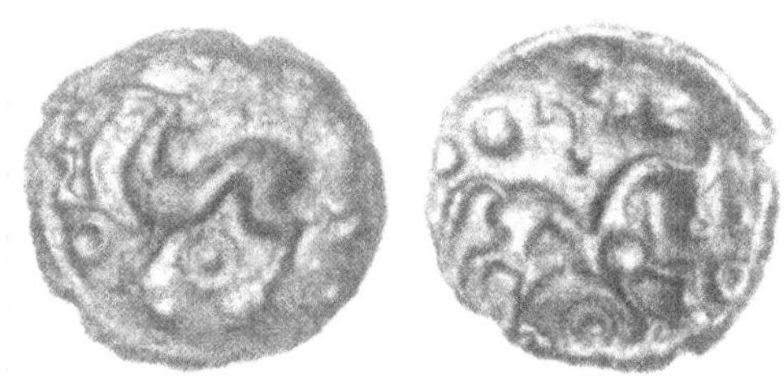

Figure 8. Bronze unit, BMC 403/407 (CCI 97.1589, Essex). Twice actual size.

In the south Thames region, probably the most obvious of all the Belgic/British relationships is represented by the Chichester cock bronze, first published in detail by Burnett (1992), and comprehensively dissected by Cottam (1999). Burnett (1992, 342) notes that the reverse of the southern British type is derived primarily from Scheers 111, probably of the Bellovaci, while Cottam (1999, 9-12) also points out similarities between some of the Chichester cock subtypes and features on Scheers 107 (Ambiani?), 110 (Caleti?) and 121 (Bellovaci?). None of the Belgic prototypes are at all common in Britain, let alone from the Chichester region, but the strength of the typological parallels is such that some connection is undeniable. An example of the related type featuring a horse on the reverse (Cottam 1999, 5, fig. 7) has recently been found at Fontaine-sur-Somme (Somme), in what is still a comparatively rare case of a coin crossing the Channel from west to east (DT 387; attribution corrected by Delestrée 2003); it is tempting to suggest that this encapsulates the ties that must have existed between the two regions in order for these complex processes of borrowing and reinterpretation to take place.

Not all of these relationships involve copying between the same metals. The 'Abingdon Zoo' silver unit (de Jersey 1998) shares virtually every detail of its obverse with the bronze Scheers 88, attributed to the Ambiani. A single example of the Belgic type is known from Britain (curiously, from South Ferriby), although another bronze unit with a very similar obverse is recorded from Sonning in Berkshire (Sherlock 1956, 398 no. 6). The reverse of that coin is nearly a mirror image of another rare Ambianic type (Scheers 78), and could also be related to a bronze unit from Chilly (Somme), illustrated by Delestrée (1996, 74 no. 16). None of these bronze coins are likely to be of British origin, although the assumption that bronze coinage was never part of the south Thames coinage has been dented by the discovery of the Chichester cock and related types, and even a bronze unit of Verica (Cottam 1996). This would seem, then, to be an example of a British silver coinage imitating some elements of a complex Belgic bronze series.

There are other examples of this process. Scheers 105 (DT 352) is another bronze probably of Ambianic origin, in this case coupling the obverse of a head left with small ?snake-heads in front, with a reverse showing a charioteer crouched on the rump of a horse galloping left. Two very worn examples are recorded from Hertfordshire, but from Kent are three coins which provide an almost exact copy of the bronze type, in silver (Figure 9). One of these coins was found in excavations at the Marlowe Theatre site in Canterbury (Nash and Sellwood 1995, no. 12). Another Kentish silver type (*BNJ* Coin Register 1992, no. 193) has a different reverse, but again, very nearly the same obverse as Scheers 105. The latter type can be firmly attributed to Belgic Gaul: Scheers (1977, 572) lists five single finds and three examples in a small hoard from Amiens, while Delestrée adds two from the sanctuary site of Saint-Maur, Oise (1996, 66) and an impressive thirteen from another sanctuary at Chilly, Somme (*ibid.*, 70). As with the Abingdon Zoo silver, we can be fairly sure that these are cases of British silver imitating Belgic bronze.

Figure 9. Kentish silver copy of Scheers 105 (CCI 98.2153, Kent). Twice actual size.

One further 'Belgic' type is worth singling out here, listed among the uncertainly attributed coins in the Appendix. BMC III, 31 (Figure 10), found at Mildenhall (Wiltshire) before 1881, has only one continental provenance (Hallencourt, Somme), but another four are now recorded from Sussex: Eastbourne, Chichester, Oving and Warningcamp. Another appeared on eBay in August 2004, probably from a Hampshire source. The reverse is not dissimilar to the Chichester cock bronze, and it may be that this is another British production.

Figure 10. Bronze unit, BMC III, 31 (CCI 69.0662, Mildenhall, Wilts.). Twice actual size.

These few examples should indicate the potential complexity of the stylistic relationships between Belgic and British coinage. The significance of these relationships will be considered in more detail in the concluding discussion. There are likely to be many more such links, but beyond the very obvious cases listed here they may be difficult to confirm. It is not unreasonable to suppose that die-engravers were working from a very similar range of cultural beliefs and symbols on both sides of the Channel, and consequently it would not be surprising if some motifs occur independently on both continental and insular coinages; the difficulty lies in deciding which cases are coincidence, and which cases attest to some contact between the two areas.

Contexts

As with so many categories of Iron Age coins in Britain, there is a disappointing lack of contextual information on the majority of the Belgic imports. In many cases this is because coins have been found in ploughsoil by metal detectorists; but even those coins which have been recorded in archaeological excavations very often yield little more useful evidence.

Tables 2 and 3 list some 56 single finds with a degree – however paltry – of associated archaeological information. Only three locations – Canterbury, Hayling Island and Silchester – have more than four examples of Belgic coins, and of these only a very limited number are from useful archaeological contexts.

The temple at Hayling Island is potentially one of the most useful, although not all the associations of the coins found there have yet been published. A number of Belgic imports apparently date to phase 2 of the temple (see Table 2), but at present it is not always clear whether they belong to phase 2a – early/mid first century BC, not later than c. 30 BC – or phase 2b, from the early first century AD to c. 60 AD. King and Soffe (2001, 114, Table 7.1b) list a Veliocasses potin (Scheers 206) from a phase 2b context, but its given location – E45 – is shared with a minim possibly of Verica (Briggs *et al.* 1992, no. 67), which is unlikely to date before 25 – 30 AD. This could though be a rare instance of a Belgic import from a certain pre-conquest context. A small hoard from Hayling Island also appears to be firmly pre-conquest (see below).

location zone of origin, type, CCI	comments, details of context
Canterbury, Kent	
uncertain, cf. S94, 97.2340	silver; residual (Nash and Sellwood 1995, no. 43)
ATEVLA VLATOS, S41, not in CCI	silver plated; no further details
Ambiani, S93, 61.1660	no details (Haselgrove 1987, 449 no. 42)
Ambiani, S59, 61.1668	no details (Haselgrove 1987, 449 no. 44)
Ambiani, S80?, 91.0285	'early Roman pit fill' (on CCI index card)
Ambiani?, S178, not in CCI	no details
Ambiani?, S119, 97.2339	residual (Nash and Sellwood 1995, no. 15)
Meldi, S143, 61.1679	occupation deposit, mid C1 AD (Haselgrove 1987, 453 no. 82)
Suessiones, S198, 97.2338	'pit', period? (Nash and Sellwood 1995, no. 14)
Veliocasses, S206, 78.0108	period I, pre-Flavian (Haselgrove 1987, 446 no. 8)
GERMANVS INDVTILLI L, S216, 61.1676	fill of pit, LPRIA? (Haselgrove 1987, 452 no. 79)
uncertain, 99.0349	hearth, late C1 BC - 70/80 AD (Nash and Sellwood 1995, no. 28)
uncertain, S199 or S205, not in CCI	'late Flavian onwards' (Haselgrove 1987, 451 no. 68)
unidentified, 83.0277	'Belgic topsoil', phase 1 (Nash and Sellwood 1995, no. 56; Haselgrove 1987, 448 no. 32B)
unidentified, 97.2341	LPRIA ditch? (Nash and Sellwood 1995, no. 44; Haselgrove 1987, 447 no. 21)
unidentified, not in CCI	no details
unidentified, not in CCI	no details
Colchester, Essex	
GERMANVS INDVTILLI L, S216, 72.0609	Hawkes and Hull 1947, 142: one u/s, two in period IV layer (beginning c. 49 AD)
GERMANVS INDVTILLI L, S216, not in CCI	
GERMANVS INDVTILLI L, S216, not in CCI	
unidentifed, 78.0121	in C18 soakaway (Goodburn 1987, 15 no. 2)
Hayling Island, Hants.	
Suessiones, S27, 91.0335	gold plated; phase VII (C3/C4 AD; Haselgrove 1987, 404)
ATEVLA VLATOS, S41 (four coins, 91.0416, 433, 439, 579)	silver plated; one of these four coins is phase II (Haselgrove 1987, 403) and two are phase III/IV (Roman period; *ibid.*, 404)
Aduatuci, S190, 91.0486	details not yet published
Ambiani, S90a, 91.0431	'phase II' (Briggs et al. 1992, no. 120)
Aulerci Eburovices, LT 7021, 91.0550	details not yet published
Remi, S194, 91.0327	unstratified (Haselgrove 1987, 405)
Suessiones, S198, 91.0440	'phase II' (Briggs et al. 1992, no. 125)
Veliocasses, S206, 91.0339	'phase 2b' (King and Soffe 2001, 114)
Veliocasses, S206, 91.0563	details not yet published
Silchester, Hants.	
'Nervii', S29, 62.0088	gold plated; exc. c. 1900, no further details
uncertain, cf. S52, 91.0541	silver; period 5.31 (c. 80 AD or later) (Boon 2000, 135 no. 19)
Ambiani, S80d, 62.0203	'south gate or ditch outside' (Boon 1954, no. 19)
Ambiani, S80f, 91.0540	period 5.2 (c. 80 AD or later) (Boon 2000, 135 no. 18)
Remi, S195, 62.0246	insula XXXIV house 1 (Haselgrove 1987, 411)
Remi, S195, not in CCI	in Victorian backfill (Boon 2000, 135 no. 17)
GERMANVS INDVTILLI L, S216, 62.0209	no further information (Haselgrove 1987, 412)
unidentified, 62.0154	no further information (Haselgrove 1987, 412)
unidentified, 91.0545	period 4.10 (later 40s AD?) (Boon 2000, 136 no. 20)

Table 2. Belgic imports: archaeological contexts of single coins, major sites. Coins are bronze unless otherwise stated.

The Belgic coins from Canterbury have come from several sites both within and outside the city walls. While three or four are likely to come from genuine pre-conquest horizons, the majority are residual in later deposits. At Silchester, just one of the Belgic coins excavated in the modern series of investigations (Boon 2000, 136 no. 20) comes from an Augustan or Tiberian context. The coins from the earlier excavations, between 1890 and 1909, have no useful contextual information.

A series of 'minor' sites have smaller numbers of coins recorded (Table 3). Of these, just a single unidentified bronze unit from Puckeridge has been found in a context of c. 43 - 65 AD (Haselgrove 1987, 425 no. 22); every other coin in the table has either no further information, or is residual in a later context.

location zone of origin, type, CCI	comments, details of context
Ash, Kent	
Bellovaci, S185?, 99.2160	Anglo-Saxon grave (Faussett 1856, pl. XVII.16)
Braughing, Herts.	
Ambiani, S80d, 72.0684	unstratified (Haselgrove 1987, 432)
Folkestone, Kent	
Ambiani, S87, 97.1166	no details (Winbolt 1925, 80 no. 5)
Hengistbury Head, Dorset	
Leuci, S186, not in CCI	exc. c. 1919; no further details (Cunliffe 1987, 136, fiche 5: A7-8)
Kelvedon, Essex	
Aduatuci, S190, 73.0908	residual (Rodwell 1988, 78 no. 8)
Leicester, Leics.	
GERMANVS INDVTILLI L, S216, not in CCI	no further information (Pearce 1948, 279 as "*Gallo-Roman*. temp. Augustus")
Puckeridge, Herts.	
Ambiani, S80d, not in CCI	possibly re-identified?
unidentified, 73.1019	period II, c. AD 43-65 (Haselgrove 1987, 425 no. 22)
unidentified, not in CCI	no details; possibly re-identified?
Richborough Castle, Kent	
Ambiani, S59, not in CCI	exc. 1931, Richborough V, 37377; no further details
Ambiani, S81, 64.0125	exc. 1931, Richborough II, 2495 (Allen 1968, 187 no. 10); no further details
Bellovaci, S185, 61.1777	Richborough II, 2494; BMC III, 468; 'surface clearing'
St Albans, Herts.	
unidentified, not in CCI	unstratified (Neal et al. 1990, 110 no. 14)
Watchfield, Oxon.	
Leuci, S186, 99.2158	C6 AD grave (Scull 1992, 179, 182)

Table 3. Belgic imports: archaeological contexts of single coins, minor sites. All coins are bronze.

location zone of origin, type, CCI	comments, details of context
Penzance, Cornwall	
1 S190 cl. II, 2+ S186 cl. II, & central Gaulish?	no further details (Allen 1995, 24 no. 30)
Hayling Island, Hants.	
Aulerci Eburovices, LT XXVIII 7034 (two)	in hoard with Carnutes bronze; 'phase 2a' (King and Soffe 2001, 118)
Faversham, Kent	
Veliocasses, 6+ S165	no further details (Allen 1960, 277)
Lancing Down, West Sussex	
GERMANVS INDVTILLI L, S216, not in CCI	in (Flavian?) temple deposit, or in Roman grave? (Haselgrove 1987, 291-294)
Wanborough, Wiltshire	
uncertain, Debord (1987) cl. II	possibly with Dobunnic silver? (Allen 1960, 249; 1961, 111, 130)

Table 4. Belgic imports: coins in hoards.

The few hoards which contain Belgic coinage mostly add little to our knowledge (Table 4). One has been excavated, at Hayling Island: a group of four Carnutes bronze units with two bronzes of the Aulerci Eburovices, found in the south-east corner of the "inner phase 2a enclosure" (King and Soffe 2001, 118), and thus presumably dating to the mid or late first century BC.

Distributions

Figures 11-19 show the distribution of single finds and hoards of Belgic coins in Britain.

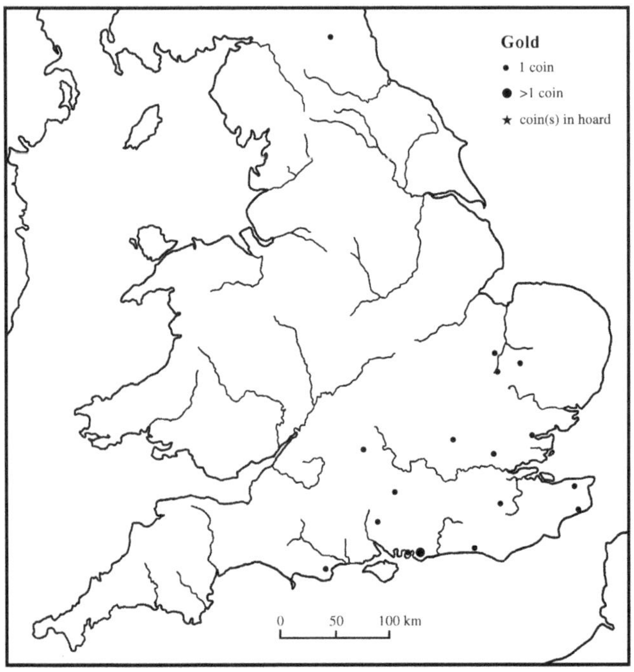

Figure 11. Distribution of Belgic gold in Britain.

Both gold (Figure 11) and particularly silver (Figure 12) are concentrated mostly in the area south of the Thames: there seems to have been relatively little penetration of Belgic precious metal coinages into the north Thames territories (although clearly the Gallo-Belgic gold coinages did reach the north Thames region in considerable numbers (Cunliffe 1981, 62-67)). Apart from a couple of coins excavated at Canterbury, silver imports are limited to the territory of the Atrebates, which might perhaps reflect the predilection of the south Thames region for that metal.

The distribution of the bronze imports is rather more complex. The general maps of struck and cast bronze (Figures 13-14) suggest at least three concentrations of these imports in Britain: in north-east Kent, around Chichester, and – slightly less clearly – in the Braughing/Puckeridge area of Hertfordshire. The problem with these apparent concentrations, however, is that all three can be explained as the result of current metal-detecting activity and, in particular, the vagaries of recording. The rash of findspots in north-east Kent is testimony to the diligence of David Holman in recording detector finds from the county (Holman 2000). The concentration of finds around Chichester reflects intensive metal-detecting on the Westhampnett bypass and on several other highly productive sites nearby, coupled with a willingness on the part of most of the detectorists involved to sell their finds more or less as soon as they come up. The Braughing/Puckeridge concentration is a slightly less intensive version of the same phenomenon.

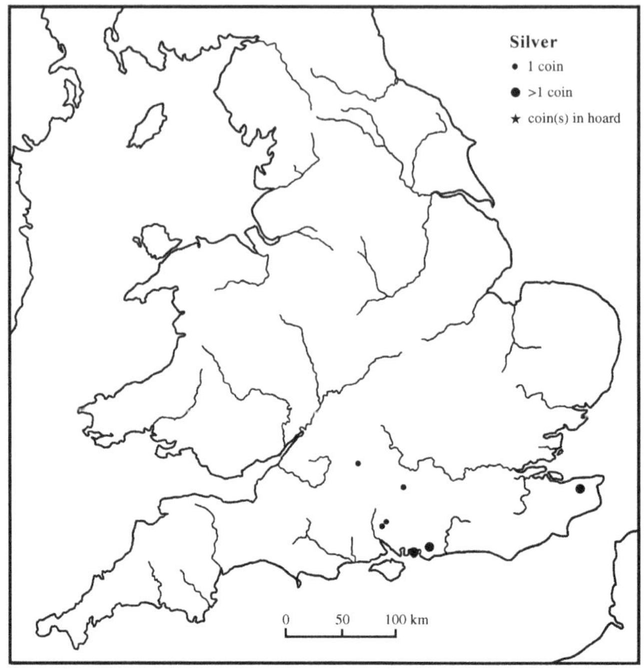

Figure 12. Distribution of Belgic silver in Britain.

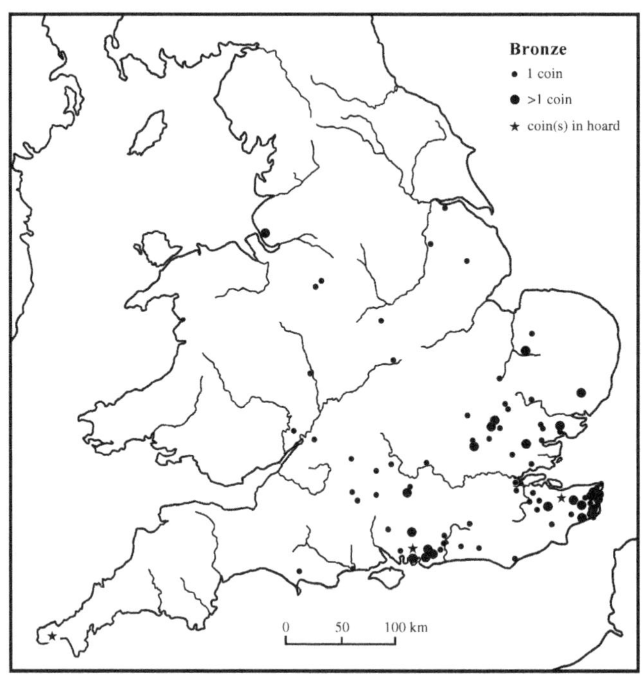

Figure 13. Distribution of Belgic struck bronze in Britain.

The circumstances of current metal-detecting activity and differential recording thus combine to produce what may be a deeply misleading pattern of finds. There may be other areas of the south-east rich in finds of Belgic coins, but because interest is less focused on those areas – and because these are usually bronze coins, often in poor condition and difficult to identify – they are by and large unreported. Biases in distribution maps are always likely to be present in some form or other, but in this case they seem particularly marked, and as such they complicate any interpretation of the data.

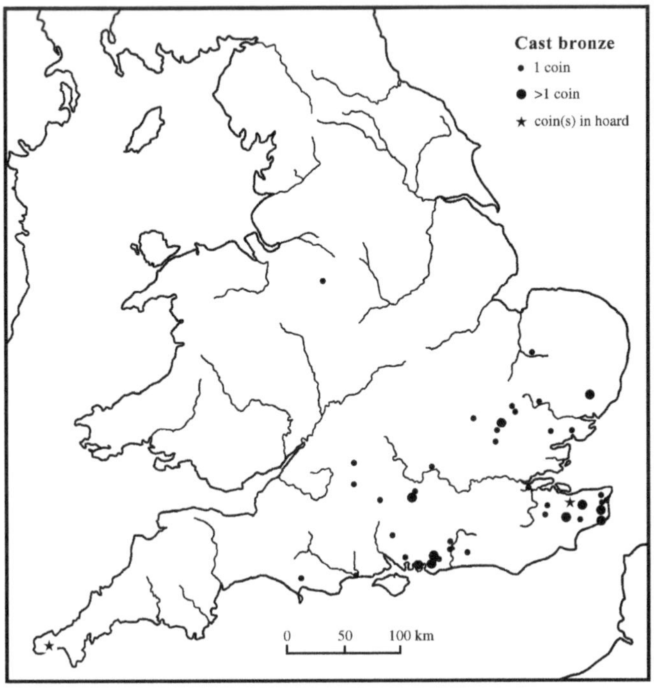

Figure 14. Distribution of Belgic cast bronze in Britain.

Bearing in mind these problems, we may be able to refine the general picture by concentrating on various aspects of the bronze coinages. On the whole there is little difference between the distribution of struck and cast, the latter being simply rather less common. There is no obvious association of cast imports with those areas north and south of the Thames where this style of bronze coinage had been in use – indeed there is far more imported cast bronze at Chichester than there is insular material (Cunliffe 1981, 72-73), although this may of course simply reflect the period during which the Chichester sites were flourishing. The only notable difference between the distributions of struck and cast bronze imports seems to be a more abrupt decline in the spread of cast coins beyond the core territories of the south-east, although even here only a handful of struck bronze coins are known from the so-called "peripheral" tribes.

The various regional divisions of Belgic Gaul suggested by Haselgrove, and described above, have been used to construct Figures 15-18. The distribution of imports from both the western zone – dominated by the coins of the Ambiani – and the southern zone (the Remi and the Suessiones) simply reflect the overall distribution of the bronze coinage, each clearly showing the three focuses of Chichester, north-east Kent and Braughing/Puckeridge. Coins from the eastern zone (Figure 17) are comparatively much rarer, and little can be inferred from the handful of recorded findspots.

The central zone (primarily the Nervii and the Aduatuci) provides a slightly more interesting pattern (Figure 18). Neither Chichester nor north-east Kent are particularly well-represented, but there does appear to be some bias towards the territory of the Trinovantes, in the eastern part of the north Thames region. Again this consists of only a few coins at present, but on this basis it seems to be genuinely different to the distribution of the bronze imports from the remainder of Belgic Gaul.

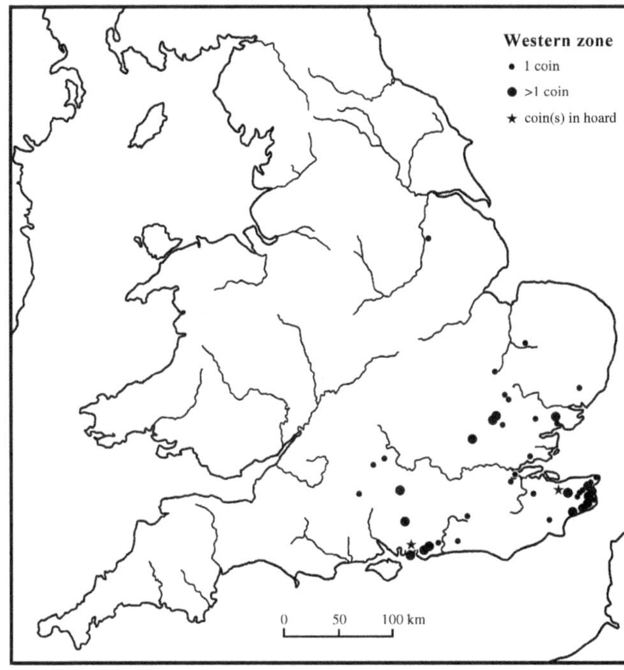

Figure 15. Distribution of western Belgic bronze in Britain.

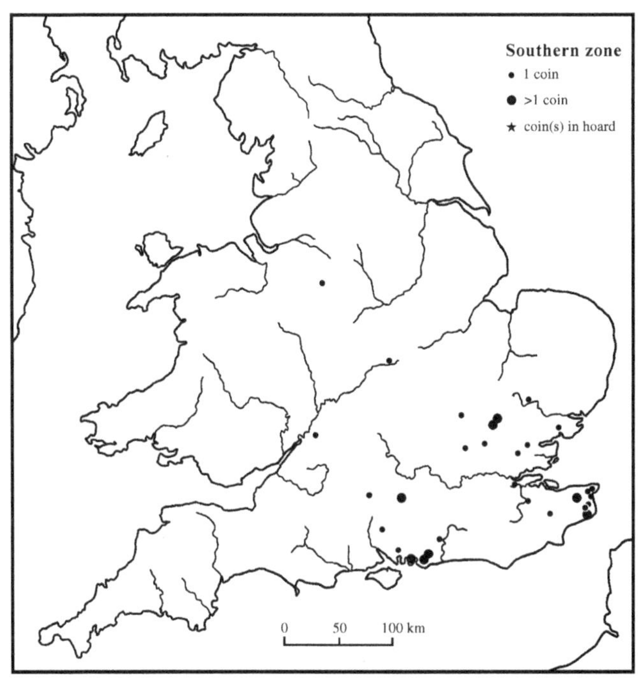

Figure 16. Distribution of southern Belgic bronze in Britain.

The thirteen examples of the very late Germanus Indutilli L type are widely scattered, almost from the south coast to the Humber (Figure 19), although there is a slight concentration in north-east Kent, as well as the three coins found in the excavations of the 1930s at Colchester. It may be significant that none are recorded from Chichester or Hayling Island, the implication being that most Gaulish imports were lost at these sites before the Germanus brass unit became widespread. The lack of this coinage in the area of Braughing and Puckeridge is perhaps more surprising, since its late date would not disqualify it from arriving along with the significant quantities of Belgic and other Gaulish pottery imports recorded at Braughing before c. 10 AD (Bryant and Niblett 2001, 103-104).

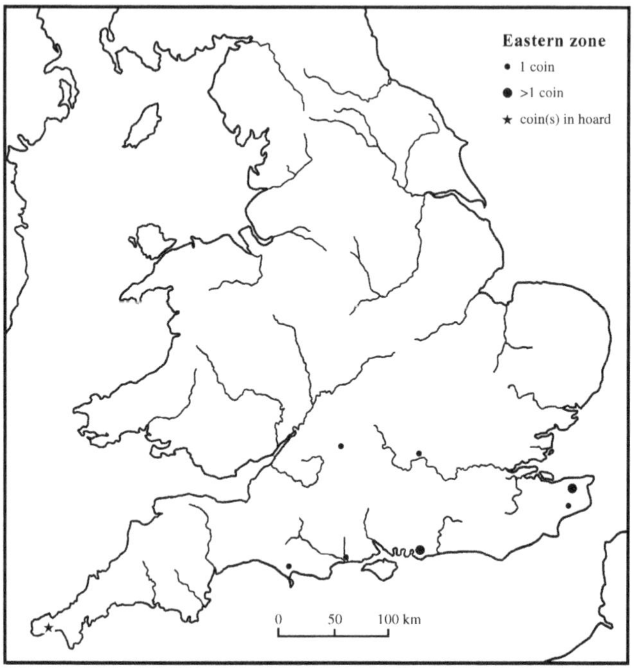

Figure 17. Distribution of eastern Belgic bronze in Britain

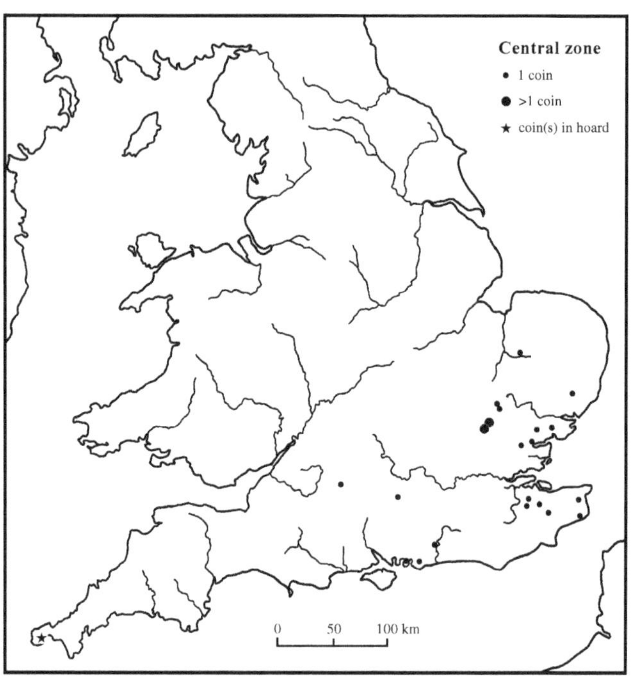

Figure 18. Distribution of central Belgic bronze in Britain.

Given the problems of modern biases in recording, is there anything else that can usefully be drawn out of these distribution maps? The general maps of bronze imports (Figures 13-14) seem to show more coins than might be expected in west Berkshire. If this too is not the reflection of better than average recording, in this case by the West Berkshire Heritage Service at Newbury Museum, then it might be significant in the context of the Abingdon Zoo silver, based on bronze Belgic prototypes.

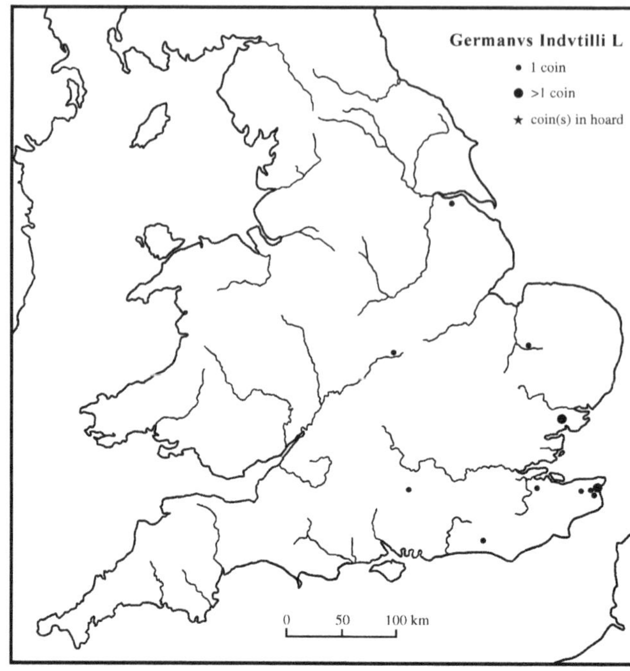

Figure 19. Distribution of Germanus Indutilli L in Britain.

Discussion

Given the size of our data sample, it is somewhat frustrating that so many aspects of the importation of Belgic coins into Britain remain elusive. The problem, simply, is that most of the coins are what Haselgrove (1987, 42-43) classifies as second or third order data: not recovered in archaeological excavation, and not always precisely spatially recorded. However detailed the grid reference, the value of an isolated metal-detected ploughsoil find more or less stops with its findspot; very few of these finds have any contextual evidence which might just allow a little speculation on, for example, the date at which the coin was deposited. The same is unfortunately true for most archaeological finds prior to c. 1970, which coupled with a stubborn reluctance on the part of most Iron Age coinage to turn up in sealed Iron Age contexts means that excavated coins often contribute little more information than their detected counterparts. The vagaries of recording – amply demonstrated in the distributions analysed above – also contribute to the overall difficulties of interpretation.

So what conclusions can we safely draw? Above all, that significant quantities of Belgic bronze coinage were imported into south-east Britain in the later first century BC. Given the difficulties of identifying much of this material, and the poor condition of a large part of it, our sample of just over 300 coins is likely to reflect only a very small proportion of the coinage actually imported in the late Iron Age and early Gallo-Roman period. Not surprisingly, Kent seems to have been a principal beneficiary of these imports, although its unusually well-recorded dataset should not be ignored. Even so it is likely that there was repeated contact between Kent and the tribes just across the Channel, in particular the Ambiani, as other forms of archaeological evidence would suggest (Cunliffe 1991, 130). Indeed the quantity of imported Belgic bronze may contradict Cunliffe's suggestion (*ibid.*, 147-148) that following Caesar's campaigns, "the tribes of Kent were peripheral to the economic expansion enjoyed by those north of the Thames," if we can assume some sort of economic function for most of the imports.

The Ambiani and their neighbours may have also looked further westwards for their insular contacts, to judge by the concentration of finds around Chichester, and we cannot ignore the much-debated presence of the Belgae in this area (Cunliffe 1991, 108-110; Rudd, Van Arsdell, this volume). The relatively high proportion of continental material at Hayling Island temple suggests some form of well-developed link in place at least until c. 30 BC. If – and it is still a fairly big if – if we can link some of the indigenous numismatic developments of this area, such as the Chichester cock bronze, with Caesar's Belgae "who came to plunder... and later settled down" (*de Bello Gallico* V, 12), then potentially the link could have been established much earlier, and well before the conquest of Gaul. This raises the intriguing possibility that local imitations of Belgic and other continental types were produced before the Gallic War, and are therefore some of the earliest struck coins produced in Britain. Our problem as ever is the lack of precise dating at this period. The possible prototypes for the Chichester cock bronze – including Scheers 107, 110, 111 and 121 – are apparently not recorded from useful archaeological contexts in Belgic Gaul (Haselgrove 1999), and so do not provide very helpful dating evidence for the insular developments. The precise status of the producers of the various Chichester coinages remains still more unclear: were they really Belgic immigrants who had settled in the region, or were they actually indigenous inhabitants who chose to reproduce or imitate some of the motifs they encountered on Belgic coinage, either through trading contact or perhaps because they had active social or political relationships across the Channel? The current evidence does not allow us to decide.

Close proximity to the south-east coast was evidently not a prerequisite for contact with Belgic coinage, as indicated by the finds at the Braughing/Puckeridge complex and, rather more intriguingly, in West Berkshire. The scattering of imported bronze and the presence of a local silver copy of an Ambianic type surely suggests a particular relationship between this region and some part of Belgic Gaul, perhaps developing through marriage and other social ties and maintained for at least a decade or two after the Gallic War. As with the North Thames bronzes and those found around Chichester, there is a strong sense – yet to be confirmed by close archaeological dating, it must be admitted – that these early, innovative developments were more or less over by c. 30 BC, by which time the inscribed coinage of a single ruler had become the norm in all of these areas. By that time too, of course, the production of Belgic coinage itself was very nearly over, and although imports must have continued up to the Roman conquest of Britain and beyond, the fact that the native Belgic coinage was being quite rapidly phased out must have both restricted its availability as a model for British coinage, and perhaps also reduced its suitability as such a model.

Appendix. Gazetteer of Belgic coins found in Britain.

The gazetteer on the following pages lists the c. 327 Belgic coins found in Britain and recorded in the Celtic Coin Index, or elsewhere, up to the end of 2003. The information is mostly self-explanatory but brief details of the columns are as follows:

County

Listed by the first three letters, e.g. KEN for Kent, with the following exceptions:

ESU	East Sussex
GRL	Greater London
HEW	Hereford and Worcestershire
NHA	Northamptonshire
NHM	Northumberland
WSU	West Sussex

Locality/reliability

Findspot listed by parish (where known). The reliability indicator varies from 1 (reliable or almost certainly reliable) through 2 (probably reliable) to 3 (unreliable). Coins with a reliability indicator of 3 are not plotted on the distribution maps and have not generally been considered in the discussion above.

Grid reference

A four figure reference is provided. For some coins a more precise location may be recorded in the Celtic Coin Index.

Find/date

Type of find and date, where known: md (metal detected), exc. (excavated) or unk. (unknown).

Gazetteer

Reference to previously published gazetteers: Allen 1960 (abbreviated as 'O'); Haselgrove 1978 ('I'); Haselgrove 1984 ('II'); Haselgrove 1989 ('III').

CCI

Unique CCI reference number. In almost every case the presence of a number in this column indicates that an image of the coin is maintained in the Celtic Coin Index.

Inscription, type, references etc.

Lists the commonly accepted reading of the inscription, whether or not this is visible on the particular coin in question. Basic information on type is provided, in most cases with reference to Scheers 1977 (abbreviated as 'S') and Allen 1995 (BMC III).

county	locality	rel.	grid ref.	find	date	gazetteer	CCI	inscription, type, references etc
a) gold and base gold (see text)								
Meldi								
CAM	Ely	1	TL5380	md	2001	-	02.0004	/ROVECA, S28
Nervii (Gallo-Belgic XE)								
HAM	Silchester	1	SU6362	exc.?	c. 1900	O, 172	62.0088	plated; S29 cl. I, LT XXXV 8760
KEN	Kent	2	-	unk.	c. 1977	II, 151	99.2161	S29 cl. II, LT XXXV 8746
NOR	Ashill	3	TF9005	md	1979	-	87.0775	supposedly this type, but no image
-	Sussex	2	-	unk.	c. 1900?	I, 123	61.0377	S29 cl. I, LT XXXV 8760
Remi or *Suessiones*?								
ESS	Maldon	1	TL8507	md	1996	-	01.0926	S152, cl. VI
KEN	Canterbury	1	TR1558	exc.	1986	-	-	S152, bronze (Haselgrove, pers. comm.; Stour Street)
KEN	Dover	1	TR3141	md	c. 1998	-	98.0376	S152 cl. II, Doyen cl. VIII or X
KEN	Kent	2	-	md	c. 1999	-	00.0918	S152, ?cl. IV, Doyen cl. IX
WIL	Upavon	3	SU1355	md?	c. 1990	-	02.0379-86	S152, various classes
	alleged small hoard, but from unreliable source							
WIL	Wiltshire	2	-	md	c. 2001	-	01.1636	S152, cl. uncertain
WSU	Chichester	1	SU8604	md	c. 1995	-	95.3383	S152 cl. VIII, Doyen cl. XVIII
WSU	Chichester	1	SU8604	md	c. 1995	-	95.3384	S152 cl. IV, Doyen cl. IX
WSU	Chichester	1	SU8604	md	1995	-	96.1683	S152 cl. II, Doyen cl. VIII
Suessiones (Gallo-Belgic XF)								
HAM	Hayling Island	1	SU7202	exc.	1977	II, 151	91.0335	/CRICIRV, plated; S27 cl. II
KEN	Tonbridge	1	TQ5946	unk.	bef. 1907	O, 173	92.0067	S27 cl. I, LT XXXII 7941
Treveri								
CAM	Fordham	2	TL6370	unk.	bef. 1971	I, 124	-	S30 cl. IV, LT XXXVI 8815
GRL	Hainault	1	TQ4591	md	1991	-	-	VOCARANT/VOCARANT, base gold; S30 cl. II, LT XXXVI 8823; info. DJ Holman
HAM	Winchester	1	SU4829	md	2000	-	00.1961	very base gold; S30, cl. VI?
NHM	Hexham	1	NY9364	md	1993	-	97.1370	plated; S16, BN 6818
OXF	Steventon	1	SU4792	unk.	c. 1855	I, 124	-	S16, LT XXXVIII 9296; electrum
Veliocasses								
DOR	Wareham	1	SY9287	md	1989	-	01.0989	S25 cl. II, LT XXIX 7239
unattributed type								
ESU	Brighton	2	TQ3104	unk.	c. 1873?	O, 275	-	S23, Treveri? (Sills 2003, 212); Selsey?
HER	St Albans	1	TL1507	unk.	bef. 1916	II, 151	78.0110	S23, Treveri? (Sills 2003, 212); no image
b) silver								
unattributed type: ATEVLA VLATOS								
HAM	Hayling Island	1	SU7202	exc.	1977	II, 151	91.0416	plated; S41 cl. II, BMC II, 566
HAM	Hayling Island	1	SU7202	exc.	1978	II, 151	91.0433	plated; S41 cl. I, BMC II, 566
HAM	Hayling Island	1	SU7202	exc.	1978	II, 151	91.0439	plated; S41 cl. I, BMC II, 566
HAM	Hayling Island	1	SU7202	md?	c. 1983	III, 70	91.0579	plated; S41 cl. II, BMC II, 566
KEN	Canterbury	1	TR1558	exc.	bef. 1965	I, 127	-	plated; S41, BMC II, 566
WSU	Chichester	1	SU8604	md	c. 1993	-	94.1106	S41 cl. I, BMC II, 566
other silver types								
HAM	Pitt	1	SU4528	md	1991	-	00.0115	S54, LT XXXVIII 9401; Treveri
HAM	Silchester	1	SU6362	exc.	1980s	III, 70	91.0541	cf. S52, petit billon type
HAM	Winchester	2	SU4829	unk.	bef. 1800	II, 151	63.0264	S51 cl. I; Allen 1965, 92 no. 20
KEN	Canterbury	1	TR1558	exc.	1980	II, 151	97.2340	uncertain, possibly Belgic; cf. S94
WIL	Wanborough	1	SU2082	unk.	bef. 1936	O, 249	61.0063	pseudo-legend; Debord 1987 cl. II
WSU	Chichester	1	SU8604	unk.	bef. 1920	O, 281	-	S55, LT XXXVIII 9383; Treveri?

c) bronze

county	locality	rel.	grid ref.	find	date	gazetteer	CCI	inscription, type, references etc
Aduatuci?								
BER	Mortimer	1	SU6363	md	2000	-	00.0762	cast; S190 cl. IV, BMC III, 519
ESS	Chelmsford	1	TL7006	md	c. 1995	-	95.3436	S217 cl. III (as G-R bronze), BMC III, 42 (or Eburones?)
ESS	Colchester	1	TL9825	unk.	bef. 1941	O, 269	-	S217? Colchester, but not in BMC III
ESS	Great Chesterford	2	TL5042	md	1999	-	99.1384	cast; S190 cl. IIIb, BMC III, 520
ESS	Kelvedon	1	TL8648	exc.	1972	I, 131	73.0908	cast; S190 cl. IV, BMC III, 519
ESS	Maldon	1	TL8507	md	c. 1996	-	99.1247	S217 cl. III (as G-R bronze), BMC III, 42 (or Eburones?)
ESS	Saffron Walden	1	TL5338	md	c. 1996	-	96.1767	cast; S190 cl. IV, BMC III, 519
HAM	Bramley	1	SU6458	md	1994	-	-	cast; S190 cl. IV, BMC III, 519 (Fulford and Creighton 1998, 340)
HAM	Hayling Island	1	SU7202	exc.	1980	II, 152	91.0486	cast; S190 cl. IV, BMC III, 519
HER	Braughing	1	TL3925	unk.	bef. 1890	O, 276	69.0641	S217 cl. III (as G-R bronze), BMC III, 42 (this coin; or Eburones?)
HER	Puckeridge	1	TL3823	md	2002	-	03.0905	cast; S190 cl. IV, BMC III, 519
KEN	Ashford	1	TR0142	md	2001	-	01.0363	cast; S190 cl. IV, BMC III, 519
KEN	Boughton M'chelsea	1	TQ7751	md	c. 1987	III, 72	88.0067	cast; S190 cl. IV, BMC III, 519
KEN	Dover	2	TR2847	md	c. 1997	-	97.1912	cast; S190 cl. IV, BMC III, 519
KEN	Maidstone	1	TQ7655	md	c. 2002	-	02.1105	S217 cl. III (as G-R bronze), BMC III, 42 (or Eburones?)
KEN	Thurnham	1	TQ8257	md	1999	-	00.1328	cast; S190 cl. IV, BMC III, 519
KEN	Woodnesborough	1	TR2956	md	1997	-	97.1955	cast; S190 cl. IV, BMC III, 519
NOR	Hockwold	1	TL7287	md	c. 1986	III, 72	87.0684	cast; S190 cl. IV, BMC III, 519
SUF	Charsfield	1	TM2556	md	c. 1994	-	94.1067	cast; S190 cl. IV, BMC III, 519
WIL	Clatford	1	SU1568	md	2003	-	03.0820	cast; S190 cl. IV, BMC III, 519
WSU	Amberley	1	TQ0313	md	2000	-	00.0761	cast; S190 cl. IV, BMC III, 519
WSU	Chichester	1	SU8604	md	c. 1994	-	94.1107	cast; S190 cl. IIIb, BMC III, 520
Ambiani								
BER	West Ilsley	1	SU4784	md	c. 1998	-	99.0253	S122, LT XXXIV 8526
BUC	Buckinghamshire	2	-	md	c. 1994	-	94.0441	S103 cl. II, BMC III, 42
CAM	Cambridge	1	TL4458	md	c. 1994	-	95.0721	S80g
ESS	Colchester	1	TL9925	exc.	1976	II, 152	78.0109	S93?
ESS	Colchester	1	TL9925	md	1992	-	95.0181	S59, BMC III, 24
ESS	Essex	1	-	md	1988	-	90.0827	VOCIIC /,S80b, BMC III, 17
ESS	Essex	1	-	md	1994	-	96.1572	S80j, BMC III, 14
ESS	Essex	1	-	md	c. 1998	-	98.0383	S80f, BMC III, 15
ESS	Fingringhoe	1	TM0519	md	1995	-	00.0825	S89, BMC III, S22; or British?
ESS	Great Chesterford	1	TL5042	md	c. 1994	-	95.1157	cf. S64, cf. BMC III, 22; or British?
ESS	Orsett	1	TQ6481	md	c. 2001	-	02.0044	S65 cl. VI
HAM	Hayling Island	1	SU7202	exc.	1978	-	91.0431	S90 var. a, LT XXXIV 8503
HAM	Petersfield	1	SU7423	md	1995	-	97.1366	S90?
HAM	Petersfield	1	SU7423	md	2002	-	02.0787	S64 cl. II
HAM	Silchester	1	SU6362	exc.	1873	O, 276	62.0203	S80d, BMC III, 19
HAM	Silchester	1	SU6362	unk.	1974	I, 129	74.0240	cf. S87 cl. II for rev., but obv. head l., not two boars
HAM	Silchester	1	SU6362	exc.	1980s	III, 70	91.0540	S80f, BMC III, 15; pierced
HER	Braughing	1	TL3925	unk.	bef. 1919	O, 276	69.0642	S59, BMC III, 27 (this coin)
HER	Braughing	1	TL3925	unk.	bef. 1919	O, 276	69.0643	S63, BMC III, 28 (this coin)
HER	Braughing	1	TL3925	unk.	bef. 1919	O, 276	69.0645	S83, BMC III, 13 (this coin)
HER	Braughing	1	TL3925	unk.	bef. 1890	O, 276	69.0646	cf. S64 cl. I, or British?; BMC III, 22 (this coin); Evans N14
HER	Braughing	1	TL3925	unk.	bef. 1919	O, 276	69.0647	S59, BMC III, 26 (this coin)
HER	Braughing	1	TL3823	exc.	1971	III, 71	72.0684	S80d, BMC III, 19
HER	Braughing	1	TL3925	md	1990s	-	97.1857	S125, attribution uncertain
HER	Braughing	1	TL3925	md	1990s	-	97.1878	S80d, BMC III, 19
HER	Braughing	1	TL3925	md	1998	-	00.1377	S59, BMC III, 24
HER	Braughing	1	TL3925	md	c. 2002	-	03.0473	S80f, BMC III, 15

county	locality	rel.	grid ref.	find	date	gazetteer	CCI	inscription, type, references etc
Ambiani (continued)								
HER	Braughing	1	TL3925	md	c. 2002	-	03.0474	S80e?
HER	Puckeridge	1	TL3823	exc.	1971	I, 129	-	/A, S80d, BMC III, 19
HER	Puckeridge	1	TL3823	md	c. 1983	III, 71	83.0367	S66
HER	St Albans	1	TL1407	md	c. 1997	-	97.1922	S59, BMC III, 24
HER	St Albans	1	TL1407	md	c. 1997	-	97.1923	S59, BMC III, 24
HER	St Albans	1	TL1407	md	c. 1997	-	97.1924	S64 cl. I
HER	St Albans	1	TL1407	md	c. 1997	-	97.1925	S78
HER	St Albans	1	TL1407	md	c. 1997	-	97.1926	S80c, BMC III, 20
HER	St Albans	1	TL1407	md	c. 1997	-	97.1927	S80c, BMC III, 20
HER	St Albans	1	TL1407	md	c. 1997	-	97.1928	S80d, BMC III, 19
HER	St Albans	1	TL1407	md	c. 1997	-	97.1929	S80f, BMC III, 15
HER	St Albans	1	TL1407	md	c. 1997	-	97.1931	S105
HER	St Albans	1	TL1407	md	c. 1997	-	97.1932	S125, attribution uncertain
HER	St Albans	2	TL1407	md	c. 1990	-	03.0585	S80h, BMC III, S19
HER	Thorley	1	TL4718	md	1997	-	97.2097	S105
HEW	Worcester	1	SO8484	unk.	bef. 1892	O, 277	62.0204	S80j, BMC III, 14
HUM	South Ferriby	1	SE9921	unk.	bef. 1958	O, 277	61.1807	S88
KEN	Acrise	1	TR2042	md	1999	-	00.1364	S82
KEN	Broadstairs	1	TR3969	md	1993	-	94.0331	cf. S64 cl. I, cf. BMC III, 22; British?
KEN	Canterbury	1	TF1457	exc.	1955	O, 276	61.1660	S93
KEN	Canterbury	1	TR1457	exc.	1955	O, 276	61.1668	S59, BMC III, 24
KEN	Canterbury	1	TR1457	exc.	1990	-	91.0285	S80?
KEN	Canterbury	1	TR1457	exc.	bef. 1965	I, 130	-	S178; attribution uncertain
KEN	Canterbury	1	TR1457	exc.	1980	II, 152	97.2339	S119; attribution uncertain
KEN	Canterbury	1	TR1457	exc.	2000	-	01.1824	S89 var., BMC III, 21?
KEN	Canterbury	1	TR1457	exc.	2000	-	01.1825	S60
KEN	Dover	1	TR2847	md	1997	-	97.2049	S64
KEN	Dover	2	TR3141	md	c. 1997	-	97.1911	S80a
KEN	Folkestone	1	TR2437	unk.	1892	O, 276	69.0644	VOCIIC /, S80b, BMC III, 17 (this coin)
KEN	Folkestone	1	TR2437	exc.	1924	-	97.1166	S87 cl. I
KEN	Folkestone	1	TR2437	md	c. 1998	-	00.1337	S81
KEN	Folkestone	1	TR2437	md	1988	-	01.1776	S90c
KEN	Folkestone	1	TR2437	md	2000	-	01.1859	S75 var., BMC III, S26 var.
KEN	Folkestone	2	TR2235	md	1995	-	03.0077	S95, BMC III, S22
KEN	Goodnestone	1	TR2653	md	2001	-	01.1805	S91 var.?
KEN	Goodnestone	1	TR2653	md	2001	-	01.1833	S81?
KEN	Harrietsham	1	TQ8753	md	1983	III, 75	84.0765	possibly S82
KEN	Kent	1	-	md	c. 2000	-	00.1824	S80j, BMC III, 14
KEN	Kent	1	-	md	c. 2002	-	03.0309	VACIICO/, S80e, BMC III, 18
KEN	Meopham	1	TQ6466	md	c. 1993	-	98.0395	S80f, BMC III, 15
KEN	Minster in Thanet	1	TR3264	md	2000	-	01.1846	NEREI MVTINVS/, S79
KEN	Richborough Castle	1	TR3260	exc.	1931	O, 276; I, 131	-	S59; *Richborough* V, 37377
KEN	Richborough Castle	1	TR3260	exc.	1931	O, 276	64.0125	S81
KEN	Richborough Castle	1	TR3260	unk.	1935	-	95.0033	/VIIRICIVS, S109 cl. II var. (horse r.)
KEN	Sandwich	1	TR3457	md	c. 1992	-	92.0713	S80c, BMC III, 20
KEN	Sandwich	1	TR3357	md	1985	-	92.0716	/VIIRICIVS, S109 cl. I
KEN	Sandwich	1	TR3457	md	1980s	-	94.0262	S65 cl. VI var.
KEN	Sandwich	1	TR3357	md	c. 1992	-	94.0268	S80b, BMC III, 17
KEN	Sandwich	1	TR3357	md	1980s	-	94.0380	S80f, BMC III, 15
KEN	Sandwich	1	TR3357	md	1989	-	95.0141	S80j, BMC III, 14
KEN	Sandwich	1	TR3357	md	1980s	-	-	S76; info. DJ Holman
KEN	Sholden	1	TR3552	md	2001	-	01.1783	S91 var.
KEN	Springhead	1	TQ6272	md	c. 2002	-	03.0022	S89 or 95?
KEN	Sutton	1	TR3149	md	1998	-	99.0810	cf. S80 types
KEN	Whitfield	1	TR3146	md	1993	-	96.2303	S60
KEN	Whitfield	1	TR3045	md	c. 1997	-	97.1910	S59, BMC III, 24
KEN	Woodnesborough	1	TR3156	md	1980s	-	94.0350	S81
KEN	Worth	1	TR3355	md	1980s	-	94.0311	VOCIIC /, S80b cl. II, BMC III, 17
KEN	Worth	1	TR3355	md	1992	-	94.0344	S81

county	locality	rel.	grid ref.	find	date	gazetteer	CCI	inscription, type, references etc
Ambiani (continued)								
KEN	Worth	1	TR3355	md	1980s	-	95.2771	S81
KEN	Worth	1	TR3355	md	1980s	-	95.2774	S89, BMC III, S22; or British?
KEN	Worth	1	TR3355	md	1991	-	-	S80d or 80e? info. DJ Holman
KEN	Worth	1	TR3355	md	1997	-	98.1163	S90, var. a, LT XXXIV 8503
KEN	Worth	1	TR3355	md	1997	-	98.1169	S80b, BMC III, 17
KEN	Worth	1	TR3355	md	2001	-	01.1840	S80e, var. a, BMC III, S21
LIN	Knaith	1	SK8284	md	2000	-	01.1572	S133
LIN	Lincolnshire	3	-	unk.	bef. 1945	I, 130	61.1662,	S113, BMC III, 16
	2 coins in hoard or collection?						61.1665	/VIIRICIVS, S109
LIN	Tupholme	1	TF1468	md	2000	-	00.1772	S80j, BMC III, 14
NOR	Norfolk	2	-	md	c. 1998	-	99.0271	S80j, BMC III, 14
NOR	Norfolk	2	-	md	c. 2003	-	03.0837	S59, BMC III, 24
STA	Cheddleton	1	SJ9651	unk.	1877	O, 279, 284; I, 135	96.1696	S121, BMC III, S28 (this coin)
SUF	Freckenham	1	TL6573	md	c. 1992	-	94.0016	S65 cl. V
WIL	Winterbourne	2	SU1834	md	2001	-	03.0626	S65, cl. VI
WSU	Chichester	1	SU8604	md	c. 1995	-	95.0717	S80h, BMC S19
WSU	Chichester	1	SU8604	md	c. 1994	-	95.1131	/VIIRICIVS, S109 cl. II
WSU	Chichester	1	SU8604	md	c. 1996	-	97.1198	S122
WSU	Horsham	1	TQ1730	md	c. 2001	-	01.1416	S122 var.
WSU	Houghton	1	TQ0112	md	c. 1995	-	95.3172	S80h, BMC S19?
WSU	Westhampnett	1	SU8806	md	c. 1995	-	95.1415	S59, BMC III, 24
WSU	Westhampnett	1	SU8806	md	1995	-	95.3919	S92
WSU	Westhampnett	1	SU8806	md	1997	-	01.0988	S90a
WSU	Westhampnett	1	SU8806	md	1997	-	99.0689	S64 var.
Atrebates								
HEW	Weston u. Penyard	1	SO6423	md	c. 1994	-	94.1256	ANDOBRV/, S46 cl. I, BMC III, 33
KEN	Goodnestone	1	TR2553	md	1994	-	95.0240	ANDOBRV/, S46 cl. I, BMC III, 33
KEN	Sandwich	1	TR3357	md	1985	-	94.0383	RVBIOS/, S136 (or Morini?)
KEN	Worth	1	TR3355	md	1980s	-	94.0307	RVBIOS/, S136 (or Morini?)
LIN	Lincolnshire	3	-	unk.	bef. 1945	I, 130	61.1661	ANDOBRV/, S46 cl. I, BMC III, 33
	hoard or collection?							
WSU	Chichester	1	SU8604	md	c. 1993	-	94.1102	ANDOBRV/ GARMANOS, S46 cl. II, BMC III, 35
Aulerci Eburovices								
HAM	Hayling Island	1	SU7202	exc.	1976	I, 130	78.0105-106	LT XXVIII 7034
	2 in hoard with 4 coins of Carnutes							
HAM	Hayling Island	1	SU7202	exc.	1981	III, 70	91.0550	LT XXVIII 7021? very corroded
KEN	North-east Kent	1	-	md	c. 1992	-	92.0631	LT XXVIII 7020? very worn
WSU	Chichester	1	SU8604	md	c. 1993	-	94.1082	cast; BN 9199-9202
Bellovaci								
ESS	Great Chesterford	1	TL5043	unk.	c. 1934	O, 280	61.1778	cast; S185 cl. III, BMC III, 469
KEN	Ash	1	TR2858	exc.	1762	I, 132	99.2160	S185 cl. II, BMC III 466? (I, 132 as S200)
KEN	Richborough Castle	1	TR3260	exc.	c. 1928	O, 280	61.1777	cast; S185 cl. II, BMC III, 468 (this coin); *Richborough* II, 2494
LIN	Lincolnshire	3	-	unk.	bef. 1945	I, 130	61.1666	S130
	hoard or collection?							
MER	Liverpool	2	SJ3490	unk.	bef. 1864	O, 277	-	S123
	one or more in hoard?							
OXF	Aston Upthorpe	1	SU5482	unk.	bef. 1938	O, 278	69.0655	S120 cl. I, BMC III, 32 (this coin)
SUF	Charsfield	1	TM2556	md	1994	-	95.0030	cast; S185 cl. II? BMC III, 466
WSU	Chichester	1	SU8604	md	1999	-	01.0386	S120 var., BMC III, 32 var.
Caleti?								
HER	St Albans	1	TL1407	md	1990	-	92.0606	S110
LIN	Lincolnshire	3	-	unk.	bef. 1945	I, 130	61.1670	S110
	hoard or collection?							

county	locality	rel.	grid ref.	find	date	gazetteer	CCI	inscription, type, references etc
Leuci								
BUC	Great Marlowe	1	SU8486	unk.	c. 1930	O, 279	-	cast; S186
COR	Penzance two or more in hoard?	1	SW4730	unk.	1888	-	96.1692-1693	cast; S186 cl. Ij, BMC III, 412, 414 (these coins)
DOR	Dorchester	1	SY6990	md	c. 1994	-	94.1438	cast; S186 cl. II?, BMC III, 426
DOR	Hengistbury Head	1	SZ1790	exc.	c. 1919	III, 71	-	cast; S186
HER	North-east Herts.	1	-	md	c. 1995	-	95.0745	cast; S186 cl. Ib, BMC III, S416
KEN	Canterbury	1	TR1653	md	1978	III, 72	79.0082	cast; S186 cl. I
KEN	Kent	2	-	unk.	bef. 1964	I, 132	64.0127	cast; S186 cl. Ih, cf. BMC III, 412
KEN	Lyminge	1	TR1540	md	1992	-	94.0388	cast; S186 cl. Ie, BMC III, 410
KEN	North-east Kent	1	-	md	1995	-	96.1637	cast; S187, BMC III, 302
OXF	Watchfield	1	SU2490	exc.	1983	III, 72	99.2158	cast; S186 cl. I
WSU	Chichester	1	SU8604	md	c. 1995	-	95.3407	cast; S186 cl. Ia, BMC III, 398
WSU	Chichester	1	SU8604	md	1995	-	96.1633	cast; S186 cl. II, BMC III, 426
WSU	Chichester	2	SU8604	md	1995	-	96.3446	cast; S186 cl. I, cf. BMC III, 412
WSU	Chichester	2	SU8604	md	1995	-	96.3447	cast; S186 cl. Ic, BMC III, 405
Lexovii								
WSU	Chichester	1	SU8604	md	c. 1994	-	95.1132	LIXOVIATI/, LT XXVIII 7143, BMC III, 147
Meldi								
KEN	Canterbury	1	TR1457	exc.	c. 1950	O, 277	61.1679	EPENV/EΠHNOS, S143, BMC III, 102
OXF	Oxfordshire	1	-	md	c. 2001	-	01.1076	ROVECA/POOYIKA, S28 cl. III var. a, BMC III, S80
WSU	Chichester	1	SU8604	md	c. 1995	-	95.3406	EPENV/EΠHNOS, S143, BMC III, 102
Nervii								
COR	Penzance 1 coin in hoard	1	SW4730	unk.	1888	O, 277	96.1690	/VARTICEO, S190 cl. IIa, BMC III, 38 (this coin)
HER	Braughing	1	TL3925	md	c. 1998	-	98.2306	S190, cl. Ib
HER	Puckeridge	1	TL3823	md	c. 1983	III, 71	83.0403	VERCIO/VER IO, S145, BMC III, 39
Remi								
BED	Lilly Hoo	1	TL1227	unk.	bef. 1864	O, 277	69.0640	cast; S191, BMC III, 506 (this coin)
ESS	Brentwood	1	TQ5993	md	c. 1994	-	95.0499	REMO/REMO, S146, BMC III, 53
ESS	Colchester	1	TL9825	md	c. 1992	-	92.0622	cast; S191, BMC III, 483
GLO	Cheltenham	1	SO9422	md	c. 1993	-	94.0064	REMO/REMO, S146, BMC III, 53
HAM	Hampshire	2	-	md	c. 1999	-	00.1097	REMO/REMO, S146, BMC III, 53
HAM	Hayling Island	1	SU7202	exc.	1977	II, 152	91.0327	cast; S194, BMC III, 477
HAM	Silchester	1	SU6362	exc.	1874	O, 279	62.0246	cast; S195, BMC III, 511
HAM	Silchester	1	SU6362	exc.	c. 1980	III, 71	-	cast; S195, BMC III, 511
HER	Puckeridge	1	TL3823	md	c. 1983	III, 71	83.0399	REMO/REMO, S146, BMC III, 53
KEN	Abbey Gate	1	TQ7558	md	1997	-	97.2326	REMO/REMO, S146, BMC III, 53
KEN	Northbourne	1	TR3254	md	1990	-	95.0097	cast; S191, BMC III, 483
KEN	Richborough	1	TR3260	md	1995	-	95.0938	cast; S191, BMC III, 483
KEN	Shorne	1	TQ6974	md	1991	-	94.0398	cast; S191, BMC III, 483
KEN	Worth	1	TR3355	md	2001	-	01.1837	cast; S193, BMC 507
NHA	Nobottle	1	SP6763	md	c. 1984	III, 44	85.0001	REMO/REMO, S146, BMC III, 53;. III, 44 as Cunobelin
STA	Leek Moor	1	SJ7770	unk.	bef. 1940	O, 277	96.1699	cast; S191, BMC III, S524 (this coin)
WSU	Chichester	1	SU8604	md	1995	-	96.3441	cast; S191, BMC III, 483
WSU	Chichester	2	SU8604	md	1995	-	96.3444	cast; S194, BMC III, 477
WSU	Chichester	2	SU8604	md	1995	-	96.3445	cast; S195, BMC III, 511
WSU	Chichester	1	SU8604	md	c. 1996	-	97.1254	TISIOS REMOS/, S147 cl. II, BMC III, 66
-	Sussex	1	-	md	c. 1993	-	94.0606	cast; S191, BMC III, 483
Suessiones								
BER	Newbury	1	SU4767	md	c. 1988	-	88.0005	cast; S198 cl. I, BMC III, 444
ESS	Chelmsford	1	TL7006	md	c. 1995	-	95.3440	AEIOYIYIIA/ΔEIVICIAC, S155 cl II

county	locality	rel.	grid ref.	find	date	gazetteer	CCI	inscription, type, references etc
Suessiones (continued)								
HAM	Compton	2	SU4725	md	c. 1995	-	96.1295	cast; S198 cl. I, BMC III, 444; possibly in imported soil?
HAM	Hampshire	2	-	md	c. 1984	-	99.0442	cast; S196 cl. II, BMC III, 471
HAM	Hayling Island	1	SU7202	exc.	1978	II, 152	91.0440	cast; S198 cl. I, BMC III, 444
HAM	Purbrook	1	SU6708	md	c. 1995	-	95.0350	cast; S198 cl. I, BMC III, 444
HER	Braughing	1	TL3925	unk.	1868	O, 277	69.0650	cast; S198, cl. I, BMC III, 444 (this coin)
HER	Braughing	1	TL3925	md	2000	-	00.1168	cast; S198, cl. I, BMC III, 444; several?
HER	Braughing	1	TL3925	md	1990s	-	97.1879	/CAΔOY?, S151, BMC III, 76
HER	Braughing	1	TL3925	md	1999	-	03.0773	S156, BMC III, 109
HER	Puckeridge	1	TL3823	md	1972	I, 129	73.0909	/CRICIRV, S27, BMC III, 86
HER	Puckeridge	1	TL3823	md	c. 1997	-	01.0912	cast; S198 cl. I, BMC III, 444
HER	St Albans	1	TL1407	md	c. 1997	-	97.1933	/CAΔOY?, S151, BMC III, 76
HER	Ware	1	TL3514	md	c. 1992	-	92.0723	cast; S198 cl. I, BMC III, 444
KEN	Ashford	1	TR0142	md	c. 2001	-	01.0362	cast; S198 cl. I, BMC III, 444
KEN	Canterbury	1	TR1558	exc.	c. 1979	II, 153	97.2339	cast; S198 cl. I, BMC III, 444
KEN	Dover	1	TR2947	md	1996	-	96.3167	cast; S198 cl. I, BMC III, 444
KEN	Dover	2	TR3141	md	c. 1997	-	97.1913	cast; S198 cl. I, BMC III, 444
KEN	Ebbsfleet	1	TR3363	md?	c. 1991	-	91.0548	cast; S198 cl. I, BMC III, 444
KEN	Kent	1	-	md	1991	-	94.1401	/CRICIRV, S27, BMC III, 86
KEN	Minster in Thanet	1	TR3363	md	1991	-	-	cast; S198 cl. I, BMC III, 444; info. DJ Holman
KEN	Sandwich	1	TR3357	md	1980s	-	94.0261	/CRICIRV, S27, BMC III, 86
SUF	Clare	1	TL7745	md	c. 1996	-	96.2835	cast; S198 cl. I, BMC III, 444
WSU	Arundel	1	TQ0107	md	c. 1999	-	99.1197	cast; S198 cl. I, BMC III, 444
WSU	Chichester	1	SU8604	md	c. 1996	-	97.1197	cast; S196 cl. I, BMC III, S507
WSU	Tangmere	1	SU9006	md	c. 1999	-	99.1196	cast; S198 cl. I, BMC III, 444
WSU	Westhampnett	1	SU8806	md	c. 1994	-	95.1416	S154 cl. II, BMC III, 80
WSU	Westhampnett	1	SU8806	md	1995	-	95.3335	cast; S198 cl. I, BMC III, 444
WSU	Westhampnett	1	SU8806	md	1995	-	96.1353	cast; S198 cl. I, BMC III, 444
-	Sussex	1	-	md	c. 1996	-	97.0196	cast; S198 cl. I, BMC III, 444
Veliocasses								
ESS	Coggeshall	2	TL8522	md	c. 1980	-	92.0218	S163 cl. Ia
ESS	Saffron Walden	1	TL5338	unk.	bef. 1958	O, 278	-	cast; S165
HAM	Hayling Island	1	SU7202	exc.	1977	II, 152	91.0339	cast; S206 cl. I (or lower Normandy for S206 type)
HAM	Hayling Island	1	SU7202	exc.	1981	-	91.0563	cast; S206 cl. I
KEN	Canterbury	1	TR1558	exc.	c. 1978	I, 132	78.0108	cast; S206 cl. uncertain
KEN	Canterbury	1	TR1454	md	1994	-	95.0265	S163 cl. Ib
KEN	Faversham hoard of six or more?	1	TR0161	unk.	bef. 1955	O, 277	61.1729-730 65.0157 65.0159 96.1694-695	cast; S165 cl. I, BMC III, S9-S11, S14 (these coins) see also Sittingbourne
KEN	Folkestone	1	TR2235	md	2000	-	00.1773	S163, cl. uncertain
KEN	Sandwich	1	TR3357	md	1980s	-	94.0276	S163 cl. Ic
KEN	Sittingbourne	2	TQ9063	unk.	bef. 1955	O, 277	61.1732	cast; S165 cl. I; perhaps really from Faversham hoard?
WSU	Chichester	1	SU8604	md	c. 1989	-	90.0830	S163 cl. II, BMC III, 1
WSU	Chichester	1	SU8604	md	c. 1995	-	95.3411	SVTICOS/ RATVMACOS, cast; S164 cl. IV
WSU	Chichester	1	SU8604	md	c. 1996	-	97.1255	cast; S206 cl. I
WSU	Clapham	1	TQ0909	unk.	1953	O, 280	61.1659	cast; S206 cl. I
WSU	Westhampnett	1	SU8806	md	1996	-	99.0688	S163 cl. Ie
WSU	Westhampnett	1	SU8806	md	1999	-	02.0439	S163 cl. Ie
unattributed type: /GERMANVS INDVTILLI L								
CAM	Fordham	1	TL6370	md	c. 1999	-	00.0917	S216, BMC III, 263
ESS	Colchester 3 examples in exc.	1	TL9925	exc.	1930s	O, 278	72.0609 + 2	S216, BMC III, 263; *Camulodunum*, 142

county	locality	rel.	grid ref.	find	date	gazetteer	CCI	inscription, type, references etc
GERMANVS INDVTILLI L (continued)								
HAM	Silchester	1	SU6362	exc.?	bef. 1900	O, 278	62.0209	S216, BMC III, 263
KEN	Canterbury	1	TR1557	exc.	c. 1950	O, 278	61.1676	S216, BMC III, 263; exc. at 10 Castle St
KEN	Sandwich	1	TR3357	md	1980s	-	94.0263	S216, BMC III, 263
KEN	Sandwich	1	TR3357	md	1980s	-	-	S216, BMC III, 263; info. DJ Holman
KEN	Thurnham	1	TQ8058	md	2001	-	01.1784	S216, BMC III, 263
KEN	Woodnesborough	1	TR3156	md	c. 1986	-	-	S216, BMC III, 263; info. DJ Holman
KEN	Worth	1	TR3355	md	1998	-	99.0807	S216, BMC III, 263
LEI	Leicester	1	SK9017	exc.	c. 1936	III, 71	-	S216, BMC III, 263
LIN	Owmby	1	SK9785	md	c. 1997	-	97.1693	S216, BMC III, 263
WSU	Lancing Down	1	TQ1706	unk.	1838	O, 278	-	S216, BMC III, 263
	one in hoard (temple deposit?) with British coins							
other uncertainly attributed types								
ESU	Eastbourne	1	TV6199	md	1996	-	99.1878	BMC III, 31; British?
HER	Braughing	1	TL3925	md	c. 1998	-	98.2305	ECCAIOS/ECCAIOS, S176, cl. II, LT XXX 7485
HER	Braughing	1	TL3925	md	2000	-	02.0070	ECCAIOS/ECCAIOS, S176, cl. I, BMC III, 113
HER	St Albans	1	TL1407	md	c. 1997	-	97.1930	/IMONIO, S104, LT XXXIV 8507
KEN	Canterbury	1	TR1557	unk.	1869	O, 279	69.0651	cast; BMC III, 442 (this coin)
KEN	Canterbury	1	TR1557	exc.	c. 1978	-	99.0349	cast; S199 or 205
KEN	Dover	1	TR2847	md	1997	-	-	as *BNJ* 60 (1990), no. 159; info. DJ Holman; poss. not Belgic
WIL	Mildenhall	1	SU2169	unk.	bef. 1881	O, 279	69.0662	BMC III, 31 (this coin); British?
WSU	Chichester	1	SU8604	md	c. 1996	-	97.1234	cast; S213, BMC III, 317
WSU	Chichester	1	SU8604	md	c. 1996	-	97.1223	cast; "Durocasses", BN 7936
WSU	Chichester	1	SU8604	md	1997	-	98.2030	/IMONIO, S104, LT XXXIV 8507
WSU	Chichester	1	SU8604	md	c. 1996	-	97.1226	BMC III, 31; British?
WSU	Oving	1	SU9005	md	1995	-	96.3529	BMC III, 31; British?
WSU	Tangmere	2	SU9006	md	1997	-	97.1377	S210, BMC III, S397; Suessiones? or Senones?
WSU	Warningcamp	1	TQ0307	md	2003	-	03.0851	BMC III, 31; British?
uncertain/unidentified types								
BER	Sonning	1	SU7180	unk.	c. 1840	I, 128	70.0070	probably Ambianic type
DOR	Dorchester	1	SY6990	unk.	c. 1953	II, 150	61.1658	too worn for identification; not Armorican (as II, 150)
ESS	Colchester	1	TL9925	exc.	1973	III, 71	78.0121	cast; too worn for identification
ESS	Colchester	1	TL9925	md	c. 1996	-	97.1218	Ambiani? very worn
ESS	Essex	1	-	md?	c. 1990	-	90.0833	S80e (Ambiani)? extremely worn
ESS	Essex	1	-	md	c. 1997	-	98.0382	very worn
ESS	Essex	1	-	md	c. 1997	-	98.0384	very worn
ESU	Bexhill on Sea	1	TQ7407	md	2003	-	03.1142	possibly BMC III, S561 type?
GRL	Kew Bridge	1	TQ1977	md	1998	-	99.0679	cast; uncertain type, possibly not Belgic
HAM	Silchester	1	SU6362	exc.	c. 1874	O, 190, 268	62.0154	head l./horse l.; Belgic?
HAM	Silchester	1	SU6362	exc.	1985	III, 71	91.0545	cast; possibly Belgic type
HER	Puckeridge	1	TL3823	exc.	1971	I, 118	73.1019	probably a Belgic type
HER	Puckeridge	1	TL3823	exc.	1971	II, 152	-	S80d or 80e? not identified in exc. report
HER	St Albans	1	TL1107	exc.	1982	III, 74	-	"uncertain Belgic"
HUM	Kirmington	1	TA1011	md	1997	-	97.1301	boar standard on both sides
KEN	Aldington	1	TR0735	md	1992	-	95.0919	too worn for identification
KEN	Canterbury	1	TR1457	exc.	1982	III, 72	83.0277	cast; too corroded for identification
KEN	Canterbury	1	TR1457	exc.	c. 1979	II, 153	97.2341	cf. Scheers, Seine-Maritime 301; could be from elsewhere in Gaul?
KEN	Canterbury	1	TR1457	exc.	bef. 1982	II, 154	-	"probably Belgic Gaul"
KEN	Canterbury	1	TR1457	exc.	1980	II, 154	-	possibly Belgic type
KEN	Eastry	1	TR3054	md	1996	-	97.1963	helmeted head r./horse l.
KEN	Worth	1	TR3355	md	1980s	-	94.0295	possibly S80a cl. I (Ambiani)?
KEN	Worth	1	TR3355	md	1980s	-	95.2742	cast; possibly S186 (Leuci)?

county	locality	rel.	grid ref.	find	date	gazetteer	CCI	inscription, type, references etc
uncertain/unidentified types (continued)								
LEI	Leicester	1	SK5804	unk.	bef. 1960	O, 277	61.1677	too worn for identification; Scheers has as possible S87
LIN	Lincolnshire hoard or collection?	3	-	unk.	bef. 1945	I, 130	61.1657, 1663-64	too worn and corroded for identification
LIN	Owmby	1	SK9883	md?	bef. 1975	II, 154	92.0527	Mack 445b; possibly a Belgic type? or British? cf. Evans G12 for rev.
NOR	Norfolk	2	-	md	c. 1998	-	99.0272-279	seven coins, incl. one cast; all very worn; possibly from one site?
WIL	Avebury	1	SU1070	unk.	c. 1900	I, 133	82.0582	or central Gaulish potin?
WSU	Chichester	1	SU8604	md	c. 1994	-	95.0717	head l./horse l.
WSU	Chichester	1	SU8604	md	c. 1996	-	97.1252	too worn for identification

Coins deleted from previous gazetteers

This section includes only coins which have been explicitly identified as Belgic types in previous gazetteers; it does not include all the coins listed as "uncertain British or Gaulish", or suchlike.

BED	Upper Stondon	1	TL1535	unk.	1878	O, 276	-	British; Evans G12
ESS	Colchester	1	TL9825	exc.	1970	I, 128; II, 152	72.0598	Allen 1985, M3:B1; probably British
ESS	Harlow	1	TL4712	exc.	c. 1971	I, 36; II, 152	73.0512	new Addedomaros bronze
ESS	Tilbury	1	TQ6376	md	1986	III, 70	88.0161	north Thames type, snake/horse and rider
ESS	Wickford	1	TQ7693	exc.	c. 1970	I, 129	72.0599	probably British
HAM	Hayling Island	1	SU7202	exc.	c. 1977	II, 152	91.0447	Kentish type, VA 167 (Briggs et al. 1992, no. 121, as S83)
HAM	Hayling Island	1	SU7202	exc.	c. 1979	II, 153	91.0499	more likely British? (Briggs et al. 1992, no. 15)
HAM	Silchester	1	SU6362	exc.	c. 1873	O, 276	-	repeat of Boon (1954), either no. 5 or 14?
HAM	Silchester	1	SU6362	exc.	c. 1873	O, 277	62.0210	possibly central Gaulish
HER	Braughing	1	TL3823	exc.	1971	III, 71	72.0597	cf. S66bis, but perhaps north Thames?
HER	Puckeridge	1	TL3823	exc.	1971	I, 131	73.1015	British, stater core?
KEN	Canterbury	2	TR1558	unk.	bef. 1958	O, 276	64.0126	British; probably Kentish type
KEN	Canterbury	1	TR1558	exc.	1976	I, 132	-	two potins listed; probably just one (78.0108, S206)
NOR	Brettenham	1	TL9484	unk.	bef. 1864	O, 277	69.0533	British; Evans G12
SUF	Coddenham	1	TM1354	md	1980	III, 71	-	probably British

Bibliography

Allen, D. F. 1960: The origins of coinage in Britain: a reappraisal. In S. S. Frere (ed.), *Problems of the Iron Age in southern Britain* (London, Institute of Archaeology Occasional Paper 11), 97-308.

Allen, D. F. 1961: A study of the Dobunnic coinage. In E. M. Clifford, *Bagendon, a Celtic oppidum: a record of the excavations of 1954-56* (Cambridge, Heffer), 75-149.

Allen, D. F. 1965: Les pieces d'argent minces du comte de Hampshire: nouveau lien entre la Gaule celtique et la Grande-Bretagne. *Revue Numismatique* (series 6), 7, 79-93.

Allen, D. F. 1968: The pre-Roman coins. In B. W. Cunliffe, *Fifth report on the excavations of the Roman fort at Richborough, Kent* (Oxford, Society of Antiquaries Research Report 23), 184-188.

Allen, D. F. 1985: The Belgic coins. In R. Niblett, *Sheepen: an early Roman industrial site at Camulodunum* (CBA Research Report 57), fiche 3:B1-3.

Allen, D. F. (ed. M. Mays) 1995: *Celtic coins in the British Museum III: bronze coins of Gaul* (London, BMP).

Bean, S. 1991: Two unpublished types of Celtic coin. *Celtic Coin Bulletin* 1, 7-8.

Blockley, K., Blockley, M., Blockley, P., Frere, S. and Stow, S. (eds), *Excavations in the Marlowe Car Park and surrounding areas. Part II: the finds* (The Archaeology of Canterbury volume V) (Canterbury Archaeological Trust).

Boon, G. C. 1954: The ancient British coins found at Silchester. *Antiquaries Journal* 34, 70-73.

Boon, G. C. 2000: The coins. In M. Fulford and J. Timby, *Late Iron Age and Roman Silchester. Excavations on the site of the forum basilica 1977, 1980-86* (Society for the

Promotion of Roman Studies, Britannia Monograph 15), 127-179.

Briggs, D., Haselgrove, C. and King, C. 1992: Iron Age and Roman coins from Hayling Island temple. *British Numismatic Journal* 62, 1-62.

Bryant, S. R. and Niblett, R. 2001: The late Iron Age in Hertfordshire and the north Chilterns. In J. Collis (ed.), *Society and settlement in Iron Age Europe* (Sheffield), 98-110.

Burnett, A. 1992: A new Iron Age issue from near Chichester. *Spink Numismatic Circular* 100, 340-342.

Cottam, G. L. 1996: Further confirmation of a Kentish alliance? - light shed by a new bronze unit of Verica. *British Numismatic Journal* 66, 113-116.

Cottam, G. L. 1999: The 'cock bronzes' and other related Iron Age bronze coins found predominantly in West Sussex and Hampshire. *British Numismatic Journal* 69, 1-18.

Creighton, J. 2000: *Coins and power in late Iron Age Britain* (Cambridge, CUP).

Cunliffe, B. W. (ed.) 1981: *Coinage and society in Britain and Gaul: some current problems* (London, CBA Research Report 38).

Cunliffe, B. W. 1987: *Hengistbury Head, Dorset I: the prehistoric and Roman settlement 3500 BC - AD 500* (Oxford, OUCA monograph 13).

Cunliffe, B. W. 1991 (3rd ed.): *Iron Age communities in Britain* (London, Routledge).

Debord, J. 1987: Une production tardive en argent de l'atelier monétaire gaulois de Villeneuve-Saint-Germain (Aisne). In *Mélanges offerts au Docteur J.-B. Colbert de Beaulieu* (Paris, Le Léopard d'Or), 235-252.

de Jersey, P. 1997: Armorica and Britain: the numismatic evidence. In B. W. Cunliffe and P. de Jersey, *Armorica and Britain: cross Channel relationships in the late first millennium BC* (Oxford, OUCA monograph 45, Studies in Celtic coinage 3), 72-103.

de Jersey, P. 1998: Abingdon Zoo: a new Celtic silver unit from Berkshire. *Spink Numismatic Circular* 106, 150-151.

de Jersey, P. 1999: Exotic Celtic coinage in Britain. *Oxford Journal of Archaeology* 18, 189-216.

Delestrée, L.-P. 1996: *Monnayages et peuples gaulois du Nord-Ouest* (Paris, Errance).

Delestrée, L.-P. 2003: Un nouveau bronze de l'ile de Bretagne en Gaule Belgique. *Cahiers Numismatiques* 40 (June, no. 156), 39-40.

Delestrée, L.-P. and Tache, M. 2002: *Nouvel Atlas des Monnaies Gauloises. I, de la Seine au Rhin* (Paris, Commios).

Doyen, J.-M. 1987: Les subdivisions «aux segments de cercles» du type BN 8030: état de la question. In *Mélanges offerts au Docteur J.-B. Colbert de Beaulieu* (Paris, Le Léopard d'Or), 315-330.

Evans, J. 1864: *The coins of the ancient Britons* (London).

Faussett, B. 1856: *Inventorium Sepulchrale* (London).

Fulford, M. and Creighton, J. 1998: A late Iron Age mirror burial from Latchmere Green, near Silchester, Hampshire. *Proceedings of the Prehistoric Society* 64, 331-342.

Goodburn, R. 1987: The Celtic coins. In N. Crummy (ed.), *Colchester Archaeological Report 4: The coins from excavations in Colchester 1971-9* (Colchester Archaeological Trust), 15-16.

Haselgrove, C. 1978: *Supplementary gazetteer of find-spots of Celtic coins in Britain, 1977* (Institute of Archaeology, London, Occasional Paper 11a).

Haselgrove, C. 1984: Celtic coins found in Britain 1977-82. *Bulletin of the Institute of Archaeology, University of London* 20, 107-154.

Haselgrove, C. 1987: *Iron Age coinage in south-east England: the archaeological context* (Oxford, BAR 174).

Haselgrove, C. 1989: Celtic coins found in Britain 1982-1987. *Bulletin of the Institute of Archaeology, University of London* 26, 1-75.

Haselgrove, C. 1999: The development of Iron Age coinage in Belgic Gaul. *Numismatic Chronicle* 159, 111-168.

Hawkes, C. F. C. and Hull, M. R. 1947: *Camulodunum. First report on the excavations of Colchester 1930-39* (OUP, Society of Antiquaries Research Report 14).

Holman, D. 2000: Iron Age coinage in Kent: a review of current knowledge. *Archaeologia Cantiana* 120, 205-233.

King, A. and Soffe, G. 2001: Internal organisation and deposition at the Iron Age temple on Hayling Island, Hampshire. In J. Collis (ed.), *Society and settlement in Iron Age Europe* (Sheffield), 111-124.

Mack, R. P. 1964 (2nd ed.): *The coinage of ancient Britain* (London, Spink and Seaby).

Nash, D. and Sellwood, L. C. 1995: The Celtic coins. In K. Blockley et al. (eds.), *Excavations in the Marlowe Car Park and surrounding areas. Part II: the finds* (Canterbury Archaeological Trust), 922-926.

Neal, D. S., Wardle, A. and Hunn, J. 1990: *Excavation of the Iron Age, Roman and medieval settlement at Gorhambury, St Albans* (English Heritage Archaeological Report 14).

Pearce, B. W. 1948: Coins. In K. M. Kenyon, *Excavations at the Jewry Wall Site, Leicester* (Oxford, Society of Antiquaries Research Report 15), 279-282.

Rodwell, K. A. 1988: *The prehistoric and Roman settlement at Kelvedon, Essex* (CBA Research Report 63/Chelmsford Archaeological Trust Report 6).

Scheers, S. 1977: *Traité de numismatique celtique II. La Gaule Belgique* (Louvain, Peeters).

Scheers, S. 1982: Les monnaies trouvées au fanum de Chilly (Somme) de 1978 à 1980. *Revue Archéologique de Picardie* 4 (1982), 92-118.

Scull, C. 1992: Excavations and survey at Watchfield, Oxfordshire, 1983-92. *Archaeological Journal* 149, 124-281.

Sherlock, R. J. 1956: A nineteenth century manuscript book on coins. *British Numismatic Journal* 29, 394-399.

Sills, J. 2003: *Gaulish and early British gold coinage* (London, Spink).

Winbolt, S. E. 1925: *Roman Folkestone* (London, Methuen).

The Belgae in Hampshire

Robert Van Arsdell

When this paper was originally presented in Oxford, the recent movement to assign coins to the Belgae was described as a third attempt to identify these people in the archaeological record. This was not completely accurate, however, since a much earlier first attempt was not discussed at the meeting.

This first attempt began in the sixteenth century, when antiquarian writers speculated about the territory of the Belgae (Camden 1590, 151-152). Later editions of Camden's *Britannia* (1789, vol. 1, 54) identify the Grim's Ditch near Woodyates as a Belgic construction. In the eighteenth century, William Stukeley tried to establish a date for Stonehenge, and in doing so pursued the matter of the Belgae further. He suggested (Stukeley 1724, 181; 1776, 189) that the Wansdyke was a Belgic structure, partially because of the rudeness of its construction. Stukeley also noted (1740, 4) that the Wansdyke was cut by the Roman road to Bath, and therefore suggested that it must have predated the Romans. Believing that sarsen stones would not have been moved across the Wansdyke for military and political reasons, he thus pronounced Stonehenge to be a pre-Roman work.

Stukeley went on (1740, 64) to suggest a date of 460 BC for the construction of Stonehenge. He assumed that a compass orientation was built into its design, and calculated the date using William Herschel's estimate of the wandering of the earth's magnetic pole. Stukeley then suggested that Diviciacus had constructed the Wansdyke in about 100 BC.

In a mid-nineteenth century article, Edwin Guest (1851) elaborated on Stukeley's work, and published a map of the Belgae in southern Britain. This identified certain ditches as Belgic constructions. He accepted Stukeley's idea that the Wansdyke was the result of a later, or in his words "second" Belgic invasion, but not that Diviciacus was the builder.

All of this early work was made largely redundant by General Pitt-Rivers, when he published his excavations of the Wansdyke (Pitt-Rivers 1892). Finds of Samian pottery and other Roman objects beneath the bank proved that the earthwork was at least Roman in date, and probably later. Although Pitt-Rivers did not excavate across the junction of the Roman road and the Wansdyke, it was clear that the pre-Roman date suggested by Stukeley and Guest was incorrect.

Pitt-Rivers unintentionally launched the second attempt to identify the Belgae in the archaeological record. At Rotherley, a village "of the Roman age but of British construction" (Pitt-Rivers 1888, 65), he identified a new form of wheel-thrown pottery. In the excavation report (*ibid.*, 142ff.) he published finds of the "bead rim" pots which were to loom so importantly in the study of the Belgae many years later.

In 1913, Maud Cunnington identified three phases of occupation at Casterley Camp in Wiltshire (Cunnington 1913-14, 83-85): an early occupation of "pit dwellers"; a second phase of pre-Roman invaders (who used bead rim pottery); and a final Roman phase. That archaeologists would have had their minds fixed on invasions at the outbreak of the World War I is hardly surprising. Cunnington's suggestion (*ibid.*, 84) that bead rim pottery was introduced during an "invasion by a new race, or tribe, of superior culture" would be enlarged upon by other invasion-minded archaeologists in the coming decades. Bushe-Fox (1925, 33) found more examples of bead rim pottery at Hengistbury Head and Swarling, and he suggested that these pots, in association with Belgic and Arretine pottery and La Tène III fibulae, could represent the invasion of the Belgae.

Hawkes and Dunning (1930, 153-154) took the idea further still, asserting that the bead rim pottery should be considered together with the coinage of Commios, and that both could be assigned to a second Belgic invasion of Britain at the close of the Gallic War. They noted (*ibid.*, 278) affinities to bead rim pottery in Gaul as part of the evidence, suggesting that the pottery of Normandy had been the inspiration for the style introduced by the Belgic invaders.

Almost immediately afterwards, Cunnington (1932) attacked this expansion of her earlier contribution. She argued that the La Tène III fibulae were too widely distributed in Britain to be of any use in identifying the Belgae, and that the bead rim pottery need not be an imported style. She objected particularly strongly to the suggestion that the introduction of the potter's wheel necessitated an invasion. Her retort to Hawkes and Dunning – "but no sooner does the Briton (or the potter in Britain) presume to make use of a wheel, than his unfortunate pots are robbed of their native parentage; and thus orphaned are obliged to seek new ancestry, and find it in Normandy" – (Cunnington 1932, 27-28) is still a valid warning to all those interpreting archaeological evidence.

Hawkes and Dunning (1932) attempted to rebut Cunnington's attack with a restatement of their evidence. They also clarified their distribution map of bead rim pottery (which confusingly included Roman types in the initial publication), but the damage was done. The idea that bead rim pottery revealed the Belgae in Britain never received acceptance, though it is worth noting that 'never received acceptance' and 'was wrong' are not the same thing.

For many years after 1932 the debate on the location of the Belgae fell silent. Some fifty years later it was resurrected by Barry Cunliffe (1984), launching a third attempt to identify the tribe in the archaeological record. Cunliffe suggested that Hawkes and Dunning's ideas deserved a second look, particularly those concerning Commios. Cunliffe also identified some exotic pottery forms, such as tazze and quoit-shaped pedestal vases, with links to Normandy. The issue of the Belgae was then raised again by Cunliffe (1991, 108), noting that the Aylesford-Swarling culture was usually accepted as evidence of the Belgae in Britain, but could not be identified anywhere pre-dating the Gallic War. He pointed out that Caesar specifically mentions Belgic invasions (*de Bello Gallico*, V, 12), and suggested that one approach to solving the problem would lie in identifying where the Romans thought the Belgae lived. The answer, of course, was Venta Belgarum, now Winchester. Cunliffe and de Jersey (1997, 106) again raised the issue, noting the presence of exotic pottery forms found near Chichester which bore affinities to pottery from Normandy.

Sharples (1990) showed some reluctance to accept this partial resurrection of the ideas of Hawkes and Dunning. Although not directly debating the issues raised by Cunliffe, Sharples noted that i) most of the exotic imports to Hengistbury did not penetrate far inland, and thus Hengistbury need not have been a conduit for continental trade to southern central Britain; ii) trade need not have been an impetus for cultural or settlement changes inland from the coast during the first century BC; and iii) that the changes identified could have been the result of an evolution in manufacturing techniques, or trade within Britain (in other words a totally domestic phenomenon as opposed to a core-periphery relationship with Rome). These ideas essentially mirrored those of Maud Cunnington (1932).

By 1997, the attempt to find the Belgae, after three tries, remained at something of a stalemate. While the evidence for an invasion was identified, it was slim and equivocal. The influence of the Belgae on the archaeological record, if there was such an influence, was seen to be marginal. The thrust of the arguments for a Belgic presence could easily be parried by Cunnington's famous retort to Hawkes and Dunning.

The recent fourth attempt to identify the Belgae relies largely on numismatic evidence. It is important to realize that numismatic proofs, especially in the field of Celtic coinage, are virtually impossible to make. The usual procedure is to analyse all the forms of evidence: findspot distributions, typology, related archaeological work, the writings of ancient authors, metrology, metallurgy, die-cutting, image-borrowing and so on. Usually a worker is fortunate if a convergence is found amongst three or four kinds of evidence. At least one form of evidence will normally be in contradiction. And woe to the researcher who finds a new variety of coin with strong typological affinities to the coinage of one tribe, but with a single findspot well within the territory of a different tribe. Whichever way she or he decides the issue, somebody else will immediately adopt the opposite position.

The problems of identifying the Belgae in the coin record are made more difficult by the appearance of a number of suspected modern forgeries during the past decade. There is always a need for great caution when a large number of new types of coin are discovered in a short period. Numismatists have been recording new Celtic coins since the time of Camden, and new discoveries should be subject to some scepticism at first.

In a series of articles, Philip de Jersey (1997a; 1997b; 2001) and Chris Rudd (2001) have taken up Cunliffe's challenge and have tried to find the Belgae in the numismatic record. In his 1997 articles, de Jersey included a map with a region around Winchester labelled "Belgae?". A later map by Rudd (2001, 2) eliminated the question mark from the label. Later in 2001, de Jersey (2001b, 6) stepped back from the "Belgae" identification and suggested the more neutral-sounding "Solent" should be used. He also suggested that the coin types for the Solent region would include the Cheriton staters, some uninscribed silver types of unusual style, and the copper "Chichester cock" type. These were all reasonable suggestions. During the same period, Rudd used the "Belgae?" maps to identify additional types as coins of the Belgae in his sales lists. These too were reasonable suggestions.

There has, however, been no comprehensive attempt to identify the convergence of several types of numismatic evidence to prove that these truly are the coins of the Belgae. As the idea that the Belgae struck their own, distinctive coinage gains credence through repetition, it is easy to overlook the fact that no proof has been given.

One might think that the problem can be solved by the application of the numismatic methods which have served so well in the past. Unfortunately, this is not the case. Many of the coins are represented by only a few examples, and the number of recorded findspots is even smaller. Mapping many types together is questionable, because the coins do not fall into neat, easily identifiable typological groups. Furthermore, one of the most common types, the Cheriton stater, is largely found in hoards, not spread about the countryside in a large number of isolated finds. Findspot distribution maps derived from this kind of date are unreliable, and difficult to interpret.

The typological evidence is often equivocal as well. Rudd list 26, no. 31 (*Tangmere Stub Tail*), list 29 no. 32 (*Cog Wheel Wreath*), and list 52 no. 32 (*Qc Corkscrew*) all look similar to the coinage of the Atrebates: one could easily turn the findspot versus typology argument against the Belgae. Including a moderate percentage of typologically equivocal types in the findspot distribution maps would invalidate the results.

Since conclusive "proofs" are not in the offing, a second, less rigorous path to a temporary solution may be suggested. A subset of types can be selected for distribution analysis. The types should have noticeable typological differences from the coins normally associated with Allen's British Q series and its derivatives. They should be plausibly genuine ancient coins, and they should have reasonable numbers of findspots, not dominated by hoards.

When these criteria are applied, only a small number of types fit the bill. For gold coins, Rudd list 29 no. 33 (*Ratham Sun Ring*), list 54 no. 34 (*Danebury Scrolls*) and list 31 no. 29 (*South Coast Cog Wheel*) could be selected. This is a rather unhappy group, however, because the typological affinity to British Q is still arguably evident. For silver, Rudd list 27 no. 55 (*Chichester Lyre*) and list 30 no. 28 (*Hayling Moon Head*) could be selected. Finally, for copper, Rudd list 28 no. 78 *(Chichester Cock*) and list 60 no. 35 (*Chichester Horse*) would be chosen; the copper coins have the least typological affinity to British Q.

The findspot distribution maps for these gold, silver and copper types are shown in Figures 1-3. Only "dot maps" can be drawn, since too little data is available to plot reliable trend-surface maps; which in itself should be a cause for caution. The numbers on the maps denote the tally of finds in a single locality, rather than indicating a hoard. The black squares indicate single finds.

The first point to be examined is whether these coins have the same distribution as Pitt-Rivers's bead rim pottery. The main distribution of the pottery in Hawkes and Dunning's map (1932, 415) lies to the west of the Avon, with a small number of pots about the Test. Even if more recent data are added to show additional finds of bead rim pots to the east, the difference from the coin distributions is plain: the coins are not found to the west, and thus the purported Belgae/Solent coins do not have the same distribution as the bead rim pottery.

The second point to discuss is whether these coins have a distribution distinct from that of the roughly contemporary Atrebatic coinage. The trend surface map for Atrebatic B (the uninscribed triple-tailed horse type, roughly equivalent to British Q and its derivatives) is given in Figure 4. These extremely common types completely cover southern central Britain east from the upper reaches of the Test. Significantly, they also include the Chichester region. All three of the Belgae/Solent distributions fall within that of Atrebatic B. The area around Chichester has a high concentration of Belgae/Solent findspots; and it's also a high spot in the distribution of Atrebatic B. A weak argument might be made that the Belgae/Solent types are found only on the west side of the Atrebatic B distribution, but even this is not entirely true. Overall, the Belgae/Solent types do not have a findspot distribution distinct from Atrebatic B.

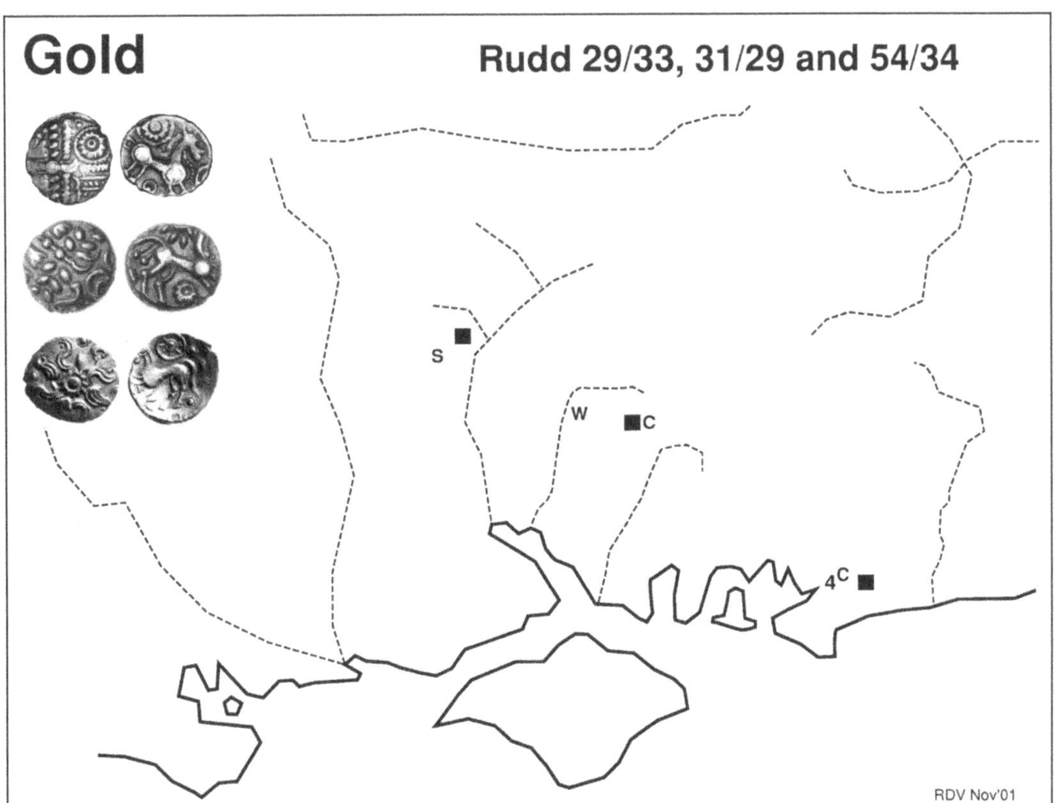

Figure 1. Distribution of gold Belgae/Solent issues.
Locations marked (left to right): Stockbridge, Winchester, Cheriton, Chichester.

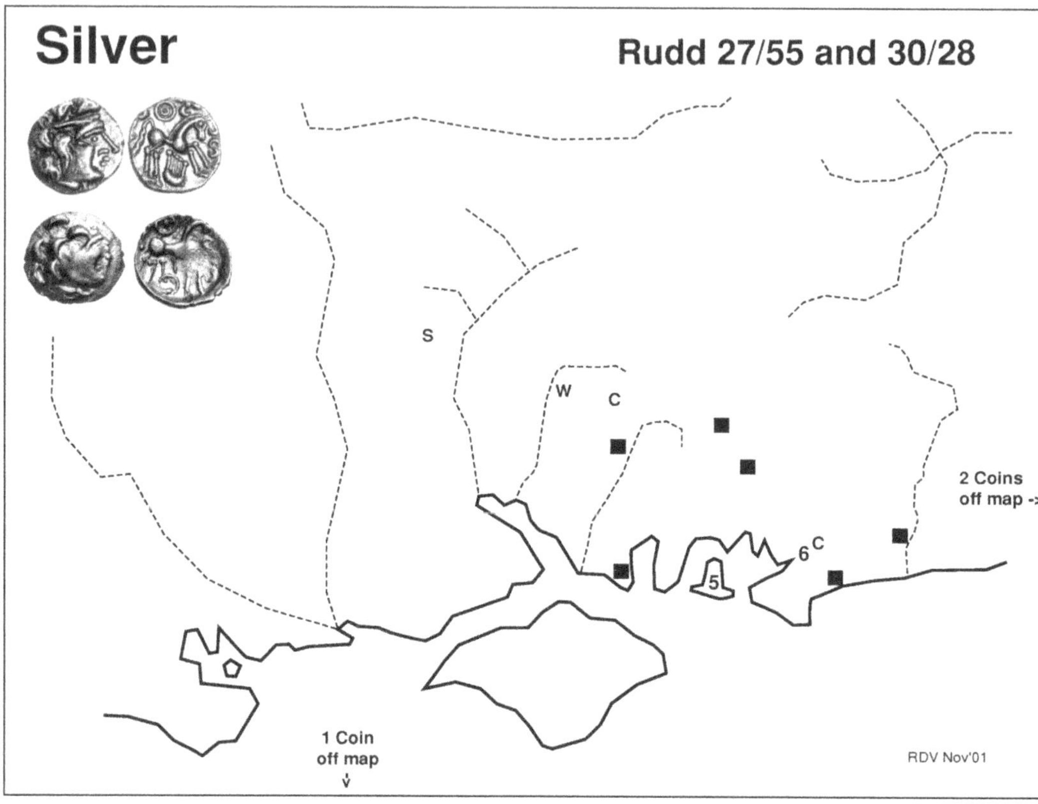

Figure 2. Distribution of silver Belgae/Solent issues.
Locations marked (left to right): Stockbridge, Winchester, Cheriton, Chichester.

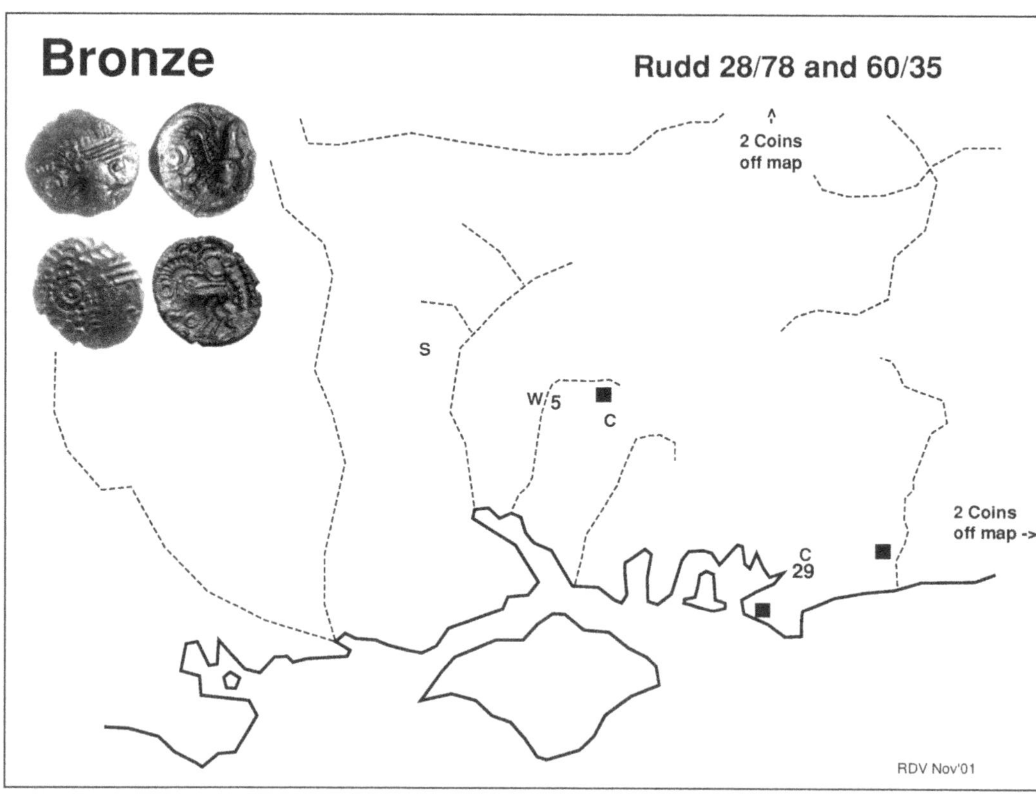

Figure 3. Distribution of bronze Belgae/Solent issues.
Locations marked (left to right): Stockbridge, Winchester, Cheriton, Chichester

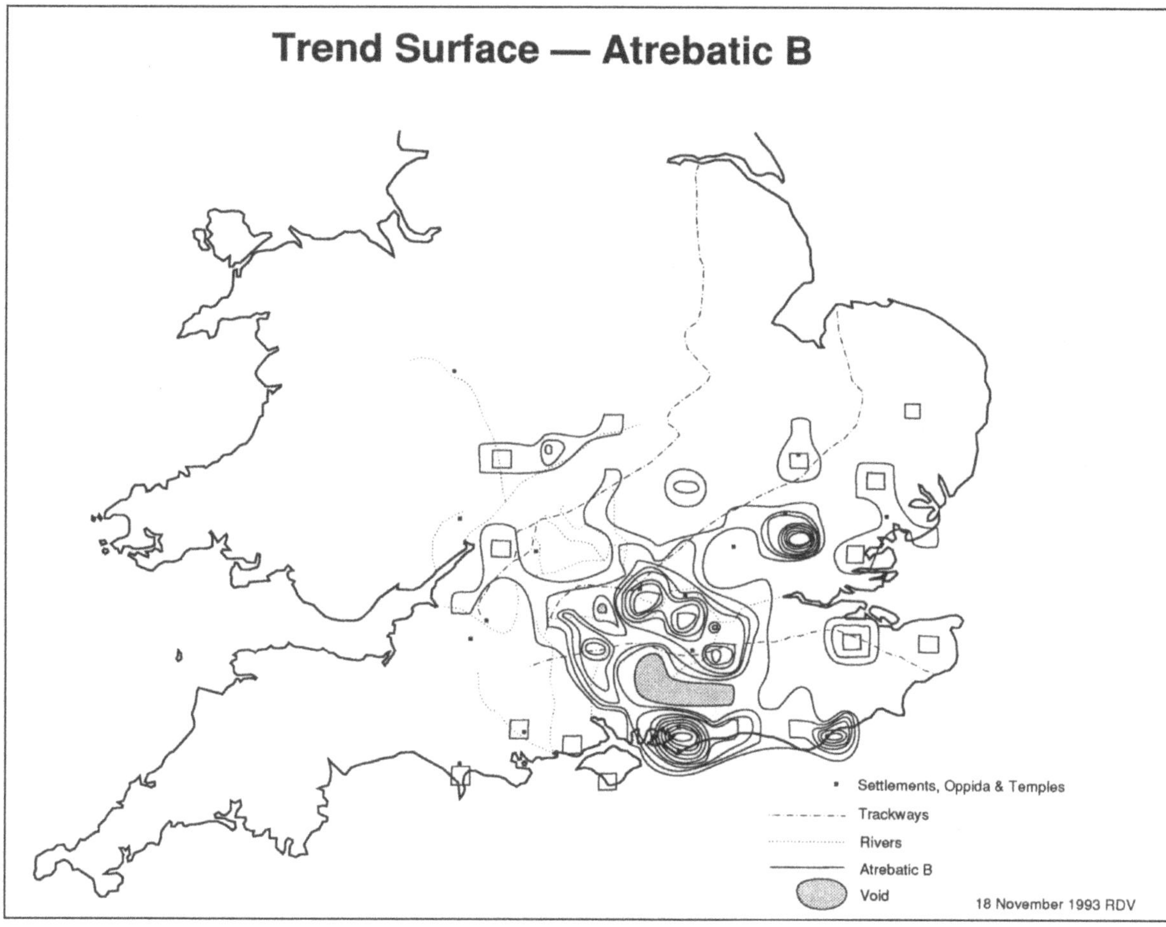

Figure 4. Trend surface map for Atrebatic B.

It is perplexing that Chichester appears with a high concentration of Belgae/Solent coins. Chichester is outside the Belgic region on the recent maps discussed above (de Jersey 1997b; Rudd 2001). One could argue that these are not the coins of the Belgae, but instead those of the Regni. A rebuttal might be offered that they are still the coins of the Belgae, but have been found in Regnan territory. Given the difficulty of such speculation, it is perhaps wise to fall back on a neutral "Solent" term, as de Jersey (2001, 6).

But the neutral term does not move us any closer to identifying the issuing authority for these coins, a key goal of all numismatic research. Given the evidence as it is today, however, it is impossible to assert that the Belgae of Winchester or the Regni of Chichester should be preferable to the Atrebates. I would suggest that there is some plausibility to the idea that the Belgae or the Regni could be identified in the numismatic record. There are typological anomalies (and affinities to Gaulish coinage) identified by Rudd and de Jersey that could be important. But to date, the evidence to distinguish these coins from the coinage of the Atrebates is slim, and certainly no proof is available. Until further work is done, and better evidence is provided, it would be preferable to consider these coins are part of the Atrebatic series. A similar line of reasoning would suggest that the Cheriton staters should remain with the Durotriges, until better information is forthcoming.

Bibliography

Bushe-Fox, J. P. 1925: *Excavations of the late-Celtic urn-field at Swarling, Kent* (London, Reports of the Research Committee of the Society of Antiquaries of London, 5).

Camden, W. 1590: *Britannia* (London, Bishop).

Camden, W. (enlarged by R. Gough) 1789: *Britannia* (London).

Cunliffe, B. W. 1984: Relations between Britain and Gaul in the first century BC and early first century AD. In S. Macready and F. H. Thompson (eds), *Cross-Channel Trade between Gaul and Britain in the pre-Roman Iron Age* (London, Society of Antiquaries Occasional Paper (New Series) 4), 3-23.

Cunliffe, B. W. 1991 (3rd ed.): *Iron Age communities in Britain* (London, Routledge).

Cunliffe, B. W. and de Jersey, P. 1997: *Armorica and Britain* (Oxford, OUCA Monograph 45).

Cunnington, M. E. 1913-14: Casterley Camp. Being an account of excavations carried out by Mr. and Mrs. B. H. Cunnington. *Wiltshire Archaeological Magazine* 38, 53-105.

Cunnington, M. E. 1932: Was there a second Belgic invasion (represented by bead-rim pottery)? *Antiquaries Journal* 12, 27-34.

de Jersey, P. 1997a: Who made money in Celtic Britain? *Chris Rudd list* 26.

de Jersey, P. 1997b: Mint sites of Celtic Britain. *Chris Rudd list* 28, 1-2.

de Jersey, P. 2001: Where and when? *Chris Rudd list* 56, 2-7.

Guest, E. 1851: On the "Belgic ditches", and the probable date of Stonehenge. *Archaeological Journal* 8, 143-157.

Hawkes, C. F. C. and Dunning, G. 1930: The Belgae of Gaul and Britain. *Archaeological Journal* 87, 150-335.

Hawkes, C. F. C. and Dunning, G. 1932: The second Belgic invasion. *Antiquaries Journal* 12, 411-430.

Pitt-Rivers, A. 1888: *Excavations in Cranborne Chase, near Rushmore, on the borders of Dorset and Wilts. 1880 – 1888. Vol. II, Excavations in barrows near Rushmore. Excavations in Romano-British village, Rotherley. Excavations in Winkelbury Camp. Excavations in British Barrows and Anglo-Saxon cemetery, Winkelbury Hill* (London).

Pitt-Rivers, A. 1892: *Excavations in Cranborne Chase, near Rushmore, on the borders of Dorset and Wilts. Vol. III, Excavations in Bokerley and Wansdyke, Dorset and Wilts., 1888-1891* (London).

Rudd, C. 2001: Tribal or regional? *Chris Rudd list* 55, 2-3.

Sharples, N. 1990: Late Iron Age society and continental trade in Dorset. In A. Duval, J.-P. Le Bihan and Y. Menez (eds), *Les Gaulois d'Armorique* (Revue Archéologique de l'Ouest suppl. 3) 299-304.

Stukeley, W. 1724: *Itinerarium curiosum* (London).

Stukeley, W. 1740: *Stonehenge, a temple restor'd to the British druids* (London).

Stukelely, W. 1776 (2nd ed.): *Itinerarium curiosum* (London).

The Belgae and Regini

Chris Rudd

Before I talk about the coins of the Belgae and Regini I must speak of tribal names. I'm worried about them. They are an endangered part of Britain's prehistory. They are at risk of dying of neglect. Like the prehistoric earthworks that are being destroyed each year by modern farmers, road builders and property developers, Britain's tribal names are gradually being eroded by modern scholarship. The Romans showed them more respect than we do.

The numismatic erosion of tribal names began 141 years ago when Sir John Evans correctly identified the 'difficulty of defining the territory occupied by the different tribes' and sensibly proposed that ancient British coins should be classified by region rather than by tribe (Evans 1864, 36). In 1987 Colin Haselgrove developed a system of geographical classification and in 1996 Richard Hobbs used a similar format when he catalogued the British Museum collection of Iron Age coins.

Rationally, I can see the wisdom of regional cataloguing (see below, Figures 5, 7) and I concede that it is prudent scholarly practice. Emotionally, I feel outraged that our ancestral tribal names are treated with such disdain by professional archaeologists and academic numismatists. Every year Britain spends millions of pounds in preserving ancient monuments, in excavating ancient sites, in recording ancient remains and in displaying ancient artefacts in museums. Rightly so. They are part of our national heritage and, as such, should be protected, conserved and celebrated. I suggest that Britain's ancient tribal names are also part of our national heritage and therefore equally deserving of protection, conservation and celebration. For example, I'd like to see a few thousand pounds invested in tribal road signs such as 'Welcome to Norfolk, land of the Eceni' or 'You are now in Gwent, ancient home of the Silures.'

Thanks chiefly to Claudius Ptolemaeus and the authors of the Antonine *Itinerary* and the Ravenna *Cosmography*, more than thirty of Britain's tribal names have survived at least two thousand years (Figure 1). Some are even embedded in modern place names. For example, Devon is derived from the Dumnonii, Dorset and Dorchester take their names from the Durotriges, Kent and Canterbury come from the Cantiaci (or Cantion). Such venerable tribes, distinguished by the longevity of their linguistic influence, are worthy of our respect.

I suspect that there were a number of smaller tribes and sub-tribes about whom we know nothing today. For example, Caesar tells us that the Cenimagni, Segontiaci, Ancalites, Bibroci and Cassi surrendered to him (*BG* 5.21). We may reasonably identify the Cenimagni with the Eceni of East Anglia, but who and where were the other four tribes? Nobody else mentions them. 'Presumably they were located in south-eastern Britain and were later absorbed by a larger confederation' say Rivet and Smith (1979, 250). Or maybe they were simply too small to be mentioned by later Roman commentators and cartographers.

The ebb and flow of tribal boundaries, together with possible deletions or revisions of tribal names that may have occurred between the first century BC and the mid second century AD, when Ptolemy compiled his *Geography* (Figure 1), are sometimes used as an excuse for not classifying Iron Age coins by Iron Age tribal names. This excuse might be acceptable for the smaller tribal groups which may (or may not) have been absorbed by larger groups by the time of the Claudio-Flavian colonization of Britain. But this excuse is inexcusable today when applied to larger tribal groups, especially those which achieved the status of *civitas* or *municipium* under the Romans, such as the Eceni and Corieltauvi in the east, the Catuvellauni and Trinovantes north of the Thames, the Cantiaci and Atrebates south of the Thames, the Belgae and Regini on the south coast, and the Dobunni and Durotriges in the west and south-west. This excuse is inexcusable today because it leans precariously on the 'old archaeology' of successive waves of mass migrations from Belgic Gaul – militant migrations which supposedly caused so much insular warfare, economic havoc, social turmoil and political instability that one couldn't possibly rely on the tribes of south-east Britain staying in their territories from one decade to another, let alone for a whole century prior to AD 43; that tribal boundaries were constantly shifting, with hillforts changing hands like pieces of chess; and that tribal nomenclature was consequently ever liable to change. This excuse also assumes that everyday life in rural Britain underwent a momentous upheaval when Claudius trundled his elephants up to Camulodunon in AD 43, that tribal infrastructures had disintegrated by AD 150 and that the Romans were incredibly careless or insensitively callous when they named their *civitas* capitals. We now know that such assumptions are unsafe.

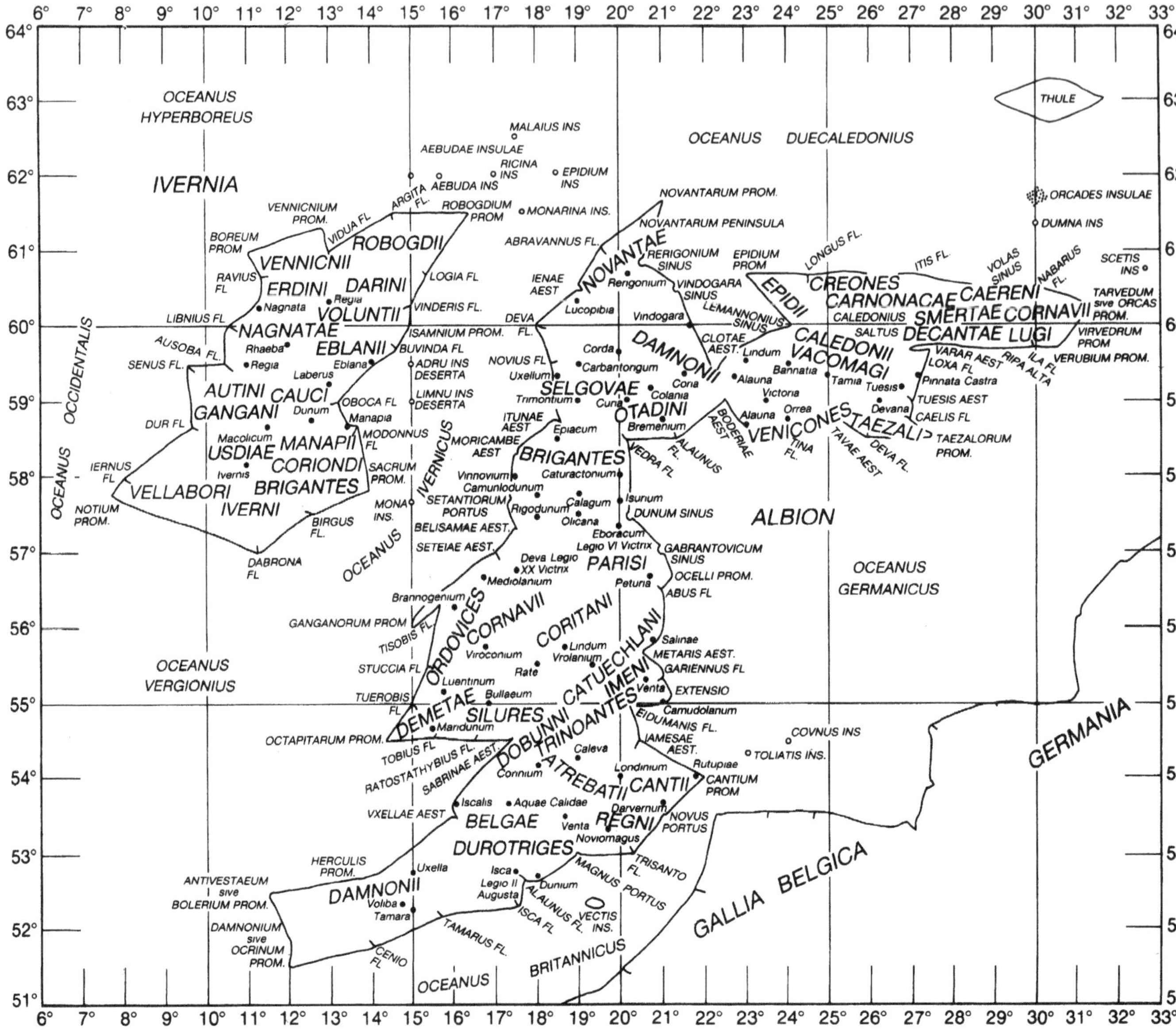

Figure 1. Britain (Albion) and Ireland (Ivernia) according to the Geography of Claudius Ptolemaeus. Note the presence of Belgae, Regni, Venta (Winchester) and Noviomagus (Chichester). Just as we have revised Ptolemy's 'Coritani' to read 'Corieltauvi' in the light of recent scholarship, so too should we amend his 'Regni' to 'Regini', as recommended by Kenneth Jackson in 1948 (map: Jones and Mattingly 1990).

Boundaries and names

Firstly, the 'new archaeology' suggests that there was an influx of influence from Gallia Belgica and Armorica in the first century BC (Cunliffe and de Jersey 1997), that there were no mass migrations during this period and that there was two-way cross-Channel commerce rather than one-way Gallic conquest – traders, not invaders. Moreover, many of Britain's so-called Iron Age 'hillforts' are now thought to have had more peaceful purposes or to have fallen into disuse in the first century BC. This 'less invasive, more persuasive' trend in pre-Roman scholarship has two corollaries: less tribal mobility, more tribal stability. Tribal rulers were doubtless vying for power all the time and sometimes raiding each other's territory. But the bulk of the population – the farmers and their families – stayed settled in their settlements from birth to death. Just as they did in medieval England, if not more so. The Durotriges remained mainly in Wessex. The Dobunni remained mainly in the Cotswolds. The Cantiaci remained mainly in Kent. Just as they did in Roman times, if not more so. With no mass migrations from Gaul in the first century BC, and no massive Gallic invasions, why should there be any large-scale movements of people in south-eastern Britain between 100 BC and AD 43? Why should we imagine entire tribes might be loading up their ox carts and pack horses and leaving their homes to move to neighbouring regions? There was apparently enough good land for crops and cattle for every tribe during this period and there don't appear to have been any major insular threats to tribal health or tribal security, with the possible exception of a burgeoning cross-Channel traffic (Britain to Gaul) in slaves (Figures 2, 10). This indeed could bring terror into the homes of enfeebled tribes and cause whole families to move to safer areas and stronger kingdoms, especially when the Roman demand for slaves increased. But was the slave trade in late Iron Age Britain ever as huge and horrendous as the American slave trade in sixteenth and seventeenth century west Africa? (Cunliffe 2005, 601). Big enough and bad enough to cause major movements of population within Britain? I'm not sure about that.

Figure 2. Cantian Wine Carriers, a silver unit of the Cantiaci, c.50-30 BC, found at Springhead, Kent (CCI 02.0715). It shows two men carrying a large, two-handled, Roman-style wine amphora between them. The two cabled bars with a ring at each end – one above the amphora, the other held by the man on the right – may represent slave chains and could perhaps be the first contemporary image of Britain's Iron Age slave trade.

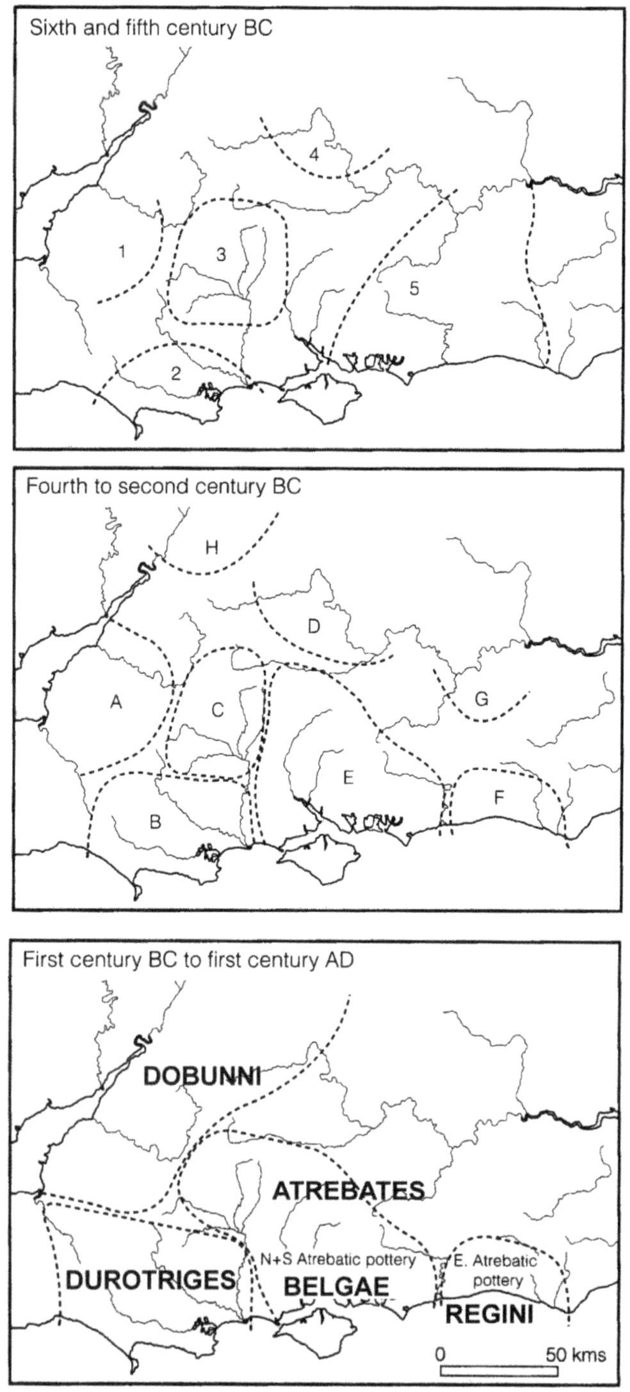

Figure 3. The great antiquity of tribal boundaries is supported by archaeology. 'Reviewing the evidence overall, it is a reasonable supposition that the tribes known to us at the time of the Claudian invasion can be traced back as geo-political entities to the Middle Iron Age, and in some areas possibly even earlier' (Cunliffe 2005, 134; source of maps: Cunliffe 2005, 592, third adapted by author).

Secondly, if we accept that there is unlikely to have been any large-scale movement of population in south-eastern Britain (east of the Severn to Humber line) between 100 BC and AD 43, then we should also accept that there are unlikely to have been many large-scale shifts in tribal boundaries during this period. A few, yes; a lot, no. Where is the archaeological evidence to support any such changes in tribal limits? Where is the numismatic evidence? Just because certain types of late Iron Age coins travel across tribal limits does not imply that people were moving house, nor that tribal boundaries were moving either. Tribal groupings in late Iron Age Britain seem to have been based on one or two major settlement centres within each area (Figure 9), and tribal boundaries appear to have been largely determined as much by major geographical features such as rivers and marshes (both of sacred significance) as by socio-economic forces. Britain's medieval county boundaries have remained comparatively constant for almost a thousand years, despite many massive internal power struggles and many massive socio-economic changes. Similarly, I see no logical reason why most of the big tribal boundaries of late Iron Age Britain may not have been defined many centuries prior to AD 43 (Figure 3), perhaps even in the Bronze Age.

Thirdly, if we can curb our healthy academic scepticism for a moment and imagine that maybe – just maybe – Britain's major tribal groups remained pretty constant for a couple of hundred years, say, from 100 BC to AD 150, then we might also be able to open our mind to the possibility that tribal names had an equally long life, much longer perhaps than we currently think.[1] Some names describe the nature of the territory (e.g. Cantiaci 'people of the corner land') and others the perceived character of the people (e.g. Catuvellauni 'men good in battle'). Other names are more obscure (e.g. Corieltauvi, Eceni and Dobunni) and may be suggestive of a more ancient origin, possibly 'pre-Celtic'. This shouldn't surprise us. Some British river names also appear to be possibly 'pre-Celtic' (e.g. Stour 'strong'). The same comment applies to the prehistoric names for the island (Albion 'the land') and its inhabitants (Pritani 'figured folk, tattooed people'). Both seem to have been current many centuries before AD 43. Moreover, the late Iron Age coins of certain tribes display symbols which could be described as 'tribal emblems' or 'tribal heraldry' (Figure 4); these may indicate a long-term tribal consciousness, a group awareness that 'we are these people', which again may be seen as evidence of the cohesion, durability and longevity of Britain's tribal groups, tribal boundaries and tribal names (Stevens 2002).

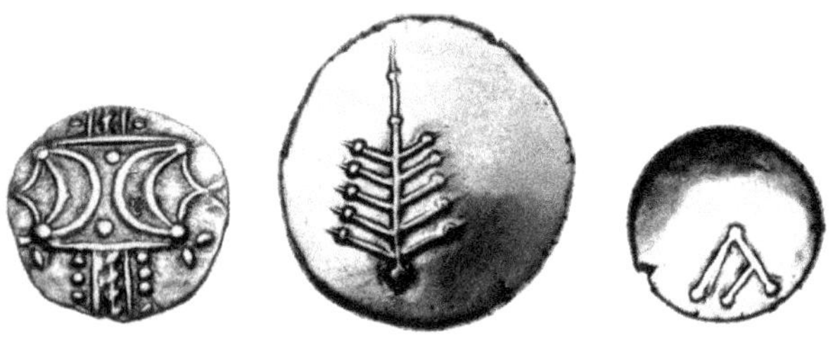

Two moons of the Eceni (VA 730) | 'Tree of life' of the Dobunni (VA 1105) | Letter A for Atrebates? (VA 353-5)

Figure 4. Certain recurring symbols may be interpreted as 'tribal emblems' or 'tribal heraldry' and may indicate a tribal awareness that 'we are these people'. Obvious examples are the opposed crescent moons of the Eceni and the 'tree of life' – possibly the budded branch of a coppiced ash tree – of the Dobunni (which is exclusive to them). The letter A seen on a gold quarter stater of Commios (VA 353-5) might similarly refer to his Atrebatic ancestry, though it might also be a dynastic symbol.

Fourthly, the 'new archaeology' would prefer us to consider the Claudian invasion of Britain more in terms of a colonization or annexation, part of an ongoing process of romanization that had been initiated as far back as 54 BC by Julius Caesar, developed by Augustus and merely consummated by Claudius and his successors (Creighton 2000; Manley 2002). There is a growing body of archaeological evidence to support this view. It would appear that there may have been Roman traders, Roman soldiers and Roman officials in Britain well before AD 43 and that the Claudian intervention was enthusiastically welcomed by some tribal rulers and their people – even actively encouraged and materially endorsed by such chieftains. Whether we accept this view or not, the plain fact is that the British tribal system didn't suddenly fall apart in AD 43. It simply came under new management. In many ways this was a 'friendly takeover' by a multinational corporation whose chief executive officers had been negotiating with Britain's company directors for many years previously, sometimes openly, sometimes secretly. Shares had been exchanged, big loans had been given, heavy investments had been made, many deals had been done, many contracts had been signed. The CEO's flying visit in AD 43 was, to a degree, a diplomatic gesture only and merely ratified an arrangement that had already been agreed. After AD 43 business in Britain was pretty much as usual and continued to be controlled by many of its former directors and managers (or their sons), some of whom became fabulously rich as a direct result of the takeover by Denarius.com – a takeover that would have been much harder to pull off if there had not been substantial internal leverage at the highest levels of British management. If this wasn't the reality, how could a tiny minority of Roman soldiers and administrators control two million Britons for over three hundred years? The Roman invasion was largely by invitation and the Roman conquest was partly by co-operation.[2]

Fifthly, I think that the naming of *civitas* capitals of Roman Britain was probably done carefully and with due consideration for native feelings and local customs. The naming of people and places was not only of political significance in ancient cultures, but of religious and supernatural significance too. There was potent magic in a name and the process of naming was a powerful ritual, not lightly undertaken. In fact, the naming of *civitas* capitals will almost certainly have been conducted in conjunction with regional chieftains and with proper respect for local traditions; the creation of several client-kingdoms in Britain implicitly supports this view. Just as Romano-British inscriptions indicate that there was a widespread conflation of ancient British deities with Roman deities, so too the naming of *civitas* capitals in Roman Britain must have been a thoughtful and respectful act of union, rather than a random imposition by Roman administrators (Jones and Mattingly 1990, 41). Moreover, the naming of *civitas* capitals will have been logical and traditional. For example, if the people around Wroxeter hadn't already been called the Cornovii, it wouldn't have been named *Viroconium Cornoviorum*; and if the people around Cirencester hadn't already been called the Dobunni, it wouldn't have been named *Corinium Dubonnorum*; likewise Silchester, Exeter, Caerwent and Caistor St Edmund. Furthermore, I think we can assume that the Roman tribal capitals at Winchester (*Venta Belgarum*) and Chichester (*Noviomagus Reg(i)norum*) were named with the same Roman logic. The people living around Winchester were known as 'Belgae'. The people living around Chichester were known as 'Regini'. It seems strange that I should need to be so boringly heavy handed about hammering this home, but it is necessary because generations of archaeologists, prehistorians and numismatists have elected to ignore the obvious, because the obvious doesn't fit their evidence.

To sum up my introduction to the coins of the Belgae and Regini, I must reiterate that many if not most of Britain's larger tribes were probably of ancient origin, possibly much older than we may imagine; that tribal boundaries probably didn't fluctuate hugely between 100 BC and AD 100; that tribal names probably didn't change much either during this period; and that the names of Roman *civitas* capitals probably provide a reliable guide to tribal territories of the time. My prime point is that we should show more respect for our ancestral tribal names, especially when we are cataloguing Iron Age coins. For example, why classify the coins of the Durotriges as 'south-western' when we can be reasonably certain that they were issued by the Durotriges? Don't get me wrong. I'm not against regional labels. What I resent is the indiscriminate dismissal of tribal names. I'm happy to use regional labels in conjunction with tribal names

(Figures 5-7), but not on their own (Rudd 2001). Philip de Jersey (2001) says: 'I'm happy to use tribal names in conjunction with regional labels, but not on their own. Are the two positions really so very far apart?' No, they are not. Philip and I stand united on the same firm ground.

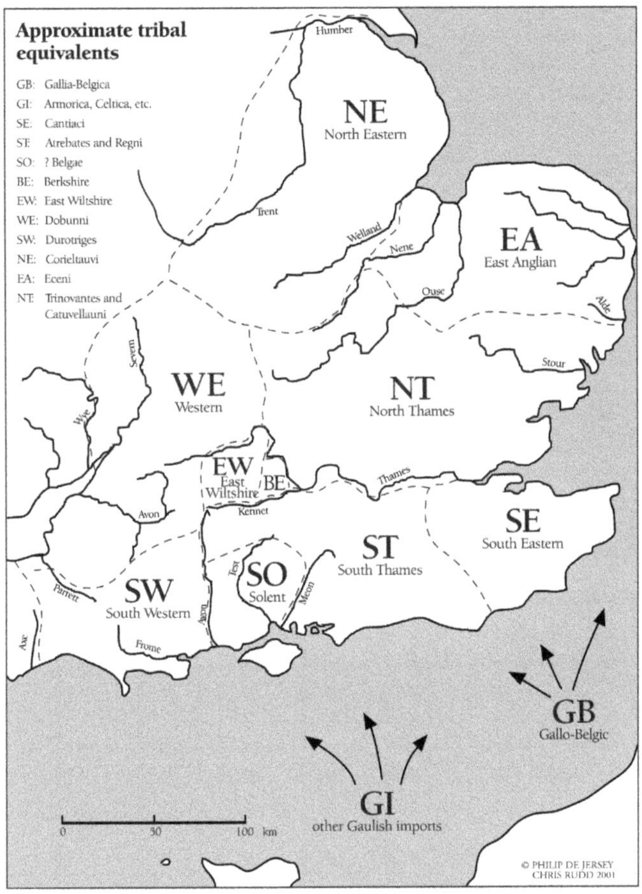

Figure 5. Regional classification of Celtic coins found in Britain. 'Across southern Hampshire, the situation is complicated by the possible presence of a distinct coin-issuing authority in the first century BC, here defined as the Solent zone (SO). This area seems to focus on the Test valley; and may extend as far north as the Danebury region of Hampshire, while in the south it is unclear whether it should include the Isle of Wight; further work may suggest that the island should be treated separately' (de Jersey 2001).

The Belgae

In 1994 I noted that 'There seems to be a small tribal group between the Atrebates and Durotriges, occupying the Petersfield-Portsmouth-Chichester triangle. Their first coinage may have been the Chichester Cock bronze units (Evans G9), followed by Cheriton Smiler gold staters (VA 1215), Petersfield Wreath Face gold quarters (Evans D9), Danebury Ex-Type silver units (VA 292), plus Hayling Island types.'[3]

In 1997 I wrote: 'Under the heading of Belgae, a Roman cantonal name from Ptolemy's *Geography* II, 3, 13, the Antonine *Itinerary*, Iter VII, XII, XV, and the Ravenna *Cosmography*, 106, I am now placing those early uninscribed coins that cluster around Danebury, Winchester, Hambledon, Portsmouth and Chichester – some strongly influenced by Gallic prototypes. They seem to sit more comfortably here, within a twenty-mile hinterland of the east Solent and Southampton Water, rather than with the Atrebates or Durotriges (see Dr Andrew Burnett's paper on Chichester Cock bronze, Spink *Num. Circ.*, December 1992, which first alerted me to the possibility of a discrete Belgic group)... My regrouping of these very rare, little studied, south-coast coins is tentative and I accept that the Chichester types may belong to a people who later became known as the Regni, Regini or Regnenses.' (*Chris Rudd list* 26, March 1997, 8).

PHASE	DURATION	MAIN FEATURES
1	mid/late C2 BC	earliest imports; early Gallo-Belgic A and B
2	late C2 BC	later Gallo-Belgic A and B, earliest potin (Thurrock)
3	early C1 BC	flat linear potin, earliest Gallo-Belgic C
4	c. 80 - 60 BC	Gallo-Belgic C and D, earliest British derivatives
5	c. 60 - 50 BC	Gallo-Belgic E and F, British derivatives (eg Whaddon Chase)
6	c. 50 - 20 BC	early silver, struck bronze, latest potin; earliest inscribed types (eg Commios, Addedomaros)
7	c. 20 BC - 10 AD	includes Tasciovanos, Dubnovellaunos, Tincomaros
8	c. 10 - 40 AD	includes Cunobelin, Verica
9	c. 30 - 45 AD	includes Epaticcus, Caratacus, Amminus
10	post 43 AD	?Durotriges cast bronze, ?Prasutagus

Figure 6. Ten phases of British Iron Age coins (de Jersey 2001, based on Haselgrove (1987) with modifications by Creighton (2000)).

During the past decade I have seen nothing and heard nothing which has persuaded me to abandon my idea of the Belgae minting coins in Hampshire, though it does require some justification and modification. On the contrary, over the last ten years I have seen an increasing quantity of south-coast coins which don't appear to have been issued by the Atrebates or Durotriges and which might be attributed to the Belgae or Regini.

In 2001 my Belgae proposal was challenged in Oxford by Robert Van Arsdell, a great numismatist whose work I enormously admire. He spent most of his playful talk kicking at sandcastles I hadn't built and wasn't defending – the Belgic invasion theories of various distinguished archaeologists, most of them dead (see Van Arsdell, this volume). He dismissed the evidence of Cheriton gold staters because they came mainly from hoards and because some had been condemned as spurious.[4] He discarded the evidence of extremely rare types because he feared some of them could be modern forgeries, implying (albeit unintentionally) that I'd been peddling counterfeits. And he discounted the evidence of Chichester Cock bronzes (Figure 55) as 'a failed coinage experiment in the Atrebatic/Regnan series.'[5]

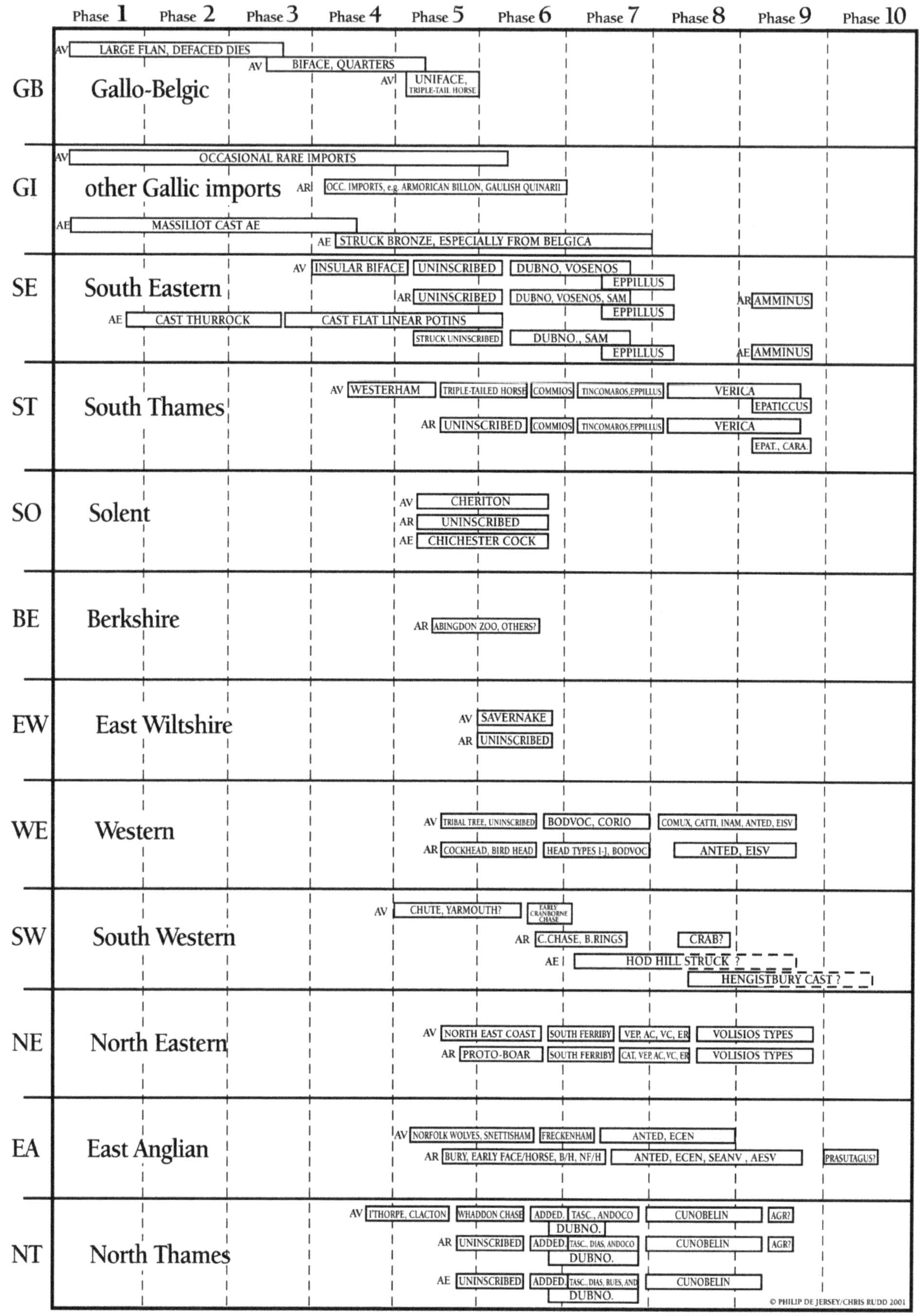

Figure 7. Main phases of Celtic coinage in Britain, classified by region and chronology (de Jersey 2001).

I'm not sure that Van Arsdell's jests merit a response. But more seriously, in his masterwork *Celtic Coinage in Britain* (1989), he makes the Regini subservient to the Atrebates – a complete travesty of the truth. And, like almost everyone else, he altogether ignores the Belgae in Hampshire – an understandable omission in view of the paucity of Belgic coins available to him in 1989, but unacceptable today. This paper, therefore, has three aims: one, to show that there are many south-coast coin types which cannot comfortably be classed as Atrebatic or Durotrigan. Two, to suggest that these distinctly different coin types were issued by the Belgae or Regini. And three, to question the commonly held assumption that the coins of the Regini and Atrebates can be 'treated numismatically as one tribe.' My study area is southern England, particularly the south coast, bounded by Brighton in the east and Bournemouth in the west, and London to Swindon in the north (Figure 8). My period is c. 60 - 30 BC. My material is selected uninscribed coins found chiefly in east Hampshire and West Sussex. And my prime focus is on recorded findspots.

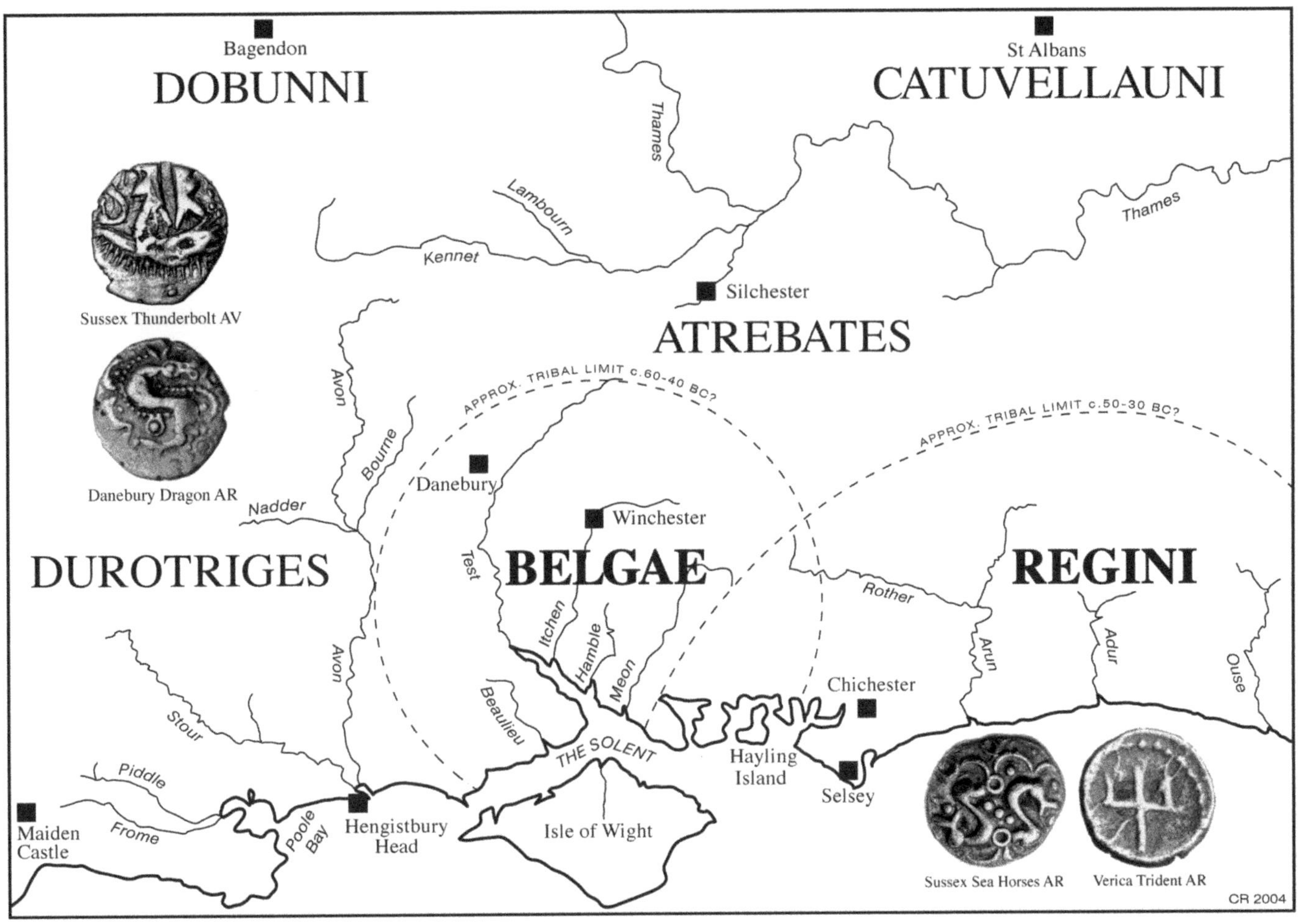

Figure 8. The Belgae and Regini were maritime peoples, enriched by local fishing, salt production and overseas trade. Some of their coins depict dolphins, sea-horses, sea-dragons, boats, galley prows and tridents. Both tribes were flourishing well before the Roman occupation. The growth of the Commian dynasty, perhaps based at Selsey, then Chichester, probably marked the decline of the Belgae, who seemed to have ceased minting coins by c. 30 BC.

As a working hypothesis I am assuming that the tribal territory of the Atrebates was centred on Silchester (*Calleva Atrebatum*), bounded by the Thames and Kennet in the north and the Harroway in the south (there isn't a scrap of literary, archaeological, epigraphic or numismatic evidence to indicate that the land of the Atrebates extended further south, let alone to the south coast); that the tribal territory of the Durotriges was centred on Maiden Castle and then Dorchester (*Durnovaria*), bounded by Christchurch harbour in the east and the Axe in the west; that the tribal territory of the Belgae was centred initially on Danebury and the Solent and latterly on Winchester (*Venta Belgarum*), bounded by Bosham harbour in the east and the Avon in the west, including Hayling Island and possibly the Isle of Wight too; and that the tribal territory of the Regini was centred at first on Selsey Bill and then Chichester (*Noviomagus Reginorum*), bounded by the Pevensey Levels in the east, the Wey in the north and the streams flowing into Bosham harbour in the west (Cunliffe 1973; Figures 59, 60).

I am aware that the tribal boundaries I have outlined are thoroughly speculative, especially those of the Belgae and Regini, but I hope to demonstrate that each of these two tribal regions contains distinctive coinages. I also realise that the majority of the coins I've selected are excessively rare (only one to five specimens recorded by the Celtic Coin Index) and are therefore statistically insignificant. Individually, one cannot draw worthwhile conclusions from plotting the findspots of such scarce types. However, when considered cumulatively, the provenances of these rare coins begin to form some reliable clusters and repetitive patterns of distribution (Figure 107).

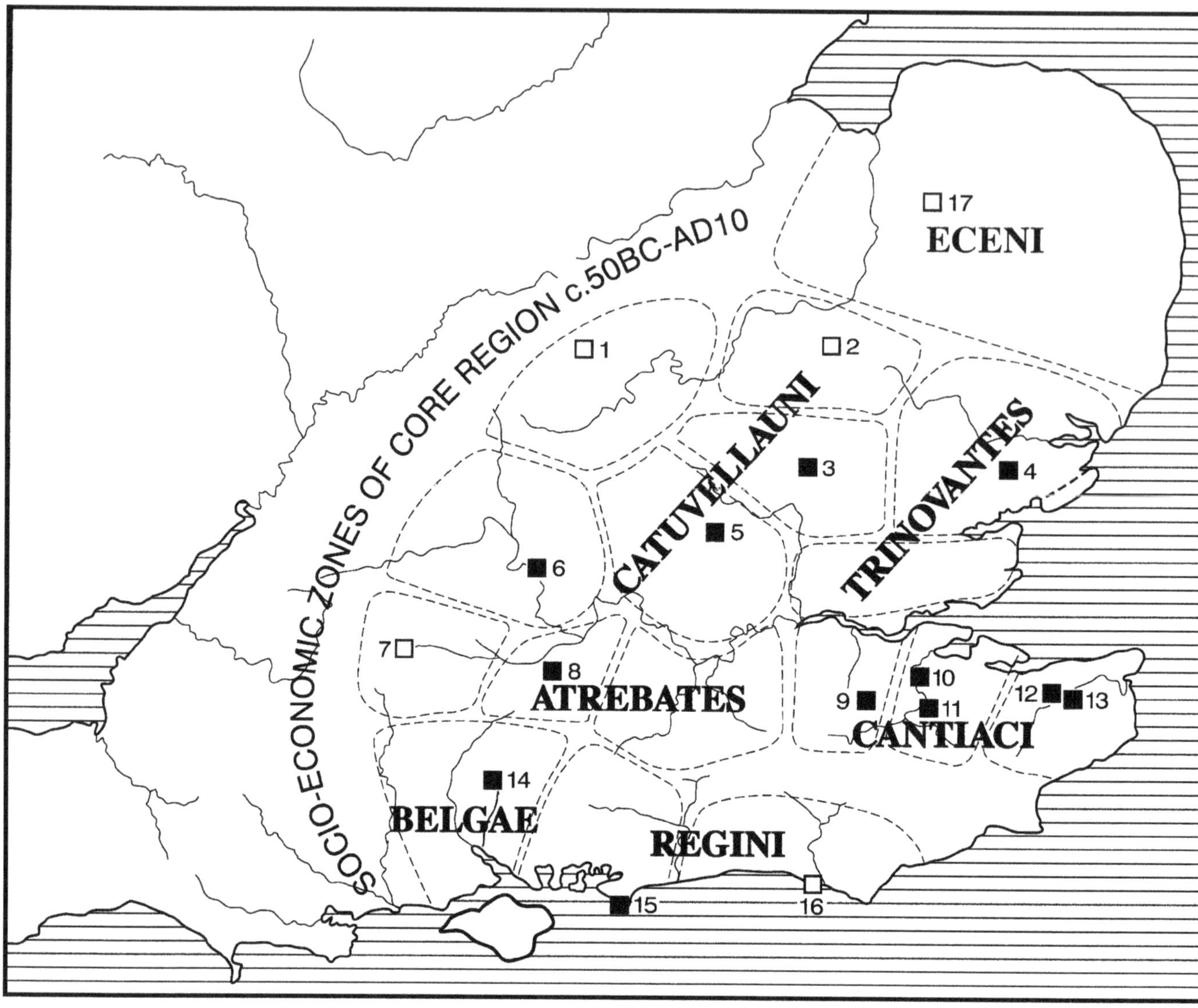

Figure 9. With their proximity to Gaul, plus an abundance of natural harbours and inland waterways, the Belgae and Regini held key trading positions in relation to the other tribes of south-east Britain, particularly in the first century BC. This map shows socio-economic zones in Cunliffe's 'core region' in the period c.50 BC – AD 10 and how they help define the tribal boundaries. Black squares denote nucleated settlements with some evidence of urban functions; open squares are possible nucleated settlements. 1 Duston, 2 Cambridge, 3 Braughing, 4 Colchester, 5 Verulamium, 6 Dyke Hills, 7 Marlborough, 8 Silchester, 9 Oldbury, 10 Rochester, 11 Loose, 12 Bigbury, 13 Canterbury, 14 Winchester, 15 Selsey, 16 Castle Hill, Newhaven, 17 Woodcock Hill, Saham Toney (Cunliffe 1981 with modifications).

My notions about the Belgae in Hampshire and the Regini in Sussex are based primarily on my personal observation as a coin dealer over a period of twelve years, buying coins directly from the people who find them and carefully noting where they are found. At first I accepted Van Arsdell's tribal attributions without question, including what he said about which tribes were dominant north and south of the Thames. Then gradually, over the years, I began to notice that the findspots quoted to me by finders didn't always match the attributions quoted by Van Arsdell, especially with some of the rarer coin types of the south-coast. How, for example, could Willett's Nipple gold quarter staters (VA 1229; Figure 64) possibly be classed as Durotrigan (as Van Arsdell states) when the ones that I was buying were all found around Chichester? How could Danebury Corded silver units (VA 292; Figures 10, 43) possibly be classed as Atrebatic when the majority of specimens have come from Clanfield, which is over thirty miles from the capital of the Atrebates? Despite such glaring inconsistencies, I have continued to be guided by some of Van Arsdell's overly simplistic tribal elisions. Right up until November 2004 my sales catalogue still had a section labelled 'Atrebates and Regni' and said they were 'two south Thames tribes, numismatically classed as one'. It's time for such numismatic wrongs to be righted.

I don't wish to compound the confusion that Van Arsdell has perpetrated and that I have perpetuated. So I'll keep the salient issues simple. The two key questions are these: is there a distinctive group of coins within the territory of the Belgae? And is there a distinctive group of coins within the territory of the Regini? I believe the answer to both questions is 'yes'. Apart from commenting briefly on the few main types of each region, I'll let the coins and their findspots speak for themselves.

Figure 10. The head on this Danebury Corded silver unit (VA 292) has features in common with the head on Chichester Cock bronze (BMC 657-659), such as the swept-back hair, the straight hairline, the aural ring and the oral curve. Moreover, the rings in front of the face – there are three in all, linked by a beaded line – may represent a slave chain (see Figure 2).

I make no apology for presenting so many little maps with so few dots and rings on them. That's the nature of these uninscribed coins of the south-coast hinterland. Very few have been found. Even fewer have been reported. And fewer still have reliably recorded provenances. The coins I have selected for study are by no means comprehensive or even representative. I have left out coins which have no recorded findspots. And I have excluded Westerham South gold staters (VA 202), Qa gold staters (VA 210, 212, 214), Qb gold staters (VA 216) and the commoner types of Qc gold quarter staters (VA 220, 222, 226), firstly because their distribution has already been adequately charted by others, and secondly because these early uninscribed gold coins travel extensively across tribal boundaries.

Belgae gold staters (Figures 11-15)

Three main types of gold staters occur exclusively in the region of the Solent and nowhere else: the Yarmouth Type (VA 1220), Chute/Cheriton Transitional (VA 1210) and Cheriton Smiler (VA 1215). Yarmouth staters are mostly from a hoard on the Isle of Wight and have four radial lines in front of the horse; four similar radial lines can also be seen on some Hampshire Thin Silver coins and thin silver coins of Picardy, but not on coins of the Atrebates or Durotriges. Chute/Cheriton Transitional staters come chiefly from the Cheriton hoard and Fareham district, but never from the territory of the Durotriges. Cheriton Smiler staters are mostly found within fifteen miles of Portsmouth, but never in the heartland of the Durotriges. The modern forgeries of Cheriton Smiler staters are now widely recognised and can no longer be used as an excuse for excluding the genuine coins from this discussion. Van Arsdell catalogues all three of these gold stater types as Durotrigan, but I can see no logical reason for associating them with a tribe whose centre was sixty miles away in Dorset and whose core coinage of Cranborne Chase silver and billon staters (VA 1235) developed directly from Chute gold staters (VA 1205), not from these base-gold off-shoots in east Hampshire.

The small maps which follow throughout this paper are based on data from the Celtic Coin Index kindly supplied by Philip de Jersey in October 2004. The interpretations of them are mine, not his. Individually these maps prove nothing. However, when examined together, they show frequently recurring findspots and cluster patterns. They are suggestive, not conclusive. Where several finds have been made in close proximity I combine them for the sake of clarity and emphasis, e.g. 1 Chichester, 1 Ratham and 1 Westhampnett = 3 Chichester area. ● denotes single find, ⦿ found in hoard, ○ ten or more finds. The coins are not shown to scale.

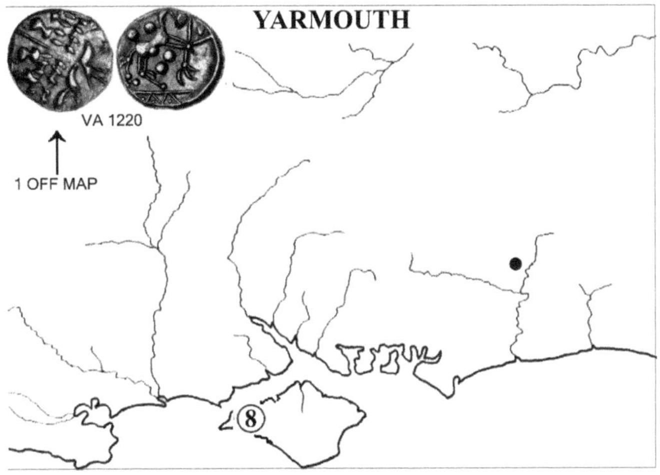

Figure 11. Fourteen Yarmouth gold staters: 8 Yarmouth, IOW (hoard), 1 each Wisborough Green, Weston under Penyard (Herefordshire), 4 unprovenanced.

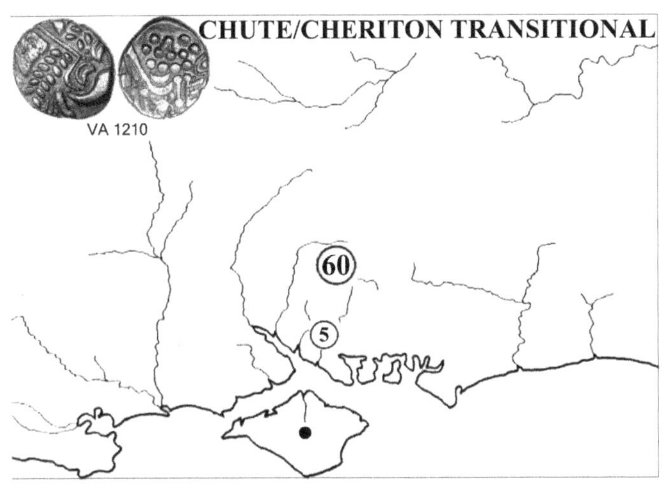

Figure 12. Seventy-five Chute/Cheriton Transitional gold staters: 60 Cheriton (in hoard), 5 Fareham area, 1 Isle of Wight, 9 unprovenanced.

Belgae gold quarters (Figures 16-23)

We have two main types of gold quarter staters to consider: the Sussex Thunderbolt (VA 143) and the Petersfield Wreath Face (BMC 568). The Sussex Thunderbolt seems to be the earlier of the two – heavier and generally more golden in colour – and has a much wider circulation, extending from Kent to Gloucestershire, with a small scattering along the south bank of the Kennet. However, the main concentration is solidly in east Hampshire, with the largest single group coming from the Cheriton hoard. Six have also been found in the Chichester area, which might suggest that the influence of the Belgae was perhaps greater at this time, and later contracted.

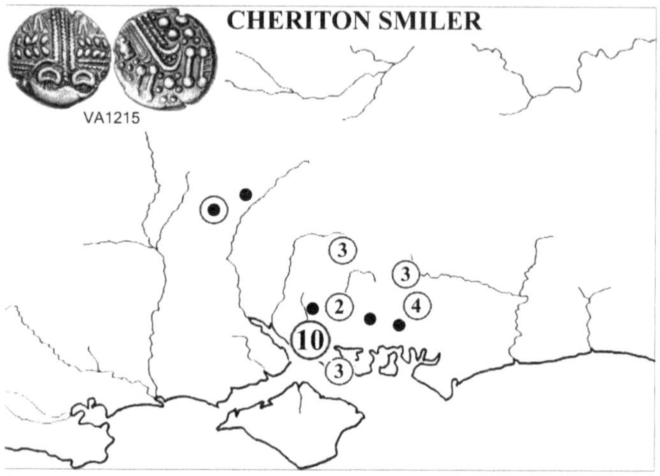

Figure 13. Cheriton Smiler staters.

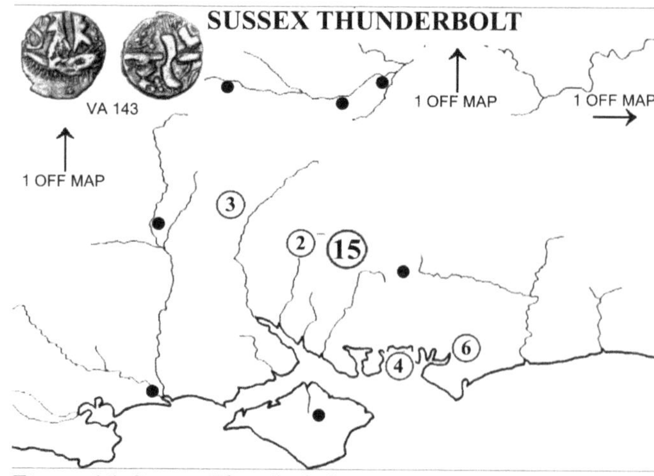

Figure 16. Sussex Thunderbolt quarter staters.

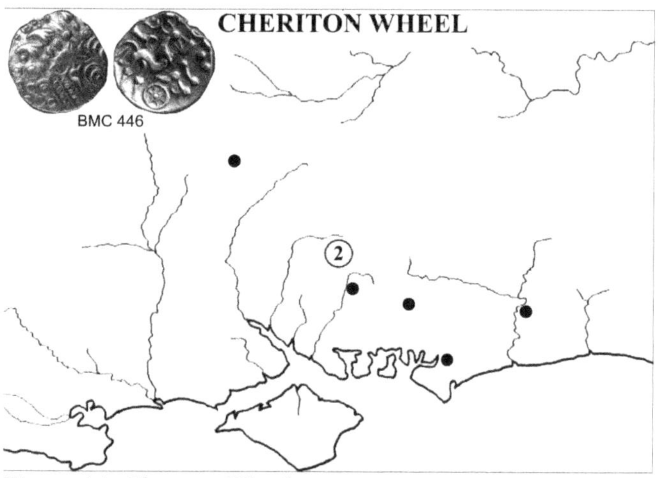

Figure 14. Cheriton Wheel staters.

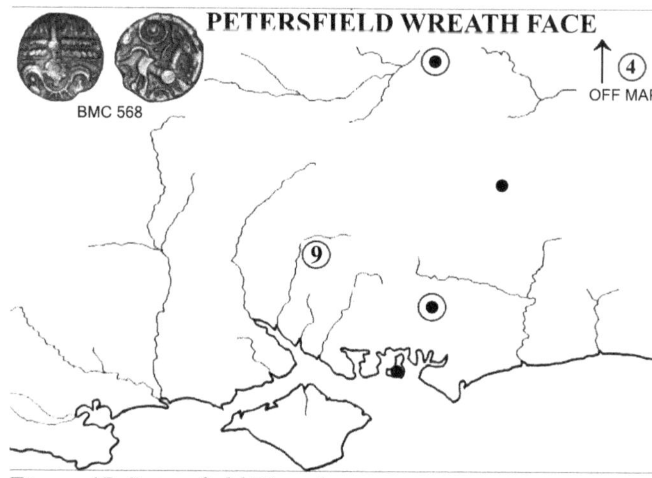

Figure 17. Petersfield Wreath quarter staters.

Figure 15. Cheesefoot Head staters.

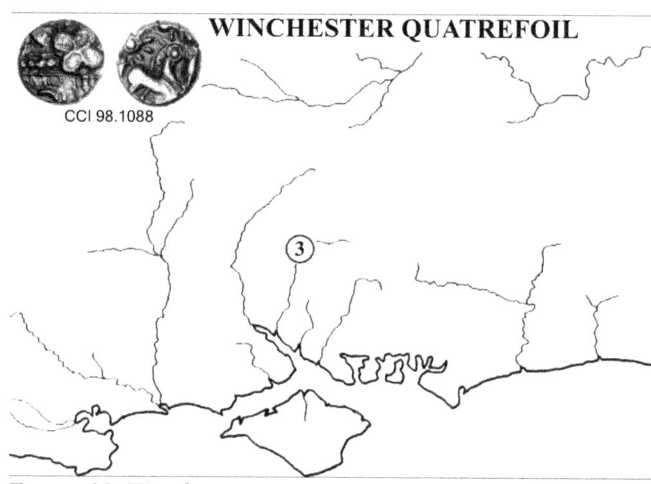

Figure 18. Winchester Quatrefoil quarter staters.

Figure 13. Fifty-six Cheriton Smiler gold staters: 10+ Wickham (in hoard), 4 Compton (3 hoard), 3 Cheriton (2 hoard), 3 Petersfield (hoard?),3 Portchester/Portsmouth, 2 Hambledon, 1 each Horndean, Shedfield, Rowlands Castle, Danebury (hoard), Wherwell, 26 unprovenanced.

Figure 14. Nine Cheriton Wheel gold staters: 2 Cheriton (hoard), 1 each Tangley, Compton, Corhampton, Greatham, Chichester, 2 unprovenanced.

Figure 15. Eight Cheesefoot Head gold staters: 2 Hurstbourne Tarrant (hoard), 1 each Cheesefoot Head, Corehampton, Upton Grey, Hayling Island, 2 unprovenanced.

Figure 16. 82 Sussex Thunderbolt gold quarter staters: 15 Cheriton (in hoard), 6 Chichester area, 4 Hayling Island, 3 Danebury (hoard), 2 Winchester (hoard?), 1 each Langrish, Downend (IOW), Hengistbury Head, Old Sarum, Brimpton, Hungerford, Reading, Amersham, Andoversford (Glos.), Rochester (Kent), 41 unprovenanced.

Figure 17. Twenty-nine Petersfield Wreath Face gold quarter staters: 9 Clanfield area (hoard?), 4 Essendon, Herts. (in hoard), 1 each Waltham St Lawrence (hoard), Guildford (hoard?), Compton (hoard), 13 unprovenanced.

Figure 18. Three Winchester Quatrefoil gold quarter staters recorded, all from near Winchester (hoard?).

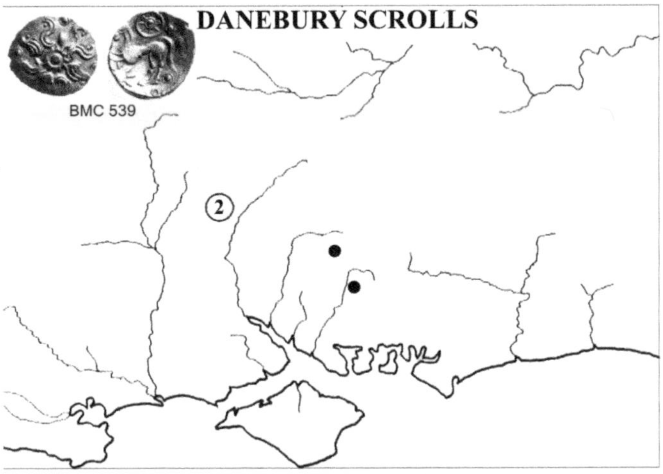

Figure 19. Danebury Scrolls quarter staters.

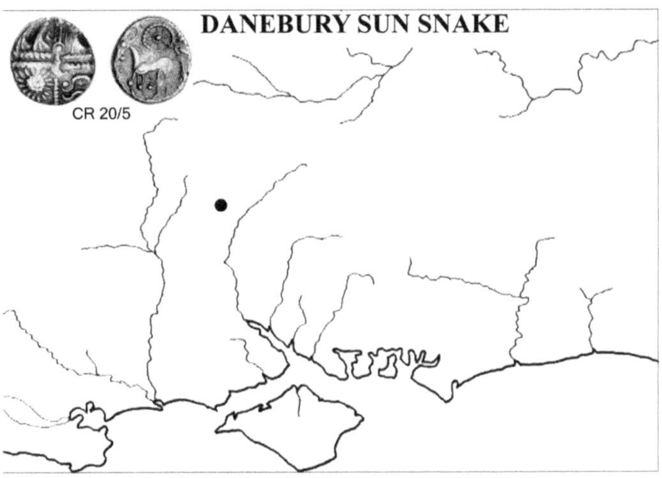

Figure 20. Danebury Sun Snake quarter stater.

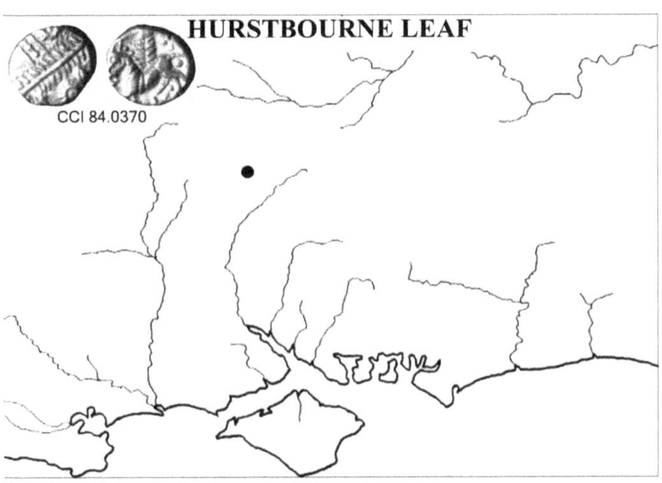

Figure 21.Hurstbourne Leaf quarter stater.

Figure 22. Hayling Cross quarter stater.

Figure 23. Hayling Leaves quarter staters.

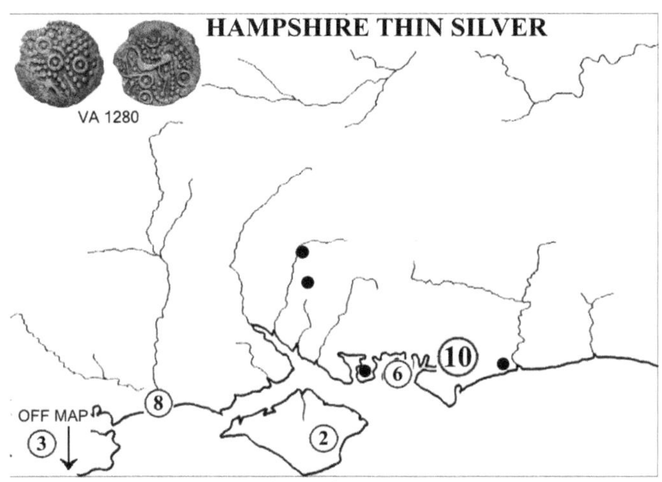

Figure 24. Hampshire Thin Silver units.

Figure 19. Five Danebury Scrolls gold quarter staters recorded: 2 Danebury (hoard), 1 each Cheriton (hoard?), Corhampton, 1 unprovenanced.

Figure 20. One Danebury Sun Snake silver unit, from Danebury.

Figure 21. One Hurstbourne Leaf quarter stater, from Hurstbourne Tarrant (in hoard?).

Figure 22. One Hayling Cross gold plated quarter stater, from Hayling Island.

Figure 23. Two Hayling Leaves gold plated quarter staters: 1 Hayling Island or Chichester, 1 Slough.

Figure 24. Thirty-eight Hampshire Thin Silver units: 10 Chichester area, 8 Hengistbury Head, 6 Hayling Island, 3 Le Catillon, Jersey (in hoard), 2 Newchurch, IOW, 1 each Winchester, Owslebury, Portsmouth, Climping, 5 unprovenanced.

Van Arsdell calls the Sussex Thunderbolt a 'Kentish Geometric Type' and wonders if it is imported from Gaul. My Sussex name is equally misleading. With the benefit of more findspots we can now see that it belongs with the Belgae in Hampshire. I don't think it is accidental that the Sussex Thunderbolt, like other *au bateau* quarter staters (VA 69, 1225, 1242, 1249 and Sills 460-461), apparently features a boat on the obverse. The boat design may be a deliberate attempt to foster cross-Channel and inter-tribal payments (Cunliffe 2005, 134; Sills 2003, 349, 350). The Petersfield Wreath Face is even more obviously Belgic, with most of the finds made in the Clanfield district. Like many gold quarter staters of the Regini, it has a dumpy, undished flan and is more coppery than the Qc gold quarters normally ascribed to the Atrebates (VA 220, 222, 226).[6]

Belgae silver units (Figures 24-47)

The following twenty-three silver units fall broadly into two categories: a few Solent types (five) and many Danebury types (eighteen). By far the most important of the Solent types are the Hampshire Thin Silver coins (VA 1280) which come in a variety of designs, all with paper-thin flans and all decorated with beaded lines. They are unmistakably derived from less abstract prototypes struck by the Ambiani, c. 60 - 50 BC (Figure 106) and are generally found between Chichester and Hengistbury Head, including two from the Isle of Wight. Van Arsdell puts them with the Durotriges, but I think their design and distribution both favour the Solent area as the most likely source. The same may be said of four much rarer Hayling Island silver units: Haying Moon Head (*BNJ* 1992, pl. 2.36), Hayling Stalk Lips (BMC 630), Hayling Head Back (*BNJ* 1992, pl. 1.31) and Hayling Two Boars (*BNJ* 1992, pl. 1.20). They may all have been minted on Hayling Island or near Chichester.

Of the eighteen different types of silver units found at Danebury seven feature animals (mostly boars and horses), three have geometric designs and eight are head/horse types. The animal and geometric types may be the earliest and have mostly been found only at Danebury, which suggests that they were probably minted at Danebury for use in that district. Does this mean that there was a separate little kingdom at Danebury within the Belgae tribe? Or does it mean that Danebury was the early capital of the Belgae – a capital that later transferred to Winchester?

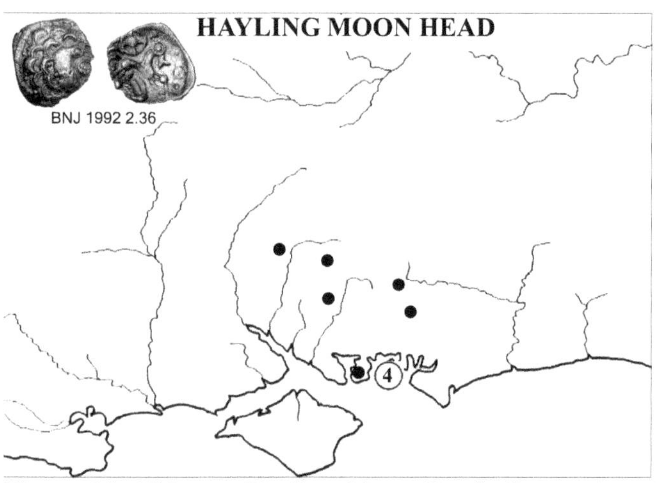

Figure 25. Thirteen Hayling Moon Head silver units: 4 Hayling Island, 1 each west of Cheriton, Droxford, Petersfield, Pitt, Portsmouth, Compton, 3 unprovenanced.

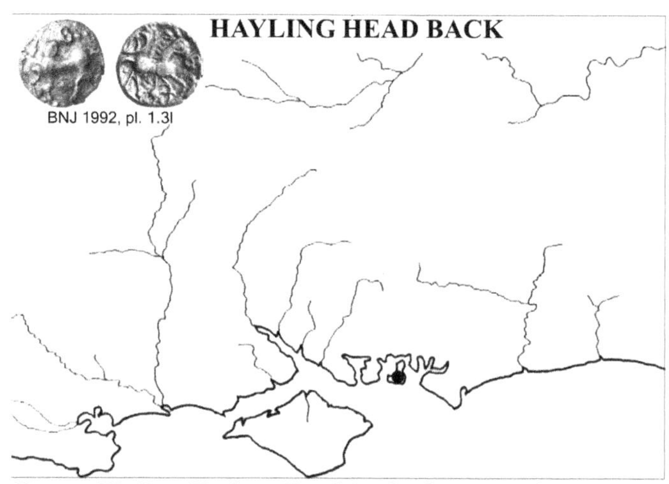

Figure 27. One Hayling Head Back silver unit, from Hayling Island.

Figure 26. Six Hayling Stalk Lips silver units: 4 Hayling Island, 2 Danebury (in hoard).

Figure 28. Two Hayling Two Boars silver units: 1 Hayling Island, 1 unprovenanced.

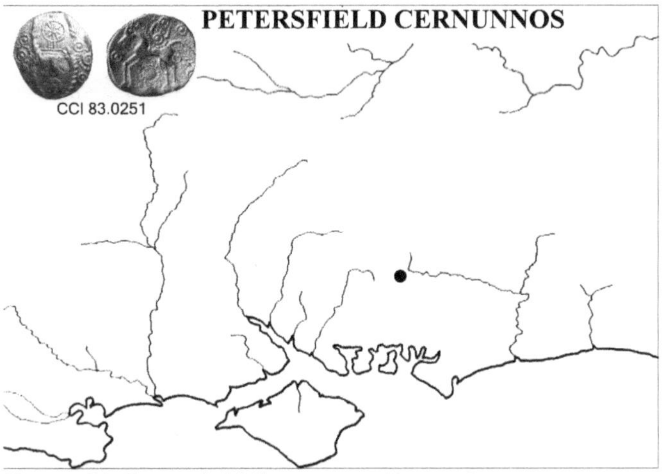

Figure 29. Petersfield Cernunnos silver unit.

Figure 30. Danebury Beast silver units.

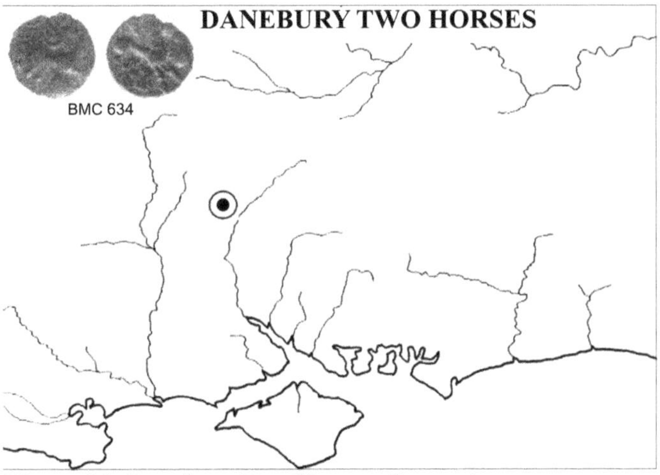

Figure 31. Danebury Two Horses silver units.

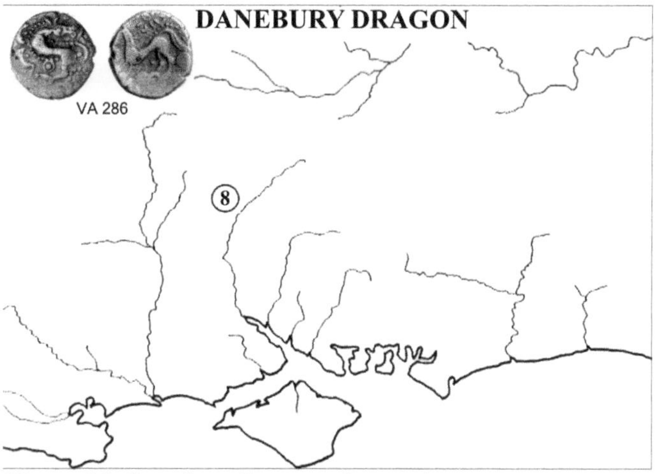

Figure 32. Danebury Dragon silver units.

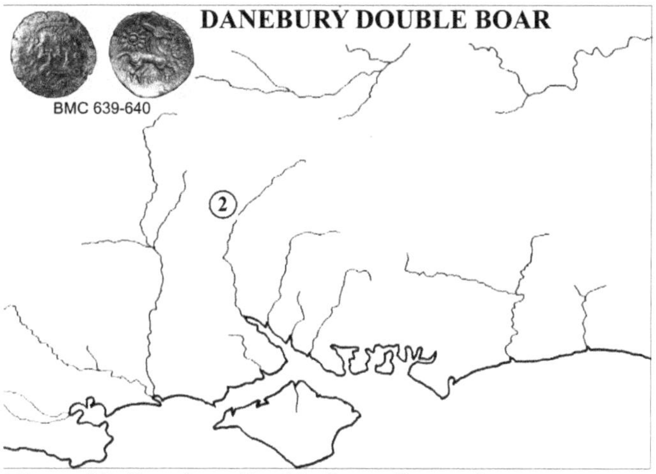

Figure 33. Danebury Double Boar silver units.

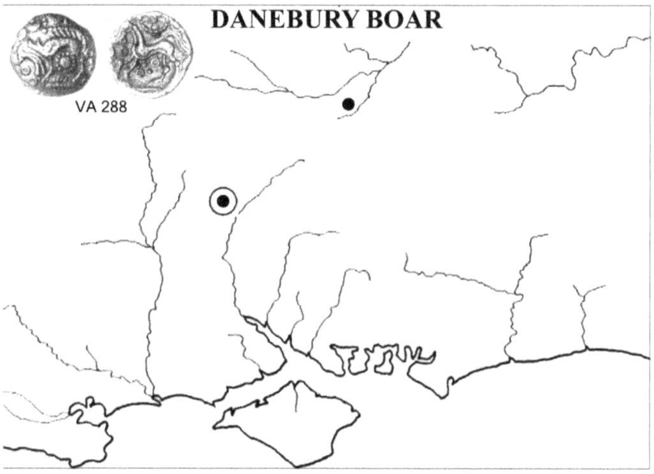

Figure 34. Danebury Boar silver units.

Figure 29. One Petersfield Cernunnos silver unit, from Petersfield.
Figure 30. Two Danebury Beast silver units: 1 Danebury (in hoard), 1 unprovenanced.
Figure 31. One Danebury Two Horses silver unit, from Danebury (in hoard).
Figure 32. Nine Danebury Dragon silver units: 8 Danebury (in hoard), 1 'Hampshire'.
Figure 33. Three Danebury Double Boar silver units: 2 Danebury (in hoard), 1 unprovenanced.
Figure 34. Four Danebury Boar silver units: 1 Danebury (in hoard), 1 Silchester, 2 unprovenanced.

Figure 35. Winchester Boar silver unit.

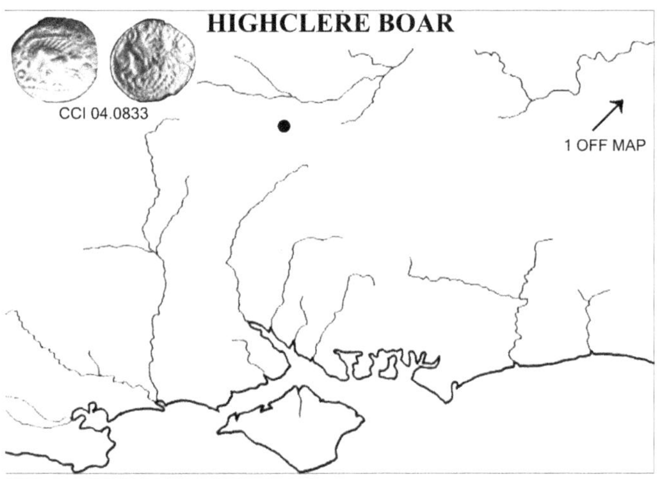

Figure 36. Highclere Boar silver units.

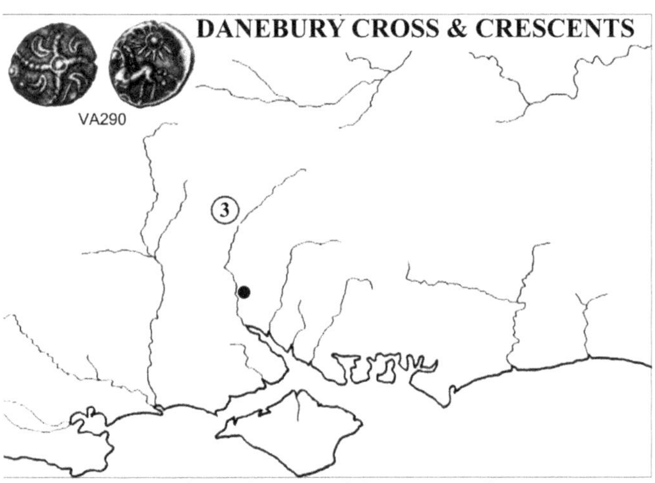

Figure 37. Danebury Cross and Crescents silver units.

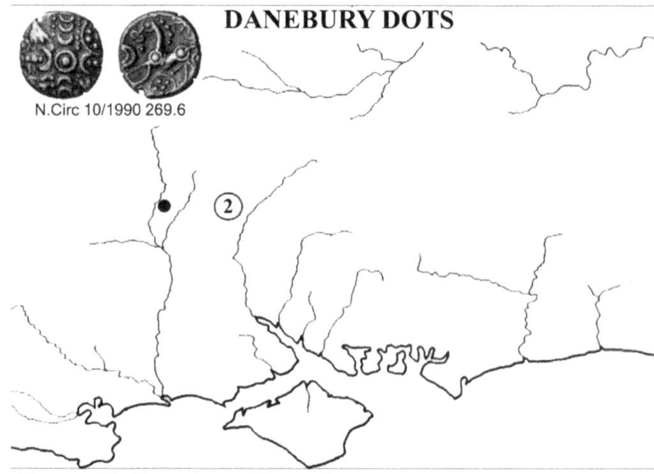

Figure 38. Danebury Dots silver units.

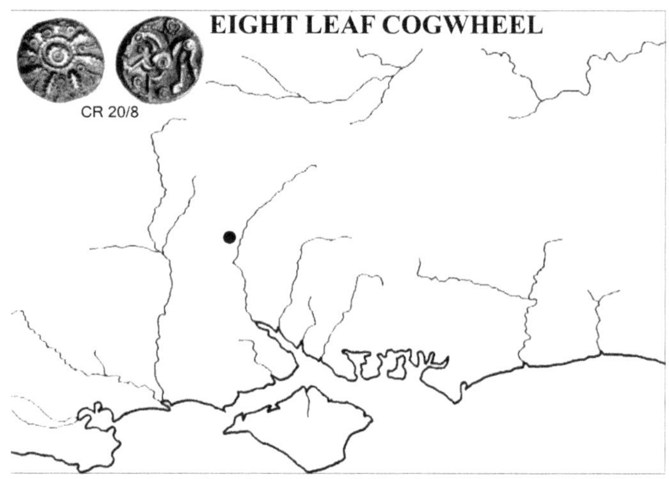

Figure 39. Eight Leaf Cogwheel silver unit.

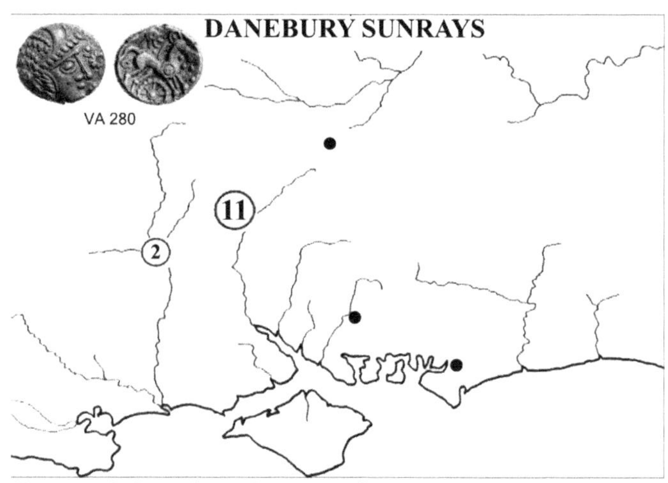

Figure 40. Danebury Sunrays silver units.

Figure 35. Three Winchester Boar silver units: 1 Winchester, 2 unprovenanced.
Figure 36. Three Highclere Boar silver units: 1 each Highclere, Braintree (Essex), 1 unprovenanced.
Figure 37. Five Danebury Cross and Crescents silver units: 3 Danebury (in hoard), 1 Romsey, 1 unprovenanced.
Figure 38. Three Danebury Dots silver units: 2 Danebury (hoard), 1 Amesbury.
Figure 39. One Eight Leaf Cogwheel silver unit, from Houghton.
Figure 40. Twenty-two Danebury Sunrays silver units: 11 Danebury (in hoard), 2 Salisbury, 1 each Fair Oak, Hambledon, Chichester, 6 unprovenanced.

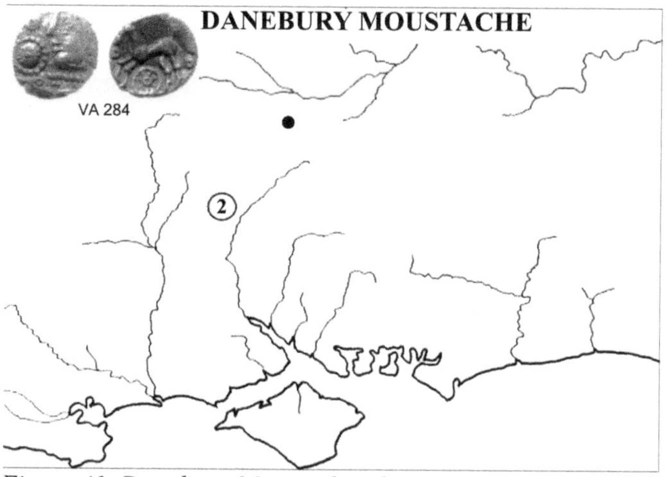

Figure 41. Danebury Moustache silver units.

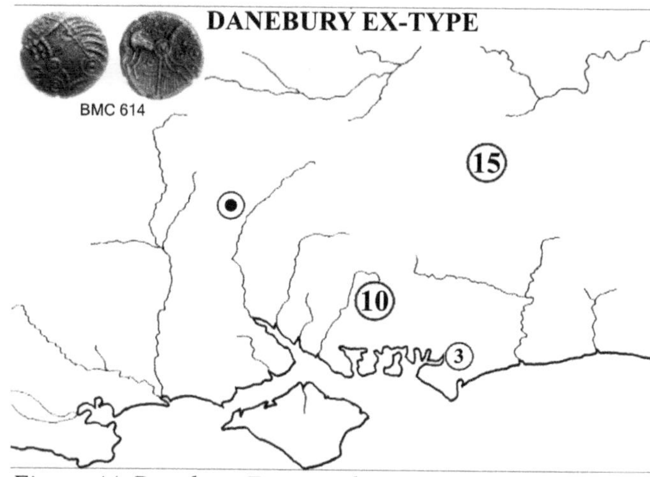

Figure 44. Danebury Ex-type silver units.

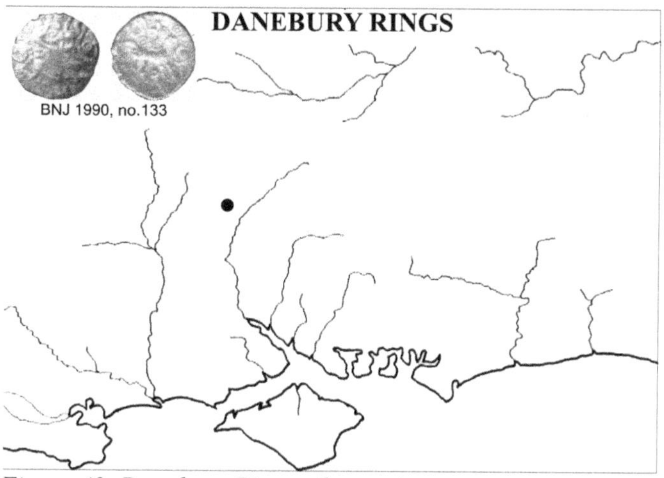

Figure 42. Danebury Rings silver units.

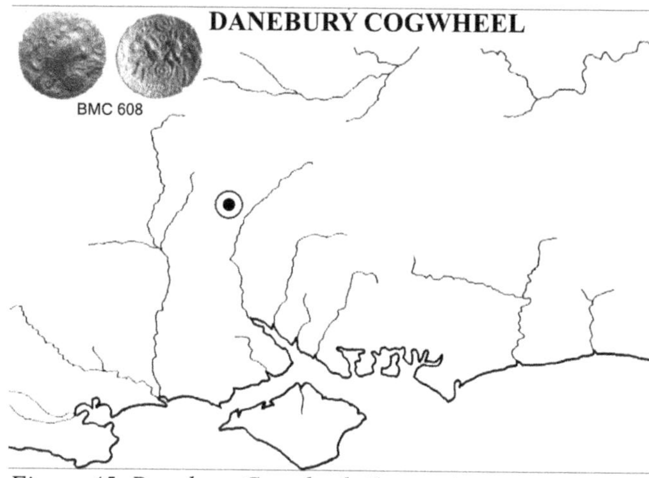

Figure 45. Danebury Cogwheel silver unit.

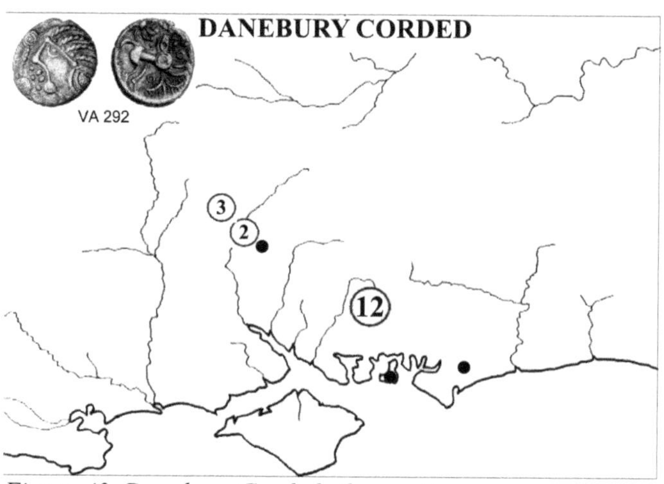

Figure 43. Danebury Corded silver units.

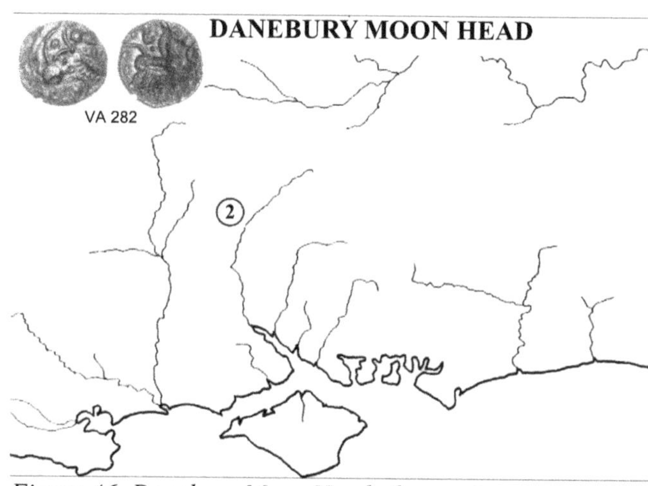

Figure 46. Danebury Moon Head silver units.

Figure 41. Six Danebury Moustache silver units: 2 Danebury (in hoard), 1 south of Newbury, 3 unprovenanced.
Figure 42. Two Danebury Rings silver units: 1 '15 miles from Danebury', 1 unprovenanced.
Figure 43. Twenty-three Danebury Corded silver units: 12 Clanfield (hoard?), 3+ Danebury (hoard?), 2 Stockbridge (hoard), 1 each Ashley (near Winchester), Hayling Island, Tangmere, 3 unprovenanced.
Figure 44. Fifty-five Danebury Ex-Type silver units: 15 Wanborough (in hoard), 10 Clanfield (hoard?), 3 Chichester, 1 Danebury (hoard), 26 unprovenanced.
Figure 45. One Danebury Cogwheel silver unit, from Danebury (in hoard).Head looks Dobunnic or east Wiltshire.
Figure 46. Two Danebury Moon Head silver units, both from Danebury (in hoard). Head looks Dobunnic or east Wiltshire.

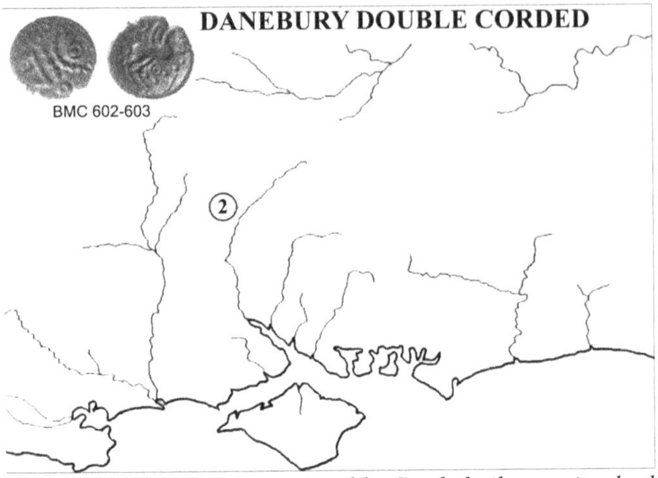

Figure 47. Two Danebury Double Corded silver units, both from Danebury (in hoard). Head looks Dobunnic or east Wiltshire.

Three of the eight Danebury head/horse types – Danebury Sunrays (VA 280), Danebury Corded (VA 292), Danebury Ex-Type (BMC 614) – are distributed more widely than the animal and geometric types. Most Danebury Corded coins come from Clanfield, not Danebury; and the coin that presumably follows it, Danebury Ex-Type, has a much more easterly bias, with fifteen specimens in the Wanborough hoard. Strictly speaking, Danebury Ex-Type is an inscribed coin, though the meaning of the letters EX is unknown. Danebury Corded may have been the last of the silver coins struck at Danebury and Danebury Ex-Type was probably minted somewhere near Portsmouth or Chichester, not at Danebury, and could well have been the final issue of the Belgae. Van Arsdell attributes all his Danebury silver coins to the Atrebates - but why? Danebury is only twelve miles from *Venta Belgarum*, the later centre of the Belgae, whereas *Calleva Atrebatum*, capital of the Atrebates, is twenty-five miles away from Danebury – twice the distance. Why fight the logic of geography?

Belgae silver half units (Figures 48-54)
There are at least seven silver half units which could reasonably be described as British Belgic. One of them, Hayling Comets (*BNJ* 1992, pl. 1.19), might be an Isle of Wight type, though I think Hayling Island or Chichester might also be considered as possible mint sites for this little coin. Five of the silver half units are excessively rare Danebury types which, like the full units, are restricted almost exclusively to Danebury. And the last silver half unit shown here, Clanfield Anemone (VA 1662), is most frequently found alongside the Petersfield Wreath Face gold quarter stater (BMC 568) and Danebury Ex-Type silver unit (BMC 614), and could be contemporary with them. Van Arsdell quirkily attributes the Clanfield Anemone to 'Dubnovellaunus in Essex,' presumably on account of its crossed wreath and crescents motif – an understandable mistake. But of course this is clearly a Solent type, not Trinovantian.

Belgae bronze units (Figures 55-57)
Chichester Cock bronzes (BMC 657) and related types have been thoroughly investigated by Andrew Burnett (1992) and Geoff Cottam (1999), and I have no new information to add to the wealth of data they have assembled, with the exception of the recently discovered Chichester Wolf Cock (*Chris Rudd list* 63, no. 38). Both Burnett and Cottam propose that these bronze coins 'were produced some time in the mid or late first century BC'. I agree with them, but would prefer c. 60 - 50 BC rather than later. I think that they were among the first coins minted in the Solent area. Moreover, the fact that they seem to have been struck at or near Chichester might indicate that Chichester, and perhaps the Selsey peninsula too, were originally held by the Belgae. Alternatively, one could argue that these Chichester bronzes were the first coins made by the Regini: the Roma-derived helmet-type silver units of West Sussex – for example, Sussex Helmet (*Chris Rudd list* 15, no. 8) – could be cited in support of this view (the helmeted Chichester Cock head was also ultimately derived from Roman Republican Roma types). But a Roma-derived helmet-type silver unit, Mossop Helmet (*Chris Rudd list* 78, no. 31), has also recently been found at Danebury (Belgae territory). Moreover, the cluster of findspots around Winchester (*Venta Belgarum*) suggests that the Chichester bronzes belong to the Belgae, not to the Regini, and definitely not to the Atrebates, as Van Arsdell would have us believe.

Regni or Regini ?
Before discussing the coins of this tribe, let me quickly settle the question of what this tribe should be called – Regni or Regini? In 1948 Kenneth Jackson convincingly argued that the correct ancient British name was Regini, meaning 'the tall ones' or 'the proud, stiff ones.' (1948, 58). This interpretation was later endorsed by Leo Rivet and Colin Smith (1979, 445-46). However, more than half a century later, archaeologists and numismatists are still talking about the 'Regni', completely ignoring the expert advice of distinguished Celticists and philologists who know a lot more about the language of Iron Age Britain than we do. Getting the name right is of crucial importance with regard to this tribe, because Regni or Regnenses has been misinterpreted as referring to the Roman kingdom of Togidubnus (Cogidubnus), implying that the tribe was a Roman creation or, as Van Arsdell (1989, 111) puts it: 'The Atrebates/Regni occupied the territory that is today Berkshire, Sussex and parts of Hampshire. *Whether two distinct tribes occupied separate areas is not known because the Regni are virtually unknown to history until the Roman period*' [my italics]. The misnomer of Regni suppresses the truth: the Regini were in Britain long before the Romans and, until their short-lived subjugation by the Catuvellauni around AD 42, were probably the dominant tribe south of the Thames, not the Atrebates.

Regini gold staters (Figures 58, 61)
I shall not attempt to sort out who minted Westerham South, Qa or Qb gold staters or the commoner types of Qc gold quarters. I shall simply say that I suspect that they were produced by at least two mints (Selsey and Silchester?) and that I'd be amazed if there is any evidence to suggest that the Atrebates were in overall control of the production and distribution of all of these gold coins. My guess is that the shots were being called from Selsey, not Silchester. So I'll focus again on the south coast.

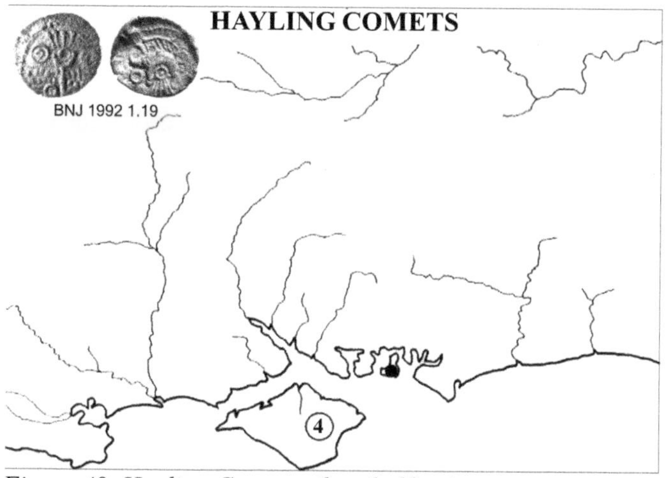

Figure 48. Hayling Comets silver half units.

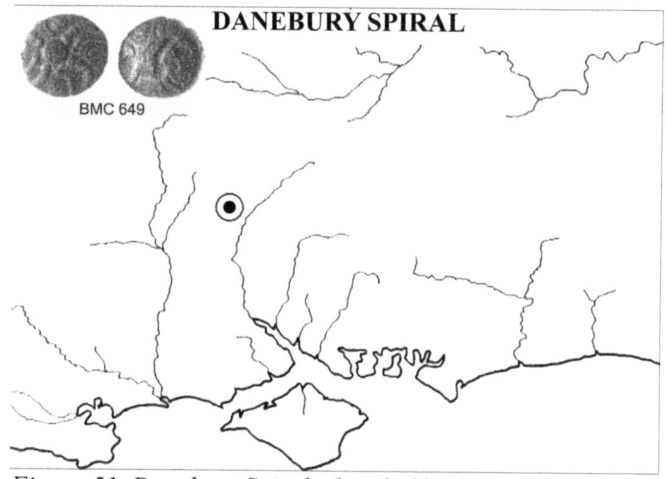

Figure 51. Danebury Spiral silver half units.

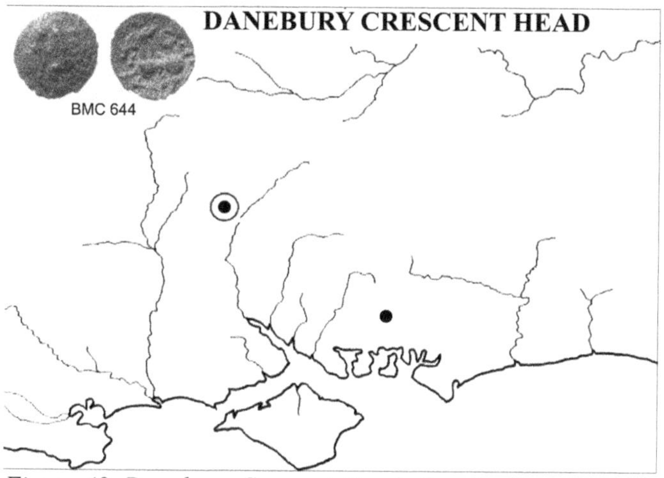

Figure 49. Danebury Crescent Head silver half units.

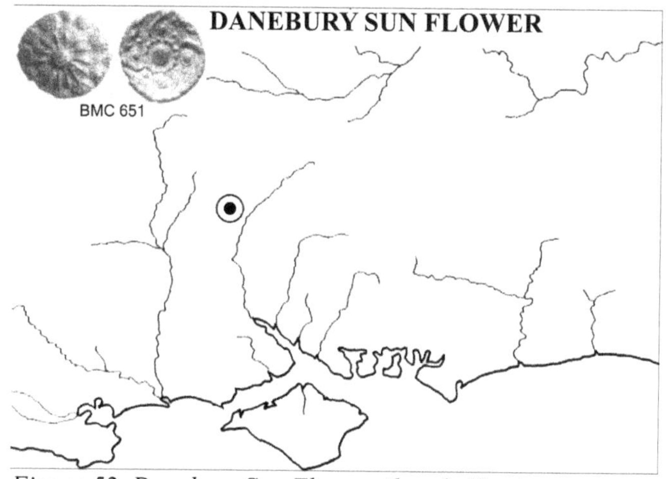

Figure 52. Danebury Sun Flower silver half units.

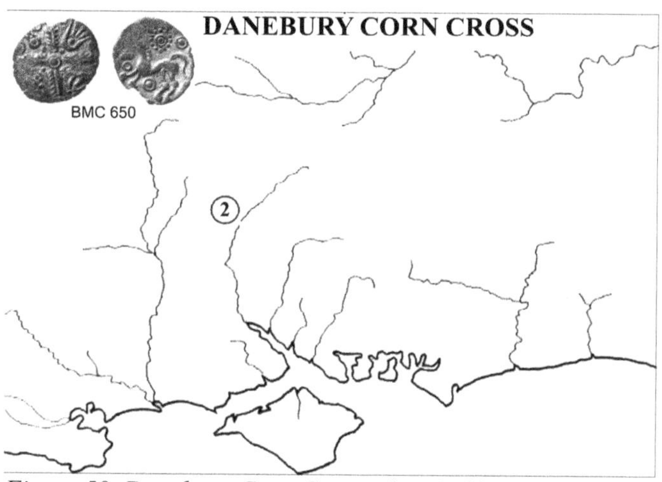

Figure 50. Danebury Corn Cross silver half units.

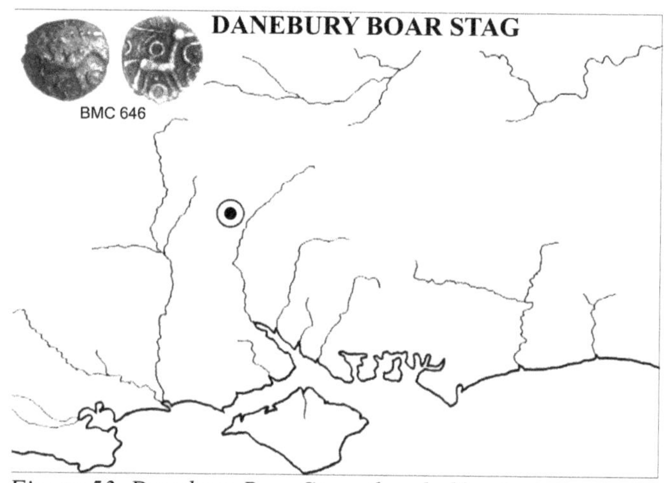

Figure 53. Danebury Boar Stag silver half units.

Figure 48. Five Hayling Comets silver half units: 4 Newchurch, IOW (hoard?), 1 Hayling Island.
Figure 49. Two Danebury Crescent Head silver half units: 1 Danebury (in hoard), 1 Blendworth.
Figure 50. Three Danebury Corn Cross silver half units: 2 Danebury (in hoard), 1 unprovenanced.
Figure 51. One Danebury Spiral silver half unit, from Danebury (in hoard).
Figure 52. One Danebury Sun Flower silver half unit, from Danebury (in hoard).
Figure 53. Two Danebury Boar Stag silver half units: 1 Danebury (in hoard), 1 unprovenanced.

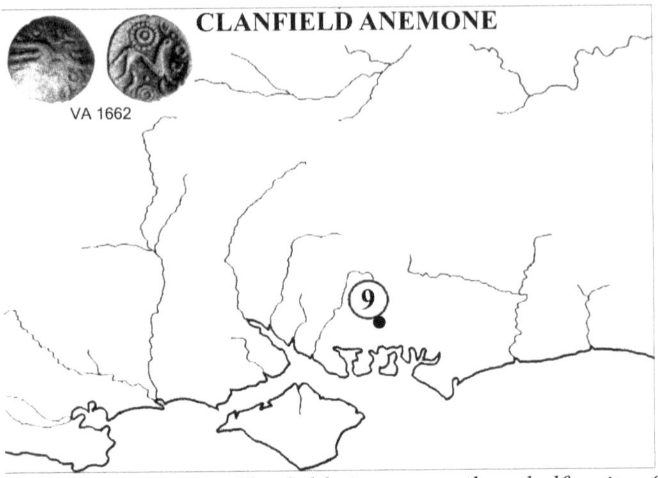

Figure 54. Sixteen Clanfield Anemone silver half units: 9 Clanfield (hoard?), 1 Horndean, 6 unprovenanced.

Figure 56. Eight Chichester Horse bronze units: 4 Chichester area, 1 each Winchester, Fontaine-sur-Somme (northern France), 2 unprovenanced.

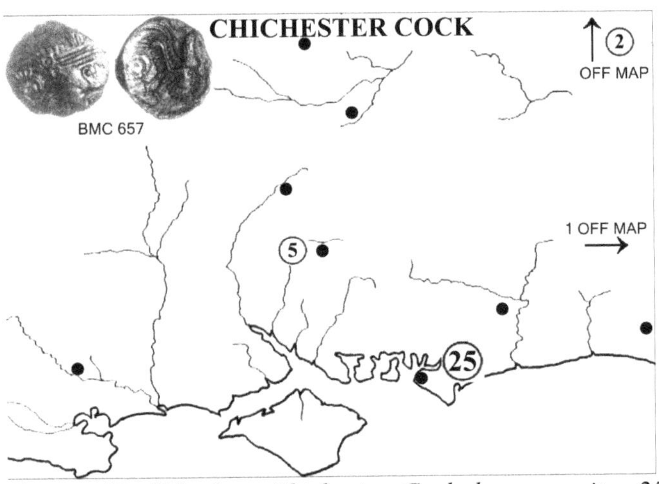

Figure 55. Fifty-four Chichester Cock bronze units: 25 Chichester area, 5 Winchester area, 1 each Bedfordshire, north-west Essex, Shapwick (hoard?), Lewes, Silchester, Tichborne, Whitchurch, Worth (Kent), Abingdon, Bignor, Wittering, 13 unprovenanced.

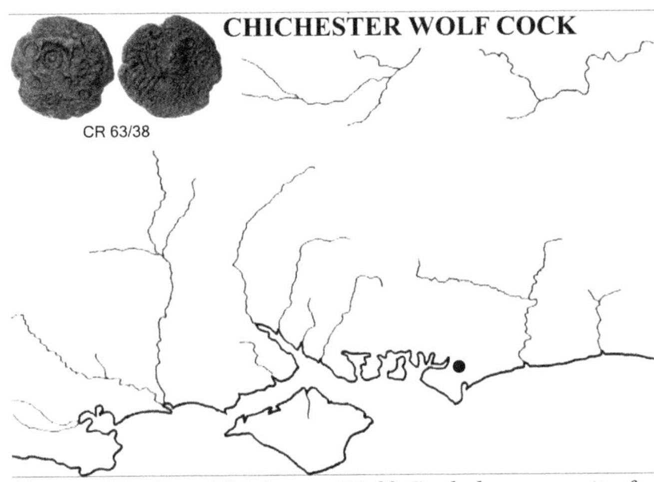

Figure 57. One Chichester Wolf Cock bronze unit, from Chichester.

Are there any uninscribed gold staters that have been found within the region of the Regini and that have not been encountered in the territory of the Atrebates? Yes, there are. They are called Climping staters, after the hoard site at Climping, West Sussex (DCMS *Treasure Annual Report* 2000, 106-107, and *Chris Rudd lists* 68, no. 18, 72 no. 20), and they appear to be southern imitations of Catuvellaunian Whaddon Chase staters.[7] At least fifty have been recovered from the hoard, with sixty or more Qa and Qb staters (mostly with very worn dies), but sadly only eighteen coins have been declared, despite repeated attempts to persuade finders to fulfill their legal obligations (Rudd 2005).

Figure 58. Climping gold staters (top CCI 03.0633, bottom CCI 03.0620).

Regini gold quarters (Figures 62-77)

There are at least sixteen gold quarter staters which are found in West Sussex, mostly around Chichester, which might qualify as coins of the Regini tribe. The main types are the Selsey Diadem (VA 78 'imported, uncertain tribal origin, possibly struck in Britain'), Phallic Geometric (VA 1227 'Durotrigan'), Willett's Nipple (VA 1229 'Durotrigan'), Ratham Ring Pole (BMC 538) and Selsey Tramlines (VA 254 'Atrebatic').

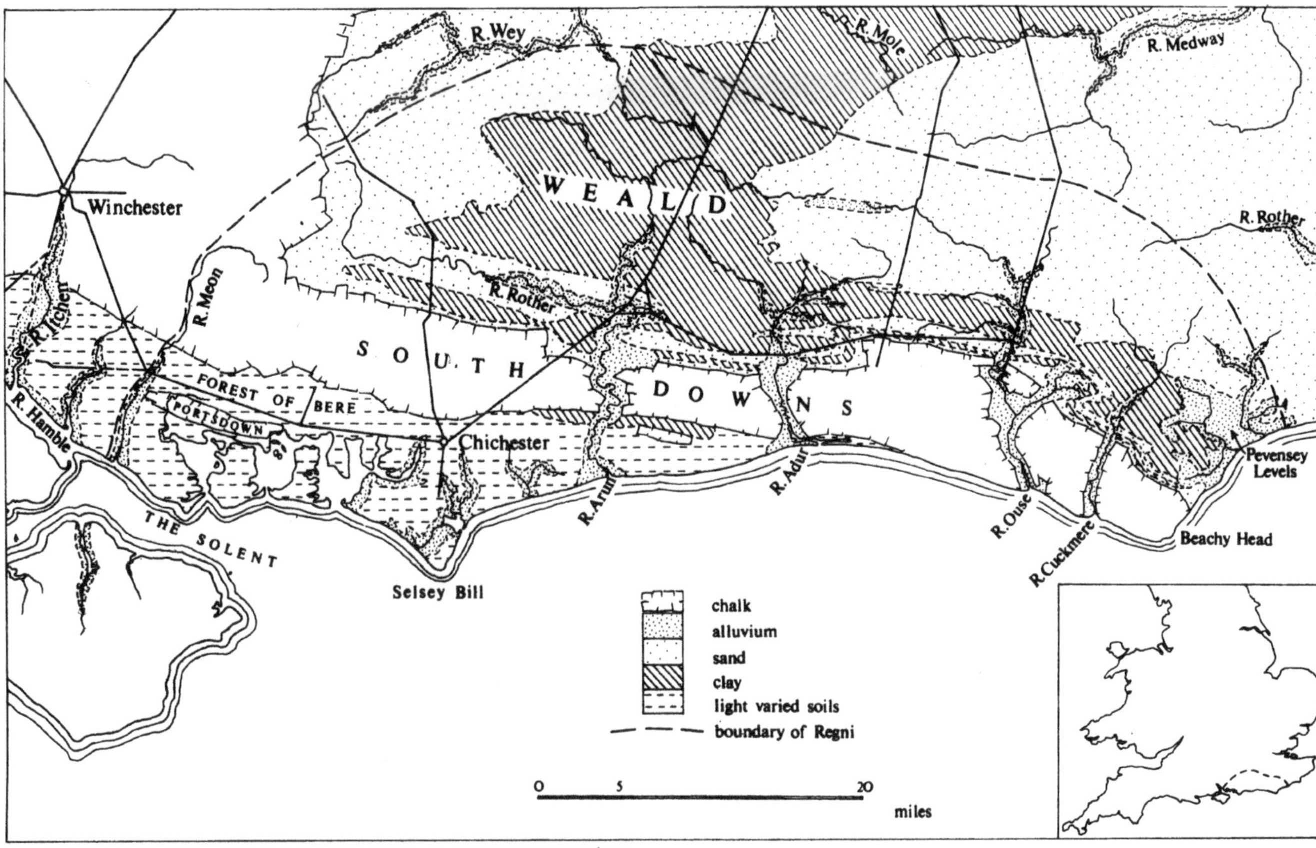

Figure 59. The territory of the Regini in the Roman period (Cunliffe 1973). With the exception of the Ashdown Forest hoard, no significant groups of Regini coins have been found east of the Arun; which might indicate that the region of the Regini ended at the Arun in the late Iron Age (see Figure 107).

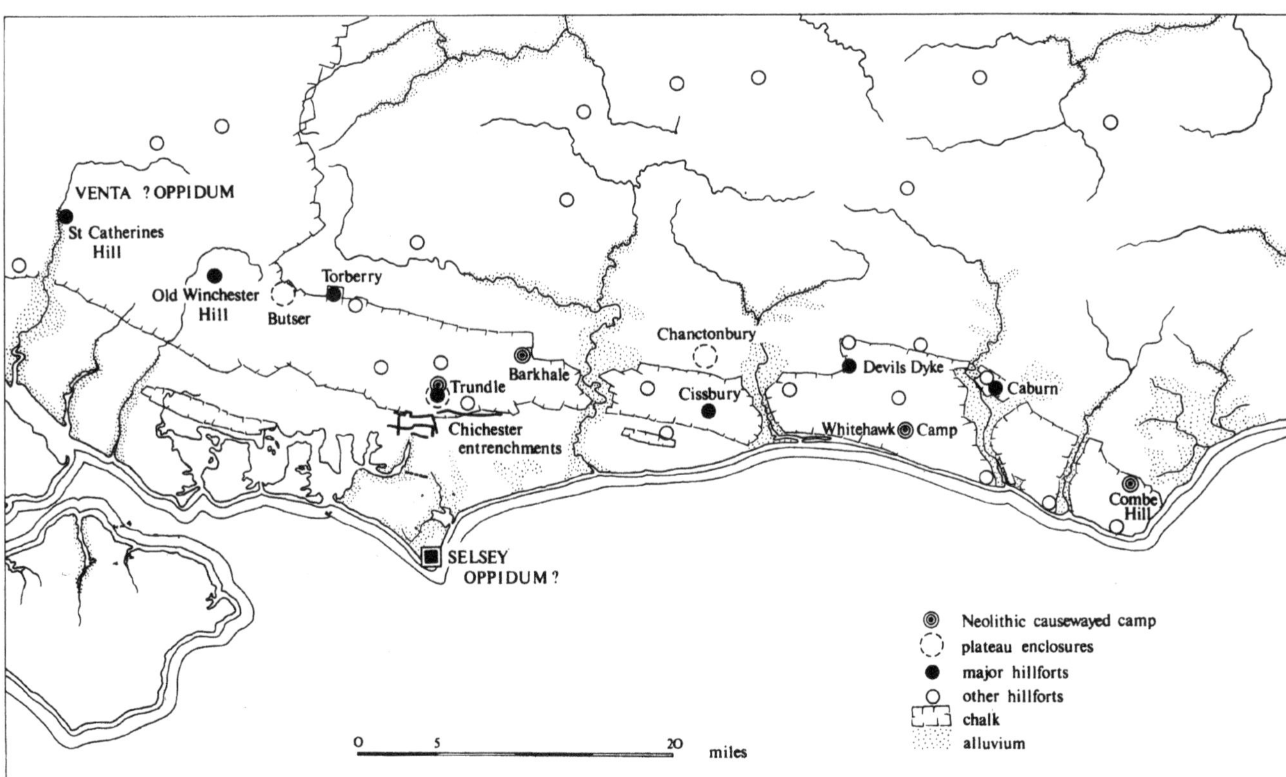

Figure 60. Pre-Roman settlement in the territory of the Regini (Cunliffe 1973). At some point in the second half of the first century BC the capital of the Regini may have moved from Selsey to Chichester.

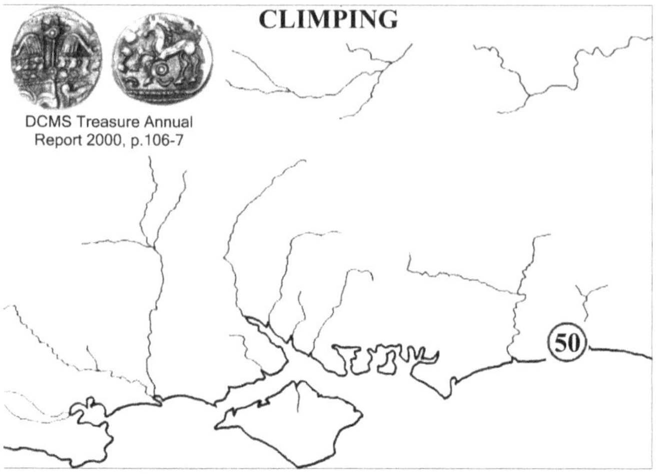

Figure 61. Climping staters.

Figure 62. Selsey Diadem quarter staters.

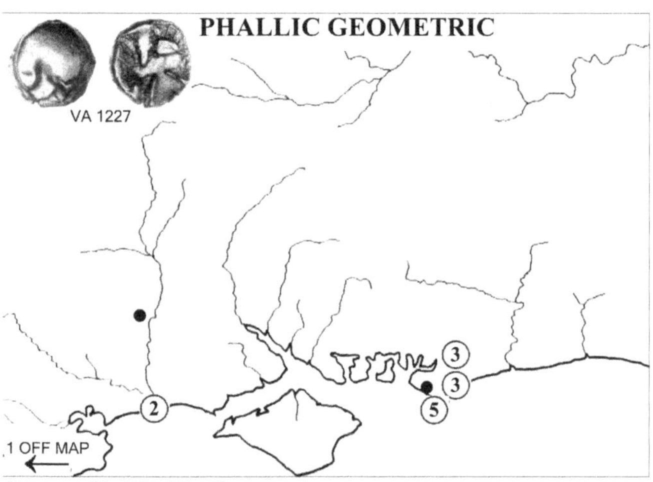

Figure 63. Phallic Geometric quarter staters.

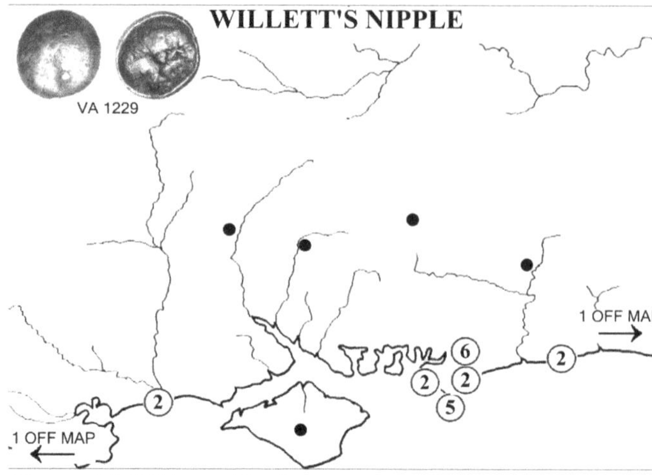

Figure 64. Willett's Nipple quarter staters.

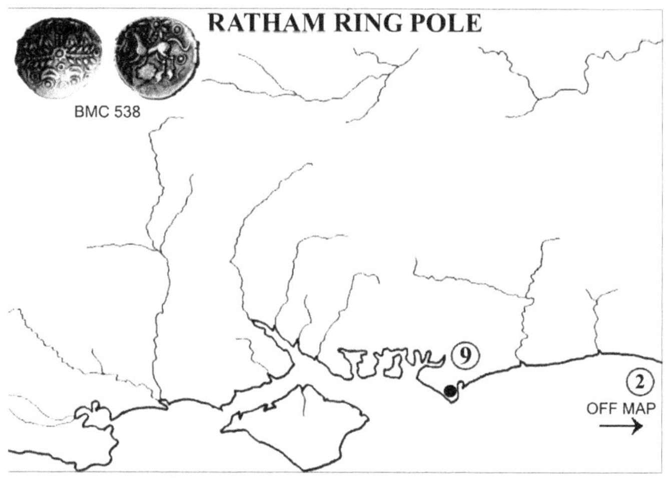

Figure 65. Ratham Ring Pole quarter staters.

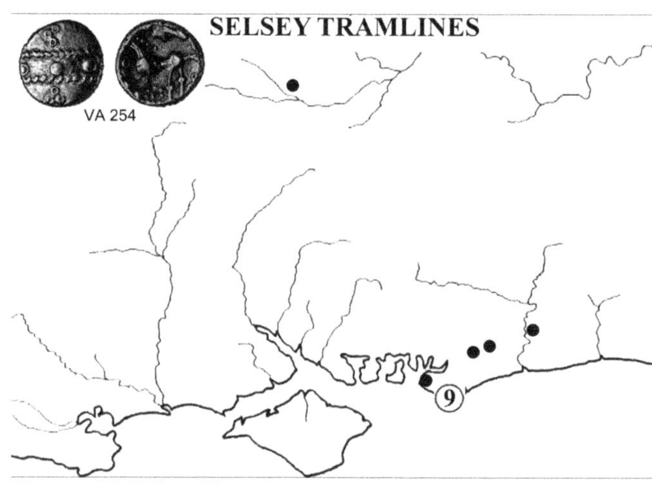

Figure 66. Selsey Tramlines quarter staters.

Figure 61. Thirty Climping gold staters: 8 Climping (hoard), 22 unprovenanced, but probably from same hoard.
Figure 62. Eight Selsey Diadem gold quarter staters: 6 Selsey (hoard?), 2 Chichester area.
Figure 63. Thirty-two Phallic Geometric gold quarter staters: 5 Selsey, 3 Chichester area, 3 Bognor Regis (hoard), 2 Christchurch/Hengistbury Head, 1 each Fordingbridge, Bracklesham Bay, Carn Brea, Cornwall (in hoard), 16 unprovenanced.
Figure 64. Forty-three Willett's Nipple gold quarter staters: 6 Chichester area, 5 Selsey, 2 East Wittering (in hoard?), 2 Bognor Regis (in hoard), 2 Hengistbury Head, 2 Worthing, 1 each Arlington, Oakhanger, Stockbridge, Winchester, Isle of Wight, Wisborough Green, Carn Brea, Cornwall (in hoard), 17 unprovenanced.
Figure 65. Seventeen Ratham Ring Pole gold quarter staters: 9 Chichester area, 2 Eastbourne, 1 Selsey (in hoard?), 5 unprovenanced.
Figure 66. Twenty-six Selsey Tramlines gold quarter staters: 9 Selsey (hoard?), 1 each Bury, Fontwell, Tangmere, West Wittering, Chieveley, 12 unprovenanced.

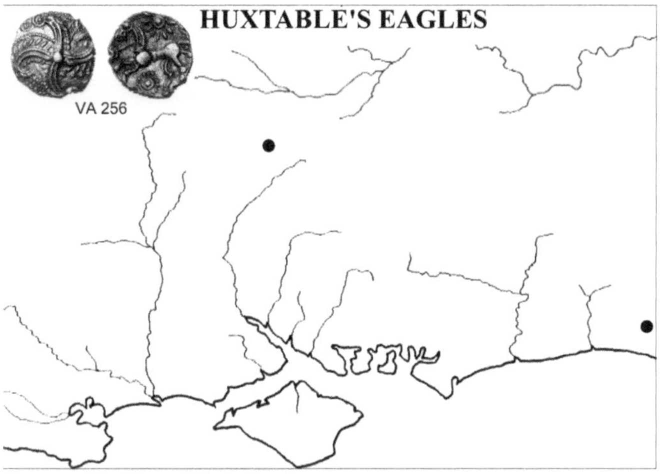

Figure 67. Huxtable's Eagles quarter staters.

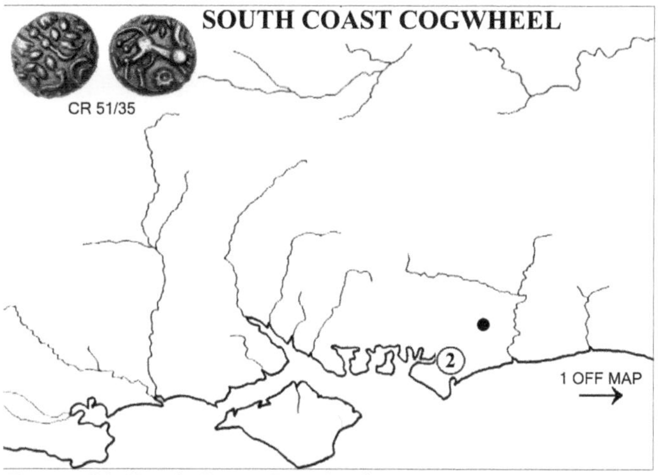

Figure 70. South Coast Cogwheel quarter staters.

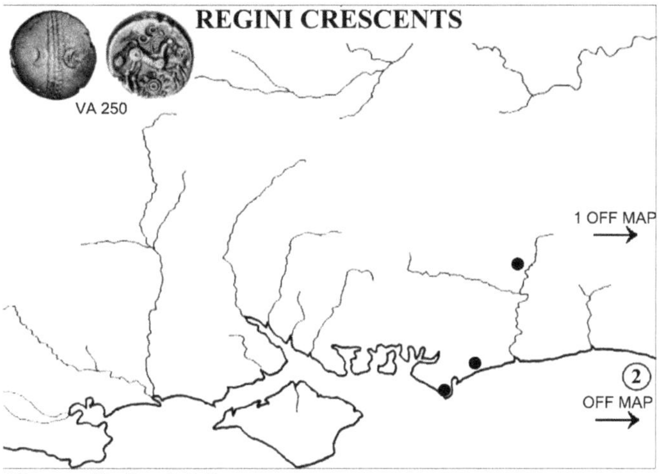

Figure 68. Regini Crescents quarter staters.

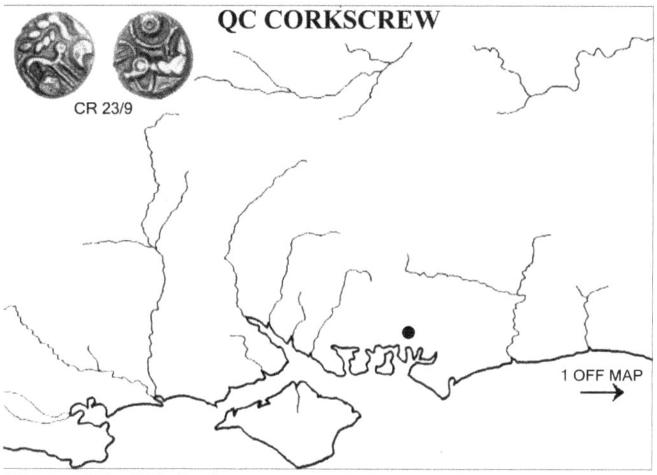

Figure 71. QC Corkscrew quarter staters.

Figure 69. Three Wheeler quarter staters.

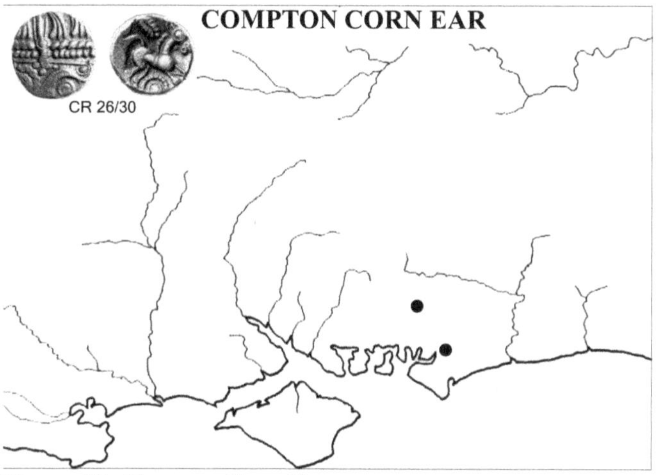

Figure 72. Compton Corn Ear quarter staters.

Figure 67. Five Huxtable's Eagle gold quarter staters: 1 near Lewes, 1 Ashmansworth, 3 unprovenanced.
Figure 68. Fourteen Regini Crescents gold quarter staters: 2 Eastbourne (1 in hoard), 1 each Ashdown Forest (in hoard), Bognor Regis, Selsey (in hoard?), Wisborough Green, 8 unprovenanced.
Figure 69. Three Three Wheeler gold quarter staters: 1 Selsey (in hoard?), 2 unprovenanced.
Figure 70. Five South Coast Cogwheel gold quarter staters: 2 Chichester area, 1 Slindon, 1 Eastbourne, 1 unprovenanced.
Figure 71. Three QC Corkscrew gold quarter staters: 1 Funtington, 1 Eastbourne, 1 unprovenanced.
Figure 72. Two Compton Corn Ear gold quarter staters: 1 Compton, 1 Chichester.

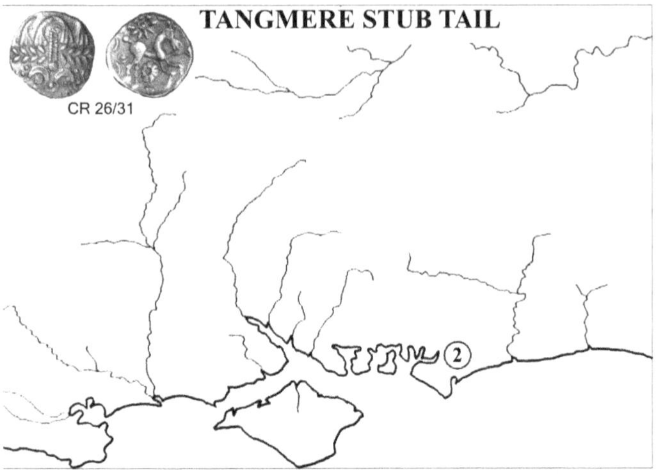

Figure 73. Tangmere Stub Tail quarter staters: 2 Chichester area, 1 unprovenanced.

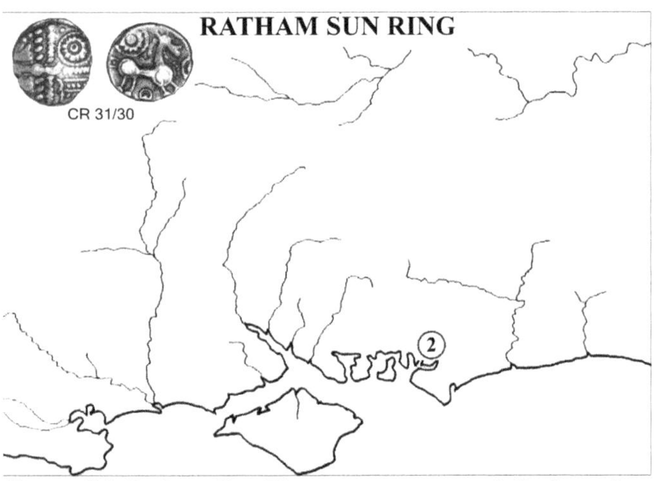

Figure 74. Ratham Sun Ring quarter staters: 2 Ratham, 1 unprovenanced.

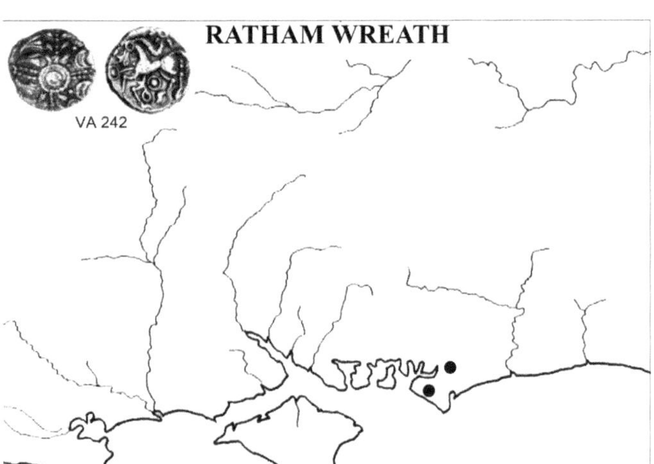

Figure 75. Ratham Wreath quarter staters: 1 Chichester, 1 Bracklesham.

Figure 76. Ratham Rose quarter stater: 1 Ratham, 1 unprovenanced. Regini or Belgae.

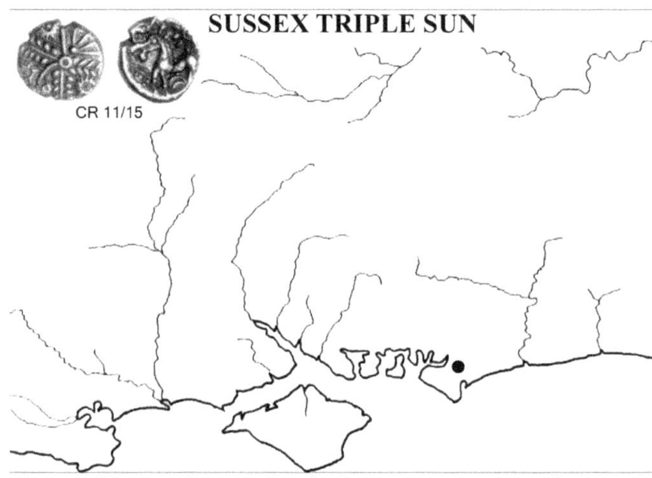

Figure 77. One Sussex Triple Sun quarter stater, from near Chichester.

One of the main distinguishing features of these uninscribed south-coast quarters is that most of them are struck on smaller, lighter and thicker flans than the commoner types of Qc quarters (VA 220, 222, 226) which are usually attributed to the Atrebates. Only one specimen of these sixteen different types of south-coast gold quarter staters has ever been found in Atrebatic territory and it is difficult to comprehend why the majority of them are automatically catalogued as Atrebatic.

Regini silver units (Figures 78-91)

The three most frequently recorded silver units of the Regini are the Sussex Lyre (BMC 635), Arundel Moon Man (*BNJ* Coin Register 1992, no.39) and Ashdown Forest (VA 264 'early Atrebatic type'). Almost all provenanced specimens of the Sussex Lyre (Figure 78) and Arundel Moon Man (Figure 79) have been found exclusively in West Sussex and nowhere else; not a single example has been found even remotely near the region of the Atrebates. These are unquestionably south-coast types and have no connection whatsoever with the Atrebatic mint at *Calleva*. By contrast the Ashdown Forest type has a more northerly and easterly distribution and could have been issued by a separate *pagus*.

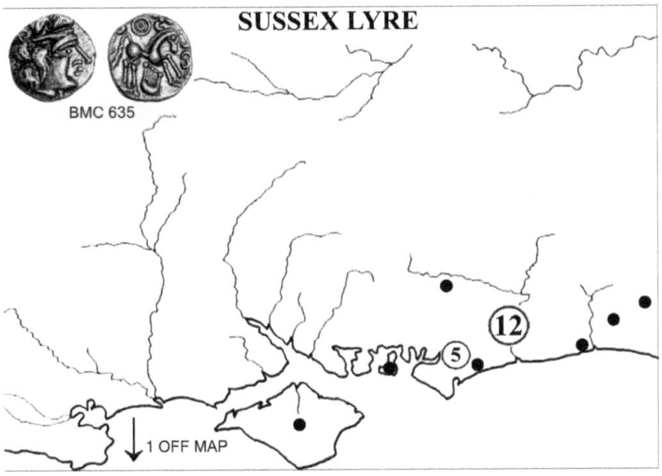

Figure 78. Thirty-eight Sussex Lyre silver units: 5 Chichester area, 1 each Bognor Regis, Hayling Island, Ditchling, Isle of Wight, Arundel, Harting, Poynings, Shoreham by Sea, Le Catillon, Jersey (hoard), 24 unprovenanced (but many of these may be from an undeclared hoard of at least 12 found 'east of Chichester' – probably near Arundel – in 1994).

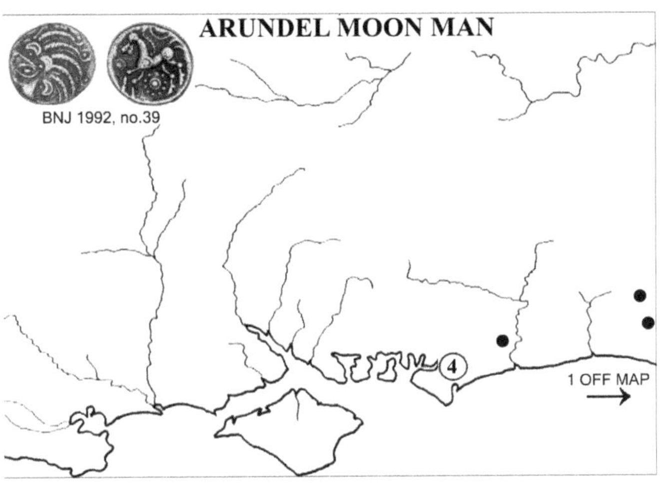

Figure 79. Eleven Arundel Moon Man silver units: 4 Chichester area, 1 each Arundel, Alciston, Lewes, Plumpton, 3 unprovenanced.

The other ten silver units of the Regini illustrated here are mostly centred on West Sussex. The Chichester Boar (BMC 577) is the most widely scattered and seems to be an early type. Andrew Burnett associated it with the Chichester Cock bronze units (BMC 657-659), which are also widely scattered, but they show a more westerly bias than the Chichester Boar. The Chichester Lyre (*Chris Rudd list* 27, no. 55) appears to be a degraded version of the Sussex Lyre and might be Belgic rather than Reginian; it is impossible to be precise about such tribal attributions, firstly because there are so few provenanced examples and secondly because Chichester figures prominently in the distribution patterns of certain coin types of both the Belgae and Regini. Moreover, several distinctive coin types seem to turn up in both tribes, in comparatively close geographical proximity; for example, the Petersfield Cernunnos (Figure 81) which I have assigned to the Belgae, and the Chichester Cernunnos (Figure 82) which I have assigned to the Regini. All I can declare with any degree of confidence is that none of these south-coast silver units is of Atrebatic origin – not a single one of them.

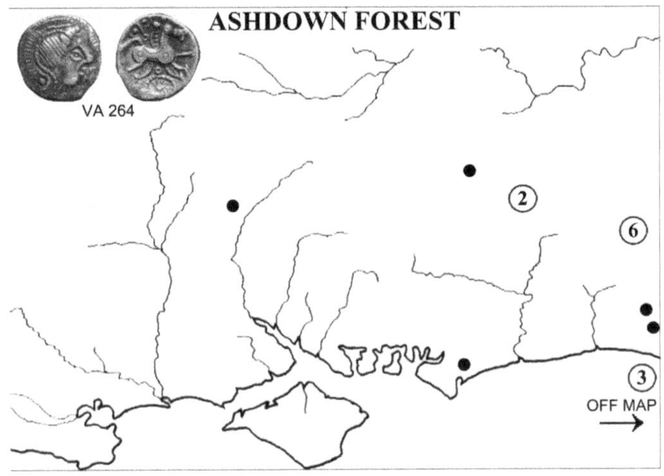

Figure 80. Twenty-one Ashdown Forest silver units: 6 Ashdown Forest (hoard), 3 Pevensey (hoard?), 2 Farley Heath (hoard?), 1 each Firle, Lewes, Danebury (in hoard?), Wanborough (in hoard?), Westhampnett, 5 unprovenanced.

Figure 81. Petersfield Cernunnos (SCMB 769, 1982), a unique silver unit which might be attributed to the Belgae.

Figure 82. Chichester Cernunnos (CCI 99.1271), a unique silver unit which might be attributed to the Regini, though it is very similar to the Petersfield coin. There is a boar between the antlers.

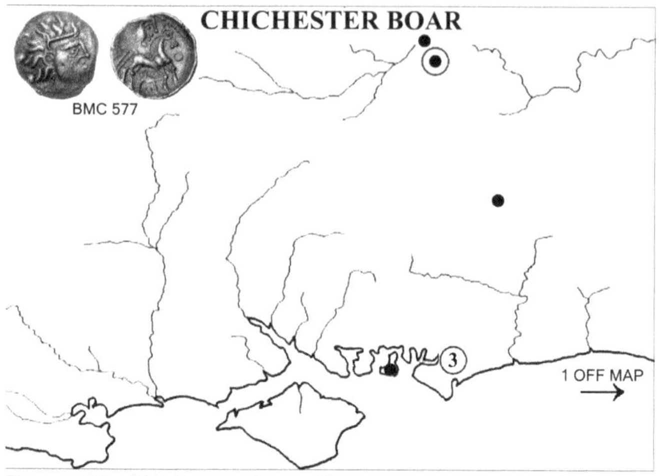

Figure 83. Chichester Boar silver units.

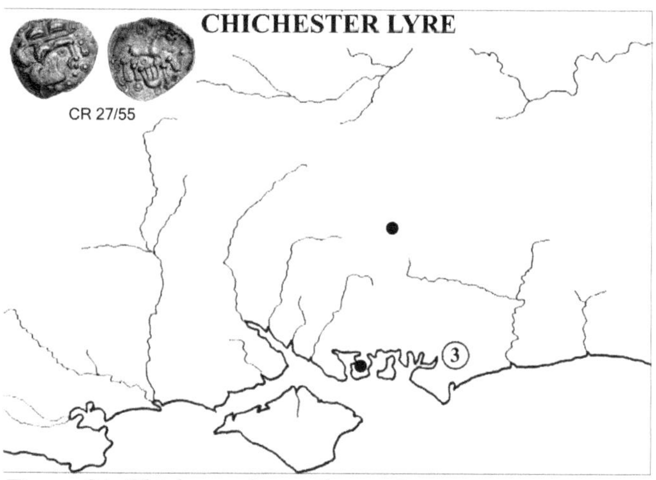

Figure 84. Chichester Lyre silver units.

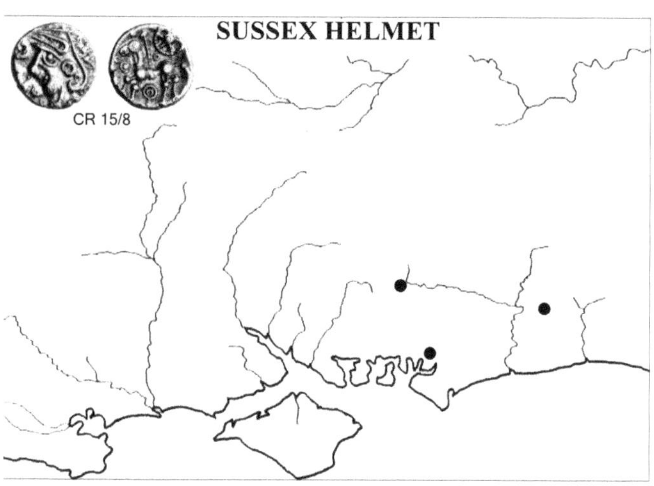

Figure 85. Sussex Helmet silver units.

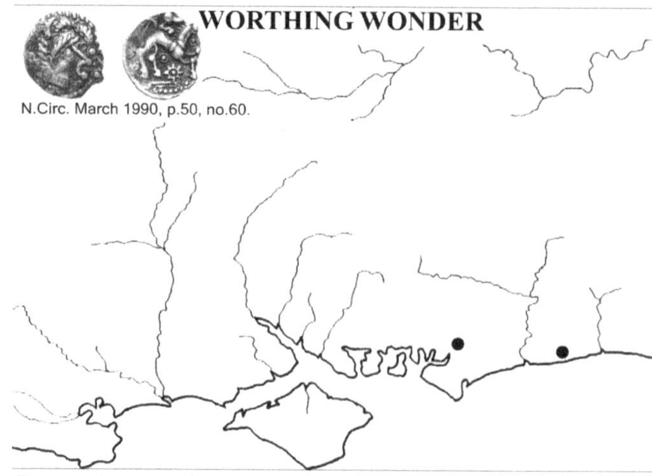

Figure 86. Worthing Wonder silver units.

Figure 87. Patching Moon Hair silver units.

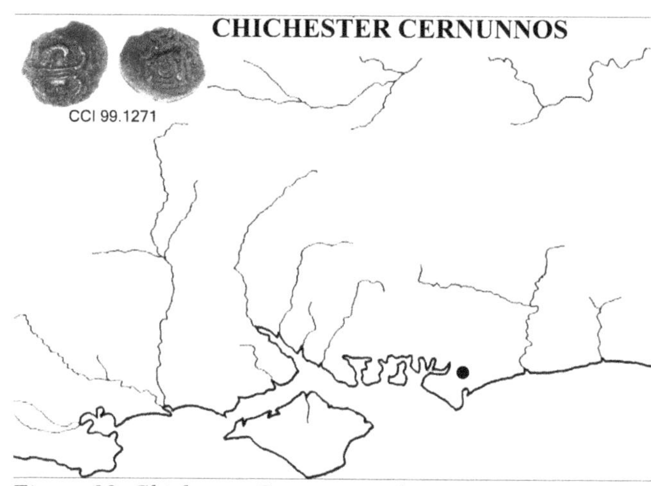

Figure 88. Chichester Cernunnos silver unit.

Figure 83. Twelve Chichester Boar silver units: 3 Chichester area, 1 each Hayling Island, Alciston, Godalming, Waltham St Lawrence (hoard), Wargrave, 4 unprovenanced.
Figure 84. Seven Chichester Lyre silver units: 3 Chichester area, 1 Portsmouth, 1 Selborne, 2 unprovenanced.
Figure 85. Three Sussex Helmet silver units: 1 each Ratham, Thakeham, Petersfield.
Figure 86. Two Worthing Wonder silver units: 1 Worthing, 1 Chichester.
Figure 87. Two Patching Moon Hair silver units: 1 Patching, 1 East Ashling.
Figure 88. One Chichester Cernunnos silver unit, from Chichester

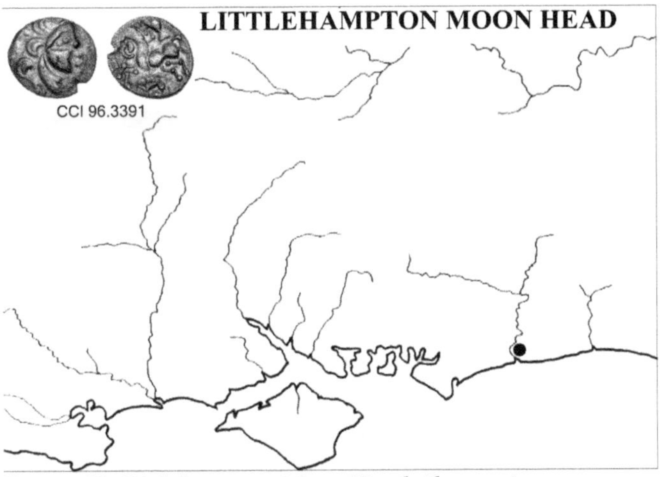

Figure 89. Littlehampton Moon Head silver unit.

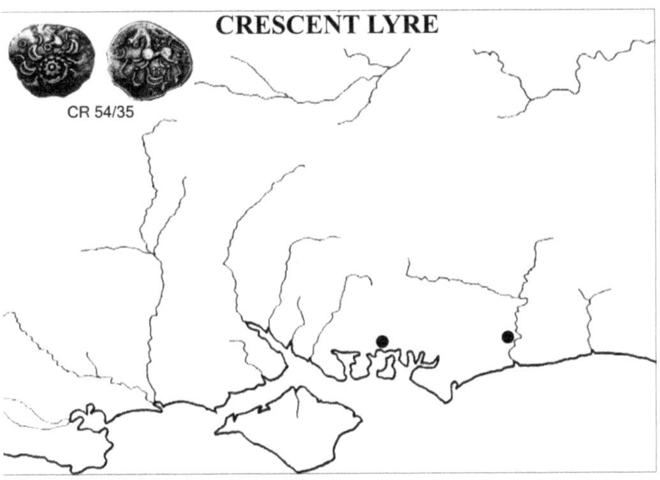

Figure 90. Crescent Lyre silver units.

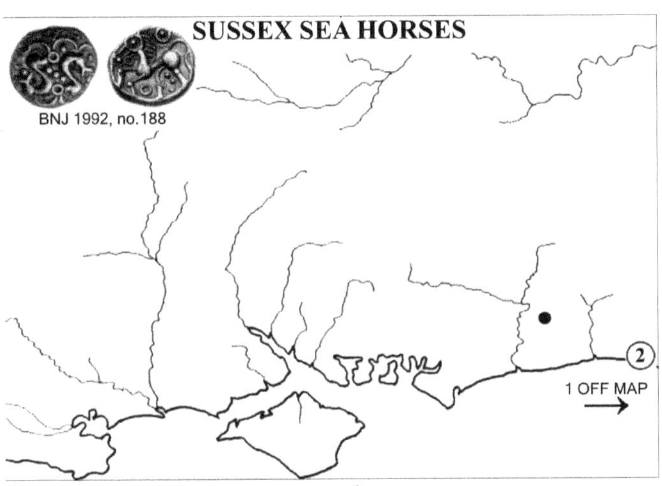

Figure 91. Sussex Sea Horses silver units.

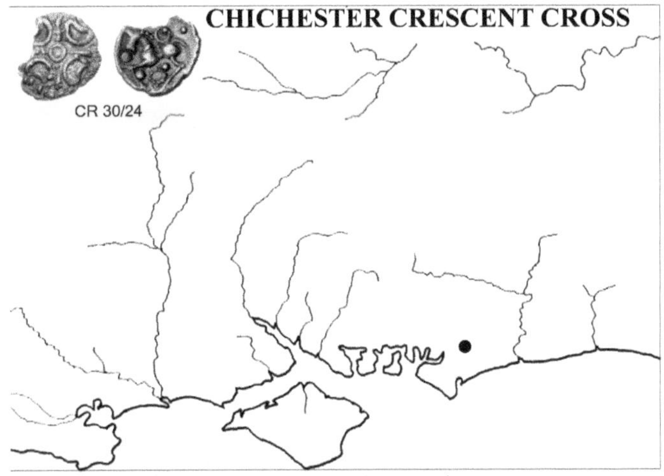

Figure 92. Chichester Crescent Cross silver minim.

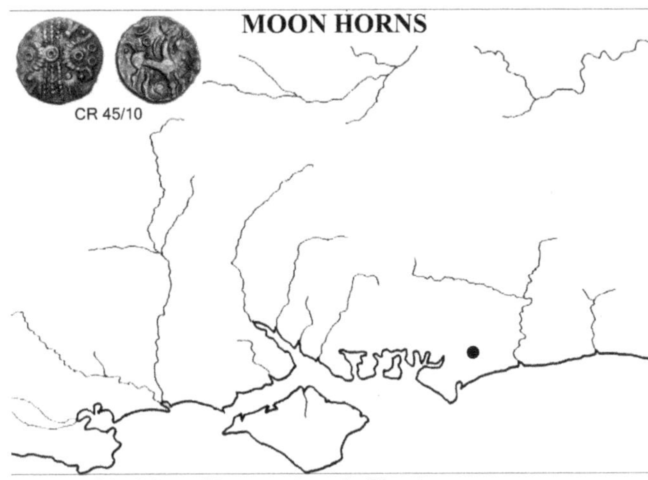

Figure 93. Moon Horns silver half unit.

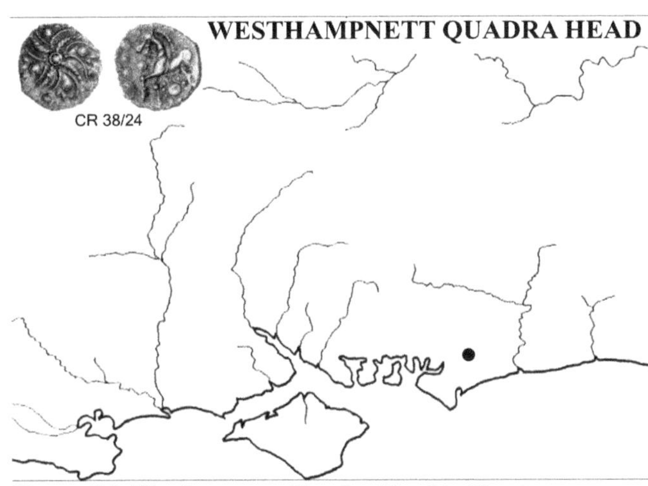

Figure 94. Westhampnett Quadra Head half unit.

Figure 89. One Littlehampton Moon Head silver unit, from Littlehampton. 'Possibly an Armorican issue, although the style and weight suggest a British production' (P. de Jersey, pers. comm.).
Figure 90. Two Crescent Lyre silver units: 1 Havant, 1 near Arundel.
Figure 91. Six Sussex Sea Horses silver units: 2 Newhaven, 1 Eastbourne, 1 Storrington, 2 unprovenanced.
Figure 92. One Chichester Crescent Cross silver minim, from Westhampnett.
Figure 93. One Moon Horns silver half unit, from Tangmere.
Figure 94. One Westhampnett Quadra Head silver half unit, from Westhampnett.

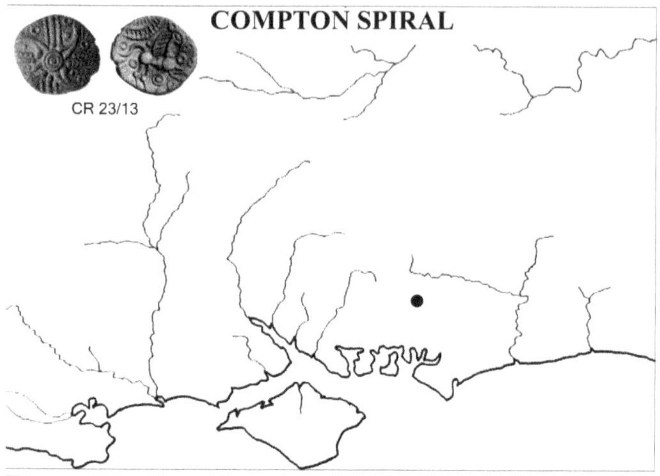

Figure 95. One Compton Spiral silver half unit, from Compton.

Figure 96. Three Chichester Star silver half units: 1 Ratham, 1 Petersfield, 1 unprovenanced.

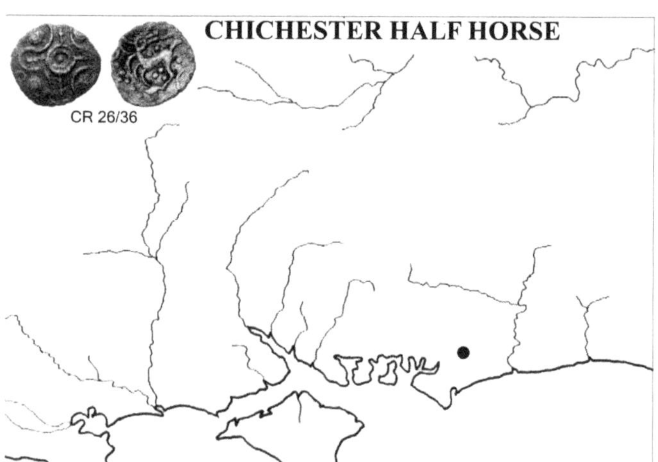

Figure 97. One Chichester Half Horse silver half unit, from Tangmere.

Regini silver half units (Figures 92-97)
My attribution of these six silver half units to the Regini is almost entirely arbitrary; they could all be Belgic. With the exception of the Chichester Star (Figure 96), each type is represented by only one recorded specimen which has only been published in my catalogue. I have given them to the Regini simply because all six have been found closer to Chichester than to Danebury or Winchester. That's good enough for my purposes, because all I want to demonstrate, yet again, is that they are south-coast issues which cannot by any rational calculation be associated with the Atrebates.

Regini and Atrebates – one tribe or two?
Van Arsdell says (1989, 111): 'Traditionally, the Atrebates/Regni have been treated numismatically as one tribe, and *there is no reason to change this approach* [my italics]. Only one coinage circulated in the tribal territory.' In the previous pages I have presented thirty-five reasons why this approach should be changed and why the old tradition should be forgotten: namely thirty-five uninscribed coin types that are found mostly along the coast of West Sussex, especially around and to the east of Chichester; that can all justifiably be attributed to the Regini (or some perhaps to the Belgae); and that *do not* circulate in the territory of the Atrebates or indeed anywhere near it. The only way one can counter this argument is by claiming that the Atrebates controlled the coast of West Sussex in the mid first century BC, that the powerful maritime *oppidum* of Chichester (Figure 103) was under the thumb of land-locked Silchester (forty miles away) during the period that these thirty-five coinages were struck, and that the Romans blundered badly when they named this south-coast capital *Noviomagus Reg(i)norum,* instead of *Noviomagus Atrebatum.*

Despite being so dismissive about the 'one tribe, one coinage' concept, I must concede that there is overwhelming numismatic evidence of some kind of trade agreement between the Regini and the Atrebates – an agreement which may date from the mid first century BC and which may at times have developed into a political alliance and defence coalition. How much of this mutual pact was due to economic or military coercion by one side or the other is uncertain, but intermarriage between royals and nobles is a distinct possibility. However, we can be fairly sure that the alliance wasn't a permanent one and that a lot of jockeying for power took place between 50 BC and AD 43. And I think we can also be fairly sure that the two tribes maintained their individual tribal identities and tribal cultures, that there were no mass migrations from one tribe to another, that there was no large-scale 'ethnic cleansing', and that the two tribes didn't share all of their coins for all of the time. And, most important to our present discussion, there doesn't seem to be any archaeological or numismatic evidence that the Regini were dominated by the Atrebates, as Van Arsdell unequivocally implies in *Celtic Coinage of Britain.*

In this outstanding and authoritative book Van Arsdell names 27 different uninscribed coins as 'Atrebatic' types (half of which have never been found in Atrebatic territory), and he classifies 158 different coins as 'Atrebatic' (including Danebury types, Kentish types and Regini types found solely on the south coast). What evidence does he offer for his belittlement of the Regini? None, as far as I can see. So let's ask some more specific questions.

- What evidence is there that the Atrebates were sole producers of Westerham South gold staters (VA 202) or that the Regini were junior partners in the production of them?[8]

- What evidence is there that the Atrebates had more control over the minting of Qa and Qb gold staters (VA 212, 216) and that substantially more of both have been found in the territory of the Atrebates than in the region of the Regini?

- What evidence is there that the Atrebates struck more Qc gold quarter staters (VA 220, 222, 226) than the Regini did? I have already shown that there are many rare types of Qc gold quarters that are found chiefly, if not exclusively, in the region of the Regini and that the Atrebates are unlikely to have struck any of them. So what about these three common types of Qc quarters?

- What evidence is there that the Atrebates issued more uninscribed silver coins than the Regini did? In fact, did the Atrebates issue *any* uninscribed silver coins of their own? If so, which types can confidently be attributed to their Silchester mint? I have already demonstrated that there are many rare types of uninscribed silver coins that are found chiefly, if not exclusively, in the region of the Regini and that the Atrebates are unlikely to have issued any of them.

- What evidence is there that the Atrebates wielded power over the Regini – monetary power, economic power, military power, political power or social power – during the period that both tribes were minting uninscribed coins? Is there any archaeological evidence of Atrebatic superiority between, say, 60 BC and 45 BC? Is there any numismatic evidence? Any historical evidence? Any epigraphic evidence? Any literary evidence? Just because there is no surviving documentary evidence of the Regini before the Roman occupation of Britain doesn't mean that the Regini didn't exist before AD 43 or that they were in some way inferior to the Atrebates. Van Arsdell (1989, 111) says: 'Whether two distinct tribes occupied separate territories is not known because the Regni are virtually unknown to history until the Roman period.' But the Durotriges, the Eceni, and the Corieltauvi are also 'virtually unknown to history until the Roman period'. Does Van Arsdell similarly doubt that these tribes existed before the Romans encountered them, or that they 'occupied separate territories', or that they were weak tribes? Incidentally, it should be remembered that Julius Caesar never once mentions the British Atrebates by name. Ancient documentary evidence of the Atrebates in Britain comes from precisely the same three classical sources as those that inform us of the Regini in Britain and are not a jot more extensive or more authoritative (Rivet and Smith 1979; Jones and Mattingly 1990).

- What evidence is there that Commios went directly to Silchester when he left Gaul and that he didn't disembark on the south coast and establish his power-base at Chichester? Barry Cunliffe states that Commios 'probably landed somewhere in the Solent region' (Cunliffe 2005, 142).

- What evidence is there that Commios I and Commios II (if indeed there were two, as has been suggested) ruled their kingdoms from Silchester and not Chichester?

- What evidence is there that more coins of Commios were issued at Silchester than Chichester or that Silchester was the principal mint of Commios? As a dealer buying directly from finders, I get the impression that some coins of Commios show a distinctly southern bias. For example, the Commios Moon Head silver minim (BMC 759-760) is found mainly around Chichester and in the land of the Belgae.

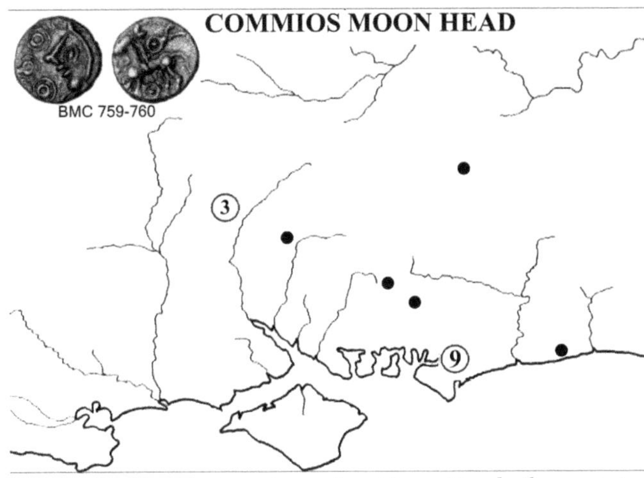

Figure 98. Twenty-two Commios Moon Head silver minims: 9 Chichester area, 3 Danebury (in hoard?), 1 each Butser Hill (in hoard?), Wanborough (in hoard), Weeke, Compton, Worthing, 5 unprovenanced.

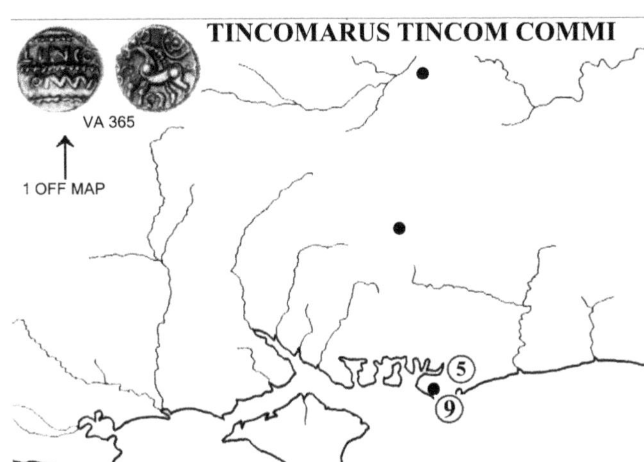

Figure 99. Twenty-three Tincomarus Tincom Commi gold quarter staters: 9 Selsey (hoard?), 5 Chichester area, 1 each East Wittering, Alton, Waltham St Lawrence (in hoard), Brough, Cumbria, 5 unprovenanced.

- What evidence is there that Tincomarus ruled from Silchester or that his main mint was at Silchester? Again, my hands-on experience as a dealer indicates completely the reverse and I have selected two coin types to illustrate this: the Tincomarus Tincom Commi gold quarter stater (VA 365) and

Tincomarus Diadem (VA 473). The findspots of both types (Figures 99-100) indicate that they are coins of the Regini, not the Atrebates. Simon Bean's comments on the geographical distribution of the coins of Tincomarus confirm this: 'The majority of the Celtic types of Tincomarus are distributed in the vicinity, or to the south of the South Downs, with a concentration in the Chichester region... The recurrent theme... is the pre-eminence of the Chichester region...' (Bean 2000, 137-38).

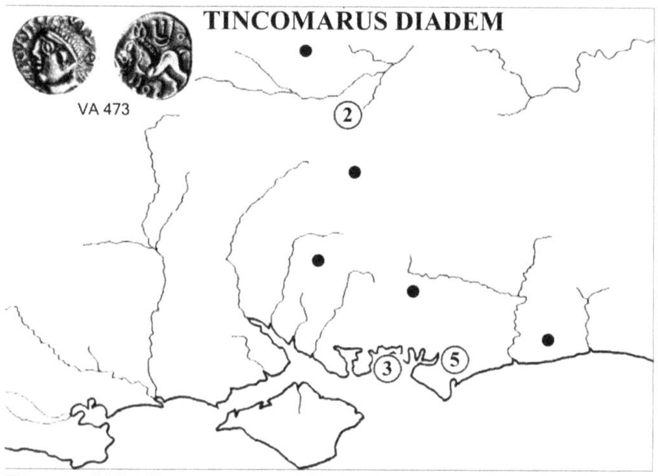

Figure 100. Twenty-seven Tincomarus Diadem silver units recorded: 5 Chichester area, 3 Hayling Island, 2 Silchester, 1 each Blewbury, Tichborne, Basingstoke, Findon, Harting, 12 unprovenanced.

- What evidence is there that any son of Commios I or Commios II, apart from Eppillus, ruled primarily in the territory of the Atrebates and had his main mint at Silchester? Even Eppillus didn't say he was king of the Atrebates and merely claimed to be king of *Calleva* (Figure 101). Even then, his reign wasn't a long one or exclusively Atrebatic; he also took control of some Cantiian territory, either as an act of expansion or as a result of expulsion from *Calleva*. I think that Van Arsdell (1989, 142-48) is entirely correct in classifying some of the coins of Eppillus as 'Atrebatic', but I believe that he exaggerates the importance of this ruler when he says 'Eppillus assumed the Atrebatic/*Regnan* leadership' [my italics]. Where is the evidence that Eppillus was ever king of the Regini?

Figure 101. This silver unit (VA 415) can reasonably be catalogued as 'Atrebatic' because, for a while at least, Eppillus ruled solely in the kingdom of the Atrebates, though he was probably the son of a Reginian ruler.

- What evidence is there that Verica ruled both the Regini and the Atrebates from a single royal court at Silchester or that he favoured the Atrebates in preference to the Regini? Chichester was probably his 'home town' – the place of his birth and growth (unless, of course, he grew up in Rome) – and he probably regarded himself first and foremost as Reginian (albeit Roman educated, perhaps), rather than Atrebatic. His hold on the northern kingdom may have been considerably less secure.

- What evidence is there that Epaticcus and Caratacos (Figure 102) considered the Regini less important, less powerful or less desirable for Catuvellaunian colonization than the Atrebates?

Figure 102. What makes us imagine that Epaticcus and Caratacos were ever welcome in the territory of the Atrebates or the region of the Regini? As the corn-ear gold stater of Epaticcus (VA 575) makes abundantly clear, they were both Catuvellaunian despots. If they weren't, why did Verica travel all the way to Rome for emergency aid? When the Romans chased Caratacos out of southern Britain, I'm sure that the Regini at least were glad to see the back of him. In our romantic view of Caratacos as a 'freedom fighter' we tend to overlook the likelihood that he was as much a colonizer as Claudius was.

For over fifty years the Regini have been cast in the role of second-class citizens by everyone who has written about them; not just numismatists, but archaeologists too. But why has everyone jumped to the conclusion that it was a total takeover by the Atrebates and that the merger (if it actually happened) resulted in the Regini being submerged? I guess it is because everyone knows that Commios was made king of the Atrebates in Gaul (*BG* 4.21) and that he may have been Atrebatic by birth, though we can't be absolutely certain of this. Therefore the natural assumption is that when he crossed the Channel he became king of the Atrebates in Britain too, and that the Regini were subsequently overwhelmed by the Atrebates. I think this is a false assumption. I think there is another way of interpreting the situation – a way which doesn't involve the dismissal of the Regini and which may explain why the Belgae became numismatically invisible to us.

It is all too easy to criticize the creative work of other people, especially when it contains many imaginative insights as well as much solid science, as Van Arsdell's *Celtic Coinage of Britain* undoubtedly does. So, to compensate for my negative reaction to his treatment of the Regini and the Belgae, I'll now float a few positively creative ideas of my own, no less speculative than his. I'll quickly sketch an alternative historical scenario for the south coast in the first century BC/AD.

An alternative scenario

The first scene in my alternative scenario is directly inspired by John Creighton's intriguing proposal that Commios didn't flee to Britain, but was sent by Caesar to establish a pro-Roman kingdom in southern Britain, subsidized by Roman gold (Creighton 2000, 59-64). Let's speculate. Let's explore Creighton's novel concept and see where it leads us.

In 51 BC, after his submission to Mark Antony, Commios sets sail for Britain, accompanied by his family, his close friends, his personal bodyguard of trusted warriors, a small troop of cavalry and several chests of Roman gold. His mission is part political, part commercial – primarily to consolidate treaty agreements made by Caesar in 54 BC with southern chieftains (for example, to ensure the continued payments of tribute money, some of which may have lapsed or been late), and secondarily to develop Britain's growing cross-Channel trade with Roman merchants, which is why Caesar's financiers are willing to fund the mission.

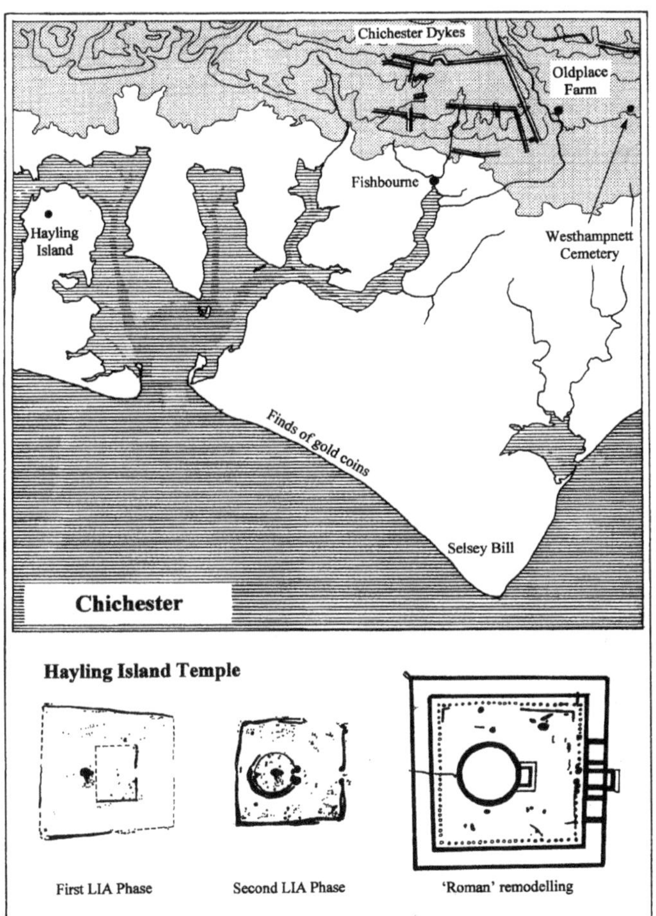

Figure 103. The location of the Chichester entrenchments, Westhampnett cemetery and Fishbourne Roman palace and the development of the Hayling Island temple (Creighton 2000).

Commios heads for the Solent, disembarks in Chichester harbour, sets up his first base on the Selsey peninsula and soon starts meeting various tribal leaders, druids and trade delegates from the Regini, Belgae and Atrebates, many of whom have been told of his arrival several weeks in advance and most of whom welcomed the news. After a difficult six years of living with invasion threats, sending young men to fight in France (many didn't return), paying tribute money to Caesar, coping with political uncertainty and accommodating an influx of foreign migrants (many couldn't even speak British), the southern chieftains were now delighted to be joined by such a powerful Gallic leader – an international hero in his own lifetime – well placed with the Romans, with investment funds to prove it.

There are many reasons why the Chichester/Selsey peninsula (Figure 103) was carefully selected as the ideal long-term location for the court of Commios and his successors and as a focus for his political and commercial activities, and why it was infinitely preferable to an inland site, such as Silchester. First and foremost was the fact that Chichester was surrounded by friendly tribes, with the Regini to the east (whose capital it was), the Belgae to the west and the Atrebates to the north. Chichester was well out of reach of Cassivellaunos and over sixty miles away from *Verlamio*, capital of the marauding Catuvellauni, now led by the ambitious young Addedomaros; whereas Silchester and the Atrebates were uncomfortably close to the Catuvellauni, with only the Thames between them. Secondly, Chichester was fast becoming the Marseilles of southern Britain, the centre of a massive import-export trade (Figures 8, 106, 108), much of it recently acquired from the Durotrigan harbours of Christchurch and Poole, which had lost their Brittany business in the Gallic War. Thirdly, Chichester was close to many highly important and highly profitable specialist businesses, such as the extensive saltworks around the fringes of the harbour inlets to the west and the extraction of iron from ferruginous sandstone in the Weald (Cunliffe 1973). Fourthly, Commios could see the potential of Chichester as a major outlet for the lucrative trade in British slaves. Fifthly, Chichester and the Solent hinterland were rapidly turning into a cosmopolitan commercial complex, full of migrant merchants from Belgic and Armorican tribes, as indicated by their imported coins. Being a multilingual, silver-tongued negotiator with a unique network of contacts on both sides of the Channel, Commios quickly spotted the profit opportunities of this situation – opportunities that land-locked Silchester couldn't begin to match. Sixthly, Chichester was near an important druid centre on Hayling Island (Figure 103) and Commios was well aware of the value of maintaining friendly relations with the druids. Finally, from the point of view of the Romans, Chichester was close enough to Gaul for them to keep an eye on Commios and the gold they had given him (just in case he decided to 'go native' again), whereas Silchester wasn't. From every angle, *Noviomagus* 'new market'[9] was the new boom town of the south coast, eclipsing the old Regini capital of Selsey, which was now starting to fall into the sea. There simply couldn't be a better place for Commios to consolidate the southern tribes for Rome, to make a lot of money for himself and his backers, and to build a brighter future for his family.[10]

Within a couple of months of landing on the south coast Commios negotiates a number of agreements with the king of the Atrebates and establishes a secondary base for himself and his followers at Silchester. He mints gold coins bearing a three-tailed horse at both Chichester and Silchester and it isn't long before the Commian dynasty, now deeply entrenched at Chichester, dominates the tribal policies and economies of the Regini, the Belgae and the Atrebates. But Commios himself doesn't live long enough to reap the rewards of all his wheeling and dealing. With Roman consent he is succeeded by his eldest son, also called Commios, who continues to implement the political and commercial strategies planned by his father, Caesar and Mark Antony. Still based mainly in his southern kingdom of the Regini, Commios II issues gold coins bearing his name at Chichester and Silchester; one of the gold quarter staters (Figure 4) carries the letter A to remind people that, although he is king of the Regini, he comes from the royal family of the Atrebates in Gaul, and that he is now also king of the Atrebates in Britain. This is a period of great expansion and great wealth for the Regini, whose new capital at Chichester continues to grow, whose commerce with Gaul continues to increase and whose alliance with the Atrebates continues to bear fruit, because they help defend them from cross-border raids by the Catuvellauni.

Commios II has three sons: Tincomarus, Eppillus and Verica. The eldest, Tincomarus, inherits the southern and northern kingdoms but keeps his royal seat at Chichester, as requested by Augustus. His younger brother, Eppillus, becomes jealous of his success, marries a daughter of Tasciovanos and captures *Calleva* with the help of the Catuvellauni. The Atrebates feel betrayed by this treachery, as do the Regini, and between them they eventually manage to dislodge Eppillus from Silchester. He then moves into Kent, again with the aid of the Catuvellauni, but his reign there is also of brief duration. Around AD 10 Tincomarus dies and is succeeded by Verica, the youngest son of Commios II. Verica lives up to his name 'over king', regains the northern kingdom for the Regini and rules wisely for a remarkable thirty years. The length and strength of Verica's reign, and the huge wealth he accumulates on his vast royal estate at Chichester, are rivalled only by Cunobelinus, king of the Catuvellauni and Trinovantes for thirty years. Like Commios I, Commios II and Tincomarus, Verica's power-base was always securely anchored at Chichester, from where he could control naval and merchant shipping, cross-Channel imports and exports (especially the export of slaves to Roman traders), and the deployment of his armed forces around the tribal boundaries of the Regini, Belgae and Atrebates. Verica was born in the land of the Regini and, though educated in the ways of the Romans, regards himself as a man of the Regini.

Around AD 35 the Atrebates are invaded by Epaticcus (Figure 102) the brother of Cunobelinus, and Verica is unable to prevent him taking Silchester, though he manages to hang onto much of his Reginian kingdom for the next seven years, thanks to the strength of his army and the loyalty of the Regini. Eventually Catuvellaunian warriors cross over the ancient Harroway track and penetrate into the northern territory of the Regini. Epaticcus is killed in the fighting that follows, but is rapidly replaced by a nephew – a son of Cunobelinus called Caratacos 'the beloved' (Figure 102) who hates the Romans and Roman sympathisers, such as the Regini, most of whose overseas income now comes from Italy. Indeed, by AD 40 several Roman merchants now live in Chichester, which is partly garrisoned by Roman soldiers. Verica knows that Caratacos is a brilliant cavalry commander, as cunning as he is courageous, and fears that his Catuvellaunian horsemen might one day defeat the Regini and capture *Noviomagus* itself. Verica therefore hurries to Rome with his bodyguard and asks Claudius for help. The rest, as they say, is history.

Verica returns to Britain with Aulus Plautius, who lands half his invasion force at Richborough in Kent and half at Chichester harbour, much to the relief of the Regini, who are pleased to have their old king safely home. Verica dies shortly afterwards and is replaced by his eldest son, Togidubnus (Figure 104) who has grown up in Rome and served in the Roman army with General Vespasianus. Like his father, grandfather and great-grandfather, Togidubnus makes his home at Chichester and later builds a splendid palace for himself at Fishbourne – the finest regal residence outside Italy. He is now the richest man in Britain and, thanks to Roman patronage, one of its most powerful rulers (Henig 2002). For a hundred years the Regini have remained loyal to Rome. This is their reward.

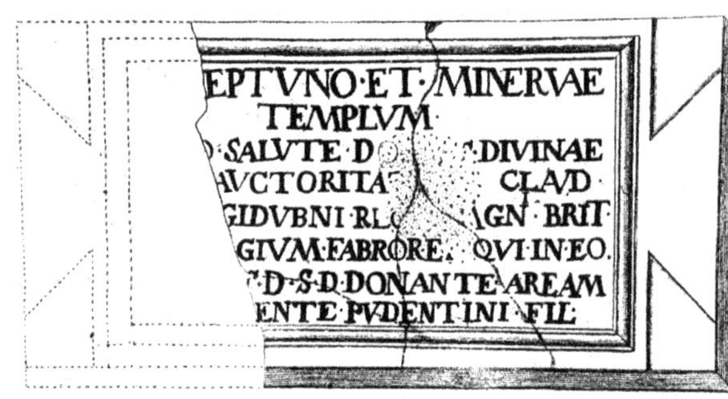

Figure 104. This slab of Purbeck marble, found at Chichester and dating to the Flavian period or earlier, refers to Togidubnus, king of the Regini, who was 'consistently loyal down to our time' (Tacitus Agricola *14). The inscription reads: 'A temple to Neptune and Minerva and for the safety of the divine house (of the emperor) by the authority of Ti. Claudius Togidubnus, [Great King] in Britain, (erected by) the guild of fabri and its members at their own cost. [Pud?]ens son of Pudentinus, donated the site' (*RIB, *I, 91). This inscription indicates the importance not only of Togidubnus, but also of Chichester and the Regini.*

What role did the Belgae play in this partly imaginary, century-long scenario? I don't know and can but guess. I get the feeling – and it is only a feeling – that as the power of the Regini and Atrebates swelled under the Commian dynasty the influence of the Belgae declined (Figure 8). Was their *floruit* the heyday of Danebury, which ceased to be occupied circa AD 20? Or did they enjoy a renaissance when Gallic War migrants settled in the Solent hinterland? I think the answer is 'yes' and 'yes'.

Looking at the arc of defended enclosures to the east of the Avon and its Bourne tributary – Buckland Rings, Ampress, Castle Hill, Castle Piece, Gorley Hill, Frankenbury, Figsbury Rings and Bury Hill – I surmise that the western boundary of the Belgae may once have followed a similar line, and that the outer northern limit might be defined by the Harroway and defended by Bury Hill, Balksbury, Cadbury, Andyke, Tidbury Ring, Norsebury Ring and Oliver's Battery. Looking at the distribution of uninscribed coins, I guess that the Belgae's eastern boundary could be Bosham harbour, rather than the Meon, as suggested by Cunliffe (Figures 9, 59). In fact, the Belgae may even have occupied the northern portion of the Chichester/Selsey peninsula in the first half of the first century BC; if we believe that the Chichester bronze coins were struck c. 60 - 50 BC, then this begins to look like a possibility. It also seems to be confirmed by the easterly bias of Hampshire Thin Silver coins in the Solent (Figure 24).

If the Belgae were ever in charge of the Chichester area in the first half of the first century BC, they certainly weren't in the second half. Cheriton staters (Figures 12, 13) and Petersfield Wreath Face quarters (Figure 17) don't encroach on Chichester; and stylistically they are distinctly different from wreath/horse coins of the Regini and Atrebates. They are also lighter in weight and more cuprous. They have to be Belgic productions, not Atrebatic, not Durotrigan.

I believe that the advent of Commios on the Chichester/Selsey peninsula – do we seriously think he sailed up the Thames to Silchester under the nose of Cassivellaunos? – signalled the beginning of the decline of the Belgae as a military force on the Solent; that their focus of political influence gradually retracted northwards to their heartland of Danebury and Winchester; and that they had stopped producing their own coins by c. 30 BC (if the Belgae had issued inscribed coins, there would never have been any numismatic doubt about them as a coin-producing tribe). I believe that the Belgae became allied to the Regini and Atrebates, but it was probably an alliance of compliance on the part of the Belgae, not a union of equal partners.

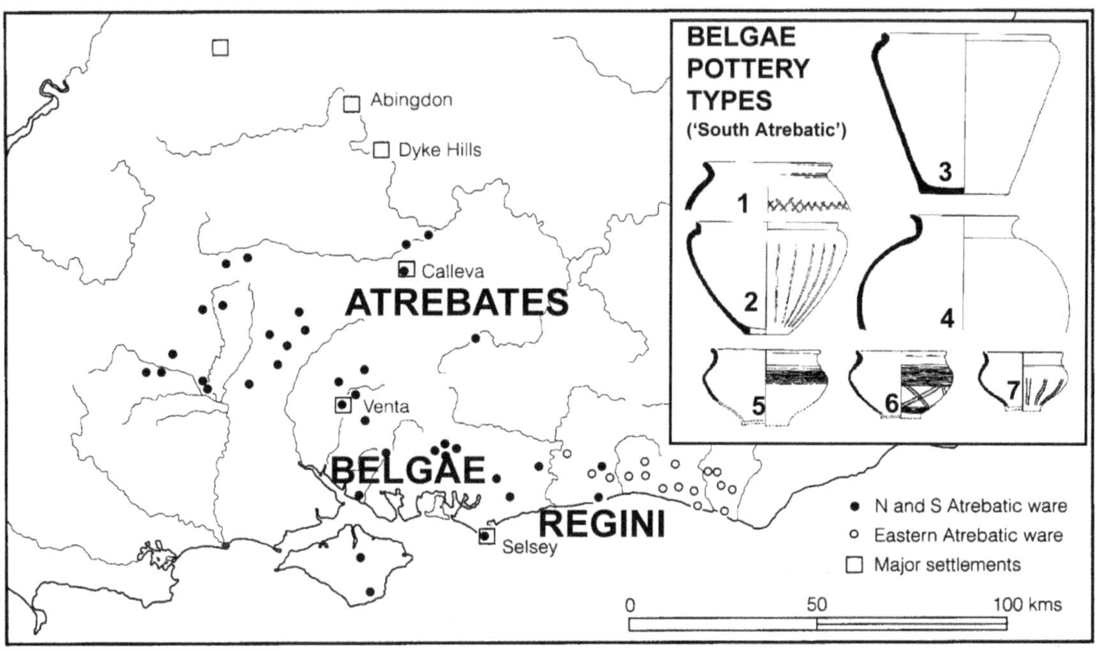

Figure 105. The three ceramic style-zones of southern Britain, c.50 BC – AD 43, with seven typical pottery types of the Belgae in Hampshire: 1 Winchester, Hants; 2-4 Horndean, Hants; 5-7 Chalton, Hants. (source: Cunliffe 2005, 171, 645, adapted by author).

Conclusions

Julius Caesar tells us: 'The interior of Britain is inhabited by people who claim, on the strength of an oral tradition, to be aboriginal; the coast by immigrants from Belgica who came to plunder and make war – nearly all of them retaining the names of tribes from which they originated – and later settled down to till the soil' (*BG* 5.12). Is Caesar right or is he wrong? Were there Belgae in Britain or not? And, if so, where?

The *Ordnance Survey Map of Southern Britain in the Iron Age* tells us that there were tribes in Britain called Parisi, Catuvellauni and Atrebates. The map of Gaul tells us that tribes called Parisi, Catalauni and Atrebates were also in Gallia Belgica. I conclude that Caesar is right. People from Belgica did migrate to Britain. But did some of them settle on the south coast?

Ptolemy's *Geography* (Figure 1), the Antonine *Itinerary*, and the Ravenna *Cosmography* all record that there was a place in Roman Britain called *Venta Belgarum*. Rivet and Smith (1979, 492) state that *Venta Belgarum* means 'market of the Belgae' and identify this place as 'the Roman city of Winchester, Hampshire, capital of the *Belgae*'. Common sense suggests that the Romans wouldn't have named a city after the Belgae unless there were Belgae living there and that they had been there for quite some time – probably for at least a century or so. I therefore conclude that the people living around Winchester in the first century BC/AD were called 'Belgae' because they had migrated from Belgica in Gaul and that they may reasonably be referred to as 'Belgae' in my coin catalogues[11]. But is there any archaeological evidence for the Belgae in southern Britain?

Cunliffe (2005, 169, 171) notes that there were three style-zones of pottery in southern Britain, c. 50 BC – AD 43, which emerged from indigenous traditions: 'These may be defined as an Eastern Group, extending along the Sussex coastal plain and downs approximately to the Arun; a Southern group, covering the rest of Sussex and Hampshire west to the Test; and a Northern group, centring on Salisbury Plain and spreading north to the edge of the Thames valley…The three broadly defined ceramic zones probably owe their identity partly to the indigenous folk tradition and partly the distribution ranges of the production centres, but it is conceivable that *the regionalization in the later period also reflects a political fragmentation and realignment* [my italics]'. Cunliffe labels these three ceramic style-zones 'Eastern Atrebatic', 'Southern Atrebatic' and 'Northern Atrebatic', thus reflecting the current belief that the Atrebates controlled all the territory from the Thames to the south coast between c. 50 BC and AD 43. However, looking at these three different ceramic style-zones from my numismatic viewpoint, I'd respectfully suggest that they could just as well be branded 'Regini', 'Belgae' and 'Atrebates' (Figure 105). In other words, there is archaeological evidence for distinctively different pottery in the Solent hinterland, produced by indigenous people who could arguably be called 'Belgae'.

Manley (2002, 39-40) has described further archaeological evidence which suggests that 'communities were arriving from the Continent and settling.' This includes early cremation graves at Owslebury, Hampshire, displaying an intrusive burial rite (Collis 1968), and possibly the earliest cremation cemetery of the southern Iron Age at Westhampnett,[12] east of Chichester (Fitzpatrick 1997). At this site, between about 90 and 50 BC, burials took place using a rite which was strongly influenced by contemporary traditions across the Channel (*ibid.*, 208). Perhaps most significantly of all, the excavators of the Silchester basilica have suggested that a planned Iron Age street pattern probably dates from the last two decades of the first century BC, and may imply a settlement of colonists from north-west Gaul (Fulford and Timby 2000). Evidently there is some archaeological evidence for the Belgae in southern Britain, especially in the Solent hinterland. But is there numismatic evidence?

Briggs, Haselgrove and King (1992, 41) state that 'The Hampshire region evidently had particularly close ties with Belgic Gaul, which was the source of nearly 45 per cent of the Gaulish coins found at Hayling Island, while Picardy and Upper Normandy between them provided models for several important early southern coinages, including British O, British Q, and the thin silver series'. Burnett (1992) and Cottam (1999) both confirm that the Chichester Cock bronze coins found in the Solent hinterland are derived from prototypes made by the Belgae in Gaul.

There is further numismatic evidence. Cunliffe and de Jersey (1997, 90) write: 'The importance of this region [Chichester] in the early numismatic history of southern Britain is only gradually being realized, principally as the result of metal-detecting finds of the past decade... the area seems to have produced a very early bronze coinage, based on a Belgic issue... which of course immediately brings to mind the possibility of Belgic settlement in this area.'

John Sills notes that 'The number of [Insular Cf gold] quarters from the Selsey region suggests that the series was struck on or near the coast, and the Hampshire hoards are consistent with payments being made to hinterland tribes…Whether they were used to buy military service or to pay tribute, or both, the implication is that *a Belgic colony on the south coast* [my italics] either came under threat from indigenous tribes in the decade or so before the Gallic Wars, or issued gold to finance expansion inland' (Sills 2003, 349). Sills also speaks of a currency zone in 'the coastal strip between West Sussex and Dorset *colonized by Belgic migrants* [my italics]. These new colonies may have developed independently of their parent tribes, and it is possible that a group based around Selsey and Chichester came under pressure from hinterland tribes and was forced to strike its own gold coinage' (*ibid.*, 350).

For twelve years metal detectorists have been telling me that they find an unusually high proportion of Gaulish coins in the area around Chichester, most of which were minted by the tribes of Gallia Belgica. And finally, findspots recorded by the Celtic Coin Index tell me that there are more than forty different types of uninscribed British Iron Age coins found mainly in East Hampshire (Figures 11-57) – *more than forty different coin types that are found almost exclusively in east Hampshire (the region of Venta Belgarum) and nowhere else.* I conclude that there is numismatic evidence for the Belgae in the Solent hinterland.

To sum up this amble through the southern counties here is a seven-point credo. Like so much in Iron Age numismatics, it is an article of faith rather than a statement of fact.

1. I believe that the tribes of the Pritani are much older than we imagine and that the ethnic roots of some of them may be buried in the Bronze Age or even earlier.
2. I believe that tribal boundaries and tribal names may also be older than is commonly thought and that some of the names may be 'pre-Celtic'.
3. I believe that at least three different major tribes issued coins south of the Thames: people in West Sussex (the Regini), people in northern Hampshire (the Atrebates) and peoples in the Solent hinterland (later known collectively as the Belgae).
4. I believe that the Belgae may first have been established around Danebury hillfort and that they were later strengthened by a small but influential influx of migrants, before and during the Gallic Wars, who settled around Chichester and Portsmouth.
5. I believe that the Regini provided the power-base of the Commian dynasty, first at Selsey, then at Chichester; that they were in alliance with the Atrebates (also of Belgic origin) and that they dominated the Belgae of Hampshire who stopped minting coins around 30 BC.
6. I believe that the Atrebates came to prominence with Commios I and Commios II who took control of Silchester and minted coins there and that they later fell under the sway of the Catuvellauni during the reign of Eppillus.
7. I believe that it is seriously misleading, historically as well as numismatically, to clump the Belgae, the Regini and the Atrebates together and to call them all 'Atrebatic'. This artificial marriage of convenience may make for tidy cataloguing but it doesn't seem to be supported by either archaeology or the distribution of coin finds.

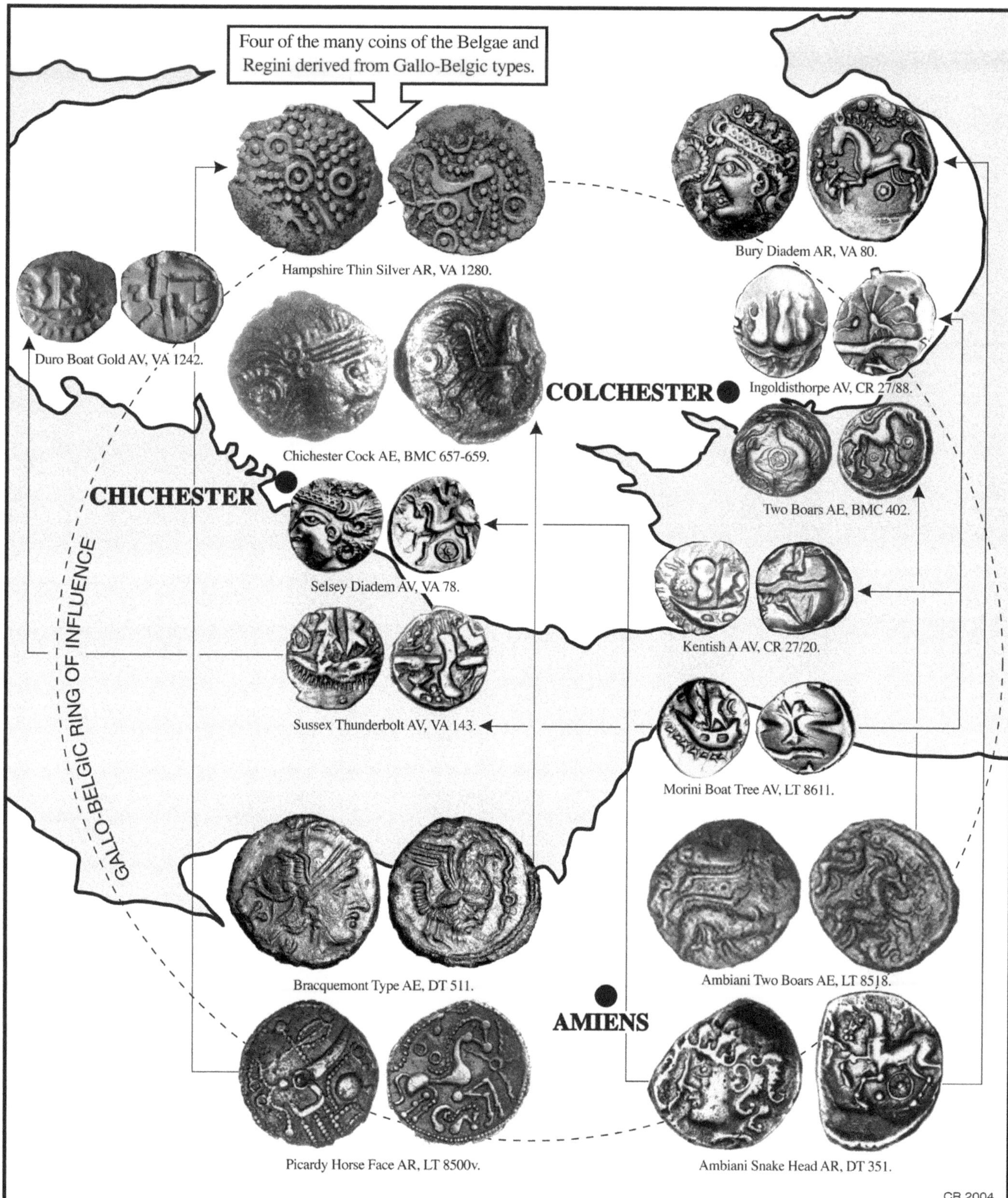

Figure 106. Regular cross-Channel commerce, in evidence since 3000 BC, intensified with the development of a monetary economy in the first century BC. We see here a few of the numerous British coins directly inspired by the influx of Gallo-Belgic influence, including coins of the Belgae and Regini. The influence of Ambianic coins in particular is felt not only on the south coast (e.g. Hampshire Thin Silver and Selsey Diadem), but also in Essex and East Anglia (e.g. Two Boars and Bury Diadem). In many ways the economic growth of Chichester is paralleled by that of Colchester. Both profited from cross-Channel trade in the first century BC. Both became Britain's most important political centres in the first century AD. The success of Camulodunon is well known. The achievement of Noviomagus, capital of the Regini, was perhaps as spectacular, but has yet to be recognised.

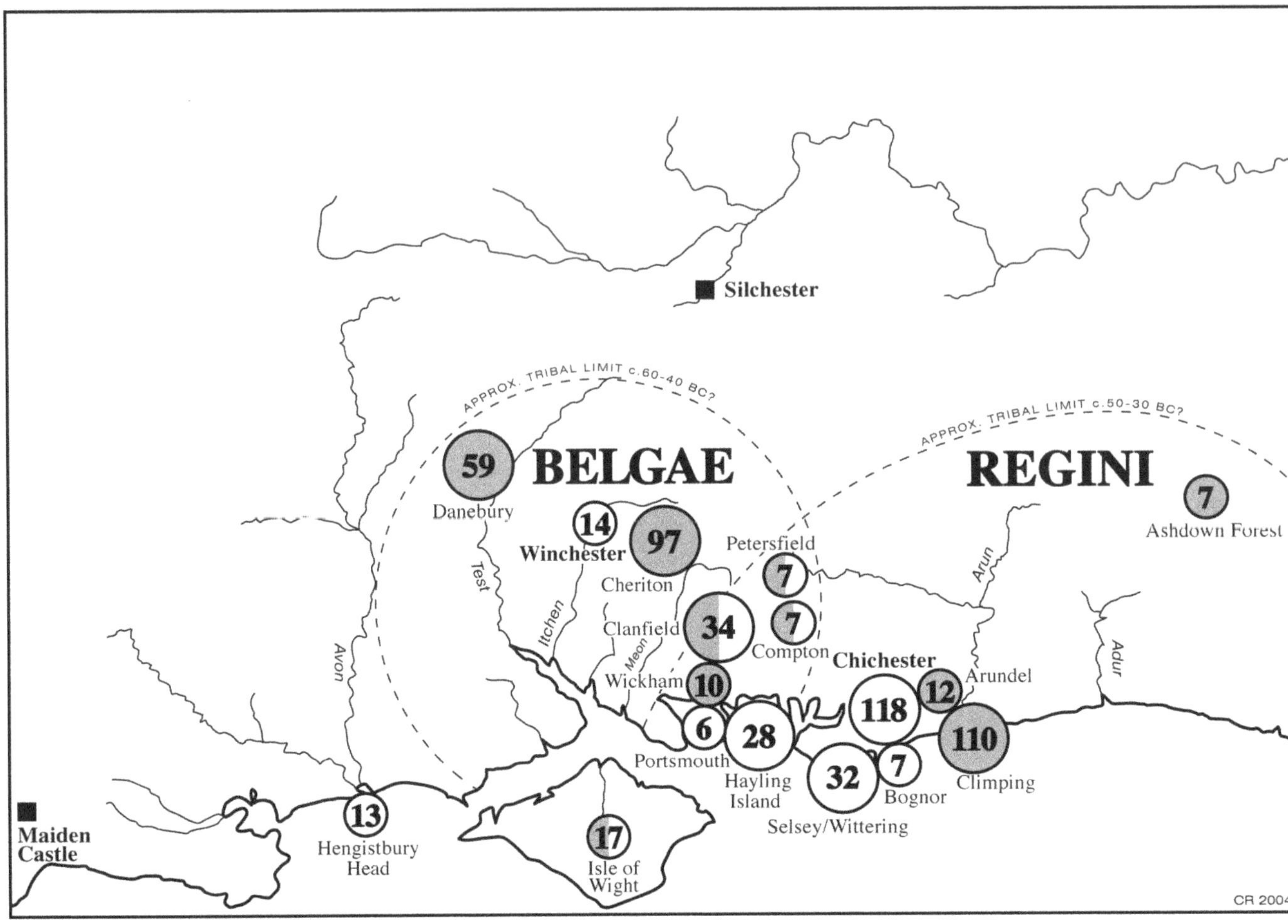

Figure 107. The seventeen most productive cluster-districts for uninscribed coins in the study area, excluding Wanborough, are Chichester (118), Climping (110), Cheriton (97), Danebury (59), Clanfield (34), Selsey/Wittering (32), Hayling Island (28), Isle of Wight (17), Winchester (14), Hengistbury Head (13), near Arundel (12), Wickham (10), Petersfield (7), Compton (7), Bognor (7), Ashdown Forest (7) and Portsmouth (6). Shaded rings denote hoards, half-shaded rings signify partial or possible hoards. Unlike trend surface maps which can be hard to read and notoriously misleading, this quantified cluster map clearly identifies concentrations of uninscribed coin finds and allows us to distinguish between hoards and cumulative single finds. For example, we can quickly see that most Belgae coins are found in a crescent from Danebury to Hengistbury Head, with no significant quantities in the cusp; the distribution maps of individual coin types mirror this pattern, with virtually no coins found between the Meon and Avon. We can also see that the main groups of Regini coin finds are tightly bunched around Chichester and that no significant groups occur east of the Arun, apart from the Ashdown Forest hoard coins, which look isolated. Most importantly, we can perceive from this cluster map that no significant groups of uninscribed Belgae coins or uninscribed Regini coins filter northwards into Atrebatic territory.

The Belgae won't go away. They have made a comeback and they are here to stay. As for the Regini, I shall leave them for others to sort out. Meanwhile, it would be good if we called them by their correct name – Regini, not Regni. Even better if we gave them some coins of their own – for example, those uninscribed types that are found only in their region. And better still if we placed their name before that of the Atrebates, as may be indicated by a greater weight of coin finds in the southern kingdom, especially around Chichester, and as confirmed by the subsequent elevation of Togidubnus as high-king over the Atrebates. His palace was near Chichester, not Silchester.

I leave you with a tentative table of tribal attributions for the main southern coin types and rulers (Figure 109). Of necessity it can only be tentative because the majority of the most fundamental questions – some of which I have asked here, others which I have barely alluded to – all these basic questions, plus myriads more, currently remain unanswered. The great thing about innovative thinkers like Robert Van Arsdell, who publish their thoughts freely and fearlessly – sometimes with a reckless disregard for the few facts available and the many fantasies of others – is that they force the rest of us to think. Thank you, Bob!

Figure 108. The maritime prowess and prosperity of the Regini may be symbolized on this Verica Galley silver unit (CCI 04.0501).

PHASE	DURATION	BELGAE	REGINI	ATREBATES	REGINI and ATREBATES
4 5	c.80-60 BC c.60-50 BC	Yarmouth AV STATER VA 1220	Phallic Geometric AV QUARTER VA 1227		Westerham South AV STATER VA 202
			Willett's Nipple AV QUARTER VA 1229		
5 6	c.60-50 BC c.50-20 BC	Chichester Cock AE UNIT N.CIRC. DEC.1992	Climping AV STATER CR 68/18		British Qa/Qb AV STATERS VA 210-216
		Sussex Thunderbolt AV QUARTER VA 143	Selsey Diadem AV QUARTER VA 78		Selsey Dahlia AV QUARTER VA 220-222
		Chute/Cheriton AV STATER VA 1210	Ratham Ring Pole AV QUARTER BMC 538		Bognor Cog Wheel AV QUARTER VA 226
		Cheriton Smiler AV STATER VA 1215	Selsey Tramlines AV QUARTER VA 78		Commios I COINS ISSUED?
		Petersfield Wreath AV QUARTER BMC 568-570	Regini Crescents AV QUARTER VA 250		
		Hampshire Thin AR UNITS VA 1280	Chichester Boar AR UNIT BMC 577		
		Hayling Moon Head AR UNIT BNJ 1992, pl.1.31	Sussex Lyre AR UNIT BMC 635		
		Danebury Sunrays AR UNIT VA 280	Arundel Moon Man AR UNIT BNJ 1992, no.39		
		Danebury Corded AR UNIT VA 292	Ashdown Forest AR UNIT VA 264		
6	c.50-20 BC	Danebury Ex-Type AR UNIT BMC 614-628			Commios II AV/AR VA 350-358
		Clanfield Anemone AR HALF UNIT VA 1662			
7	c.20BC-AD10		Tincomarus AV/AR VA 460-564	Eppillus AV/AR VA 405-422	
8	c.AD10-40				Verica AV/AR VA 460-564
				CATUVELLAUNI in ATREBATES	
9	c.AD30-45			Epaticcus AV/AR VA 575-585	
				Caratacus AR VA 593-595	
10	post AD 43	Togidubnus NO COINS ISSUED			

CR 2004

Figure 109. Proposed interim tribal attribution of principal uninscribed southern coin types and southern rulers, pending a more thorough examination of their distribution and dating.

Notes

[1] Jones and Mattingly (1990, 37-41) note that most place-names in Roman Britain were Celtic or British, not Latin: 'One of the most striking features of Romano-British place names is that the vast majority were entirely Celtic or British in origin... In fact, only about 50 of the known place names were wholly or partly Latin.'

[2] See for example the views of Francis Pryor, who is adamant that everyday life in Britain was not overturned overnight by the arrival of the Romans: 'Was Iron Age Britain very different from Roman Britain? I believe that it wasn't, for the simple reason that, setting aside short-lived introductions such as towns, the army and the imperial administration, *Roman Britain was Iron Age Britain.*' (Pryor 1994, 49-50).

[3] *Numismatic jottings* (MS notebook), 29.10.94. However, I was not the first person to wonder if the Belgae of Hampshire minted coins of their own. In 1864 Sir John Evans, speculating on the source of Westerham South gold

staters (VA 202) and Chute gold staters (VA 1205), wrote: 'Whether the coins were struck by the Belgae or Durotriges, or by both, I will not pretend to determine, though I think it must have been by the tribe last mentioned.' (1864, 38).

[4] Late in 1991 a new variety of Cheriton type gold stater (a variant of VA 1215) surfaced on the south coast. Within two years about forty had apparently been sold – all in 'mint state' condition, all struck from the same pair of dies and mostly, it would seem, from the same trade source. In December 1993 Robert Van Arsdell, who exposed the Haslemere forgeries in the 1980s, challenged the authenticity of these new Cheriton staters at the New York International Numismatic Convention and phoned me on 12 December to express his concerns. Initially, I and a few other dealers were not convinced by Van Arsdell's objections, due to misleading misinformation we had been given about the alleged 'excavation' of the so-called 'hoard'. However, scholarly opinion supported his challenge and Philip de Jersey said 'I think the evidence that they are fakes is now overwhelming' (pers. comm., 14 January 1994). I therefore asked metallurgist Peter Northover to analyse nine of the suspect coins. He concluded that all nine were modern forgeries (P. Northover, *Analysis of Cheriton-style staters*, 5 June 1994). Today, a decade later, there is now no doubt that Van Arsdell's suspicions were fully justified.

[5] If Chichester Cock bronzes were 'a failed coinage experiment', as Van Arsdell alleged in 2001, then it must have been quite an extensive 'experiment'. Geoff Cottam (1999) identifies two different types of 'cock bronze'. He says that Type 2 'is a large issue of coins struck from a minimum of ten obverse and nine reverse dies' and that 'taking a figure of 10,000 coins as the potential life of an obverse die, this would give an estimate for the output of base metal coins of 200,000, to which estimate we should probably ascribe a lower limit of around 100,000 and an extreme upper limit in the region of half a million.'

[6] These dumpy, undished flans have also been noted by Simon Bean (2000, 54, 58).

[7] The similarity between Climping Type gold staters and Whaddon Chase gold staters (VA 1470-76) is close, the only substantial difference being that the Climping horse faces left and has different ornaments around it. The metal content of Climping staters is also almost identical to that of Whaddon Chase staters. In order to check the authenticity of the hoard (some people had some doubts about it shortly after its discovery in August 2000) I had two coins from it analysed by Peter Northover (pers. comm. 1.2.2001) – a Climping Type stater (46% gold, 34% silver, 19% copper) and a British Qb stater (53% gold, 29% silver, 18% copper). A Climping Type stater was later analysed by the British Museum (DCMS *Treasure Annual Report 2000*, p. 107, published July 2002), producing a similar alloy content (50% gold, 35% silver, 15% copper), comparable to that of Whaddon Chase staters analysed by the British Museum Like Peter Northover, the British Museum's 'research lab found that the metal composition, corrosion, and surface condition of the coins were all consistent with them being ancient, genuine coins, and with their having been found with the other British Qas and Qbs. There were similar corrosion products and soil deposits on both the Climping staters and the others' (Jonathan Williams, pers. comm. 24.9.2004).

[8] 'It is probable that all four Westerham style issues were struck under the authority of Cassivellaunus and are the coinage of the British coalition against Caesar' (Sills 1997).

[9] If Selsey was the 'old market' then we can see how Chichester came to be named 'new market'. I think the 'new' refers to the pre-Roman shift in tribal capital, rather than to the Roman restructuring of the *civitas* capital. The Celtic word *magos* originally meant 'field' and was later used to denote a market-place. It occurs in *Caesaromagus* 'Caesar's market' (Chelmsford, Essex) and the other British *Noviomagus*, the Roman settlement at Crayford, Kent. The word is also found frequently in Gallic place-names, such as *Argantomagus*, 'field or market of silver' (Orne) and *Rotomagus* 'field of races' or 'market of the wheel' (Rouen) (Rivet and Smith 1979, 287, 427, 428; Delamarre 2003, 214).

[10] Having been pardoned by Mark Antony (*BG* 8.48) why would Commios, one of the most famous and most successful men in all of Gaul, creep furtively away to a life of obscurity and penury in Britain? It just doesn't make sense and is out of character with the many other descriptions of Commios and his actions contained in Caesar's Gallic War commentary. The case for Commios being set up in Britain by Caesar in well argued by John Creighton (2000, 59-64).

[11] 'The fact that in Gaul the name *Belgae* was applied to a collection of tribes, not an individual tribe, suggests that the British *Civitas Belgarum* was an artificial creation of the Roman government' (Rivet and Smith 1979, 267). This may or may not have been the case. However, if there hadn't been people in this area that were commonly identified with tribes from Gallia Belgica, the name *Belgae* would not have been given to then, however 'artificially'. And, just because there wasn't a single tribe in northern Gaul called *Belgae*, doesn't mean that there may not have been a single tribe – perhaps a long established single tribe – in Hampshire called the *Belgae*. Moreover, the name itself is of Celtic origin, not Roman (*ibid.*).

[12] The Westhampnett site, commonly called 'Tangmere' by detectorists, produced more single finds of Iron Age coins in the 1990s than any other south coast site, many of them sadly the sour fruits of nighthawking. Some of these Tangmere coins were not made locally, such as a rare Domino V-Type gold stater (VA 829-3 variant) 'found in a spring near the side of a wooden temple at Tangmere, West Sussex, December 1996' which 'could have been an offering to a spring deity' (May 2002). Other Tangmere coins had been imported from Gaul (Cunliffe and de Jersey 1997; de Jersey; 1999). These finds of imported Gallic coins from Tangmere underline the international status of Chichester in the first century BC/AD.

Acknowledgements

I thank Robert Van Arsdell for prodding me to justify my 'Belgae' and to question his 'Atrebates,' Philip de Jersey for providing the findspots and helpful comments, Nick Bendy for producing the distribution maps, and Elizabeth Cottam for editing this and pulling it all together.

Picture credits

I am grateful to the following people for kindly granting me permission to reproduce their illustrations: **1** Barri Jones and David Mattingly, *An Atlas of Roman Britain*, Oxbow Books, 1990; **5, 6, 7** Philip de Jersey, *Chris Rudd list* 56, March 2001; **3, 9, 59, 60, 105** Barry Cunliffe, *Iron Age Communities in Britain,* Routledge, 2005 and *The Regni,* Duckworth, 1973; **81, 82** Celtic Coin Index, Oxford; **103** John Creighton, *Coins and Power in Late Iron Age Britain,* Cambridge University Press, 2000.

Bibliography

Bean, S. C. 2000: *The Coinage of the Atrebates and Regni* (Oxford, OUCA Monograph 50).

Briggs, D. Haselgrove, C. and King, C. 1992: Iron Age and Roman coins from Hayling Island temple. *British Numismatic Journal* 62, 1-62.

Burnett, A. M. 1992: A new Iron Age issue from near Chichester. *Spink Numsimatic Circular* 100, 340-342.

Collis, J. R. 1968: Excavations at Owslebury, Hants: an interim report. *Antiquaries Journal* 48, 18-31.

Cottam, G. L. 1999: The 'cock bronzes' and other related Iron Age bronze coins found predominantly in West Sussex and Hampshire. *British Numismatic Journal* 69, 1-18.

Creighton, J. 2000: *Coins and Power in Late Iron Age Britain* (Cambridge, CUP).

Cunliffe, B. W. 1973: *The Regni* (London, Duckworth).

Cunliffe, B. W. 1981: Money and society in pre-Roman Britain. In B. W. Cunliffe (ed.), *Coinage and society in Britain and Gaul: some current problems* (CBA Research Report 38), 29-39.

Cunliffe, B. W. 2005 (4th ed): *Iron Age communities in Britain* (London, Routledge).

Cunliffe, B. W. and de Jersey, P. 1997: *Armorica and Britain* (Oxford, OUCA Monograph 45).

de Jersey, P. 1999: Exotic Celtic coinage in Britain. *Oxford Journal of Archaeology*, 18, 189-216.

de Jersey, P. 2001: Where and when? *Chris Rudd list* 56, 2-7.

Delamarre, X, 2003 (2nd ed.): *Dictionnaire de la langue gauloise* (Paris, Errance).

Evans, J. 1864: *The coins of the ancient Britons* (London).

Fitzpatrick, A. 1997: *Archaeological excavations on the Route of the A27 Westhampnett Bypass, West Sussex, 1992. II: the Cemeteries* (Salisbury, Wessex Archaeology Report 12).

Fulford, M and Timby, J. 2000: *Late Iron Age and Roman Silchester: Excavations on the site of the forum-basilica 1977, 1980-86* (Britannia Monograph 15).

Haselgrove, C. 1987: *Iron Age coinage in south-east England: the archaeological context* (Oxford, BAR 174).

Henig, M. 2002: *The heirs of King Verica* (Stroud, Tempus).

Hobbs, R. 1996: *British Iron Age coins in the British Museum* (London, BMP).

Jackson, K. 1948: On some Romano-British Place-Names. *Journal of Roman Studies* 38, 54-58.

Jones, B. and Mattingly, D. 1990: *An Atlas of Roman Britain* (Oxford, Oxbow).

Manley, J. 2002: *AD 43, the Roman invasion of Britain* (Stroud, Tempus).

May, J. 2002: Detective work on a domino stater by a consortium of sleuths. *Chris Rudd list* 64, 3-5.

Pryor, F. 2004: *Britain AD: a quest for Arthur, England and the Anglo-Saxons* (London, Harper Collins).

Rivet, A. L. F. and Smith, C. 1979: *The Place-Names of Roman Britain* (London, Batsford).

Rudd, C. 2001: Tribal or regional? *Chris Rudd list* 55, 2-3.

Rudd, C. 2005: Climping report to HM Coroner for West Sussex, 17.5.05, and Treasure Valuation Committee, 9.8.05.

Sills, J. 1997: The earliest British coins: dating the undated. *Chris Rudd list* 27.

Sills, J. 2003: *Gaulish and early British gold coinage* (London, Spink).

Stevens, W. F. 2002: Tribal emblems on late Iron Age coinage – numismatic statements of tribal unity. *Coin News* Nov. 2002, 23-24.

Van Arsdell, R. D. 1989: *Celtic Coinage of Britain* (London, Spink).

The silver coinage of Tasciovanos

Rainer Kretz

Introduction

In contrast to his gold and to a lesser degree his bronze issues, Tasciovanos's silver coinage has to date received scant attention. Even studies aimed at identifying classical prototypes for some of the issues appear to have largely concentrated on his bronze coinage (Henig 1972; Scheers 1982; 1992). The main reason is most probably that until the advent of metal detecting in the late 1970s, the silver issues of Tasciovanos had been exceedingly rare. By 1980 only 39 silver coins had been recorded with the Celtic Coin Index, a number that has since risen to 248, a six fold increase (P. de Jersey, pers. comm.). Remarkably, the number of types attributed to this ruler had also remained unchanged until the 1980s. In his monumental work *The coins of the ancient Britons*, Evans (1864) lists a total of nine types of silver unit directly attributable to Tasciovanos (excluding the Sego and Dias issues), with his later supplement (1890) containing no further additions. When Mack (1953) published his own study almost ninety years later, the number of recorded silver types had remained static. Van Arsdell's 1989 catalogue raised the total number to ten by adding an uninscribed unit (V1698), which had recently come to light. Since then the growth in metal detecting has been instrumental in the steady uncovering of additional new types, thus enabling this study to comprise a total of sixteen types of Tasciovanos silver together with one Sego and two Dias issues.

This investigation is aimed at surveying Tasciovanos's complex and wide-ranging silver issues in some detail. Above all it will seek to establish the likely phasing of the different issues and in the process examine potential prototypes, both Celtic and classical, which may have inspired the iconography here displayed. In addition, it will take a closer look at the relationship between Tasciovanos's silver and other Celtic coinages, the range and type of the inscriptions associated with these coins and examine whether any regional trends in the distribution of the various types can be observed.

Earlier work

Camden, on the advice of Mr Powell, 'a person admirably skilled in that language' considered the Celtic word *Tascia* to signify a tribute penny (Pegge 1776, 22). Following his lead, Pettingal proposed that it was the '... tribute, paid by the *Tag* or British prince of each province, to the Roman conquerors' (Pettingal 1763, 9).

Pegge was the first to identify Tascia as a personal name. He saw Tascio (sic) as a 'provincial artist, entertained in the service of the British prince Cunobelin...' and concluded that he must have been the mint-master of Cunobelin (Pegge 1776, 55). In dividing the coins of Cunobelin into six classes, Pegge mistakenly included seven coins now deemed to be issues of Tasciovanos (*ibid.*, table II, classes V and VI/1).

Birch (1845) seems to have been the first to correctly interpret the recorded inscriptions as the personal name Tasciovanus, thus employing a later version of the name (Kretz 1998, 4) and combining it with the hypothetical Latinised ending *-us*. This form was subsequently adopted by Evans (1864, 228) and has continued in use to the present day, although the available evidence from the North Thames region seems to suggest that *-os* remained the common ending for Celtic personal names until well into Cunobelin's reign, when the ending *-us* finally makes its appearance in both nominative (V2063, BMC 1883) or genitive forms (V1951, V2055).

The earliest detailed work on the series is that of Evans. He makes little attempt at classification, other than differentiating in the broadest terms between those coins carrying Tasciovanos's name, those carrying the Verulamium mint signature and others inscribed SEGO and DIAS (Table 1). Evans comments on the classical origin of some of the designs and speculates that this may have been due to the employment of foreign artists or those educated abroad (Evans 1864, 243-244). He also correctly observed that the 'butting bull' type (V1794) had been copied from an Augustan denarius and that from its style and resemblance to the coins of Cunobelin, it probably belonged to the latter part of Tasciovanos's reign (*ibid.*, 242).

Allen tentatively suggested a grouping based both on the Verulamium mint and stylistic criteria, placing the copy of

Augustus's denarius (V1794) last in the series (Allen 1944, 14). He did not address the silver again but, as part of his study of the bronze types from the Romano-British temple at Harlow, arranged twenty-two types of bronze belonging to the wider Tasciovanos group (i.e. also including Sego, Dias, Rues and Andoco) into eight categories by focussing on legends and combinations of legends (Allen 1967, 2). Although he does not specifically say so, a similar split may equally have been applied to the silver.

Rodwell (1976, 249-261) closely followed Evans's original classification, whereas Haselgrove based his division on the different combinations of legend and the varying degrees of Roman influence (Haselgrove 1987, 255-256, 258-259).

More recently Van Arsdell has divided the silver issues into three separate coinages reflecting his treatment of Tasciovanos's three main stater series, whilst placing the SEGO and DIAS issues into a separate 'interregnum' period. His arrangement focuses almost entirely on stylistic considerations, with the Celtic types forming the first coinage while the more Romanized issues make up the second and third (Van Arsdell 1989, 363-393).

This paper identifies a total of five groups of Tasciovanos silver, based in the main on stylistic and typological criteria but also supported by orthographical and metrological factors, with an additional two groups containing the more controversial SEGO and DIAS types. The coinage of Andoco, whilst closely related to that of Tasciovanos, is considered to be that of either a co-ruler or client king. Consisting of gold, silver and bronze it was a coinage of high quality and considerable importance in its own right and as such has been dealt with in some detail elsewhere (Kretz 2002).

Whilst some of the classifications have been relatively straightforward, others are of necessity more tenuous and open to different interpretation. This study should therefore be seen as a first step towards a comprehensive classification of Tasciovanos's silver and it is acknowledged that the passage of time together with any future discovery of new types may cause us to revise some of the suggestions put forward in this paper.

Finally, I should like to acknowledge the huge debt owed to Dr Philip de Jersey, whose exemplary study of 'Cunobelin's silver' (de Jersey 2001) together with his constant encouragement and support have inspired me to carry out a similar examination of the silver coinage of Tasciovanos. As can be expected when dealing with father and son, there are many parallels between the two coinages and it seemed only natural to base my own work on a tried and tested formula.

Evans (1864, 1890)

I. T's name only	II. Mint name (VER)	III. SEGO	IV. DIAS
B1	C1, C2	F1	G1
D1?, D4, D5			
E1, E2, E3			

Allen (1944)

I.	II.	III.	RICON series	SEGO	DIAS
B1	C1, C2	E1	D4?	F1	G1
E2, E3	D1?				

Rodwell (1976)

I. T's name only	II. Mint name (VER)[1]	III. T's name plus DIAS or SEGO
B1	C1?, C2?	F1
E2, E3	D1?	G1

Haselgrove (1987)

Series I.	II. (DIAS)	*III. (RVES)*[2]	IV. (SEGO)
Class 1 B3	G1, G2		F1
Class 2 (some Roman influence)			
B1, C1, C2, D1, D4, D5			
Class 3 (pronounced Roman influence)			
E1, E2, E3			

Van Arsdell (1989)

I.	II.	III.	SEGO	DIAS
A1	B1	D1, D4, D5	F1	G1
C1	C2	E1, E2, E3		

Table 1. Earlier classifications of Tasciovanos's silver, with reference to classes adopted in this paper.

The coins

A. Early issues

Two types stand out from the remainder due to their distinctive Celtic style: one uninscribed, the other with an archaic form of legend (Figure 1).

A1

A2

Figure 1. Group A issues. All die reconstructions are shown at approximately twice actual size, from drawings by the author.

A1 (V1698, BMC 1654)

Obv.: Abstract head with curly hair l., forehead, nose and brow formed by one continuous ridge. Tight rows of braided hair sometimes interspersed with rows of pellets; rosette in front of forehead with ?ringed pellet above. Stylised cloak or patterned border below and behind.

Rev.: Horned horse stepping r., pellets under head vary from none to three, both head and shoulder formed by ringed pellets. Bucranium flanked by pellets with two or perhaps three ringed pellets above horse, stylised wheel of variable size below, some pellets in the field, unidentified object behind the horse.

A2 (V —, BMC 1656-57)

Obv. Back to back crescents within cruciform wreath pattern, wreaths ending in ringed pellets. Stylised horses' mouths and outline 'teardrops', sometimes accompanied by a pellet, in opposing quadrants. 'Teardrops' can face inward or outward and the arrangement of the motifs may vary. There appears to be a border formed by a circular outer wreath.

Rev. Prancing horse of fine Celtic style l., head composed of ringed pellet. Rosette above horse, annulets or ?ringed pellets in front and behind, sometimes pellet under horse's head. Legend TASCI or TASC in archaic-style lettering below the horse.

The two types stand aside from the remainder on account of their largely undiluted Celtic style, the iconography employed, their average weights of below 1.00g and in the case of A2 the archaic form of the legend. Another notable feature of the earliest issues is that Group A and its immediate successor B1 were struck from unusually large dies, when compared to most of the remainder of Tasciovanos's silver.

Unknown to Allen, A1 is the typological descendent of some uninscribed issues he grouped together as British LX (Allen 1960, 124, 133, pl. XI). Whilst the obverse design has ultimately evolved via two closely related early British LX types, i.e. LX6 (V1546) and LX7 (V1549), the immediate precursor of A1 is most probably Allen's LX8 (V1552). Both obverses are variations of the same theme and share typologically and stylistically closely related reverses. The same is also true for an early bronze unit (V1615), which Van Arsdell (1989, 351) has attributed to Addedomaros. The recorded findspots however point strongly towards a Catuvellaunian origin, and it is conceivable that V1615 could be an early issue of Tasciovanos or perhaps just predate him. A horse of similar posture to A1 and also featuring a head composed of a ringed pellet can be found on an early Tasciovanos quarter stater (V1688).

In the absence of an inscription, it is the presence of the bucranium above the horse which most strongly identifies this issue with Tasciovanos. A bucranium flanked by pellets is a key motif on the obverses of Tasciovanos's earliest staters (VA 1680, 1682; see Kretz 1998) and second series quarter staters (V 1690, 1692; Kretz 2001a), and a strong indicator that A1 is likely to represent his first silver issue. Van Arsdell (1989, 367) was therefore most probably correct in assigning this type to Tasciovanos, a classification upheld by Hobbs (1996, 117; BMC 1654). Curiously, this was to remain his only silver type to feature the bucranium.

The use of this motif on Tasciovanos's coinage seems to be confined to the last two decades of the first century BC. Towards the latter part of that period, it also occurs on Andoco's gold issues (V1860, 1863; Kretz 2002, 271). It then once again re-emerges on a couple of early Cunobelin issues, a silver (de Jersey 2001, 4, type A4) and a bronze unit (V1965), after which it finally disappears from the North Thames stage (*ibid.*, 5).

It is unclear what animal is portrayed on the reverse. Hobbs (1996, 117) refers to it as a horse, but it clearly has horns. It could potentially be a goat but has an unusually long tail. On balance, it is most probably a mythical creature - a horned horse. The image has been adapted from its British LX8 prototype (V1552), which shows a similarly styled, goat-like creature. Curiously, a similar animal, identifiable as an indigenous Ibex, occurs on silver coins (LT 2879) (c.100-75 BC) of the Cavares, who inhabited the departments of Vaucluse, Drôme and Isère in South-East Gaul. On the face of it, such an association would seem rather fanciful, yet there are many instances of both motifs and coins travelling over considerable distances.

Stylistically closely related to the previous type, A2 is the first of Tasciovanos's inscribed silver units. The obverse features an early version of the 'crossed wreaths' theme with stylised horses' mouths and outline 'teardrops' in opposing quadrants. The former motif, more commonly associated with an Addedomaros stater (V1620) and associated quarter (V1623) is a rare motif on Tasciovanos's coinage but can be found on an early quarter stater (BMC 1638-39). The latter is associated with a number of his quarter staters, but especially early ones like my types I/A (BMC 1638), I/B (V1688) and I/C (V1694) (Kretz 2001a, 7). The reverse shows an elegant Celticized horse, stylistically so similar to that on an early quarter stater (V1688), that the two types give every indication of originating from the same hand. A2 also has strong parallels with and may have formed the prototype for many of the Essex issues of Dubnovellaunos in gold, silver and bronze (Table 2). Below is the legend TASC or TASCI in large and uneven Gallo-Latin script, yet balancing the design extremely well. The archaic style of the inscription once again suggests a close link with the above mentioned quarter stater (V1688) and the two types therefore give every indication of being contemporaneous.

Type	**Links**
A1	O/ earlier north Thames parallels, i.e. British LX6 (V1546) and LX7 (V1549) but immediate precursor probably LX8 (V 1552). Uncertain bronze V1615 perhaps a parallel development, with Dubnovellaunos bronze V1669 following a little later. Bucranium characterizes Tasciovanos's earliest stater issues (V1680, V1682) R/ adapted from LX8 (VA 1552) featuring a goat-like creature, perhaps ultimately modelled on a silver issue of the Cavares (LT 2879) c.100-75 BC, portraying an ibex.
A2	O/ close to quarter stater V1688, detached horses' mouths motif also occurs on Addedomaros stater V1620 and quarter stater V1623 R/ stylistically close to quarter stater V1688 and may have formed prototype for some Essex issues of Dubnovellaunos e.g. V1660, V1663 and V1665
B1	O/ bronzes V1705, 1707 and 1709 show more stylized versions of the same theme R/ similar to Tincomarus staters V 375 and V376 and Verica staters V460 and V500, ultimately all modelled on same Republican denarius
B2	O/ Eppillus silver unit V415 probably modelled on the same Roman prototype R/ style of horse similar to some Tasciovanos quarter staters e.g. V1692, BMC 1641
B3	O/ prototype for E1? Style of head similar to rare Andoco silver unit (CCI 98.0155 and 03.0702)
B4	O/ similar to Tasciovanos quarter staters e.g. V1690 and V1692 R/ a wingless Capricorn occurs on Eppillus silver unit V443
C1	O/ shared with C2, similar to Eppillus quarter stater V437, Verica later uses almost identical obverse for minim V559
C2	O/ shared with C1, remainder as for C1 R/ design shared with V1851
D1	R/ similar to bronzes V1713 and V1826 and Sego silver BMC 1663, a similar boar also occurs on an Eppillus silver unit V416
D3	O/ broadly the same design as quarter stater V1786
D4	O/ D3 design in slightly modified form R/ design broadly the same as V1786
D5	O/ Similar design to Tincomarus's incuse tablet e.g. V375/376 and V385
E1	O/ close to Augustan head on bronze V1814, uncertain relationship with B3 R/ similar butting bull occurs on Tincomarus minim V383-5
E3	R/ similar Pegasus occurs on bronze V1818 and Eppillus quarter stater V435
F1	O/ close similarities to D5 (V1800) R/ design shared with C2 (V1747)
G1	O/ same geometric design as bronze V1810 and Tincomarus/?Verica minims V383, V560 and V561 R/ similar horse to bronze V1812
G2	R/ close to D1 and bronzes V1713 and V1826

Table 2. Relationships between Tasciovanos's silver and other Celtic coinages.

A1 and A2 occupy a unique position within Tasciovanos's silver on account of their unusually low mean weights of below one gram (Table 3), a feature shared with their immediate precursors British LX7 and LX8. Of all the other types, only B1 comes close to this weight. The die links for A1 and A2 (Figure 2) indicate a relatively simple production process while suggesting that more than one pair of dies were in use on occasions.

Type	*No. of coins*	*Weight*
A1	8	0.88
A2	8	0.91
B1	15	1.05
B2	1	1.4
B3	5	1.23
B4	7	1.14
C1	12	1.38
C2	19	1.16
D1	15	1.23
D2	14	1.22
D3	12	1.21
D4	14	1.26
D5	34	1.23
E1	12	1.24
E2	12	1.19
E3	9	1.24
F1	7	1.16
G1	15	1.17
G2	18	1.20
All coins	237	1.19

Table 3. Mean weights of Tasciovanos's silver (excluding plated coins).

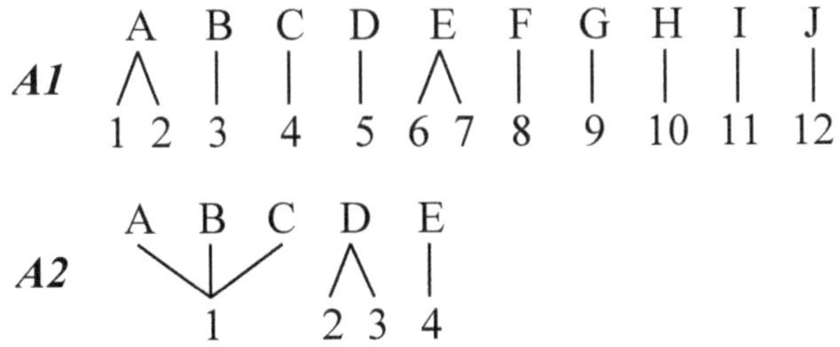

Figure 2. Die-links for Group A.

B. Middle issues

This group contains a loose assembly of relatively early types rather than a coherent group of typologically related issues, and as such cannot be considered entirely satisfactory (Figure 3).

B1 (M158, V1745, BMC 1667-68)

Obv.: Celtic-style bearded head with droopy moustache l., hair arranged in succession of beaded crescents infilled with lines of beads, two pellet crosses in front of face, all within pellet border.

Rev.: Mounted warrior wearing body armour and holding javelin galloping r. Rosettes above and below tail and above horse's head, sometimes pellet above horse's rump and javelin. Inscription TASCIA in archaic style lettering with TAS below horse and CIA in front.

B2 (M —, V —, BMC—)

Obv.: Upturned crescent with ringed pellet in cusp, the interior hatched with beaded lines. Star above, flanked by ring, double pellet and two single pellets arranged symmetrically on either side, exergual line connecting both ends of the crescent, uncertain lettering below. Fragments of the first two letters are visible which may prove to read TA.

Rev.: Horse r., crescent above, star in ring or ?wheel in front, triangular motif below.

B3 (M —, V —, BMC —)

Obv.: Celticized Roman-style laureate head with lentoid eye r., probably TAS in front, annulet under chin and pellet border around.

Rev.: Horse of crude style with flowing mane and drooping tail left, probably VIR above.

B4 (M —, V —, BMC 1666)

Obv.: Cruciform arrangement of wreath and outline 'teardrops' with back to back crescents in centre. Letter and pellet in each of the four quadrants spelling TASC in two different arrangements; pellet border. One variant has a tiny pellet between the crescents.

Rev.: Winged, horned and bearded Capricorn r., ring and sometimes pellet above, occasionally pellet in front. Unclear whether legend below is VER, VIR or both; pellet border.

In a way this group consists of misfits, which cannot be easily accommodated within any of the other four categories of Tasciovanos's silver. They have one thing in common in that all of them share stylistic features suggesting a relatively early production date. Of the four issues only B3 has a pronounced regional bias, being largely concentrated in Berkshire. Another feature common to all of them is that they bear legends. Three of them carry the ruler's name, while a forth - B2 - may ultimately prove to do so. In addition two of the types, B3 and B4, are inscribed VER or

VIR on the reverse, thus setting the trend for the more flamboyant VER legends to follow.

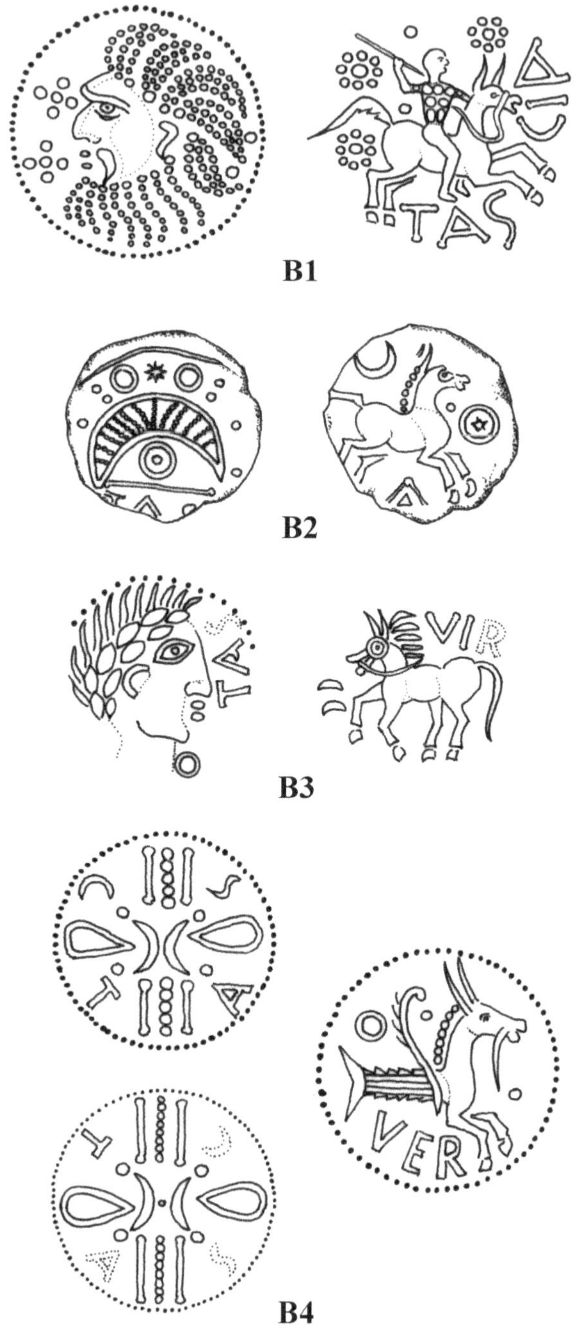

Figure 3. Group B coins.

Some of the earlier examples of B1 are masterpieces of Celtic engraving and represent one of the artistic high points among Tasciovanos's silver. Although the wild Celtic head on the obverse in combination with the archaic-style legend at first seem to indicate an early date, the reverse's close similarity to the second stater series (V1730, 1732, 1734, 1736) strongly suggests a position early on in the second phase. This is also borne out by the low mean weight, which at 1.05g is intermediate between the earliest types at below 1.0g and B1's successors, weighing around 1.15g or more. It is further supported by the style of legend, which on at least some of the dies employs more orthodox Roman letters than the previous type. Judging by the style and composition of the reverse, it is not inconceivable that this issue may have formed the prototype for the second phase stater series and a bronze (V1750), which is probably broadly contemporary with it. The obverse of this coin may be an illustration of the Celts' habit of washing their hair in lime-water in order to bleach and stiffen it, until it differed in no respect from the manes of horses (Diodorus Siculus *History* 5, 28).

B2 is a recent discovery of which only one example is recorded. Unfortunately only a tiny portion of the legend is visible but it is just possible that the first two letters might be T and A. Although at this stage we cannot be certain that this is indeed one of Tasciovanos's issues, the style of the horse, which is extremely close to some of his quarter staters (e.g. V1692, BMC 1641), points strongly in this direction. Weighing in at 1.4g, this coin is unusually heavy when compared to the other three types from this group. If future finds were to be of similarly heavy weight, this may indicate a closer relationship with C1, the only other type to regularly weigh around 1.4g.

The obverse of B2 is probably modelled on a Roman denarius though it is difficult to be certain as to exactly which one. The strongest contenders are perhaps two Republican denarii (Crawford 390/1 and 494/20a), but an Augustan issue (RIC I, 300) dating to 19 BC also remains a possibility (Table 4). The design of the obverse is echoed by a silver unit of Eppillus (V415) with REX CALLE above and below a large crescent. As B2 stylistically looks the earlier interpretation of the Roman original and appears closer to it in spirit, it quite possibly predates the Eppillus issue.

The most obscure type within this group is undoubtedly B3, the obverse of which shows a Celticized Roman-style head - most probably that of Augustus - while the reverse carries a strange and somewhat amateurish depiction of a horse, which in this guise does not occur on any other Tasciovanos issue. At first sight the obverse gives every indication of having been the prototype for the much more accomplished and thoroughly Romanized E1, but stylistically and in terms of the poor quality of the engraving on B3, there might be a greater gap in time between the two issues than the very similar obverses would have us believe.

I have placed B4 at the very end of this group on account of its classicized reverse. It could equally be argued that it should form part of the extensively Romanized issues of group E, but I felt on balance that the obverse's similarity to some of Tasciovanos's second phase quarter staters, such as BMC 1641-43, suggests a broadly similar timeframe of production. The inspiration for the reverse most probably comes from Augustan denarii featuring a Capricorn bearing cornucopiae on its back (RIC I, 126/128). It would seem that the Celtic engraver copied this to him unfamiliar feature from a worn specimen, thus interpreting the cornucopiae as a wing. Hobbs (1996, 117) mistakenly refers to the animal as a 'winged griffin'.

An example of B2 has been analysed by Northover (1992, 294, C306) and was found to contain 98.25% silver, 0.24% gold and 0.68% copper. It is one of only three published metallurgical analyses for the silver units belonging to the wider Tasciovanos complex. The analysis suggests that the most likely source for silver of this quality would have been melted down Republican and early Imperial denarii (*ibid.*, 257).

The die links for group B are extremely simple with only rare occasions when more than one pair of dies was in use (Figure 4). The average weights tend to fluctuate with B1 close to the low weights of Group A, while as we have seen the single specimen of B2 is rather heavier than one might have expected (Table 3). The weights of B3 and B4 are broadly in line with the majority of Tasciovanos's silver issues.

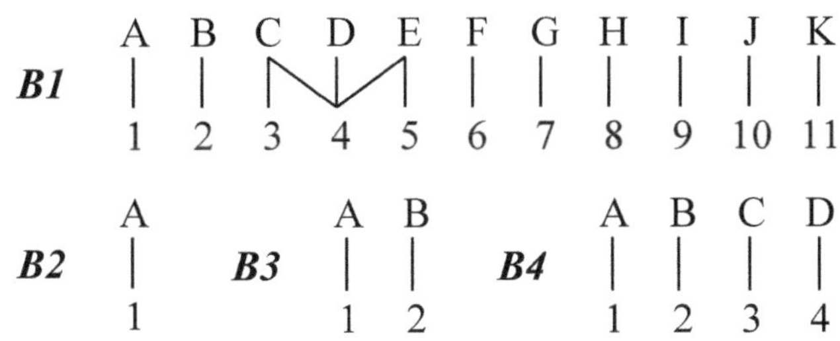

Figure 4. Die-links for group B.

Type	Prototype
B1	R/ probably denarius of P. Crepusius, 82 BC (Crawford 361)
B2	O/ possible prototypes incl. denarii of L. Lucretius Trio, 76 BC (Crawford 390/1), P. Clodius, 42 BC (Crawford 494/20a) and P. Petronius Turpilianus, 19 BC (RIC I, 300)
B3	O/ general resemblance to the laureate head of Augustus, but difficult to be more precise
B4	R/ possibly an Augustan denarius, 18-17/16 BC (RIC I, 126/128)
C1	O/ probably inspired by the late Republican/Augustan fashion to include an inscription within a border on an otherwise blank surface, cf. M. Agrippa, 38 BC (Crawford 534/3), Mark Antony, 33 BC (Crawford 542/1-2), Augustus, 19-18 BC (RIC I, 525)
C2	O/ see C1 R/ perhaps adaptation of Augustan denarius, 43 BC (Crawford 490/1 and 3)
D1	R/ possibly denarius of M. Volteius, 78 BC (Crawford 385/2)
D2	R/ ultimate model possibly silver staters of Maroneia (Thrace) 386-347 BC (SNG Copenhagen 606), perhaps via a Roman gemstone
D3	R/ possibly adapted from denarius of Cn. Plancius, 55 BC (Crawford 432/1), or quinarius of C. Antius C. F. Restio, 47 BC (Crawford 455/3)
D4	R/ possibly denarius of Q. Titius, 90 BC (Crawford 341/1) or denarius of Augustus by P. Petronius Turpilianus, 19 BC (RIC I, 297) but neither particularly convincing; intaglio?
D5	R/ possibly adapted from Republican denarius showing rider's cloak flowing in the wind e.g. denarius of A. Licinius Nerva, 47 BC (Crawford 454/1 and 2) or earlier denarii depicting the Dioscuri etc.
E1	O/ Augustus's laureate head (same as reverse) R/ Augustus's 'butting bull' Lugdunum type, 11-10 BC (RIC 187a/188a) (Evans 1864, 241-242; Allen 1944, 14; Scheers 1982, 620). Almost identical images of the bull can be found on Greek silver of the fourth century BC
E2	O/ Possibly the denarius of Q. Pomponius Rufus, 73 BC (Crawford 398/1) or quinarius of Mn. Cordius Rufus, 46 BC (Crawford 463/4b) (Laing 1991, 23) or the denarius of M. Plaetorius Cestianus, 67 BC (Crawford 409/1), though none especially convincing R/ possibly denarius of Lucius Papius, 79 BC (Crawford 384/1) (Henig 1972, 217) but not convincing; more likely a Greek original or gem
E3	O/ possibly the denarius of Lucius Papius, 79 BC (Crawford 384/1) (Henig 1972, 217), but more likely a Greek original or gem R/ perhaps Augustan denarius by Petronius Turpilianus, 19 BC (RIC I, 297) (Laing 1991, 20) (Henig 1972, 220)
F1	R/ perhaps adaptation of Augustan denarius, 43 BC (Crawford 490/1 and 3)
G2	R/ possibly denarius of M. Volteius, 78 BC (Crawford 385/2)

Table 4. Classical prototypes for Tasciovanos's silver.

C. VER in ring issues

Two types stand aside from the remainder on account of their plain obverses, boldly inscribed VER for Verulamium,[3] which in all likelihood was also the location of the mint (Figure 5).

The presence of the mint signature coupled with the almost identical obverses has singled out these two types since the early work of Evans, with his classification subsequently being upheld by Allen. More recently Van Arsdell has elected to separate them, placing C1 (V1699) in his first and C2 (V1747) in his second coinage (Table 1). The latter is unusual in lacking any reference to Tasciovanos, yet it is hard to see who else might have been responsible for its issue and an association with this ruler remains the most likely option.

C1 (M161, V1699, BMC 1670-73)

Obv.: VER within pellet border.

Rev.: Horse r. on double exergual line, rosette above rear, legend TASCIA with TAS under horse, CI in front and inverted A above.

C2 (M162, V1747, BMC 1674-76)

Obv.: VER within pellet border.

Rev.: Helmeted horseman wearing diadem r., exergual line and corded border. One variant is recorded which has a small star both in front and below the horse and lacks the exergual line.

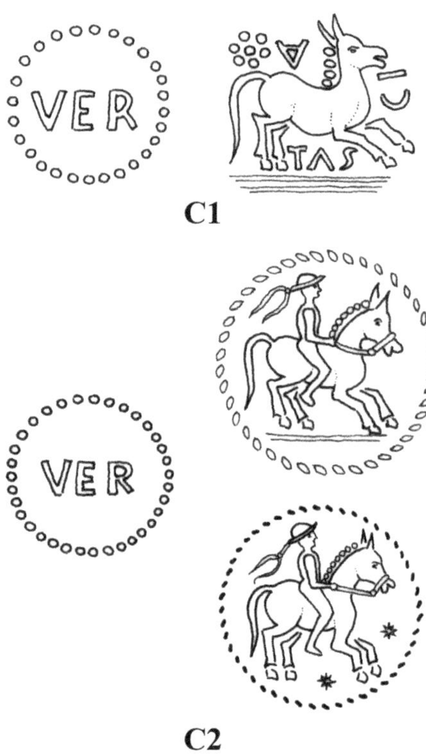

Figure 5. Coins in group C.

Although the immediate impression is that of a homogenous group, there may be a greater distance in time between the two issues than is at first apparent. Stylistically, the reverse of C1 appears to be earlier than the more heavily Romanized reverse of C2. In addition, there is also the weight issue, with C1 being on average almost 20% heavier than C2 (Table 3), although with only twelve records, this figure must be viewed with a degree of caution. A relatively early date for C1 is also indicated by the antiquated legend TASCIA, employing the letter 'A' instead of the later 'O', a form of spelling which on the stater issues went out of fashion towards the end of the first series (Kretz 1998, 4).

The obverses of both types are boldly branded with the name of the mint, which here takes precedence over the ruler's name, but we can only guess as to the reasons why. Unfortunately, the recorded provenances are too few and the findspots too widely scattered to offer much help in this respect. Although no firm guide to their chronology, the droopy-tailed horse reflects the prevailing fashion within the early second series gold coinage, as is evidenced by similar horses on both the stater (Kretz 2001b, 239) and quarter stater (Kretz 2001a, 8-9) issues.

The image may represent the king himself, whose sovereignty is portrayed here by the addition of the regal diadem. Evans (1864, 25) thought it strange that this decoration, which is ultimately of Eastern origin, should be associated with a British ruler.

Despite their almost identical obverses C1 and C2 are not die-linked. The number of pellets making up the circular border on C2 is greater than on C1, with the engraving also generally of a higher quality. The die chain of C2 must be treated with a degree of caution as a combination of very similar obverse dies coupled with poor quality images makes accurate determination extremely difficult.

The die links for this group are again simple with C1 being unusual in having been struck from a ratio of five obverse to three reverse dies (Figure 6).

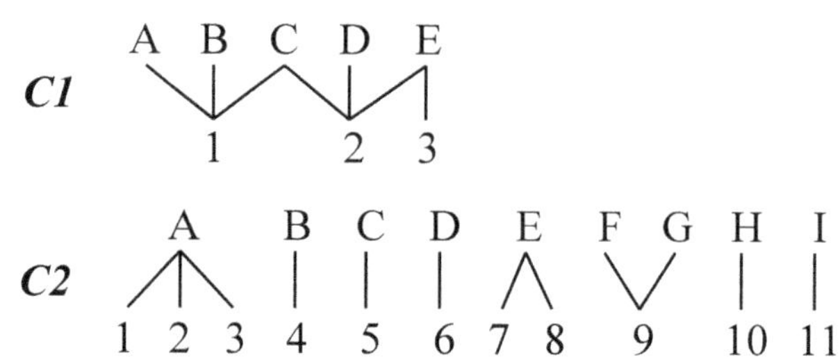

Figure 6. Die-links for group C.

D. Tablet issues

All five types share some form of tablet as the main obverse feature and thus form a relatively homogenous group (Figure 7). The reverses feature Romanized representations of typically Celtic themes, with the exception of D4, which depicts a largely classical Pegasus.

D1 (M164, V1796, BMC 1661-62)

Obv.: Box containing X within cruciform wreath pattern, small pellets marking the four corners, V-E-R-L in the four segments, sometimes two pellets flanking each letter, pellet border.

Rev.: Boar with erect bristles r., small star below, legend TAS above, pellet border.

D2 (M —, V —, BMC 1655)

Obv.: Inscribed square or rectangular tablet, either i) with or ii) without annulets at the four corners, set within a cruciform pattern of a wreath crossed by a corded line, both usually ending in ringed pellets. The barely recognizable and garbled inscriptions appear to be abbreviations of Verulamium and may read VER, VIR, VE, VII and perhaps VI in retrograde.

There are indications of a possible second legend and what might be the letters A and C towards the periphery of the four quadrants. If confirmed, this would most probably spell TASC.

Rev.: Horse with long trailing reins r., ring above head and ring or ringed pellet above rump. Exact nature of legend in front of horse is unclear but on present evidence it most probably reads VER or VIIR.

D3 (M —, V —, BMC —)

Obv.: TA·SCI or TASC in tablet with concave ends, placed at right angles across wreath of two plain and one corded lines, curved lines terminating in pellets emerge from the four angles, short horizontal line at each end of the tablet, pellet border.

Rev.: Stag or ?ibex l., ringed pellet sometimes flanked by two pellets above, legend VER/?VIR with or without pellet in front, ringed pellet below, pellet border.

D4 (M165, V1798, BMC 1664-65)

Obv.: TASC in tablet with concave ends, placed at right angles across wreath of two plain and one corded lines which may terminate in an arc or perhaps a large annulet, short horizontal line at each end of the tablet and small star or pellet in each of the quadrants, ?pellet border.

Rev.: Pegasus l., usually with pellet triad in front and a small star or pellet both above rump and below horse, sometimes within a pellet border. Some dies feature additional pellets while others show Pegasus having horns.

D5 (M166, V1800, BMC 1677-80)

Obv.: TA·SC, TASC, or TASG in rectangular tablet of varying size with either square or concave ends, surrounded by border of three circles (inner and outer plain, middle beaded). Sometimes there are just two circles (inner plain and outer beaded).

Rev.: Helmeted horseman l., carrying an elliptical, decorated shield with a central boss on his left arm, either i) with or ii) without a lowered lance in his right hand. Cloak flowing behind which on later dies is transformed into a diadem; exergual line below and pellet border.

All the types in this group share a common design element in the shape of a box or tablet as the central obverse feature. This is at first uninscribed and set within the traditional crossed wreaths. As both the tablet and the inscription gain in importance, the remainder of the design is progressively simplified until finally only the inscribed tablet surrounded by a border remains. The name-in-tablet style is unparalleled within both the Roman and Gaulish coinages. It is probably the most distinctive innovation in coin design in late first century BC Britain and constitutes a major indigenous development. A recent comprehensive investigation into this phenomenon by Williams (2002) has persuasively demonstrated that the origin of the tablet most probably lies in Roman manufacturers' stamps on imported amphorae and ceramics.

The majority of the five types still exhibit traditional Celtic iconography, albeit in a Romanized form, with only one reverse (D4) being classically inspired and a second (D2) potentially so (Table 4).

Like the previous group, D1 is yet another type where the mint signature takes precedence over the king's name. Here the back to back crescents usually central to the crossed wreaths arrangement (cf. A2 and B4) have been modified into the letter X and set within a square box with concave sides. Boars similar to the one on the D1 reverse also occur on Tasciovanos's bronzes V1713 and V1826, and on G2.

D2 appears to carry references to Verulamium on both sides and at first seems to lack any mention of Tasciovanos. However, there are traces of what may be letters within the four quadrants of the obverse, which may turn out to be a secondary legend. The two fragments visible look like the letters A and C. If confirmed by future discoveries, these are likely to form part of the legend TASC and would thus confirm D2's association with this ruler.

Unusually for Tasciovanos's issues, the obverse dies of D2 are often poorly engraved, making it is extremely difficult to decipher the letters contained within the tablet. The quality of the die-cutting is extremely uneven and the general impression is one of a hastily conceived and executed issue. It seems odd that, at a time when the propaganda value of legends was increasingly being recognized, Tasciovanos's mint would be allowed to issue coins whose engraving was so obviously inferior and not fit for its intended purpose. The horse with trailing reins on the reverse was most probably inspired by an earlier classical source. A similar theme occurs for instance on Greek silver staters from Maroneia belonging to the fourth century BC (Table 4). Whilst these are unlikely to have formed the direct model for D2, it is clear that this motif must have travelled a considerable distance in both space and time before finally finding its way into the design repertoire of a British engraver.

Although pure speculation, it is conceivable that the image of the horse with trailing reins - having either thrown off its rider or simply broken free - might have been intended to convey a symbolic message. If so, this image may be directly related to the demise of Andoco some time towards the end of Tasciovanos's second stater series (Kretz 2002, 270-271) and probably not long before D4 was issued. This event confirmed Tasciovanos as the supreme ruler of the Catuvellauni, a fact he shortly thereafter celebrated with the issue of the RICON series.

The obverse of D3 is closely associated with the RICON staters and quarters, with the closest match being the quarter V1786. The animal portrayed is usually referred to as a stag (e.g. Chris Rudd list 54, no. 69), but is quite possibly modelled on something more exotic like an ibex. On some dies its body is slim and long-legged, whilst on others it is stocky with short legs. Although the images are often poor, the animal appears to have horns rather than antlers.

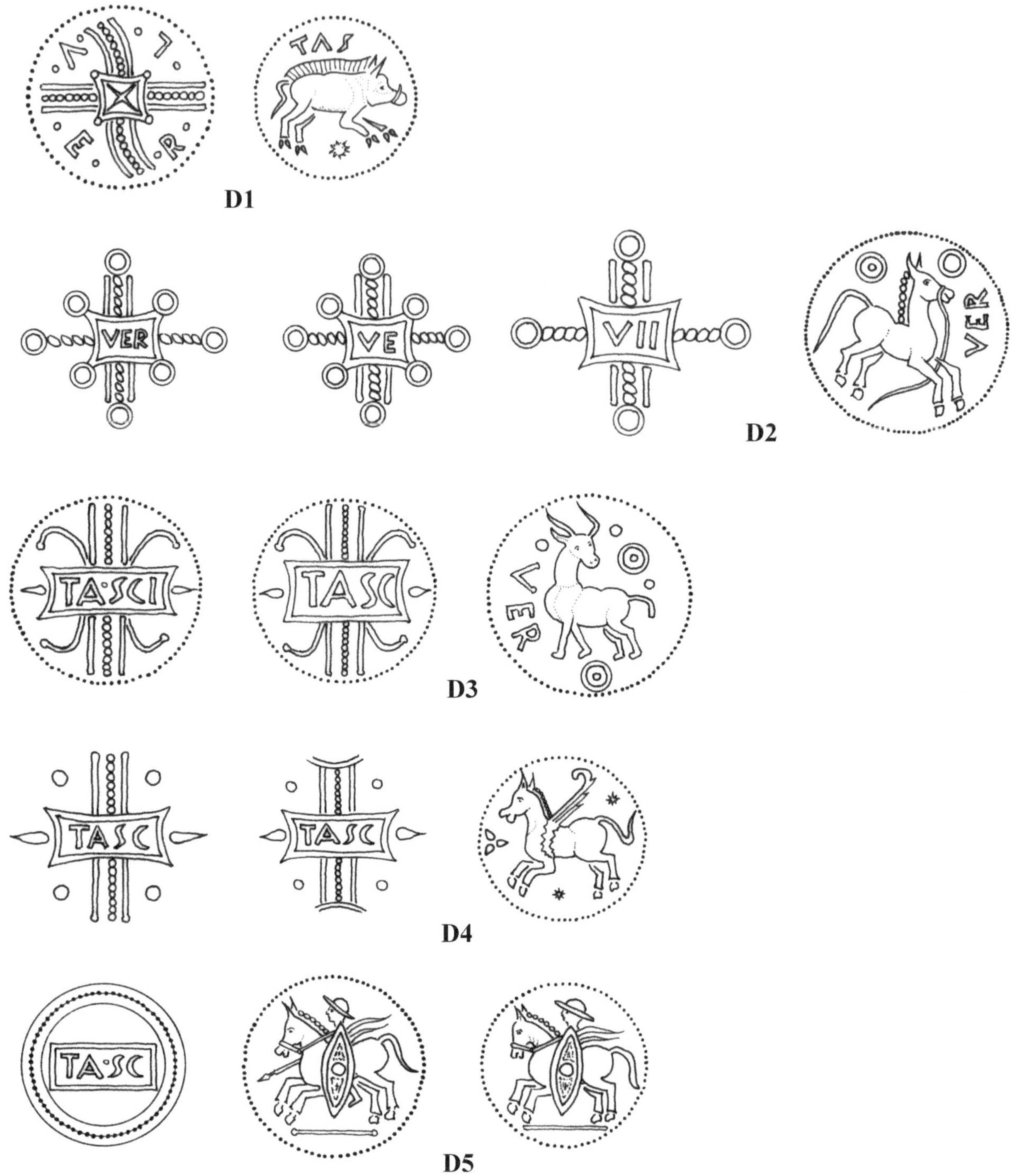

Figure 7. Coins in group D.

The obverse of D4 is a variation on the previous type and the reverse based on the RICON quarter stater reverse (V1786). Some dies show Pegasus having grown horns like an antelope, a fact already noted by Evans (1864, 236-237).

D5 is a rather variable type, with both obverses and reverses exhibiting a number of minor variations. It features a much simplified obverse, retaining just the inscribed tablet and placing it within a new border design - the triple circle. The reverse shows a horseman, carrying a large elliptical shield and occasionally a lowered lance, with his cloak flowing behind him. His brimmed helmet is of the same design found on many second series and 'RICON' type staters. There are several reverse dies towards the very end of the series which lack the flowing cloak and show a diadem trailing from the back of the helmet instead (see for example Chris Rudd list 30, no. 62). This unusual feature is also found on types C2 and F1 which may be indicative of all three types belonging to broadly the same period. The intention may have been to identify the rider as Tasciovanos (Evans 1864, 252).

D5 is by far the most common variety of Tasciovanos's silver with twice the number of examples (43) recorded as the next most common type C2 (21). The reasons behind the popularity of this type are unclear but may have something to do with the simple but powerful branding on the obverse coupled with the warrior-like reverse image. Assuming that Tasciovanos was directly involved in the selection and issue of his coin types, it is not too difficult to see why he should have favoured D5. This type features a powerful combination of images, which go a long way towards conveying his importance and authority, whist still retaining an essentially Celtic feel. Interestingly D5 is one of only two silver issues from the wider Tasciovanos group (the other is F1) of which several examples have been found south of the Thames in Kent, an indication that this must have acted as an effective tribal barrier.

There are instances within Group D (types D3 and D5) where dies contain additional pellets within the inscription, i.e. TA·SCI and TA·SC respectively. There are similar occurrences in type G1, where the obverse's secondary inscription may read CO or C⊙, in G2 where the reverse legend is TASCI⊙, and in the RICON series of staters (V1780), where one die is inscribed TASCIOV RIGON· (BMC 1628) and another TASCI⊙ RIC⊙N (BMC1629-30). The most likely explanation is that these carefully placed pellets are mintmarks of some kind, aimed at aiding the recognition of certain dies or batches of production. A similar phenomenon, in the form of pellets and crosses has been observed amongst Cunobelin's gold (Allen 1975, 3-4) and silver issues (de Jersey 2001, 7).

The average weights of the five D types are remarkably consistent, ranging from 1.21g to 1.26g, a difference of just 0.05g (Table 3). Despite the increased number of dies for D5, the die links are still not particularly complex (Figure 8). However, it is interesting to note that the reverse dies (6) outnumber the obverse dies (3) in D3, whilst the opposite is the case in D4 where the obverse dies (12) outnumber the reverse dies (7).

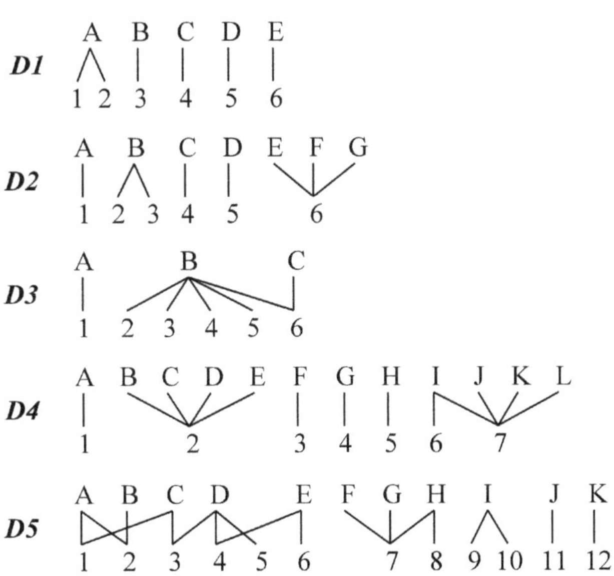

Figure 8. Die-links for group D.

E. Extensively Romanized issues

A group of three types differentiated by their thoroughly Romanized obverses and reverses (Figure 9).

E1 (M163, V1794, BMC 1681-82)

Obv.: Roman-style laureate head r., TASCIA in front with A lacking crossbar, pellet border.

Rev.: Butting bull l. with bushy tail raised above its back, star above shoulder, pellet border. One variant is recorded which has legend TASCI below the exergual line.

E2 (M160, V1792, BMC 1658-59)

Obv.: Eagle standing l. with head turned back, sometimes tiny pellet triad to the left of head, three options for legend TASCIO: i) TAS in front and CIO behind; ii) TA in front and SCIO behind; iii) TASCI behind and O in front. Pellet border.

Rev.: Griffin r. with left front leg raised, standing on exergual line. Either pellet-in-ring in front of head or single pellet under beak, pellet triad under belly, pellet border.

E3 (M159, V1790, BMC 1660)

Obv.: Griffin r. surrounded by border of three circles (inner and outer plain, centre beaded).

Rev.: Pegasus stepping l., various options for inverted legend TAS: i) T behind rear legs, A under horse and S between forelegs; ii) T under horse, A between forelegs and S under head; iii) TA under horse and S between forelegs; iiii) T under horse and A and S between forelegs. Pellet border.

These three types stand out from the remainder of the silver on account of their extensive Romanization, with both obverses and reverses displaying images closely modelled on Roman/Classical prototypes (Table 4). Some doubts remain about the inclusion of E1 within this group. I suspect it may ultimately prove to belong to an earlier period, possibly even predating group D. There are two reasons why I am doubtful about its apparently late date. The first is the inscription, which in TASCIA employs a form of spelling, which on the stater coinages went out of use towards the end of the first series to be replaced by TASCIO, which is also the legend employed by E2. Within Tasciovanos's silver the only other examples of the TASCIA legend are B1 and C1, two relatively early types. The second reason is that both obverse and reverse are direct copies of a Roman original with little attempt at adaptation or innovation. E2 and E3 on the other hand both display images which have undergone a degree of evolution and are probably several stages removed from any likely model in the form of a Roman denarius.

As Evans (1864, 241-242) noted 140 years ago, there can be little doubt that the model for E1 was a series of Augustus's Lugdunum (Lyon) types, struck around 11-10 BC (RIC I, 187a/188a), which show Augustus's laureate head on the obverse and a similar butting bull on the reverse, a theme perhaps ultimately derived from Greek silver coins of the fourth century BC. Assuming the copies were produced within a few years of the original, this would give us a date of around 5 BC or a little later for E1. Such a date would in my view be too early for the remainder of Group E. If we are correct in thinking that the degree of Romanization is a valid factor in determining chronological order, E2 and E3 are likely to represent the last mainstream issues produced by Tasciovanos's mint. Interestingly, at least one of the reverse dies of type E1 is inscribed TASCI below the exergual line, thus making it the only silver type to carry the ruler's name on both sides.

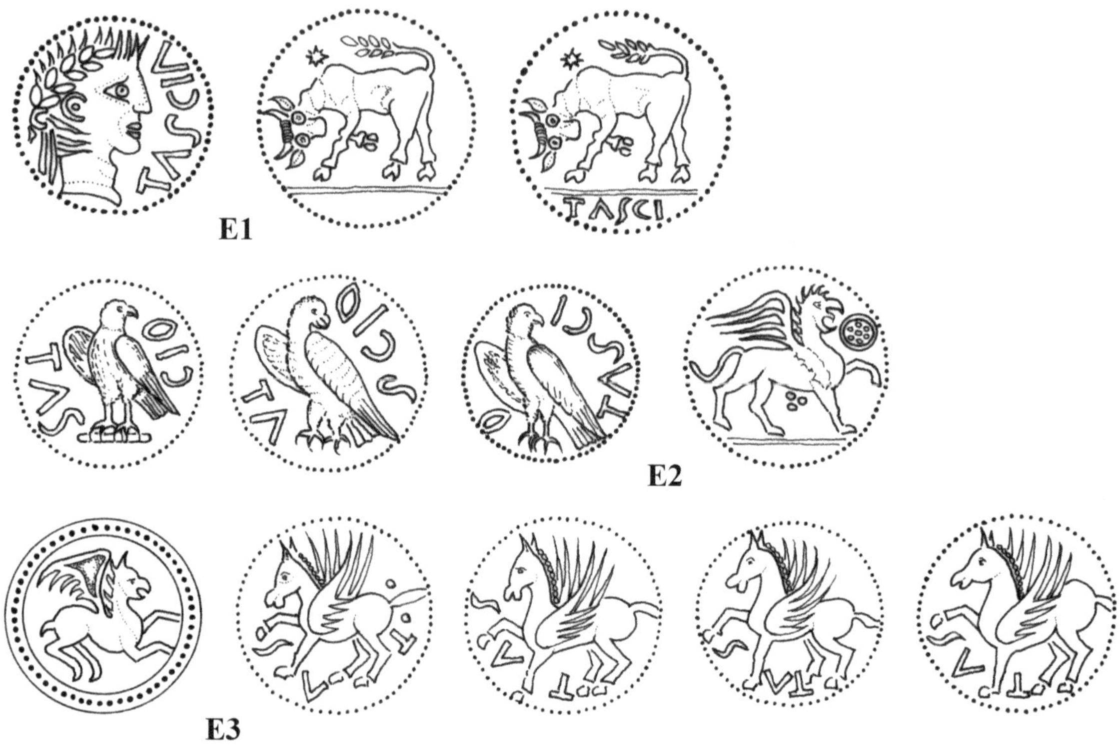

Figure 9. Coins in group E.

Eagles in similar, though not identical poses to the obverse of E2 are depicted on Republican denarii of M. Plaetorius Cestianus (67 BC; Crawford 409/1) and Q. Pomponius Rufus (73 BC; Crawford 398/1), as well as on a quinarius of Mn. Cordius Rufus (46 BC; Crawford 463/4b), but none is likely to have been the direct model for this type. The same is true for the griffins depicted on the reverse of E2 and the obverse of E3 which are far removed from the creature featured on the denarius of Lucius Papius (79 BC; Crawford 384/1).

The Pegasus portrayed on E3 is noticeably different to those featured on D4 and quarter stater V1786. Its probable prototype is a denarius of Augustus struck by Petronius Turpilianus in 19 BC (RIC I, 297), which shows a similar posture, including the stepping leg. All of this suggests that British engravers must have had a fairly extensive repertoire of both Celtic and Roman/Classical motifs at their disposal.

Strangely, at this late stage in the series the bold branding of the obverses with either the ruler's name or the tribal capital has been abandoned, the reasons for which are unclear. Whilst the obverse of E1 still carries TASCIA in bold lettering, the legends on the later examples of E2 especially are much less competently engraved. E3 carries a single, upside down, disjointed inscription of TAS, hardly the most impressive of legends when compared to some of the earlier designs.

The average weights of group E are very consistent, ranging between 1.19g and 1.24g and are broadly in line with the vast majority of Tasciovanos's silver issues (Table 3). The die links within this group are once again not particularly complex (Figure 10).

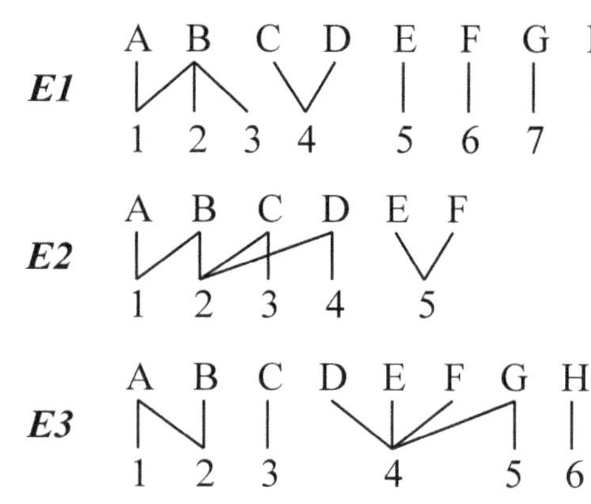

Fig. 10. Die-links for group E.

F. SEGO type

A silver unit belonging to the wider SEGO series (Figure 11).

F1 (M196, V1851, BMC 1684)

Obv.: SECO or SEGO in rectangular tablet, usually with exaggerated corners. Two borders: i) pellet circle; ii) interwoven lines, one plain the other beaded.

Rev.: Helmeted horseman wearing diadem, sometimes on exergual line. On two of the dies the subject is surrounded by a number of annulets and the occasional pellet, while another shows the horseman within a plain field. Corded border.

F1

Figure 11. Coin in group F.

I have isolated F1 from the tablet issues (Group D) to which it typologically belongs as it also forms an integral part of the SEGO series. This consists of three closely related issues, a gold stater (V1845), a quarter stater (V1848) and silver unit F1. To these Van Arsdell (1989, 387) has added a bronze (V1855) and Holman (1999, 196) a further uncatalogued variant. However, these later attributions are based on an indistinct legend and a handful of Kentish provenances, and for the time being must be considered unproven.

This rather short-lived and extremely rare series is one of apparent paradoxes. The stater is the only coin in the series referring to both Tasciovanos and Sego, having a prominent tablet inscribed TASCIO on the obverse and a less conspicuous SEGO legend on the reverse. The quarter stater, which is typologically so close to the previous type that it must belong to the same series, also has a tablet inscribed TASCIO on the obverse, yet makes no mention of SEGO. By way of contrast, the silver unit has SEGO prominently displayed within the obverse tablet but lacks any reference to Tasciovanos. Finally, bronze V1855 is thought to bear the legend SEGO on the reverse with its uncatalogued variant possibly just carrying the letter 'S'. Of Tasciovanos's many and varied issues, those belonging to the SEGO group have a distinctly different distribution to the remainder, being predominantly found in the far east of Kent, a region from where other issues of Tasciovanos are either absent or at best extremely scarce (Holman 1999, 196-198).

Recent research has indicated that that inscriptions referring to SEGO are not confined to Tasciovanos but may also be found on the coinages of Cunobelin and Amminus (*ibid.*, 196). Cunobelin's bronze 'ship' type (V1989) carries the reverse legend SE while a silver issue of Amminus bears the reverse legend SEC (LT LV D36; Scheers 1975, pl. XVI.273). On present evidence the distribution of both these types is once again centred on Kent (Holman 1999, 196-197), which led Muckelroy *et al.* (1978) to speculate that coins bearing legends starting with SE... might have been intended for circulation in Kent. Several of the SEGO legends on record appear to read SECO rather than SEGO. A similar ambiguity has also been noted in the coinages of both Tasciovanos and Cunobelin (Kretz 2000b, 98-100; de Jersey 2001, 12-13), thus supporting Allen's (1980, 123) view that no clear distinction was made between the letters G and C.

The three coin types in question each have their own distinctive style and do not appear to originate from a single workshop/mint. However, they are separated by a sufficient length of time to account for any apparent stylistic changes and I therefore feel that at this stage a mint name, however unlikely, cannot be ruled out entirely. It is worth remembering that Tasciovanos's son and heir Cunobelin, whilst employing the tablet to promote his own name, also frequently uses it to denote his capital/mint at Camulodunum, eg. on V1910, V1913, V1918 and V1977.

As all the coins carrying a SEGO type legend have a predominantly Kentish distribution, they may be connected to one or more major events, most probably of a military nature. There is a distinct possibility that such an event took place in Kent during Tasciovanos's reign and was subsequently commemorated by him with a special issue in gold, silver and possibly bronze. Although there is no reference to Verulamium, the typological and stylistic evidence suggests that this series was most probably struck in or around Tasciovanos's capital for subsequent distribution in Kent. The victory celebrated and the message conveyed may have been of such importance that years later both Cunobelin and Amminus paid homage to it on their own coinages, thereby associating themselves with an important event in their tribal history. Alternatively, they may each have celebrated their own Kentish achievements, military or otherwise, by following an already established pattern.

So what might SEGO mean? Ellis Evans (1967, 254-255) equates the element *Sego* mainly with 'strength' and 'vigour' but also with 'victory', while others including Schmidt (1957, 265), Lambert (1994, 32) and most recently Delamarre (2001, 228-229) all translate it primarily as 'victory'. It is well attested in Britain in personal names, e.g. *Segovax* (one of Caesar's four kings of Kent; *De Bello Gallico* V, 22); tribal names, e.g. *Segontiaci* (a tribe mentioned by Caesar and presumably located in S.E. England; *De Bello Gallico* V, 21); and place names, e.g. *Segontium* (the Roman fort at Caernarvon; Rivet and Smith 1979, 454).

It has also been suggested that SEGO may be a title meaning 'Powerful' or 'The Powerful One' (Holman 1999, 197). If it is indeed an epithet, I feel 'The Victorious' would perhaps be a more fitting alternative. On the other hand, Sego may simply be a noun meaning 'Victory'. This series may therefore record an important military event such as the annexation of Kentish territory late in Tasciovanos's reign, the successful outcome being celebrated with a small scale 'victory' issue for distribution in the new dominion. It would thus constitute a message similar to that contained on the closely related and broadly contemporaneous RICON stater (V1780), with *rigon/ricon* perhaps meaning 'Great or Supreme King' (Kretz 2000, 98).

The obverse of F1 follows very much in the tradition of Group D and is especially close to D5.[4] The reverse is modelled on C2 with some additional rings and the odd pellet in the field. Although one of the reverse dies (no. 3) appears to be an almost direct copy of C2, there is no evidence of any die-linking between the two types.

The average weight of F1 is similar to that of Group G and slightly lower than the bulk of Tasciovanos's silver (Table 3). The die links are again extremely simple, as one would expect from such a small issue (Figure 12).

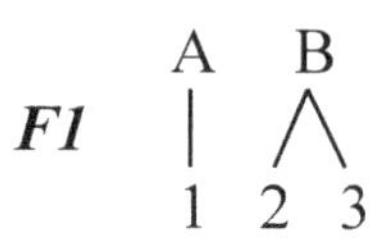

Figure 12. Die-links for group F.

G. DIAS issues

Two types linked by their legends and the use of squares in their obverse designs (Figure 13).

G1 (M188, V1877, BMC 1683)

Obv.: Two interlocking squares, one usually beaded, the other plain with concave sides, sometimes pellets in the outer angles. DIAS in tablet in the centre, letter C above and either O or pellet-in-ring below. Pellet border.

Rev.: Horse l., triskeles or three-pointed star in front, upturned crescent above and legend VIR or VER below. Pellet border.

G2 (M —, V —, BMC 1663)

Obv. Cross contained within square saltire, surrounded by an inner and outer pellet circle enclosing a serpentine border.

Rev. Boar r., TASCI⊙ inverted above and DIASV, DIASS or DIAS below.

G1 inscribed DIAS CO/VIR and a bronze (V1882) inscribed TASC DIAS/VIR have been known since Evans's time and suggest a close connection between Dias, Tasciovanos and Verulamium. Evans (1864, 249-250) judged from the character and style of G1 that the type was struck either under Tasciovanos or shortly thereafter, and speculated that DIAS might be an abbreviation of the Gaulish name DIASVLOS, a chieftain of that name being recorded from the Gaulish tribe of the Aedui (RIG 135).

Since Evans's far-sighted observations little progress has been made in determining the exact origin of this series, the discovery of the first example of G2 in archaeological excavation in 1972 once again reiterating the already established association with Tasciovanos. Since then further discoveries of G2 have produced two variants of the DIAS legend, i.e. DIASS and DIASV. These seem to point in much the same direction as Evans's original hunch and the most credible interpretation today is still that of a personal name such as Diasulos.

Figure 13. Coins in group G.

Unfortunately, such a formation is as unusual as it is problematic. According to Schmidt (1957, 193) it would appear not to be bithematic, i.e. composed of two elements as was common with Celtic personal names. Names commencing with *Dia-* are extremely rare but do occur in the Gaulish tribal name of the *Aulerci Diablintes* and the personal name *Diarilos* (RIG 132). In addition there is a record from far away Dacia (modern Romania) of the personal name *Diassu-marus* (Schmidt 1957, 193), the first element of which bears a strong resemblance to some of the legends found on G2. A potential, albeit partial, attestation separated by many hundreds of miles from southern Britain must of course be treated with considerable caution, but it is a timely reminder that the presently favoured reconstruction *Diasulos* is not necessarily a foregone conclusion and that an alternative formation such as *Dias(s)umaros* must remain a possibility.

Typologically, the distinctive geometric designs of the Group G obverses stand apart from the remainder of Tasciovanos's silver issues and represent a new development. However, the inscribed tablet employed by G1 indicates a close link with Groups D and F, as does the unusual serpentine border on the obverse of G2, which is probably modelled on the F1 obverse. The reverse of G1 portrays the type of horse typically found on some of Tasciovanos's quarter staters (V1690/1692), while the reverse of G2 takes its theme directly from D1. The similarities between the obverses, together with the borrowing of outdated reverse designs, suggest that Groups F and G may belong to broadly the same period, with the latter probably representing the last silver issues within the series.

The obverse of G1 carries a curious secondary inscription in the form of the letters C and O above and below the DIAS legend, but the purpose and meaning of these additional letters remain unknown. On one die (B) the letter 'O' takes the form of a ringed pellet, a feature also found on the reverse of G2, where the O in TASCIO is represented in the same way. Similar instances occur elsewhere in Tasciovanos's coinage (see discussion of D3 and D5 above). It is thought that these strategically placed pellets may represent some form of mintmark.

Interestingly, one of the obverse dies (A) of G1 appears to have undergone a degree of selective re-cutting. Coins struck from this die show traces of other letters underneath the DIAS legend (e.g. CCI 94.0894). The third letter of the original inscription was almost certainly an 'S' while the fourth letter was quite possibly a 'C'. If this interpretation is correct, it would suggest that this die might originally have been inscribed TASC before it was re-cut in the name of DIAS. Whether this might indicate the gift of a recently cut but unused die from Tasciovanos to his co-ruler or the re-cutting of such a die on Tasciovanos's death, we can unfortunately only guess at.

Recently a coin with the same design as G2 but with a new type of legend has been described by de Jersey (2004). Instead of the usual reference to Dias on the reverse, it bears the inscription CAT or possibly CATII, with the extended front legs forming the final two letters. Whether CAT might represent the beginning of the tribal name Catuvellauni or CATII records a personal name remains unclear. The coin in question is a plated unit of relatively poor workmanship and as such unlikely to be a product of the official mint. Until future discoveries confirm its status, it should therefore be treated with caution.

Evans's enlightened guess that G1 was struck either under Tasciovanos or shortly thereafter remains probably still the most likely scenario. It also seems likely that Dias was not just a member of the ruling Catuvellaunian dynasty but may conceivably have been a brother or son of Tasciovanos. Unlike the much rarer Sego issues, Dias's coinage has survived in substantial numbers akin to those of the more plentiful silver issues of Tasciovanos. There are only two Tasciovanos issues (C2 and D5) with greater recorded numbers than G1 and G2. This together with the heavy concentration of Dias issues in the Catuvellaunian heartland around Verulamium leads me to believe that he might perhaps have been a late co-ruler destined to inherit the core Catuvellaunian territories on Tasciovanos's death. This would also go some way to explaining why there are no Dias issues in gold. In any case, subsequent events prevented any such plans from becoming reality and Dias quickly disappeared from the numismatic record.

One example each of G1 and G2 has been analysed. G1 was found to contain 98.59% silver, 0.15% gold and 0.64% copper (Northover 1992, 294, C313) with G2 composed of 97.58% silver, 0.08% gold and 1.36% copper (*ibid.*, C352, where incorrectly described as V1877). The analyses once again suggest that the most likely source for silver of that quality would have been melted down Republican and early Imperial denarii (*ibid.*, 257).

The average weights of Group G are similar to Group F and in line with the bulk of Tasciovanos's silver (Table 3). The die links are once again extremely simple (Figure 14).

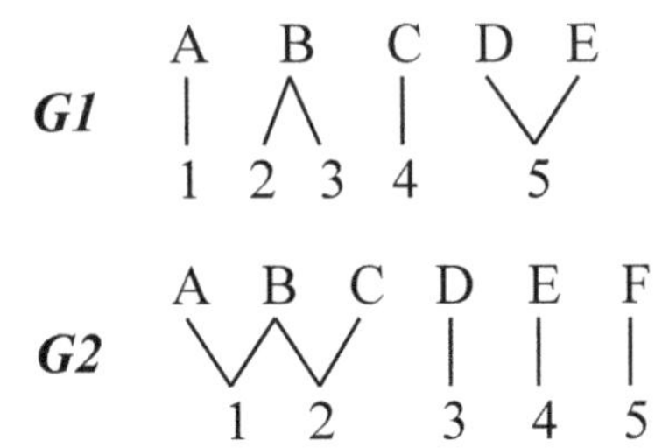

Figure 14. Die-links for group G.

Contexts

Information on the contexts of Tasciovanos's silver is, regrettably, extremely scarce. Out of a total of 302 coins listed in this study just eight have been recovered in archaeological excavation, yet even in these cases the available information is strictly limited (Table 5). Some coins remain unpublished, while those that have been published provide us with little if any useful information towards establishing a relative chronology for Tasciovanos's silver.

Metal detector finds are equally problematic and either lack contextual information altogether or, in one or two exceptional cases, allow only the broadest chronological phasing to be established.

Tasciovanos's silver is only rarely found in hoards. However, there are hoarded coins from Watford, Bourne End and Berkhamsted (all in Hertfordshire) but unfortunately the records are too poor to be of any real value (Table 6). Other sites with multiple finds of Tasciovanos's silver, but possibly not from hoards include St. Albans (Herts.), Foxton (Cambs.) Evenley (Northants.) and Raunds (Northants.).

Distributions

We now have an adequate number of provenances for Tasciovanos's silver issues to assist us in building up a meaningful picture of its overall pattern of distribution.

Unlike the silver coinage of his successor Cunobelin, which extends across the Catuvellaunian, Trinovantian and Cantian territories (de Jersey 2001, fig. 13), the distribution of Tasciovanos's silver issues is firmly centred on the

Catuvellaunian core, with the river Thames forming an effective southern boundary (Figure 15). There are only a handful of finds from neighbouring territories, most of which are on an insignificant scale. One notable exception is a concentration of findspots in Kent to which we will return in due course.

site	type	CCI no.	comments
Baldock, Herts.	C1	72.0066	exc. 1971, site A, feature 334 - found in quarry, probably filled 70-90 AD (Goodburn 1986, 91, no.7)
Baldock, Herts.	G2	93.0551	exc. 1981 at Upper Walls Common, no further details
Cambridge, Cambs.	A1	99.1155	exc. c.1980, context 225, sf 104, no further details
Harlow, Essex	B1	90.0293	temple exc.; sf 713
Harlow, Essex	B4	90.0348	temple exc.; sf 843
Harlow, Essex	C2	90.0521	temple exc.; sf 1290A
Harlow, Essex	E1	90.0268	temple exc.; sf 643
Tring, Herts.	G2	74.0148	exc.1972 at Pendley House, Cow Roast; CR 72, layer 3, sf 19

Table 5. Details of Tasciovanos's silver found in excavation.

site	type	CCI no.	comments
Berkhamsted, Herts.	D4	02.1165	also included Tasciovanos gold and Cunobelin gold and silver
	D4	95.0576	
	D5	98.0400	
	G2	96.1099	
Bourne End, Herts.	D5	00.0044	probably identical with the Watford hoard
	D5	00.1831	
	D5	01.1605	
	D5	03.0375	
	G2	03.0291	
	G2	03.0890	
near Watford, Herts.	A1	95.0732	also included Tasciovanos and Andoco gold and Cunobelin silver
	B4	94.0762	
	D2	94.0689	
	D2	94.0690	
	D2	94.0691	
	D2	94.0706	
	D2	94.0761	
	D2	94.0893	
	D3	94.0692	
	D3	94.0970	
	D3	94.0777	
	D4	94.0764	
	D5	94.0693	
	D5	97.2307	
	E2	94.0779	
	G1	94.1460	
	G2	94.0688	
	G2	94.0734	

Table 6. Details of Tasciovanos's silver found in 'hoards'.

Especially puzzling is the lack of provenances from Trinovantian territory. It is in stark contrast to the generally accepted view that Tasciovanos held Camulodunum for at least a short period early in his reign, as is suggested by a rare stater (V1684) and quarter stater (V1694), both of which carry the CAMVL legend. Of the seven provenanced CAMVL type staters (2) and quarter staters (5) on record, four have been found in Hertfordshire, one in Buckinghamshire, and one each in Surrey and Greater London. Although the sample is small, it would seem to indicate that the issues bearing the CAMVL legend were not specifically produced for distribution amongst the Trinovantes but may have merely served some kind of commemorative purpose.

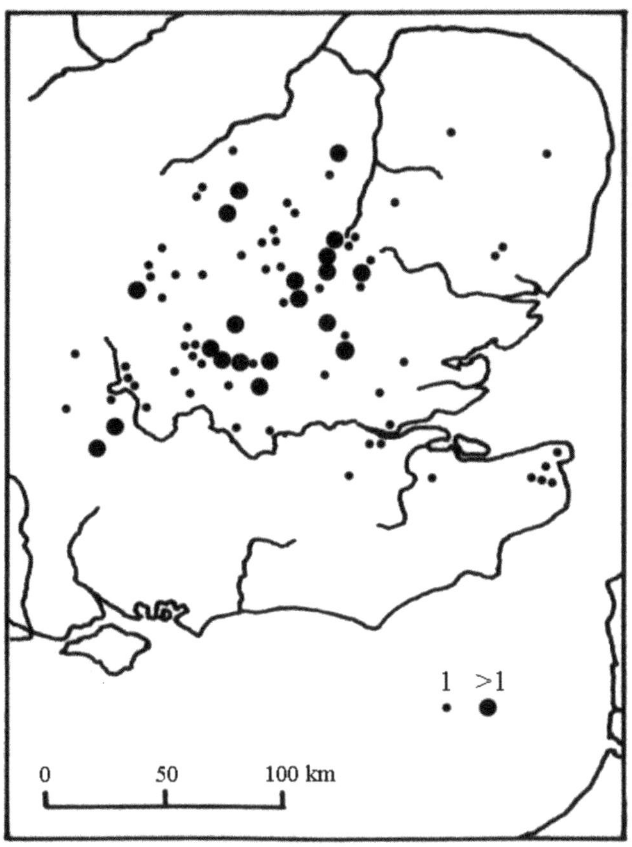

Figure 15. General distribution of Tasciovanos's silver.

A cursory inspection of the provenances of Tasciovanos's remaining gold issues reveals a similar picture. Of almost 200 provenanced Tasciovanos staters and quarter staters (including plated and cores) recorded in the Celtic Coin Index, only about nine were found in core Trinovantian territory, with another nine originating in the ill-defined border regions between the Catuvellauni, Trinovantes and Iceni. More surprisingly still, just a single quarter stater is recorded from Colchester itself. This is hardly the level of finds one would expect had Tasciovanos been in control of the Trinovantian capital for any significant length of time.

The distribution by inscription (Figure 16) is based on Evans's division of Tasciovanos's coinage of 140 years ago, which continues to remain a valid means for grouping and analysing the silver. Whilst a recent analysis of Cunobelin's silver based on the different legends showed relatively well differentiated distribution patterns (de Jersey 2001, fig. 14), such trends are much less obvious in Tasciovanos's case. It would appear however that the issues bearing Tasciovanos's name have the widest-ranging distribution of the four groups, whilst those carrying the mint signature seem to be more concentrated within core Catuvellaunian territory.

Unusually, the DIAS issues (Group G) are more or less confined to the Catuvellaunian tribal area, with a heavy concentration of findspots around Verulamium (Figure 17). This may suggest that Dias became co-ruler late in Tasciovanos's reign, perhaps briefly inheriting the Catuvellaunian throne upon the latter's death, before vanishing from the historical record. His precarious position and lack of political authority may explain why his issues only circulated within a relatively confined area.

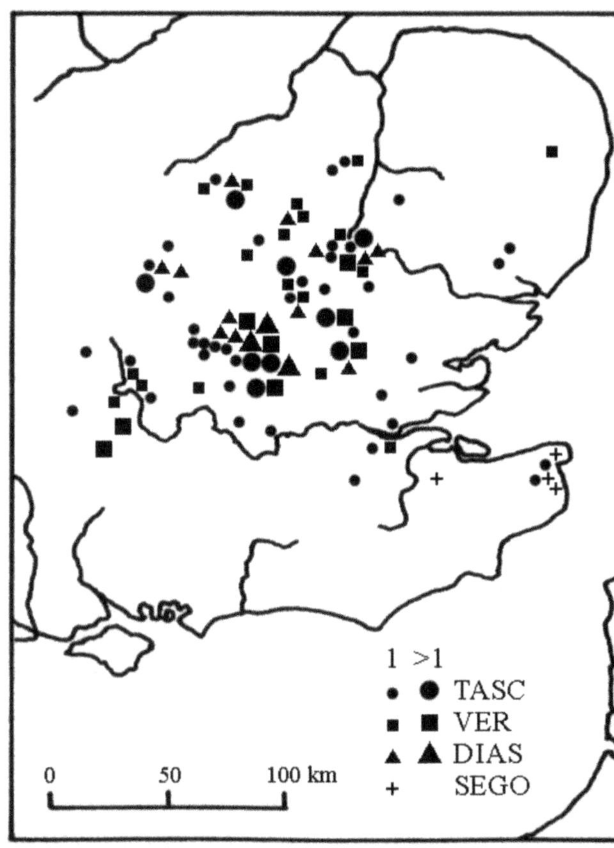

Figure 16. Distribution of Tasciovanos's silver by inscription.

Particularly worth noting is the distribution of the SEGO type (F1) of which all provenanced examples have been found in Kent and especially in the east (Figure 18), a pattern also replicated by other Sego issues (Holman 1999, 196).

The individual distributions of the remaining five groups of Tasciovanos's silver are for the most part not especially informative. They generally show a distribution firmly centred on the Catuvellaunian territories, with a scattering of outlying finds. Group A, comprising the earliest silver, conforms to this pattern (Figure 19). At this point in time there is no obvious concentration of finds in or around any of the major identified settlements like Verulamium, Wheathampstead or Braughing. Although we only have a handful of provenances for each type, it is perhaps worth pointing out that the distribution of A1 at present shows a western bias whereas A2 tends to be found more towards the east. Of the six provenanced examples of A2 only one was found in traditional Catuvellaunian territory (St. Albans, Herts.) with another possibly close by in Harlow (Essex), and of the remainder, two are from Suffolk and one each from Cambridgeshire and Essex.

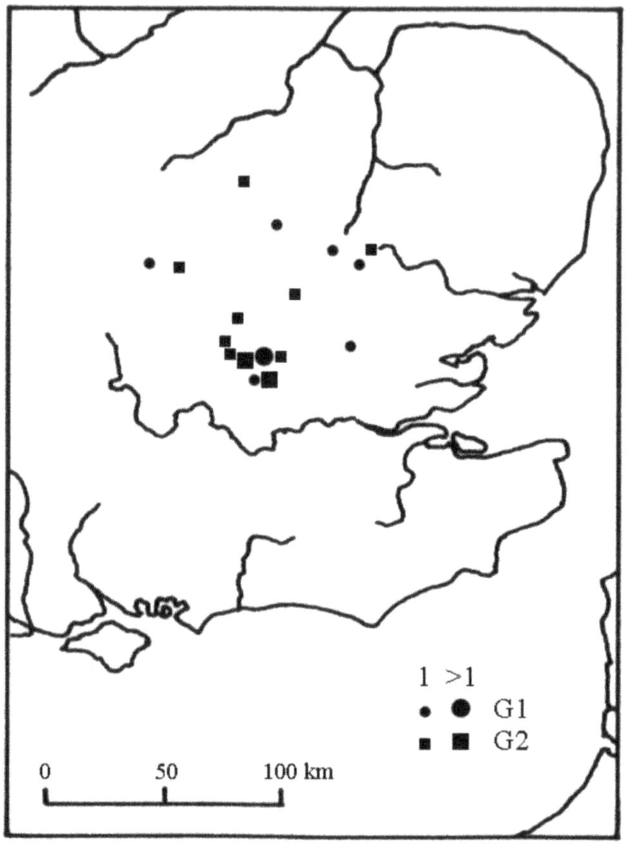

Figure 17. Distribution of group G (Dias) coins.

A similar pattern is exhibited by Group B, which shows the wider Verulamium area almost devoid of finds, with B3 largely concentrated on Berkshire (Figure 20). Although there are only five examples of this type on record, the distribution – three coins in Berkshire and one each in Bedfordshire and Kent – does hint at the possibility of B3 having been a small-scale issue struck for a specific purpose and aimed at distribution on the south-western fringes of Tasciovanos's kingdom. This would at least go some way towards explaining how such a stylistically odd and crudely produced type came to be issued by the Catuvellaunian mint. It is hoped that future finds may throw further light on this intriguing question.

Group C, though not particularly rare, suffers from a lack of provenances, which makes any interpretation difficult (Figure 21). The nature of its design suggests that it was most probably centred on Verulamium.

Group D is the first to show a heavy concentration of finds in and around Verulamium (Figure 22). Unusually, one of the types (D5) also has a number of findspots in Kent. This, the most common type of Tasciovanos's silver, is typologically closely related to the SEGO type (F1) and likely to be contemporaneous with it. It is possible that D5, which boldly carries the ruler's name on the obverse, may have been issued in Kent in tandem with F1 to underscore an important military success.

Figure 18. Distribution of group F (Sego) coins.

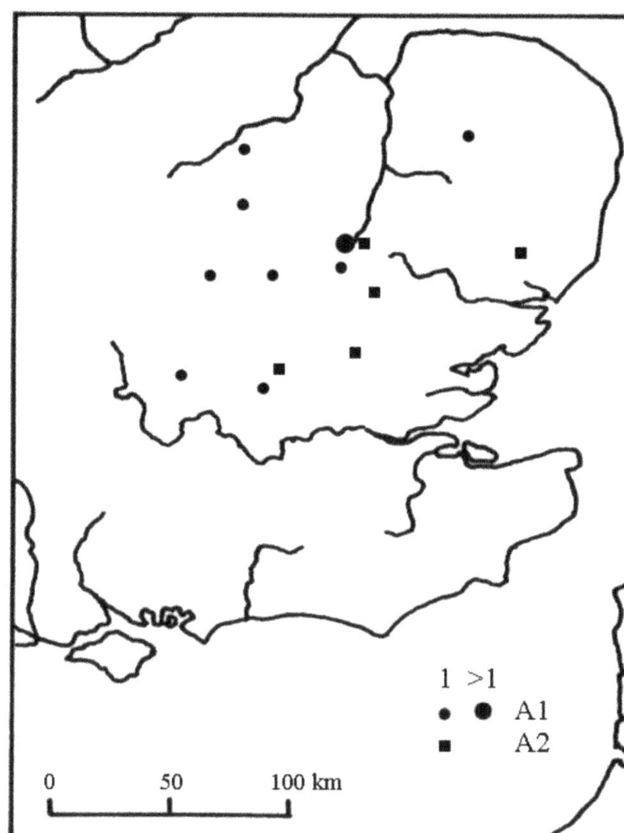

Figure 19. Distribution of group A coins.

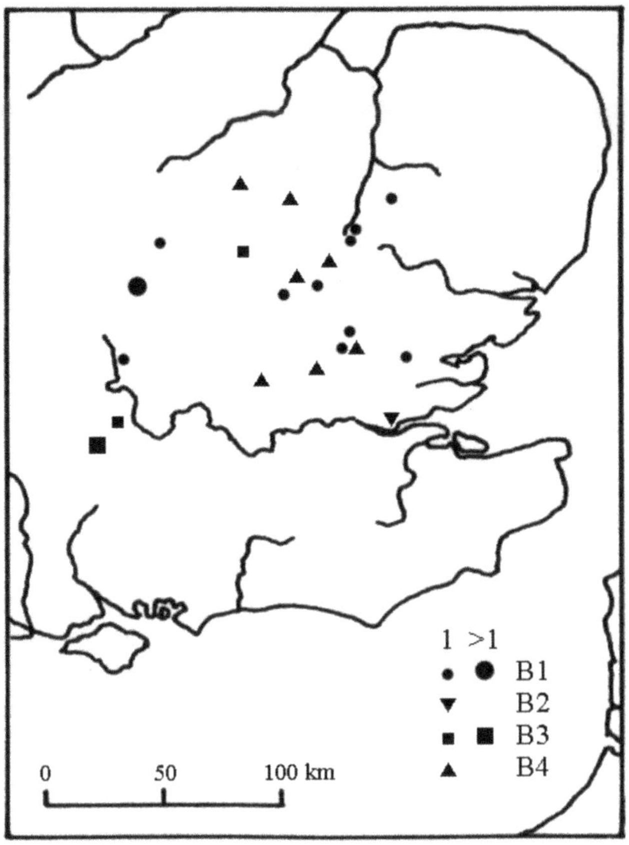

Figure 20. Distribution of group B coins.

Figure 21. Distribution of group C coins.

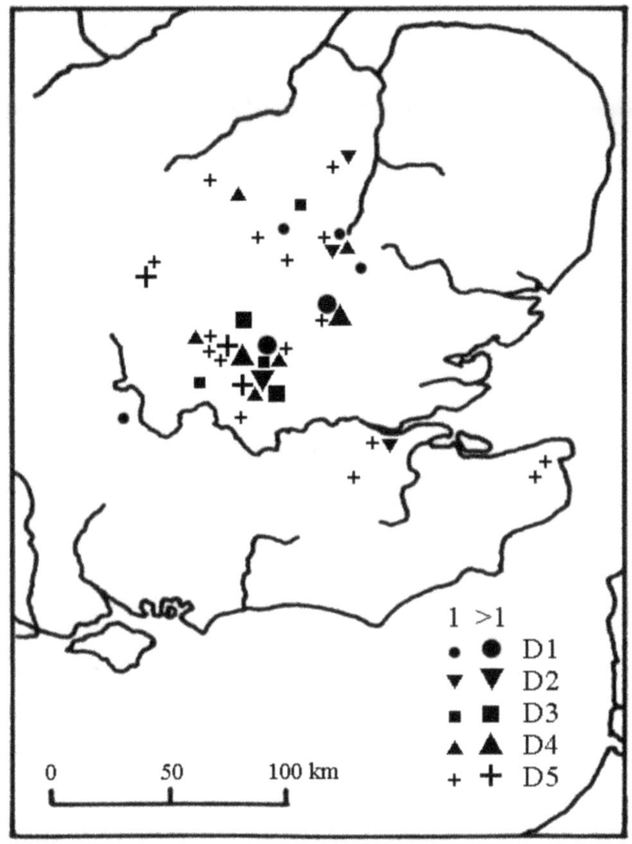

Figure 22. Distribution of group D coins.

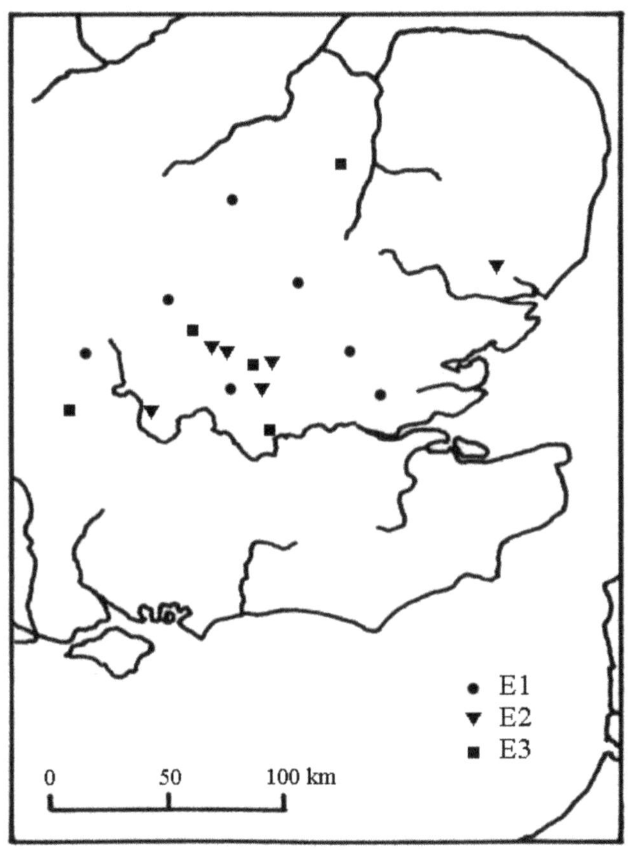

Figure 23. Distribution of group E coins.

Group E again shows a concentration of finds in the wider Verulamium area together with a number of outlying findspots, which include Berkshire and Oxfordshire (Figure 23).

Synthesis

Tasciovanos's silver issues belong for the most part to the late first century BC. They form part of the wider North Thames series, the earliest examples of which were last studied in some detail by Allen (1960, 124, 133; 1964, 2) who provisionally classified them as 'British LX'.

Some of Allen's British LX group are typologically related - either directly or via intermediate types - to the 'Whaddon Chase' series (British L) and it is amongst these that we must look for the uninscribed precursors to the earliest silver of Tasciovanos (Allen 1967, 2). Although one or two types from the LX group may conceivably form part of Tasciovanos's earliest silver, we are at present unable to accurately identify them as such. Consequently, this study has concentrated on those types which can be ascribed to Tasciovanos with at least a reasonable degree of certainty.

The complex nature of Tasciovanos's silver coinage and the existence of a number of closely related issues carrying other names associated with his own has been appreciated since Evans. Although further progress has been made in studying detailed aspects of the North Thames coinage in the meantime, we are still a long way from understanding the sequence of events before, during and following Tasciovanos's reign. Until such time when the remainder of the available material has been studied in some detail, we are unlikely to gain a fuller understanding of this difficult period. Thus this study is but a first step towards a thorough examination of Tasciovanos's silver and it is accepted that future studies and new discoveries will undoubtedly result in a reassessment of some of the ideas put forward here.

Of the seven identified groups, A is undoubtedly the earliest, exhibiting a largely undiluted Celtic iconography together with an average weight of less than 1.00g and in the case of A2 an archaic-style legend. A1 appears to be a direct linear descendant of Allen's British LX6, LX7 and LX8, whereas A2 shows strong stylistic links to a number of Tasciovanos's early quarter staters, especially V1688. Of added interest is the close resemblance between the reverse of A2 and many of Dubnovellaunos's Trinovantian issues in all metals (Table 2), hinting at near contemporaneity between the two rulers.

Unless unidentified silver types of Tasciovanos are lurking somewhere within British LX, Group A consisting of just two types would appear rather small and insignificant when compared to the first stater issue (V1680, 1682, 1684), of which six distinct types have been identified (Kretz 1998, 2-7). This might indicate that the production of silver coins was a fairly recent development and that at this early stage silver may have played a relatively minor role compared to the gold issues.

The widely scattered distributions of Groups A and B show no major concentration of finds centred either on Verulamium or any of the other candidates for an earlier Catuvellaunian stronghold, such as Wheathampstead and Braughing. It suggests that at this early stage in Tasciovanos's reign Verulamium had not yet been appointed the tribal capital it was shortly to become, and this is further supported by Wheeler's view (Wheeler and Wheeler 1936, 41-46) that the intensive pre-Roman occupation of the site only began c. 15-10 BC.

One of the mysteries of Tasciovanos's coinage is a stater (V1684) and quarter stater (V1694) carrying the CAMVL legend. These are usually thought to be evidence that Tasciovanos held Camulodunum for at least a short period sometime during his reign. However, such a scenario is neither supported by the available provenances for the CAMVL types, nor by those for the remainder of Tasciovanos's gold or indeed silver issues. Consequently, any potential occupation by Tasciovanos of Camulodunum must for now be considered unproven.

There is an obvious temptation to connect the CAMVL issues with the start of Cunobelin's reign, but the timing of the two events cannot be easily reconciled. There can be little doubt that the CAMVL issues are relatively early, probably belonging to the very end of the first series of staters (V1680/1682). Assuming that Tasciovanos's rule lasted for about 30 years, this would give a tentative date of c. 20 BC – 10 AD for his reign, which is broadly in line with convention. At a guess the first series might have lasted for about five or ten years, thus producing a date of c. 15-10 BC for the CAMVL issues. This compares with a generally accepted starting date for Cunobelin's rule of c. 10 AD, a discrepancy of some 20-25 years which at present cannot be bridged. Whatever the significance of the CAMVL types, we must for now accept that we are still some way from finding the answer.

The four types of Group B, although typologically extremely variable, all give the impression of belonging to the early part of the series and predating groups C, D and E. All four types display early features in their iconography, composition or lettering, yet the first signs of classical influence upon Celtic coin design are already much in evidence. Stylistically, B1 appears the earliest and this is supported by its low mean weight (1.05g), which is intermediate between Group A and B1's successors. B3 is undoubtedly the oddest of any of Tasciovanos's silver issues, appearing rather crude in terms of design and execution when compared with the remainder. It also has a rather odd distribution with the majority of the coins originating in Berkshire.

The two Group C types form a homogenous unit, characterized by obverses boldly inscribed VER within a pellet circle, a simple and highly effective design. The ruler's name is now either subservient or missing and any Celtic features have all but disappeared. Unusually and for reasons unknown to us, the available records indicate that C1 is almost 20% heavier than C2, making it by far the heaviest type within Tasciovanos's silver.[5] Group C is thought to have been struck approximately midway through the series.

Group D forms perhaps the most cohesive of the five mainstream groups, featuring a central tablet, which is usually inscribed. Variations of the popular 'crossed wreaths' obverse design continue in use for much of the series, while the reverses feature animals in one form or another, some of which are of classical origin (Table 4). This group belongs to the latter part of Tasciovanos's silver with the majority of types contemporaneous with the RICON series of staters (V1780) and quarter staters (V1786, BMC 1650), and at least two types (D3 and D4) being typologically derived from it. D4 in particular is so close to quarter stater V1786 as to be almost a copy of it. D5 forms the most common variety of Tasciovanos's silver and is the only mainstream silver type with a minor distribution in Kent. The name-in-tablet style is an important indigenous British development, unknown in this particular form from either the Roman or Gaulish coinages and without doubt one of the most distinctive design features to appear on late first century BC Iron Age coinage (Williams 2002).

Both the obverses and reverses of Group E display images closely modelled on Roman/Classical prototypes (Table 4). The extent of the Romanization and lack of any surviving Celtic features suggests that much of Group E belongs to the very end of Tasciovanos's mainstream silver issues. The only exception here might be E1, the obverse of which bears a strong resemblance to B3. Conveniently, the Augustan prototype for E1 struck at Lugdunum (Lyon) in 11-10 BC gives us a useful fixed point for this issue. Assuming that E1 was produced within a few years of the original, it may date from around 5-1 BC. If correct, it would most probably predate E2 and E3, which are more likely to belong to the first decade AD.

The silver coinage of Tasciovanos is firmly centred on the traditional Catuvellaunian territories with the river Thames forming an effective southern boundary. Of particular note is the lack of findspots in Essex and Suffolk, including the Trinovantian capital Camulodunum. Although the evidence is inconclusive, the distribution of Tasciovanos's issues by inscription (Figure 16) suggests that the types bearing his name have a slightly wider-ranging distribution than those featuring the Verulamium mint signature.

A particularly puzzling feature of Tasciovanos's silver issues is the seemingly idiosyncratic use and arrangement of the legends. Some coin types are inscribed on either one or very rarely both sides with his name, others exhibit the ruler's name on one side and the mint signature on the other, and just two types (C2 and D2) are inscribed with the name of the mint only (one of them on both sides), thus lacking any reference to Tasciovanos at all. As Evans (1864, 252) observed, 'It would seem that, in certain cases, the name of the town was allowed to take precedence over that of the prince....', a phenomenon which can also be observed in the coinage of Cunobelin.

I believe the legend arrangements were deliberate rather than accidental and suspect that they may have served some deeper purpose no longer obvious to us. Perhaps the different types were intended to convey specific messages to their users or targeted at certain regions or groups under Tasciovanos's control? Unfortunately, the distribution maps do not offer much help in this respect. Allen (1967, 3) thought that the coins where the mint name stands alone may have been struck at Verulamium after Tasciovanos ceased to rule. I think this unlikely from a typological point of view, as both silver units in question exhibit features consistent with an earlier date.

Several issues exist which combine Tasciovanos's name with those of others, including Sego, Andoco, Dias and Rues. These have traditionally been interpreted as personal names identifying subordinate kings, co-rulers or simply associates of Tasciovanos. Van Arsdell (1989, 362, 384-385) saw these names as indicative of an interregnum period, a hypothesis that has not met with general acceptance. I have since demonstrated (Kretz 2002) that Andoco's coinage is most probably that of a client king, ruling a separate though affiliated area possibly centred on Baldock (Herts.) for perhaps 5-10 years, his reign coinciding with Tasciovanos's second stater series (V1730-1736). Whilst the questions raised by the Sego and Dias issues form an integral part of this study, the coinage of Rues has yet to be studied in greater detail.[6]

The Sego series is represented by F1, the sole constituent of Group F. Although arguably part of Group D (tablet types), it has been given separate status here due to forming an integral part of the Sego series of gold, silver and possibly bronze.

Chronologically, F1 belongs to the very end of Group D, although its reverse copies the earlier C2. This order receives further support from the SEGO stater (V1845), the obverse design of which is based on the RICON stater (V1780) whilst employing a similarly outdated reverse type. All the issues featuring Sego-type inscriptions appear to be centred on Kent, and this together with the possible interpretation of *sego* as 'the victorious' or simply 'victory' may suggest that all these types commemorate one or more important military events in Kent.

Although Group G is once again typologically and stylistically closely related to Group D, it was quite possibly issued by an individual other than Tasciovanos and is therefore treated separately here. On G1 the die cutter has taken the usual 'name-in-tablet' concept one step further and combined it with a complex geometric pattern. G2 drops the inscribed tablet but further explores the geometric theme, while its reverse resurrects an earlier D1 reverse. These developments suggests that chronologically the Dias types follow on from Group D, thus belonging to the final stages of Tasciovanos's reign and/or the period immediately thereafter. It is particularly noteworthy that Dias's silver issues have survived in substantial numbers, akin to some of the more plentiful types of Tasciovanos. This together with the heavy concentration of findspots in the Catuvellaunian heartland may suggest that he was a late co-ruler destined to succeed Tasciovanos.

The non-existence of reliable fixed points for dating purposes, together with our lack of knowledge about the frequency of the issues or the intervals between them, makes any attempts at accurate dating extremely hazardous and open to question. It is possible for example that the coinage of Tasciovanos was compressed over a shorter period of time than is generally assumed. However, judging by the abundance of types produced and their survival rate, whilst making due allowances for the greatly enlarged territories and increased trade/prosperity under Cunobelin, it seems unlikely that Tasciovanos's reign could have been far short of the thirty or more years of his successor.

Yet another problem is the starting point of Cunobelin's reign. Evans (1864, 223) believed that there were reasons for supposing that Cunobelin commenced his rule over the Trinovantes in Tasciovanos's lifetime, perhaps around 5 BC, and that they may have ruled together, one over the Catuvellauni, the other over the Trinovantes for a period of about 10 years. More recently de Jersey (2001, 29) has given qualified support to the idea of a short overlap. Such a scenario is persuasive in that it would explain why Cunobelin's earliest silver is confined to the territory of the Trinovantes (*ibid.*, fig. 15), and account for the stylistic similarities between his first silver issues and the earlier Iron Age coinages of the North Thames region (*ibid.*, 27).

This study's aim is to provide a broad chronological framework for the silver, which in turn relates to and interlinks with previously identified stages in the development of Tasciovanos's gold issues (Kretz 1998; 2000; 2001a; 2001b; 2002). Figure 24 illustrates the form such a development might have taken, based on the limited information presently available. Although it paints a broad-brush picture of the suggested phasing for the various groups, this should not be interpreted as a period of continuous production with one type or one group following another in an almost seamless fashion. In reality this process would have been considerably more complex and it is entirely likely that some types were issued simultaneously or even recurrently as and when the need arose.

Tasciovanos	**A →→→**	**B→→→**	**C→→? D→→→→→→→?**	
			E→→→→→→→→?	
Sego				**F→→?**
Dias				**G→→→?**
	c. 20 BC	10	0	c. 10 AD

Figure 24. Proposed phasing of Tasciovanos's silver.

In contrast to Tasciovanos's later stater issues (Kretz 2001, 101; 2001b, 240) the die-links for the silver do not indicate any periods of unusually high activity, but suggest that for the most part small-scale issues were produced at irregular intervals. The rarity of some of the types, e.g. B2, B3 and F1, in combination with their often distinct distribution, suggests they were limited issues struck for a specific purpose. Whilst there is evidence for the operation of two separate, albeit closely associated mints/workshops in the striking of some of Tasciovanos's staters (Kretz 2001b, 235) and quarter staters (Kretz 2001a, 8), no such division could be identified for the silver.

Until further evidence comes to light at some future date, progress on any of the issues here raised is unlikely. However, little by little our understanding of this difficult period improves, as is illustrated by the recent discovery of a new type of Cunobelin quarter stater carrying the reverse legend DVBN (Williams and Hobbs 2003, 55-56). This has for the first time confirmed the long suspected connection between these two individuals and is most probably indicative of Cunobelin succeeding Dubnovellaunos as ruler of the Trinovantes, although the details of that event remain as obscure as ever.

There is clearly a long way to go until we can claim to have a better understanding of the events surrounding Tasciovanos's reign. It is therefore to be hoped that the present interest in the Celtic series and the momentum of scholarship which has developed over the past decade or two will be maintained into the future and that we will see more detailed studies on related subjects to further illuminate this poorly understood period in British history.

Notes

[1] Although the text is unclear, it is assumed that Rodwell (1976, 254) refers to these three types as they had all been recorded at that point in time.

[2] Not applicable to this study.

[3] Although the later Roman spelling *Verulamium* is used here, the numismatic evidence would suggest that the British form was *Verlamio(n)* (cf. V1808).

[4] Obverse die A features a tablet within a pellet border (CCI 87.0502).

[5] With the possible exception of B2, the single specimen of which weights 1.4g.

[6] de Jersey (2001, 29) notes that only 33% of Rues findspots are located in Hertfordshire, with the remainder spread into Trinovantian territory and beyond.

Appendix. Gazetteer of Tasciovanos's silver

The gazetteer contains details of all examples of Tasciovanos' silver recorded in the Celtic Coin Index (CCI) at the Institute of Archaeology, Oxford, or otherwise known to the author, up to the end of 2003.

In addition to the usual bibliographic notes, the final column contains references to a number of auction catalogues, dealer's lists and museum collections with the abbreviations explained below:

BDW	Buckland, Dix and Wood auction catalogues
CNG	Classical Numismatic Group auction catalogues
CNR	Classical Numismatic Review sales lists
Cummings	John Cummings sales lists
BMC	R. Hobbs, *British Iron Age Coins in the British Museum*, 1996
Miller	David Miller sales lists
Mossop	H. R. Mossop collection, sold at Glendining's, 6. 11.1991
NCirc	Spink Numismatic Circular
Rudd	Chris Rudd sales lists
Seaby CAMB	Seaby Coin and Medal Bulletin
Vosper	Mike Vosper sales lists

References to earlier gazetteers are abbreviated as Origins (Allen 1960) and Suppl. I, II or III (Haselgrove 1978, 1984 and 1989 respectively). 'exc.' indicates the coin was found in an archaeological excavation.

CCI	wt.	dies	provenance	comments
A1				
M -, V1698, BMC 1654			**uninscribed**	
01.0409	1.0	A1	-	-
01.0410	0.9	E6	-	-
01.0550	1.00	B3	near Raunds, Northants.	-
01.1015	0.65	-	-	Rudd list 58, no. 54
02.0273	0.97	F8	Watton, Norfolk?	-
03.0456	-	-	Bledlow, Bucks.	-
03.0841	-	F8	Foxton, Cambs.	-
03.1072	-	C4	-	V1698 plate coin
86.0410	-	A2	Old Warden, Beds.	-
93.0902	-	D5	-	ex Mossop, lot 292/2
93.0903	0.92	G9	-	ex Mossop, lot 293, BMC 1654
95.0732	0.76	-	Watford, Herts.	-
98.0173	-	J12	nr. Newport Pagnell, Bucks.	-
98.2159	-	E7	King's Cliffe, Northants.	-
99.1155	-	H10	Cambridge, Cambs.	exc.
99.1259	0.81	I11	'north Thames'	Rudd list 47, no. 50
-	-	-	Castle Hill, Cambridge	exc. 1974-7, new type, Suppl. II, 129, might be 99.1155
A2				
M -, V -, BMC 1656-57			**-/TASC(I)**	
00.1627	-	D2	-	*Spink, Coins of England 2000*, no.221
01.0607	-	-	Suffolk	-
82.0301	1.13	A1	-	ex Mossop, lot 294, BMC 1656
83.0265	-	B1	Harlow, Essex?	-
90.0084	0.77	D3	near Saffron Walden, Essex	Symons 1990a, no. 62
94.1428	0.89	E4	near St. Albans, Herts.	-
96.1878	0.52	-2	-	ex Mossop, lot 295/1, BMC 1657
97.0043	0.97	E4	near Cambridge, Cambs.	Rudd list 26, no. 67
99.0312	0.7	-2	-	Vosper list 105, no. 23
99.0635	1.14	D3	Coddenham, Suffolk	Rudd list 45, no. 31
99.1680	1.14	C1	-	Rudd/Vecchi 15, 15.6.1999, lot 1632
B1				
M158, V1745, BMC 1667-68			**-/TASCIA**	
00.1815	1.1	C4	east of Cambridge, Cambs.	-
03.0845	-	D4	Letchworth, Herts.	-
68.0200	1.1	H8	Gayton, Northants.	BMC 1668
68.0201	1.02	I9	-	BMC 1667
73.0232	1.13	E5	-	-

CCI	wt.	dies	provenance	comments
B1 (continued)				
73.0233	1.17	E4	-	Fitzwilliam
84.0028	-	G7	-	-
88.0073	0.99	J10	Thorley, Herts.	Symons 1990b, no. 107,
90.0293	1.05	B2	Harlow, Essex	temple exc., Harlow Museum
93.0905	1.14	F6	Cherry Hinton, Cambs.	ex Mossop, lot 296
94.1081	1.06	C3	near Oxford	-
95.0437	-	K11	Reed, Herts.	-
96.1000	1.14	-	Evenley, Northants.	-
96.1024	1.03	-	Evenley, Northants.	-
96.1385	1.00	H8	Suffolk	Rudd list 21, no. 58
96.1661	0.87	A1	near Chelmsford, Essex	Rudd list 23, no. 45
99.0634	1.12	A1	Freckenham, Suffolk	Rudd list 45, no. 30
99.1372	0.76	-	-	Rudd list 48, no. 73
B2				
M -, V -, BMC -			**?TAS/-**	
01.1495	1.4	A1	Orsett, Essex	Although allegedly found at Orsett, Essex, this coin may actually originate from Springhead, Kent
B3				
M -, V -, BMC -			**?TAS/?VIR**	
82.0226	1.25	A1	'Roman site', Bedford, Beds.	Nat. Mus. of Wales
98.1025	1.25	B2	Compton, Berks.	*Tr. Hunting*, July 1998, p. 9
98.1142	1.23	-	Winterbourne, Berks.	-
98.1200	1.24	- 1	Winterbourne, Berks.	-
99.2013	1.2	- 1	Kent	-
B4				
M -, V -, BMC 1666			**TASC/VER**	
00.0308	1.2	C3	-	-
00.0814	-	C -	Titchmarsh, Northants	-
02.0749	1.26	B2	-	Rudd list 66, no. 69
03.0951	-	C3	near Huntingdon, Cambs.	-
90.0348	0.55	-	Harlow, Essex	plated; temple exc., Harlow Mus.
93.0923	1.17	C3	-	ex Mossop, lot 324, BMC 1666
94.0762	1.26	A1	nr. Watford, Herts.	Rudd list 11, no. 50
96.3301	1.05	D4	Ashwell, Herts.	plated; Rudd list 28, no. 158
96.3319	1.18	A1	near Cheshunt, Herts.	Rudd list 26, no. 68
98.1401	0.74	D4	Foxton, Cambs.	Rudd list 36, no. 41
99.0879	1.16	C3	-	Rudd list 46, no. 44
C1				
M161, V1699, BMC 1670-73			**VER/TASCIA**	
01.0148	1.35	D -	-	Rudd list 55, no. 154
01.1604	1.46	C1	Northants.	Rudd list 61, no. 62
02.0879	1.04	D2	-	Rudd, Liz's list 2, no.53
68.0205	1.40	C1	St. Albans, Herts.	BMC 1673
68.0206	1.37	B1	-	BMC 1671
68.0207	1.50	- 2	-	BMC 1672
68.0208	1.42	D2	-	BMC 1670
72.0066	1.52	C2	Baldock, Herts.	exc.
82.0220	1.47	E2	-	Rudd list 10, no. 49
82.0221	-	-	-	modern fake
84.0045	-	-	-	modern fake
93.0075	1.38	- 1	Oxfordshire	Rudd list 23, no. 73
94.0062	-	A1	-	Miller list 31, no. 3
94.0229	1.27	E3	-	*NCirc* April 1994, no. 2097
94.0708	1.33	A1	-	-
96.1338	-	-	-	*NCirc* Feb.'96, no.100, modern fake?

CCI	wt.	dies	provenance	comments
C1 (continued)				
99.0482	-	-	-	Sotheby's 22.4.99, lot 75, modern fake?
C2				
M162, V1747, BMC 1674-76			**VER/-**	
00.0880	1.22	E8	Sutton Courtenay, Oxon.	Rudd list 51, no. 62
00.1585	-	A1	-	-
01.0149	0.86	A3	St. Albans, Herts.	Rudd list 55, no.155
02.0468	1.14	C5	-	Rudd list 64, no.61
02.1135	1.00	- 7	St. Albans, Herts.	Rudd, Liz's list 3, no.53
03.0110	1.27	H10	-	Rudd list 68, no. 62
67.0098	1.49	-	-	Hunterian
67.0099	1.05	-	-	Hunterian
68.0209	1.30	A1	-	BMC 1675
68.0210	1.30	A1	-	BMC 1674
68.0211	0.75	D6	Dorchester, Oxon.	BMC 1676
73.0234	0.94	-	Kettering, Northants.	Kettering Mus., Midlands Syll. 17, 14
83.0304	1.14	I11	-	Symons 1993, no.10
87.0533	1.13	E7	Ditchingham, Norfolk	-
90.0521	1.87	A2	Harlow, Essex	temple exc., Harlow Museum
93.0906	1.05	- 3	-	ex Mossop, lot 297
94.1114	0.98	-	Nuneham Courtenay, Oxon.	-
94.1620	1.19	G9	-	-
97.1015	1.22	B4	St. Albans, Herts.	Rudd list 27, no. 96
98.1019	1.20	F9	-	Vosper list 99, no. 137
98.2334	-	A3	-	-
D1				
M164, V1796, BMC 1661-62			**VERL/TAS**	
00.1065	0.98	A2	-	Rudd list 52, no.62
01.0353	0.87	D5	St. Albans, Herts.	Rudd list 56, no.66
01.0497	1.34	A1	Cambridge, Cambs.	-
02.0628	1.34	E6	Puckeridge, Herts.	Rudd list 65, no.101
03.1468	1.31	D5	-	*NCirc* Dec. 2003, CC 0060
66.0105	1.20	-	-	Ashmolean
68.0214	1.32	A1	-	BMC 1661
68.0215	1.21	D5	-	BMC 1662
82.0222	1.46	B3	-	Symons 1990b, no.109
83.0382	1.24	E6	Puckeridge, Herts.	-
93.0908	1.53	B3	-	ex Mossop, lot 299
95.3740	1.16	A1	Compton, Berks.	Newbury District Museum
96.1668	0.85	A1	near St. Albans, Herts.	Rudd list 22, no. 58
96.1761	1.30	A2	Great Chesterford, Essex	Rudd list 27, no. 99
99.0024	1.3	C4	near St. Neots, Cambs.	-
D2				
M -, V -, BMC 1655			**VER(VIR)(VE)(VII)/?VER**	
01.1018	1.10	B3	-	Rudd list 58, no. 57
02.0627	1.21	A1	Springhead, Kent	Rudd list 65, no. 100
93.0904	1.25	B-	-	ex Mossop, lot 295/2, BMC 1655
93.1002	1.36	A1	Stonea, Cambs.	Birmingham Museum
94.0689	1.20	E6	Watford, Herts.	Rudd list 10, no. 53
94.0690	1.21	D5	Watford, Herts.	Rudd list 12, no. 44
94.0691	1.20	C4	Watford, Herts.	-
94.0706	1.16	B2	near Watford, Herts.	Rudd list 11, no. 48
94.0761	1.25	F6	near Watford, Herts.	-
94.0893	-	A1	Watford?	Cummings May 1994, E12
94.1180	1.19	E6	-	-
94.1234	-	-6	-	Cummings Sept. 1994, E5
94.1424	1.20	A1	-	-

CCI	wt.	dies	provenance	comments
D2 (continued)				
95.0462	1.19	G6	-	-
97.2308	1.29	D5	Foxton, Cambs.	Rudd list 30, no. 63
98.0151	1.33	A1	-	Vosper list 126, no.29
99.1814	-	-1	-	reverse only
D3				
M -, V -, BMC –			**TASC(I)/VER**	
00.0375	1.20	B5	near Dunstable, Beds.	-
00.1215	1.11	C6	St. Albans, Herts.	Rudd list 53, no. 79
00.1528	1.18	B5	-	Rudd list 54, no. 69
84.0254	1.26	B5	Watford, Herts.	shown to BM, Suppl. III, 38, new type
89.0016	1.24	B5	West Wycombe, Bucks.	Suppl. III, 36, new type
94.0692	1.05	C6	Watford, Herts.	Rudd list 10, no. 54
94.0970	1.31	B3	Watford, Herts.?	*NCirc* April 1994, no. 3988
94.0777	1.26	B2	near Watford, Herts.	Rudd list 11, no. 49
94.1184	1.27	B6	-	-
95.1163	1.27	A1	Dunstable, Beds.	-
95.1442	1.1	B5	-	Vosper list 85, no.102
99.0908	1.31	B4	Godmanchester, Cambs.	-
D4				
M165, V1798, BMC 1664-65			**TASC/-**	
00.0460	1.35	B2	Raunds, Northants.	-
00.1624	1.3	G4	-	Vosper list 115, no.14
00.1757	-	A1	-	-
00.1949	-	D2	North Hertfordshire	-
01.0914	-	I6	Puckeridge, Herts.	-
02.0498	-	C2	-	modern fake
02.0536	-	C2	-	modern fake?
02.1165	1.28	D2	Berkhamsted, Herts.	-
03.0889	1.29	L7	St. Albans, Herts.	Rudd list 73, no.56
68.0216	1.22	-1	-	BMC 1665
73.0236	1.34	-	Puckeridge, Herts.	ex Mossop, lot 300, BMC 1664
78.0023	1.22	I7	near Aylesbury, Bucks.	shown Ashmolean, Suppl. II, 129
94.0764	1.24	K7	near Watford, Herts.	Rudd list 11, no.47
95.0576	1.14	E2	near Berkhamsted, Herts	Rudd list 21, no.59
95.1073	-	H5	-	Cummings May 1995, E9
98.0152	1.23	F3	-	-
98.0388	1.27	H5	Higham, Kent?	-
98.1400	1.24	D2	Foxton, Cambs.	Rudd list 36, no.40
99.0484	1.22	J7	-	Sotheby's 22.4.1999, lot 78
99.0735	1.3	D2	-	Vosper list 106, no.17

02.0498 and 02.0536 are virtually identical, both appearing round about the same time. The former is a modern fake of what appears to be an authentic but unrecorded coin and the same is almost certainly true for the latter. I have therefore identified the obverse die (C), although the existence of a genuine specimen has yet to be established.

CCI	wt.	dies	provenance	comments
D5				
M166, V1800, BMC 1677-80			**TASC/-**	
00.0044	1.24	A1	Bourne End, Herts.	Rudd list 49, no. 44
00.0374	1.2	I10	Cambs./Herts. border	-
00.0892	-	D5	Wendover, Bucks.	-
00.1154	-	I9	Syresham, Northants.	-
00.1831	1.3	F7	Bourne End, Herts.	-
01.0150	1.28	H7	-	Rudd list 55, no. 156
01.0379	-	E4	-	-
01.0775	-	E4	Warwickshire	*The Searcher*, March 2001, p.15
01.1134	1.22	H7	St. Albans, Herts.	Rudd list 59, no. 63
01.1605	1.07	J11	Bourne End, Herts.	Rudd list 61, no. 63

CCI	wt.	dies	provenance	comments
D5 (continued)				
02.0629	1.33	H8	-	Rudd list 65, no. 102
02.0783	1.08	E6	Harston, Cambs.	-
02.0895	-	C1	Weston Turville, Bucks.	-
03.0262	1.31	F7	Wingham, Kent	Rudd list 69, no.49
03.0375	1.23	J-	Bourne End, Herts.	Rudd list 51, no.96
03.0690	-	-	Wilden, Beds.	plated
03.0995	1.2	C3	Darenth, Kent	-
66.0106	1.09	C3	-	Ashmolean
67.0101	1.51	B2	-	Hunterian
68.0217	1.62	-	Biggleswade?, Beds.	plated, BMC 1680
68.0218	1.58	B2	-	BMC 1678
68.0219	1.18	A2	-	BMC 1677
68.0220	1.16	C3	nr. Biggleswade, Beds.	BMC 1679
68.0221	1.14	-	Iver, Bucks.	BM cast
73.0237	1.28	G7	-	Fitzwilliam
73.0238	1.26	D3	Puckeridge, Herts.	ex Mossop, lot 301
73.0240	1.26	D4	Weekley, Northants.	Kettering Museum
81.0058	1.19	K12	Chatteris, Cambs.	Chatteris Museum?
91.0050	1.32	E4	Evenley, Northants.	-
91.0051	1.00	-	Evenley, Northants.	-
93.0365	1.2	I-	Buckinghamshire	*The Searcher*, June 1993, p.26
94.0359	1.21	-	Minster in Thanet, Kent	-
94.0693	1.14	F7	Watford, Herts.	Rudd list 10, no.52
94.1509	1.30	H7	-	Rudd list 13, no.58
95.0910	1.22	F7	Chevening, Kent	Rudd list 28, no.159
95.2618	1.15	I-	-	*NCirc* July 1995, no.4078
96.2897	1.2	E6	-	*The Searcher*, Sept.1996, p.25
97.0029	1.3	G7	-	Vosper list 94, no.95
97.2307	1.21	I10	nr. Watford, Herts.	Rudd list 30, no.62
98.0400	1.10	I9	Berkhamsted, Herts.	-
98.0497	1.31	F7	-	Rudd list 31, no.59
99.0653	-	H8	Buckinghamshire -	
99.0758	-	A1	-	*NCirc* May 1999, no.2014
E1				
M163, V1794, BMC 1681-82			**TASCIA/-(TASCI)**	
00.0459	1.30	F6	Raunds, Northants.	-
01.0220	1.21	E5	Brentwood, Essex	-
02.0320	1.12	B2	Amersham, Bucks.	Rudd list 63, no.66
66.0104	1.20	B3	-	Ashmolean
67.0100	1.12	G7	-	Hunterian
68.0212	1.18	A1	-	BMC 1681
68.0213	1.29	B3	-	BMC 1682
90.0268	1.32	D4	Harlow, Essex	temple exc., Harlow Museum
95.1270	-	B1	near Buckingham, Bucks.	-
96.3300	1.21	H8	Ashwell, Herts.	Rudd list 25, no.47
97.0162	1.25	C4	Witney, Oxon.	Rudd list 27, no.98
99.0313	1.4	F6	-	Vosper list 105, no.24
99.0483	1.25	A1	-	Sotheby's 22.4.1999, lot 77
99.1287	-	-	Bedfordshire?	reverse only, *Treasure Hunting*, Sept. 1999, p. 24
E2				
M160, V1792, BMC 1658-59			**TASCIO/-**	
00.0307	1.3	B1	-	-
02.0103	1.07	A1	Baylham, Suffolk	Rudd list 62, no.63
03.0060	-	-	St. Albans, Herts.	-
03.1413	-	D2	-	*The Searcher*, Oct. 2003, p.13
66.0103	1.31	C2	-	Ashmolean
68.0203	0.92	E5	Wallingford, Berks.	BMC 1659

CCI	wt.	dies	provenance	comments
E2 (continued)				
68.0204	1.15	E5	-	BMC 1658
88.0111	1.28	A1	-	Symons 1990a, no.48
94.0779	1.22	A1	near Watford, Herts.	Rudd list 11, no. 46
94.0985	1.3	D4	Tring, Herts.	Vosper list 92, no.114
95.0651	1.19	F5	-	BDW 21.3.1995, lot 451
95.3162	-	-	-	*Treasure Hunting*, Oct. 1995, p.39
96.3278	0.94	F5	-	Rudd list 24, no.135
97.1221	1.19	F5	-	-
99.0657	1.35	C3	Aston Clinton, Bucks.	-
-	-	B2	-	V1792 plate coin
E3				
M159, V1790, BMC 1660			**-/TAS**	
00.0827	1.29	C3	Stonea, Cambs.	-
02.0370	1.28	G4	Uffington, Oxon.	-
03.1361	-	E4	-	*Tr. Hunting*, August 2003, p.62
68.0202	1.31	D4	-	BMC 1660
82.0219	1.26	B2	-	Sotheby's 22.4.1999, lot 76
93.0907	1.26	F4	-	ex Mossop, lot 298
94.0026	1.24	E4	nr. Hemel Hempstead, Herts.	-
95.1269	-	H6	Whitchurch, Bucks.	found "on Roman site"
96.2382	1.03	G5	-	Rudd list 26, no.69
98.0153	1.26	A2	-	-
99.0268	-	H-	Sion Reach, in the Thames	Seaby CAMB, Aug. 1976, 326, E77
99.1598	1.24	A1	Bedfordshire	-
-	-	-	Lexden, Colchester, Essex	Stukeley 1762, XX, 8, Suppl. I, 60, probably identical with BMC 1660
F1				
M196, V1851, BMC 1684			**SEGO(SECO)/-**	
01.1887	1.2	B2	Woodnesborough, Kent	-
68.0223	1.21	B3	-	BMC 1684
87.0502	1.29	A1	Isle of Thanet, Kent	-
94.0310	0.87	B3	Worth, Kent	-
98.0148	1.25	B2	-	-
99.0025	1.3	B3	Thurnham, Kent	-
99.1373	1.01	B2	-	Rudd list 48, no.74
G1				
M188, V1877, BMC 1683			**DIAS CO/VIR(?VER)**	
00.1882	-	C4	north of Lincoln, Lincs.	-
01.0153	1.10	B3	-	Rudd list 55, no.163
01.1136	1.20	B2	Great Chesterford, Essex	Rudd list 59, no.65
03.0112	1.17	A1	-	Rudd list 68, no.64
03.0417	1.17	B2	St. Albans, Herts	Rudd list 70, no.66
03.0530	1.11	C4	-	Rudd list 71, no.61
03.0673	1.24	B2	Harston, Cambs.	-
68.0222	1.13	B2	Harlow, Essex	BMC 1683
73.0241	1.25	A1	-	Fitzwilliam
79.0014	1.12	B2	near St. Albans, Herts.	Nat. Mus. of Wales
84.0795	1.2	C4	Southoe, Cambs.	-
93.0981	1.26	C4	-	*NCirc* Sept. 1994, no.5600
94.0894	0.90	A1	-	Rudd list 12, no.45
94.1232	-	E5	-	Cummings Sept. 1994, E2
94.1460	1.29	A1	Watford, Herts.	Rudd list 14, no.23
95.1443	1.2	E5	-	Vosper list 85, no.103
95.2924	-	D5	Wappenham, Northants.	Vosper list 126, no.35
96.2691	1.22	E5	-	Rudd list 23, no.75
97.0204	-	D5	-	Rudd list 26, no.92

CCI	wt.	dies	provenance	comments
G1 (continued)				
98.2079	-	C4	-	*NCirc* Sept. 1998, no.5514
G2				
M -, V -, BMC 1663			**- /TASCIO DIAS(S)(V)**	
00.0001	-	-	-	-
00.0813	-	-	Titchmarsh, Northants.	-
00.1607	1.3	-1	-	Vosper list 114, no.6
03.0291	0.80	-	Bourne End, Herts.	fragment
03.0890	1.03	F5	Bourne End, Herts.	Rudd list 73, no.59
74.0148	1.28	A1	Tring, Herts.	exc., Berkhamsted & Dist. Arch. Soc.
83.0200	1.23	D3	St. Albans, Herts.	Nat. Mus. of Wales
93.0551	1.37	E4	Baldock, Herts.	exc., Letchworth Museum
93.0702	1.01	-	near Dunstable, Beds.	-
93.0909	1.31	D3	-	ex Mossop, lot 302
94.0075	1.26	B2	-	CNR 1994/1, no.374
94.0688	1.23	D3	Watford, Herts.	Rudd list 10, no.55
94.0734	1.22	C2	Watford, Herts.	-
95.1053	1.08	A1	-	Rudd list 17, no.24
96.1037	0.76	-	Paulerspury, Northants.	AE core?
96.1099	1.20	D3	Berkhamsted, Herts.	Vosper list 88, no.99
96.1783	1.3	C2	-	-
96.2671	1.20	B1	-	Rudd list 23, no.46
97.1645	-	-3	-	*NCirc* Oct. 1997, no.4916
98.1327	-	D3	Linton, Cambs.	-
98.2021	1.18	D3	-	Rudd list 38, no.101
98.2372	1.35	D3	-	CNG 45, 18.3.1998, lot 2730
99.0937	1.32	B2	-	Vecchi, 8.10.1986, lot 21
99.1813	-	-	-	obverse only
uncertain type				
68.0549	-	-	Colchester, Essex	*Origins*, 228, *Camulodunum* 15 as Cunobelin; BMC 1669 as Tasciovanus (sic), but probably neither

Bibliography

Allen, D. F. 1944: The Belgic dynasties of Britain and their coins. *Archaeologia* 90, 1-46.

Allen, D.F. 1960: The origins of coinage in Britain: a reappraisal. In S. S. Frere (ed.), *Problems of the Iron Age in Southern Britain*, (London, Institute of Archaeology Occasional Paper 11), 97-308.

Allen, D. F. 1964: Celtic coins from the Romano-British temple at Harlow, Essex. *British Numismatic Journal* 33, 1-6.

Allen, D. F. 1967: Celtic coins from the Romano-British temple at Harlow, part II. *British Numismatic Journal* 36, 1-7.

Allen, D. F. 1975: Cunobelin's gold. *Britannia 6*, 1-19.

Allen, D. F. (ed. D. Nash) 1980: *The coins of the ancient Celts* (Edinburgh, EUP).

Birch, S. 1845: New proposed reading of certain coins of Cunobelin. *Numismatic Chronicle* 7, 78-84.

Colbert de Beaulieu, J.-B. and Fischer, B. 1998: *Recueil des Inscriptions Gauloises IV, Les légendes monétaires* (Paris, CNRS, *Gallia* suppl. 45).

Crawford, M. H. 1976: *Roman Republican Coinage* (Cambridge, CUP).

de Jersey, P. 2001: Cunobelin's silver. *Britannia* 32, 1-44.

de Jersey, P. 2004: A new Celtic inscription? *Chris Rudd List* 75, 6-7.

Delamarre, X. 2001: *Dictionnaire de la langue gauloise* (Paris, Errance).

de la Tour, H., 1892: *Atlas de Monnaies Gauloises* (Paris).

Evans, D. E. 1967: *Gaulish Personal Names* (Oxford, OUP).

Evans, J. 1864: *The Coins of the Ancient Britons* (London).

Evans, J. 1890: *The Coins of the Ancient Britons. Supplement* (London).

Haselgrove, C. 1978: *Supplementary Gazetteer of Find-spots of Celtic Coins in Britain, 1977* (London, Institute of Archaeology Occasional Paper 11a).

Haselgrove, C. 1984: Celtic coins found in Britain 1977-82. *Bulletin of the Institute of Archaeology, University of London* 20, 107-54.

Haselgrove, C. 1987: *Iron Age coinage in south-east England: the archaeological context* (Oxford, BAR 174).

Haselgrove, C. 1989: Celtic coins found in Britain 1982-1987. *Bulletin of the Institute of Archaeology, University of London* 26, 1-75.

Henig, M. 1972: The origin of some ancient British coin types. *Britannia* 3, 209-23.

Hobbs, R. 1996: *British Iron Age Coins in the British Museum* (London, BMP).

Holman, D. J. 1999: Sego and Duno: reassessment and reinterpretation. *British Numismatic Journal* 69, 196-98.

Kretz, R. 1998: The early gold staters of Tasciovanus - a reappraisal of the first series. *Spink Numismatic Circular* 106, 2-7.

Kretz, R. 2000: The 'RICON' staters of Tasciovanos. *Spink Numismatic Circular* 108, 97-102.

Kretz, R. 2001a: The quarter staters of Tasciovanos. *Spink Numismatic Circular* 109, 6-10.

Kretz, R. 2001b: Tasciovanos' second coinage staters - a first classification. *Spink Numismatic Circular* 109, 234-43.

Kretz, R. 2002: The problem of Andoco... *Spink Numismatic Circular* 110, 267-71.

Mack, R. P. 1953 (1st ed.): *The Coinage of Ancient Britain* (London).

Mack, R. P. 1975 (3rd ed.): *The Coinage of Ancient Britain* (London).

Muckelroy, K., Haselgrove, C. and Nash, D. 1978: A Pre-Roman Coin from Canterbury and the Ship represented on it. *Proceedings of the Prehistoric Society* 44, 439-444.

Northover, P. 1992: Materials issues in the Celtic coinage. In M. Mays (ed.), *Celtic Coinage: Britain and Beyond* (Oxford, BAR 222), 235-99.

Pegge, S. 1766: *An Essay on the Coins of Cunobelin* (London).

Pettingal, J. 1763: *A Dissertation upon the Tascia, or Legend, on the British Coins of Cunobelin and Others* (London).

Rivet, A. L. F. and Smith, C. 1979: *The Place-Names of Roman Britain* (London, Batsford).

Rodwell, W. 1976: Coinage, oppida, and the rise of Belgic power in south-eastern Britain. In B. W. Cunliffe and R. T. Rowley (eds), *Oppida in Barbarian Europe* (Oxford, BAR S11), 181-366.

Scheers, S. 1975: *Les monnaies gauloises de la collection A. Danicourt à Peronne* (Bruxelles, Cercle d'Etudes Numismatiques Travaux 7).

Scheers, S. 1982: Les imitations celtiques des monnaies romaines en Angleterre et leur signification historique. In T. Hackens and R. Weiller (eds), *Actes du 9e Congrès International de Numismatique* (Louvain and Luxembourg), 619-23.

Scheers, S. 1992: Celtic coin types in Britain and their Mediterranean origins. In M. Mays (ed.), *Celtic Coinage: Britain and Beyond* (Oxford, BAR 222), 33-46.

Schmidt, K. H. 1957: Die Komposition im gallischen Personennamen. *Zeitschrift für celtische Philologie* 26, 33-301.

Sutherland, C. H. V. and Carson, R. A. G. 1984 (revised ed.): *The Roman Imperial Coinage Vol. I* (London).

Symons, D. 1990a: Celtic coinage of Britain: some amendments and additions. *Spink Numismatic Circular* 98, 48-50.

Symons, D. 1990b: Further Celtic coins from the Finney collection. *Spink Numismatic Circular* 98, 268-72.

Symons, D. 1992: British Celtic coins added to the Finney collection, 1991. *Spink Numismatic Circular* 100, 226-27.

Symons, D. 1993: The Finney collection – British Celtic acquisitions, 1992. *Spink Numismatic Circular* 101, 188-89.

Van Arsdell, R. D. 1989: *Celtic Coinage of Britain* (London, Spink).

Wheeler, R. E. M. and Wheeler, T. V. 1936: *Verulamium – A Belgic and two Roman Cities* (Oxford).

Williams, J. H. C. 2002: Pottery stamps, coin designs, and writing in late Iron Age Britain. In A. E. Cooley (ed.), *Becoming Roman, writing Latin? Literacy and epigraphy in the Roman West* (Journal of Roman Archaeology Supplement 48, Portsmouth, Rhode Island), 135-149.

Williams, J. H. C. and Hobbs, R. 2003: Coin hoards and ritual in Iron Age Leicestershire. *Minerva*, July/August 2003, 55-56.

The Iceni early face/horse series

John Talbot

Introduction

Some time ago Philip de Jersey suggested to me that the dramatic increase in material discovered in recent years, as a result of the boom in metal-detecting, meant that much could be gained from a detailed study of the Iceni early face/horse coinage (EFH). The Iron Age silver units of East Anglia have long been separated into three streams dependent upon whether the type of obverse design is a pattern, a face or a boar. In each case the reverse of the coin is a horse. Various writers have speculated about the interpretation of these streams: whether they represent a sequential continuum, or the differing product of separate groups, mints or even *pagi* within East Anglia. Recent thinking has been more towards a continuum and Philip felt that it might be possible to help clarify this, as well as to understand the relationships between the EFH coins themselves.

I took up this challenge four years ago, but it soon became apparent that it would be hard to draw conclusions about this group of coins without looking at their context in terms of the other early Iron Age coinage being used in East Anglia at the time. The project has therefore been expanded to include die studies of all of the coinage of the region; this is a long process and is still ongoing. In addition to putting the face horse series into context, familiarity with the other dies has on occasion helped to provide other linkages: one of the more satisfying of these was finding a face/horse unit (Irstead A type) whose reverse had been struck from a quarter stater die, a first for British Celtic coinage; this is discussed in more detail below. As there are still some years of work ahead of me, this paper represents a progress report, focusing upon my work to date on the early face/horse silver series.

Important studies of East Anglian coinage have been published by Derek Allen (1970) and Tony Gregory (1992), and Amanda Chadburn has published some illuminating insights based upon her studies of the major Icenian coin hoards (Chadburn 1990; 1992; Chadburn and Gurney 1991), although the main body of her work is as yet unpublished. This published work and Richard Hobbs's catalogue of the British Museum collection (1996), have been extremely valuable aids to this study, but the key resource has been the Celtic Coin Index (CCI) and the vast knowledge of its custodian Dr Philip de Jersey.

Methodology

i) A die analysis of all CCI records for EFH coins as well as other Iceni coinage.
ii) Review key collections to verify difficult dies and to add new records. Collections examined include those of the British Museum, Kings Lynn Museum, the Fitzwilliam Museum and Norwich Museum, as well as a number of important private collections.
iii) Obtain the assistance of dealers to locate coins and to help with provenances. Much help has been provided by Chris Rudd and Mike Vosper.
iv) Develop a data base which contains a detailed record of each coin and is capable of producing distribution maps, weight and other statistics for groups of coins including die groups within a type.
v) Metallurgical analysis of the key types will be undertaken by Megan Dennis as part of her researches into Iron Age silver usage in East Anglia.

During the die study a collection of images has been built up and examples of these are included in this paper to illustrate the various dies. In certain cases photographic images have been pieced together using a computer graphics program to provide a fuller picture of the die. The coins are illustrated at approximately twice actual size, but because of the variety of sources used the resulting images are not precisely to scale. They can nonetheless be used to identify the dies on most coins which are in reasonable condition. Examples of coins struck from the forged dies used to produce plated coins are shown on Figure 31.

Terminology and concordance

In the course of this article I refer to "types" of coin within the East Anglian series. For the purposes of this paper I define a type as a group of coins of the same denomination which have distinctive obverse and reverse designs. Within a type there may be differing designs on, say, the obverse, as long as these are used interchangeably with a common design or designs on the reverse. With rare exceptions individual dies are specific to a type. Separate die-linked groups within a type are referred to as subtypes if they can be separated on grounds of style, distribution or weight.

The attribution of a tribal designation to the Iron Age East Anglian coinage is speculative, and my work across the whole series has pointed to some very specific links between certain coins thought to be Icenian and the issues thought to be Trinovantian. There are also stylistic links between certain East Anglian coins and issues of the Corieltauvi. Nonetheless in accordance with common usage the term Iceni has been used freely in this paper to describe the coins specific to East Anglia.

Certain of the EFH units have been grouped together either as Bury Units or Large Flan Units. These groupings are explained within the text; they are composed of types which are closely related, although there may still be chronological or geographic separation between them.

In the paper I will refer on many occasions to die linkages. If two coins are struck from different obverse dies, but share a common reverse die, then the obverse dies can be said to be die-linked. I also refer to unlinked pairs of dies, by which I mean an obverse die and a reverse die, that have only been recorded so far from examples where they were used to strike coins in conjunction with each other.

Talbot	Gregory	VA	BMC
Bury group			
Bury A	Bury A	80-1	3524 - 3527
Bury C	Bury C	-	3528 - 3532
Bury B	Bury B	-	3533 - 3535
Bury D	-	-	-
Bury E	-	-	-
Large Flan group			
LFA	FHA		3548 - 3549
LFB	FHCc	-	-
LFC	FHCc	-	3550 - 3551
Snettisham group			
Snettisham unit	FHCa	665-7 & 665-9	3541 - 3544
Irstead A	FHCb	665-3	3538 - 3539
Irstead B	new and FHA	665-1	3536, 3537, 3547
Face/horse B group			
Saham Toney unit	FHB and FHCd	665-5	3540, 3552 - 3555

Table 1. Concordance of types.

Many of the Icenian coins form denominational groups. Within the EFH series there is a type which forms such a group with the Snettisham stater and quarter stater, as does a further type with the Irstead quarter stater and one of the Freckenham staters. I refer to these types in this paper as the Snettisham and Irstead units respectively, in order to maintain an existing well-known name, although in neither case are these likely to be accurate indications of where the coins were struck.

This paper is primarily concerned with the twelve EFH types which are listed in Table 1, with a concordance to other reference works.

Some statistical information on each of the EFH types and a number of other East Anglian types is shown in Appendix 1. This information includes the number of coins known, the number of dies used and the weight range excluding the upper 5% and the lower 30% of available records. The table identifies what appear to be the most important EFH issues which, based on the number of dies used, are Bury B, LFA, LFC and the Snettisham unit. However if the number of surviving coins is the key criterion then the most important would be the commonly-found Bury A.

General observations

Many specific observations are included in the detailed summary of each type, presented below, but some more general observations based upon the work to date are as follows:

- Denominational groups are common and, with few exceptions, these are identified by stylistic similarities on the reverse die, the obverses having denominational variation.
- The die studies show a consistency of design within a particular type and even more so within die-linked groups of coins. Certain symbols appear to have had particular importance and provide a link between different types. An example of this is the hollow star used in Bury B and LFA (see Figures 15-16 and 21). This symbol supersedes a diamond shaped device on LFA, indicating that Bury B probably post-dates LFA.
- The form and style of the ubiquitous horse and in particular its head appear to be an important design element in Icenian coinage as a whole, and may be as important in establishing linkages and in ordering the coinage as is whether the obverse of a silver unit is a boar, face or pattern. The two main horse head types are a realistic head which appears to develop into a keyhole shape, and a very distinctive Y-shaped head, which itself has two forms. The two main types continue into the inscribed series. There are also a facing head and a "spoon" shaped head, the latter being associated with, and die-linked to, the keyhole form. Most of the EFH coins fit within the pattern of development of the realistic head with the clear exception of the Saham Toney unit. It is notable that the later normal face/horse group (VA790 – 794) belongs to the Y headed group.

Hoard evidence

The EFH coins are rare in the major recorded "late" Iceni coin hoards; a summary of five of the best recorded hoards is shown in Appendix 2. These include only four EFH coins, consisting of two Irstead units, one Snettisham unit and one Saham Toney unit. There is a modest increase if two very old hoards are included, for which full records are not available:

- Wimblington (pre-1906) – one Irstead A unit, one late Snettisham unit and possibly one other, in circa 300 coins (Allen 1970, 21).
- March (pre-1839) – one Irstead B unit in c. 40 coins (Allen 1970, 21).

The predominantly gold hoard excavated at Snettisham between 1988 and 1991 comprised 47 left facing Norfolk Wolf staters (British JB), 30 Snettisham staters, 14 Snettisham quarter staters, including one of a rare subtype, and three Snettisham units (Hobbs 1996, 39).

At least two major hoards have been found in the Snettisham area in recent years which have not been properly recorded. The most famous of these is the so-called "Bowl Hoard" in which a vast assemblage of Iceni coinage was found together with material from neighbouring tribes allegedly in a silver bowl. The find caused a flood of Iceni material onto the coin market and many coins which were hitherto great rarities were seen regularly, such as Cani Duro silver units and the inscribed staters. The hoard included many EFH units including at least 53 LFC (many of which are plated), two LFA, one LFB and an Irstead unit. This however may be a considerable underestimate as it is based upon the records kept by one collector who was offered material from the hoard.

The second hoard from Snettisham allegedly contained a Bury A unit which was found with two plated LFA units, two LFC units, 50 British JB staters and six Corieltauvian coins.

Considerable quantities of silver units have also been recovered from a site in West Norfolk, including many EFH and early boar/horse units. This material is considered by John Davies (pers. comm.) to be more likely to be an assemblage from a votive site, rather than a hoard. The coins are also included in Appendix 2, and the contrast with the late hoards is apparent.

With the above exceptions, Bury coins are absent from the major well-recorded East Anglian coin hoards, but have been recorded from two Bury-specific hoards:

- Barham - two Bury A, five Bury C and a North Thames quarter stater (VA 260) (de Jersey and Newman 1997).
- Nettlestead - four Bury A and one Bury C (British Museum collection).

This summary illustrates the rarity of EFH coinage in hoards, other than the Bowl Hoard, but certain observations can be made:

- Based upon its occasional presence in the late Iceni hoards, it appears likely that the Irstead unit occurs late in the EFH group.
- Bury coins are rarely found in hoards with other coinage, but Large Flan units have been found in association with JB staters, and Snettisham units have been found with Snettisham staters and quarters and JB staters.

Weight variation and chronology

It appears likely that the relatively naturalistic Bury A is one of the earliest of the EFH group, and placing Irstead late in the series indicates that there was perhaps a gradually declining standard weight for the units over the period of their issue, and the emergence of new types can be linked to these changes. Key weight statistics are shown in Table 2.

Type	Range	Midpoint	Standard
Bury A	1.31 - 1.5	1.40	1.5
Bury B	1.2 - 1.45	1.32	1.45
LF group	1.2 - 1.42	1.31	1.4
Snett. group	1.02 - 1.3	1.14	1.3
Saham Toney	0.79 - 1.13	0.96	1.15

Table 2. Weights of EFH coins.

The standard weight is somewhat subjective and is a slightly rounded value for the top weight, excluding the heaviest 5%.

Distribution

Maps of the non-hoard distribution of the main EFH types are shown in Figures 1-9. In order to give context maps are also included for non-hoard finds of normal face/horse, Ece A and the inscribed Anted series (Figures 10-12). The following general observations can be made:

i) Bury A has a wide distribution (Figure 1), with a major focus around the upper reaches of the Yare valley, west of Norwich. Distribution in west and north Norfolk is very low but a significant number of coins have been found in central Suffolk. The distribution in Suffolk is not unique (see Anted, Figure 12), except when combined with the absences to the north, which gives a southerly bias to the distribution. The distribution of Bury B is similar (Figure 2), but is a little more dispersed into western Norfolk, and without the strong distribution in Suffolk.

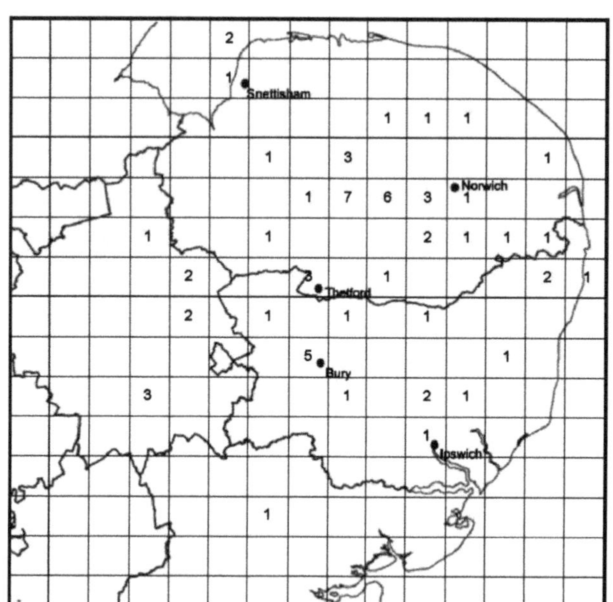

Figure 1. Distribution of Bury A.

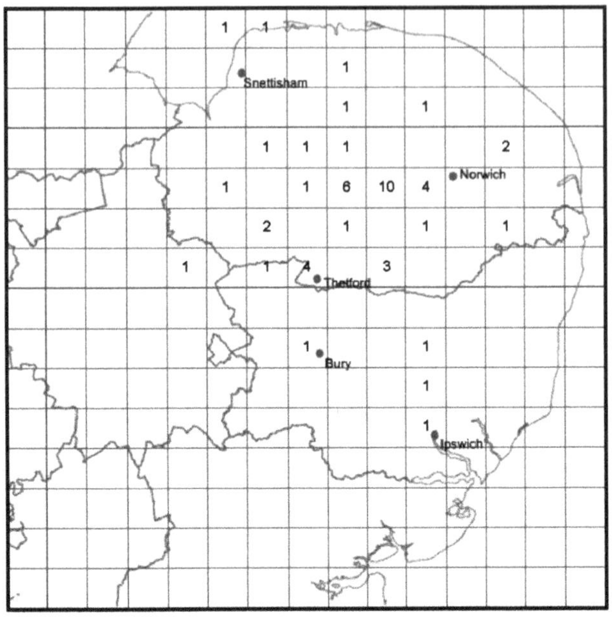

Figure 2. Distribution of Bury B.

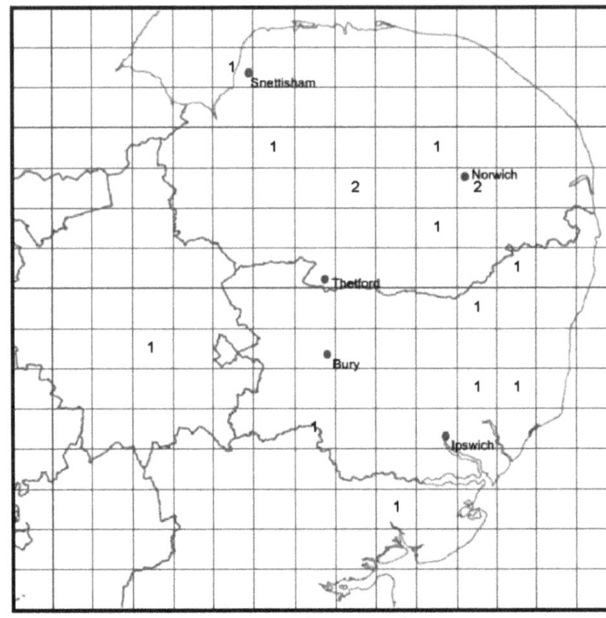

Figure 3. Distribution of Bury C.

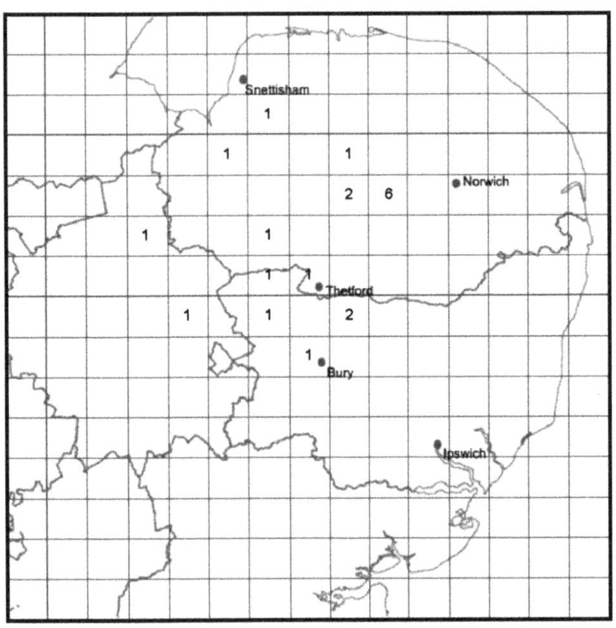

Figure 4. Distribution of LFC.

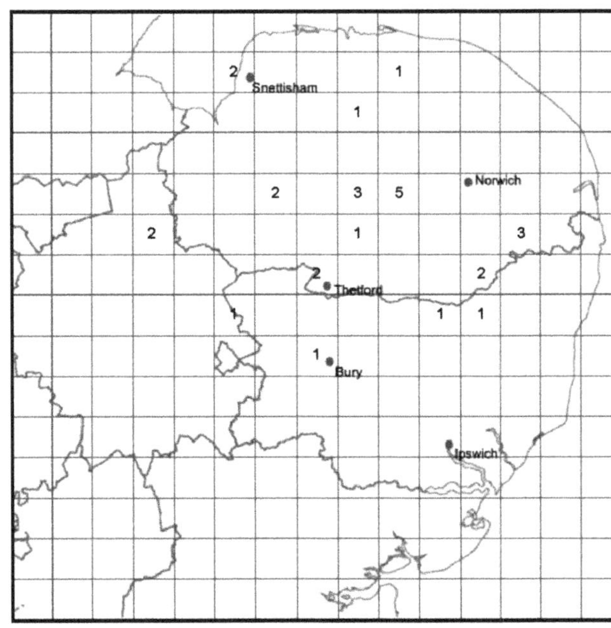

Figure 5. Distribution of LFA.

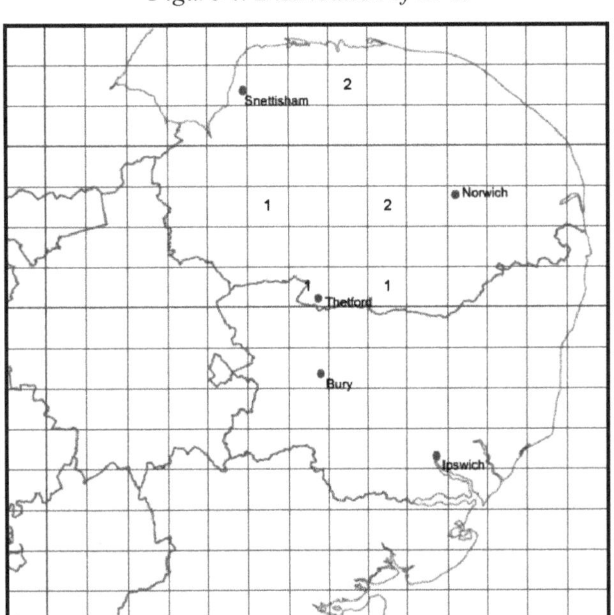

(left) Figure 6. Distribution of LFB.

ii) Bury C has a distribution biased towards eastern Norfolk, but in very low numbers (Figure 3). There is a small group of provenances around Ipswich, but this is largely a distinct die group and may be a separate type.

iii) LFC has a westerly distribution, possibly with Breckland origins (Figure 4). LFA has a strong distribution in the Waveney valley, particularly for the earliest dies, and also a central Norfolk distribution (Figure 5). LFB is very uncommon but the few recorded provenances come from central and north central Norfolk (Figure 6).

iv) Snettisham units appear to be focused on the upper Yare valley and northwest Norfolk (Figure 7), but the Snettisham quarters do not neatly overlap with the units, which though having a strong focus on the Yare valley also focus on the Breckland. Numbers for the Irstead types (Figure 8) are low but indications are that these are western issues.

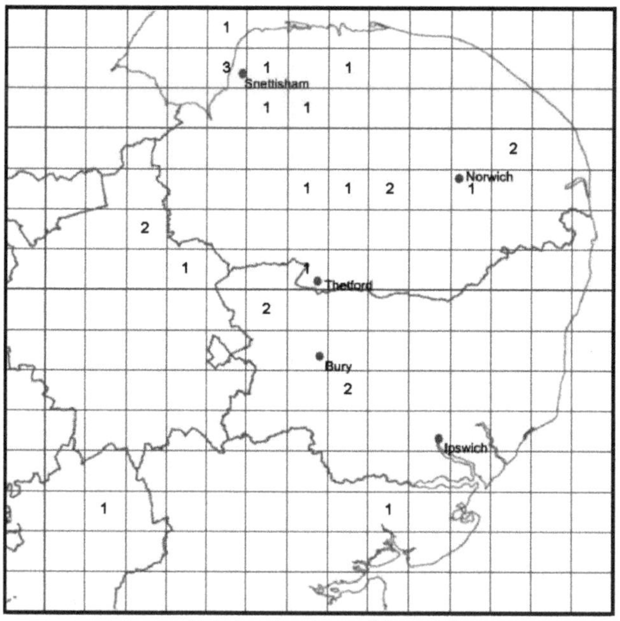

Figure 7. Distribution of Snettisham units.

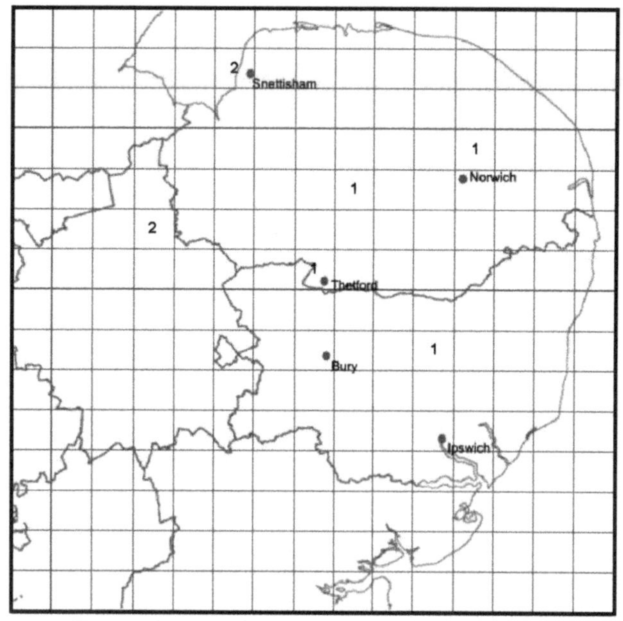

Figure 8. Distribution of Irstead A types.

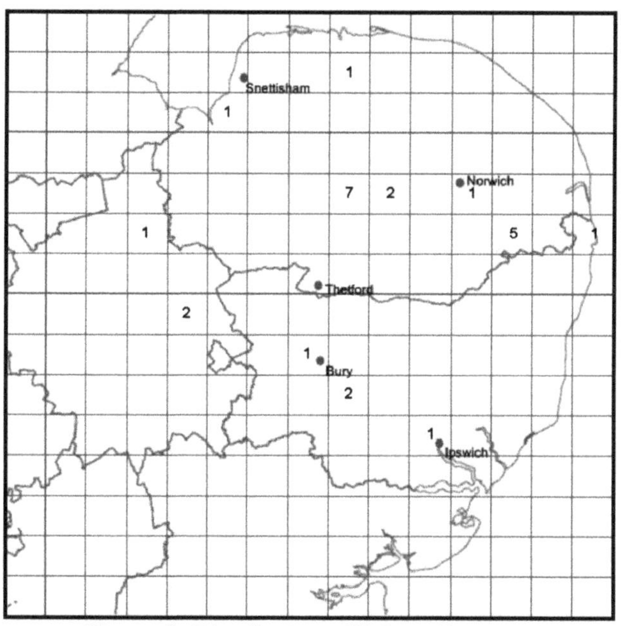

Figure 9. Distribution of Saham Toney units.

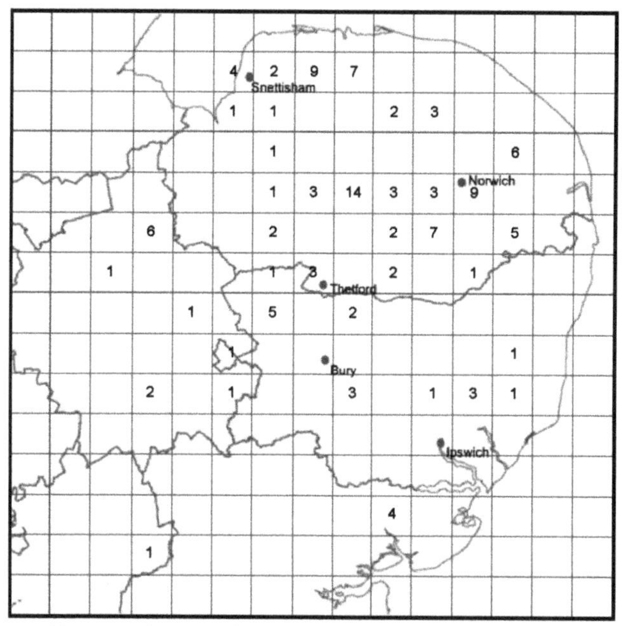

Figure 10. Distribution of normal face/horse units.

Detailed comments on the various EFH types

More detailed notes on my work in progress for each type within the EFH series are set out below. These notes should be read in conjunction with the reconstructed die images shown in the accompanying figures. Included in the notes are various tables showing the die groups within a type: where the tables have numbers in brackets, these refer to hubbed dies used on plated coins, where the original die is included elsewhere in the table.

The Bury group

The five types grouped under this heading include the EFH coins with the most realistic form of representation. They appear likely to be the earliest of the EFH group. Their name derives from the first examples being found in the Bury St Edmunds area. They are now known to have circulated much more widely, but the name has been retained as it is in common usage.

Bury A (Figure 13)

These are dished silver units on large flans, often found in excellent condition. The silver appears to be very pure, but no analyses are yet available.

The realistic diademed head faces left, with a two headed "serpent" forming a reversed S before the face. The hair is in distinctive ringlets. The realistic horse faces left, with a mane made up of small S shaped devices which also form a cross to the left of the horse. There is a large pellet below the horse and a pellet ring with pellet above, partly encircled by four or five smaller pellets or rings. Some dies have a small additional ring just above the back.

The obverse has stylistic linkages to the Selsey quarter staters (VA 78) and to the obverses of certain Ambiani silver units (eg DT 351).

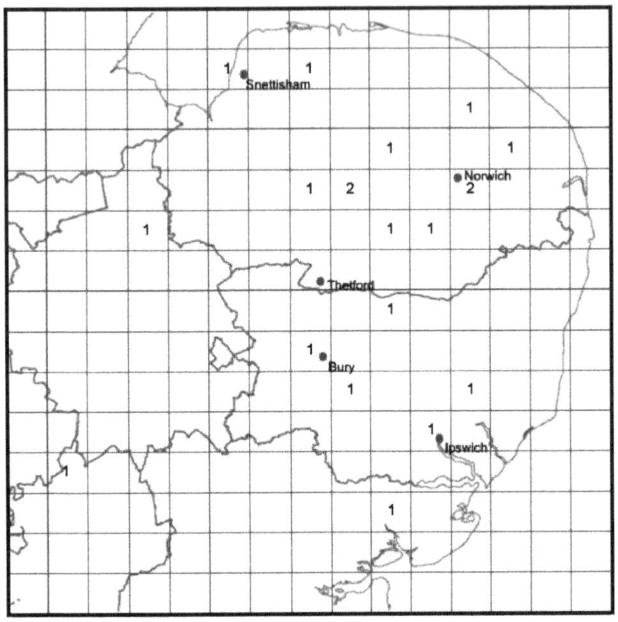

Figure 11. Distribution of Ece A units.

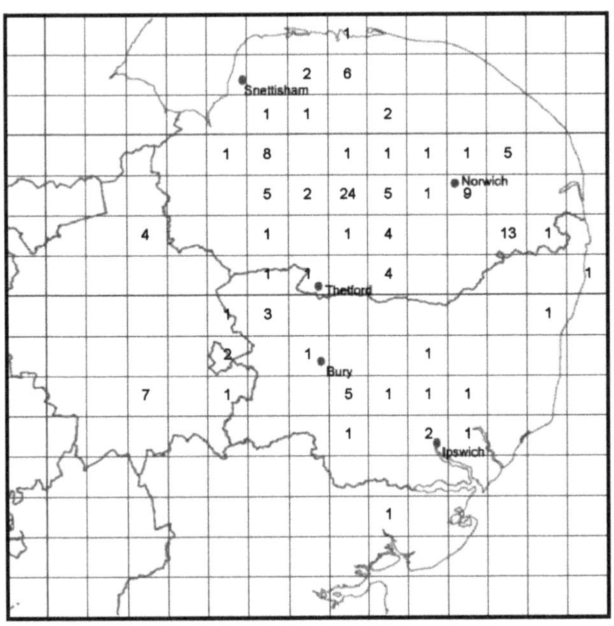

Figure 12. Distribution of Anted units.

There are two die groups:

1. Obverse A and two reverse dies (1 and 2). There is only one example of reverse die 2, a coin which shows some signs of obverse die re-cutting. Sixteen of the coins fall into this group.

2. Five obverse (B – F) and six reverse dies (3 – 8) with considerable cross-linking between the dies. Unusually, reverse die 3 links to all obverse dies in the group. There is no apparent variation from group 1, except for the obverse where the head is on a slightly larger scale. The dies do not show a neat time progression, and it appears likely that at least two reverse dies were in use at any one time. One hundred and four of the 128 known non-plated coins fall into this group. The group contains reverse dies with and without a ring above the horse, but there is no discernable significance to this variation.

In addition, there are nine coins from three unlinked pairs of dies. Two of these pairs appear very similar to dies in group 2 (H/10 and J/11); the third (G/9) has an obverse similar to die F but the reverse is a very energetic horse reminiscent of certain Bury C dies. There is only one recorded find spot, near Ipswich. It is possible that these coins are plated although none are recorded as such, and I have only been able to examine photographs.

There does not appear to be any significant weight variation between the die groups. Bury A is the heaviest and, excluding plated coins, is the commonest of all EFH types. There are 128 recorded coins and new examples are regularly seen with dealers. All known coins come from only nine obverse and eleven reverse dies and the resulting averages of fourteen and twelve examples per die are much higher than that of any other EFH type. The numbers of coins per die are approaching the same levels as the normal face/horse series and are only significantly exceeded by the late inscribed coins and the symbol series. Two dies are particularly common: obverse E with 40 known coins and reverse 3 with 38 (seventeen coins in common).

The design of Bury A remained relatively consistent and there is an unusually high degree of inter-linkage between the dies compared to other EFH types. Plated coins are relatively frequent, with nine examples from four obverse and five reverse forged dies. This is a greater number of forged dies than occurs with any other type in the EFH series. There are no die linkages within the plated coins, except that obverse die PC has two reverse dies F3 and F4. None of the plated coins are struck from hubbed dies and their reverse dies appear to be based upon the very common die 3. PD/F5 (CCI 98.2166) has been assumed to be plated, based on its appearance, but is not recorded as such.

As noted above Bury A appears to be focused on the upper Yare valley. There is a weak northern or western distribution, but it occurs in volume well to the south of most EFH coins, particularly in central Suffolk.

Bury C (Figure 14)
A small group of only 34 recorded coins, with seven obverse and seven reverse dies. These include three unlinked pairs of dies, the remainder forming a single die-linked group. New dies continue to emerge and it is likely that several remain to be found.

The head faces right with a helmet which includes ornate decoration starting around the ear and rising over the head. There is only one recorded example of die A, very similar to a retrograde Bury A with an S-shaped "serpent" before the face. Dies C, G and H are alike with four pellets before the face; this feature is reduced, apparently to only one pellet, on the remaining dies, although full details cannot be seen on all of them. An off-struck die G shows a pattern of circles or torcs around what would otherwise appear to have been the perimeter of the die.

The realistic horse faces left and, where it can be seen, the tail always appears to comprise a solid line with a shadowing line of pellets. The surrounding decoration shows considerable variation:

- Ring containing seven pellets above with single pellet below and various pellets above (die 7).
- Spoked wheel and various pellets above with single pellet below, evocative of Bury A (dies 4 to 6).
- Die 3 has a pellet and two rings below, and similar above, with a wing shape emerging from the lower pellet – appearing reworked as a solid ovoid in later versions of the die. The only example of die 2 is similar but with more rings above and the same signs of recutting over an earlier device. The only example of die 1 is poor but appears likely to be closest to this type; it is not recut.

The die groups are shown in Table 3.

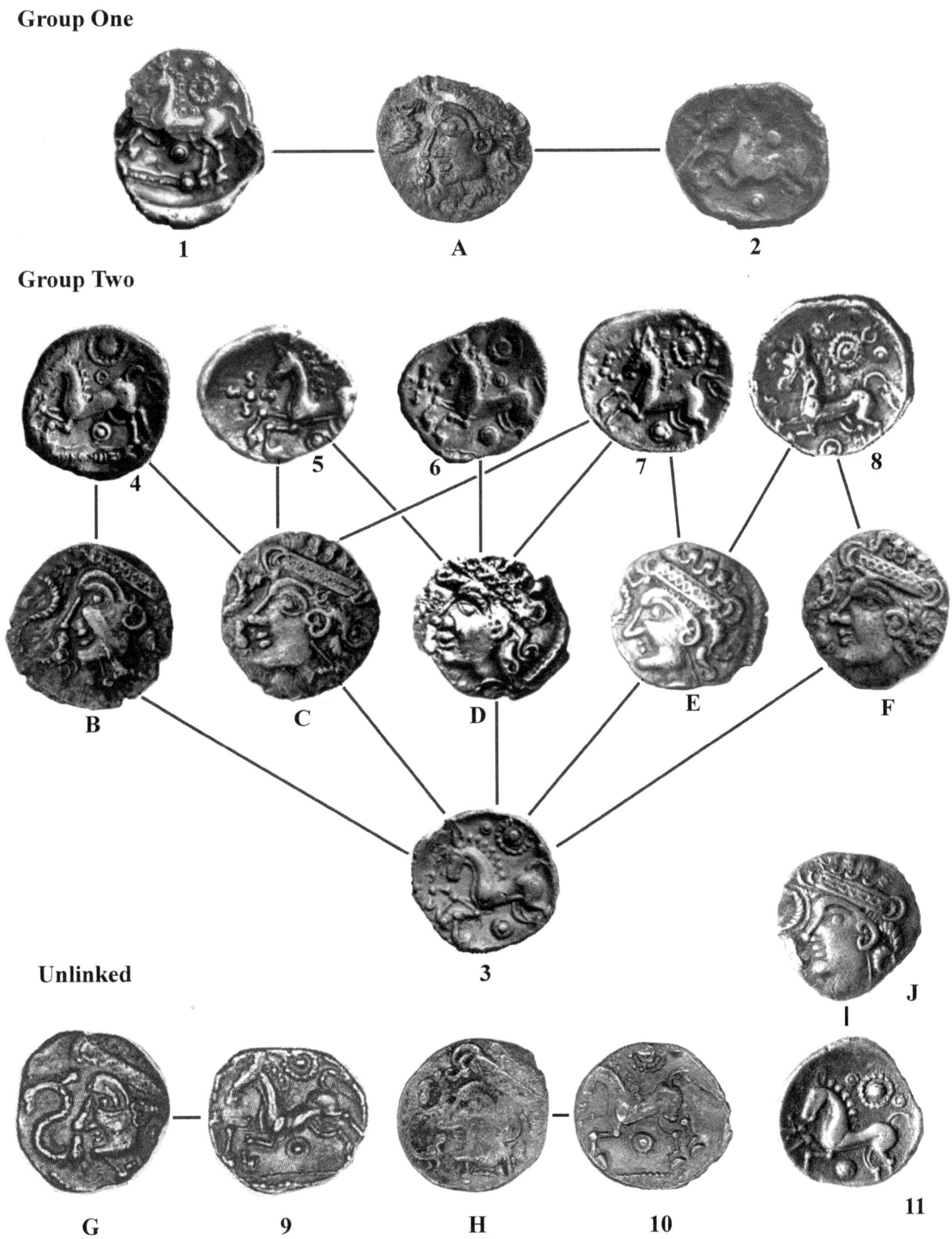

Figure 13. The Bury A type.

Group no.	Obverse dies	Reverse dies	Number known	Weight range
1	A	1	1	
2	B	2	2	
3	C, D, E	3, 4, 5	18	1.3 – 1.39
4	F	6	1	
5	G	7	12	1.23 – 1.45

Table 3. Die groups for Bury C.

The distribution is problematic given the few provenances, but shows a bias towards East Norfolk. It is possible that die group 5 originates in the Ipswich region as five of the seven coins with a provenance have been found in that area, although of these four are hoard coins.

Figure 14. The Bury C type.

Bury B (Figures 15 and 16)
The third largest group of EFH coins with 82 recorded examples, as well as five plated coins. There is an exceptionally large total of 34 dies, second only to the Snettisham unit among the EFH types and almost equivalent to boar/horse B (VA 657); however, there are 176 recorded examples of the latter.

The diademed head faces right, with five torc-like braids of hair rising from the diadem. There is a large pellet at either end of the diadem with a snake-like projection rising from the rear pellet. The ear is covered by a spiral-like guard and there are "ringlets" between the ear and nose, and one in front of the nose. Some dies show a ladder effect on the side of the head (see dies A and B).

The realistic horse faces right with detailed reins, decorated "harness" bands and a leaf-shaped tail. There is a large wheel shape above, which takes a variety of forms (see below), and there is usually a small ring immediately above the horse. There are various additional decorations above including a spiral star. There is a device in the form of a cross in front of the horse and a pellet-ended hollow star below; many dies show an angled exergue or track marks which rise up to meet the upper parts of the forward rear leg (see dies 4 and 9).

There are three types of wheel on the reverse:

1. Central pellet with a ring of outer pellets, many of which are connected by spokes.
2. As 1 but with solid inner ring and no spokes.
3. As 2 but outer ring of pellets more distant and with spokes.

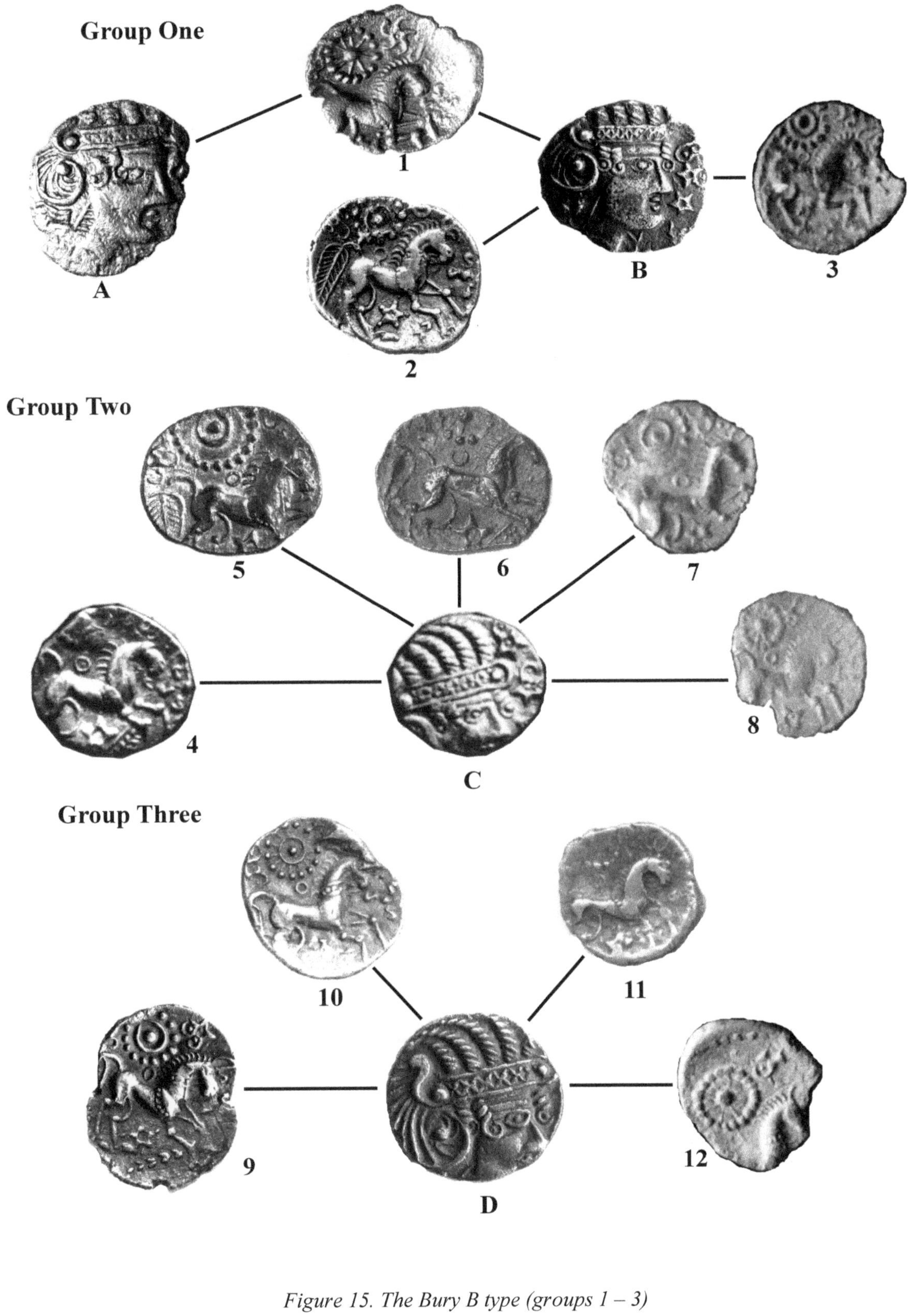

Figure 15. The Bury B type (groups 1 – 3)

There are four main die groups which account for 78 of the 87 recorded coins (see Table 4). In addition there are three other unlinked pairs of dies, one of which is uniface (H/24, J/25, 26), and a small group of three dies (G/22, 23).

The core distribution pattern for Bury B is a vertical, north to south, central band of Norfolk, but with little of the penetration into Suffolk shown by Bury A. There appears to be a focus on the upper Yare valley, particularly for die groups 3 and 4. Sample sizes are small but die group 2 appears to have a more easterly bias and die group 1 possibly a bias to the west.

Group Four

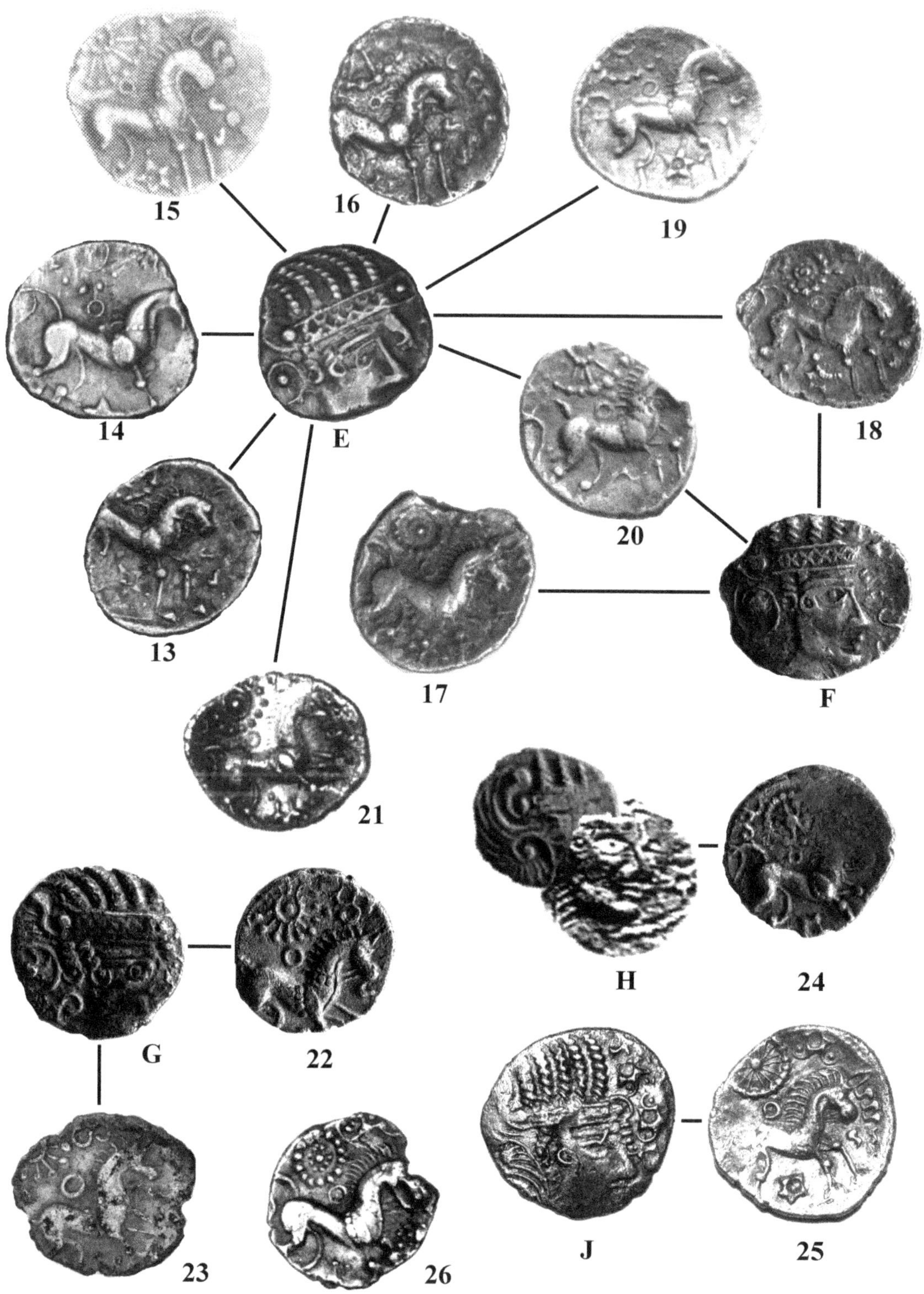

Figure 16. The Bury B type (group 4).

Group number	Obverse dies	Reverse dies	Number of coins	Weight range	Reverse ring type
1	2	3	7	1.41 – 1.49	2, 1
2	1	5	15	1.15 – 1.41	1, 2
3	1	4	17	1.22 – 1.41	1, 2, 3
4	2	9	39	1.25 – 1.4	3, 2
Plated	3(1)	3	5		1, 3

Table 4. Die groups for Bury B.

There are no major differences to distinguish each die group but the following observations can be made:

- The horses are shown with either their front legs prancing, or standing, and in die groups with examples of both, the former precedes the latter. This has been used as the basis for the chronological order of the first four groups. The unlinked dies have not been arranged chronologically.
- Group 1 appears to be heavier than the later three major groups which all appear to be of similar weight.
- Obverse dies in group 1 generally display the full face whereas the later groups tend only to show the upper part of the head. This is particularly noticeable in the case of the common die E in group 4 which continued to be used until it was very worn.
- The form of the large wheel on the reverse dies may be significant, as there is some correlation to die group and chronology.

There is a marked contrast between the die analysis of Bury B and that of Bury A. Bury B has considerably more dies – 34 compared to 20 – spread amongst a smaller surviving sample of coins, and it is to be expected that an appreciable number of dies are still to be found. The greater number of dies and the larger number of die groups indicate that the two types had a very different production pattern.

Five plated coins have been recorded. There are five different dies and in addition a strike either directly or otherwise from "official" die E.

An important feature of Bury B is the hollow star motif, which may appear on every die, and which is also an important design element on LFA, where it does not appear on early dies, and LFB. The concentric circle patterns on the reverse also are repeated in the LFA group.

The relatively high number of surviving coins and the large number of dies used suggest that the type was produced over either over a lengthy period or from a diverse number of sites. The absence of plated coins appears to point more towards diverse production points rather than longevity.

Bury D (Figure 17)
A small group of coins with nonetheless a clear West Norfolk distribution and a weight range of 1.25 – 1.38g. There are only eleven coins in total and these are struck from a single obverse die (possibly two, but assumed to be only one with slight recutting) and five reverse dies.

The head faces left with a large eye, a Bury A-like ear, "braided" hair and a beard incised into the chin, surrounded by ring and pellets. The horse faces left with a realistic head, ornate bridle detail and a leaf-like tail. In front is a pellet in pellet ring and below is a pellet in ring. Above are a variety of concentric circle designs evocative of Bury B, and there are two small ringed pellets immediately above the horse's back.

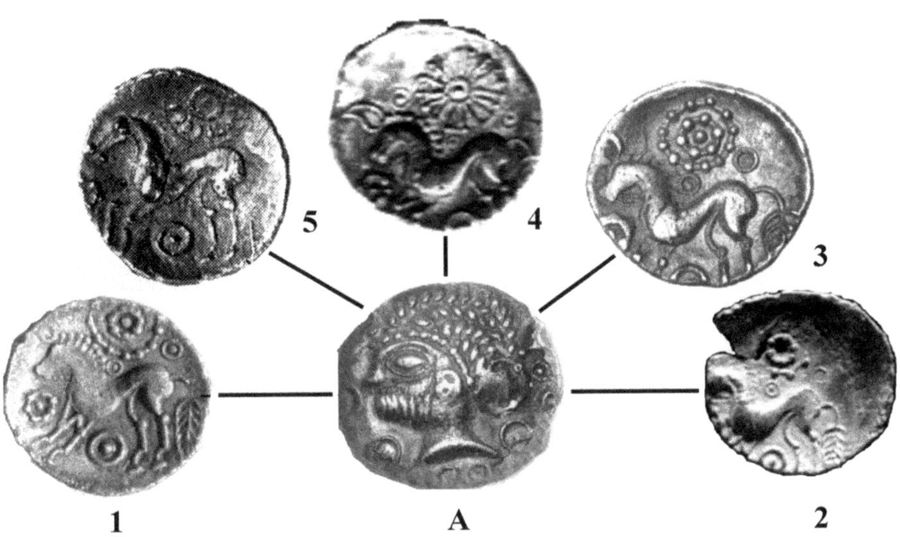

Figure 17. The Bury D type.

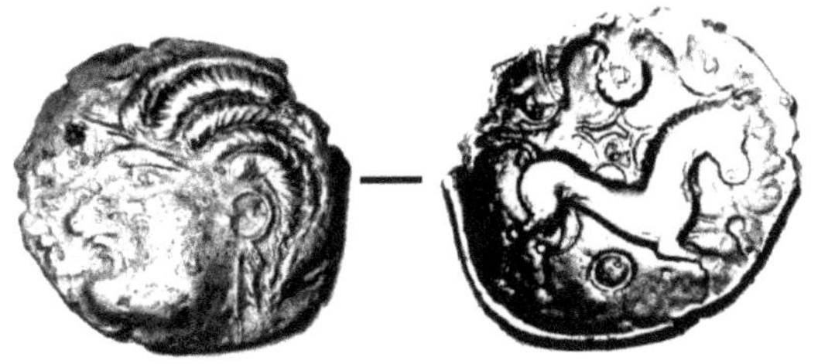

Figure 18. The Bury E type.

Bury E (Figure 18)
This type appears to be related to the Bury series. There are only two coins known, both from a single reverse die but differing obverse dies. Both coins have a South Norfolk provenance, and the only recorded weight is 1.18g.

One die shows a left-facing head with locks of hair swept backwards. The design before the face may be as on Bury A and there is a vertical line below the ear, also as Bury A. There is only a very poor strike from the other die which appears to be left-facing. The horse has a realistic head and faces right with a hollow five-armed star above it. Above the star is a pellet in ring, or a cog, with wing-like arms rising then falling to either side. There is a ring with two pellets below the horse.

Figure 19. Single coins.

General observations on the Bury group
The Bury coins generally have a more realistic form of representation than the other EFH types, and this is particularly the case for Bury A and Bury C. These two types appear closely related and, although much of the detail is different, the basic design of the horse is very similar (see Bury A die 6 and Bury C die 4). The Bury C obverse die A has a serpent before the face and looks like a retrograde Bury A, while the remaining C dies are more distinctive.

Bury A and C have different distributions but, importantly, have been found together in two hoards. It appears reasonable to speculate that these two types were in circulation at the same time and represent regional issues of central and eastern East Anglia respectively.

Bury B is a more stylised type than A or C and, with the exception of die group 1, is also lighter in weight. This coinage also uses the hollow star decoration which occurs on several of the large flan units. It appears likely that Bury B is later than Bury A and Bury C, and that during the intervening period the area in which these coins were destined to circulate had moved somewhat to the north.

The remaining Bury types are less comfortable bedfellows and have been classified with the Bury coins as they are clearly early types and share a number of decorative elements on the reverse, particularly with Bury B. Bury D is appearing in gradually mounting numbers in West Norfolk although Bury E remains at only two known examples. It appears likely that Bury D was a local issue within West Norfolk circulating at roughly the same time as Bury B. I have assumed that Bury E was a local issue at the same time, based upon its Norfolk provenances and the use of the hollow star, although it has a similarity to certain Trinovantian issues.

The suggested chronological order of Bury A and C being in issue together, then being followed by B, makes their alphabetic names illogical but I have not sought to confuse matters by suggesting changes to such well known nomenclature.

Figure 19, left, shows three coins each known from a single example, which may well be Icenian and which appear to relate to the Bury series and in particular to Bury C. The top coin is recorded as VA 81 by Van Arsdell (1989) and the other two are otherwise unclassified.

The Large Flan deeply-dished units
This is an important group of early coins characterized by a more stylised obverse than the early Bury coins, but retaining a relatively realistic reverse. They are struck on large flans and are deeply dished. As yet none of these coins appear to be directly related to coins of other denominations.

Large Flan A (LFA) (Figures 20 and 21)
Deeply-dished silver units on a large flan, very thin towards the edges and often found broken.

There are two main types of obverse:

1. The head is left-facing with a scroll from the forehead. Below the scroll are a variety of concentric rings, spokes and pelleted rings similar to Bury B reverses. Between the scroll and the shoulder is either a hollow star (as Bury B) or a diamond. Behind the head the hair ends in a tight scroll.

2. As 1 but a scroll descends from the mouth to echo that from the forehead, and between the two the Bury B type design is replaced by a large ring and pellet. There are only three dies of this type, with only one example known of each. Dies A and B are very similar and are the only two LFA dies with a clearly defined ear, which is in a similar style to that used on Bury A.

The reverse has a realistic horse facing to the right. Above the horse is a ring and pellet from which lead two upward, divergent arms, each ending in a ring and pellet, with a ring and pellet between them. To the lower left is either the hollow star or a diamond. Below the horse are either two or three vertical ringed pellets, the diamond or a single ring and pellet.

The 67 recorded coins include four which are plated: three from the same pair of dies and the fourth a uniface coin apparently hubbed from reverse die 21. From the remaining coins I have identified ten obverse and 25 reverse dies, of which thirteen of the reverse and five of the obverse dies have only a single recorded example.

There is only one major die group for this type and it includes 50 of the 63 non-plated coins. In addition there are four other pairs of dies, not otherwise linked, and six reverse dies coupled with unidentified, much worn obverses.

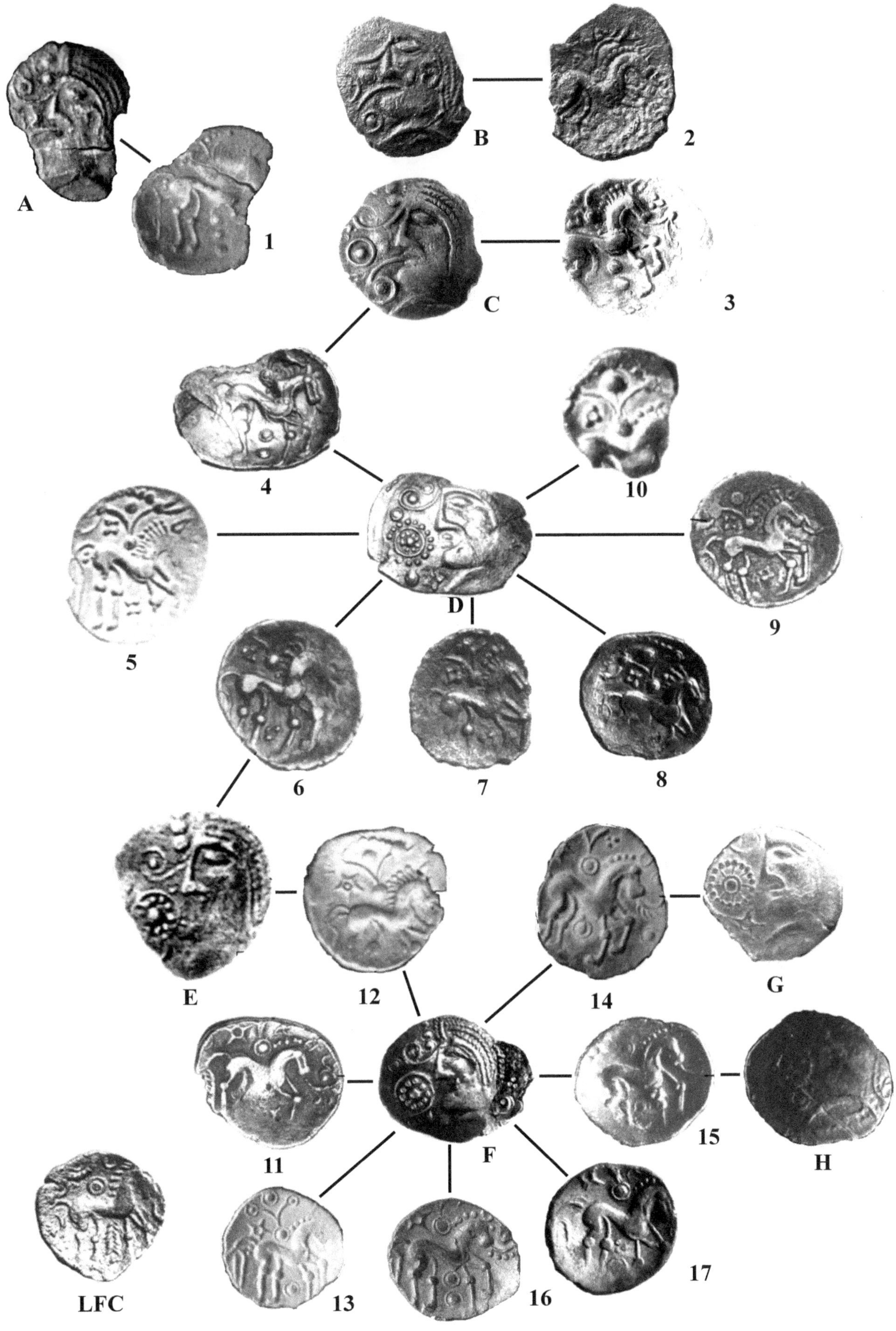

Figure 20. The LFA type.

Figure 21. The LFA type (continued).

Within the die group there appears to be an orderly, stylistic progression of reverse dies, the earliest being die 3 with at least two rings vertically below the horse. A key design element is a diamond-shaped device which is subsequently superseded by a hollow five-pointed star. The link between the two main elements of the die group is provided by only one coin linking die E to die 6, but the link is unequivocal. The coins not so far die-linked to the main group, appear likely to be either very early coins (dies A/1 and B/2), or late coins often struck with worn out obverse dies.

One coin has been identified which provides a die link between the early LFC reverse die 1 and an LFA obverse. This important coin, CCI 78.0085, was found at Saham Toney and whilst it does not appear to be a forgery, its current location is unknown. Unfortunately the obverse image of this coin is poor and the LFA die cannot be identified with certainty, although there are similarities to die F. The LFC die is shown on Figure 23 and is a strike from the earliest die of that series, but there is not a neat chronological continuum, as it is not a late impression from die F which itself is not the last die in the LFA series. Assuming that the coin is not plated it suggests that LFC is later than LFA, that there was a period of overlap and that there was at least some production at a common site.

The full scale of LFA and all linkages within the type cannot yet be ascertained. New dies are still being regularly discovered and there is a low recovery rate of coins compared to original die numbers (only 2.5 coins per reverse die). Thus the series is likely to be bigger than can presently be seen. Indications are, however, that the type is the result of a continuous sequence of minting from linked dies.

The uniface group of reverse dies, 20 to 25, have unidentifiable worn obverses. I suspect that several of these will eventually prove to be from a worn die F. There is also a uniface example from earlier in the group, the reverse being a relatively unworn strike from die 5 (CCI 98.1379). The obverse cannot be die D, and an examination of the coin suggested it was not plated, nor did it produce any clues as to the original obverse die.

Other unusual features of the series include:

- Dies K/19 (CCI 02.0733), which are so far unlinked to other dies, are anomalous in having a hollow star in place of the scroll on the obverse, and before as well as above the horse on the reverse. The reverse is very odd in giving the appearance that the hollow star in front of the horse overlies an earlier "flame" emerging from its mouth.

- Reverse dies 12 and 13 both show signs of having had an earlier version of the start of the tail which now crosses through a pellet.

- Many reverse dies, particularly those with uniface obverses, are very similar in the layout of the horse's body but differ in the ancillary detail. This may be the result of hubbing key design elements, but further work needs to be done before any firm conclusions can be reached.

The distribution of non-hoard coins is very interesting, showing a clear easterly distribution around the Waveney valley for the early coins of the type and some later coins, but with a central Norfolk distribution for most of the later coins.

Large Flan B (LFB) subtypes I, II and III (Figure 22)
Subtypes I and II were formerly included within early face/horse Cc, and subtype III is recorded as BMC 387. There are only sixteen coins (including two plated), from five obverse and eight reverse dies, which fit into the three distinct and unlinked subtypes. The weight of the coins is 1.26 – 1.38g and there is no clear weight variation between the subtypes.

The limited number of coins available suggests a distribution in northern and central Norfolk, with a pattern slightly more northerly and easterly than LFC, but the sample size is extremely small.

Subtype I: the obverse has a right-facing head with an eye, a ring and pellet within a pellet ring or ring before the face, and distinctive lines of pelleted poles seemingly randomly from or before the face (A and B). The reverse has a realistic-headed horse facing left. There is a branch and two pelleted poles below and a bucranium-like object above. The other decoration includes hollow, pellet ended five-pointed stars (dies 1 -3).

Subtype II: the obverse is very different to subtype I, the right-facing head having a large eye, with an arc of pellet rings behind the hair, a scroll from the forehead and a large pellet ring before the mouth. These obverse dies are stylistically close to LFC or the Snettisham unit (C and D). The reverse is as subtype I but with only a single branch below the horse (dies 4 – 7). Subtype II has a plated example which shares a reverse die with a solid coin (PA/4).

Subtype III: the obverse is ambiguous, but appears to be a left-facing head with braided hair and a row of large pellets below. The reverse is as subtype I, but with a branch and single pelleted pole below. Above the horse is a large ring and pellet, possibly with wing-like extensions to either side. The remaining field is well decorated with devices including smaller ring and pellet motifs and slender serpentine forms. Before the horse's head may be a cross similar to that on Bury A. There are only three known examples which all appear to be from the same pair of dies.

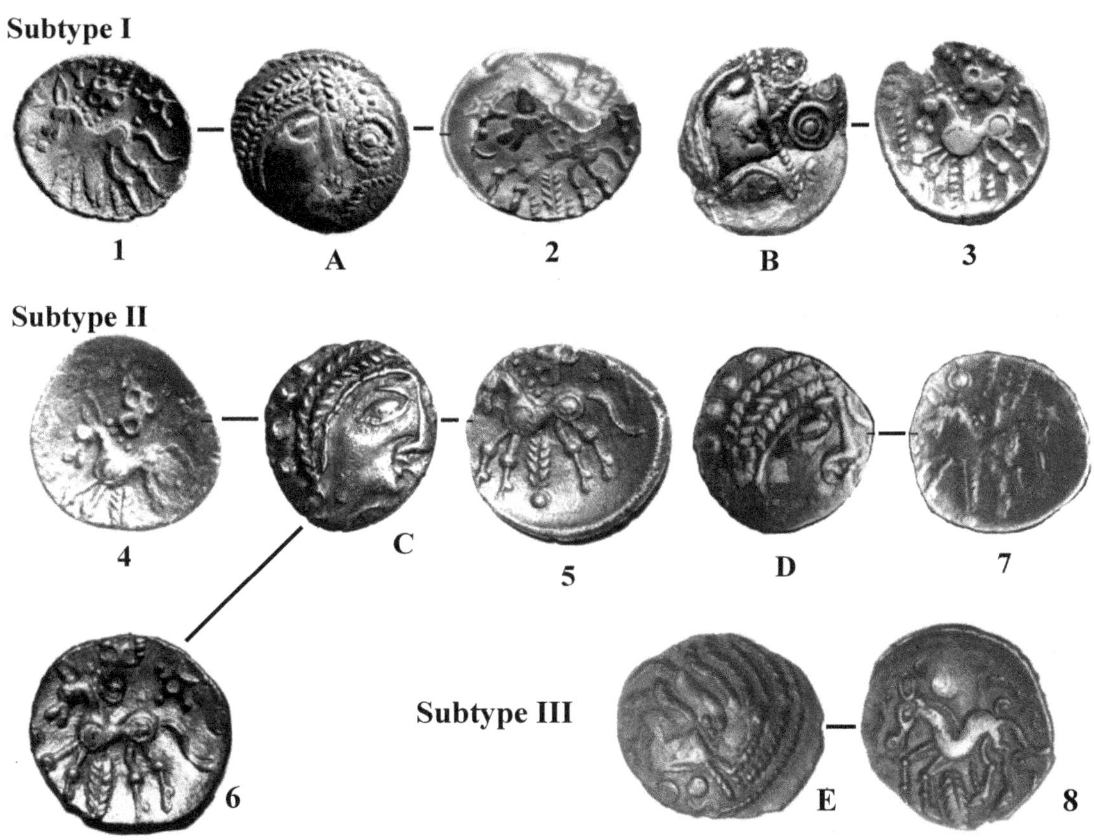

Figure 22. LFB, subtypes I, II and III.

Large Flan C (LFC) (Figure 23)
A group of dished, large flan silver units. There are many die styles, but the type is distinguished by a right-facing head on the obverse and, on the reverse, a right-facing horse over a pole or branch, with a ringed pellet and a larger wheel or ring of some form above and with a variety of other decoration. Many obverses have a large and well defined eye.

Group	No. coins	Obverse dies	Reverse dies	Weight
1	38	4	2	1.22 – 1.47
2	47	4	5	1.15 – 1.39
3	19	7	9	1.07 – 1.35
Plated	31	4 (4)	0 (4)	1.26 – 1.48

Table 5. Die groups for LFC.

There are 135 recorded coins, of which at least 31 are plated, and, of the 99 with a recorded provenance, 77 (including all but one of the plated coins) come from either the hoards found at Snettisham or the assemblage at the West Norfolk site. The coins form into four groups (Table 5).

Die groups 1 and 2 appear to represent a chronological progression. This assumption is based upon the style of the reverse dies, which show a gradual change through the two groups; the die-link to LFA at the beginning of group 1; and evidence of average weight declining through the groups. Each of the two groups is fully die-linked except for a link in group 2 which is questionable as the connection is a strike from a very worn die E; this linkage is thus shown by a dotted line on Figure 23.

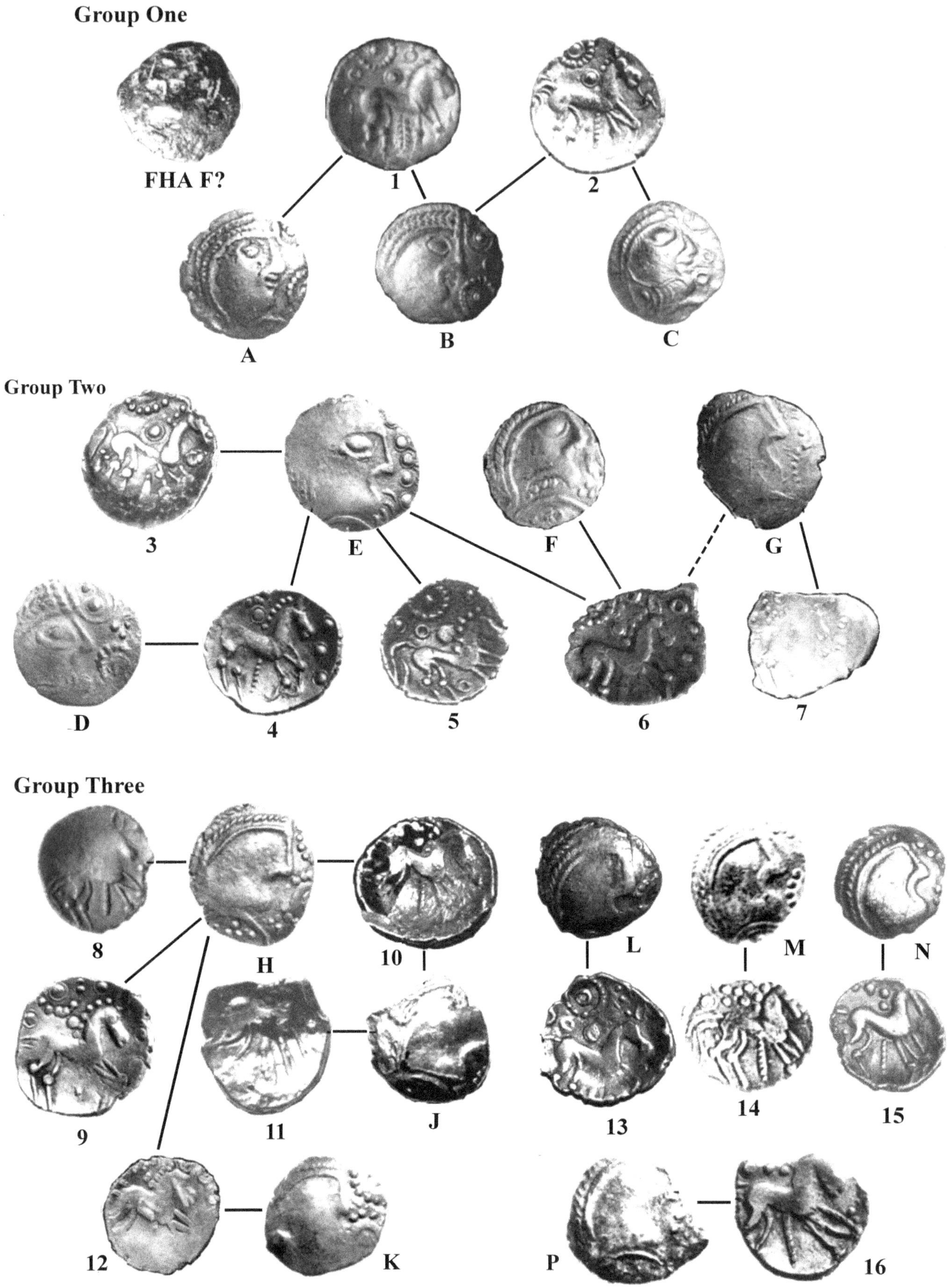

Figure 23. The LFC type.

The distribution of the coins does not appear to vary between the groups, with a clear west Norfolk pattern which, after excluding hoard coins, appears focused on the Breckland.

Group 3 is a stylistically similar group of dies which are generally cruder than those in the other groups. Only twelve of the 19 coins in this group are die-linked. The group is assumed to be the last in the type as they are generally lighter, and the obverse and reverse styles of group 3 are encountered at the end of group 2. This latter point is not certain, however, due to the poor linking coin referred to above.

The obverse dies of groups 1 and 2 show remarkable variation. At the start of the sequence is a LFA die, probably die F, and at the end of the sequence there appears to be a group 3 type. The other 6 dies, which all have a clearly defined eye, include three with a forehead scroll and a pellet ring below, die C with a "pipe" from the mouth and the very common die E with a line of pellets down the front of the face. At least four of the dies have beards in various forms (C, D, E, F and probably B). The last die of group 2 and all seven obverse dies of group 3 have a common style with a pelleted forehead scroll, a substantial pellet ring below and no eye.

The reverse dies show less variation. The normal pole under the horse is represented in die 1 as a leaf or branch; dies 1 and 2 have a four-armed device before the horse which, where visible, is replaced by several ringed pellets in the later dies. Towards the end of group 2 and throughout group 3 the reverse dies become generally cruder and the neat ringed pellet and wheel above the horse are replaced by a greater number of often larger pellets and sometimes a much larger pellet ring. The single-rooted tail is replaced by a cruder double-rooted tail. Die 5 from group 2 has two pellets and a ring above the back, and is unique in LFC in having a ring below instead of a pole. This upper portion of this die is extremely close in design to die 13. A recently recorded example of a die 5 coin has been discovered to be a very fine plated coin, but other examples seen of this somewhat anomalous die appear to be solid.

Towards the end of group 2 the coin flans are frequently very irregular (see examples on Figure 23), and give the appearance of having been struck without the usual care. This lack of care does not recur to the same degree in group 3, which includes a number of unlinked pairs of dies, perhaps indicating that the group may not be sequential, but may represent geographic or chronological dispersion. The latter appears more likely given the stylistic continuity within the group and the lack of any distribution difference, based upon recorded provenances.

It is interesting that most of the many identified plated coins are copies of coins from group 1. The 38 non-plated coins in this group compare to 28 known plated copies. There is a likelihood that this may even understate the quantity of plated coins as some of them have proved hard to separate from the "genuine" coins. These plated coins are predominantly produced from three "official" dies, or hubbed copies thereof. The fact that most plated coins are based upon group 1 may indicate that this group had the longest period of circulation. It also supports the idea that group 2 may have been a rushed issue, at least in part, and that group 3 is the result of small and/or intermittent production. Such conclusions are speculative and need to be treated with caution as it seems that many of these plated coins may well emanate from one, or possibly two, inadequately recorded Snettisham hoards.

General observations on the Large Flan group of units

These coins are a fascinating and key element within the EFH series. The two main types, LFA and LFC, have proved to be large and complex issues, with new dies regularly being found and many more likely to be discovered.

Present evidence suggests that the series followed Bury A, but was first issued before Bury B. They appear to have been the contemporaneous production of two or more separate "mints", principally in western and central East Anglia. Present evidence also indicates that FHA may have started in the Waveney valley and then moved westwards, whereas the related LFC is more likely to be a Breckland issue. These issues appear to have had a reasonably consistent weight and to have been produced in volume.

The Snettisham group

This large group of units is probably a continuing and developing single series with some regional sub-issues. Stylistically it has been separated into Snettisham and Irstead units, each of which is divided in turn into two subgroups. Certain of the subtypes form denominational groups with issues of gold coinage. It is probable that the early boar/horse units (BMC 3440) are closely related to this group.

The Snettisham unit (Figures 24 and 25)

This group consists of 78 coins, which form five die groups, plus six unlinked pairs of dies and one reverse die unlinked except to an unidentifiable obverse. In total I have so far identified 15 obverse dies and 26 reverse dies and of these twelve reverse and seven obverse dies are known from only one example each. It is very likely that some of the die groups will coalesce as more examples are found. New dies are still being encountered and clearly the series was large and complex (Table 6).

The coins have a dispersed distribution across west and central Norfolk, but with concentrations in northwest Norfolk and the upper Yare valley, the latter being also a major focus for the Snettisham quarter stater. Snettisham units are generally struck on a smaller flan, and less dished, than the Large Flan group. Their weight distribution at 1.03 – 1.3g is almost exactly in line with the Irstead unit. The last eleven reverse dies take on a number of different features, but as they link to the earlier dies through die M they are treated as a continuation of the group, although they are described separately at end of this section.

The obverse is a right-facing head which is large relative to the size of the flan, with a large eye, no ear, a lens before the mouth and a "scroll" curving away from the forehead. Certain dies show decoration below the scroll, such as the pelleted ring on die E and the concentric circle design on die H. The obverse is clearly related to, and probably derived from, LFB type II and many of the LFC obverses.

On the first eighteen reverse dies there is a right-facing horse

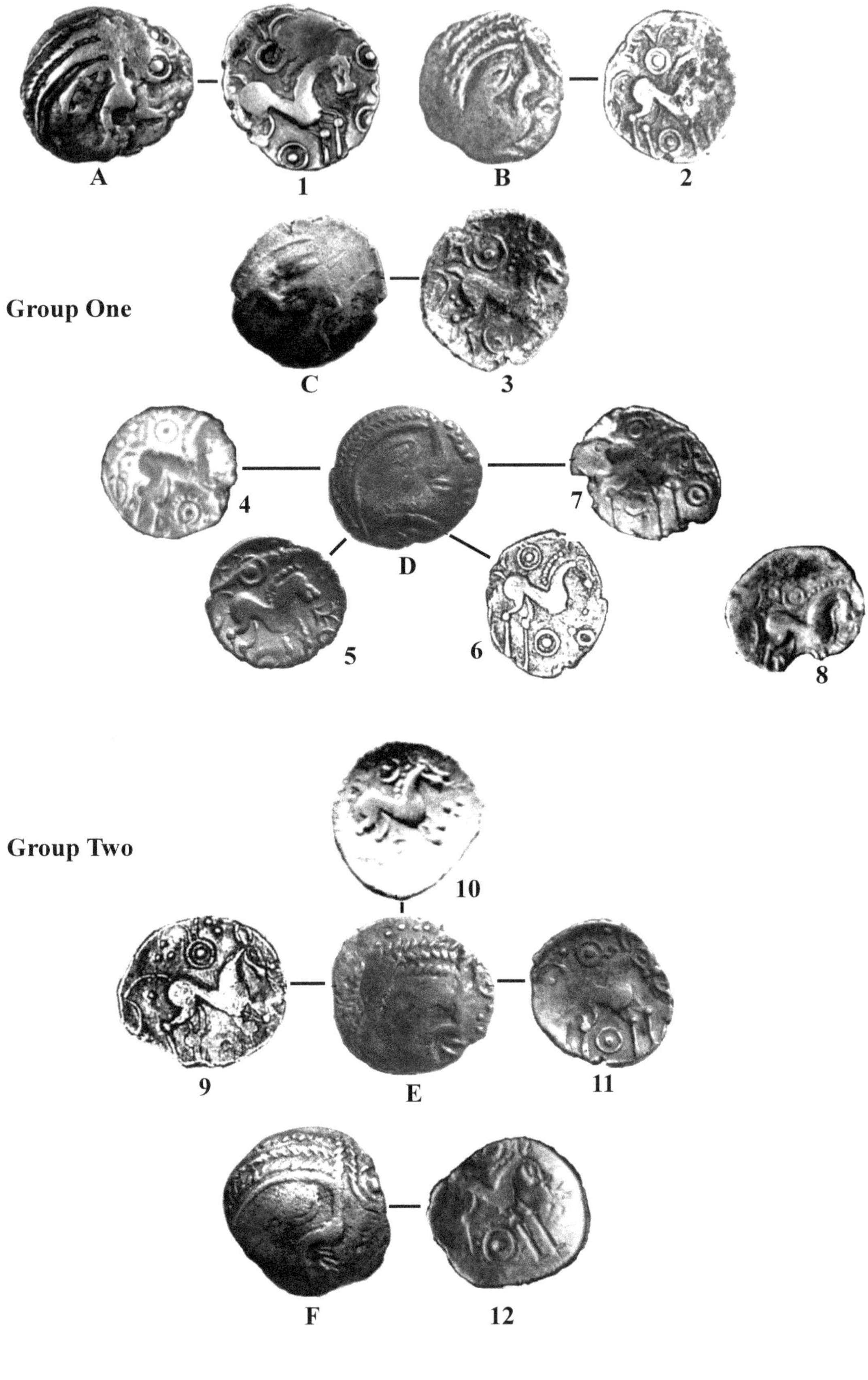

Figure 24. The Snettisham unit (groups 1 and 2)

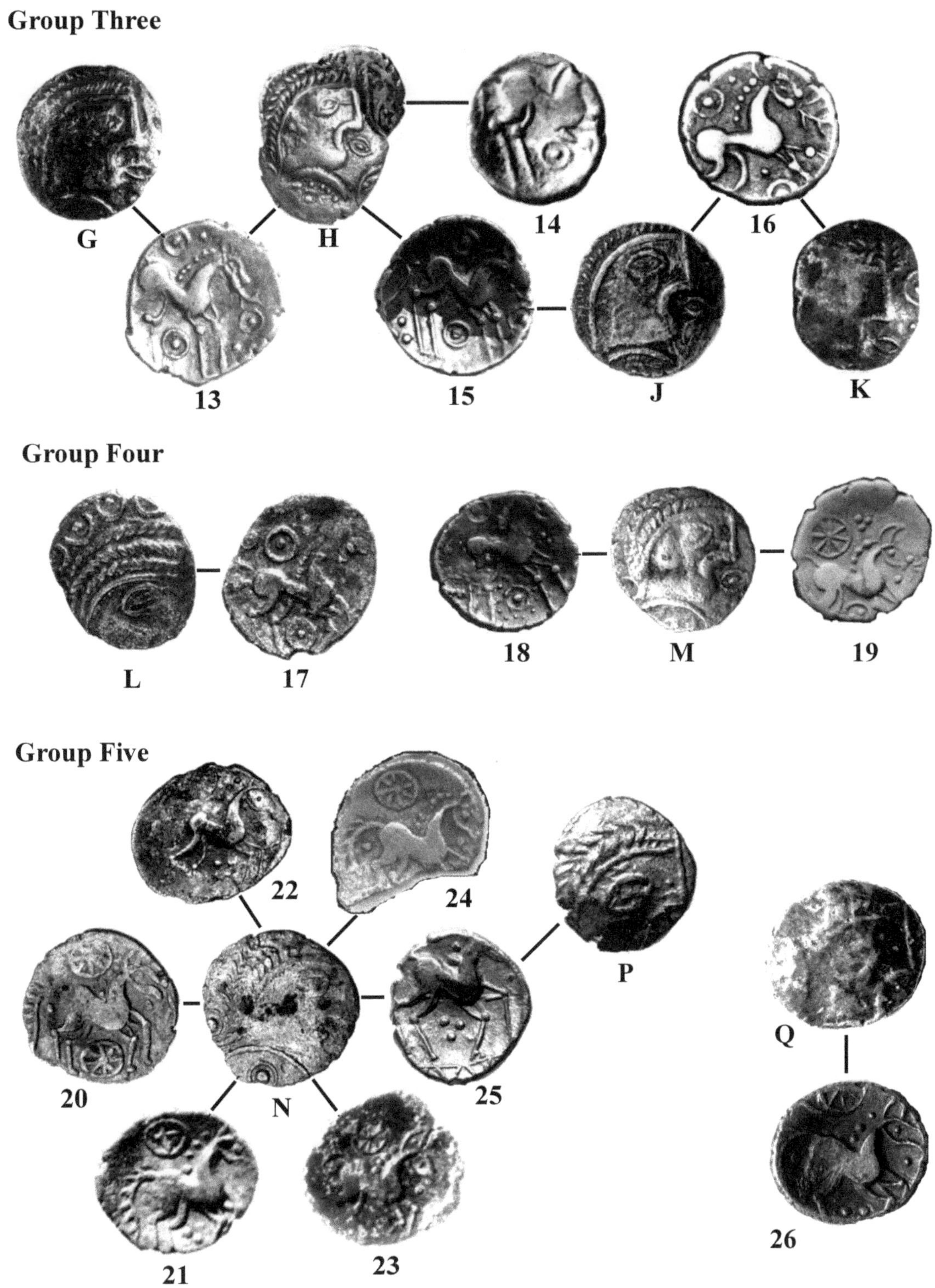

Figure 25. The Snettisham unit (groups 3 – 5).

with "fire" streaming from the mouth and a variety of manes (dotted, solid or absent). Below the horse is a pellet in ring, some with an outer ring of pellets, while below the head is another pellet in ring; the tail is leaf-shaped. The horse's head appears to be transitional, with the earlier dies having realistic heads which then develop into the open keyhole shape. Above the horse is a pellet in ring, which in most cases appears to have two outward branching lines. The full design is not visible but is evocative of that ending in two rings on the Snettisham stater and on LFA. The form of decoration to the left of the upper pellet in ring may divide the units into two subtypes: dies 1 to 8 show a kite in this position, but subsequent dies have a pellet triplet either side of the upper pellet in ring.

Comparative weights reveal little, although the kite coins may be slightly heavier and have been assumed to be the earliest.

These reverse designs are very close in ornamentation and style to those of the Snettisham stater and certain of the Snettisham quarter staters, and thus appear to form the different denominations of a single series, although the gold coins do not share the "kite" symbol found on the early units. These different denominations were found together in the 1988 – 1991 Snettisham hoard. The reverses have much in common with certain of the LFA reverses, which appear to be the forerunners to this group.

The final eight reverse dies are different, although they die-link to the earlier dies through obverse die M. They also have a right-facing horse, but it is closer to Irstead A than to the 18 earlier dies. It has an open keyhole head, but most dies have a spoked wheel above, without tangential lines, and a pellet triangle below. There are at least three variants: die 21 has another spoked wheel instead of pellets below the horse, die 19 has a ring containing two or three pellets below and a pellet triangle in addition to the wheel above, and the spoked wheel above the horse on die 26 has the tangential line which also occurs in the Irstead A units.

Only fourteen coins are known from the final group of eight reverse dies, which share four obverse dies, including the linking die M. Condition is generally poor, particularly of the obverses. All the dies are linked with the exception of reverse 19, which is linked to obverse die M, and the unlinked Q/26. The weight range of this final group of coins is lower than the earlier coins but the difference is not meaningful in view of their poor condition and the low sample size.

The final obverse dies also vary from the earlier dies. Dies N, P and Q are cruder and have no lens before the mouth. Die N has a pronounced shoulder with a pellet in ring below it; this area is not visible on the other dies.

These final coins appear to be transitional between the Snettisham units and the Irstead unit. More is likely to be learned as additional coins come to light.

Group	No. coins	Obverse dies	Reverse dies	Weight
1	10	D	4 - 7	1.11 – 1.14
2	10	E	9 - 11	0.97 – 1.21
3	30	G, H, J, K	13 - 16	1.07 – 1.3
4	8	M	18 - 19	1.1 -1.2
5	12	N, P	20- 25	0.92 – 1.12

Table 6. Die groups for the Snettisham units.

Irstead A (Figure 26)
A fully die-linked group of 33 coins from four obverse and four reverse dies, and in addition two Irstead quarter stater dies have also been used in the group. The weight range of 1.02 – 1.3g is as the Snettisham unit.

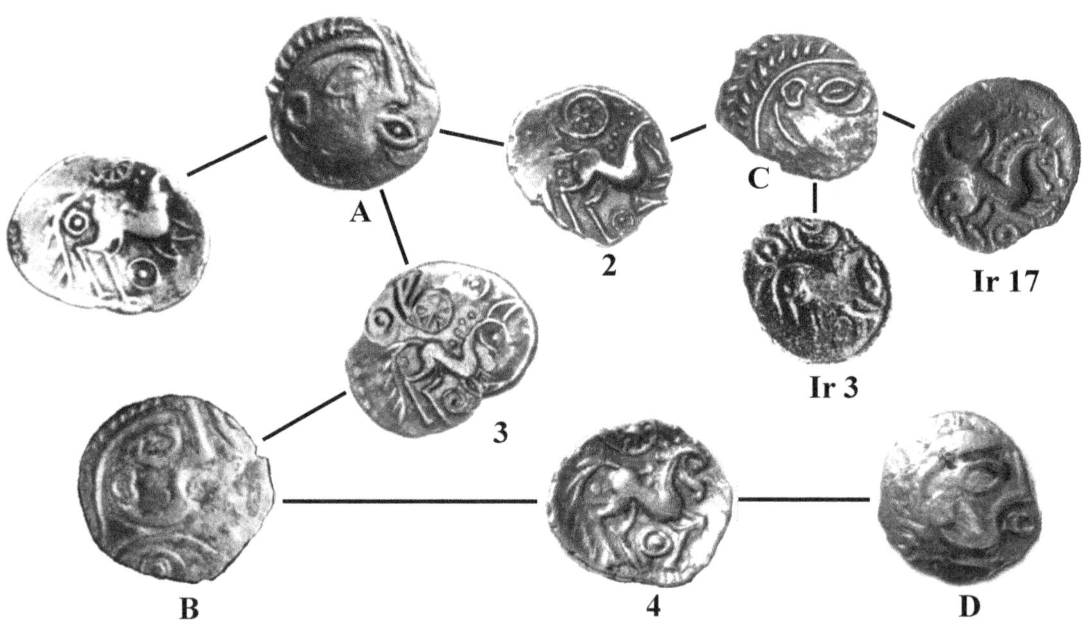

Figure 26. The Irstead A type.

The basic obverse is a right-facing crude head with a large eye and ear, no lips and a lens or eye before the mouth. There is a scroll from the forehead as in LFA and the Snettisham unit. Die C, which is rather more elongated than the other dies, has been found paired with a reverse die of the Irstead quarter stater in a silver unit from the Fring Hoard (CCI 92.0806) and another unit possibly from the Snettisham area.

The basic reverse is a right-facing horse with an open keyhole head and a spoked wheel above with a tangential line from its base rising behind in a wing-like shape. There is a pellet in ring below and a pellet below the tail, except in die 1, which has a pellet in ring below the tail.

With the exception of the upper decorative elements the reverse of this unit is extremely close in design to the Irstead quarter stater and the Freckenham stater VA626-1, and together they appear to form a denominational group. The argument for this is enhanced by the discovery of the die-links between the quarter stater and the unit.

Subtype I

A 1 B 2

Subtype II

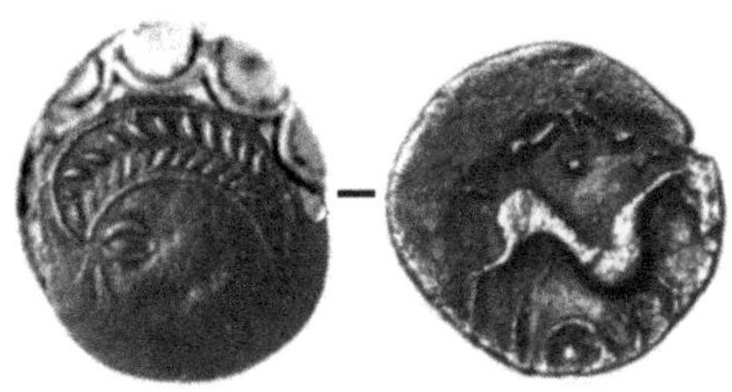

C 3

Figure 27. The Irstead B type.

Irstead B (Figure 27)
This is a small, anomalous group of only five coins, which appear to fit best within the Irstead group, although there are similarities to the Snettisham quarter stater reverses. The group differs from other Irstead or Snettisham units in having a left-facing head which has close similarities to that of LFA. Even within this small group there are two subtypes.

Subtype I consists of three coins known from two pairs of unlinked dies. Two coins are provenanced and these are both from the Fenland area. The coins are light, at only 0.87 – 0.94g.

The head is left-facing, very large for the flan, with a scroll from the forehead (as FHA) and three pellets in a ring before the nose. The horse faces right, with an open keyhole head, a pellet in ring below, triple pellets below the tail, and a spoked wheel above; at least one of the dies has triple pellets below the head. The reverse is generally evocative of other Irstead units.

Subtype II has only two known examples which share an obverse die, but only one of the coins has an identifiable reverse die. The one coin with a provenance was found at King's Lynn and the coins weigh 1.1g and 1.18g. The obverse is a left-facing head with a "swagged" line above the hair and probably a scroll before the face. The identifiable reverse has a right-facing horse with pellet in ring below and a rayed pellet ring above.

It is probable that this small group of units is a regional variation of the Irstead series produced in, or adjacent to the Fens.

General observations on the Snettisham group
This group appears to mark a key stage in the development of the coinage of the Iceni. Not only was there a change in the "standard" weight but the coinage begins to be issued with a range of related other denominations. I believe that further work is likely to show that the early boar/horse unit (BMC 3440) is closely related to the Snettisham group of units. Die analysis and comparative work in respect of the other denominations is either complete or in progress but a full account of this is beyond the scope of this paper. In order to show the obvious relationship between many of these coins I include on Figure 29 images of several of the types. This includes a rare fractional unit related to the Irstead A unit.

Saham Toney units (Figure 28)
An unusual group of 49 coins, including one plated, in which there are three very different styles of obverse die, linked to three equally different reverse styles. The coins have a small flan and are low in weight at 0.79 – 1.13g, with no variation in weight discernable between either the obverse styles or the die groups.

Obverse die styles in suggested chronological order are:
1. A right-facing head with pellets for hair, an exaggerated nose, and clearly defined ear, eye and beard (dies B, C, D, G and H).
2. A distinctive right-facing head with a pronounced eye, ornate curl below the ear and a very pointed chin. The hair is unusual, being formed of elongated pellets around the outer circumference of the upper head, leading to Chris Rudd's evocative name of Soham "Dead Head" (dies A, F and J).
3. What appears to be a full or three-quarter frontal face with hair and beard in the striated form of style 1's beard. The only recorded example of this head is broken and not in good condition, but the layout appears reasonably clear (die E).

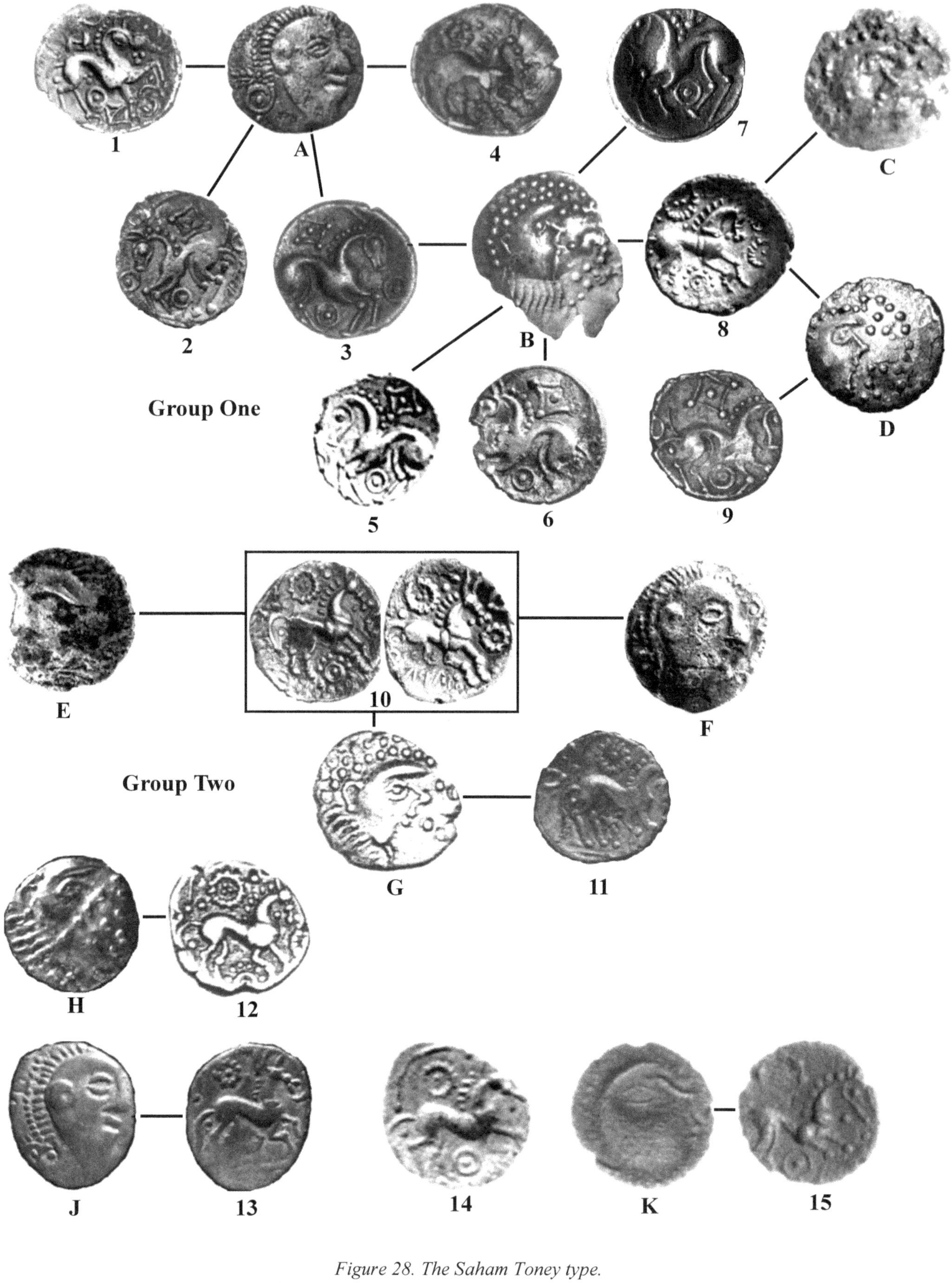

Figure 28. The Saham Toney type.

Reverse die styles are:

1. A unique right-facing stepping horse with elaborate decoration including a pellet in ring, a pellet triangle and a Z device below, a pellet triangle below the head, an H device above and a unique head form (die 1).
2. A stylised right- or left-facing horse with a keyhole type head, a pelleted kite above surmounted by a single line arc and a pellet in ring below, before and behind (dies 2, 3, 5, 6, 7 and 9).
3. A right-facing horse with Y-type head, triple or single pellet in pellet ring above and pellet in ring with outer pellet ring below. There is some variation between dies, with die 10 being unusual in having a six-armed star beneath the horse. Dies 9 and 11 clearly show indications of a single line arc above the horse (dies 4, 8, 10, 11, 12 and 13).

Obverse die style 1 has very clear stylistic links with dies cut for the Trinovantian coinage of Tasciovanos; an example of the Trinovantian unit VA 1745 may well be the work of the same artist responsible for certain of the Icenian dies. There are two main die groups and two unlinked pairs of dies (Table 7).

Group	Obv. dies	Rev. dies	No. coins
1	A - D	1 - 8	35
2	E - G	10 - 11	5
	H	9	1
	J	12	1

Table 7. Die groups for Saham Toney units.

There is only one clearly plated coin, from unique dies (Figure 31). There is also an unusual coin in the BM collection (K/15, CCI 96.1974), which is related to a uniface unit (die 13, CCI 96.2071); these have similarities to style 3 reverses and are thus somewhat speculatively included as Saham Toney units.

Reverse die 10 is presently known from three coins and displays an interesting history. The earliest example is a good strike from the die and shows that the die displayed very similar features to others in the series, such as die 12. The second shows some damage to the die below the rear of the horse, and the final example shows a remarkable transformation with considerable recutting to the area below the horse. The recutting is hard to interpret but appears to be a crude attempt at lettering.

This type has no obvious connecting features with other EFH coins, but there are similarities with the normal face/horse group which uses the Y-type horse head, as does reverse style 3 above, and a pelleted kite below the horse rather than above as in reverse style 2. The Y-head was used extensively within the uninscribed pattern/horse group and in the inscribed coins, but this small group of face/horse coins may include its first appearance in the Icenian coinage. The distribution of the coins has a generally southern bias and seven of the 26 non-hoard coins with a known provenance have been found in the vicinity of Saham Toney in central Norfolk.

Conclusion

In order to make sense of the coinage I have been developing a working hypothesis as to how the various early coinages interrelate.

Phase One (early local issues)

Bury A was the first silver coinage to appear. These units had a standard weight of 1.5g. They were probably minted in the upper Yare valley in some volume over a relatively short period of time; they circulated over a wide area and must have become well known across most of East Anglia as there were many attempts at forgery. The dies are very fine and there was probably Ambianic influence in the design and manufacture of the coins. During the same period the Bury C coinage was also minted, probably at two sites, one in west Norfolk and the other in the Ipswich area.

The earliest of the gold coinages locally produced in volume was the right facing Norfolk Wolf (British JA). This does not appear to have any linkage with a silver unit and its distribution has a more northerly bias than the main Bury units.

Phase Two

Other large flan silver coinages then started to appear on a local basis across East Anglia, initially with a similar standard weight to the Bury A, which subsequently dropped to 1.4g. The design of these beautiful coins had much more local input and they were produced in some volume from a number of distinct sites in western, central and north eastern East Anglia.

The earliest type may have been LFA, probably in the Waveney valley; production of this type may well have moved westwards with time. During the course of this issue the LFC series was started in the Breckland area and Bury B was issued as a successor to Bury A in the upper Yare valley.

The LFC coins appear to have a particular story to tell as later coins in the series show signs of high volume and rapid production: the quality of the finished coins deteriorated and many were poorly produced on irregularly-shaped flans. There were many plated copies of these coins. Subsequently there was a gradual decline in the standard weight of the Breckland coins down towards 1.35g, and issues were more intermittent.

The Bury B series was produced in volume from a large number of dies in four main die groups. The more easterly distribution of die group 2 coins suggests that at least one of the die groups represents geographic rather than chronological separation.

There is so far nothing to link this substantial production of silver coinage with the use of gold staters or quarters. I am however looking forward to completing work on the left facing Norfolk Wolf stater (British JB). A full analysis of these coins is still underway, but they were produced in profusion, different die groups appear to have distinct regional distributions, and certain die groups show the same signs of decline in weight and quality as LFC.

Phase Three (denominational coinage)

The silver coinage started to be issued at the lower standard weight of approximately 1.3g, and in conjunction with a gold coinage of staters and quarter staters. The earliest issue was probably the Snettisham unit, with related gold, and a major centre for this coinage was the upper Yare valley. Later issues were the Irstead and early boar/horse (BMC 3440 – 44) silver coinages, with a standard weight of some 1.3g, and the related gold coinages were varieties of Freckenham staters and quarter staters.

My work to date suggests that after the Snettisham series two distinct mints were producing markedly different Freckenham gold staters, and that each had a related silver coinage, although the silver coinages may have been produced at additional sites. The silver units related to mint A appear to be the Irstead unit followed by boar/horse B (BMC 3455 – 72) and for mint B the early boar/horse (BMC 3440 – 44) followed by boar/horse C (BMC 3473 – 3511).

The above developments appear to represent a logical progression, but do not take into account the Saham Toney group of EFH coins which are anomalous in weight and style. A full analysis of the subsequent development of the coinage is beyond the scope of this paper, but I have been using an outline which seeks to make sense of the stylistic groupings within the coinage which appear to have continued through most of the period of production. In this model the realistic-headed horse units develop into the open-headed coins, including those inscribed Anted and Ecen. Similarly, the Y-headed coins, starting with the Saham Toney type, develop into two separate groups which include the early pattern/horse, normal face/horse, Ece and the Saenu coinages.

This is very much work in progress and is not intended to be definitive, but provides a basis for categorising the types and gives a tentative structure to the series. I have included photographs of the reverses of a selection of coins which illustrate the working hypothesis as Figure 30.

One of the more contentious aspects of this hypothesis is the continuation of the normal face/horse series alongside the inscribed coinage, and its lack of continuity with EFH coinage. The hypothetical order of the later coins is based upon my die analysis of many of these types and their occurrence in the late hoards. Preliminary analysis indicates that the hoards were deposited after the final production of the coinages referred to above and that they have a similar mix of these Icenian coins. Therefore I have used the ratio of hoard to non-hoard provenances as a rough measure of time in circulation before deposition, and hence age. On this basis certain die groups of normal face/horse coins appear very late, notwithstanding a much lower survival rate of coins per die than the common inscribed coinage. I have so far die-checked some 95% of recorded Icenian coins and completion of this work will help to clarify these issues, as will the completion of Amanda Chadburn's study of the late hoards.

Another contentious assumption is that the Y-headed coins form a separate group and are not directly derived from the early Icenian coinages. My assumption is that these coinages are derived from types commonly referred to as Trinovantian; indeed the Y-head itself can be found in the coinage of Tasciovanus (see VA 1732). In the course of looking at the various Icenian dies it has become apparent that a number of types are closely related to coins of the Trinovantes, and in particular to issues ascribed to Addedomaros, Dubnovellaunos, Tasciovanus and Cunobelin (eg Talbot 2003). Further work is needed in respect of these possible links which all appear to be related to Y-headed coins and the Ece A coins with the facing horse's head (VA 760).

The apparent linkages of the Y-headed coinage with that of more southerly groups is matched by apparent links between the main open-headed coinages and the coinage of the Corieltauvi, most obviously in the boar/horse silver units. Unfortunately straightforward explanations are rare, and the position is complicated by obvious stylistic links between the normal face/horse series (Y-headed) and certain Corieltauvian coins. These regional linkages will clearly be a fruitful area for future research.

The working model creates an alternative theoretical structure to try to make sense of some of the anomalies which are emerging. However as I complete die sequences for the other early coinages, and as new types and dies emerge, I am encountering further evidence of local production and variation, and I suspect that the reality of Iron Age coin production in East Anglia may be more complex and may have more local elements than can be described at present. Nonetheless the main issues can now be explained as being bursts of activity, often in parallel. The Iceni coinage has often been seen as an extended chain of successive issues over what must have been a long period of time. The coinage can now be rationally interpreted in a different way, and in fact it may have been issued over a much shorter period, or if over a longer period, then on an intermittent basis. Work is continuing on trying to weave the few clues as to the timing of the early issues into a rational overall hypothesis.

This paper on the early face horse coinage represents the area of my work on the coinage of the Iceni that is the most complete; even so it remains work in progress. One of my hopes is that by publishing my work to date on this series, readers may identify dies or die-links from their own records or collections which have not yet been found by me, and which will help me to complete as full a picture as is currently possible of this fascinating coinage.

Snettisham unit

Snettisham quarter

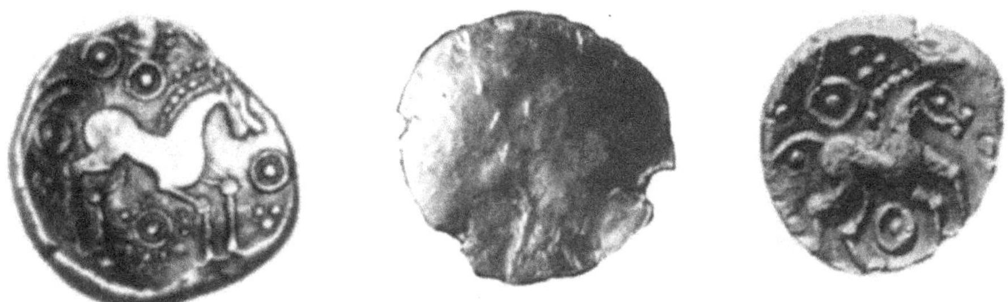

Snettisham stater

Irstead 1 quarter

Irstead A unit

Undescribed fractional unit

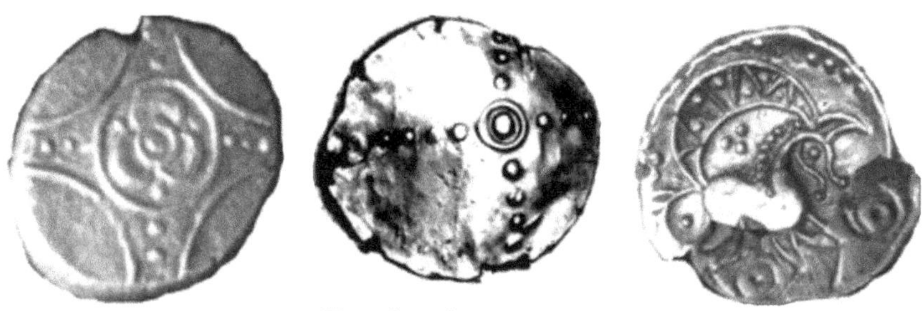

Freckenham stater

EBH unit

Freckenham stater

Figure 29. Examples of Snettisham, Irstead and boar/horse coinages.

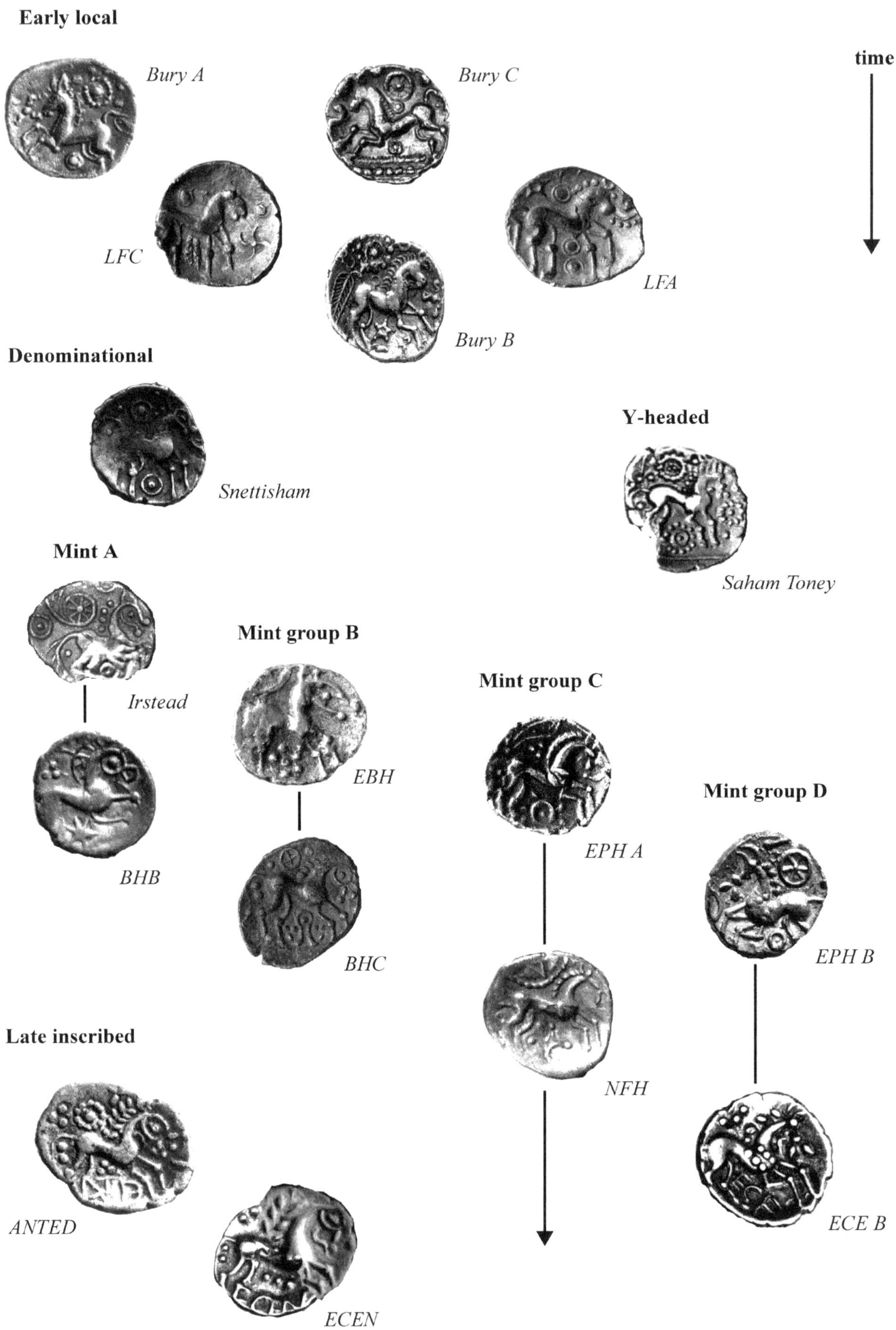

Figure 30. Hypothetical structure of Icenian coinage.

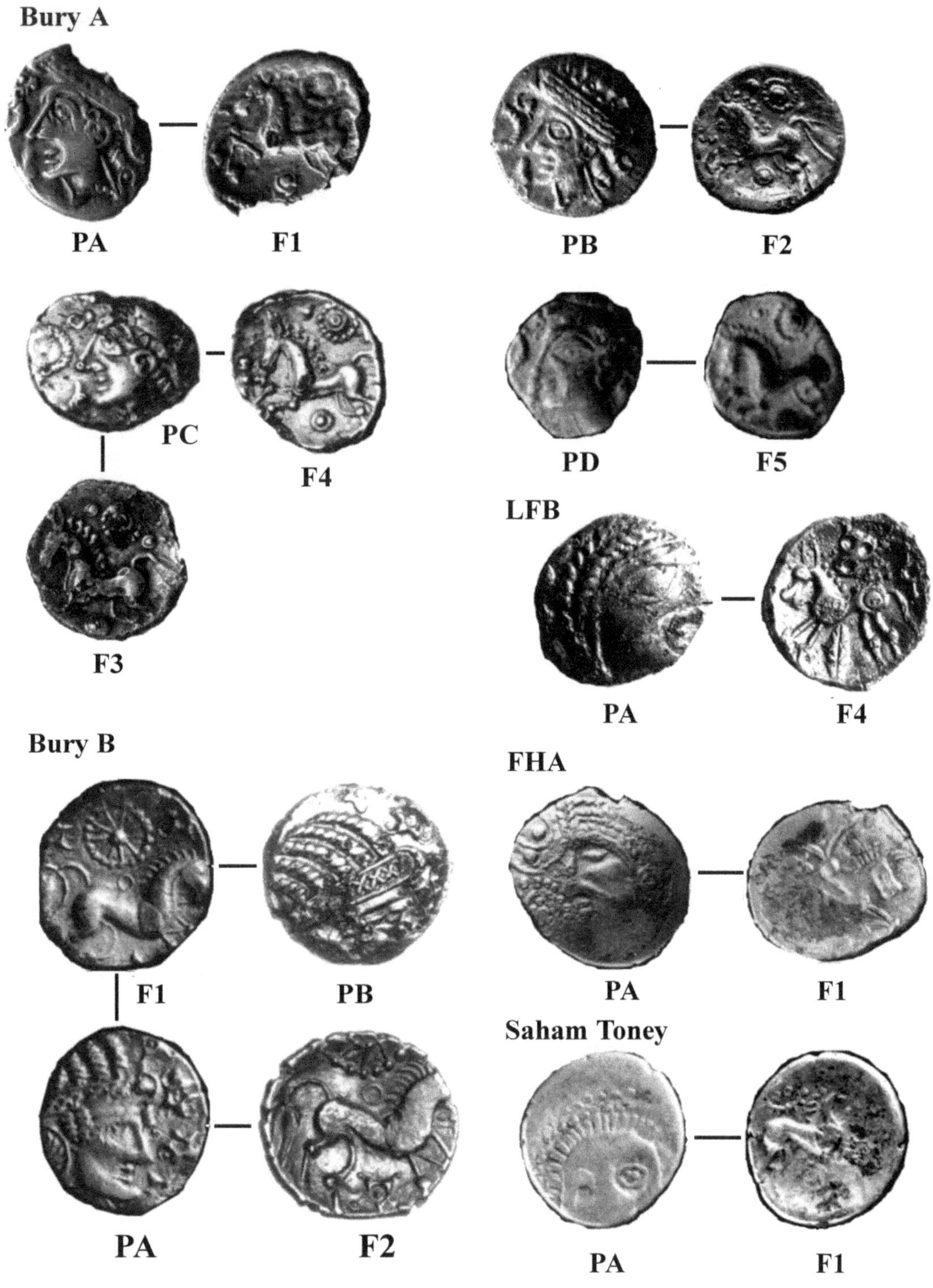

Figure 31. Examples of plated coins.

Appendix 1. Iceni coin and die numbers: work in progress.

Type	Traditional ref.	Standard coins			Weight	Plated coins			Coins per die	
		Total coins	Obv. dies	Rev. dies		Total coins	Obv. dies	Rev. dies	Obv.	Rev.
Bury										
Bury A	Bury A	128	9	11	1.31 - 1.5	9	4	5	14.2	11.6
Bury C	Bury C	34	7	7	1.18 - 1.45				4.9	4.9
Bury B	Bury B	87	9	25	1.2 - 1.45	5	2 (1)	3	9.7	3.5
Bury D		11	1	5	1.25 - 1.38				11	2.2
Bury E		2	2	1	1.18 only				1	2
LF group										
LFA	FHA	63	10	25	1.2 - 1.41	4	1	1	6.3	2.5
LFB1		7	2	3	1.3 - 1.42				3.5	2.3
LFBII		4	2	4	1.26 - 1.39	2	1	(1)	2	1
LFBIII	BMC 387	3	1	1	1.08 and 1.36				3	3
LFC	FHCc	104	14	16	1.14 - 1.41	31	4 (4)	0 (4)	7.4	6.5
Snettisham group										
Snet U	FHCa	78	15	26	1.02 - 1.3				5.2	3
Ir A U	FHCb	33	4	4	1.02 - 1.3				8.2	7.2
Ir B U	BMC 3536	5	3	3	0.94 - 1.18				1.6	1.6
EBH	BMC 3440	35	3	8	0.94 - 1.16				11.6	4.4
Saham Toney type										
Saham T.	BMC 3540	48	10	15	0.79 - 1.13	1	1	1	4.8	3.2
For comparison										
BHB	BMC 3455	176	14	24	0.96 - 1.22	10	6	7	12.6	7.3
NFH	Note 1	1182	73	87	1.18 - 1.29	29	13(4)	14(3)	16.2	13.6
ECE B	Note 2	456	10	23	1.18 - 1.3	3	1	2	45.6	19.8
ECE A	VA760	348	8	11	1.2 - 1.3				43.5	31.6
ECEN	Note 3	1141	23	42	1.19 – 1.3	18+			49.6	27.2
SYM	Note 4	104	2	6	1.21 - 1.29				52	17.3

Note 1 VA 790, 792 and 794
Note 2 VA 762, 764 and 766
Note 3 VA 730, 732, 734, 740, 754 and 756
Note 4 VA 750 and 752

Appendix 2. Comparison of Icenian hoards.

	Forncett	Honingham	Fring	Field Baulk	Lakenheath	Total	West Norfolk	Total population
BURY A							1	119
BURY C								31
BURY B							2	79
BURY D								9
BURY E								2
LFA							2	58
LFB							2	11
LFC							18	100
SNET U	1					1		72
SNET Q							7	70
IR A U			2			2	4	29
IR B U							3	5
EBH							6	28
Saham Toney		1				1		44
BHA	3	1		3		7		45
BHB	3	4	2	4	3	16		176
BHC	19	13	3	26	19	80	14	311
EPH A	1					1	5	74
EPH B	2	4		1	2	9	2	84
NFH	65	84	29	172	88	438	17	1182
OTHER	-	-	-	-	2	2		N/A
INSCRIBED	242	234	117	666	301	1560		N/A
ROMAN	45				67	112		N/A
TOTAL	381	341	153	872	482	2229		

Bibliography

Allen, D. F. 1970: The coins of the Iceni. *Britannia* 1, 1-33.

Chadburn, A. 1990: A hoard of Iron Age silver coins from Fring, Norfolk and some observations on the Icenian coin series. *British Numismatic Journal* 60, 1-12.

Chadburn, A. 1992: A preliminary analysis of the hoard of Icenian coins from Field Baulk, March, Cambridgeshire. In M. Mays (ed.), *Celtic coinage: Britain and beyond* (Oxford, BAR 222), 73-81.

Chadburn, A. and Gurney, D. 1991: The Fring coin hoard. *Norfolk Archaeology* 69, 218-225.

de Jersey, P. and Newman, J. 1997: Iron Age coins from Barham, Suffolk. *British Numismatic Journal* 67, 93-95.

Delestrée, L.-P. and Tache, M. 2002: *Nouvel Atlas des Monnaies Gauloises. I, de la Seine au Rhin* (Paris, Editions Commios).

Gregory, A. 1992: Snettisham and Bury: some new light on the earliest Icenian coinage. In M. Mays (ed.), *Celtic coinage: Britain and beyond* (Oxford, BAR 222), 47-68.

Hobbs, R. 1996: *British Iron Age coins in the British Museum* (London, BMP).

Talbot, J. 2003: A new example of the "Eyelash Crescent" Iceni stater. *Chris Rudd list* 69 (May 2003), 6-7.

Van Arsdell, R. D. 1989: *Celtic Coinage of Britain* (London, Spink).

An Iron Age coin weight from Rotherwick, Hampshire

Jeffrey May

The purpose of this paper is to comment more fully on what has now been mentioned several times in the literature as the first certain example of an Iron Age coin die from Britain. The object is a small cylinder of bronze, with the negative impression of the obverse of a Gallo-Belgic stater on one end. It first came to notice at Seaby Coins (now the Classical Numismatic Group) of New Bond Street. It was shown to the British Museum, where the metal was analysed by Mr Mike Cowell, and, confident that it was ancient, the Museum acquired it. Dr Jonathan Williams noted it as a coin die in the British Museum Magazine in 1994 (Williams 1994, 12-13), and it was accepted as a die elsewhere (de Jersey 1996, 11).

The object was said to have been found near Basingstoke in Hampshire, in 1993. It is now possible to give the circumstances of the discovery, the precise findspot, and to speculate on the possible implications of the findspot. It is also possible to suggest an alternative function for the piece.

Description

The cylinder (Figure 1) is c. 15mm long and c. 18mm in diameter. The ends are flat, and the edges are slightly rounded. One end shows an indistinct negative impression of the features commonly seen on the obverses of early Gallo-Belgic staters, notably the face, wreath and curls ultimately derived from the Apollo head of the gold staters of Philip II of Macedon and kindred pieces.

The impression (Figure 2) was probably made by hammering an actual coin on to the cylindrical block, the latter perhaps first softened by heating – the process known as hubbing. The resulting obverse design appears reversed, that is left-facing, and the original coin was therefore a right-facing Gallo-Belgic type. The cylinder surface is very worn, suggesting that the original coin was itself worn, and the type is more easily identified from an impression than from the cylinder itself. It would have been suitable for producing the small size of Gallo-Belgic right-facing stater classified by Derek Allen as type Aa (Allen 1960, 100), and by Scheers as class IV (Scheers 1977, 244 and pl. III.59). Indeed Dr Williams (pers. comm.) has established die links with two such coins in the British Museum (no. 2131, BM 1767, and no. 11712, BM 1766), and more recently has shown me a photograph of another die-linked example, from Gamels Hall, Hertfordshire, now in Hertford Museum.

There are a few tiny flecks of gold adhering to the cylinder, both on the ends and on the side. The base of the cylinder is plain, although there is a circular mark of smoother metal approximately 6mm in diameter at the centre, and two or three other linear marks across the surface. It is not clear whether these represent hammer marks.

Figure 1. Iron Age coin weight from Rotherwick, Hampshire. Height c. 15mm, diameter c. 18mm. Photograph by British Museum Photographic Services.

Mr Cowell has kindly allowed me to make use of his unpublished analysis (Cowell 1993). His report and subsequent letter note that:

"The surfaces... are patinated, and there are also adhering patches of soil. The working face also has a black finish which extends partly down the sides. There was no fluorescence under ultraviolet light. The patination seems to be deeply penetrating, judging by the appearance of the surface where some areas on the edge of the working face have broken away. A small taper section was attempted on the edge of the non-working face, but uncorroded metal was not exposed after approximately 1mm of material had been removed... providing good evidence of the corrosion penetration.

The body metal of the die was analysed non-destructively by X-ray fluorescence. Because of the surface patination, the analysis was approximate, or semi-quantitative, and revealed the composition as a leaded tin-bronze with traces of arsenic and antimony. The tin content could be as high as 15%, although this could only be confirmed by drilling into the object and removing a corrosion-free sample."

Cowell concluded that the composition is consistent with a date in the Iron Age, although he noted that the composition of Iron Age copper-based metalwork is not specifically distinctive, and therefore the attribution cannot be absolutely certain.

Optical microscopy revealed small fragments of gold foil or leaf on the surface of the object, both on the sides and the ends. These fragments were confirmed as gold with examination and analysis by the scanning electron microscope. A gold particle on the face was found by SEM to be a gold/silver alloy containing 74% gold, 18% silver, 5% copper and 3% lead. Cowell notes, however, that these figures may be subject to errors due to contamination from corrosion products of the copper alloy, and that the copper reading and possibly the lead too could be affected by this. There is also the possibility of surface enrichment of the gold, since the SEM only analyses a very thin layer on the surface. Nonetheless, the gold composition is similar to the alloys used for the early Iron Age coinage, and is closest, perhaps, to Gallo-Belgic Aa quarter staters.

Figure 2. Impression taken from coin weight (scale in millimetres). Photograph by J. May.

Cowell agreed that the piece seemed almost certain to be a die, but that the absence of much deformation or damage suggested that it had not been used extensively. He also noted that the diameter of the cylinder and the size of the Gallo-Belgic stater impression suggested that it was a forger's die, rather than an official one. The presence of small fragments of gold on the sides and the ends suggested that it had been in close proximity to gold foil or leaf, although it seemed less likely that the gold fragments had been transferred to the surface through striking plated forgeries, since they ought then to be confined solely to the end or working face.

SEM examination also revealed some dendritic structure preserved in the corrosion on the working face, which strongly suggested that the object was cast, and also that it had probably not been extensively worked.

The discovery of the piece

The object had been bought by Mr Eric McFadden, then Senior Director of Seaby's, from another dealer. At that time, Ms Bridget Roe was a member of Seaby's staff, and it was she who notified me of the find soon after it had arrived in New Bond Street. I visited Seaby's, and as it seemed likely that the piece would be sold abroad and perhaps lost to British numismatics, Mr McFadden generously allowed me not only to make notes on the piece, but also to make impressions of each end of the cylinder. This was done with Xantopren L, a silicone-based elastomeric impression material marketed by Bayer, which seemed neither to leave deposits on the cylinder, nor to remove any of the flecks of gold from its surface.

The object was said to have been found near Basingstoke, but no further details regarding provenance were forthcoming at that stage. It was obviously important, however, to try and establish a more exact findspot, not least because the context might throw some light on function if, for example, it had come from a late Iron Age settlement site which might produce further evidence of minting. I therefore wrote to the anonymous finder pleading for more information. Mr McFadden kindly sent my letter to the dealer from whom he had obtained the piece. In due course I was telephoned by Mr David Morgan, of Swaffham, Norfolk, who most helpfully confirmed that he had bought the object from the actual finder, and had later sold it to Seaby's. Mr Morgan had also established that the finder was willing to furnish further details, and provided me with his name and telephone number.

The trail led to Mr David Walsh of Sandhurst, who explained that he had found the cylinder with a metal detector in the ploughsoil of a field at Rotherwick, some eight kilometres north-east of Basingstoke, on about the 8th August 1993. He had sold it to Mr Morgan at a metal detectorists' rally at Newbury, Berkshire, on 22nd August. He also mentioned that he had other finds from nearby fields, including an Iron Age plated stater, some lumps of silver-coloured metal, and a Bronze Age 'axehead'. In March 1996 I had an opportunity to visit Rotherwick with Mr Walsh, and was shown the precise findspot, together with those of the other finds.

The cylinder was found in an arable field just north of Rotherwick church, and east of Frog Lane (Figure 3). Mr Walsh remembered its position clearly, to within about ten metres, some 75m east along a track from Frog Lane to Rooks Farm, and 25m south into the field (SU 71115644). There were no other finds of Iron Age or Romano-British date from the field, and only a small amount of medieval material.

In another arable field nearby, however, north of the track leading west from Frog Lane towards Mill Lane and close to the edge of Winnells Copse, Mr Walsh found a plate

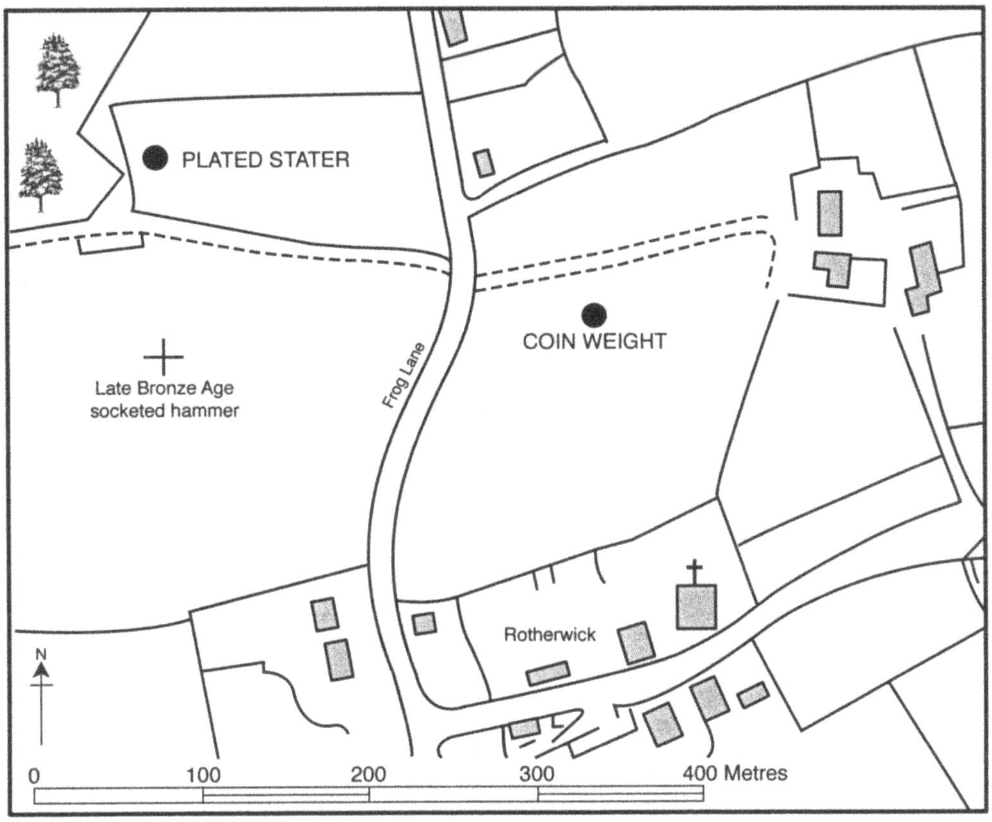

Figure 3. Location of the Rotherwick coin weight and plated stater.

forgery of a Gallo-Belgic stater (SU 70865655). This findspot is c. 250m north-west of the location of the cylinder. Again there were no other finds of Iron Age or Romano-British date in the field.

The other finds are less relevant to this story. The 'axehead' was a Late Bronze Age socketed hammer, similar to those in a hoard from the Isle of Harty, Kent (Smith 1956). It came from the field south of the track to Winnells Copse. The silver-coloured metal lumps came from a field bounded by Mill Lane on its northern and eastern sides, about 1km further north-west at SU 701562. Here Mr Walsh had also found a few Roman bronze objects, including three coins. It seems unlikely that the metal lumps were related to activities connected with the use of the other finds.

The plated stater

The plated stater (Figure 4) is in poor condition, having suffered erosion of metal around its entire circumference. Its diameter is now between 8 and 9mm. Gold plating, however, is still present on most of the obverse and reverse sides, although worn off in places, particularly at the high points.

The type appears to be Scheers's Gallo Belgic C, class V (Scheers 1977, 270, pl. IV.87). The obverse has downward pointing wreath leaves and a face which has largely disintegrated. On the reverse, there is no trace of the usual pellet beneath the horse, but it could have been lost through erosion of the flan edge. The large pellet below the horse's neck is presumably the top of the left foreleg.

The stater was analysed by Dr Matthew Ponting at the Department of Archaeology, University of Nottingham. The copper core comprised 91.66% copper, 7.26% tin, and tiny amounts of iron and lead. The plating consists of 83% gold, 9% silver and 8% copper. This alloy is slightly finer than that of the gold flecks on the cylinder, but both are comparable with the alloys of early Gallo-Belgic staters. The stater was acquired by the writer, and is also now in the British Museum.

Figure 4. Plated stater from Rotherwick (scale in millimetres). Photograph by J. May.

The location

Rotherwick lies on a north-south ridge between the valleys of the rivers Lodden and Whitewater, which meet some nine kilometres to the north before flowing on towards the river Thames (Figure 5). The low-lying, unexcavated Bullsdown hillfort is 4.5km to the north-west, and beyond it, 9 km in the same direction, is the late Iron Age oppidum of Calleva.

The fields in this area have been intensively metal-detected by Mr Walsh, and it seems unlikely that any of the finds came from an Iron Age settlement. The writer saw no sign of pottery scatters, albeit from a fairly quick examination. The lie of the land, however, invites some speculation. The highest point of the Rotherwick ridge is marked by the modern road, Frog Lane. It seems possible that this road could mark a prehistoric route linking the Pilgrim's Way, some 6km to the south, with the Bullsdown hillfort or with Calleva, via a crossing of the river Lodden in the area of Stratfield Saye Park. Prehistoric routes or trackways, however, are notoriously difficult to identify to general satisfaction; nevertheless the finding of the cylinder and the more-or-less contemporary plated stater on the other side of Frog Lane is suggestive.

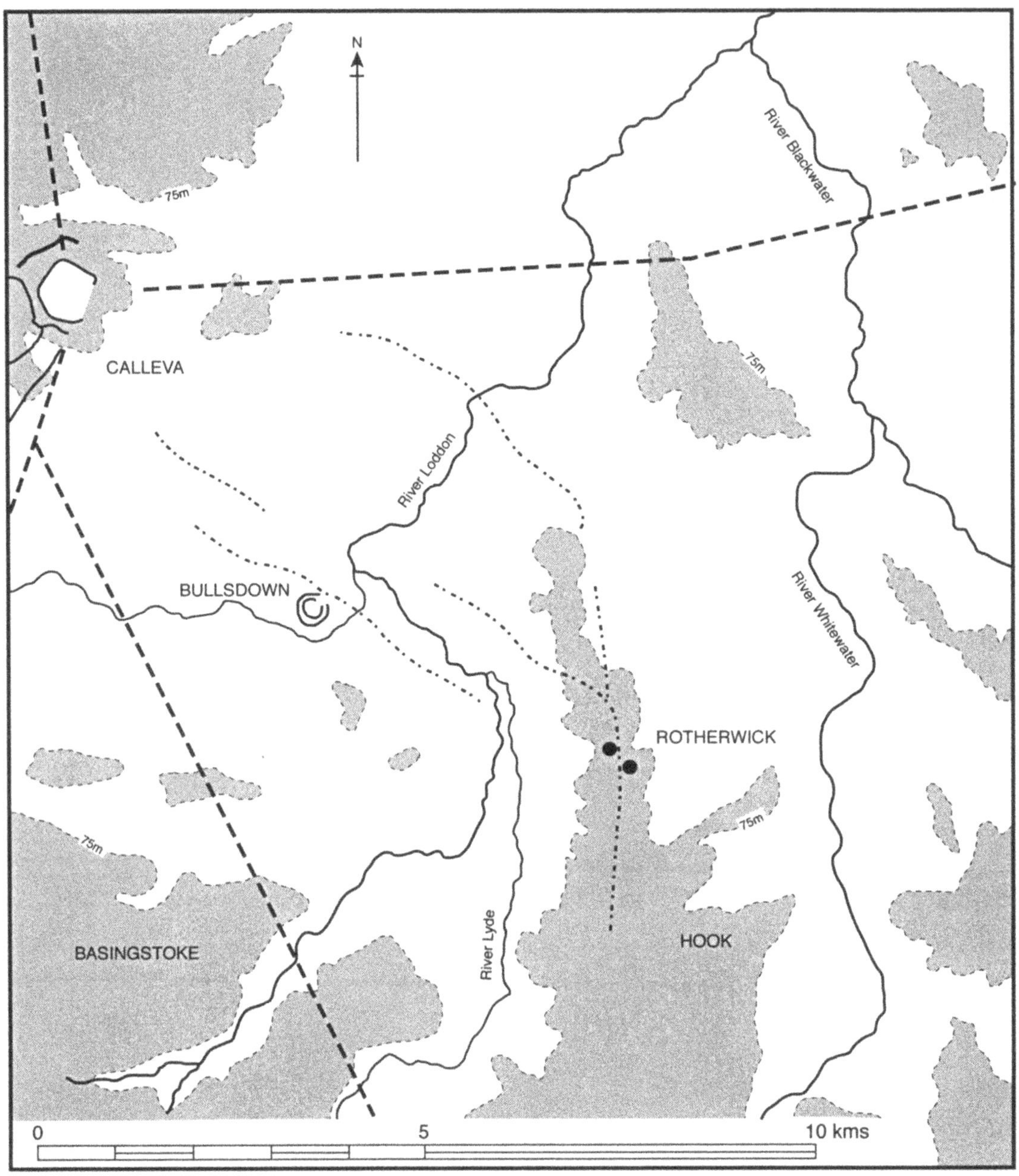

Figure 5. Location of the Rotherwick coin weight in relation to Bullsdown and Silchester.

The function of the cylinder

First thoughts suggested the obvious possibility that the object is a pile die. Its diameter, though, is too small for an official die, since it is clear from the varied positions of coin designs on the flans, that obverse dies were usually much larger than the coin blanks. With our piece, parts of the design run off the edge of the cylinder. The design impression is very weak, and it seems likely that it was produced by a very worn coin, rather than that it had become worn through use.

Exactly how the flecks of gold came to adhere to the cylinder sides, however, is puzzling. It seems certain that the object was never gold plated, although gilding on copper alloy or on silver is known from the British Iron Age, as on the late La Tène beaked brooch from Dragonby (Olivier 1996, 234, fig.11.1 no. 3, and cover).

There are, unfortunately, no genuine Iron Age dies from Britain to compare our piece with. The corroded iron rods from E. M. Clifford's excavation at Bagendon, Gloucestershire (Clifford 1961, 147, 192 & pl. 46), albeit associated with possible mint debris, are trussle dies, if dies at all. On the continent, the old find from Avenches in Switzerland (Keller 1862) seems closest to the Rotherwick piece, although the copper alloy die is here set in an iron sleeve to slow its deterioration in use. Two obverse dies, from Mont Beuvray and Saint Symphorien d'Ancelles, both for striking silver coins, are listed by Delestrée and Duval (1977).

The proximity of the Rotherwick plated stater at first sight might help the argument in favour of a die, particularly since it is of a type not too far removed from the impression on the cylinder. But the lack of use-wear or damage noted, and the provenance of the piece far from any known Iron Age site and unassociated with any of the debris commonly supposed to represent minting, argues for caution.

An alternative explanation is that the cylinder is a coin weight, rather like the weights with coins or coin impressions in their ends known from the Saxon period (Williams 2000). The metrology of the Rotherwick piece supports this interpretation. The weight of our cylinder is 33.96 grams, or perhaps a little more if one allows for the small amount of corrosion and metal loss around the edges. If the cylinder was indeed a weight, it is by no means certain that it was intended for weighing only the Gallo-Belgic type depicted on it. But taking this particular type of small-flan stater, the mean weight of the admittedly few examples that I have had access to, is 6.87 grams. Our Rotherwick piece would therefore correspond to within 0.39 of a gram to the mean weight of five such staters. That degree of correspondence seems more than mere coincidence. Indeed, if one allowed for a little weight loss on the Rotherwick cylinder, the correspondence would have been extremely precise.

If the Rotherwick object is a coin weight, we might imagine that the staters were weighed in stacks of five at a time, which is a number that could well suit a small balance, such as those implied by the Iron Age balance arms from Verulamium (Wheeler and Wheeler 1936, 176 and fig. 24.5) and Gussage All Saints (Wainwright 1979, 110, fig. 85.3045). Weighing in stacks of five would have been quicker than weighing staters individually, yet the number is still manageable and the presence of any plated coins in the stack would be revealed by their lighter weight. Could this be how the Rotherwick plated stater came to be discarded?

As a final speculation, we might imagine that counting in fives could have been a naturally convenient practice in Iron Age Britain. Multiply by ten and we have the number of cavities in the pellet-mould tray from Verulamium (Frere 1983, 31 and pl. Ib). And among the Corieltauvi to the north at least, the standard in minting the earliest gold staters seems to have been in the ratio of fifty staters to the Celtic pound of 309 grams (May 1994, 12-13). Maybe at least some regions of Britain had prematurely adopted a decimal system along with the Gallo-Belgic euro.

Acknowledgements
I am most grateful to Dr J. Williams for permission to publish the piece and for first establishing the die links; to Mr M. Cowell and Dr M. Ponting for permission to quote their analyses of the weight and the plated stater, and to the former for permission to use his photograph of the weight, Figure 1; to Dr M. Spratling for discussing Iron Age balances; and to Dr P. de Jersey for inviting me to participate in the conference, where several helpful suggestions came forth.

Bibliography

Allen, D. F. 1960: The origins of coinage in Britain: a reappraisal. In S. S. Frere (ed.), *Problems of the Iron Age in Southern Britain* (London, University of London, Institute of Archaeology, Occasional Paper 11) 97-308.

Clifford, E. M. 1961: *Bagendon, A Belgic Oppidum. Excavations 1954-1956* (Cambridge, Heffer).

Cowell, M. 1993 (unpublished): *Report on the examination of a coin die purporting to be Iron Age*. British Museum, Department of Scientific Research, 7 October 1993.

de Jersey, P. 1996: *Celtic Coinage in Britain* (Princes Risborough, Shire Archaeology 72).

Delestrée, L.-P. and Duval, A. 1977: Un coin monétaire inédit du Mont-Beuvray. *Antiquités Nationales* 9, 45-47.

Frere, S. S. 1983: *Verulamium Excavations Vol.II* (London, Reports of the Research Committee of the Society of Antiquaries, 41).

Keller, F. 1862: Notice of a die for striking Helvetian or Gaulish gold coins; found at Avenches, Switzerland. *Archaeological Journal* 19, 253-258.

May, J. 1994: Coinage and the settlements of the Corieltauvi in East Midland Britain. *British Numismatic Journa*l 64, 1-21.

Olivier, A. C. H. 1996: Brooches of silver, copper alloy and iron from Dragonby. 231-64 In J. May, *Dragonby. Report on Excavations at an Iron Age and Romano-British Settlement in North Lincolnshire* (Oxford, Oxbow Monograph 61, vol. 1) 231-264.

Scheers, S. 1977: *Traité de Numismatique Celtique, II, La Gaule Belgique* (Paris, Les Belles Lettres).

Smith, M. A. 1956: Isle of Harty. *Inventaria Archaeologica* 1956, GB 18.3 nos. 22-3.

Wainwright, G. J. 1979: *Gussage All Saints. An Iron Age Settlement in Dorset* (London, H.M.S.O., Department of the Environment Archaeological Report 10).

Wheeler, R. E. M. and Wheeler, T. V. 1936: *Verulamium. A Belgic and Two Roman Cities* (London, Reports of the Research Committee of the Society of Antiquaries 11).

Williams, G. 2000: Anglo-Saxon and Viking coin weights. *British Numismatic Journal* 69, 19-36.

Williams, J. 1994: Ancient British forger's coin-die. *British Museum Magazine* 20, 20.

The Silsden hoard: discovery, investigation and new interpretations

Gavin Edwards and Megan Dennis

In memory of my father, Arthur Ronald Edwards, 1920 – 2002, who never ceased to enjoy the pursuit and discovery of new knowledge and understanding.

Discovery and recovery

On the 1st August 1998 Mr Jeff Walbank of Silsden discovered the first of 28 items that have collectively become known as the Silsden hoard (Walbank 1999). The process of recovery was made possible through the skilled use of a metal detector and took several months to complete. While this might suggest the items were spread over a large area, the main difficulty in recovery was due to varying soil conditions. The finds all came from a relatively discrete area, supporting the view that they were originally deposited as the result of a single event.

On the 15th December 1998 the Silsden hoard was declared Treasure and was officially recorded as consisting of the following:

1 gold stater of Cunobelin, linear type (VA 1910)
4 gold staters of Cunobelin, wild A series (VA 1931)
3 gold staters of Cunobelin, wild B series (VA 1933)
4 gold staters of Cunobelin, plastic A series (VA 2010)
1 gold stater of Cunobelin, plastic B series (VA 2020)
6 gold staters of Cunobelin, classic A series (VA 2027)
1 gold stater of Epaticcus (VA 575)
6 gold staters inscribed IISVP RASV (VA 920)
1 gold stater inscribed VOLISIOS DVMNOVELLAVNOS (VA 972)

1 Roman iron finger ring set with an intaglio

Site history

From the dispersed nature of the individual find spots (Figure 1) it is apparent that the hoard was disturbed after its original deposition, presumably as a result of plough action. There is visual evidence of post-medieval ridge and furrow and the somewhat elongated nature of the scatter is in line with the direction of ploughing. It is difficult to be certain how much ploughing the soil has been subjected to, as the soil type is not well suited for arable use. The land is now used as pasture, and it is generally believed that the last major episode of ploughing took place during the Second World War.

To test if the items were coming from a detectable archaeological context a small trial trench was excavated near the centre of the scatter. The results were inconclusive but did confirm that the items were being recovered from a depth of c. 15 - 20cm, well within that which would be expected to be disturbed by ploughing. It was during this trial excavation that one of the staters was recovered.

As part of the initial investigations of the surrounding area, Rob Vernon, of the Department of Archaeological Sciences, Bradford University, undertook a magnetometry survey. This identified a number of anomalies, but it has not yet been established if these are archaeological in origin or the result of local geology.

Archaeological context of discovery

There is very little evidence to determine the exact extent and nature of Iron Age activity within the immediate area. The site lies on the south-west flank of Rombalds Moor, a distinctive area of upland which is well known for a wide range of prehistoric sites, including an extensive group of carved rocks. Considerable quantities of lithic and other artefactual evidence have been recovered from the uplands to provide clear evidence of human activity stretching from the Mesolithic through to the Bronze Age. Rombalds Moor seems to have been an important landscape displaying both ritual and settlement activities. There is some evidence of early Iron Age activity, but then there seems to have been a general abandonment of the upland zone and a move towards the valley zones in the middle and late Iron Age.

Below the main upland zone of Rombalds Moor there are a number of earthwork sites that have in the past been dated to the Iron Age. Fragmentary remains of Iron Age 'walling' are also known but in all cases there is no independent dating evidence to confirm this. That there must have been an Iron

Age presence is largely assumed and this assumption relies heavily on the presence of a significant number of beehive querns that have been recovered as stray finds or built into walls. Looking at their distribution it seems to confirm the general impression that a widespread movement towards the valley zones had already taken place by the late Iron Age (Figure 2).

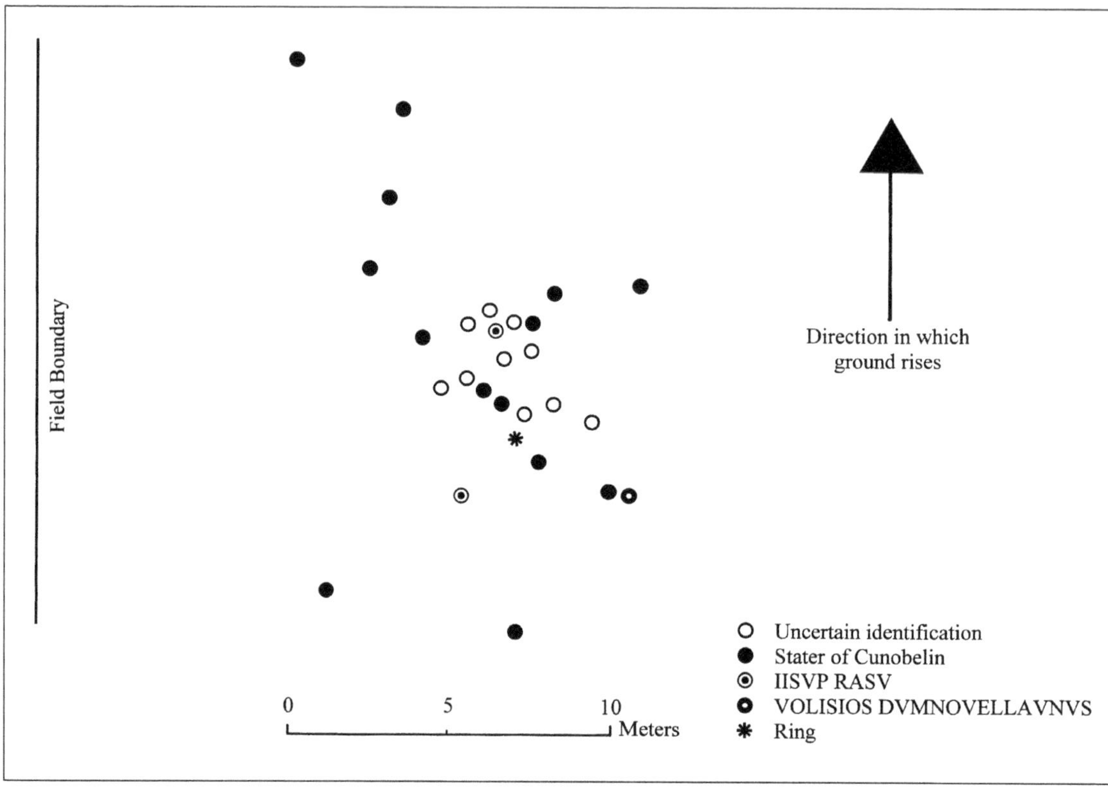

Figure 1. Findspots of objects comprising the Silsden hoard.

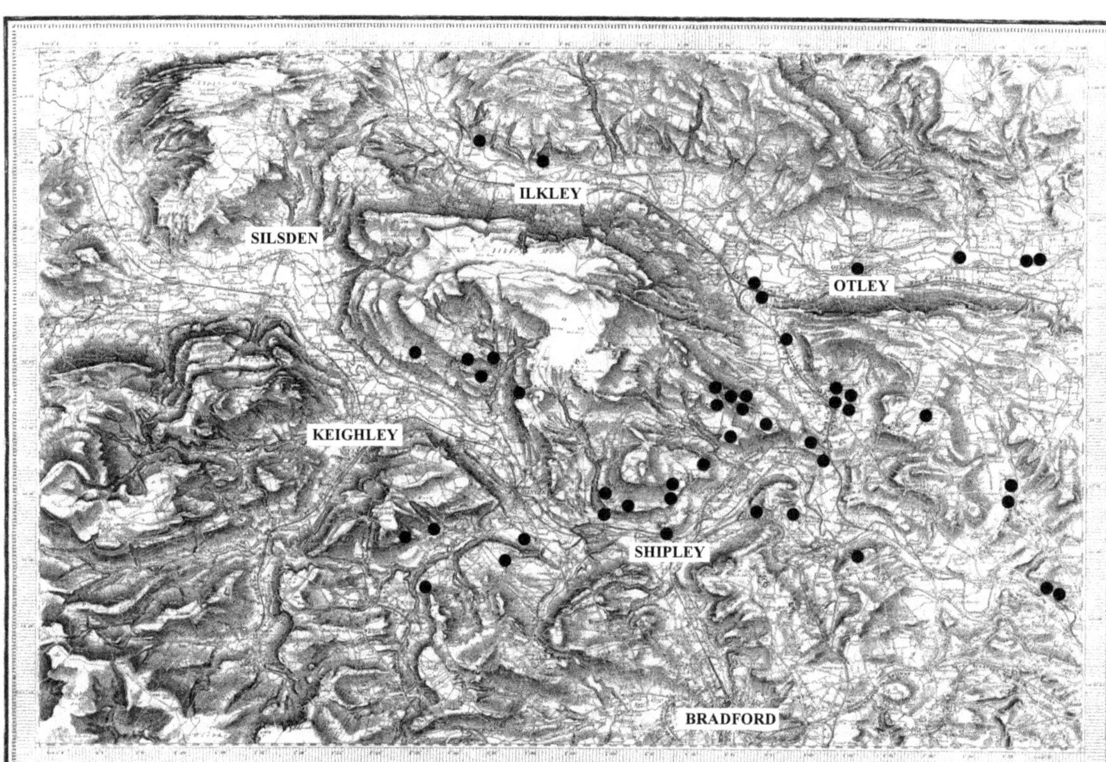

Figure 2. Local distribution of Iron Age beehive querns.

Another indicator of a significant Iron Age presence is the Roman fort at Ilkley. Founded in AD 79 as part of the military conquest of the Brigantes, it was to remain garrisoned almost continuously throughout the Roman occupation. Although sited on the northern side of Rombalds Moor, in the Wharfe valley, it was clearly an integral part of the whole infrastructure of Roman control and was probably strategically positioned in response to potential threats from major centres of Brigantian opposition.

While there is some evidence to imply an Iron Age presence in the area, the Silsden hoard seems to suggest that it might be far greater, and more important than has previously been recognized. What the nature of that presence might be is presently the subject of on-going work but one of the earliest results has been the discovery of two broken portions of beehive quern (not shown on Figure 2). These were found built into the dry stone walling surrounding the field in which the hoard was found and are not thought to have been moved far from their original find spots.

The existence of the Silsden hoard and the unique nature of its contents could not possibly have been anticipated. It was clearly a find of great importance, and considerable potential, requiring as much detailed examination as possible. It was to that end that the Department of Archaeological Sciences, Bradford University and the Bradford Museum Service agreed to a programme of physical and metallurgical analysis of the gold staters. This programme of analysis, carried out under the supervision of Gerry McDonald and Rick Jones, investigated new techniques for the analysis of gold alloy coins and raised opportunities for further work at the Department of Materials, Oxford University.

Scientific Investigation

Methodology

A selection of the coins, including one of each type, excluding single examples, were analysed by Peter Northover and Chris Salter at Oxford University. Each of the selected coins was analysed by microprobe as previously described (Northover 1992, 277).

An electron probe microanalysis with wavelength dispersive spectrometry was carried out using the CAMEBAX automated instrument. Coins were prepared by mounting within brass holders. Small areas of the coin edge were then ground and polished. Depending on the alignment of the coin in the holder and the size and curvature of the coin an area of up to several millimetres square was prepared. The final polish was achieved with a 1μm diamond paste that allowed the coins to be examined metallographically before analysis in the instrument. This metallographic examination helped to verify the authenticity of the coins.

The electron microprobe was operated under the following conditions: an accelerating voltage of 25kV, an absorbed electron current at the sample of approximately 30nA, and an X-ray take-off angle of 40°. Thirteen elements were analysed including tin, lead, iron, cobalt, nickel, copper, zinc, arsenic, antimony, sulphur, silver, bismuth and gold. The detection limits for most of these elements are 100-200ppm (parts per million), but are 300ppm for gold and 0.10% for arsenic.

Three analyses were taken from the small prepared area (less than $2mm^2$ in size) on each coin. Each analysis derived from an area of 50μm. The mean analysis was then calculated. Previous analysis at Bradford had suggested that several of the coins were severely heterogeneous, but unfortunately the semi-destructive nature of the Oxford methodology made it impossible to investigate this any further. The colour differences visible on the surface of the coins demonstrate how clearly the gold is segregated within them.

A technological examination had previously been carried out at Bradford. The coins were weighed, measured, photographed, examined under a video microscope and die alignments recorded. This second part of the scientific program was carried out on all coins.

Results

This unique integrated approach led to some interesting findings. The analyses were collated to provide an average result for each coin, with the severely heterogeneous noted.

Coin Number	Coin Type	% Gold	% Silver	% Copper
2	IISVP RASV	30.27	10.32	58.93
10*	IISVP RASV	29.92	10.21	59.59
13*	Cunobelin classic A	34.91	8.49	56.31
14	Cunobelin plastic A	42.68	10.28	46.84
18	IISVP RASV	30.03	12.74	56.89
19	Cunobelin classic A	42.76	14.19	42.80
20	Cunobelin wild B	42.13	8.22	49.49
21	Epaticcus	40.01	5.23	54.27
23	Cunobelin wild A	44.21	12.12	43.47

Table 1. Analytical results for the Silsden coins.
** coin is severely heterogeneous*

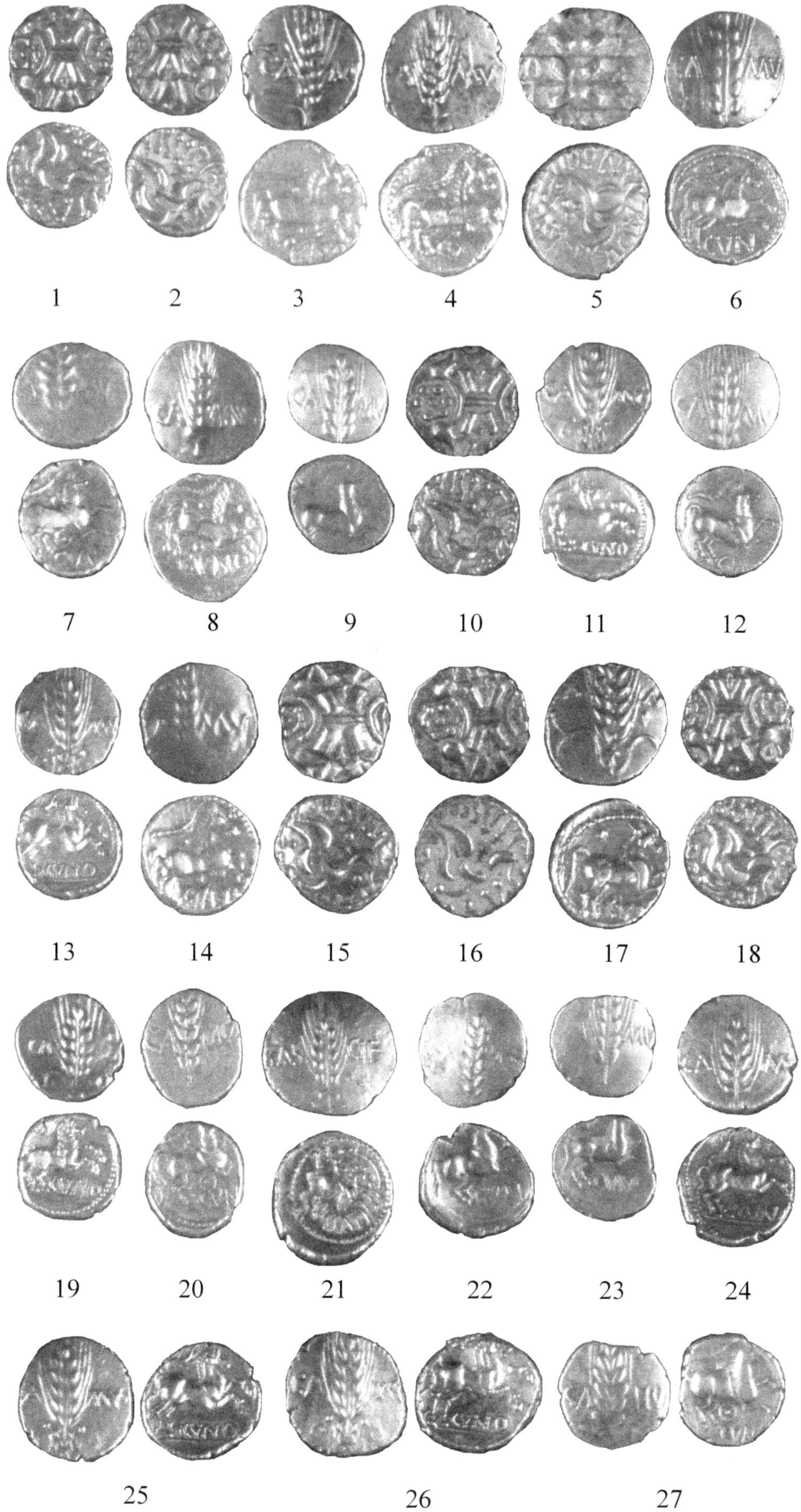

Figure 3. Coins from the Silsden hoard. Shown at actual size.

Discussion

The results show good agreement with other published analyses of Iron Age coinage (Cowell et al. 1987; Burnett and Cowell 1988; Cowell 1992; Northover 1992), confirming their authenticity (Figure 4). The examination of the prepared coins before analysis had revealed surprisingly little corrosion. This is interpreted as a result of the stable burial conditions in a field which has lain fallow since the Second World War. The coins have not been subjected to the ravages of modern fertilisers or pesticides and changes in conditions from yearly ploughing, which produces the high levels of corrosion in most recently discovered Iron Age coins.

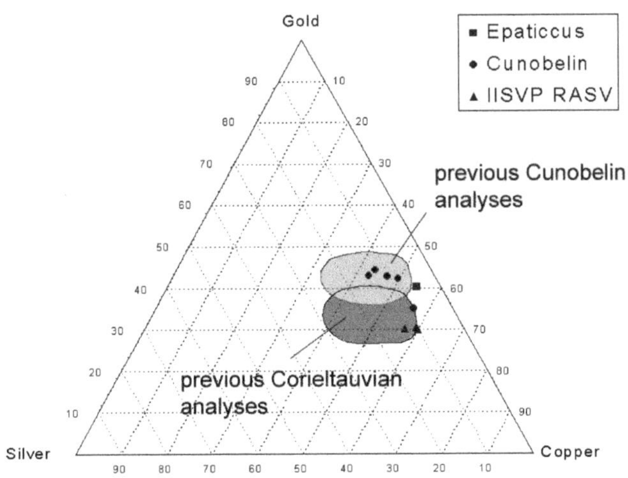

Figure 4. Ternary diagram of Silsden hoard analyses.

Cunobelin classic staters

The Cunobelin classic staters from Silsden are slightly underweight (Figure 5), with a significant group of coins at 4.8 - 5.0g that require further interpretation and examination. The most likely reason for this decrease in weight is the age of the staters when they were deposited. They have become more worn by being in circulation for a longer period than is usual. The control of coin weight appears to be important throughout what has been described as the 'episodic manufacture' of the Cunobelin staters (Allen 1975). Allen (*ibid.*) calculated that the weight of Cunobelin staters was maintained at 5.4g with 1 - 2% error. The slightly lower mean mass of the Silsden coins does not suggest that the coins were below weight when produced. Rather it can be interpreted that the coins had been used for a considerable length of time before deposition.

IISVP RASV staters

The second largest group of coins were the IISVP RASV Corieltauvian coins. Comparing the weights of the Silsden IISVP RASV coins with the few records of this rare coin in the Celtic Coin Index revealed that these coins have a wider weight range than seen for the much more common Cunobelin staters (see Figure 5; IISVP RASV weights range from 4.4 – 5.6g, whereas Cunobelin staters all fall between 4.8 - 5.6g). This may suggest that the Corieltauvian moneyers had less control over the weight of their coins, perhaps because they were minting in stressful circumstances. The analysis above (see Figure 4) shows that the IISVP RASV staters contain more copper than the Cunobelin coins. It may be interpreted that this is due to the cutting off of southern contact and raw materials after the Roman invasion. The sudden invasion in the south must have had some impact on earlier trading routes, perhaps slowing down or stopping altogether the movement of precious metals into more peripheral areas. The only option open to the Corieltauvi would be to add more copper to their later issues. This suggests that the IISVP RASV coins are late in the Corieltauvian sequence, a conclusion strengthened by the work of Williams (2000) linking the IISVP RASV and Icenian ESVPRASTO series and the work by Cottam (forthcoming) on the Corieltauvian coinage as a whole.

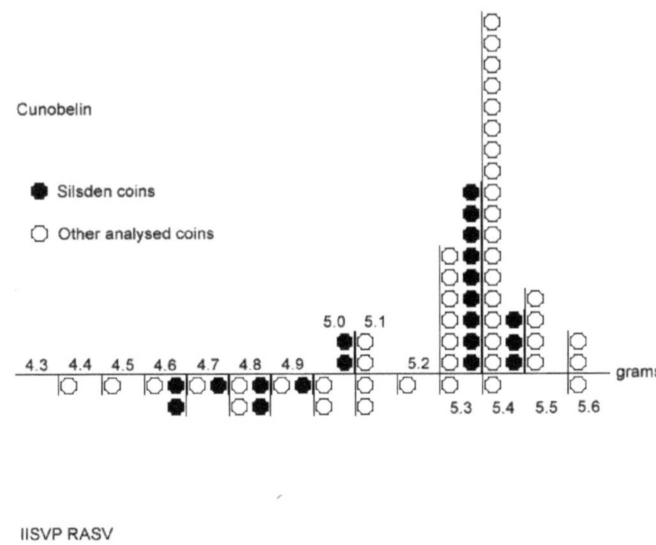

Figure 5. Weights of Cunobelin and IISVP RASV staters.

Die Alignments

Further exciting evidence was uncovered during the investigation to suggest the late date of the IISVP RASV series, and to strengthen Allen's interpretation of the classic coins as the latest in the sequence of Cunobelin stater types (Allen 1975). During the technological examination of the coins in the hoard the relationship between the obverse and reverse images was recorded.

For most of the coins this resulted in a variety of alignments, except for the Cunobelin classic series and IISVP RASV issues (Figures 6, 9). These reveal a more consistent relationship between the obverse and reverse designs. This could have been achieved by careful positioning of the dies during striking. For the production of coins on as large a scale as Cunobelin (Allen 1975), however, this would prove very time inefficient. More likely perhaps is the use of a hinged die or similar alignment mechanism. Hinged dies are known from later Roman periods (Zograph 1977; Figure 7) and may be illustrated in frescoes in the House of Vettii at Pompeii (Ogden 1908; Figure 8).

This apparent change in production, occurring at the same time as the adoption of realistic Romanised art styles in the southern coinages of Britain, is strongly suggestive of the uptake not only of Roman imagery, but also manufacturing techniques during the latest stages of Iron Age coinage in Britain.

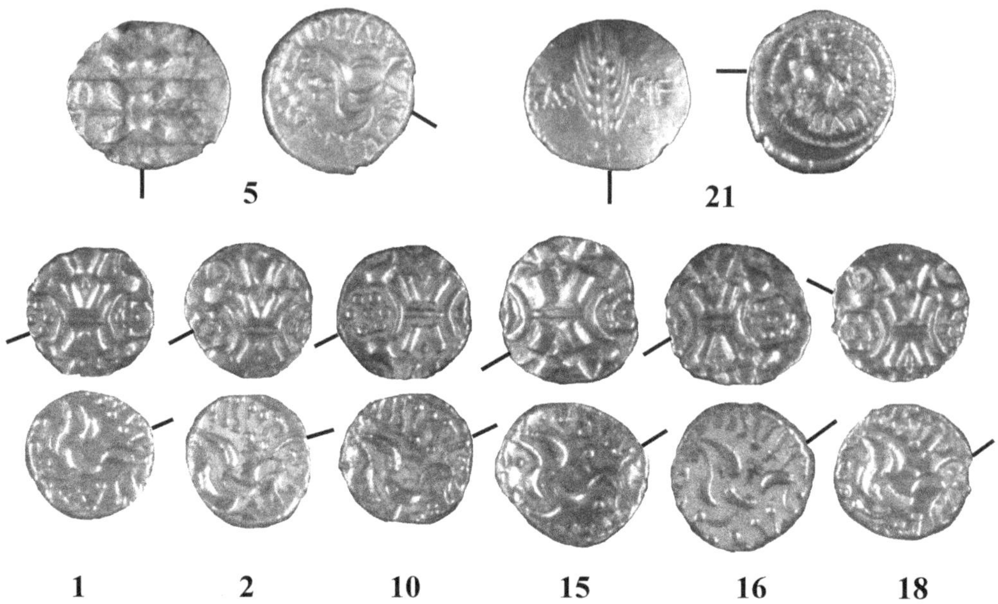

Figure 6. Die alignments of the Silsden coins: Volisios Dumnovellaunos (5), Epaticcus (21) and IISVP RASV (bottom row). As the obverse of the IISVP RASV issues could also be rotated through 180 degrees, the die alignments are based on the orientation of the horse's tail on the reverse.

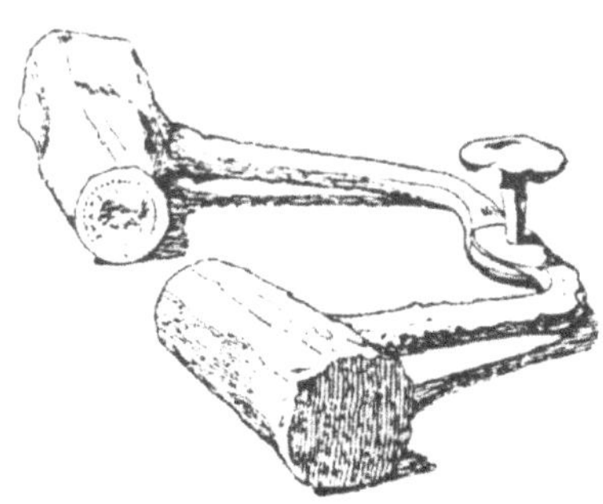

Figure 7 (left). Roman hinged dies (Zograph 1977).
Figure 8 (right). Fresco from the House of the Vettii, Pompeii (Coarelli 2002, 300).

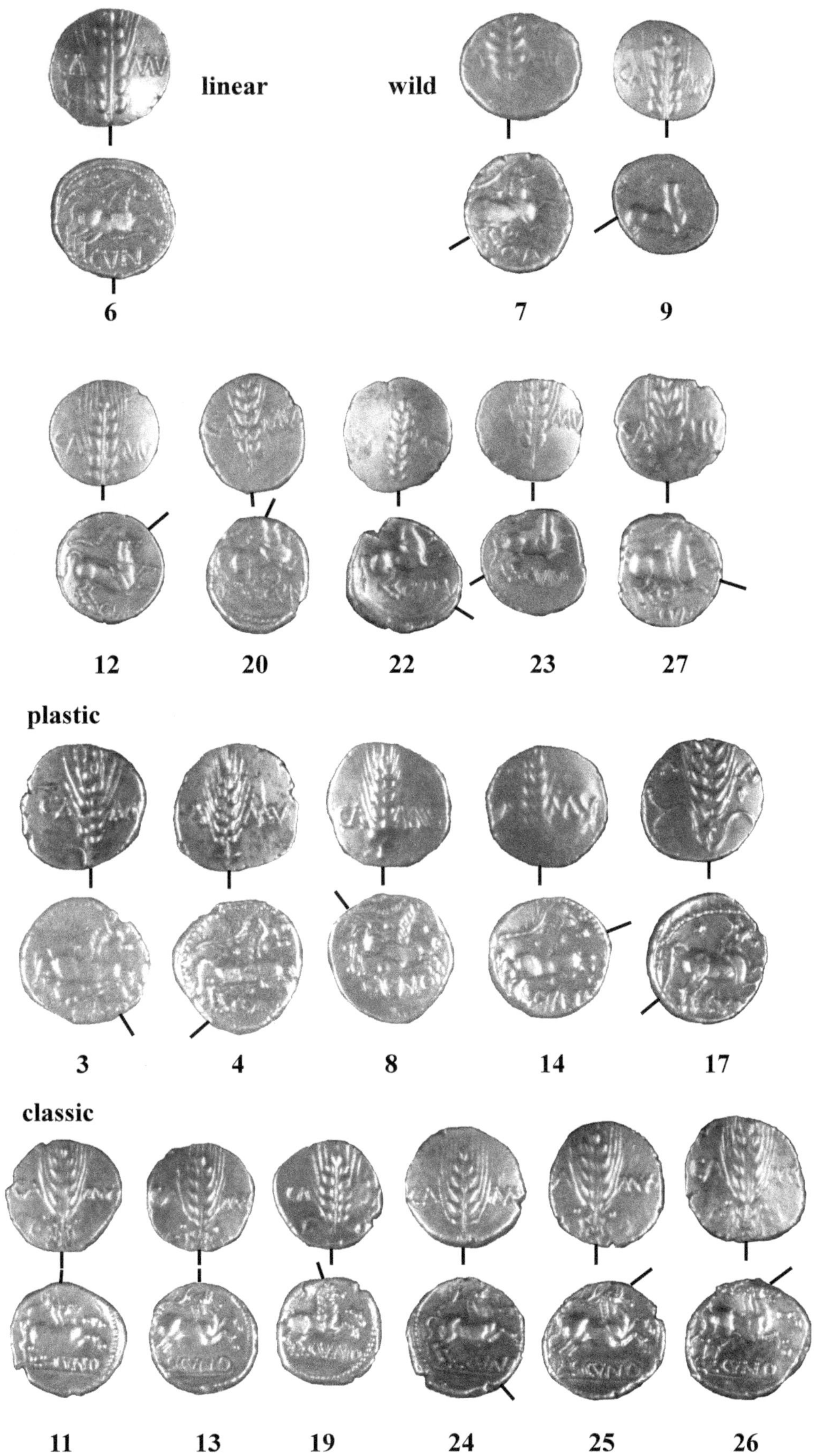

Figure 9. Die alignments of Cunobelin's staters in the Silsden hoard.

Metallurgy and meaning
The work on the Silsden hoard has demonstrated the importance of continuing programs of analyses to enable more accurate interpretation of the coins of the late Iron Age. The examination of the 27 coins has demonstrated clearly the late date of both the Cunobelin classic staters and the Corieltauvian IISVP RASV coins.

Work is continuing on corroboration of the die alignment results, and to interpret them along with numismatic and archaeological evidence. One area that should be reassessed is the recording of die alignments on the coins, which may be useful not only in the identification of changes in manufacturing techniques but also in die link studies and the dating of problematical types.

Dating evidence
The dating of the Silsden hoard is somewhat problematic as there are three quite distinct elements to be considered.

1) Gold staters of Cunobelin and Epaticcus
The dating of the staters of Cunobelin and that of Epaticcus can rely upon well-established and accepted chronologies (Allen 1975). What is particularly surprising about the coins in the Silsden hoard is the inclusion of such a wide range of Cunobelin issues. Hoards of Cunobelin staters are rare even in their normal area of distribution, and so far the only other hoards to contain a comparable range of coins are those found at Somerton and Shotley, Suffolk (Burnett 1994; de Jersey and Newman 1995).

Accepting that there is a chronological sequence to the production of Cunobelin's staters, the range of issues would suggest that the Silsden hoard is representative of a considerable proportion of Cunobelin's long reign. The presence of Cunobelin's classic series A staters, and one of Epaticcus, raises the possibility that this portion of the hoard had been accumulated right up until the time of the Roman invasion in AD 43. Just as for the Somerton and Shotley hoards, which are located on the edges of Cunobelin's main distribution area, it is interesting to speculate if the ultimate deposition of the hoard at Silsden, so far north, was in some way directly linked to the Roman invasion.

2) Gold staters of the Corieltauvi
The dating of Corieltauvian coinage is less certain, as indeed is the initial extent of Roman control over their territory (Cunliffe 1991, 199-210). It was originally thought that Corieltauvian coin production ceased soon after the Roman invasion, but observations on the distribution of VOLISIOS coinage by Jeffrey May (May 1992, 104-105), the recent links suggested by Jonathan Williams (Williams 2000) between inscribed Corieltauvian coinage and that of the Iceni, and the forthcoming publication of the coinage by Geoff Cottam (Cottam forthcoming) suggest a different picture. In some areas Corieltauvian coin production may have continued after the initial phase of Roman conquest. This would certainly seem to be supported by the Silsden coins, where the Corieltauvian types show fewer signs of wear compared to many of those of Cunobelin. The reduction in size and weight and the increased copper content of the IISVP RASV staters, as mentioned above, also strengthen this argument. If controlled die alignments are a late development in production technology then the presence of aligned dies for the IISVP RASV series also suggests they are a later issue.

While the exact chronology of inscribed Corieltauvian coinage is still debated, it is probably safe to place the IISVP RASV issues near the end of the series. Whether the production of these late issues took place before, during or after events relating to Roman military action following the Boudiccan revolt will, for the moment, have to be the subject of speculation.

3) Roman iron finger ring set with an intaglio
In terms of dating the hoard, the most significant aspect of the ring is the earliest possible date of manufacture attributed to it by Dr Martin Henig of the Institute of Archaeology, Oxford University. He dates the ring to the time of Nero, 53 – 61 AD, which fits in very well with a revised dating of the inscribed Corieltauvian coinage. Unfortunately without any conclusive stratigraphical association between the ring and the staters it is still possible that it is an unrelated deposition. It is, however, very hard to believe that two such unique and unexpected depositions should occur in the same place as a result of a random effect.

Taking all three elements of the hoard together it is still possible that they were deposited separately, but the close physical proximity of each to the other can leave little doubt that they are in some way linked. The hoard was probably acquired, accumulated and ultimately deposited together in the third quarter of the first century AD.

Iron Age Coinage in Brigantian Territory
The Brigantes are not known to have produced any coinage of their own, but this is not the first time that coins from other tribal areas have been recovered from within their territory. The presence of such a significant group of Cunobelin staters is indeed the first to be recorded, but two other hoards containing Corieltauvian coinage have been found in relatively close proximity. The Honley and Lightcliffe hoards were both found within 25km of the Silsden hoard and in what would appear to be topographically very similar settings (Figure 10). While only consisting of a single gold stater there is one other reported find that seems to be of particular relevance.

All three discoveries were made during the nineteenth century, which deprives us of any detailed locational information, and unfortunately many of the coins are now lost. For the hoards the most authoritative assessment of their contents is still that established by Graham Teasdill (1961) and which is summarized as follows.

Honley Hoard
Found in 1893, the Honley hoard consisted of five silver Corieltauvian issues of VOLISIOS, and 18 Roman coins: 12 silver denarii of the Republic from Valeria (133 – 126 BC) to Brutus (c. 43 BC) and 6 Imperial silver and brass coins of Nero (54 – 68 AD) and Vespasian (69 – 79 AD). It also contained other items of Roman manufacture including a first century AD bronze fibula.

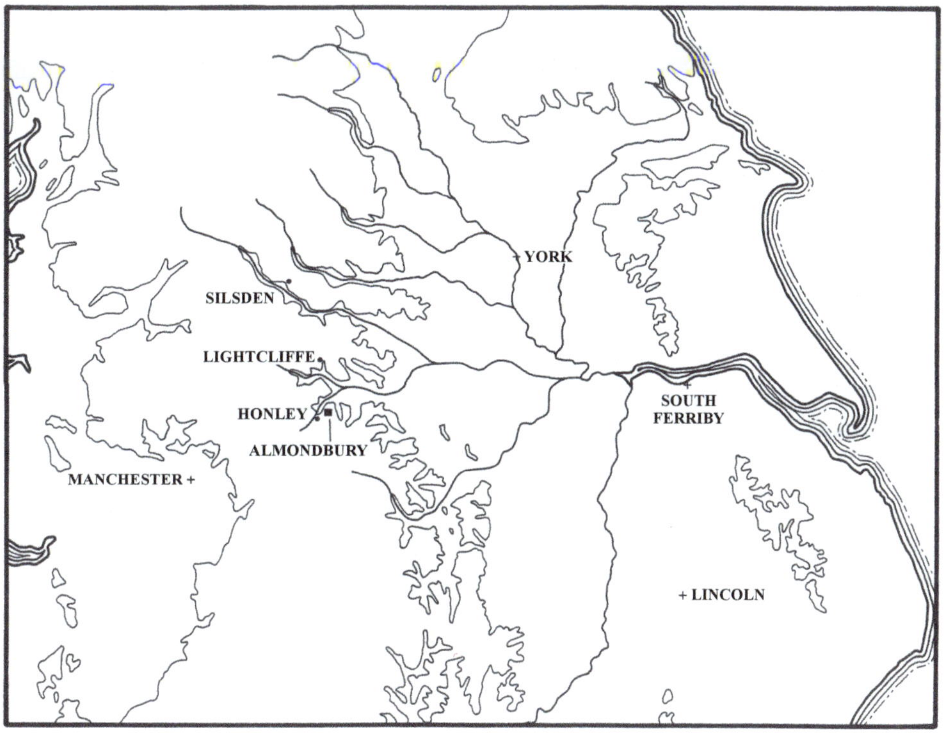

Figure 10. Location of the Silsden, Honley and Lightcliffe hoards.

Lightcliffe Hoard

Establishing the contents of this hoard is particularly problematic as a number of conflicting accounts have to be reconciled and the Almondbury hoard, once thought separate, has to be amalgamated with the other objects. Workmen digging for gravel found the Lightcliffe hoard between 1827 and 1831. The hoard is thought to have consisted of as many as 200 Roman silver coins and 18 gold staters including inscribed issues of VEP CORF, IISVP RASV and VOLISIOS. Most of the Roman coins were never fully recorded, but 39 of them were listed and range from Aelia (133 – 126 BC) to Caligula (37 – 41 AD).

Gold Stater of Verica

In 1890 Evans reported (Evans 1890, 511) that a gold stater of Verica had been found at Keighley. Whether this should be taken to mean within the town of Keighley itself or simply in the vicinity is uncertain, but the location of the Silsden hoard is less than 4 miles from Keighley town centre. Being so far removed from its normal distribution area the credibility of this find has often been called into question. With the discovery of the Silsden hoard its authenticity would now seem to be safer. The presence of this additional gold stater from the south of Britain supports the hypothesis for an important late Iron Age centre located somewhere within the immediate area.

Discussion

Such a remarkable and unique hoard containing a combination of Iron Age coinages, together with a mid-late first century AD Roman iron finger ring, raises many questions about the processes that brought such an assemblage together. In the case of the staters there is also a need to provide some explanation as to how they came to be deposited so far from their normal areas of distribution.

Taking the staters on their own it is self evident that they form two quite discrete groupings; one originating from the south of Britain and the other from the north-east. If, as increasingly seems to be the case, IISVP RASV staters post-date those of Cunobelin, it suggests that there might be a geographical and chronological sequence to the composition of the hoard. The first part involved the staters of Cunobelin and Epaticcus, the second the addition of the Corieltauvian staters, with a possible third element represented by the Roman iron finger ring. After collation these objects were then all deposited in Brigantian territory.

One possible mechanism by which this might have occurred has already been suggested for the Honley and Lightcliffe hoards. Occurrences of Corieltauvian coinage in Brigantian territory are still the subject of speculation, but in both cases it is generally accepted that they were deposited by Corieltauvian refugees (May 1992). From what they were fleeing, and when, is something that has not been adequately debated, but the assumption seems to be that their flight was in reaction to Roman military advances (*ibid.*). If this is indeed the case then it would not be unreasonable to suggest that the Silsden hoard represents two separate removals from Roman military advances, the first probably being related to the initial Roman invasion in 43 AD.

On that basis it is possible that the staters of Cunobelin, Epaticcus and the earlier recorded stater of Verica were deposited shortly after the Roman invasion. This would however imply that the Corieltauvian staters were deposited separately, or that the later chronology being suggested for Corieltauvian coinage is incorrect and that the IISVP RASV types were contemporary with those of Cunobelin. The alternative to this is that the staters of Cunobelin and Epaticcus remained in circulation until after the later production of the IISVP RASV staters. This may be possible if an individual or group of refugees removed them to Corieltauvian territory from the south of Britain. Then at a later date, having acquired additional north-eastern staters, the refugees fled for a second time into Brigantian territory. Looking at the historical framework of events this second stage of flight could have taken place following the Boudiccan revolt, or even as late as the final Roman conquest of the north which started around 70 AD.

While the exact chronology of events will probably never be known, it does seem to suggest that the Silsden hoard was accumulated over a period of time, and that there are three quite distinct elements to its composition and deposition that need to be accounted for:

a the assemblage of 'southern' tribal coinage
b the addition of Corieltauvian coinage, and possibly the Roman iron finger ring
c final deposition in Brigantian territory

With such a limited number of hoards to work with it is impossible to come to any definitive interpretation. If the hypothesis that refugees deposited the Silsden, Honley and Lightcliffe hoards is accepted, then it opens up some further possibilities.

As has already been suggested an individual or group of refugees having to flee on two consecutive occasions could have assembled the hoard. If that is the case then the mechanism by which the hoard was assembled is more likely to have been that of accumulation, not the product of on-going trade or exchange. Individual items were received or acquired on a regular basis and were then retained permanently.

This gradual accumulation makes it less likely that the hoard was assembled as a source of bullion. The inclusion of the iron finger ring also argues against this interpretation, but while in Corieltauvian territory, it is hard to understand why the potential gold source of the southern coins was not utilised. To keep the coins implies that they had a different but higher value than that represented by their gold content. Indeed it might be possible to argue that there is an implied equality between the two groups of staters. Their true value is in what they represented, not their gold content. The metallurgical content of staters was simply a function of availability/control over resources, and aesthetic and technological imperatives regarding their production.

Such a mechanism also has very interesting implications for the length of time it would have taken to assemble the Silsden hoard. If the different issues of Cunobelin do indeed cover most of his reign, and the Corieltauvian coinage can be attributed to post-Roman invasion, possibly up to and beyond the Boudiccan revolt, then the accumulation of the Silsden hoard took 40-50 years, or even longer. If such an estimate were correct, then in practical terms this would suggest that there is also a hereditary dimension to such hoards.

The rather unusual and wide date range of Roman issues in the Honley and Lightcliffe hoards might be demonstrating the same phenomenon. If so the time period obviously covers many generations, making the accumulation and ownership of such hoards something that is more likely to be associated with a family or clan than an individual. For the Honley and Lightcliffe hoards it appears that the accumulators only had access to Roman coinage before acquiring Corieltauvian staters. This suggests that they were also twice displaced refugees, but from which region is unknown. All three hoards would suggest a remarkable willingness on the part of the Corieltauvians to accept their presence and to allow them to become integrated into their society. However with so few occurrences of mixed coinage from anywhere else in the country this was probably not usual and only occurred as a result of some exceptional circumstance. One obvious unifying factor would have been a refusal to submit to Roman rule following their invasion of the south, or possibly a joint involvement in military resistance to further Roman advances.

The fact that all three hoards were deposited in Brigantian territory suggests that having once again fled from the Romans the refugees then hoped to join with the Brigantians in a further stand against the invaders. As the Roman military conquest of the north was completed so rapidly, and then enforced almost permanently thereafter, the opportunity to do so never arose.

While not denying a more conventional interpretation of coinage as a function of trade/gift exchange (Haselgrove 1996) or the political/military ambition (Kent 1981; Nash 1987) of those who issued them, with the Silsden hoard it might be more important to consider the purpose and motivation of the individual, or individuals, who were able to acquire and accumulate such an assemblage. Rather than seeing access to coinage as the mechanism by which individuals were able to interact within a wider social context, perhaps the act of acquiring them was an expression of individuality. Possession of such items demonstrated something about the owner: not an accumulation of wealth, but of status through proven ability or intention.

Such an interpretation would suggest that staters were not intended to be exchanged, except possibly through a redemption or recall mechanism from the individual back to the issuing authority. These gold coins are in some way symbolic or representative of a specific relationship between the individual and the issuing authority, something that may have no origins in, or relationship to tribal affiliations. It may be a form of recognition for individual achievement or a demonstration of allegiance to the issuing authority, either in its own right or to some common cause or purpose. Essentially, to hold the coins and to be able to show them was an expression of self that engendered an appropriate reaction, either recognition of status/ability, or as supporting a common cause.

Taking that to be the case the Silsden hoard could then be representative of southern tribal refugees moving into the portion of Corieltauvian territory which remained outside direct Roman control following the invasion of 43 AD. There they seemed to have been accepted, either because they had a transferable skill or status that the Corieltauvi recognized, or because they had a common cause against the Romans. For a while it might even have been the case that the Romans were not perceived to be an on-going threat and that there was an attempt to re-establish an independent Iron Age identity. This ambition might have been shared with the Iceni, giving rise to the similarities in inscriptions of later issues. With so little certainty about the meaning of such inscriptions an alternative interpretation may, however, be suggested. Rather than identifying an individual, some may refer to a deity, cause, or collective ambition to which those who produced and accepted the coins wished to associate themselves.

The bronze fibula in the Honley hoard and the iron finger ring in the Silsden hoard could very well be an indication of on-going and potentially peaceful contacts with the Romans. However, having been able to link into the distribution of Corieltauvian staters the southern tribal refugees still continued to retain their original coinage, probably in the hope or belief that a successor to the issuing authority from which they received them would one day be able to re-establish itself. Under such circumstances they would then have been able to return to their original homeland and regain the full symbolic meaning and value of their coins. It was probably the same reaction to further Roman military action that applied when they had to flee again, this time into Brigantian territory. Again it was probably hoped that the situation would reverse itself but within a very short period of time it must have become self evident that it would not.

Perhaps the individual or individuals who deposited the Silsden hoard were killed or died before they could realise any exchange value, but it would seem more likely that there was a votive element behind its deposition. If staters are representative of a special relationship between those who hold them and the issuing authority that produced them, then they would have carried considerable symbolic and emotional value which would have far outweighed any recoverable material value. Once it was realised that the issuing authority and all that it represented was incapable of re-establishing itself, then the continued retention and ultimate disposal of such staters would have carried considerable significance. This disposal or deposition was probably intensely private and would not necessarily involve, or produce, what could archaeologically be recognised as a votive context.

Conclusions

The Silsden hoard is indeed a most perplexing assemblage of artefacts. It can be interpreted along more conventional lines, such as the earnings of a Celtic warrior or the booty of a Roman legionnaire, but its unique make up does seem to demand the exploration of alternatives. The recovery, examination and interpretation of the Silsden hoard has added validity to the Lightcliffe and Honley hoards and the Verica stater from Keighley. The scientific examination has reinforced the interpretation of the Cunobelin Classic and IISVP RASV issues as being late in the late Iron Age British sequence. The change in die technology identified by studying the hoard has added weight to this argument and suggests there is further work to do on the identification of detailed manufacturing techniques. In addition to the above, the Silsden hoard also invites discussion on a much more theoretical basis, raising a number of issues that now need further consideration. These can be summarized as follows:

1) that following the invasion in AD 43, a portion of Corieltauvian territory remained outside Roman control and attempted to maintain an independent identity possibly in association with the Iceni

2) that certain hoards were accumulated over a number of generations and are representative of the status and ownership of a family, or clan, rather than an individual

3) that staters were not readily transferable and were representative of a special relationship between those who received them and the issuing authority who produced them

4) that the metallurgical content of staters was influenced by the availability of resources and the aesthetic/technological requirements of their production

5) that equal significance should be placed on the acceptance of staters as there is on the initial production and distribution by the issuing authority

6) that if the special relationship between those holding staters and the issuing authority is broken the disposal of staters took on special significance

In conclusion it is only through the continued communication and close co-operation between metal detectorists and archaeologists, and the integration of theoretical and physical analysis, that we can ever hope to increase our understanding of the late Iron Age coins of Britain, their function, role within society, their chronology, and what they can tell us about the complex interaction of the Roman and Iron Age communities.

Acknowledgements

The authors would like to acknowledge the support and enthusiasm of the following: Jeff Walbank, Bradford Museum Service, Department of Archaeological Sciences, University of Bradford (especially Gerry McDonnell, Rick Jones and Rob Vernon), Department of Materials, University of Oxford (especially Peter Northover and Chris Salter), Catherine Johns of the British Museum, Martin Henig of the Institute of Archaeology, Oxford University and Philip de Jersey of the Celtic Coin Index.

Bibliography

Allen, D. F. 1975: Cunobelin's gold. *Britannia* 6, 1-19.

Burnett, A. 1994: Somerton, Suffolk, Treasure Trove. *British Numismatic Journal* 64, 127-128.

Burnett, A. and Cowell, M. 1988: Celtic coinage in Britain II. *British Numismatic Journal* 58, 1-10.

Coarelli, F. (ed.) 2002: *Pompeii* (New York, Riverside).

Cottam, G. forthcoming: *The inscribed coinage of the Corieltauvi.*

Cowell, M. 1992: An analytical survey of the British Celtic gold coinage. In M. Mays (ed.), *Celtic coinage: Britain and beyond* (Oxford, BAR 222), 207-233.

Cowell, M., Oddy, W. and Burnett, A. 1987: Celtic coinage in Britain: new hoards and recent analyses. *British Numismatic Journal* 57, 1-23.

Cunliffe, B. W. 1991 (3rd ed.): *Iron Age communities in Britain* (London, Routledge).

de Jersey, P. and Newman, J. 1995: Staters of Cunobelin from Shotley, Suffolk. *British Numismatic Journal* 65, 214-215.

Evans, J. 1890: *The coins of the ancient Britons. Supplement* (London, Quaritch).

Haselgrove, C. 1996: Iron Age coinage: recent trends. In T. Champion and J. Collis, *The Iron Age in Britain and Ireland: recent trends* (Sheffield, JR Collis Publications), 67-85.

Kent, J. 1981: The origins of coinage in Britain. In B. W. Cunliffe (ed.), *Coinage and society in Britain and Gaul: some current problems* (London, CBA Research Report 38), 40-43.

May, J. 1992: Iron Age coins in Yorkshire. In M. Mays (ed.), *Celtic coinage: Britain and beyond* (Oxford, BAR 222), 93-111.

Nash, D. 1987: *Coinage in the Celtic world* (London, Seaby).

Northover, P. 1992: Materials issues in the Celtic coinage. In M. Mays (ed.), *Celtic coinage: Britain and beyond* (Oxford, BAR 222), 235-299.

Ogden, W. S. 1908: The Roman mint and early Britain. *British Numismatic Journal* 5, 1-50.

Teasdill, G. 1961: *Coin finds of the Huddersfield District* (Huddersfield, Tolson Memorial Museum Handbook 16).

Walbank, J. 1999: Yorkshire's golden harvest. *The Searcher* May 1999, 43-44.

Williams, J. H. C. 2000: The silver coins from East Anglia attributed to King Prasutagus of the Iceni: a new reading of the obverse inscription. *Numismatic Chronicle* 160, 276-281.

Zograph, A. N. 1977: *Ancient coinage part I: the general problems of ancient numismatics* (Oxford, Tempus Reparatum).

www.ingramcontent.com/pod-product-compliance
Ingram Content Group UK Ltd.
Pitfield, Milton Keynes, MK11 3LW, UK
UKHW061846041026
15591UKWH00015B/938

9 781841 719672